MARKETING FOR HEALTH CARE ORGANIZATIONS

MARKETING FOR HEALTH CARE ORGANIZATIONS

PHILIP KOTLER

Northwestern University

ROBERTA N. CLARKE

Boston University

PRENTICE-HALL, INC., Englewood Cliffs, New Jersey 07632

Library of Congress Cataloging-in-Publication Data

KOTLER, PHILIP.
Marketing for health care organizations.

Includes bibliographies and index.
1. Medical care—Marketing. 2. Social service—Marketing. I. Clarke, Roberta, (date). II. Title.
[DNLM: 1. Health Services—organization & administration—United States. W 74 K87m]
RA410.56.K68 1987 362.1'068'8 86-18733
ISBN 0-13-557562-1

Editorial/production supervision and interior design: Kim Gueterman
Cover design: Bruce Kenselaar
Manufacturing buyer: Ed O'Dougherty
Cover photo by Tom Grill, Comstock

Printed in the United States of America

10 9 8 7 6 5 4 3 2

ISBN 0-13-557562-1 01

Prentice-Hall International (UK) Limited, *London*
Prentice-Hall of Australia Pty. Limited, *Sydney*
Prentice-Hall Canada Inc., *Toronto*
Prentice-Hall Hispanoamericana, S.A., *Mexico*
Prentice-Hall of India Private Limited, *New Delhi*
Prentice-Hall of Japan, Inc., *Tokyo*
Prentice-Hall of Southeast Asia Pte. Ltd., *Singapore*
Editora Prentice-Hall do Brasil, Ltda., *Rio de Janeiro*

To Milton Kotler, for your continuously perceptive research into the health care market

To Allen and Aaron Michel and to all of my students who have taught me as much as I have taught them

CONTENTS

PREFACE

Marketing has passed beyond the point of being a "hot topic" in health care. It is now recognized as a necessary management function in a highly competitive, resource-constrained, and sometimes hostile environment. Unfortunately, there are still too many health care managers who allude to the need to "market" their organizations' services, while merely pursuing a few promotional activities in search of a quick fix. Clearly, few health care marketing problems are amenable to quick solutions. Most of these problems require a deep understanding of the environment, the market and the way it segments itself, and the organization's goals for each segment. Moreover, these problems require the health care marketer to master well-established marketing concepts such as positioning, the marketing mix, channels management, consumer behavior, and marketing budgeting. All of these concepts have proved useful to health care organizations as the managers have incorporated marketing into their managerial functions.

And they *have* incorporated marketing. At the time of the writing of this book, there are over 2,000 high-level marketing executives working in U.S. hospitals. Other types of health care organizations may also have one or more managers responsible for marketing the organization. The number of health care marketing consultants has grown to over 700, and four national associations are competing to serve managers with an interest in health care marketing.

But what is marketing? As defined in this book, *marketing is the effective management by an organization of its exchange relations with its various markets and publics.* Health care organizations have numerous markets: patients, physicians, regulators, alternative delivery systems such as HMOs and PPOs, reimbursement agencies, employers, business roundtables, and other organizations seeking to change the way health care is organized, delivered and paid for, as well as innumerable markets relevant to a specific service or product. Marketing is the organization's undertaking of analysis, planning, implementation, and control to achieve its exchange objectives with its target markets.

Through decades of working in business markets, marketers have formulated a conceptual system that yields systematic insight into the structure and dynamics of market exchanges. The transposition of this conceptual system to the health care industry poses a number of challenges calling for creative translation. The vast amount of marketing literature has focused on product marketing; yet the products of the health care organizations are largely services. This effects not only product definition but also the concept of distribution and channels.

The traditional marketing theories regarding pricing strategies and behaviors, while becoming far more relevant in the now-competitive health care environment, are still unable to be directly translated into many health care situations; regulated pricing, a market in which demand can be created by supply, and a historical consumer unconcern and ignorance of prices calls for a tailored approach to pricing.

And the perspective of health care as a "right" brings with it ethical imperatives and considerations that are not generally issues in traditional marketing thought. Health care organizations that have historically held nonprofit status are, in some instances, rapidly moving toward a for-profit orientation and simultaneously trying to determine what responsibilities they still have to serve the unserved and underserved segments. For-profit health care providers may not consider these issues at all; or they may, by contrast, act very much like their nonprofit brethren. And yet other health care and social service organizations maintain a not-for-profit focus and then wonder if even the best of marketing strategies will allow them to survive in a competitive resource-scarce environment.

The purpose of this book is to apply the conceptual system of marketing to the marketing problems of health care and social service organizations. The text has been tailored to address the marketing problems which health care managers are likely to encounter.

The book is divided into five parts. Part I (Understanding Marketing) explains the nature, role, and relevance of marketing to health care organizations. Part II (Organizing Marketing) shows how marketing can be organized in health care organizations to carry out marketing analysis, planning, and control. Part III (Analyzing Marketing Opportunities) describes the major concepts and tools available to health care organizations to understand their customers, markets, and environments. Part IV (Planning the Marketing Mix) discusses the four major instruments—product, price, place, and promotion—that constitute the organization's strategic and tactical means for attracting and retaining customers. Part V (Supporting the Marketing Effort) describes marketing strategies for attracting two major input resources—people and funds.

Each chapter begins with an appropriate story that sets the theme of the chapter. The chapters include boxed exhibits of interesting developments, examples, and illustrations concerning health care and social service marketing.

There are innumerable unnamed individuals who contributed to this book. The students who allowed the classroom to be the testing ground for new applications of marketing concepts to health care were more helpful then they will ever know. Two research assistants in particular, Linda MacCracken and Venessa Di Fleuneri, aided in handling details of manuscript development. David Franzblace, a Boston University Health Care Management Program alumnus, deserves credit for submitting a steady stream of examples of health care marketing from all over the country. Faculty colleagues from the marketing departments of the J. L. Kellogg Graduate School of Management at Northwestern University provided valued input. And excellent manuscript reviews were provided by William Flexner, DBA (Flexner and Associates), Professor Duncan Neuhauser (Case-Western Reserve School of Medicine), and Dr. Mitchell Rabkin (CEO of Boston's Beth Israel Hospital). To all these individuals, we offer our thanks.

Philip Kotler

Roberta N. Clarke

PART I
Understanding Marketing

1

MARKETING'S ROLE IN HEALTH CARE ORGANIZATIONS

Most hospitals and health care organizations face a variety of marketing problems. Some have arisen recently due to decreased funding and changing reimbursement policies by the government, employer groups and third parties, to regulatory policies affecting the organization's ability to provide service, and to changing marketplace characteristics. Other problems have been troubling health care organizations for many years, but are only now being recognized and addressed. Consider the following examples:

Generally untrained in marketing and subsequently in issues of pricing, hospital CEOs nowadays deal with a host of pricing decisions:

> What pricing structure should the hospital negotiate with HMOs and PPOs? How much of a volume discount must be offered?
>
> In order to compete with the walk-in medical clinic nearby, should the hospital cut its price to patients seen in the Emergency Service for non-emergent problems?
>
> As the lowest cost (and priced) hospital in town, the hospital is in a unique position to promote this advantage to price-sensitive businesses, insurers, and alternative delivery systems. Will this negatively influence consumers, who often equate price with quality?

Independent nonprofit home health care agencies throughout the country are fearful of the increasing competition developing in their field. The advent of DRG reimbursement has decreased the average length of stay in hospitals across the country, leading to a greater need for hospital aftercare. In an effort to "follow" their patients as well as to spread their overhead, hospitals the agencies have served in the past are now setting up their own home health services in direct competition with the independent agencies. Proprietary home health agencies that had been ineligible for Medicare certification are now eligible due to changes in federal policies. As a result, proprietary home health agencies now find it to their financial advantage to attract patients who have traditionally been the primary market of the nonprofit home health agencies.

Local health regulatory agencies (HSAs) had been charged with the responsibility of regulating what health services were offered by which organizations in the best interests of the local community. However, some HSAs realized that they could not make these regulatory decisions intelligently because their knowledge of the community was limited to traditional demographic data that did not necessarily indicate what health services the community wanted and needed.

Osteopathic hospitals have historically had to deal with lack of awareness and misunderstanding of osteopathic medicine. This image problem has resulted in difficulties in attracting not only patients, but also physicians.

Neighborhood health centers were initially set up to serve disadvantaged communities, based on the philosophy that the government had a responsibility to make high-quality health care available to everyone, including those individuals who could not afford to pay for this care. As government funding for programs aimed at the disadvantaged has declined in recent years, neighborhood health centers have found themselves having to rely increasingly upon their patient base, which cannot afford to pay for the care provided to them. Many neighborhood health centers wonder if they will be able to survive without substantial external funding.

Many inner city hospitals, built in the early twentieth century to serve rapidly expanding, vibrant urban populations, now find the neighborhoods in which they are located considered unsafe, aging, and deteriorating. These hospitals often experience trouble attracting a financially viable mix of patients because their location is considered unattractive by the suburban and wealthier urban populations with better third-party insurance. Moreover, since these hospitals primarily serve their local populations, which are often poor, it is incorrectly assumed that the quality of medical care delivered reflects the status of the local population.

The effectiveness of many long-standing health promotion campaigns has been called into question. Efforts to increase the usage of safety belts, to decrease alcohol consumption, and to maintain a generally healthy life style have failed significantly to affect the behavior of the majority of the country's population. Future funding for such programs is now being tied more closely to proof that the campaigns will achieve some reasonable level of success. In order to increase their chances of producing successful campaigns, many health promoters have started to look to marketing for help.

A great variety of health care organizations are facing marketing problems (as well as marketing opportunities). These organizations are confronting a multitude of changing variables in the marketplace: increased regulation, decreased outside funding, more aggressive competition, drastically changing reimbursement policies, a growing shortage of certain necessary clinical skills and an oversupply of others, a wave of entrepreneurial ventures by both health care providers and nonproviders, and a more critical consumer or patient population. Board members, public authorities, business roundtables, citizen organizations, and provider groups are seriously questioning managers of health care organizations about their organizations' missions, objectives, and strategies. One result is that these managers are being forced to see what marketing might offer to keep their organizations viable and able to respond to future challenges.

At the same time, many health care managers are approaching the marketing function with caution. Although most health care organizations have readily accepted such business functions as finance, accounting, planning, and public relations, some have been skeptical about marketing. Marketing connotes "big business"—commercialism and Madison Avenue gimmickry—particularly to those with little actual exposure to the marketing function. In addition, marketing appears to conflict directly with the antisolicitation rules contained in the professional ethics of most clinical professions. Board members of health care organizations who use marketing techniques daily in their work cannot determine how marketing would be applied in a health care setting. Traditional third-party reimbursement policies do not recognize the value of marketing and therefore do not reimburse for it. The burden of proof of the relevance and utility of marketing to the health care organization falls on the marketer.

In this chapter, we will cover the following topics, which managers of health care organizations often raise about marketing:

1. What is marketing?
2. Why should health care organizations be interested in marketing?
3. What are the distinctive characteristics of marketing in health care organizations?
4. What are the major marketing problems health care organizations face?
5. How are health care organizations using marketing today?
6. What are the major criticisms and benefits of marketing?
7. What is the essence of a marketing orientation?

WHAT IS MARKETING?

The term *marketing* has been widely misunderstood by health care administrators and professionals. Most commonly, it has been viewed as a glorified version of public relations.[1] For that reason, the public relations function in some health care organizations has been inappropriately charged with the responsibility for marketing. This has been done when marketing has been defined as selling, advertising, and promotion.

A second area sometimes confused with marketing is fundraising or development. It is not surprising that marketing has been aligned with these two functions, since public relations and development have traditionally been the two most sophisticated marketing capabilities in health care organizations.

A range of other health care management areas have been affiliated with marketing: community relations, outreach, public information, and community affairs. All these areas tend to be promotional in nature, again demonstrating the tendency for health care organizations to define marketing in terms of selling, informing, advertising, and image making.

It is much less common to see a health care organization define marketing in terms of planning. Yet the activities planners perform—the collection and analysis of population and provider data—are similar to some of the activities necessary for good marketing. Planning is viewed as internal to the organization. It is often not recognized as having marketing components because marketing is perceived as being external to the organization.

This view of marketing is not surprising, since the most visible part of marketing is promotion. Americans are subjected to an overwhelming array of print and broadcast advertisements, to mailed promotion, telephone solicitations, billboards along highways, and a retail environment designed for selling. It may therefore come as a surprise to many administrators that the most important part of marketing is *not* selling; selling is the tip of the marketing iceberg. In fact, if the appropriate products and services are offered, and pricing, distributing, and promoting them is done effectively, these goods and services will sell very easily without requiring an intense amount of promotion and hard sell. Peter Drucker, one of the leading management theorists, summarized marketing this way: "The aim of marketing is to make selling superfluous."[2]

Marketing is a central activity of modern organizations. To survive and succeed, organizations must know their markets, attract sufficient resources, convert these resources into appropriate products, services, and ideas, and effectively distribute them to various consuming publics.

This is as true of health care and social service organizations as it is of commercial, profit-oriented businesses. These tasks are carried on in a framework of voluntary action by all the parties. The organization does not employ force to attract resources, convert them to products and services, or distribute them. The modern organization relies mainly on offering and exchanging values with different parties to elicit their cooperation. In short, modern organizations rely on exchange mechanisms to achieve their goals.[3]

Exchange is the central concept underlying marketing. Through exchanges, various social units—individuals, small groups, organizations, whole nations—get the inputs they need. By offering something attractive or needed, they acquire what they need in return. Since both parties agree to exchange voluntarily, both see themselves as better off afterward.

There are situations peculiar to the health and welfare fields where the exchange does not appear to be voluntary on both sides, e.g., the involuntary hospitalization of a mentally ill patient. However, in cases of this sort, the voluntary exchange does exist between the service-providing organization and a third party, such as a relative, a physician, or a court-appointed guardian or judge. These third parties play the relevant decision-making role in the voluntary exchange process.

A professional marketer is someone who is skilled at understanding, planning, and managing exchanges. The marketer knows how to research and understand the needs of the other party; to design a valued offering to meet these needs; to communicate the offer effectively; and to present it at the right time and place. A marketer would define marketing in the following way:

> **Marketing** is the analysis, planning, implementation, and control of carefully formulated programs designed to bring about voluntary exchanges of values with target markets for the purpose of achieving organizational objectives. It relies heavily on designing the organization's offering in terms of the target markets' needs and desires, and on using effective pricing, communication, and distribution to inform, motivate, and service the markets.

Several things should be noted about this definition of marketing. First, marketing is defined as a managerial process involving analysis, planning, implementation, and control. Marketing can also be looked at as a social process in which the material and service needs of a society are identified, expanded, and served by a set of institutions.[4] We will not use the social process view of marketing in this book because it is less relevant to managers and administrators facing very practical marketing problems.

Second, marketing manifests itself in carefully formulated programs, not just random actions to achieve desired responses. If a charitable organization simply asks a group of volunteers to go out and collect money, this is likely to produce disappointing revenue. The volunteers are without direction as to whom to call on, what to say about the organization, and how much to ask for. Their effort is more like selling than marketing. Marketing precedes any selling and manifests itself in carefully formulated plans and programs.

Third, marketing seeks to bring about voluntary exchanges of values. Marketers seek a response from another party, but it is not a response to be obtained by any means or at any price. Marketing is the philosophical alternative to force. The marketer seeks to formulate a bundle of benefits for the target market of sufficient attractiveness to produce a voluntary exchange. A group dental practice, seeking to attract new patients, might offer free examinations for children, special hours for elderly patients, and a host of other benefits to those who utilize their practice.

Fourth, marketing means the selection of target markets rather than a quixotic attempt to serve every market and be all things to all people. The mission statements of health care organizations ordinarily forbid the organization from turning away individuals in need of any service vaguely related to the organization's offerings. In contrast, marketers routinely distinguish among possible market segments and elect to address a limited number of them on the basis of how the organization can best fulfill a specific mission or objective. A child welfare agency in need of funds does not send letters to all citizens. Rather, it buys mailing lists containing the names of people who, because of education, income, and other characteristics, are more likely to support a local social service agency.

Fifth, the purpose of marketing is to help organizations ensure survival, continued health, and the flexibility necessary to operate in a regulated environment through serving their markets more effectively. In the business sector, the major objective is profit. In the health care sector, other objectives may prevail: a city health department may want to improve the level and distribution of health services; a regional hypertension program may want to provide a greater number of people with free blood pressure tests; and a community hospital may want to make available more and better cardiovascular health promotion programs to its middle-aged service area. Of course, many health care organizations also seek to make a profit (which may be called a surplus or reserves) in order to guarantee the financial flexibility required for the organization's health.

Sixth, marketing relies on designing the organization's offerings in terms of the target market's needs and desires, rather than in terms of the seller's personal tastes. Efforts to impose on a market a product, service, or idea that is not matched to the market's needs or wants are likely to fail. Companies that design products they feel are good for the market without consulting the market beforehand often find they have few customers. In the health care sector, the same holds true. Hospitals that design industrial health programs without studying the attitudes and medical needs of local businesses often find subsequent usage of these programs disappointing. Effective marketing is user-oriented, not seller-oriented.

Seventh, marketing utilizes and blends a set of tools called the *marketing mix*—product/service design, pricing, communication, and distribution. Too often the public equates marketing with only one of its tools such as advertising. But marketing is oriented toward yielding results, and this requires a broad conception of all the factors influencing buyer behavior.

WHY SHOULD HEALTH CARE ORGANIZATIONS BE INTERESTED IN MARKETING?

Different industries and organizations develop their initial interest in marketing at different times. Organizations that enjoy a sellers' market, one marked by an abundance of customers or incoming resources, tend to avoid or ignore marketing. Organizations typically become aware of marketing when their market undergoes a change. When buyers (patients or clients), funds, or other resources needed by the organization become scarce, the organization becomes concerned and receptive to nontraditional solutions such as marketing.

One might note a difference here between profit-oriented and nonprofit health care organizations. Some are incorporated as for-profit organizations, but in fact act like nonprofit organizations. They seek not to maximize profit as their primary objective but to place service objectives as top priority. These for-profit organizations, acting as they do like nonprofit organizations, are in contrast to profit-oriented organizations whose top priority it is to maximize profit, ROI or some other financial indicator. In the current highly competitive, difficult financial environment, many health care organizations, incorporated as nonprofit, act very similarly to the majority of for-profit incorporated organizations.

Profit-oriented health care organizations manage the resource attraction effort (the attraction of funds) and the resource allocation effort (the provision of goods and services) with one exchange model. Duncan Neuhauser, the noted health policy analyst, calls this the "cash and carry" model (see Figure 1–1).

Organizations that fit this model have always had to attract the market's usage in order to generate revenue. As a result, they have often

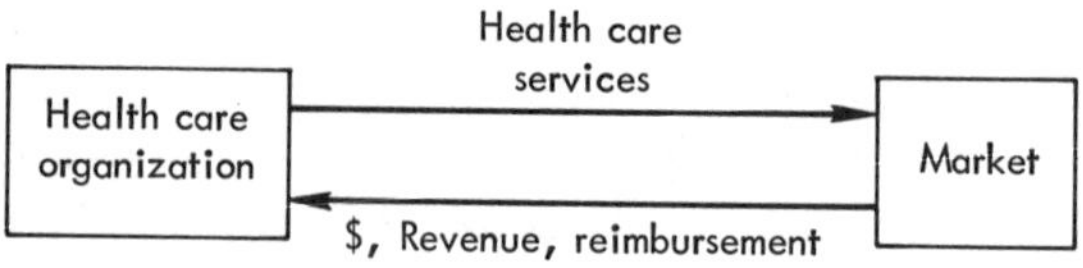

FIGURE 1–1 The Cash and Carry Model

tended to be more sensitive to marketing. Nonprofit organizations have traditionally divided the resource attraction and allocation efforts between two exchanges (see Figure 1–2). If the organization attracted sufficient funds and resources from donors, it did not also have to generate substantial market use. Marketing activities, although not recognized as such, were more prone to focus on donors than on the user or consuming market.

One major factor that has caused this to change is that funds from donor sources have not kept pace with the financial needs of nonprofit health care organizations. Moreover, with the advent of Medicare, Medicaid, and better third-party insurance over the past two decades, significant revenue was also generated as a result of the market consuming the health services offered. With donors providing fewer funds and the consuming market generating more funds through third-party payors, traditional nonprofit organizations have increasingly focused their efforts on attracting usage by the market in order to generate revenue.[5] See Figure 1–3 for the more complex third-party payor model.

A second reason why health care organizations have become interested in marketing is the impact of the regulatory process. Even if such an organization has a wealth of funds and resources, and therefore does not depend upon market usage for survival, it may not be allowed to operate as it wishes. For example, an inpatient rehabilitation center may find that the regulatory agency does not allow it to expand its busy stroke unit without simultaneously closing down its underutilized spinal cord injury beds. A community mental health center may be man-

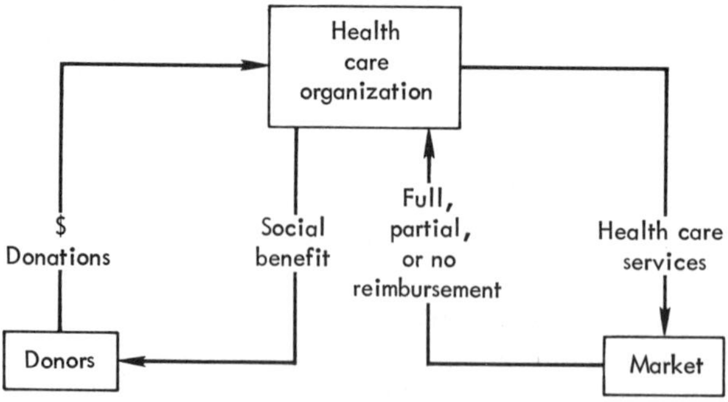

FIGURE 1–2 The Philanthropic Model

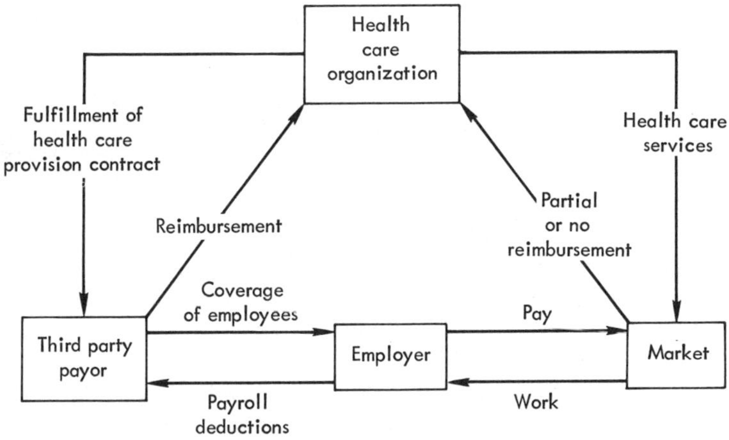

FIGURE 1–3 The Third-Party Payor Model

dated to serve more socially and economically deprived patients if it is to maintain its approved service area. Under traditional cost-based reimbursement, a hospital could be penalized with lower per day reimbursement if its census was not sufficiently high. And regulated pricing systems penalize an underutilized unit carrying heavy fixed costs, because it cannot pass on those costs through increased charges. (By 1987, all Medicare hospital payments will be broken down into 467 categories, called "diagnosis related groups," for each of which the government will pay a flat fee.)

The effect of rulings and decisions by federal and local regulatory bodies is to pressure health care organizations to seek high market utilization and utilization by specific groups. This forces upon the organization the need to market its services to these groups. Most of these regulatory pressures first arose in the 1970s and have continued with the more recent wave of pricing regulations. Combined with the relative decline in donor funds over the past decade, they have thrust marketing into prominence in health care management.

THE DISTINCTIVE CHARACTERISTICS OF MARKETING IN HEALTH CARE ORGANIZATIONS

Marketing in the health care sector does not involve new marketing principles so much as new and challenging settings for the application of these principles. Nonprofit health care organizations have distinct marketing concerns because of their nonprofit status. As identified by Weinberg and Lovelock,[6] two of these are multiple publics and multiple objectives.

Nonprofit organizations normally have at least two major publics to address from a marketing standpoint: their patients or clients, and their donors or sources of funds. Additionally, all health care organizations have to deal with other publics as well, such as medical, nursing, and other professional staffs; regulatory agencies, reimbursement agencies, employer groups, and related government and business agencies. Business organizations also deal with a multitude of publics, but their tendency is to think about marketing only in connection with one of these publics, their customers.

Nonprofit organizations, whether providing health care or other services, tend to pursue several important objectives simultaneously rather than only one, such as profits. The mission statement of the Peninsula General Hospital Medical Center (see Exhibit 1–1) contains a wide variety of objectives, such as: to provide a high quality of medical care, to educate health professionals, to provide an attractive atmosphere in which employees can work, to provide home care and rehabilitation services, to provide outpatient services for those without a private physician, and to serve as an area referral center. In addition, the hospital must have sufficient financial resources to achieve its missions.

EXHIBIT 1–1 An Example of Multiple Objectives

Mission, Goals and, Objectives of Peninsula General Hospital Medical Center

Mission

Peninsula General Hospital Medical Center is a voluntary, nonprofit institution, organized as a non-stock corporation under the Laws of Maryland. Where needs exist, and resources permit, its mission is to provide a primary, secondary and tertiary diagnostic and treatment center for the delivery of health care services and programs within its service area of Somerset, Wicomico, and Worcester Counties, Maryland; portions of Sussex County, Delaware; and Accomac County, Virginia; and, generally, for the lower Delmarva Peninsula.

Goals

The goals of Peninsula General Hospital Medical Center are:

1. To serve as an acute care hospital for its service area and as a referral center for specialized medical care services for the lower Delmarva Peninsula.
2. To encourage and stimulate a high level of medical competence.
3. To provide the personnel and facilities necessary to discharge its Mission.
4. To participate in educating persons in health professions and occupations.

5. To participate in the planning and coordinating of future health care services.
6. To assure the financial resources necessary to discharge its Mission.
7. To offer care in the most efficient, effective and cost conscious manner possible.

Objectives

The objectives of Peninsula General Hospital Medical Center are:

1. To assist in the provision of quality acute inpatient care services which will include medical, surgical, psychiatric, obstetric, and pediatric care.
2. To provide critical care services for patients in keeping with the latest medical techniques.
3. To provide emergency care to patients who fall victim to accident or illness.
4. To assist in provision of specialized medical care services in order to serve as an areawide health referral center.
5. To provide the specialized services and facilities which physicians of the area require to support their own diagnostic and treatment procedures.
6. To encourage and support the Medical Staff in developing excellence in the rendition of medical care in the region, both within PGHMC and throughout the service area.
7. To assist in provision of outpatient diagnosis and care to improve health and to reduce, where possible, the need for inpatient admission.
8. To assist in provision of a family outpatient service which will offer a means for those without a private physician to receive primary care and enter the health care system.
9. To assist in provision of rehabilitation services aimed at restoration of the impaired.
10. To assist in the provision of home care and related services.
11. To participate in the planning of future health care services and programs.
12. To participate in developing the overall coordination, distribution and provision of regional health programs and services.
13. To cooperate in the recruitment of the required professional and technical specialists for the regional service area.
14. To provide the clinical facility for educational programs in conjunction with educational institutions.
15. To provide educational programs for PGHMC employees to the full extent of the Hospital's educational resources.
16. To establish a continuing program to provide funds necessary to attain PGHMC goals and objectives.
17. To provide an employment atmosphere which will enable personnel to function effectively and attain personal satisfaction.

SOURCE: Mission statement of the Peninsula General Hospital Medical Center, Salisbury, Maryland. By permission.

The result is that it is nearly impossible to formulate strategies that will satisfy all the objectives. Management must do its best to choose among alternative strategies. Business organizations also have multiple objectives, but they tend to be dominated by the drive for profit.

Other concerns characteristic of all health care organizations, whether profit-oriented or not, are these:

1. Most health care organizations are engaged in the production of services rather than goods. Services are intangible, inseparable, variable, and perishable. A medical group practice offers an intangible service called health care; its delivery is inseparable from its deliverers (physicians, nurse-practitioners); its quality is variable with respect to who delivers it; and it is perishable in that an empty nurse-practitioner's office or idle physician means a loss of the associated revenue, since a service cannot be stored. Service marketers must keep these characteristics in mind when developing marketing strategies and plans. Moreover, production and consumption of the service occur simultaneously, so the consumer must be integrated into the production process.
2. Health care organizations are usually subject to close public scrutiny because they provide needed public services, are subsidized, are often tax-exempt, and are increasingly regulated. They experience political pressures from various publics and are expected to operate in the public interest. For example, when a neighborhood mental health center published and distributed a glossy multipage brochure describing its services, many citizens publicly objected to a community service organization spending its limited funds for promotional purposes.
3. The majority of dollars expended for health care are reimbursed by third parties. This results in less consumer price sensitivity than is found in most other industries. Without having to bear the responsibility of paying for the health care sought, individuals may be willing to purchase not only higher-priced health care, but more care than they may need.
4. One major effect of federal and particularly local regulatory bodies on health care organizations has been to limit their choice of marketing strategies. Health care organizations cannot necessarily determine their own product line or service policy; in some cases, it is dictated to them. For example, Brigham and Women's Hospital in Boston, as part of the conditions under which it was granted permission to build a new facility, was required to add a 40-bed rehabilitation unit to its acute care hospital. Regulatory agencies may also require health care organizations to serve certain markets, to charge certain prices (particularly with DRGs and in states that have rate-setting commissions), and to provide services in certain locations.
5. Generally, business organizations have a triangular power structure, with ultimate authority for the organization in the hands of one person or group at the top. In most health care organizations, power is split between two groups: the administration and the clinical staff, such as nurses and

physicians. This sometimes causes problems in selecting marketing strategies, because the strategies one group finds optimal might be rejected by the other.[7] Exhibit 1–2 describes such a situation.

EXHIBIT 1–2

The Dual Hierarchy of Power: Obstetrics Example

In the early 1970s, maternity patients began demanding changes in the ways their babies were delivered. Many insisted that their husbands accompany them through labor and delivery, even if the delivery were by caesarean section. Some also wanted the labor and delivery to proceed in one birthing center without having to experience the physical discomfort of being moved from a labor area to delivery room. These patients were willing to "shop around" at various hospitals until they found one that met their wishes.

Hospital administrators, who were responsible for keeping the hospital census up, saw that it was in the hospitals' best interest to offer these alternatives to maternity patients. Otherwise, they risked losing the patients to other hospitals which offered these choices.

However, many physicians would not agree with the administrator's suggestion that the hospital expand its obstetric protocols in accordance with the demands of maternity patients. Obstetricians often felt that nonprofessionals were inappropriately dictating to them how to practice their medical specialty. Moreover, the concepts of birthing centers and husbands in delivery rooms contradicted the training of most obstetricians. Anesthesiologists protested that the presence of a lay person in an operating room during a caesarean birth added to the risk of infection, of surgical error due to distraction, and was unnecessary for either the mother or baby.

The inability of administrators and physicians to agree on this matter led to a stalemate on obstetric service marketing strategy for many hospitals. The dual hierarchy of power necessitated that both parties be in agreement on any strategy before it could be implemented. Shortly thereafter, when some obstetricians began losing their patients to other obstetricians offering the expanded set of delivery alternatives, they experienced pressures for change similar to those felt by the hospitals' administrators. Only then could the hospitals implement their desired obstetric marketing strategy because both groups—administrators and physicians—believed the strategy to be in their best interests.

THE MAJOR MARKETING PROBLEMS HEALTH CARE ORGANIZATIONS FACE

Each health care organization needs to identify the specific marketing problems it faces. The organization might be surprised at the number of problems it discovers. Recently, a large hospital in Chicago undertook a marketing inventory and identified the following problems:

1. Its overall number of patient admissions was falling.
2. Certain medical departments, such as psychiatry and pediatrics, were grossly underutilized.
3. The hospital had a particularly low rate of admissions in the summertime because its "product mix" was stronger in serving illnesses and accidents likely to arise in the winter season.
4. The neighborhood was changing from a predominantly white middle class neighborhood to one of poor blacks and Latinos, whose medical needs and financial resources were radically different.
5. The hospital had a poor image among the newer groups in the community as being elitist and indifferent to their problems.
6. Two newer hospitals in the suburbs had attracted away several physicians and patients who formerly had used this hospital.
7. Physician morale was at a low level as a result of complaints from patients about poor nursing care and poor food, as well as lack of physician amenities such as generous office space and secretarial help.
8. Nurses' morale was also low as a result of low pay, poor schedules of working hours, and sharp words from the physicians. The hospital needed additional nurses but had trouble recruiting them.
9. Patients reported during exit interviews that they thought the nursing care and food were poor and that their rooms were overly hot and depressing.
10. The development office was finding it increasingly hard to attract large contributors to help meet the hospital's expenses.
11. The volunteers' office was finding it increasingly hard to attract additional women volunteers, as more women entered the labor force.

Marketing arises when an organization forms an idea of a desired level of transactions it wants with a target market. At any point in time, the actual demand level may be below, equal to, or above the desired demand level. Marketing management's task is to influence the level, timing, and character of demand in a way that will help the organization achieve its objectives.

Demand may be in any one of eight states; each presents a different marketing challenge.[8]

1. *Negative demand.* A market is said to be in a state of negative demand if a major part of the market dislikes the product and in fact may even pay a price to avoid it. There are people who have a negative demand for vaccinations, dental work, vasectomies, and psychiatric care. The marketing task is to analyze why the market dislikes the product, and whether a marketing program can change the market's beliefs and attitudes through

product redesign, lower prices, modified access, and more positive promotion.

2. *No demand.* Target consumers may be uninterested in or indifferent to the product. Medicaid recipients may be uninterested in a health promotion program aimed at discouraging their "shopping around" from one physician to another. The employees in a company may not have sufficient concern to use a free hypertension testing program set up by their employer. The marketing task is to find ways to connect the benefits of the product with the person's natural needs and interests.
3. *Latent demand.* A substantial number of consumers may share a strong desire for something that cannot be satisfied by any existing product or service. There is enormous latent demand in health care for cures for cancer, aging, heart disease, and any number of debilitating diseases. More likely to be satisfied in the near future is latent demand for nonharmful cigarettes, for 100 percent effective convenient birth control with no side effects, and for total dental cavity prevention. The marketing task is to measure the size of the potential market and to develop effective goods and services that will satisfy the demand.
4. *Falling demand.* Every organization, sooner or later, faces falling demand for one or more of its products. Sanitariums for people with tuberculosis, syphilitic paresis, and other now-treatable diseases have been all but eradicated due to the enormous decline in demand, and the outpatient units of some psychiatric hospitals have experienced a decrease in usage as people increasingly seek mental health services in their own community. The marketer must analyze the causes of market decline and determine whether demand can be restimulated through finding new target markets, changing the product's features, expanding the product line, or developing more effective communications. The marketing task is to reverse the declining demand through creative remarketing of the product. If this cannot be done, then the marketing task becomes one of recognizing the best time to discontinue offering the product so that valuable resources will not be wasted.
5. *Irregular demand.* Many organizations face demand that varies on a seasonal, daily, or even hourly basis, causing problems of idle capacity or overworked capacity. Demand for primary care in emergency rooms is higher on evenings and weekends when physicians' offices and neighborhood health centers are not open. Pediatricians face very busy schedules at the beginning of the school year and in late spring (pre-summer camp physicals), but are often idle in the summer. Hospital operating rooms are heavily booked during the week and underbooked during the weekend. The marketing task is to find ways to alter the time pattern of demand through flexible pricing, promotion, access and other incentives.
6. *Full demand.* Organizations face full demand when they are pleased with the amount of business they have. The marketing task is to maintain demand at its current level in the face of the ever-present possibility of changing market preferences and more vigorous competition. The organi-

zation must keep up its quality and continually measure market satisfaction to make sure that it is doing a good job.

7. *Overfull demand.* Some organizations face a demand level higher than they can or want to handle. Home health organizations frequently have requests for more home health aide services than are available. State Medicaid offices may find more people wishing to avail themselves of Medicaid benefits than the office is budgeted for. Inner-city emergency rooms are often overcrowded, usually with non-emergent patients. The marketing task, called *demarketing,* requires finding ways to discourage demand temporarily or permanently.

   Generally demarketing seeks to reduce overall demand and consists of such steps as raising prices and reducing promotion, access, or service. Selective demarketing consists of trying to reduce the demand coming from those parts of the market which are less profitable or less in need of service. Demarketing in this context does not aim to destroy demand, but only to reduce its level.[9]

8. *Unwholesome demand.* Products considered unwholesome will attract organized efforts to discourage their consumption. Demarketing campaigns in this context, sometimes called *unselling campaigns,* have been conducted against cigarettes, alcohol, hard drugs, large families, and abortion. The marketing task is to get people who like or wish to use something to give it up. Antiproduct marketers use the same tools as demarketers, although the former are also more likely to use emotional communication and reduced availability to discourage consumption.

HOW HEALTH CARE ORGANIZATIONS USE MARKETING TODAY

Health care organizations vary greatly in their awareness and use of modern marketing ideas. Some organizations, primarily those that provide diagnostic and treatment services directly to patients (hospitals, physicians' private practices, most mental health and social service agencies, home health agencies) are applying marketing ideas actively. Others, such as government agencies and offices (regulatory agencies, state Medicaid offices, federally funded health research groups), have shown little awareness or interest in marketing. Whether a particular organization or an institutional sector adopts marketing depends on the depth of its marketing problems, management and staff attitudes toward marketing, and other factors. Similar organizations may exhibit responses to marketing that range from open hostility or indifference to great enthusiasm.

A few years ago, health professionals scorned the idea of marketing, imagining that it would lead to ads such as "This week's special for cardiac patients—fluoroscopy and cardiac catheterization—only $1,295." Hospital administrators argued that patients did not choose hospitals, their doctors did. So marketing, to be effective, would have to be directed at physicians. Some hospitals today still refuse to consider marketing and, in the words of one administrator, "would rather use prayer." There has been much contention about the value of marketing, some of which has been publicly aired in media like the *Wall Street Journal* (see Exhibit 1–3.)

EXHIBIT 1–3

Hospitals Turning to Bold Marketing to Lure Patients and Stay in Business

In Glenview, Ill., Glenbrook Hospital runs an $18,000 newspaper advertising campaign, its first ever. One full-page ad boasts that Glenbrook's emergency room has "a superb staff and the very latest equipment." The result: within a month, emergency-room visits shoot up one-third.

In Dallas, Baylor University Medical Center constructs a $12.5 million professional building. The adjacent facility offers doctors low-cost rental space, a fully equipped exercise club, a post office, a dry cleaner, three restaurants and a hotel. The result: within four years, the hospital's medical staff expands to 800 from 700, and 230 physician tenants in the office building account for more than half of the medical center's patients.

These efforts typify a bold, new marketing thrust by U.S. hospitals. Under tremendous competitive pressure to attract patients, hospitals are turning to a host of promotional techniques, ranging from low-key, "image" advertising to high pressure hustling. The latter includes discounts and drawings for free cruises for patients and leased Mercedes for physicians. Observes Philip Kotler, marketing professor at Northwestern University's Graduate School of Management: Hospital marketing "is one of the hottest topics in the health-care world."

NEW TREND

Hospitals used to look askance at the idea of advertising and marketing, but they can no longer afford to. Staying in business has become top priority.

The federal government estimated the U.S. has 130,000 excess hospital beds costing $2 billion a year because of overbuilding, shorter hospital stays, more outpatient surgery and the low birth rate. "As hospitals get fewer patients," says Prof. Kotler, "they have to make sure they're doing the right job—that their doctors are happy and their patients are happy."

There's also growing public clamor to check runaway health costs by closing unneeded hospitals and restricting expansion. Recognizing that it's too expensive to continue to be all things to all people, many hospitals see marketing strategies as the key to their economic survival. One hospital marketing director says: "We're going to push cancer treatment like crazy, like it hasn't been pushed before."

MARKET RESEARCH

In marketing new or existing services, hospitals are going to great lengths to find out what patients want and how they view the institution.

A $6,000 marketing survey last year uncovered some public-image problems for Orlando Regional Medical Center in Orlando, Fla. Whitecollar residents "thought this (center) was a poor people's county hospital, when it's actually the largest private, nonprofit hospital in all of Florida," recalls James Davis, Orlando's marketing director.

To counter the impression and attract these affluent, potential patients, the Orlando center is launching a $40,000 physicial-fitness program this fall. It's building an outdoor running track and installing lockers, showers and an exercise room in a renovated building. Participants will receive a complete physical, professional monitoring of their progress and diet and exercise classes. And Mr. Davis says television commercials for the program will stress that "we aren't a county hospital."

WEEKEND ADMISSIONS

Sunrise Hospital in Las Vegas changed admitting practices by physicians by luring patients directly. In 1976, the Humana Corp. unit faced a low occupancy rate on weekends, caused by doctors' reluctance to work then. So patients who entered Sunrise on weekends received a 5¼% discount and later, a chance for a $4,000 cruise anywhere. The 68 weekly drawings alone cost the hospital about $280,000. But the 50% increase in weekend admissions boosted net income $600,000.

While appealing directly to the public is important, most hospital marketers acknowledge that physicians are still their main source of patients. Hospitals are using market research to pinpoint medical staffers who admit the largest number of patients. They are also devising an array of merchandising tools, occasionally including some questionable ones, to retain doctors and recruit new ones.

In Southern California, a health planner charges that some "overbedded" hospitals are taking extreme measures to recruit doctors. They're offering leased luxury cars, paid vacations in the Bahamas, free office space and even cash bounties for maintaining a high volume of admissions. "We have indications that up to 16 of the 39 hospitals in Orange County may be involved" in these questionable marketing practices, contends Stanley Maddock, executive director of the Orange County Health Planning Council.

At the moment, however, most hospitals market to physicians in a much more low-key fashion.

St. Luke's Hospital in Phoenix ranked fifth among the six Arizona hospitals performing open-heart surgery in 1974. Currently, it ranks first in volume—the result of intense marketing to surgeons. Among other things, the medical center built another operating room and an additional heart-catherization laboratory, used for diagnostic procedures. "We put money into it and built up a heck of an open-heart program," recalls Orlando's Mr. Davis, formerly the marketing director at St. Luke's.

Marketing advocates say that when aggressive marketers such as St. Luke's take business from others, rival institutions will be forced to find different, medically necessary services in which to specialize. Hospitals that don't eventually will go out of business. "Experts are predicting that between 1,000 and 1,500 hospitals (of the 7,000 in the U.S.) will close in the next five years," says Prof. Kotler. One reason they'll fold, he adds, is that instead of marketing, these hospitals "do nothing but pray."

Letter to the Editor

Your Sept. 11 article regarding "bold" marketing approaches used by hospitals to increase their utilization reflects the sickness of our health care delivery systems. As an employer who provides excellent and competitive health care benefits to thousands of employees, we are studying and implementing programs to contain health costs. The practices you describe can only add to higher health care costs without any beneficial result to the sick. We are increasingly concerned with abuses such as unnecessary surgery, overly long hospital stays, sloppy billing and overly high charges.

The description of methods used to lure patients to hospitals on weekends so they can spend unnecessary days filling beds is disheartening. Not only are physicians reluctant to work on weekends, as the article states, but hospitals are not staffed to provide more than basic patient support and emergency services. Weekend admissions often benefit no one but the hospital. Moreover, the practice of pursuing "heavy admitters" by offering paid vacations, free office space and cash bonuses is reprehensible.

Your article closes with a quote from Prof. Kotler that those hospitals that do not market "do nothing but pray." Let all of us who are interested in providing good health care at realistic cost levels pray for those hospitals that only pray and, presumably do not resort to the practices described. Let us also pray for a return to common sense in the health care industry. And with our prayers, let us aggressively work to eliminate the shameful practices described in the article.

Sherman D. Rosen
Corporate Director
Compensation and Benefits
Hart Schaffner & Marx
Chicago, Ill.

SOURCE: Joann S. Lublin, *The Wall Street Journal,* September 11, 1979, p. 34. Reprinted by permission of *The Wall Street Journal,* Response to September 11, 1979, article in "Letters to the Editor," *The Wall Street Journal,* Monday, October 1, 1979, p. 31.

Nevertheless, many hospitals have taken their first tentative steps toward marketing. Some have embraced it intelligently, with great understanding. A few have rushed in with more enthusiasm than understanding, believing it to consist of clever promotional gimmicks. For example:

> Sunrise Hospital in Las Vegas ran a large advertisement featuring the picture of a ship with the caption, "Introducing the Sunrise Cruise, Win a Once-in-a-Lifetime Cruise Simply by Entering Sunrise Hospital on Any Friday or Saturday: Recuperative Mediterranean Cruise for Two."
>
> St. Luke's Hospital in Phoenix introduced nightly bingo games for all patients (except cardiac cases) producing immense patient interest as well as a net annual profit of $60,000.
>
> A Philadelphia hospital, in competing for maternity patients, let the public know that the parents of a newborn child would enjoy a candlelight dinner with steak and champagne on the eve before the mother and child's departure from the hospital.
>
> A number of hospitals, in their competition to attract and retain physicians, have added "ego services," such as saunas, chauffeurs, and even private tennis courts.

Fortunately, hospitals are now beginning to apply marketing to a broader set of problems. Where should the hospital locate a medical office building or free-standing ambulatory care unit? How can the hospital estimate whether a service will draw enough patients? What strategy should the organization adopt to attract certain categories of patients? How can the hospital attract more consumers to preventive care services, such as annual medical checkups and cancer screening tests? How can hospitals successfully compete against nursing registries in the recruitment of nurses who are in short supply? What marketing programs can build goodwill or attract more contributions?

Clearly, the interest in hospital marketing is growing. An increasing number of hospital administrators are now attending marketing seminars to learn more about marketing research, competitive analysis, promotion and advertising, pricing, and new service development. Although job titles may be misleading, a study by the American Hospital Association indicates that over half of its hospitals have a director or vice-president of marketing, or an existing manager who has responsibility for marketing. Other hospitals have assigned marketing responsibility to a board of directors marketing committee. And some hospitals have budgeted significant funds to be used for the hiring of marketing consultants and the implementation of marketing activities.

MAJOR CRITICISMS AND BENEFITS OF MARKETING

Marketing has always had negative connotations: Plato, Aristotle, Thomas Aquinas, and other early philosophers thought of merchants as unproductive and acquisitive. In modern times, marketers have been accused of getting people to buy what they do not want or need. Customers are seen as victims of high-pressure and sometimes deceptive selling.[10]

Until recently, most professions banned their licensed members from engaging in any explicit marketing activities in pursuit of clients. Codes of professional ethics proscribed direct client solicitation, advertising, and price competition. In the late 1970s, however, the Supreme Court held that these bans in codes of professional ethics had the effect of reducing competition through depriving organizations of the right to inform potential clients about their services and depriving potential clients of useful information about the organizations. As a result, advertising and certain other marketing practices have now been allowed in several professions. Medically related professions such as optometry and dentistry have in some cases aggressively adopted marketing and advertising policies.

But the issue is not yet settled. The American Medical Association, following litigation with the Federal Trade Commission regarding the AMA's ban against solicitation of patients by physicians and by organizations employing or utilizing physicians, still maintains a questioning stance regarding marketing. Health care organizations employing other medical professionals as well, such as nurses, psychologists, social workers, and various types of therapists, are uncertain what constitutes appropriate marketing behavior in light of changing professional ethics. Administrators of health care organizations feel that they must proceed cautiously with marketing activities lest their public or professional staff challenge them.

Marketing Wastes Money

A frequent criticism of health care marketing activity is that it is too expensive or wastes valuable health care dollars. This is particularly true of nonprofit health care organizations. The marketing expenses of charitable organizations are carefully watched to guarantee that they do not get out of line. One article weighing the criticisms against health care marketing reported that "people think it's pretty awful to spend hospital money on advertising" and "spending money on ads makes some people wonder about hospital management concerns."[11]

Health care organizations, of course, should not add costs that do not produce an adequate return. The marketing benefits organizations are seeking to achieve should be measured against their cost. At this stage, health care organizations are far more prone to underspend on marketing. For example, airlines spend roughly 14 percent of their revenues on promotion (which does not include other marketing functions such as market research and general marketing management); health care organizations do not allocate even one-tenth of that amount,[12] although this is changing rapidly.

Marketing Is Intrusive

A second objection to marketing is that it often intrudes itself uninvited into people's lives. It does so in at least two different ways: through market research and through promotion. Market research in any consumer industry is invasive; market researchers may enter people's homes to ask about likes and dislikes, beliefs and attitudes, income and other personal characteristics. Moreover, in health care, the research is more likely to cover sensitive areas individuals would prefer not to reveal to strangers.

The outcome of market research should be favorable to the market. Marketing research is carried out primarily to learn the needs and wants of people so that the organization can deliver greater satisfaction to its target publics. Yet health care organizations should be sensitive to the public's desire for privacy and confidentiality.

One neighborhood health center engaging in market research asked questions relating to contraceptive use, history of aborted pregnancies, possible drinking problems, and use of "soft" drugs such as Valium. There is widespread concern among the public that this information might find its way into the wrong hands.

A second area in which marketing is intrusive is promotion. Complaints about the public's inability to escape the constant barrage of promotional hype have been around for over a decade. Usually, public ire has been directed at the sheer volume of promotion produced every day. One physician, for example, reported receiving 502.75 pounds of unsolicited mail in one year.[13] But certain promotional efforts have received particular criticism due to their subject and objectionable approach. One advertisement, which was broadcast nationally during the network news shows around dinnertime, said: "It's time we discussed seriously something which concerns us all: diarrhea." The content of the advertisement plus the poor choice of timing caused such an uproar that it was quickly removed from the airwaves.

Health care organizations seeking to promote their services might run into the same objections. Advertisements for colitis treatments, cancer care, and gynecological services, while providing useful information, may be offensive. Because health care deals with such personal matters, health care organizations must be particularly careful to weigh the public's sensitivity against the organizations' need to inform their markets.

Marketing Is Manipulative

A third criticism is that organizations will use marketing to manipulate the target market. Many smokers resent the antismoking ads put out by the American Cancer Society as trying to manipulate them through fear appeals. They also reject as manipulative the information now being promoted by the American Lung Association recommending that nonsmokers protect their lungs by not allowing smoking in their personal breathing space.

Administrators should be sensitive to the possible charge of manipulation when they implement a marketing program. In the majority of cases, the health care organization is seeking some public good for which there is widespread consensus. In other cases, the charge of manipulation may be justified and such efforts, unless they are checked, will bring a "black eye" to the organization and to marketing.

Marketing Will Lower the Quality of Health Care

A common concern of many professionals is that marketing will lower the quality of health care. A former president of the American College of Surgeons offered the following statement to a conference addressing the issues of health care marketing and advertising:

> The state and national medical organizations should continue their vigilance in searching out misleading advertising which would exploit patients and lower the quality of medical care. . . . The Federal Trade Commission assumes quality of medical care. . . . The Supreme Court of the United States being more professionally oriented is obviously concerned about the impact of advertising on the quality of medical and other professional services. . . . To be sure, the public needs information concerning physicians, their work and their fees, at the same time the public needs protection from the unscrupulous and the incompetent practitioner anxious to prey on the uninformed.[14]

The assumptions made by those who fear that marketing will lower health care quality are that (1) many health care providers who advertise will do so deceptively, and (2) those providers who advertise are likely to be incompetent medically. While there is no evidence to support either of these assumptions, the beliefs are widely held among professionals. A former official of the American Medical Association stated: "A distinction was made between competent, qualified, conscientious physicians and the medicine show pitchmen, itinerant snake oil peddlers, and advertising quacks. Good doctors didn't solicit patients or participate in any of these kinds of hucksterism."[15]

The real issue underlying the stated concern about poor-quality health care is the fact that poor quality health care is being delivered, whether or not marketing is involved. Second, if medical professionals promote their services, as in other industries, there will be a need to monitor the promotion to ensure truthful and fair representation of services offered.

Marketing Will Cause Health Care Institutions to Compete

Marketing was not an accepted concept in health care management until the early 1980s. Another unacceptable term was "competition." A group of hospital administrators attending a seminar on health care marketing in the mid-1970s objected to the possibility that they might compete with each other, saying: "Hospitals don't compete. There is a sisterhood of hospitals. Hospitals help each other."

Of course, where it is easy to do so, health care organizations do help each other. One nursing home, filled to capacity, may refer an attractive (privately insured) patient to another nursing home that needs more patients. Health care organizations work together in the form of state and regional associations, voluntary associations, shared services, and so on. But health care organizations also compete. For example, two rehabilitation centers with underutilized spinal cord injury units each may send a liaison nurse to an acute care hospital's discharge planner in an attempt to persuade the discharge planner to refer the hospital's spinal cord injury patients to that particular rehabilitation center. The personnel manager of a large local company may be approached by three mental health centers, all of which are competing to obtain a contract to provide an employee assistance program to the company.

Competition occurs when two or more organizations seek to involve the same individual or group in a particular exchange process. Because the supply of certain health care services has exceeded the demand for them, health care organizations seeking full utilization of these services necessarily find themselves in competition. That competition is not necessarily bad. It may result in the elimination of unneeded services, in greater efficiency, and in greater responsiveness to the market's demands. But health care managers are wrestling with some ethical considerations:

> Is it acceptable for a health institution to expend community resources to increase its power, dominance or influence by increasing the inpatient census when that may cause another institution to decline? Many influential people in the field feel quite strongly that hospitals should not use precious resources to devour each other. They feel that there is little room for divisive competitive promotion today.[16]

The fact is that, with or without conscious marketing efforts, most health care providers will compete because of an excess in the supply of many services. The purposeful use of marketing techniques will allow more effective and efficient competitive strategies to be developed. It should also cause health care organizations to recognize when they cannot, under any circumstances, compete effectively, thus preventing them from wasting precious resources on services destined to fail.

Marketing Will Create Unnecessary Demand for Health Care

Unnecessary usage of health care services already exists. This fact is attested to by the existence of PSROs, Utilization Review, third-party-sponsored second opinion programs for surgical procedures, new reimbursement regulations in a few states featuring total revenue ceilings, and examinations of average lengths of stay. It is feared that the promotional techniques of marketing will create even further unnecessary demand.

There is reason to believe that effective marketing may create more demand. What is unclear is whether this demand is unnecessary. If people respond to a marketing campaign to have their blood pressure checked, the additional demand created would be viewed positively. On the other hand, if a plastic surgeon gained more patients for cosmetic surgery as a result of advertising, the evaluation of this additional demand might be more mixed. Some health professionals would view this as unnecessary surgery, raising health care expenditures and exposing the patient to potential iatrogenic illness.

The possibility has also been raised that health care organizations will seek to create unnessary demand in order to deal with competitive pressures. Exhibit 1–4 is an example of a comic public discussion of the creation of unnecessary demand. However, two protections could exist against the creation of additional unnecessary demand. One is requiring the patient to bear greater responsibility for payment of health services. Demand in the for-profit sector is regulated by price. The same mechanism could work in the health care sector for other than catastrophic illness. Second, mechanisms such as second opinion and inpatient admission review programs and revenue caps already exist for addressing unnecessary demand.

EXHIBIT 1–4

How to Solve the Hospital Problem

WASHINGTON—The real problem of hospital prices, the experts tell us, is not the patients but the empty beds. A hospital can keep down costs if it is absolutely full. But it starts to lose money if it doesn't have enough sick people to care for.

A recent news item said that Sunrise Hospital and Medical Center in Las Vegas is trying to solve the problem through a lottery. Sunrise seemed to be doing good business during the week, but it was suffering from a lack of patients on weekends. So the Las Vegas hospital came up with a unique plan.

If you check in on Friday or Saturday your name goes in a hat for a lottery. Every Monday morning, a certified public accountant draws a name from the hat and the winner is given the choice of five different Mediterranean cruises worth $4000. The winner has a year to claim the prize and if for some reason he or she never leaves the hospital, the prize goes to the patient's estate. I did not make this up.

The director of the hospital said the lottery has been an overwhelming success and weekend admissions are up by 40 percent.

While this is an innovative idea there are others that we can think of which would cut hospital costs and fill the empty rooms that are costing all of us so much money. One idea would be for a hospital to hook up a hotline with all the doctors accredited to the hospital. Each doctor would have a quota to fill as to how many patients he must supply to the hospital. As soon as a bed became empty the doctor would be notified that a hospital patient was needed and he would be obligated to find someone for the bed whether he needed it or not.

Suppose, for example, a patient came in with an ingrown toenail. As the doctor was treating it the hotline would ring and the administrator on the other end would say, "We need an in-patient for Room 211."

"Is it a private or semiprivate room?" the doctor would ask.

"Semiprivate, but Dr. Combs is sending over a patient with a tennis elbow so we just need one person."

"I've got a live one in my office now I can give you."

"Hurry," the administrator says, "We're losing money every minute."

The doctor goes back to the patient. "I don't know how to tell you this, but I don't like the look of this ingrown toenail. I could take it out, of course, but you might lose your toe."

"What's the alternative?"

"I'd like to put you in Our Lady of Deficits Hospital for observation. I think that with adequate hospital care and a nurse around the clock, we could observe which direction the nail is growing and possibly save the foot."

"How long will I be in the hospital?" the patient asks.

"I'll take him for a week," the administrator says. "Dr. Friedkin owes us three patients and he's promised us a pregnancy."

The doctor goes back to the patient.

"I'd like to keep you in the hospital for a week to avoid liver damage."

Of course, the quota system is not the only alternative to keeping hospitals full. Taking a leaf from Holiday Inns, the hospital could offer rooms for patients and put in cots for their children at no extra charge.

They could also offer "second honeymoon weekends" for couples wanting to get away for a few days with free X-rays and Epsom salt baths thrown in.

The main reason there are so many empty hospital beds has not been mentioned by anybody; and that is the poor quality of the food. After a meal or two in an average hospital most patients want to get dressed and leave.

There is a solution for this. Most independent surveys show there is 50 percent more surgery done in this country than is necessary—mainly because we have 50 percent more surgeons.

To cut down on surgery and also improve the quality of hospital food, HEW should provide retraining programs for surgeons and teach them how to cook.

Hopefully these surgeon-chefs, once they learned their trade, could make hospital cuisine the best in the land, and patients would extend their stays in their rooms as long as their Blue Cross would let them.

SOURCE: Art Buchwald, "How to Solve the Hospital Problem," *The Boston Globe,* May 3, 1977, p. 24. Reprinted courtesy of *The Boston Globe.*

Finally, marketers recognize that consumers cannot be sold something they do not need or want. Needed health services are not at issue; the question of unnecessary demand really revolves around whether a health care service that a patient wants but does not need, as determined by some clinically objective measure, is unnecessary.

Major Benefits

Organizations in a free society depend upon voluntary exchanges to accomplish their objectives. Resources must be attracted, employees motivated, patients and clients found. Proper incentives are a key step in stimulating these exchanges. Marketing is the applied science most concerned with managing exchanges effectively and efficiently. Marketing is designed to produce three principal benefits for the organization and its publics:

1. *Improved satisfaction of the target market.* The majority of health care organizations operate in a highly competitive environment. Yet they have historically lacked the marketing skills to develop satisfactory services for their patients or other markets. The result can be bad word-of-mouth and low repeat usage which ultimately hurts these organizations. Certain health care organizations, particularly those which are rural, isolated in deprived urban centers or those which are focused primarily on the social services, may operate in a less competitive environment or in an environment where the demand for the service exceeds the supply. These organizations may lack the motivation to satisfy their markets and may deliver unsatisfactory services which consumers may accept if they believe there

are no alternatives. Marketing, in stressing the importance of measuring and satisfying consumer needs and wants, tends to produce an improved level of client service and satisfaction.

2. *Improved attraction of marketing resources.* Health care organizations, in striving to satisfy a set of consumers or markets, must attract various resources, including physicians, nurses, other employees, volunteers, organizational alliances, funds, and public support. Marketing provides a disciplined approach to improving the attraction of these needed resources.
3. *Improved efficiency in marketing activities.* Marketing places great emphasis on the rational management and coordination of product development, pricing, communication, and distribution. Many health care organizations make these decisions with insufficient knowledge, resulting in more cost for a given impact or less impact for a given cost. Because the funds of health care organizations are often inadequate and undependable, the administrator must achieve the maximum efficiency and effectiveness in marketing activities.

Besides the broad benefits of greater satisfaction and increased efficiency, various benefits can be identified for specific institutions planning to adopt a marketing orientation. Recently, one of the authors addressed a conference of hospital administrators and claimed that hospital marketing would bring a revolution in hospital management in the next ten years. Specifically:

1. Hospitals will be much more sensitive and knowledgeable about community health needs.
2. Hospitals will abandon the attempt to be all things to all people and will seek differentiated niches in the market. Each hospital serving a community will focus on providing those services which are most needed and/or which are competitively viable.
3. Hospitals will be quicker to drop services and programs in which they have no competitive advantage or distinctiveness.
4. Hospitals will be more capable in developing and launching successful new services.
5. Hospitals will create more effective systems of distributing and delivering their services.
6. Hospitals will develop more creative pricing approaches.
7. Hospitals will create more patient, doctor, nurse and employee satisfaction.

THE ESSENCE OF A MARKETING ORIENTATION

Many people think that organizations which have added a marketing function necessarily have become market-oriented. This could not be further from the truth. For example, a large nursing home chain created and filled a marketing director position. It hired market research consultants and an advertising agency and ultimately spent a substantial sum of money on all these activities. Yet it still did not have a marketing orientation. Why? The best way to understand a marketing orientation is to contrast it to three other orientations organizations have, described below.

Production Orientation

Some health-care-related organizations focus on running a smooth production process, even if human needs must be bent to meet the requirements of that process. Third-party health insurance agencies and the billing offices of many health care providers often act this way, seemingly unaware that they are not processing just bills, but also patients. Patients calling to question a bill or medical procedure for which the insurance company will not pay often find themselves identified by and treated as a number rather than by name. Curt answers to complex billing questions and the lack of concern shown by the organization's employees for patients concerned about having to pay substantial sums out of pocket suggest that these employees subjugate the patient's interests to the interests and efficiency of the "system." Some physician's offices also have a production orientation. Large numbers of patients may wait long periods in physicians' waiting rooms so that physicians can maximize their efficiency in seeing patients.

A production orientation holds that the major task of an organization is to pursue efficiency in production and distribution.

Product Orientation

Many organizations are in love with their product; they believe strongly in its value, even if their publics are having second thoughts. They would strongly resist modifying it, even if this would increase its market appeal. The product orientation is a paternalistic approach to marketing. It says, "We know better than you what is good for you." The health care field is especially prone to this orientation. Health care providers are often so enamored with the quality, the sophistication, and the technology of the medical care they deliver that they do not recognize the consumer dissatisfaction and discomfort caused by medical care delivery. Physicians who insist on using all medical means available, including the newest technologies, to prolong the agonies of a terminally ill cancer patient display this orientation.

A product orientation holds that the major task of an organization is to deliver products it thinks would be good for the market.

Sales Orientation

Some organizations believe they can substantially increase the size of their market by increasing their selling effort. Rather than change their products to make them more attractive, these organizations will increase their budget for advertising, outreach, personal selling, and other forms of sales promotion. A home health agency may react to a decline in number of patients by sending liaison nurses out to visit its referring hospitals more frequently, by increasing its public relations budget, and by developing a new brochure for the agency. These sales-oriented steps might work to produce more patients in the short run, but their use in no way implies that the agency has moved into a marketing orientation that would generate more patients in the long run. A sales orientation is defined as follows:

> **A sales orientation** holds that the main task of the organization is to stimulate the interest of potential consumers in the organization's existing products and services.

Marketing Orientation

Some organizations have discovered the value of focusing their attention not on production, products, or sales, but on meeting their customers' changing needs and wants. They recognize that production, products, and sales are all means of producing satisfaction in target markets. Without satisfied markets, these organizations would soon find themselves "market-less."

"Market-centeredness" is attained through hard work. The organization must systematically study customer needs, wants, perceptions, preferences, and satisfaction, using surveys, focus groups, and other means. The organization must constantly act on this information to improve its products to better meet its customer's needs. Employees must be selected and trained to feel that they are working for the customer (rather than the boss or the system). A customer orientation will express itself in the friendliness with which the organization's telephone operators answer the phone and the helpfulness of various employees in solving customer problems. The employees in a marketing-oriented organization will work as a team to meet the needs of the specific target markets that are to be served.

Of course, different organizations within the same industry will vary in the degree to which they truly work for the customer. Consider a service industry such as the airlines. A British guidebook publisher decided to rate the quality of fourteen different airlines as an aid to travelers.[17] The staff boarded 43 transatlantic flights armed with tape-recorders and evaluated each trip on such factors as check-in service, baggage delivery, food, cleanliness, friendliness, and response to special stress situations such as asking for aspirin, and so on. The scores were combined in a weighted index with a maximum score of 100. The results showed great variation, with the best topping the list at 77 and the worst airline scoring only 36.

We define a marketing orientation as follows:

> **A marketing orientation** holds that the main task of the organization is to determine the needs and wants of target markets and to satisfy them through the design, communication, pricing, and delivery of appropriate and competitively viable products and services.

Societal Marketing Orientation

Health care organizations' primary objectives usually are humanitarian, philosophical, or regulatory, and based on some perceived human need. This poses a problem for these organizations as they become marketing-oriented and commit themselves to satisfying the market's needs and wants. The problem is that what the market needs may not be what the market wants. What a patient "needs" from a hospital is reasonable, good-quality medical care. Yet market research over the past few years has clearly shown that hospitalized patients "want" a variety of amenities not associated with their "need" for reasonable, good-quality medical care. They want smiling, empathetic nurses and staff, a wide selection of foods for their meals, color television sets (preferably one for each patient), and quick responses to their calls.

A marketing-oriented health care organization should not focus on meeting wants at the expense of addressing the market's needs as identified by their objectives or mission statements. However, an organization may meet needs as well as a range of wants simultaneously. Airlines, for example, meet not only our need for safe transportation, but also our wants for check-in service, on-flight service, food, drink, and cleanliness. It is almost always possible for health care organizations to meet a variety of wants as well as needs.

But in some situations, the market may have wants that are not proper to satisfy, either because they go against society's interests (such as driving at excessive speeds) or against the consumer's long-run interests (such as cigarette smoking). Customers may also have needs they do not recognize (such as a need for a balanced diet) that a health care organization may want to press on the consumer for the consumer's good, even though this may be costly to do. A growing number of marketers see it as their responsibility to take consumer needs, consumer wants, and society's interests into account in their marketing decision making. This orientation can be called a societal marketing orientation:

A societal marketing orientation holds that the main task of the organization is to determine the needs, wants, and interests of target markets and to adapt the organization to delivering satisfactions that preserve and enhance the consumer's and society's well-being.

Advantages of a Marketing Orientation

A marketing orientation can contribute greatly to an organization's effectiveness. That effectiveness is reflected in the degree to which an organization exhibits the five major attributes of a marketing orientation:

1. Customer philosophy. Does management acknowledge the primacy of the marketplace and of customer needs and wants in shaping the organization's plans and operations?
2. Integrated marketing organization. Is the organization staffed to carry out marketing analysis, planning, implementation and control?
3. Adequate marketing information. Does management receive the kind and quality of information needed to conduct effective marketing?
4. Strategic orientation. Does management generate innovative strategies and plans for achieving its long-run objectives?
5. Operational efficiency. Are marketing activities selected and handled in a cost-effective manner?

Each of these attributes can be measured. Exhibit 1–5 presents a marketing effectiveness rating instrument based on the five attributes. This instrument, specific to hospitals but modifiable to fit other types of health care providers, is completed by one or more managers. The instrument has been tested in a number of organizations, and very few managers score their organization in the superior range of 26 to 30 points. Most health care organizations score in the poor to fair range, indicating much room for marketing improvement. The breakdown of the total score into the five attribute scores indicates which attributes of effective marketing action need the most attention.[18]

EXHIBIT 1–5

Hospital Marketing Effectiveness Rating Instrument

Circle the one most appropriate answer for each question below.

CUSTOMER PHILOSOPHY

1. How does the organization view its markets?
   ____A. Hospital management thinks in terms of serving patient needs based on the facilities and staff physicians currently available.

____B. Management attempts to offer a broad range of hospital services, performing all of them well.

____C. Management thinks in terms of serving the needs of well-defined patient and physician segments that offer to the hospital the best prospect for long-term growth and financial return.

2. What is the status of the hospital's publicity, promotion, and community education programs?

____A. There is limited activity in this area.

____B. The hospital has a number of programs in this area, but coordination among them is limited.

____C. The hospital has a well-coordinated program of information and community outreach efforts, all under the guidance of one staff member.

3. How does the hospital attract and retain the medical staff of physicians?

____A. Primary responsibility for selection and attraction of staff resides with current staff physicians.

____B. The hospital relies essentially on specific incentives such as high salaries or special equipment to attract new staff.

____C. As part of the planning and coordination process, the hospital has developed a comprehensive system to determine and influence the factors affecting the physician affiliation decision.

INTEGRATED MARKETING ORGANIZATION

4. Is there a vice-president or director of marketing responsible for planning, executing and coordinating the marketing functions?

____A. No such individual exists.

____B. Yes, but there is little integration of this individual within the planning/decision-making process. This individual primarily provides marketing services.

____C. Yes, and the individual participates in hospital policy making as well as providing marketing services.

5. To what extent are marketing-oriented functions (e.g., planning, public relations, marketing research, advertising, promotion and fundraising) coordinated in the hospital?

____A. Not very well. There is sometimes unproductive conflict among these functions.

____B. Somewhat. There is some formal integration, but less than satisfactory coordination and control.

____C. Very well. There is effective coordination and control of these functions.

6. Is there a formal systematic procedure for evaluating potential new services and technologies?

____A. There is no formal procedure.

____B. A procedure exists, but it does not include heavy inputs from marketing.

____C. The procedure is well-developed, and includes heavy inputs from marketing.

MARKETING INFORMATION SYSTEM

7. Does the hospital conduct patient exit interviews and other surveys of patient satisfaction and suggestions?
   ____A. Rarely or never.
   ____B. Occasionally, but not on a formal basis.
   ____C. Yes, systematically, on a formal basis.
8. Does the hospital collect information regarding trends in demand for various types of treatments and the availability in the market of competitive services?
   ____A. Rarely or never.
   ____B. Occasionally.
   ____C. Yes, on a systematic, continuous basis.
9. Does the hospital have an information system containing relevant and up-to-date marketing data?
   ____A. Such information is limited, and is not maintained on an ongoing basis.
   ____B. Adequate records are maintained and updated on a routine basis, essentially in hardcopy form.
   ____C. An extensive, computer based information system is provided for systematic storage, maintenance, update and analysis of marketing data.

STRATEGIC ORIENTATION

10. Does the hospital regularly monitor and evaluate patient services in order to identify potential new services to offer and current services to curtail or drop?
    ____A. The hospital does not evaluate the marketing viability of its various services.
    ____B. The hospital occasionally evaluates its current services and studies potential new services.
    ____C. The hospital regularly evaluates its current services and systematically studies potential new services.
11. Does the hospital carry out strategic market planning as well as annual marketing planning?
    ____A. Strategic market planning is only initiated under special circumstances such as when considering facility expansion or debt financing.
    ____B. Strategic market planning is carried out regularly but is not done very well.
    ____C. Strategic market planning is carried out regularly and is done very well.
12. Does the hospital prepare contingency plans?
    ____A. No.
    ____B. Contingency plans are occasionally developed to meet a major threat.
    ____C. Contingency plans are routinely developed as part of the normal planning process.

OPERATIONAL EFFICIENCY

13. Does hospital management know the costs and profitability of its various services?
    ____A. Such information is not available.
    ____B. Limited information is available.
    ____C. Hospital management knows the costs and profitability of its various services.
14. Are marketing resources utilized effectively on a day-to-day basis?
    ____A. Such resources are either not available or are inadequately utilized.
    ____B. The resources are adequate and utilized to a significant extent, but not in an optimal manner.
    ____C. Yes. Such resources are employed adequately and effectively.
15. Does management examine the results of its marketing expenditures to know what it is accomplishing for its money?
    ____A. No.
    ____B. To a limited extent.
    ____C. Yes.

SCORING

Number of A responses	____ × 0 =	
Number of B responses	____ × 1 =	
Number of C responses	____ × 2 =	____
Total score		____

The following scale shows the hospital's level of marketing effectiveness:

0–5 = None	16–20 = Good
6–10 = Poor	21–25 = Very good
11–15 = Fair	26–30 = Superior

SOURCE: This instrument was prepared by Rick Heidtman under the supervision of Professor Philip Kotler, Northwestern University. Used with permission.

Organizations that move toward a marketing orientation take on three characteristics vital to their survival and effectiveness. They become more responsive, adaptive, and entrepreneurial. The next three chapters will define and illustrate these three characteristics of the effective organization.

SUMMARY

Marketing, once disdained by the health care field, is now a topic of great concern for health care management. Hospitals, large and small, urban and rural, specialty and general, are facing marketing problems. So are nursing homes, home health agencies, chronic care facilities, health clinics, medical group practices, HMOs, PPOs, regulatory and planning agencies, health promotion groups, and a wide variety of social service agencies. They must deal with declining or uncontrollable demand, dwindling contributions and reimbursements, and increased regulation. Marketing appears to be the management function that offers these organizations hope. Health care managers are therefore asking many questions about marketing.

Marketing is more than the use of certain tools such as personal selling, advertising, and publicity to attempt to create or maintain demand. Marketing is the skill of knowing how to plan and manage the organization's exchange relations with its various publics. It is the analysis, planning, implementation, and control of carefully formulated programs designed to bring about voluntary exchanges of values with target markets for the purpose of achieving organizational objectives. Marketing involves the organization in studying the target market's needs and wants, designing appropriate products and services, and using effective pricing, communication, and distribution to inform, motivate, and service the market.

Nonprofit health care organizations have distinct marketing concerns: multiple publics, multiple objectives, and the separation of resource attraction from resource allocation. All health care organizations have certain characteristics that call for special attention in applying marketing principles. They produce services rather than goods, and these services are intangible, inseparable, variable, and perishable. Health care organizations are subjected to public scrutiny and must be able to justify their marketing activities. Much health care is covered by third-party reimbursement, which has historically allowed consumers to demand more expensive and greater amounts of health care without having to pay for it, although this is now changing. The regulated nature of the industry limits the health care organization in its choice of marketing strategies, as does the dual hierarchy of power characteristic of most health care organizations.

Marketing's broad objective is to influence the level, timing, and character of demand in a way that helps the organization achieve its objectives. Marketers have to cope with eight possible states of demand: negative demand, no demand, latent demand, falling demand, irregular demand, full demand, overfull demand, and unwholesome demand.

Marketing has its critics as well as defenders. Its critics charge that marketing wastes money, that it is intrusive and manipulative, that it will lower the quality of health care, cause health care institutions to compete with each other, and create unnecessary demand. Its defenders say that marketing increases the satisfaction of the target markets by understanding their needs better, improves the attraction of marketing resources, improves the efficiency of serving markets by developing viable products, and pricing, communicating, and delivering them efficiently.

Marketing is not just a management function: it is a total organization orientation. Organizations may be production-oriented, product-oriented, sales-oriented, marketing-oriented or societal-marketing-oriented. Those that are marketing-oriented have five characteristics: a customer philosophy, an integrated marketing organization, adequate marketing information, a strategic orientation, and operational efficiency. These characteristics create an organization that is highly responsive, adaptive, and entrepreneurial in a rapidly changing environment.

NOTES

1. *The Human-Size Hospital,* 3, (May 1981), p. 1.

2. Peter F. Drucker, *Management: Tasks, Responsibilities, Practices* (New York: Harper & Row, 1973), pp. 64-65.

3. Kenneth Boulding, *A Primer on Social Dynamics* (New York: Free Press, 1970).

4. For a comparison of the managerial and social process definition of marketing, see Daniel J. Sweeney, "Marketing: Management Technology or Social Process?" *Journal of Marketing* (October 1972), pp. 3–10.

5. For an interesting commentary on this, see Eli Ginzberg, "The Monetarization of Medical Care," *New England Journal of Medicine* (May 3, 1984), pp. 1162–1165.

6. See Christopher H. Lovelock and Charles B. Weinberg, *Readings in Public and Nonprofit Marketing* (Palo Alto, CA: Scientific Press, 1978), pp. 416–20.

7. For a more detailed discussion of the dual hierarchy of power, see R. Clarke, "The Dual Hierarchy of Power," paper presented at Marketing for Nonprofit Organizations conference sponsored by the American Marketing Association at the University of South Carolina, Columbia, April 1982.

8. See Philip Kotler, "The Major Tasks of Marketing Management," *Journal of Marketing* (October 1973), pp. 42–49.

9. See Philip Kotler and Sidney J. Levy, "Demarketing, Yes, Demarketing," *Harvard Business Review* (November–December 1971), pp. 74–80.

10. The major critics in this connection are Vance Packard, *The*

Hidden Persuaders (New York: Pocket Books, 1957); and John Kenneth Galbraith, *The Affluent Society* (Boston: Houghton Mifflin, 1958).

11. Jeff DeBray, "Health Services Discover Marketing," *Advertising Age,* November 5, 1979, p. 50. Reprinted with permission from the Nov. 5, 1979, issue of *Advertising Age.* Copyright 1979 by Crain Communications, Inc.

12. Roberta N. Clarke and Linda Shyavitz, "Market Research: When, Why, and How?" *Health Care Management Review* (Winter 1982).

13. "Business Bulletin," *The Wall Street Journal,* May 12, 1983, p. 1.

14. George R. Dunlop, M.D., "The Availability of Health Information," background paper for Boston University Health Policy Institute Conference, November 4–5, 1977.

15. Russell B. Roth, M.D., "Medicine and Madison Avenue," background paper for Boston University Health Policy Institute Conference, November 4–5, 1977.

16. Tim Garton, "Marketing Health Care: Its Untapped Potential." In *Health Care Marketing: Issues and Trends,* Philip D. Cooper, ed. (Germantown, MD: Aspen Systems Corp., 1979), p. 65.

17. "A Guidebook to the Airlines," *Newsweek,* November 26, 1979, p. 88.

18. For further discussion of this instrument, see Philip Kotler, "From Sales Obsession to Marketing Effectiveness," *Harvard Business Review* (November–December 1977), pp. 67–75.

2

THE RESPONSIVE ORGANIZATION— MEETING CONSUMER NEEDS

Join a club that's still in its infancy, but growing fast.

Our own kind of rock group
The Cradle Club at Westminster Community Hospital is open to all expectant parents regardless of where you plan to have your baby.

One of the nicest things
about belonging to the Cradle Club is that you and your husband get to know others who are preparing for a new baby, too. You'll have a chance to meet with other members the day you visit Westminster Community Hospital to meet the staff and see where hundreds of Southern California babies get their start every year. Cradle Club members don't all deliver at Westminster Community Hospital, but they do meet here for classes, tours, coffee and conversation.

Pinning down little details
As a member you'll receive a Cradle Club certificate, be invited to enroll in our classes, tour the hospital's Maternity Wing, plus meet and discuss with other expectant parents the many exciting new experiences coming up. You'll learn everything from preparation for childbirth to the changes a baby will make in your lifestyle.

"Westminster Community Hospital! That's where I got my start!" Here's a brand-new T-shirt that a lot of well-dressed new kids will be wearing this season.

Baby Booty
Cradle Club members receive a plastic identification card that entitles them to receive special considerations that range from surprise gifts to money-saving discounts on items for mother and baby. These little extras come from local businessmen who've volunteered to be Cradle Club Sponsors . . . to help you celebrate the happiness of having a new baby.

Cradle Chit-Chat
You'll have more than your instincts to follow as a member of the Cradle Club. Every month (from the third month on) you'll receive a special Cradle Club Newsletter that zeroes in on those things you should be doing and planning for as your pregnancy progresses. They're filled with timely, expert information on everything from the latest maternity fashions to packing for the hospital, to preparing for your new baby's homecoming.

Education is a must!
Doctors, educators and parents agree that formal preparation for childbirth can make each step meaningful and gratifying. Our free classes on Preparation for Childbirth at Westminster Community Hospital encourage your understanding and participation by giving you knowledge, confidence and accurate expectations.

Membership is free
To join the Cradle Club, just clip out and mail the coupon below as soon as possible.

Sign up now!

Clip this coupon and mail to address below

Mother's Name ____________________

Father's Name ____________________

Mailing Address ____________________

City/State/Zip ____________________

Home Phone __________ Business Phone __________

Physician's Name __________ Due Date __________

Is this your firstborn? ☐ yes ☐ no Will dad be in Delivery Room? ☐ yes ☐ no

Please send me your schedule of evening classes so that I may choose the weekday evenings I wish to attend. I understand that membership in the Cradle Club or attendance at Prepared Childbirth Classes or Caesarean Delivery Classes does not obligate me to deliver at Westminster Community Hospital.

Signature __________ Date __________

Westminster Community Hospital

CRADLE CLUB SM

200 Hospital Circle, Westminster, California 92683, Telephone (714) 893-4541

CRADLE CLUB is a service mark of Humana.

Courtesy of Humana Hospital—Westminster

The Westminster Community Hospital is an example of a highly responsive organization. Traditionally, hospitals limited their offerings to prospective parents to medical services that facilitated labor and delivery plus a two- to five-day inpatient recovery period for mother and infant. However, as prospective parents demanded more services, responsive organizations provided them. Westminster Community Hospital responded by expanding its service line to include free childbirth classes, a place to socialize with other prospective parents, special discounts at relevant area businesses, a special T shirt for babies born at the hospital, and a newsletter providing information needed by expectant parents.

A **responsive organization** is one that makes every effort to sense, serve and satisfy the needs and wants of its clients and publics within the constraints of its budget and good clinical practice.

People who come in contact with responsive organizations report high levels of satisfaction. "The Visiting Nurse Association really took good care of my mother." "The new physicians' group I use makes everything so easy—they took my blood, did an X ray, and filled my prescription all in the same building." "The hospital's classes on emergencies in the home were very useful." These consumers, whether patients, friends, relatives, or healthy users of health services, are the best promotion for an organization. Their goodwill and favorable word-of-mouth reach others' ears, making it easy for the organization to attract and serve more people.

Responsive organizations manage to imbue their employees with a spirit of service to the customer. For example, employees at Disneyland and Disneyworld go out of their way to answer visitors' questions, pick up litter, and smile and be friendly. Disney, Inc., continuously interviews visitors to find out what they thought of the park, and especially of the employees' attitudes. Based on these responses, Disney, Inc., constantly tries to improve its guests' experiences at the park.

Unfortunately, most health care organizations are not highly responsive. One group would like to be more responsive, but lacks the resources or power. The organization's budget may be insufficient to hire, train, and motivate good employees, and to monitor their performance. Or management may believe it lacks the power to require employees to be service-oriented. This may happen when the employees are unionized or under civil service and cannot be disciplined or fired for being insensitive to customers; many city, state, and municipal hospitals must deal with this problem. The Veterans Administration hospitals tried to combat this with a "May I Help You?" campaign. The shortage of nurses throughout the health care sector in the early 1980s had the same effect: An organization may have been so thankful to have a full complement of nurses that it did not require them to be responsive and service-oriented.

A second group of health care organizations is unresponsive simply because they prefer to concentrate on other things. Teaching hospitals have long been accused of being more interested in teaching and medical research than in patient care. State Medicaid offices have been attacked for focusing on enforcing existing rules rather than on assessing whether these rules best serve the interests of Medicaid recipients. Organizations which are mandated to exist, such as Medicaid, and organizations which have historically viewed themselves as being above competition, such as some teaching hospitals, may behave bureaucratically and impersonally toward their clients.

Finally, there are always a few organizations that intentionally act unresponsively to the publics they are supposed to serve. Health service agencies (HSAs) have often been unresponsive to the requests of the hospitals with which they deal. Their mandate requires that they not be a fully responsive organization. Some urban hospitals have a policy of making patients who are using the emergency room for primary care wait three to four hours before being seen in order to discourage future use. They are being purposefully unresponsive.

We are going to assume that most health care organizations want to be more rather than less responsive to patients and publics. The concept of a responsive organization includes the following assumptions:

1. Each organization has a *mission*.
2. To perform its mission, the organization needs to attract resources through *exchange*.
3. The organization will undertake exchanges with a large number of *publics*.
4. The publics will respond to the organization in terms of their *image* of the organization.
5. The organization can take concrete steps to improve the *satisfaction* it creates in its exchanges with its various publics.

Each of these concepts serves as an important tool for understanding and improving organizational responsiveness.

MISSION

Every organization, whether proprietary or nonprofit, starts with a mission.

> An **organization** can be defined as a human collective that is structured to perform a specific mission through the use of largely rational means.

The mission is usually clear at the beginning. However, as the market and the environment change, the mission usually changes too. Most hospitals start with a mission to provide inpatient services to the very ill. Some have not expanded their missions to include health promotion to the well, primary care services to the ambulatory patient, occupational health services to local industry, free-standing joint ventures with physicians, and emergency medical training to local police and fire departments. These hospitals' growing responsiveness to other needs is changing their character and mission.

Years ago, Peter Drucker pointed out that organizations need to answer the following questions: *What is our business? Who is the customer? What is value to the customer? What will our business be? What should our business be?*[1] Although the first question sounds simple, it is really the most profound question an organization can ask. A health care organization should not define its business by listing the particular services it offers. It should identify the underlying need it is trying to serve.

What Is Our Business?

One home health agency spent eight months in meetings with staff, board members, and administrators trying to decide if its business was "skilled medical treatment at home" or "babysitting for the homebound."

Many general hospitals are questioning whether their business is to meet the community's need for "medical care" when people are sick, or if their business definition should be broader: meeting the community's need for "health care" for both the sick and the well. A few hospitals have even gone so far as to define their business as providing "health care from birth until death." These organizations have added chronic and extended care facilities for the infirm elderly and severely handicapped, day care services for elderly in need of supervision, home health and hospice services, and specialized programs for such problems as drug addiction, alcoholism, and recurring emotional crises.

Most medical group practices originally defined their business as the practice of medicine by a few physicians in adjacent offices, with shared management of the business. As some have grown, they have added services like health promotion programs to local community groups and industry. They have sponsored Alcoholics Anonymous meetings for alcoholics and their families, and Toughlove meetings for troubled families with teenagers, and they have sent out speakers to address schoolchildren on relevant health topics. These medical group practices have redefined themselves as community health resources.

State hospitals for the mentally ill sometimes find that the state budget and the mood of the state legislature dictate their business definition: custodial care intended to keep the patient out of harm's (and society's) way versus therapeutic care intended to reintroduce the patient back into a productive role in society.

A helpful approach to defining mission is to establish the organization's scope along three dimensions. The first is *consumer groups—who* is to be served and satisfied. The second is *consumer needs—what* is to be satisfied. The third is *technologies—how* consumer needs are to be satisfied. For example, consider the employee assistance program (EAP) of a mental health center. The companies served by this EAP want only classroom training for their supervisors in how to deal with troubled employees. This EAP's mission scope is represented by the small cube in Figure 2–1a. Now consider the mission of a much larger EAP, shown in Figure 2–1b. This EAP serves many more groups, meeting more needs, and providing services in a variety of ways.

An organization should strive for a mission that is *feasible, motivating,* and *distinctive.* In terms of being feasible, the organization should avoid the "mission impossible" syndrome shown in the following mission statement of one organization:

> To serve individuals of all ages, families and the community, with the most comprehensive set of services possible, in view of our own resources, the resources and interests of other health care providers, and the needs of the community.
>
> To provide the highest level of health care, by the most economical methods, without compromising quality, directed to prevention, diagnosis, treatment, rehabilitation, cure and education.
>
> To respect human dignity as we carry out these services, and to be responsive to all expressions of community concern.
>
> To provide needed services regardless of the individual's ability to pay.
>
> To protect the fiscal health of the organization through the usage of sound financial management principles, including the maintenance of services which, synergistically, are self-supporting, including the recovery of all costs, debt charges, principal reduction, bad debts and allowances.
>
> To be a welcome neighbor in the community.

While the sentiments contained in this mission statement are admirable—to serve all individuals of all ages regardless of ability to pay with the highest level of health care by the most economical methods while maintaining a fiscally sound self-supporting status—they are not simultaneously feasible.

A mission should also be motivating. Those working for the organization should feel they are worthwhile members of a worthwhile organization, engaged in some activity that will enhance people's lives.

Finally, a mission works better when it is distinctive. People take pride in working for or using the services of an organization that is unique or different. Imagine trying to raise funds for an organization

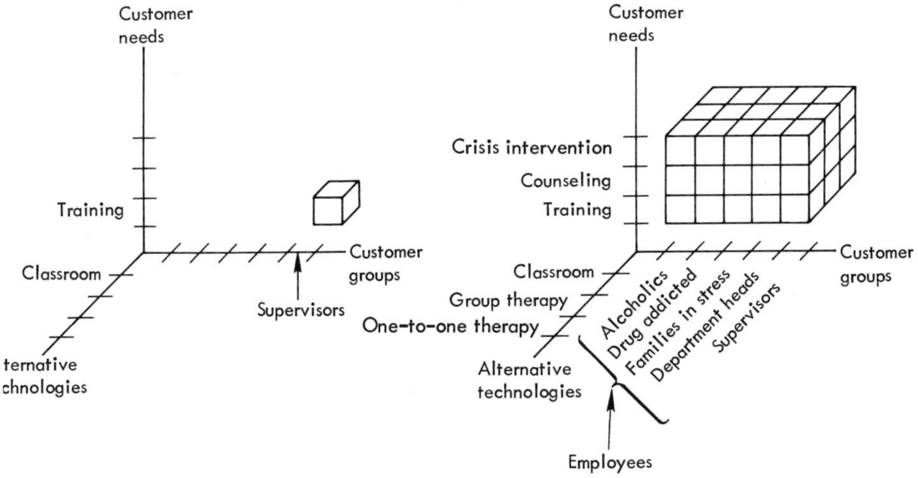

A. Highly focused EAP B. Multiservice EAP

FIGURE 2–1 The Mission Scope of Two Employee Assistance Programs

that says about itself: "We're just like every other hospital" (agency for the blind, neighborhood health center, nursing home). However, organizations should not fall into the trap of assuming that being different necessarily means being better. One social service agency prided itself on having the only urban residential facilities in the state for physically handicapped retarded adults. Unfortunately, the population this agency served was better off in suburban or rural settings, which explained why no other agency had similar urban facilities. A distinctive mission must serve the organization's clients well in order to bring the organization a loyal group of supporters.

A common fallacy among health care and social service organizations is that they are distinctive because of the high quality of their medical or clinical care. Virtually all mission statements claim to deliver the "highest quality" of medical (clinical) care, regardless of age, income, and so on. This is clearly not true. Most organizations deliver reasonable quality care, but precious few are in the vanguard. In addition, if the vast majority of health care organizations are claiming to deliver the highest quality medical care, then this claim does not differentiate them from all the other health care organizations making the same claim. It is the rare health care organization that can truly derive its distinctiveness from the high quality of its medical care.[2]

EXCHANGE

To carry on its mission, an organization needs resources. It must be able to attract and maintain patients or clients, money, materials, staff, facilities, and equipment. If these resources were not available, the organization would cease to exist. Every organization is *resource-dependent.*

Obtaining Needed Resources

How can an organization obtain needed resources? There are four possible ways:

1. The organization can attempt to develop the resources itself; members build their own facilities and find their own materials.
2. The organization can attempt to use force to obtain the resources, it can threaten resource owners or resort to theft.
3. The organization can beg for the needed resources and play on the sympathy of resource owners. This tactic (sometimes called fundraising or development, which is itself a form of exchange) may decline in effectiveness in economically difficult times.
4. The organization can offer something of value to resource owners in exchange for the needed resources. As long as an organization continues to produce value in the minds of resource owners, it is likely to attract the needed resources and survive.

The discipline of marketing is based on the last solution—that is, exchange. In modern society most organizations acquire their resources through engaging in mutually beneficial exchanges with others. The model for this is shown in Figure 2–2. The organization is seen as offering satisfactions (goods, services, benefits) to markets and receiving needed resources (goods, services, utilization, money, time, energy) in return.

Conditions for Exchange

Exchange assumes four conditions:

1. *There are at least two parties.* In the simplest exchange situation, there are two parties. In health care, because of third party reimbursement, there are often three or more. The marketer is the party more actively seeking an exchange; the marketer is someone seeking a resource from someone else and willing to offer something of value in exchange.
2. *Each can offer something the other perceives to be of value.* If one of the parties has nothing that is valued by the other party, exchange will not take place. In general, three categories of things tend to have value. The first is *physical goods*—any tangible object that is capable of satisfying a

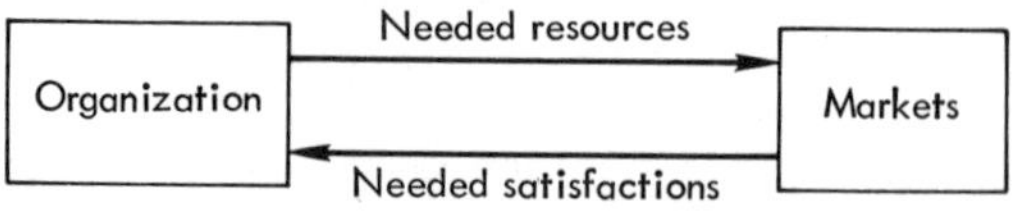

FIGURE 2–2 Organization Survival through Exchange

human want. The second is *services*—any act another person might perform that is capable of satisfying a human want. Services are usually characterized by the expenditure of time, energy, and/or skill. The third category is *money*, a generalized store of value that can be used to obtain goods or services. In the health care field, a fourth category, the *utilization of services*, has value for provider organizations because of regulatory and political pressures for efficiency.

3. *Each is capable of communication and delivery*. For exchange to take place, two parties must be capable of communicating with each other. They must be able to describe what is being offered, and when, where, and how it will be exchanged. Each party must state or imply certain warranties about the expected performance of the exchanged objects or services. In addition to communicating, each party must be capable of finding means to deliver the things of value.
4. *Each is free to accept or reject the offer*. Exchange assumes that both parties are engaging in voluntary behavior, there is no coercion. Some exchanges in health care appear not to be voluntary, such as the involuntary commitment of a patient to a psychiatric hospital. However, the decision-maker (a psychiatrist or family member, for example), acting for the patient, engages in the transaction freely, so it is a voluntary exchange.

Exchange is best understood as a process rather than an event. This process, when successful, is marked by an event called a *transaction*, which is the basic unit of exchange. A transaction takes place at a time and place, with specified amounts and conditions. Transactions themselves are a subset of a large number of events called *interactions* that make up the exchange process. Transactions are the interactions that involve the formal trading of values. When a nurse accepts a job in a physician's office, a transaction takes place. Every health care organization engages in countless numbers of transactions with other parties—patients, staff, suppliers, donors.

Exchange Analysis

Whenever two social units are engaged in exchange, it is useful to develop a diagram or map showing what is actually or potentially being exchanged between the two. Figure 2–3 presents five familiar situations. The first (Figure 2–3a) describes the classic commercial transaction. The seller offers things of value to the buyer in the form of goods and/or services; the buyer offers money in exchange. Note that the designations "buyer" and "seller" are somewhat arbitrary, for we might also say that the party with money is offering to "sell" his money for goods. In fact, if both parties were exchanging goods, a condition known as *barter*, we could not easily distinguish the buyer from the seller. In this case, both could be called *traders*. Another basic economic exchange is that between employer and employee (Figure 2–3b). The employee

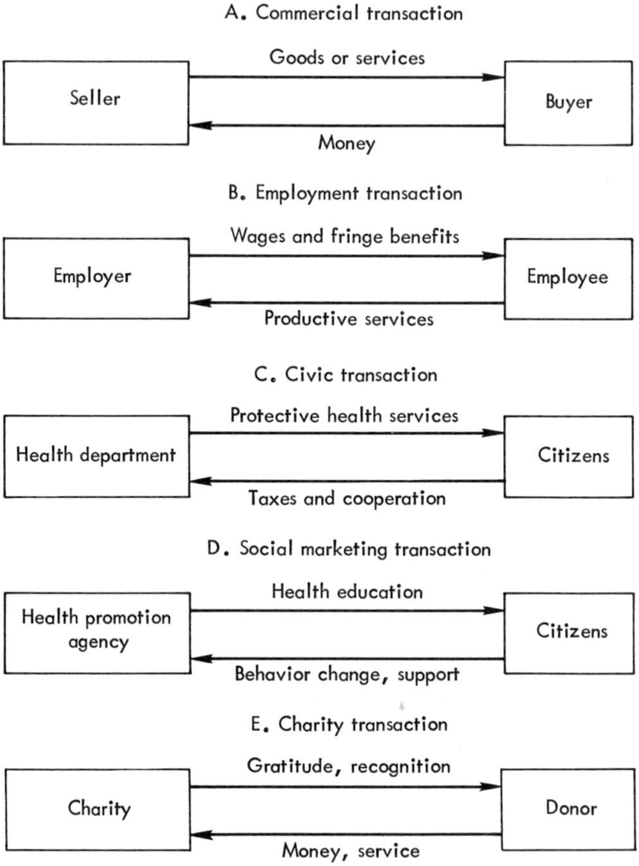

FIGURE 2–3 Examples of Exchange Transactions

offers productive services (made up of time, energy, and skill) to the employer; in exchange, the employee receives a wage and fringe benefits. There is also an overlay of psychological exchanges in this relationship, such as fear, respect, loyalty.

A third type of exchange occurs between a local health department and the local citizens (Figure 2–3c). The local health department offers protective health services such as lead paint testing; in exchange, the citizens provide taxes and cooperation. There is a question of how voluntary this transaction is, but we shall assume for the present that a social contract is voluntarily entered into between the health department and the citizens.

A fourth exchange occurs between a health promotion agency and the public (Figure 2–3d). An agency offers the public health education; in exchange, the public may change its health behavior or offer support.

A fifth exchange occurs between a charity and donors (Figure 2–3e). The charity offers the donor recognition, a sense of good conscience or well-being in return for the donor's time, money, or other donations.

Figure 2–3 shows only the basic resources being exchanged by two parties. Many health care organizations engage in much more complex exchange transactions. For example, a transaction between a hospital and one of its patients could be as shown in Figure 2–4.

Nonprovider health organizations may also have complex transactions. A health planning agency, in granting one health facility the right

FIGURE 2–4

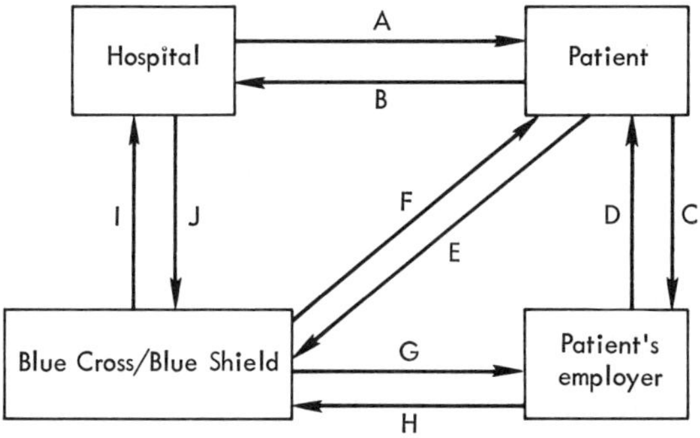

A. The hospital provides health care services to the patient.
B. The patient provides direct payment and/or guarantee of payment from a third party to the hospital. In addition, the patient provides utilization of hospital services, which the hospital seeks.
C. The patient, as an employee, provides productive work services to the employer.
D. The employer provides monetary compensation for work services, plus partial coverage for the employee's health benefits and insurance.
E. The patient provides monthly payments for health insurance, beyond that paid by the patient's employer, to Blue Cross/Blue Shield.
F. Blue Cross/Blue Shield provides guarantee of partial coverage for the patient's medical expenses.
G. Blue Cross/Blue Shield provides a mechanism by which the employer can offer health insurance to the employee group.
H. The employer provides monthly payments to Blue Cross/Blue Shield.
I. Blue Cross/Blue Shield provides reimbursement for services rendered to the hospital.
J. The hospital provides a guarantee that health services will be delivered in a cost-efficient manner so that Blue Cross/Blue Shield will not end up paying out more in reimbursements than it has attracted in payments.

to purchase a CAT scanner, simultaneously may have to refuse that option to another facility (see Figure 2–5). While these transactions are complex and therefore require a great deal of effort to manage, they are in fact a grouping of simple two-way transactions. Ultimately, exchange analysis requires (1) analyzing each individual two-way exchange, and (2) understanding the relationships between the various exchanges.

Other considerations in exchange analysis are the different weights attached to values being exchanged. A family selecting a nursing home for an elderly relative may value the nursing home's proximity to their home, a clean and pleasant atmosphere, and a strong recreational program. However, proximity may not be nearly as highly valued as the other two factors. The family may select one nursing home over another because they weigh the value of the recreation program more heavily than the value of proximity. An additional consideration is if there is any *exchange potential* at all. If the family views two nursing homes as unpleasant and poorly kept, they may be unwilling to engage in an exchange (of money for nursing home services) with either.

Predicting Exchange Outcomes

Three major theories predict how exchange situations will be resolved: economic theory, equity theory, and power theory.

Economic Theory. The basic concept in this analysis is that of *self-interest.* Individuals and organizations, when faced with two or more choices, will always favor the choice that will maximize their long-run self-interest. Put another way, people and organizations are *utility maximizers.* They will compare the benefits to the costs of a transaction and will pursue those transactions where benefits outweigh costs. The actor in an exchange process first identifies all the expected

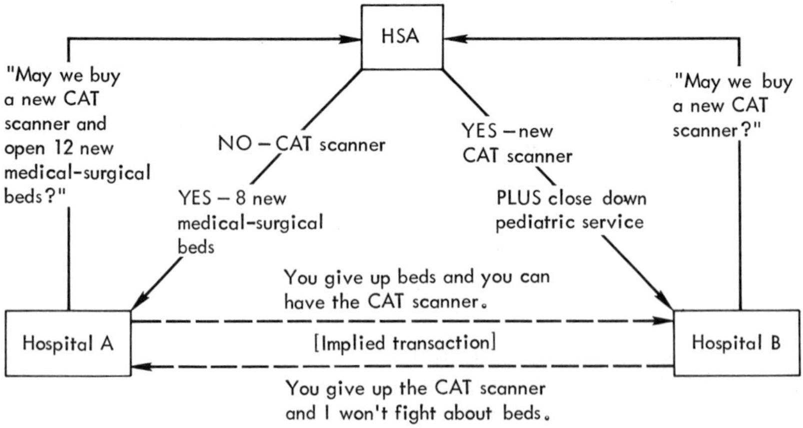

FIGURE 2–5

benefits of the potential transaction, which include money benefits, health benefits, and psychological benefits. Some attempt might be made to quantify the health and psychological benefits in terms of money. The actor then identifies all the expected costs of the potential transaction, which include money costs, psychological costs, and time and effort.

Whether an exchange will be consummated can now be predicted by this theory. There are three possible outcomes:

1. If both actors expect that their net gain will be negative no transaction will take place, for both actors will be worse off.
2. If both actors expect that the net gain will be positive, the transaction is likely to take place, because both will be better off. The only qualification here is that one or both might visualize still another transaction that will make him (them) even better off.
3. Finally, if one actor will be better off and the other worse off, a transaction will not take place unless the "better off" actor finds a way to compensate the "worse off" actor so that both will be better off. The better off actor can decide to accept a lower gain, just enough to leave the "worse off" actor with a slight positive gain.

Equity Theory. One way for two parties to reach a "transaction price" within a negotiating range is to bring in considerations of equity. The two parties may be motivated to seek a price they jointly consider to be "fair." Consider a neighborhood health center whose managers are considering hiring a physician's assistant (PA). The health center may propose that the PA's salary should have an equitable relation to the salary of a nurse-practitioner already on the staff. The PA requests a salary of $18,000. The nurse-practitioner is receiving $17,500, $1,000 more than the previous year's salary. The health center assesses the skills and training of the PA and nurse-practitioner to be roughly equal. Moreover, they note that the nurse-practitioner has been practicing for one year longer than the PA. The health center therefore offers the PA $16,750, which is close to the nurse-practitioner's salary of the previous year, but adjusted upward for inflation. If the PA accepts the position at $16,750, then the two parties have arrived at a "price" that appeals to their sense of fairness.

Power Theory. Power theory takes a different view about how the two parties will arrive at a mutually agreed upon transaction price within a negotiating range. It sees each as driven to obtain the maximum possible gain, and as willing to exploit any power it possesses to achieve that gain. If the prospective PA has more bargaining power than the health center, the final price will be closer to the PA's requested salary of $18,000. If the health center has more bargaining power, the final price will be closer to the offer of $16,750.

This leaves the question of what determines the amount of power each party has in the situation. A's power relative to B is a function of (1) how much A needs some resource that B has, and (2) how available this resource is from some alternative party.[3] In concrete terms, we can say that the PA possesses considerable power if (1) the health center badly needs to add a PA to its staff and (2) there are very few other qualified PAs available. In this case, the PA is in a seller's market and possesses considerable power to command the salary he or she wants. In general, a transaction will take place when both parties would receive a net gain. The transaction price will fall in a range between the minimum price the seller will accept and the maximum price the buyer will offer. Where the price settles will depend on equity and power considerations.

Many health care organization CEOs have had a quick immersion in power theory as they have sought to negotiate contracts with HMOs and PPOs, and in their joint ventures with physicians and other organizations. The transaction prices may include division of equity, guarantees of volume of usage, requirements regarding information processing and availability, and the like.

Exchange theory is central to being a responsive organization. *To be responsive requires analyzing the other party's needs and wants* and determining how far the organization can go toward satisfying them. An organization that is oblivious or indifferent to the needs of the other party cannot, by definition, be responsive. Let's look now at the other parties, the organization's publics.

PUBLICS

Every health care organization has several publics and must manage responsive relations with most or all of them. We define a public in the following way:

> A **public** is a distinct group of people and/or organizations that has an actual or a potential interest in and/or impact on an organization.

It is fairly easy to identify the key publics that surround a particular organization. Not all publics are equally active or important to an organization. A mutually *welcome public* is a public that likes the organization and whose support the organization welcomes. A *sought public* is a public whose support the organization wants, but which is currently indifferent or negative toward that organization. An *unwelcome public* is a public that is negatively disposed toward the organization and that is trying to impose constraints, pressures, or controls on the organization.

Publics can also be classified by their functional relation to the organization. Figure 2–6 presents such a classification. An organization is viewed as a resource-conversion machine in which certain *input publics* supply resources that are converted by *internal publics* into useful goods and services that are carried by *intermediary publics* to designated *consuming publics.* Let's look at the various publics more closely.

Input Publics

Input publics mainly supply original resources and constraints to the organization, and consist of donors, suppliers, and regulatory and third-party payor publics.

Donors. Donors are those publics who make gifts of money and other assets to the organization. A nursing school's donors consist of alumnae, friends of the nursing school, foundations, hospitals, and government organizations. A nursing school might employ a development officer or professional fundraiser. The fundraiser tries to build value in the eyes of the school's donors so that they can enjoy pride and other benefits from their association with the institution.

Suppliers. Suppliers are those organizations that sell needed goods and services to the focal organization. A local university might "sell" required academic courses to a nursing school which itself teaches no academic courses. Politicians who vote funds to government health care facilities may be considered their suppliers. In many hospitals, radiologists may be considered suppliers. They sell their professional services on contract to hospitals, but maintain their independence by incorporating as a private professional group. In a greater sense, all physicians who spend some time practicing in a hospital may be considered suppliers.

Regulatory and Third-Party Payor Organizations. The third input public consists of regulatory organizations. The regulatory publics of a nursing school include federal, state, and local government agencies, professional nursing associations, and various academic accreditation associations. The focal organization must monitor these organiza-

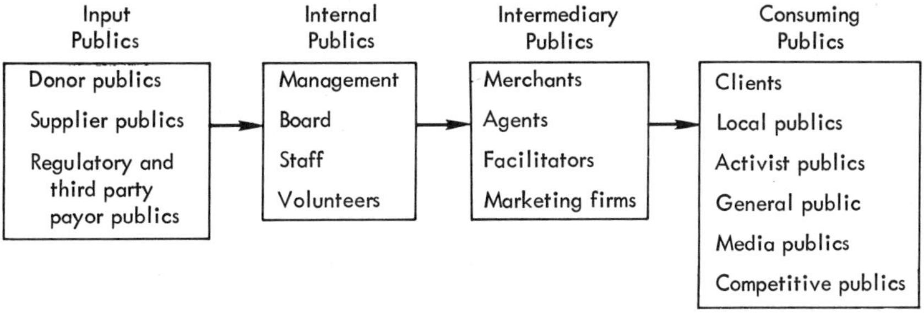

FIGURE 2–6 The Main Publics of an Organization

tions and be ready to argue against regulations that will harm its ability to create value for clients. Health care providers that do not rely entirely on self-paying patients must include third-party payors in this input public.

Internal Publics

The various inputs are managed by the health care organization's internal publics to accomplish the organization's mission. The internal publics consist of up to four groups: management, a board of directors, staff, and volunteers.

Management. Every organization has a management group that is responsible for running the organization. Reporting to the top manager, president, or chief administrator are high-level managers who are organized by function, products, markets and/or geographical area. Reporting to a nursing school dean are associate deans responsible for functions (business manager), products (dean of refresher training programs), and markets (dean of students).

The management of many health care organizations often includes a second management structure parallel to traditional management[4] composed of the clinical staff of the organization. It provides management input on both clinical and administrative matters. The medical staff of a hospital often has elected representatives who participate in the management of the hospital. Most often, these clinical representatives are not paid or are paid for less than full-time involvement in the management of the organization. However, their approval is required for successful implementation of most of the organization's management decisions.

Board of Directors. The president and management group may be responsible to a board of directors (also called trustees or overseers). Traditionally, the primary function of many boards of directors in nonprofit health care organizations was to give or raise funds for the organization. In recent years, most boards' jobs have been more clearly defined as overseeing the organization and assuring that it is operating efficiently to reach its objectives. Among the board's more important responsibilities are these:

1. The board selects or approves the chief officer of the organization.
2. The board participates in setting or approving long-range strategy for the organization.
3. The board develops or approves policies for the conduct of organizational affairs.
4. The board develops or approves compensation levels and salaries of higher management.

5. The board participates in fundraising.
6. The board considers major issues that have come before the organization.
7. The board adds members who are influential and can provide further contacts with other influentials.
8. The board legitimizes the organization in the eyes of others.
9. The board provides specialized skills and advice as would come from lawyers and business people.
10. In a hospital setting, legal precedents have determined that the board is responsible for quality of care.

Because of their important role, board members must be carefully selected. Organizations must make tradeoffs between prestigious members (who may miss a number of meetings and not be able to do much work) and working members. The managements of some health care organizations seek "window dressing" boards that do not interfere with management's plans. These are boards in name only, since they do not fulfill the primary responsibilities of a board outlined above. And many health care and social service organizations have "consumer" members, with the expectation that these board members will represent the interests of the organization's consuming publics. But the fact that a consumer has sufficient interest and commitment to spend the time on an organization's board means that the consumer board member is not representative of the organization's consumer group. Market research is actually a better means of identifying consumer needs, wants, and interests.

Staff. The staff consists of employees who generally work on a paid basis. It may include middle management, nurses, aides, social workers, skilled therapists, maintenance and housekeeping crews, telephone operators, and so on. Health care managers face the same challenges as managers in other industries in building an effective staff: defining job positions and responsibilities, recruiting qualified people, training them, motivating them, compensating them, and evaluating them.

Physicians are not a good example of staff (except in teaching hospitals, some prepaid group practice plans, and a limited but growing number of settings where physicians are salaried). Hospitals and other health care organizations provide settings where the independent physician may practice. These organizations recruit, motivate, and sometimes evaluate the physician, as they do other staff. Moreover, prospective payment and other regulatory forces have caused these organizations to seek to influence the way in which physicians practice. Nonetheless, physicians are more appropriately viewed as intermediaries than staff.

Nurses are more clearly recognized as staff in most health care settings. The perceived shortage in the early 1980s of actively practicing nurses has demonstrated to health care organizations that nurses, like other staff, are a market. To attract and motivate staff, health care organizations must give them what they want: adequate salaries, reasonable working conditions, respect, recognition, and the feeling of working for a worthwhile enterprise. In exchange, the organization can require of its staff that it perform certain duties. These duties include not only clinical and functional tasks, but also the practice of a customer service orientation. Those employees who come in contact with consumers must recognize their role as marketing representatives for their organization. An organization whose nurses are unpleasant will suffer the marketing consequence of lower census or less patient usage.

Volunteers. Many nonprofit health care organizations (and some proprietary ones) use volunteers as an important part of their operations. The volunteers usually perform less skilled work. Their unpaid work may help to keep down the operating costs of the organization, may provide services for which the organization could not otherwise pay, or may raise funds for the organization. On the other hand, volunteers are less controllable and often less productive. They may not show up for meetings, may resist doing certain tasks, and may be slow in getting work done on time. Some organizations claim to be able to accomplish more by increasing the size of the paid staff and reducing the number of volunteers. An alternative might be for the organization to improve its skill in managing and motivating the volunteers.

The competent volunteer staff manager will be skilled in attracting good, reliable volunteers and in motivating and rewarding them. A marketing approach means understanding the volunteers' needs and meeting them in a way that draws their support and hard work. Prestigious organizations may confer a bit of that prestige on their hardworking volunteers through publicity. The volunteer manager of one social service organization recognized that the majority of her volunteer market consisted of nonworking college-educated women who would want to return to paid working positions in the future. So the volunteer manager provided the volunteer staff with ongoing clinical and management training and with volunteer job tasks that could be translated into useful work experience in the (paid) labor market. Thus by offering their time on a volunteer basis, the volunteers ultimately became more marketable once they sought paid employment.

Intermediary Publics

The focal organization enlists other individuals and organizations, called *marketing intermediaries,* to assist in promoting and distributing its goods and services to the final consumers. There are four types of marketing intermediaries: merchants, facilitators, agents, and marketing firms. Because most health care organizations produce services and not products, merchants and facilitators generally play a less important role than agents and marketing firms.

Merchants. Merchants are organizations, such as wholesalers and retailers, that buy, take title to, and resell merchandise. A manufacturer of hospital laboratory equipment might make an arrangement with a merchant to buy, promote, sell, and distribute the manufacturer's product.

Facilitators. Facilitators are organizations such as transportation companies, communication firms, and real estate firms that assist in the distribution of products, services, or messages, but do not take title to or negotiate purchases. A public health department may ask local community agencies to act as facilitators by distributing its health promotion literature to the agencies' markets. It may also hire a transportation service at the normal fee to distribute the literature to community agencies across the state. Hospitals may provide free coffee and emergency training to police departments in order to use them as facilitators for attracting trauma cases.

Agents. Agent middlemen are organizations or individuals who find and/or sell to buyers the focal organization's products or services without taking possession of the product or service. In a traditional product setting, manufacturer's representatives and brokers are agents. They are hired by the focal organization and paid for their services.

In many health care settings, agents are not hired or paid directly for their services. For example, physicians may be viewed as hospital's agents. They find and admit patients to the hospital—in essence selling the hospital's services. Physicians in this role are neither hired nor paid for their agent service; however, they do receive in exchange the freedom to admit patients to and to practice medicine at the hospital. A local court that refers drug addicts convicted of crimes to a drug treatment center is an unpaid agent for that center. The term commonly used in health care for the agent's role is *referral.* Referral is one of the major forms of promotion in health care and other clinical service settings.

Marketing Firms. Marketing firms are organizations, such as advertising agencies, marketing research firms, and marketing consulting firms, that assist in identifying, developing, and promoting the focal organization's products and services to the right markets. A health maintenance organization might hire the services of these firms to identify attractive sites for new health centers, to identify and help research new services to serve the HMO's members, and to create promotional strategies for the new centers and new services.

Consuming Publics

Various groups consume the output of an organization: clients, local publics, activist publics, the general public, media publics.

Clients. Clients represent an organization's primary public, its *raison d'être.* Peter Drucker insists that the only valid definition of a business is to create a customer.[5] He would propose that hospitals exist to serve patients, hospices to serve the terminally ill, neighborhood health centers to serve neighborhood residents, and social agencies to serve the needy.

Various names are used to describe an organization's customers. The appropriate term is elusive in some cases. Consider a state hospital for the mentally ill. The patients are clearly the state hospital's consumers. A social worker in the state hospital will have certain patients as clients. The patients are not buyers in the sense of paying money for the service; instead, the citizens are the buyers, and they are buying protection for and protection from the severely mentally ill through their taxes. The citizens are also the state hospital's constituents in that the hospital also exists to serve their interests. We might conclude that the taxpayers are the state hospital's primary customers.

What this illustrates is that an organization can have a multiple set of customers, and one of its jobs is to distinguish among these customer groups. Consider this issue in relation to a health planning council. Who is the council's primary customer? Is it the general public who will benefit from the council's efforts to guarantee provision of effective and efficient health services to address identified needs? Is it local health providers who expect recognition of their cooperative planning efforts and approval of their proposals? Is it local industry which expects a decrease or leveling off in the health insurance rates it pays for employees? Is it local health care consumers who expect the council to be sensitive to their preferences in health care providers? Or is it the federal government, which expects the council to develop a more rational health care system?

Clearly, the council must take into account the interests of all these customer groups in formulating its policies, even though these interests may conflict. For example, the council may have to weigh off the interests of local health care consumers who want their favorite hospital to be able to expand its ICU service against the interests of other hospitals with existing ICU services that are not being fully utilized. A necessity of good marketing is the balancing and reconciling of the interests of diverse customer groups, rather than the constant favoring of one group at the expense of the others.

Local Publics. Every organization is physically located in one or more areas and comes in contact with local publics such as neighborhood residents and community organizations. These groups may take an active or passive interest in the activities of the organization. The residents near a hospital usually get concerned about ambulance sirens, parking congestion, and other things that go with living near a hospital.

Many health care organizations develop a community relations function whose job is to monitor the community, attend meetings, answer questions, and make contributions to worthwhile causes. Responsive organizations do not wait for local issues to erupt. They make investments in the community to help it run well and to acquire a bank of goodwill.

Activist Publics. Health care organizations are increasingly being petitioned by consumer groups, environmental groups, business roundtables and employer groups, minority organizations, and other public interest groups for certain concessions or support. Hospitals, for example, have had to deal with demands by environmental groups to install more pollution control equipment and engage in better waste-handling methods.

Organizations would be foolish to attack or ignore the demands of activist publics. Responsive organizations can do two things. First, they can train their managements to include social criteria in their decision-making. Second, they can assign a staff person to stay in touch with these groups and to communicate more effectively the organization's goals, activities, and intentions.

General Public. Health care organizations must also be concerned with the attitude of the general public toward their activities and policies. Although the general public does not act in an organized way toward an organization, as activist groups do, members of the general public do hold images of many organizations. These images then affect patronage and legislative support.

It has become increasingly clear to many health care organizations that the image of health care providers as a group has suffered. The public is voicing more complaints about the astronomical costs of hospitalization, about delays they face when trying to use certain parts of the health care system, about unempathetic treatment by health care professionals and employees, and about a general lack of sensitivity for the patient. Some of these perceptions are in fact reasonable, based on characteristics present in the health care delivery process. Health care organizations must monitor the perceptions of the public, change those characteristics in the system that lead to complaints when possible, and correct damaging misperceptions when negative attitudes have no factual basis.

Media Publics. Media publics include media companies that carry news, features, and editorial opinion—specifically, newspapers, magazines, and radio and television stations. Most health care organizations are acutely sensitive to the role played by the press in affecting their capacity to achieve their marketing objectives. An organization normally would like more and better press coverage than it gets. Getting more and better coverage calls for understanding what the press is really interested in. The effective press relations manager knows most of the editors in the major media and systematically cultivates a mutually beneficial relation with them. The manager offers interesting news items, informational material, and quick access to top management. In return, the media reports are likely to give the organization more and better coverage.

Competitive Publics

Most, although not all, health care and social service organizations face competition. Traditionally, health care organizations, especially nonprofit organizations, denied the existence of competition, feeling that this characterized the for-profit business sectors. Of course, while initial government regulatory efforts had hoped to develop a spirit of cooperation between hospitals, it is clear that most hospitals view neighboring hospitals as competitors first, and as sisters, second if at all. They compete for patients, for physicians, for alternative delivery systems contracts, for industry support, for equipment, and for regulatory approval.

An organization must be sensitive to the competitive environment in which it operates. That competitive environment consists not only of similar organizations or services, but also of more basic forces. An organization may face up to four major types of competitors in trying to serve its target market:

1. *Desire competitors.* Other immediate desires the consumer might want to satisfy.
2. *Generic competitors.* Other basic ways in which the consumer can satisfy a particular desire.
3. *Service form competitors.* Other service forms that can satisfy the buyer's particular desire.
4. *Enterprise competitors.* Other enterprises offering the same service form that can satisfy the buyer's particular desire.

Suppose a hospital is mounting a fundraising effort. The hospital seeks a few large unrestricted donations to renovate its emergency room. Consider one of the wealthy donors identified by the hospital. Suppose her decision process follows the path shown in Figure 2–7. The donor has several competing desires regarding how she uses her money: to give to charity, to travel, and to invest in an associate's new business venture. She decides to give to charity. Now she considers the best way to do this: She may give a little money to a lot of charities, a lot of money to one charity, or a little each year for fifteen years to one char-

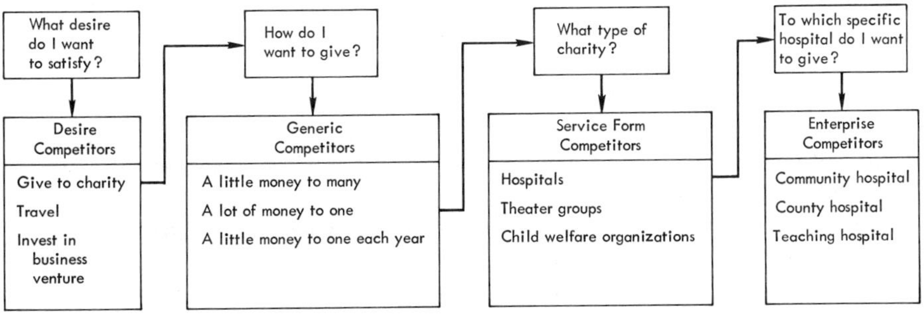

FIGURE 2–7 Types of Competitors Facing a Hospital's Fundraising Effort

ity. She decides to give a lot of money to one charity. She then considers what type of charity: hospitals, theater groups, child welfare organizations, and others. She chooses hospitals. She now must decide between specific hospitals: her full-service community hospital, the county hospital, or the major teaching hospital.

Relation Between a Public and a Market

Having demonstrated that every organization is surrounded by a multitude of publics, we can now pose the question: What is the relation between a public and a market? From the point of view of an organization, a market is *a potential arena for the trading of resources.* For an organization to operate, it must acquire resources through trading other resources. In each case, it must offer something to the market to receive in return the resources it seeks. For this reason, we define a market as follows:

> A **market** is a distinct group of people and/or organizations that have resources they want to exchange, or might conceivably be willing to exchange, for distinct benefits.

We can now see the affinities between a market and a public. A *public* is any group that has an actual or potential interest or impact on an organization. If the organization wishes to attract certain resources from that public through offering a set of benefits in exchange, then the organization is taking a *marketing viewpoint* toward that public. Once the organization starts thinking in terms of trading values with that public, it is viewing the public as a market. It is engaged in trying to determine the best marketing approach to that public.

IMAGE

Many health care organizations have said: "If only we could improve our image, everything would get better." Often, these organizations have then laden the public relations director with the responsibility of "improving our image." However, an organization does not develop a favorable image simply through its public relations efforts; its image is a function of all that it has done or can do, as well as of all that it communicates. The tendency of health care organizations to ascribe image solely to communications indicates a failure to understand how images develop.

A responsive organization has a vital interest in identifying its image with its various publics. It wants to ensure that these images facilitate rather than impede the delivery of satisfaction. Managers want to know the following things about image:

1. What is an image?
2. How can it be measured?
3. What determines the image?
4. How can an image be changed?
5. What is the relation between image and a person's behavior toward the object?

The term "image" is currently used in a variety of contexts: organizational image, corporate image, national image, brand image, public image, self-image, and so on. Such wide use has tended to blur its meanings. Our definition of image is as follows:

> An **image** is the sum of beliefs, ideas, and impressions that a person has of an object.

This definition enables us to distinguish an image from similar-sounding concepts such as beliefs, attitudes, and stereotypes, for an image is more than a simple belief. For example, the belief that the American Medical Association (AMA) is more interested in serving physicians than society would be only one element in the image one might hold of the AMA. On the other hand, people's images of an object do not necessarily reveal their attitudes toward that object. An older physician may have a positive attitude toward the AMA, while a patient advocate may not. Yet they both may hold roughly the same image of the AMA: that it is a powerful lobbying force, that it represents the interests of physicians, that it holds to traditional values, and that it is slow to change its policies. Their image of the AMA will influence their attitudes toward that group, but it is not the same as their attitudes.

Image Measurement

We will describe a two-step approach for measuring images: First, measuring how familiar and favorable the organization's image is; and second, measuring the location of the organization's image along major relevant dimensions (called the semantic differential).

Familiarity-Favorability Measurement. The first step is to establish, for each public being studied, how familiar it is with the organization and how favorably it feels toward it. To establish familiarity, respondents are asked to check one of the following:

Never heard of	Heard of	Know a little bit	Know a fair amount	Know very well

The results indicate the public's awareness of the organization. If most respondents place the organization in the first two or three categories, then the organization has an *awareness problem.*

Those respondents who have some familiarity with the organization are then asked to describe how favorably they feel toward it by checking one of the following:

Very unfavorable	Somewhat unfavorable	Indifferent	Somewhat favorable	Very favorable

If most respondents check the first two or three categories, then the organization has a serious *image problem.*

To illustrate these scales, suppose the residents of an area are asked to rate four local hospitals, A, B, C, and D. Their responses are averaged and the results displayed in Figure 2–8. Hospital A has the strongest image: most people know it and like it. Hospital B is less familiar to most people, but those who know it like it. Hospital C is negatively viewed by the people who know it, but fortunately not too many people know it. Hospital D is in the weakest position: It is seen as a poor hospital and everyone knows it.

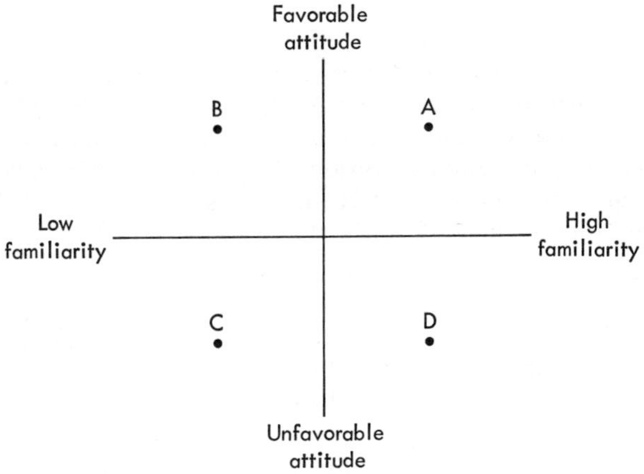

FIGURE 2–8 Familiarity-Favorability Analysis

Clearly each hospital faces a different task. Hospital A must work at maintaining its good reputation and high community awareness. Hospital B must bring itself to the attention of more people, since those who know it find it to be a good hospital. Hospital C needs to find out why people dislike the hospital and take steps to mend its ways, while keeping a low profile. Hospital D would be well advised to lower its profile (avoid news) and mend its ways. When it is a better hospital, it can start seeking public attention again.

Semantic Differential. Each hospital needs to go further and research the content of its image. One of the most popular tools for this is the semantic differential.[6] It involves the following steps:

1. *Developing a set of relevant dimensions.* The researcher first asks people to identify the dimensions they would use in thinking about the object. People could be asked: "What things do you think of when you consider a hospital?" If someone suggests "quality of medical care," this would be turned into a bipolar adjective scale, with "inferior medical care" at one end and "superior medical care" at the other. Generally, this would be rendered as a 5- or 7-point scale. A set of additional relevant dimensions for a hospital is shown in Figure 2–9.
2. *Reducing the set of relevant dimensions.* The number of dimensions should be kept low to avoid respondent fatigue. There are three basic types of scales: evaluation scales (good-bad qualities), potency scales (strong-weak qualities), and activity scales (active-passive qualities). Using these scales as a guide, or performing a factor analysis, the researcher can remove scales that fail to add new information.
3. *Administering the instrument to a sample of respondents.* The respondents are asked to rate one organization at a time. The bipolar adjectives should be arranged so as not to load all the poor adjectives on one side (so that a respondent could not sensibly rate the organization by selecting the far right or far left ranking throughout).
4. *Averaging the results.* Figure 2–9 shows the results of averaging the respondents' pictures of hospitals A, B, and C. Each hospital's image is represented by a vertical "line of means" that summarizes how the average respondent sees that institution. Hospital A is seen as a large, modern, friendly, and superior hospital. Hospital C is seen as a small, dated, impersonal, and inferior hospital.
5. *Checking on the image variance.* Since each image profile is a line of means, it does not reveal how variable the image actually is. If there were 100 respondents, did they all see hospital B, for example, exactly as shown, or was there considerable variation? In the first case, we would say that the image is highly *specific,* and in the second case that the image is highly diffused. An institution may or may not want a very specific image. Some organizations prefer a diffused image so that different groups can project their needs onto this organization. The organization will want to analyze

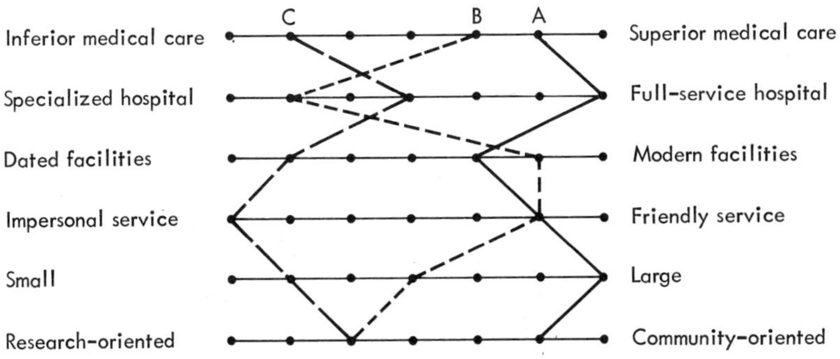

FIGURE 2–9 Images of Three Hospitals (Semantic Differential)

whether a variable image is really the result of different subgroups rating the organization, with each subgroup having a highly specific image.

The semantic differential is a flexible image-measuring tool that can provide useful information. For example, the organization can discover how a particular public views it and its major competitors. By assessing its own and the competition's image strengths and weaknesses, the organization can then take any necessary remedial steps. The organization can also discover how different publics and market segments view it. The organization can monitor changes in its image over time as well. By repeating the image study periodically, the organization can detect any significant image slippage or improvement.

Determining Image

What determines the image a person holds of an organization? There are two theories of image formation. One holds that image is largely *object-determined*—that is, that people are simply perceiving the reality of the object. If a nursing home is located next to a lake and surrounded by beautiful trees, it is going to strike people as a beautiful nursing home. A few individuals might describe it as ugly, but this would be dismissed as the peculiarity of certain individuals or their lack of real experience with the object. The object-determined view of images assumes that (1) people tend to have first-hand experience with objects; (2) people get reliable sensory data from the object; and (3) people tend to process the sensory data in a similar way in spite of having different backgrounds and personalities. These assumptions in turn imply that organizations cannot easily create false images of themselves.

The other theory holds that images are largely *person-determined.* Those holding this view argue that (1) people have different degrees of contact with the object; (2) people placed in front of the object will selectively perceive different aspects of the object; and (3) people have individual ways of processing sensory data, leading to selective distortion. For these reasons, people may hold quite different images of the same object. That is, there is a weak relation between the image and the actual object.

The truth lies somewhere in between: An image is influenced both by the objective characteristics of the object and the subjective characteristics of the perceiver. We might expect people to hold similar images of a given object or organization when the object is simple rather than complex; when it is frequently and directly experienced; and when it is fairly stable in its real characteristics over time. Conversely, people may hold quite different images of an object if it is complex, infrequently experienced, and changing through time.

Image Modification

When image research results show that the organization is in trouble, management's appropriate response is to investigate ways of modifying the image.

The first step is to develop a picture of the *desired image.* Suppose the management of hospital C wants the desired image shown in Figure 2–10. Hospital C would like the public to have a more favorable view of the quality of its medical care, facilities, friendliness, and so on. The second step is for management to develop priorities among the image dimensions (quality of medical care, newness of facilities, friendliness of service). Each dimension should be reviewed in terms of the following questions:

1. What contribution to the organization's overall favorable image would be made by closing that particular image gap to the extent shown?
2. What strategy (combination of real changes and communication changes) would be used to close the particular image gap?
3. What would be the cost of closing that image gap?
4. How long would it take to close that image gap?

For example, management might decide that it would be more effective, swifter, and less costly to improve the hospital's image of friendliness than to improve the physical facilities. An overall image modification plan would involve planning a sequence of steps through which the organization would transform its current image into its desired image.

Health care organizations seeking to change their images must have great patience, because images tend to last long after the reality of an organization has changed. The quality of medical care may have deteriorated at a major hospital, and yet it may continue to be highly regarded in the public mind. Image persistence is explained by the fact that once people have a certain image of an object, they tend to be selective perceivers of further data; their perceptions are oriented to-

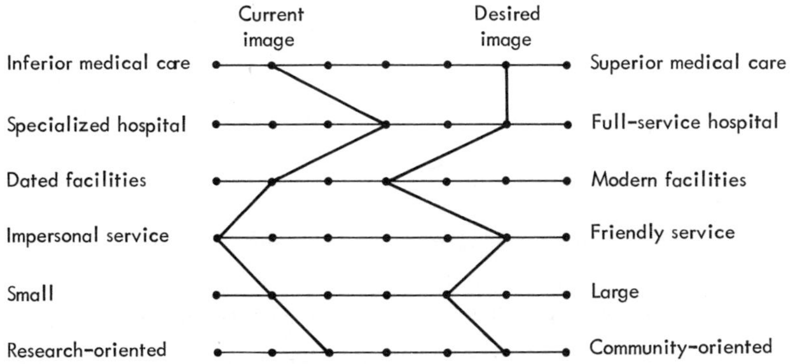

FIGURE 2–10 Current and Desired Image of Hospital C

ward seeing what they expect to see. An image enjoys a life of its own for a while, especially when people are not likely to have new first-hand experiences with the changed object.

The Relation Between Image and Behavior

Most organizations are interested in image measurement and modification because they feel that image has a great influence on people's behavior. They assume there is a close relationship between people's image of the organization and their behavior toward it. However, the connection between image and behavior is not really so. Images are only one component of attitudes. Two people may view a hospital as large and have opposite attitudes toward a large hospital. Furthermore, the connection between attitudes and behavior is also tenuous. A patient might prefer a large hospital to a small one and yet end up in the small one because it is closer to home or because the patient's physician has admitting privileges only at the small hospital.

Nevertheless, we should not dismiss image measurement and planning simply because images are hard to change and their effects on behavior are unclear. Measuring an organization's image is a useful step in understanding what is happening to the organization. And though the connection between image and behavior is not strong, it does exist. Any organization should make an investment in developing the best image it can.

SATISFACTION

Health care organizations used to think it was sufficient to deliver high-quality medical or clinical care. More recently, many health care organizations have added market satisfaction to their list of goals. Some organizations have even promoted a money-back guarantee (see Exhibit 2–1). A responsive organization makes every effort to sense, serve, and satisfy the needs and wants of its markets. Most health care organizations would like to be viewed as very responsive. Each health care organization must determine how responsive it wishes to be and develop appropriate systems for measuring and improving satisfaction in its marketplace.

EXHIBIT 2–1

Hospitals Will Guarantee Satisfaction or Money Back

After experimenting with a guaranteed services program in about 12 of its hospitals, Hospital Corp. of America, Nashville, TN, hopes to broaden the service to all of its facilities. Piloted at Plano (TX) General Hospital, the program guarantees satisfaction in all areas of hospital care, or the patient doesn't have to pay for those services. A patient with a complaint about a service must call a designated number within 24 hours of the incident. Patients can call seven days a week, 24 hours a day. The hospitals average about 10 calls a week, according to Judi H. Guthrie, manager of program development. Only about 40% of those calls are negative, she said. Another some 40% are compliments on the hospitals' service, and the other 20% are general comments. While most hospitals don't charge for unsatisfactory services, the calls with complaints are usually registered with someone with no control of the problem area, such as a business office person at discharge time, Ms. Guthrie contends. HCA's telephone line reminds patients to register their complaint within 24 hours with the patient representative answering the phone who can correct the problem. If the complaint is justified, and registered within the 24-hour time frame, the patient isn't charged for the service. The program has actually cut down on the number of credits the hospitals give, Ms. Guthrie contends. The most any of the HCA hospitals has paid in a year is $2,000, while the least is $96, she said."

SOURCE: Reprinted with permission from the July 1981 issue of *Modern Healthcare Magazine.* Copyright Crain Communications Inc., 740 N. Rush, Chicago, IL 60611. All rights reserved.

Some Hospitals Offer Services with a Money-Back Guarantee

Radford, VA.—What's this about inhospitable hospitals? If patients don't like the dinner served at the one here, they get their meal money back. Radford Community is the latest of several hospitals around the country to adopt a customer-is-always-right attitude.

Under the "Guaranteed Services" program, the adhering institutions lump it when patients don't like it—crediting the accounts of those with justifiable complaints. Specifics of the offer vary, but recompensable gripes may range from cold food to overlong waits in the ER, and there's always a staffer available to hear them. "The person on call has the authority to make any bill adjustments," says Ron Greavu, vice president of Blanchard Valley Hospital in Findlay, Ohio, where the first program was launched six years ago.

In its six-month experience with the new approach, Radford Community has found it's improved both the morale and performance of employees. Their incentive: "We've set aside $10,000 a year for the program," says community-relations director Susan Vengrin, "and what money isn't used will be divided up among the employees." She reckons the hospital has had to return only about $300 to patients since the plan started here. Valley Hospital of Las Vegas, Nev.—in the program since 1977—last year used $3,288 of the $15,000 it allotted to cover complaints about services.

But whatever the cost to these voluntary participants, Greavu of Blanchard Valley believes it'll prove worthwhile, both from a public-relations angle—demonstrating to their communities the hospitals' confidence in their staffs and services—and from the patients' standpoint—helping calm their admission jitters. Vicki Bertilino, community-relations chief at Valley Hospital, adds that it's also a good way to pinpoint problems in an institution's workings. "We've no way to find and correct many of them unless patients are prompted to tell us of them."

Besides the sites cited, the idea's being tried in Florida, Massachusetts, and Wisconsin.

SOURCE: Medical World News, copyright HEI Publishing, Inc., March 2, 1981, p. 51.

Levels of Organizational Responsiveness

There are four levels of organizational responsiveness: unresponsive, casually responsive, highly responsive, fully responsive.

The Unresponsive Organization. An unresponsive organization is at one extreme. Its main characteristics are these:

1. It does not encourage inquiries, complaints, suggestions, or opinions from its customers.
2. It does not measure current customer satisfaction or needs.
3. It does not train its staff to be customer-minded.

The unresponsive organization is typically characterized by a bureaucratic mentality. These organizations routinize operations, replace personal judgment with impersonal policies, specialize the job of every employee, create a rigid hierarchy of command, and convert the organization into an efficient machine.[7] Employees are expected to perform discrete, definable tasks but not to be responsive to consumers. Bureaucratic employees dismiss customer complaints without examination if the complaint can be justified by a bureaucratic policy. Questions of structure dominate questions of substance.

This kind of organization either assumes it knows what its publics need or that their needs do not matter. It sees no need to consult with consumers. Many hospitals were bureaucratically operated in the past when they had far more patient demand than beds. Consider the following:

> Why is it necessary to awaken a patient a couple of hours before breakfast to wash his face? . . . If it is a question of hospital routine or patient comfort, the hospital should make its routine fit the patient. . . . Why does it sometimes take many minutes for a nurse to answer a patient's light? . . . We've all seen nurses standing in the hallway talking and ignoring call lights.[8]

Whether it is the physician, nurse or aide, X-ray technician or emergency room staff, admitting clerk or billing clerk who is rude, the housekeeper who bumps the bed while cleaning, the parking garage attendant who is less than helpful when the garage is full, the health center cafeteria that turns away visitors, or the medical group practice that sees patients only during bankers' hours—all suggest that health care organizations operate for their own convenience and not that of the patients, their families and visitors.

The Casually Responsive Organization. The casually responsive organization differs from the unresponsive organization in two ways: (1) It encourages clients to submit inquiries, complaints, suggestions, and opinions, (2) it makes periodic studies of consumer satisfaction. When community health centers began to experience a decline in grant funding in the mid-1970s and had to rely more on revenue generated by patient use, they began to pay more attention to their patients and publics. Health center administrators who had formerly focused on hiring and scheduling staff, on maintaining records required by the granting organizations, and on running the operation efficiently—the earmarks of the bureaucratic mentality—now began to listen more to patients. They spent time in the waiting areas talking with patients, left their office doors open, and distributed patient satisfaction questionnaires. The result has been greater satisfaction among the organization's customers. Whether or not the increased customer satisfaction continues depends on whether the organization merely makes a show of listening or actually does something about what it hears.

The Highly Responsive Organization. A highly responsive health care organization differs from a casually responsive organization in two additional ways: (1) It not only surveys current consumer satisfaction, but also researches unmet consumer needs and preferences to discover ways to improve its service; and (2) it selects and trains its people to be customer-minded.

Most health care organizations fall short of being highly responsive. While many distribute patient satisfaction questionnaires, far fewer carry out formal, professionally designed market research on their patients' real needs and desires. Nor do they motivate and train their staffs to seek increased patient satisfaction. The staff member who is not only clinically competent but also responsive to nonclinical patient needs is not necessarily viewed as a better employee.

A health maintenance organization (HMO) recognized this failing and developed the following philosophy to guide its staff in interactions with its members.

> Our member is:
> the reason for our being. Were there no members, there would be no need for our HMO to be here today.
>
> a whole human being with a mind and a spirit as well as a body. We must not forget that the whole person walks in our doors for treatment, not just the sore throat, the aching back or the diseased organ.
>
> intelligent, questioning and able to make decisions about his or her own treatment, even if the member has no clinical training. As trained staff, we should be able to explain treatment alternatives clearly enough to the member so that the member is able to make an informed choice.
>
> dependent upon us not only for good medical care but also for sensitive personal care. We are dependent on our members for our continued existence—tomorrow, next month and next year. Our jobs and careers depend on our members.
>
> is not an interruption of our work, but rather the purpose of it. We are not doing them a favor by serving them. They are doing us a favor by giving us the opportunity to do so.

The Fully Responsive Organization. The fully responsive organization accepts or rejects consumer complaints and suggestions thoughtfully, based on what it thinks is important and what it is willing to do. The fully responsive organization is able to overcome the "we-they" distinction by accepting its customers as voting or participating members. Its major characteristics are these: (1) It encourages consumers to participate actively in the affairs of the organization. (2) It responds to consumer wishes as expressed through the ballot box or representatives.

Most health care organizations are not and do not want to be fully responsive. Some community-based health organizations have tried to be fully responsive by placing large numbers of consumers on their boards. This worked for organizations in which the consumers understood their role to be an advisory one. However, a number of organizations found themselves not only responding to, but being run by consumers. Health care managers must differentiate between their responsibility to be fully responsive versus the abrogation of their management and policymaking responsibilities. A fully responsive organization, while responding to the greatest extent possible to its consumers, is still managed by the individuals hired and charged with that responsibility.

The Concept of Satisfaction

Since responsive organizations aim to create satisfaction, it is necessary to define "satisfaction." Here is our definition:

> **Satisfaction** is a state felt by a person who has experienced a performance (or outcome) that has fulfilled his or her expectations.

Satisfaction is thus a function of relative levels of expectation and perceived performance. If the performance exceeds expectations, the person is *highly satisfied.* If the performance matches expectations, the person is *satisfied.* If the performance falls short of expectations, the person is *dissatisfied.*

To understand satisfaction, we must understand how people form their expectations. Expectations are formed on the basis of past experience with the same or similar situations, statements made by friends and other associates, and statements made by the supplying organization. The supplying organization influences satisfaction not only through its performance, but also through the expectations it creates. If it overclaims, it is likely to create subsequent dissatisfaction; and if it underclaims, it might attract fewer consumers but create high satisfaction. The safest course is to plan to deliver a certain level of performance and communicate this level to consumers.

Measuring Satisfaction

Organizations use various methods to try to measure their success in creating consumer satisfaction. The major methods are described below.

Sales-Related Methods. Many health care organizations feel that the extent of consumer satisfaction created by their activities is revealed by such objective measures as their *sales level* (more often called census or utilization in health care settings), *market share,* and/or *repeat purchase ratio.* If these measures rise or stay at an acceptable level, management draws the conclusion that the organization is satisfying its customers. A home health agency whose growing staff is fully utilized from year to year would assume it is satisfying its patients and referral sources. A maternity service that maintains a 90 percent census in a competitive market which is declining in size would also be deemed to be satisfying its patients.

These indirect measures are important but hardly sufficient. Consumers might continue to interact with an organization with which they are dissatisfied for three reasons: (1) they continue to use an unsatisfactory organization because there are no alternatives or no competitors. (2) The sales of an unsatisfactory organization may remain strong for a short time after its services are no longer considered satisfactory because of inertia in the marketplace. The consumer might rather wait to see if services will improve again before making the effort to switch to another organization. (3) Many health care organizations rely primarily on referrals. For example, community hospitals traditionally get about 70 percent of their patients through physician referrals and admissions (versus through emergency and outpatient service admissions). Nursing homes rely on hospital discharge planners and physicians, as well as other sources, for admissions. The consumer might be dissatisfied with the organization, but continue to use its services because the referral source may play the dominant role in the choice of organization. As long as the referral sources are satisfied, the organization will continue to be utilized.

Complaint and Suggestion Systems. Responsive health care organizations will make it easy for consumers to complain about unsatisfactory or disappointing services. Organizations that avoid collecting complaints do not avoid consumer dissatisfaction; it is just more difficult to identify and address problem areas.

Several mechanisms have been used to facilitate complaints. Health care organizations commonly use patient comment cards (see Figure 2–11). Some organizations, particularly inpatient facilities, use a patient advocate or ombudsman system to hear grievances and seek remedies.[9] A major teaching hospital instituted a CARE line. Anyone—patient, visitor, nurse, hospital housekeeper, physician—could dial C-A-R-E on the internal telephone system to report a problem. Sometimes a complaint or suggestion box may be positioned in a high traffic area.

Good complaint systems serve a useful purpose. By noting the frequency and type of complaints about various areas, the organization can identify and focus its corrective actions on those categories showing high frequency, high seriousness, and high remediability. Moreover, by collecting complaints over time, the organization can perform trend analysis on its various services to determine which services are improved and are receiving fewer complaints, and which are becoming problem areas.

In order to evaluate our care of patients, we want to know the opinions of those we serve. We would appreciate your cooperation in filling out and returning the attached patient survey card. Your suggestions and criticisms will help us improve our services and make the hospital experience a bit easier for tomorrow's patient. Please remember to send us your reply. If you have more comments than can be contained in the survey card, please feel free to write directly to me. Your letter will receive my personal attention.

Mitchell T. Rabkin, MD
President
Boston's Beth Israel Hospital

How Was Your Stay?

1. Was your admission to Beth Israel Hospital
   Friendly ☐ Neutral ☐ Inconsiderate ☐
2. Was our nursing service
   Excellent ☐ Satisfactory ☐ Poor ☐
3. Were the meals
   Excellent ☐ Good ☐ Fair ☐ Poor ☐
4. Was your room kept
   Very clean ☐ Fairly clean ☐ Unclean ☐
5. All in all, how would you rate Beth Israel Hospital?
   Excellent ☐ Good ☐ Fair ☐ Poor ☐
6. Do you approve of the fact that Beth Israel is a major teaching hospital of Harvard Medical School?
   Yes ☐ No ☐ Doesn't matter ☐

Your room number or floor__________

Was this your first visit? Yes ☐ No ☐

Your name__________

(Your name and address are welcome but not necessary)

Address__________

__________ Zip_____

Your doctor's name__________

Your nurse's name__________

Thank you for your help.

A major teaching hospital of Harvard Medical School.

A constituent agency of Combined Jewish Philanthropies.

Here's what I liked most!

Things I would change...

MOISTEN AND SEAL FOR MAILING

120-05B 6.82.25M

FIGURE 2–11 Patient Comment Card *Source:* Courtesy of Boston's Beth Isreal Hospital. © Copyright Beth Isreal Corporation 1985.

Complaint systems, however, have risks and limitations. First, by encouraging people to complain, the organization raises expectations. Consumers will not bother to make the effort of complaining if they think there is no chance of their complaint being addressed. Therefore, if an organization collects complaints, it ought to be prepared to address them. Second, the complaints generated by a complaint system are biased; they are not representative of the complaints that would be produced by a survey of the organization's consumers. Therefore, a complaint system is not a substitute for systematic, objective market research.

Some people are chronic complainers; their complaints tend to be overrepresented. Of more importance, most people (66 percent according to one study) do not make the effort to register their dissatisfaction formally through a complaint system. Many people resign themselves to an unsatisfactory situation, assuming that it will not happen again, or at least not to them. Some of these individuals prefer to switch to a different organization rather than "fight the system" of the organization with which they are dissatisfied.

Consumer Panels. Some organizations set up consumer panels, small groups of consumers who are questioned periodically or are free to comment at will about their feelings regarding the organization and its services. Organizations that have frequent ongoing contact with their consumers, such as HMOs and neighborhood health centers, are more likely to have consumer panels than organizations with uncertain, irregular consumer contact.

While the panel may provide valuable information to the organization, that information should be viewed critically. Like the complaints generated by a complaint system, the views of a panel are not representative. People who choose to serve on a consumer panel, whether on a paid or voluntary basis, tend to be more loyal or more extreme in their attitudes toward the organization. They differentiate themselves from the majority of the organization's consumers who have chosen not to devote their time to the organization.

Consumer Satisfaction Surveys. Recently, growing numbers of health care organizations have surveyed a random sample of consumers in order to assess satisfaction. Questionnaires are sent or telephone calls made to a random sample of past users to find out how much they liked the service and what they disliked about the service.

The questions in these surveys can take a number of forms. Consumers may be asked to *directly report* their satisfaction level by answering questions like the following:

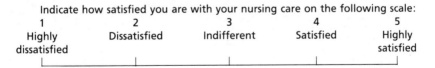

Indicate how satisfied you are with your nursing care on the following scale:

1	2	3	4	5
Highly dissatisfied	Dissatisfied	Indifferent	Satisfied	Highly satisfied

If the results are highly skewed to the left, the organization is in trouble. If the results are highly skewed to the right, the organization might conclude that it is responsive. The best interpretation of the results requires the organization to consider its satisfaction rankings in the context of the rankings of competing organizations.

The second method, *derived dissatisfaction,* is based on the premise that a person's satisfaction is influenced by his or her expectation as well as perception of the object. The person is asked two questions about each component of the health care organization—for example:

> The quality of the nursing care:
> a. How much is there now?
> (min) 1 2 3 4 5 6 7 (max)
> b. How much should there be?
> (min) 1 2 3 4 5 6 7 (max)

Suppose he circles 2 for part (a) and 5 for part (b). We can then derive a "need deficiency" score by subtracting the answer for (a) from (b), here 3. The greater the need deficiency score, the greater the degree of dissatisfaction (or the smaller the degree of satisfaction). This method provides more useful information than the previous method.

Importance/Performance Ratings. Another satisfaction measuring device is to ask consumers to rate several services provided by the organization in terms of (1) the importance of each service and (2) how well the organization performs each service. Fig. 2–12A shows how 14 services of a rehabilitation center were rated by patients. The importance of a service was rated on a 4-point scale of "extremely important," "important," "slightly important," and "not important." The rehabilitation center's performance was rated on a 4-point scale of "excellent," "good," "fair," and "poor." The ratings of all 14 services are also shown in Fig. 2–12B. This part of the figure is divided into four sections. Quadrant A shows important services that are not being offered at the desired performance levels. The rehabilitation center should concentrate on improving these services. Quadrant B shows important services the rehabilitation center is performing well; its job

A.

Service	Service description	Mean importance ratings	Mean performance ratings
1	General therapy program	3.83	2.63
2	Speech therapy	3.63	2.73
3	Occupational therapy	3.60	3.15
4	Nursing care	3.56	3.00
5	Food quality	3.41	3.05
6	Recreation program	3.41	3.29
7	Attractiveness of living area	3.38	3.03
8	"	3.37	3.11
9	"	3.29	2.00
10	"	3.27	3.02
11	"	2.52	2.25
12	"	2.43	2.49
13	"	2.37	2.35
14	"	2.05	3.33

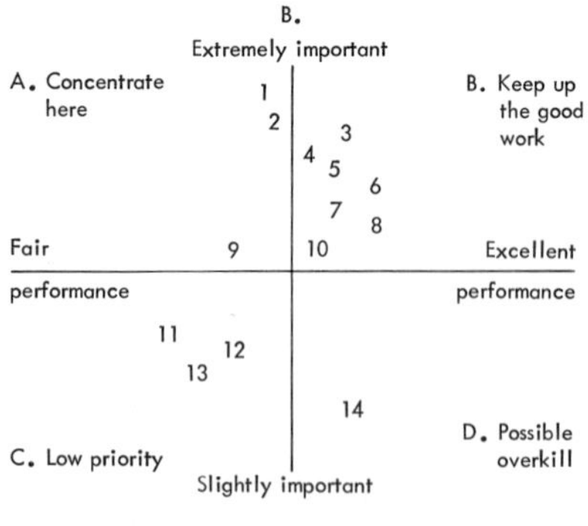

FIGURE 2–12 Importance and Performance Ratings for Rehabilitation Center Services
Source: Adapted from John A. Martilla and John C. James, "Importance-Performance Analysis," *Journal of Marketing* (Jan. 1977), pp. 77–79.

is to maintain the high performance. Quadrant C shows minor services that are being delivered in a mediocre fashion, but that need little additional attention since they are not important. Quadrant D shows a minor service that is being performed in an excellent manner, possibly a case of overkill. This rating of services according to their perceived importance and performance provides the organization with guidelines as to where it should concentrate its efforts.

Relation Between Consumer Satisfaction and Other Goals of the Organization

Some people believe that the marketing concept calls upon an organization to *maximize* the satisfaction of its customers. A more reasonable interpretation says that the organization should strive to create a high level of satisfaction for its consumers, but should weigh these efforts against the other needs of and pressures on the organization.

Consumer satisfaction can always be increased by accepting additional cost. However, in an era when public and political focus on cost containment in the health care sector is so high, such an approach would be unwise. And prospective reimbursement systems will no longer allow these costs to be passed on. A nursing home might ascertain that its patients' satisfaction level could be raised by between-meal snacks and by providing private rooms for all patients. However, while the nursing home could assume the additional cost of the snacks, it could not do so for the private rooms. Nor could it expect to pass on these costs to patients or third-party agencies.

Of particular concern to health care organizations is the weighing of immediate consumer satisfaction versus clinical needs. A hospitalized diabetic patient might be more satisfied with a higher calorie diet, but the patient's clinical need is for a low-sugar, low-calorie menu. Clearly, the organization's first responsibility is to provide the necessary clinical care. The organization seeks to satisfy many publics. Increasing the satisfaction of one public might reduce the satisfaction of another public. If all the parking spots nearest the hospital are reserved for the medical staff, the satisfaction of the medical staff is increased. Concommitantly, the satisfaction level of other hospital employees and of visitors to the hospital is reduced. Ultimately, the organization must operate on the philosophy that it is trying to satisfy the needs of different groups at levels that are acceptable to these groups within the constraint of its total resources.

SUMMARY

A responsive health care organization is one that makes every effort to sense, serve, and satisfy the needs and wants of its patients and publics within the constraints of its budget, and of the political, regulatory, and reimbursement environment. The concept of a responsive organization rests on the concepts of mission, exchange, publics, image, and satisfaction.

Every organization starts with a mission. A helpful approach to defining mission is to identify which customer groups will be served, which of their needs will be addressed, and which technologies will be used to satisfy these needs. A mission works best when it is feasible, motivating, and distinctive.

To carry out its mission, a health care organization needs resources. Marketing is based on attraction of resources through exchange. Marketing assumes that there are at least two parties; each can offer something of value to the other; each is capable of communication and delivery; and each is free to accept or reject the offer. Exchanges take place when both parties expect to be better off after the transaction.

Organizations carry on exchanges with several publics. A public is a distinct group of people and/or organizations that has an actual or potential interest in and/or impact on an organization. Publics can be classified as input publics (donors, suppliers, regulatory, and third-party payor publics), internal publics (management, board, staff, volunteers), intermediary publics (merchants, agents, facilitators, marketing firms), and consuming publics (clients and patients, local publics, activist publics, general public, media publics, and competitive publics). When the organization seeks some response from a public, we call this public a market. A market is a distinct group of people and/or organizations that has resources they want to exchange, or might conceivably be willing to exchange, for distinct benefits.

Responsive organizations are interested in their image, because it is their image to which people respond. An organization's image is the sum of beliefs, ideas, and impressions that a person or group has of that organization. Images can be measured by scaling techniques. Organizations can try to modify undesirable aspects of their image by changing their behavior and their communications.

The acid test of an organization's responsiveness is the satisfaction it creates. The more responsive organizations make use of complaint systems, surveys of satisfaction, surveys of needs and preferences, customer-oriented personnel, and customers who are given the power to influence the organization. Responsive organizations match performance to expectations, thereby creating high levels of satisfaction for their publics.

NOTES

1. See Peter F. Drucker, *Management: Tasks, Responsibilities, Practices* (New York: Harper & Row, 1973), chap. 7.

2. For further discussion, see Roberta N. Clarke and Linda Shyavitz, "Strategies for a Crowded Marketplace," *Health Care Management Review* (Summer 1983).

3. See Richard M. Emerson, "Power-Dependence Relations," *American Sociological Review* (February 1962), pp. 32–33.

4. Roberta N. Clarke, "The Dual Hierarchy of Power," paper presented at Nonprofit Marketing Conference, Columbia, South Carolina, April 1982.

5. Drucker, *Management,* p. 61.

6. C. E. Osgood, G. J. Suci, and P. H. Tennenbaum, *The Measurement of Meaning* (Urbana: University of Illinois Press, 1957). Other measuring tools exist, such as *object sorting* (see W. A. Scott, "A Structure of Natural Conditions," *Journal of Personality and Social Psychology,* 12, 4 (1969), pp. 261–78), *multidimensional scaling* (see Paul E. Green and Vithala Rao, *Applied Multidimensional Scaling,* New York: Holt, Rinehart and Winston, 1972), and item lists (see John W. Riley, Jr., ed., *The Corporation and Its Public,* New York: Wiley, 1963, pp. 51–62).

7. See Anthony Downs, *Inside Bureaucracy* (Boston: Little, Brown, 1967).

8. Quoted from a speech given by Frank Sinclair at a public relations conference of hospital administrators.

9. See "Medical Ombudsmen: More Hospitals Move to Improve Service through 'Advocates' Who Help Patients," *The Wall Street Journal,* August 27, 1976.

3

THE ADAPTIVE ORGANIZATION—DEVELOPING STRATEGIC PLANS

Organizations may be highly responsive to their clients and yet still find their survival threatened. Because of continuous changes in demographic, economic, technological, regulatory, political, reimbursement, and social forces, the market demand for an organization's services may change. New client needs and wants appear, new competition emerges, social values change, new laws and reimbursement policies are passed, and new technologies arise. The health care organization that sticks to its historical business may find itself serving the market of yesterday.

> The Perkins School for the Blind in Watertown, MA, started in the 1800s with the expressed purpose of educating blind school-age boys of normal intelligence, with no other handicaps. Over many decades, due to medical advances in identifying and treating the causes of blindness, there were fewer and fewer children with the single handicap of blindness. By the 1960s, the majority of blind people were middle-aged or older, and those children who were blind also tended to suffer from deafness, retardation, and/or a variety of other handicaps. Faced with a declining market of otherwise normal blind school-age boys, the Perkins School revamped its purpose and expanded its market to include children of both sexes with multiple handicaps.

> The National Jewish Hospital in Denver originated many years ago to serve patients with tuberculosis. Due to the public health movement and to increasing prosperity, the conditions that had fostered tuberculosis (overcrowded living conditions, poor nutrition, insanitary water and milk) began to decline. The discovery of drugs effective against tuberculosis further hastened the disappearance of the disease. The National Jewish Hospital would no longer have had patients to serve had it remained a tuberculosis hospital. It redefined its purpose as providing medical care to patients with a wide variety of respiratory diseases, such as asthma and emphysema.

The Sister Elizabeth Kenny Institute in Minneapolis was renowned for the intensive rehabilitation therapies it had developed and used for treating polio victims. With the development of the Salk vaccine in 1955 and the oral Sabin vaccine shortly thereafter, polio was virtually eliminated, and so was the need for the Sister Elizabeth Kenny Institute as a polio treatment center. However, believing that it could continue to contribute by turning its therapeutic skills elsewhere, the institute redefined its mission. It now provides its intensive therapy to individuals with major disabilities such as spinal cord injury and stroke.

In this chapter, we examine the characteristics of an adaptive organization. We define such an organization as follows:

> An **adaptive organization** is one that systematically monitors and interprets important environmental changes and shows a readiness to revise its mission, objectives, strategies, organization, and systems to align with its opportunities.

In the ideal case, a health care organization finds itself operating in a hospitable environment. It chooses appropriate objectives and develops a strategy for achieving those objectives. It develops a management structure that can effectively carry out the strategy. And it constructs workable systems of information, planning, and control that yield the data and plans needed to stay on track. The ideal case can be illustrated as follows:

Environment		Organization
Opportunities	⟶	Objectives⟶Strategy⟶Structure⟶Systems

In most cases, this ideal alignment is not realized. The main problem is that the various components change at different rates, resulting in a lack of fit. The most rapidly changing component is normally the environment. Such contemporary forces as changing demographics, increased competition, increased government regulation, altered reimbursement policies, changing social behavior and values, and new technologies have led social commentators to call this "an age of discontinuity"[1] and "future shock."[2] Clearly the health care environment's rate of change is faster than the ability of any health care organization to keep up with it. The result is that most health care organizations are less than optimally adapted to their environmental opportunities. Here is a typical situation:

Environment		Organization			
Opportunities	---	Objectives--	Strategy--	Structure--	Systems
1986		1983	1980	1977	1975

This organization is operating in a 1986 environment, but with objectives that were chosen in 1983. Basic strategy has not changed since 1980. The management structure itself has not been modernized since 1977. Finally, the organization is using systems of information, planning, and control that were designed in 1975. We can go further and predict that the organization's strategy, structure, and systems are dictating what opportunities it sees and pursues, rather than the organization studying its total opportunities and adapting its objectives, strategy, structure, and systems to work in the new environment.

To avoid this type of obsolescence, it is generally recommended that organizations look into the future and ask where the environment is going, what objectives would be reasonable in that environment, and what strategies, organizational structure, and systems would be appropriate. This set of activities is called *strategic planning.* It is a function necessary if an organization is to adapt in both the long and the short run.

Some health care organizations are already engaged in the full range of strategic planning activities, others are paralyzed. The reason for these different reactions is that organizations vary considerably in their adaptiveness to change. Some of the main factors influencing adaptability are these:

1. *Resources.* Organizations with smaller financial resources are slower to adapt because changing an organization costs money. Money is needed to carry out research on contemplated changes, to retrain management and employees, to hire specialists the organization needs, to build new internal systems for planning and control, and to inform the organization's publics about the new developments.
2. *Capital Investment.* Organizations with heavy capital investment in buildings, facilities, and equipment, such as hospitals, tend to adapt less quickly than organizations with low fixed investments, such as private medical group practices. If a hospital and a private medical group practice are both located in a declining area, the medical group practice is better able to adapt because it can move to a more attractive area.
3. *Organization constraints.* Organizations that are subject to regulatory, political, labor market, and union constraints are less adaptive in the face of needed change. Highly regulated health care organizations are going to be slower to change.
4. *Organizational leadership.* Professionally managed organizations tend to be more adaptive than organizations run by nonprofessionals or profes-

sionals trained in clinical areas. Some clinicians with substantial management skills do provide excellent leadership for health care organizations, but the majority of clinicians have a vested interest in protecting their profession. Professional managers are more interested in making the organization work than in protecting the interests of a particular profession.

5. *Organization size.* It is generally thought that very large organizations tend to be less adaptive than small organizations. Changing the direction of a battleship is much harder than changing the direction of a rowboat. However, few health care organizations are so large that it inhibits their ability to adapt. Moreover, smaller health care organizations may be so lacking in financial resources that they cannot afford to adapt easily.

We will examine the need for adaptive behavior and the tools for guiding change. Specifically, we will look at (1) the kind of environmental change that brings the need for adaptability, (2) organizational responses to change, (3) strategic planning, and (4) marketing strategy, both of which are used to help an organization adapt to its environment.

ENVIRONMENTAL CHANGE

Although an organization may currently be well matched to its environment, the possibility of environmental change poses a potential threat to its survival. Health care organizations must deal with particularly rapid and sometimes unpredictable environmental changes in federal and local regulation, reimbursement by private and government agencies, the advent of competitive entrepreneurial ventures by providers and nonprovider investors, and research or grant-dependent funding. Each election of government officials presents the possibility of major changes in the environment.

The character of an organization's environment is as much or more of a determinant of its survival than the quality of its leadership.[3] Organizational environments range from stable to turbulent. We can distinguish four types of environments.[4]

1. *Stable and unchanging.* Few health care, social service, or welfare organizations are lucky enough to find themselves operating in a stable and unchanging environment. Strategic planning plays a limited role for these organizations; successful past strategies should also be successful in the future, given that the strategies are addressing essentially the same environment. Tactical planning becomes more important in this type of environment. Current examples of this type of organization are almost nonexistent due to the major upheavals in the health care environment in the past two decades.

2. *Stable with minor fluctuations.* Some organizations operate in an environment characterized by seasonal and/or cyclical fluctuations within a fairly stable framework. A pediatric medical practice can provide a predetermined range of health care services, with adjustments in scale of operation according to seasonal demands. These changes in demand include higher demand in winter due to colds and viruses, lower demand in summer when many children are away on vacation, sudden temporary surges in demand for physicals in May and June, prior to summer camp, and in August, prior to school.
3. *Slowly changing in a predictable fashion.* Some organizations have an environment that is slowly being transformed into something new and predictable. For example, hospitals that have traditionally focused on maternity services can foresee an environment in which there is less demand for maternity services and a greater need for infertility services. With this awareness, they can make the necessary adjustments in objectives, strategy, structure, and systems.
4. *Rapidly changing in an unpredictable fashion.* Most health care organizations have experienced a succession of shocks and surprises in recent years: government constraints on hospital expansion, new forms of health care delivery (such as HMOs, PPOs, and free-standing emergency centers), major cutbacks in entitlement funds, drastic policy changes in reimbursement, the development of multi-institutional systems and chains, formerly major referral sources becoming major competitors, and rising public outcry against a variety of aspects of the health care system (primarily focused on costs). Strategic planning is much more important than tactical planning in this environment.

The health care environment seems to be growing more turbulent over time, not less. An organization that blindly maintains its usual course while its environment changes dramatically is courting disaster.

RESPONSES TO CHANGE

Most organizations, when threatened, attempt to respond. Unfortunately, the response is not always appropriate or timely. In principle, the organization can respond to a challenge in four ways:

1. *Denial.* The organization can refuse to recognize what is happening in the environment. Many community health agencies initially chose to ignore the growth of competing home health services offered by proprietary chains, community hospitals, and senior citizen homecare corporations.
2. *Opposition.* The organization can try to fight, restrain, or reverse the unfavorable developments. Thus hospitals use their trade association, with limited success, to lobby against impending legislation that dictates how much they can charge for their services and what services they can offer the public.

3. *Modification.* The organization can try to modify its own characteristics so that it is more attractive in the new environment. Some health care providers have added evening and weekend hours to meet increasing consumer demand for better access. A small number of organizations have undergone extensive modifications, the result of responding by changing their mission.
4. *Relocation.* The organization may keep its mission but shift its services to a more compatible environment. In recent years, many health care organizations have moved to the suburbs, abandoning locations in the less hospitable inner city.

Pfeffer and Salancik have identified three specific modes by which organizations can improve their survival chances in a turbulent environment:[5] controlling resources, establishing alliances, and altering the environment.

Gaining Control of Key Resources

Organizations can strengthen their positions by gaining more control over critical resources. One possibility is *vertical integration.* This has two components: trying to gain control over sources of supply (*backward integration*) or means of distribution (*forward integration*). For example, a hospital might run its own nursing school in order to ensure a constant supply of nurses (backward integration), or it might add home health services to serve its patients once they are discharged (forward integration).

Another strategy is *horizontal integration.* Hospital chains such as Humana and Hospital Corporation of America continue to acquire more hospitals as a way of increasing their resources and client base. Goldsmith,[6] based on American Hospital Association surveys, estimates that by 1979 over 80 percent of all U.S. hospitals participated in some form of shared services, and that 30 percent were involved in formal systems. Clearly, one of the greatest changes the health care field is expected to experience during this century is the transition from a cottage industry to a group of horizontally integrated systems.

Finally, an organization may pursue *diversification;* that is, it may enter additional businesses not directly related to its present business. The trend toward diversification in the health care field is sufficiently notable to have drawn major attention in the business press (see Exhibit 3–1).

The trends toward integration and diversification are likely to continue as the health care environment becomes more threatening. These strategies offer protection to the organization in a difficult environment by allowing the organization to spread its risk by depending on many markets.

EXHIBIT 3–1 Financial Cure?

Some Hospitals Are Entering Diverse Businesses, Often Unrelated to Medicine, to Offset Losses

Some hospitals are trying hard to cure their financial ills.

In Los Angeles, Northridge Hospital expects its 1981 operating surplus—comparable to a corporation's profit—to increase 12% because it owns, among other things, another hospital; a 73-bed facility to treat alcoholism and drug abuse; a restaurant, and a shopping center.

In New York, Columbia-Presbyterian Hospital hopes to cash in on Manhattan's housing shortage by building condominium apartments.

And in Dallas, Baylor University Medical Center owns four other hospitals, a construction company, an insurance concern, an office building, a hotel, a health spa and three restaurants.

Although the number of such investments by hospitals is still small, it's growing. In addition, dozens of nonprofit hospitals are spinning off profit-seeking, tax-paying businesses that sell, outside the hospital, services closely related to those already provided within the institutions.

Hospitals are running retirement-housing projects; providing home health-care services that help people stop smoking, lose weight and deal with stress; own medical-supply and laboratory-services firms, and even sell to other hospitals the management skills developed in setting up such enterprises.

Such activities reflect a significant change among the nation's 7,000 nonprofit hospitals, many of which long assumed that their tax-exempt status enabled them to ignore profitability. "For the first time, non-profit hospitals are thinking like hardheaded businessmen," says Robin E. MacStravic, an associate professor of health-services administration at the University of Washington in Seattle. "Few hospitals will survive if they rely solely on patient care for income."

The reason: Hospital costs are outpacing revenues. Many institutions are running up large deficits, and those that break even often don't have enough cash left over to replace outmoded equipment and facilities.

Meanwhile, private donations have dropped. "A good-sized hospital once got as much as $1 million a year in gifts; now, $100,000 is a lot," says Adrian Samojilowicz, the president of Community Medical Center in Scranton, Pa. In addition, endowment funds are shrinking as hospitals have been forced to dip into capital to pay their bills.

Squeezed for cash, some hospitals have turned to the tax-exempt bond market. But after a decade of heavy borrowing, "the nonprofit-hospital industry is fast reaching its debt capacity," says Thomas W. Reed, the president of Blyth Eastman Paine Webber Health Care Funding Inc., a unit of the New York securities firm. "By diversifying," Mr. Reed notes, "a hospital can be a better credit risk."

But some health experts are skeptical about the diversification trend.

"What's a hospital's competitive advantage in running a supermarket?" asks Victor R. Fuchs, a professor of economics at Stanford University. Mark Kleinman, the head of the Consumer Coalition for Health, a consumer-activist group in Washington, worries that "all this concern with making money might distract a hospital from its prime mission."

MODEST PROFITS

However, others term such worries premature. "I see a lot of businesses, but not that much money being made so far," says Robert A. Derzon, a hospital consultant with Lewin & Associates in Washington and a former high official in the Department of Health, Education and Welfare during the Carter administration. He is all for hospital diversification, but he thinks that there's more to it than just making money.

"In the old days," he says, "a hospital manager got his kick from building a bigger hospital. But in most parts of the country, there's little need now for expansion. Building new businesses is the latest kick."

Hospitals scrambling to set up new ventures disagree. "What we're doing is essential to maintain the quality our patients expect," says Larry J. Smith, vice president of Alta Bates Corp., a holding company formed by the board of trustees of the Alta Bates Hospital in Berkeley, Calif.

SERVING NEW AREAS

Other hospitals are reaching out of their immediate areas for better-heeled patients. Columbia-Presbyterian, New York's prestigious but deficit-ridden teaching and research hospital that serves many poor people living nearby in northern Manhattan, recently paid $7 million for an abandoned hospital building in the more prosperous midtown area. Through a separate company, the hospital will rent office space in the building's lower floors to its staff doctors—in the hope that they will attract richer patients who will use Columbia-Presbyterian. And to defray the cost of providing the relatively inexpensive offices, the hospital will build condominium apartments on the upper floors.

Other hospitals use new businesses as a shield against inflation. Baylor University Medical Center says it has saved hundreds of thousands of dollars by having its own construction company do work for it and for the other four hospitals now owned by the medical center. . . .

SOURCE: Michael Waldholz, *The Wall Street Journal,* August 12, 1981. Reprinted by permission of *The Wall Street Journal,*

Making sound decisions on integration and diversification requires substantial marketing information and analysis. Marketing can answer such critical questions as these: What are the opportunities and risks in the present business area? Which competitors/businesses would be best for takeover? What unrelated businesses would be attractive to enter?

Establishing Alliances

Another way for an organization to adapt to a changing environment is to form alliances with other organizations having similar interests. Health care organizations have long had these alliances in the form of *professional associations* or *trade associations* (such as the American Hospital Association, the National Association of Private Psychiatric Hospitals, or the Medical Group Management Association). The past decade has also witnessed an enormous growth of *multi-institutional systems* and *shared services* in response to an increasingly threatening environment. These alliances are not as encompassing as trade associations and often do not involve acquisition of one organization by another. Rather, they are uniquely defined relationships between two or more organizations that increase the ability of each to survive.

Altering the Legal and Social Environment

Although the health care environment is largely beyond an organization's control, health care organizations can attempt to exercise some influence on their environments. They can try to influence or alter actual and potential legislation, regulatory procedures, reimbursement policies, and social sanctions in their favor. A major purpose of professional and trade associations is to lobby in the interests of their members—to make the environment in which their members operate more favorable.

Marketing skills play an important role in these efforts, especially in the case of lobbying, which is essentially the marketing of a cause where the target audience is legislators. Effective lobbyists get to know their market (legislators), build a reputation for providing dependable information, and act to service their market. The effective lobbyist concentrates on building long-term goodwill and trust for the good of a group of organizations or individuals.

Organizations may also react singly to influence the environment in their favor. The Leonard Morse Hospital in Natick, Massachusetts, threatened by the HSA with loss of its obstetric service, organized and transported over 200 of its former obstetric patients and community residents to protest the closing at a public hearing. The hospital was allowed to keep its obstetric services. Other health care organizations have sued government bodies or sought support through the media in order to protest unfavorable conditions or decisions.

STRATEGIC PLANNING

Many health care organizations think they already have strategic planning[7] because they already have a planning function and may even have one or more staff members whose sole responsibility is to plan. However, the relationship between traditional health care planning and strategic planning is like that of second cousins: There's a blood relationship, but generally only a little similarity between the two.

Health care planning began in the 1960s as a *facilities planning* function. Organizations developed strategies around existing and planned facilities, giving little thought to other variables that might affect them. By the early 1970s, it became apparent that there was more to planning than bricks and mortar, and organizations added program planning to facilities planning: "Say, when we build our new building (facilities), let's put a backache clinic in it (program)." Both orientations assumed a continuation of the growth of the previous decades.[8]

By the early 1980s, the restraints on growth and on resources in the health care field had become apparent. Instead of planning for "new" and "more," planners began to consider market and competitive variables. They started asking questions like these: "How should our organization define itself? How should our organization achieve its mission? To whom should the organization be offering services?" Instead of planning for growth, health care organizations began to see planning as a way to meet the needs and wants of their markets, using their facilities and programs as tools for this purpose.

This is a step in the right direction, but this approach still does not encompass all the variables necessary for consideration in a strategic plan. A health care organization engaged in strategic planning would have to consider at the very least the following variables: environmental, sociological, political, legal, financial, reimbursement, economic, clinical, market, competitive, and facilities, as well as the organization's own goals and resources. A strategic plan must take into account all the variables that influence the organization's destiny.

This is strategic planning as it is defined in the corporate world, where the function has been in existence for more than a decade. It calls for a recognition and analysis of all the factors affecting the organization. It also requires predicting what will happen with regard to each of these variables: What new laws and reimbursement mechanisms will affect the health care field? What new competitive health care delivery forms will evolve, and how will they affect existing health care organizations? What will the economy do, and what impact will it have on health care usage?

These predictions are difficult to make for any organization. They are particularly difficult for health care organizations because of the turbulence that has characterized the field in the last decade. Planners, who are often responsible for or involved in the strategic planning function, have historical data from which to draw out trends. However, in a turbulent environment, where the future may be very different from the past, historical trends may be of little use. In addition, most health care planning functions do not receive a budget sufficient to allow them to collect current data that might be useful in planning for the future. Yet in spite of the difficulties inherent in strategic planning, health care organizations that want to be adaptive should make their best effort to develop and implement strategic plans.

Our definition of strategic planning reflects the current emphasis on marketing elements. As the health care field becomes more sophisticated about strategic planning over time, the definition will expand. We define strategic planning as follows:

> **Strategic planning** is the managerial process of developing and maintaining a strategic fit between the organization's goals and resources and its changing market opportunities.

Management has to pay attention to *market evolution* and *strategic fit*. All markets undergo evolutionary development: changing customer needs, technologies, competitors, methods of service delivery, and laws. The organization should be looking out of a *strategic window* watching these changes and assessing the requirements for continued success in each market.[9] There is only a limited period when the fit between the requirements of a particular market and the organization's offering is at an optimum. At these times, the strategic window is open. Later, when the organization finds that it can no longer be effective or efficient in serving this market, it should consider disinvesting and shifting its resources to new areas.

The major steps an organization must take to remain adaptive and strong in a changing environment—to engage in strategic planning—are shown in Figure 3–1. First, the organization must carry out a careful analysis of its environment, both today's environment and tomor-

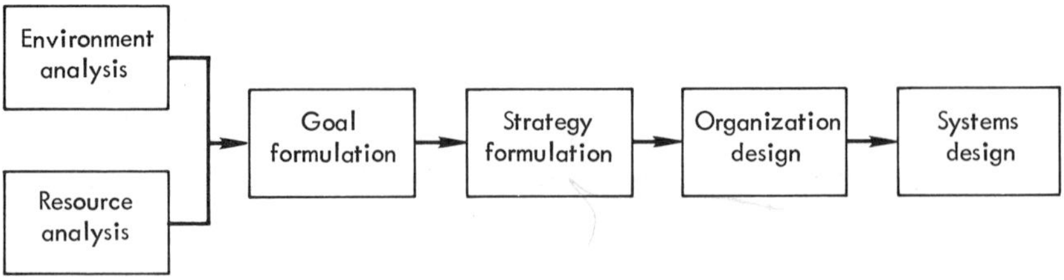

FIGURE 3–1 Strategic Market Planning Process

row's, to ascertain major opportunities and threats. Then it must review its major resources to determine what it can hope to do given its resource limitations. These two analyses lead the organization to formulate new and appropriate goals to pursue in the coming planning period. Goal formulation is followed by strategy formulation. Management chooses the most cost-effective strategy for reaching its goals. The strategy will undoubtedly point to certain changes that must be made in organization structure. Finally, to carry out the strategy effectively, the organization will turn its attention to improving its systems of information, planning, and control. When all these components are aligned, they will allow the organization to adapt to and perform in its changing environment.

We will not explore the strategic planning process in great depth here. Strategic planning is a separate subject that deserves more attention than it can be given here.[10] But some issues involved in the strategic planning process are directly tied to marketing. We will examine these issues as they relate to health care organizations.

Environmental Analysis

In order to be adaptive, the organization must identify the direction in which it wants to go. This requires examination of major environmental trends and their implications. The value of an environmental analysis lies in the identification of marketing opportunities and environmental threats.

Marketing opportunities can be assessed in terms of (1) their potential attractiveness (measured by the amount of revenue or value they might produce for the organization), and (2) their success probability (measured by the ability of the organization to develop the opportunity). Environmental threats can be similarly assessed in terms of (1) their potential severity (measured by the amount of money, prestige, or other valued resources the organization would lose if the threat materialized), and (2) their probability of occurrence.

For many years, health care organizations were not particularly interested to identifying marketing opportunities. As long as substantial funds were available, health care organizations could offer the services they wanted to offer, secure in the knowledge that funding was not a problem. But as charitable and government funds declined, health care organizations turned to identifying marketing opportunities that could produce additional revenue. Many have now become adept at assessing the potential attractiveness of a marketing opportunity, but fewer have developed the ability to identify the probability of success in developing those opportunities. Most health care organizations fail to recognize the magnitude of resources necessary to develop, implement, manage, and control new or modified programs.

For example, an area home care corporation (a semi-public agency for the elderly) that was providing homemaking services staffed by volunteers thought it could profitably expand by providing home health care services. While management recognized the need to hire nurses, it did not realize that the organization would need Medicare certification because most home health care is Medicare covered. In addition, if it was to compete against established home health agencies, such as the Visiting Nurse Association, it would have to engage in aggressive personal selling to referral sources, a costly endeavor requiring staff who would not themselves directly produce revenue. What was initially viewed as a "major opportunity for an organization like ours" later became "a bad idea, too costly and too iffy." Unfortunately, the corporation had already spent a few thousand dollars on brochures and mailings announcing this new home health care service before dropping it.

Health care organizations traditionally were little concerned about environmental threats. By and large, few major environmental threats existed in the health care environment through the 1960s. Physicians were held in reverence by the American public. Hospitals were viewed primarily as places of healing, with little thought given to costs, efficiency, or the risk of poor treatment. On the whole, the health care industry, because it was perceived as "doing good," was a protected industry. Two decades of rising costs, increasing consumerism, regulation, and competition has taken the halo away from the industry. And these trends, along with others, pose major environmental threats to health care organizations. As with marketing opportunities, health care organizations usually can realistically assess the potential severity of environmental threats, but are less able to judge the probability of occurrence.

The area home care corporation that failed to judge a marketing opportunity adequately also had difficulty assessing the probability of an environmental threat: the loss of state funds, which represented over half its total funding. Whether the state would continue the funding the following year depended upon who was elected to the legislation, whether a state tax control bill was passed, and what other interests were being strongly represented to the legislature. The home care corporation knew that loss of state funds would mean closing the agency. But it could not assess the probability of loss of state funds. Moreover, ability to react to this threat was hampered by very limited resources.

Resource Analysis

The primary reason why a health care organization should analyze its resources and capabilities is to identify its strengths and weaknesses. The premise of a resource analysis is that an organization should pursue goals, opportunities, and strategies congruent with its strengths and avoid areas where its resources are weak.

The format for a resource analysis is called a resource audit:

> A **resource audit** entails listing the organization's major resources and evaluating each as constituting a strength, a neutral factor, or a weakness of the organization.

For example, a nursing home might use a resource audit like the one in Exhibit 3–2. The checks reflect the nursing home's evaluation of its resources. One gets the sense of an organization that is well located, with good facilities, delivering care to an attractive (probably better reimbursed) patient segment. However, the nursing home seems to be understaffed, making it difficult for staff to be very service-oriented. The staff is clinically adequate, but the people are not very satisfied with their jobs. Additionally, the organization has very weak management systems, which could mean trouble if the environment becomes more turbulent.

To identify its best opportunities, a health care organization should look to its *distinctive competences,* those resources and abilities in which the organization is especially strong. The nursing home's distinctive competence seems to lie in its attractive facilities and location, which draw a better-paying market segment and result in a generally good reputation. It would not be viewed as having a distinctive medical competence given no notable clinical competence in its staff, a slight turnover problem, and a greater understaffing problem.

It is easier for an organization to work from its strengths than it is to build up a balanced set of strengths by shoring up its weaknesses. While every organization wants to correct its weaknesses, it cannot expect to develop them into distinctive competences. Furthermore, a distinctive competence may not be enough if the organization's major competitors possess the same distinctive competence. The organization should pay attention primarily to those strengths in which it possesses a *differential advantage;* that is, where it can outperform competitors. For example, the Baylor Medical Center not only has an excellent cardiac surgery service, but also has the renowned Dr. Michael DeBakey on its staff, which gives it a differential advantage in pursuing preeminence in that area.

In evaluating its strengths and weaknesses, the organization must not rely on its own perceptions, but go out and do an *image study* of how it is perceived by its key publics. For example, the management of a hospital may think the hospital is known for the high quality of its medical care. Yet an image study may reveal that it is viewed as being ill-equipped for sophisticated diagnoses, but having a very friendly nursing staff. Image research findings often reveal that health care or-

EXHIBIT 3–2 Nursing Home Resource Analysis

Note: H = high; M = medium; L = low; N = neutral

Resource	*Strength*				*Weakness*		
	H	M	L	N	L	M	H
Staff							
Clinical competence				√			
Service orientation					√		
Staff satisfaction/low turnover						√	
Full complement of nurses, aides, etc.						√	
Financial Resources							
Adequate				√			
Flexible				√			
Reimbursement Sources							
Sufficient payment per day		√					
Certain payment (few retroactive denials)			√				
Facilities							
Attractive location	√						
Attractive building		√					
Aesthetic interior	√						
Adequate size		√					
Flexible design		√					
Systems							
Adequate planning system						√	
Adequate information system						√	
Adequate control system						√	
Market Assets							
Attractive patient segment	√						
Good community relations			√				
Good general reputation		√					

ganizations have strengths and weaknesses of which they are unaware, and other strengths and weaknesses they have exaggerated.

Goal Formulation

The environmental and resource analyses are designed to provide management with the information necessary to formulate organizational goals. Due to the dramatic changes in the health care environment in recent years, we can no longer assume that goals appropriate for an organization in the past will be appropriate in the future. For instance, organizations that existed to provide social welfare, residential, and medical services to unwed mothers have all but disappeared. Some of the organizations that had provided these services recognized the need to reformulate goals and are now providing information on birth control and related services to teenagers, both male and female.

The purpose of developing a clear set of organizational goals is to keep the organization from drifting into an uncertain future. Goals enable the organization to determine what it should be doing, to develop effective plans, to create targets for performance, and to evaluate results. Without goals, anything the organization does or achieves can be considered acceptable; there is no standard for planning, control, or evaluation.

Determining what those goals should be is a difficult task. In principle, the administrator and/or the board of a health care organization can unilaterally set new goals for the next decade. Increasingly, however, top management has found it useful to involve other publics—clinical staff, referral sources, and other constituencies—in the process of goal formulation. The resulting goals are more likely to be embraced and supported because these publics were involved in their formulation.

Goal formulation involves the organization in determining an appropriate mission, objectives, and goals for the current or expected environment. The mission is the basic purpose of an organization; that is, what it is trying to accomplish. An objective is a major variable the organization will emphasize, such as financial strength, depth of clinical expertise, general reputation, or census. A goal is an objective that is made specific with respect to magnitude, time, and responsibility. We will examine these concepts below.

Mission. Health care organizations often pursue multiple objectives that are not ranked according to importance and that cannot be satisfied simultaneously. Also, most missions are not very distinctive when compared to the missions of similar—and competing—organizations. Most community hospitals, for example, have a stated mission to provide the highest quality medical and personal care to anyone who seeks it. While there is nothing wrong with this as part of a hospital's mission, it certainly does not provide a basis for distinction.

The value of having a mission, usually formally recognized in a *mission statement,* is to provide everyone in the organization with a shared sense of purpose, direction, and achievement. The mission statement should act as an invisible hand that helps widely scattered staff, clinicians, and volunteers to work independently and yet collectively toward realization of the organization's goals.

Consider a community hospital which, in addition to reasonable medical care, stresses delivering excellent personal care and amenities to the patient. This hospital would develop systems, such as primary nursing, that would allow the delivery of more personal service. It would also invest in its food service and in making its physical facilities esthetically pleasing. These actions would be taken, of course, in addition to clinical care, which is the primary reason for the hospital's existence. Contrast this situation to that of a hospital whose mission statement stresses greater medical sophistication. This hospital would invest in the acquisition of more sophisticated diagnostic equipment, the hiring of technicians to run and maintain the equipment, and the attraction of medical specialists to the staff. The whole mission of greater medical sophistication suggests that the hospital's patients will be sicker. The mission thus has implications regarding the need for a medical residency program to care for sicker patients, a changed patient age mix (probably resulting in older patients on average), a different payor mix (possibly more Medicare patients) and, under DRG reimbursement, possibly a financially less attractive group of patients.

Each mission implies a particular type of patient or market, and calls for a particular way of supplying value to that market. Developing a clear definition of its mission will lead an organization to emphasize certain things and deemphasize others. Defining mission is critical, because the definition should affect everything the organization does.

Objectives. Each organization should develop major objectives for the coming period that reflect the organization's mission. For example, the community hospital whose mission stresses personal care and amenities might include in its objectives these ideas: the attraction of patients who are not so sick they cannot appreciate the amenities, a low turnover rate among nurses, a full complement of nursing staff in order to facilitate the delivery of highly personal care, better food with more breadth in menu choice, improved physical plant, and a lower operating deficit.

In any given year, an organization may choose to emphasize certain objectives and ignore others or treat them as constraints. For example, the community hospital may be able to lower the turnover of nursing staff by raising salaries significantly. However, it is subject to the constraint of not letting the operating deficit grow beyond a certain level. Management must balance one objective against another (lowering nurse turnover vs. lowering the operating deficit) in meeting its mission. This balance may vary from year to year, depending upon management's perceptions of the major problems and opportunities the organization faces.

Goals. Objectives must be restated in an operational and measurable form called goals. The objective "low nurse turnover" must be turned into a goal such as "a 15 percent decrease in nurse turnover in the next 8 months." A goal statement permits the organization to think about the planning, programming, and control aspects of pursuing that objective. Questions arise: Is a 15 percent decrease in turnover feasible? What strategy should be used? What resources will it take? What activities will have to be carried out? Who will be responsible and accountable? All these critical questions must be answered when deciding whether to adopt a proposed goal.

Typically, the organization will be evaluating a large set of potential goals at the same time and examining them for consistency and priorities. The organization may discover that it cannot simultaneously achieve "a 15 percent turnover decrease," "a 10 percent decrease in operating deficit," and a "20 percent expansion of number of items on the menu." In this case, management may make adjustments in target levels or target dates, or drop certain goals altogether in order to arrive at a practical, achievable set of goals.

A common mistake among health care organizations unaccustomed to setting goals is to make them unduly optimistic. Instead of viewing goals as a management tool, they use goals for internal public relations—"We're so good that we should be able to fill 95 percent of our beds next year"—or as an outlet for wishful thinking. One neighborhood health center which had taken five years to sign up 3,000 members set new goals when it was planning to expand into new quarters and add new services. Within the next six months, its goals were to double its membership. Since many of the center's services were already underutilized and since the new services were likely to be used by existing members, the goal of doubling its membership did not seem justified.[11] The process of setting goals is useful only if the organization can develop strategies which make the goals attainable.

Strategy Formulation

To develop feasible strategies, a health care organization should proceed in two stages. First, it should develop a *product portfolio strat-*

egy—that is, decide what to do with each of its current major products (services). Second, it should develop a *product/market expansion strategy*—that is, decide what new products (services) and markets to add.

Product Portfolio Strategy. Most health care organizations are multiproduct organizations. They generally start with one product and over time add others. Thus, hospitals usually offer many inpatient services, several ambulatory services, plus a variety of other programs (health promotion, industrial medicine, and so on).

An organization's programs will vary in importance and contribution to the organization's mission. Some programs are large, others small; some growing, some declining; some of high quality, others not. Most health care organizations find it easier to add new programs than to remove failing ones. Existing programs always have built-in advocates: The pediatric medical staff will resist efforts to close down pediatric beds, even though pediatric admissions continue their long-term decline. In periods of economic prosperity, the organization may have enough money to satisfy everyone. The administration does not want to make enemies and settles for an inefficient allocation of resources. However, when the organization faces economic hardship, administrators are forced to make hard choices because there is not enough money to make everyone happy.

Many health care organizations have now been forced to make careful evaluations of the programs in their portfolio. The first step is to identify the key businesses, programs, or products (services) of the organization. For example, a hospital might choose to view its portfolio as consisting of its medical services—obstetrics, pediatrics, general medicine, general surgery, oncology, neurology. This is an appropriate level of analysis if each service has its own leadership, adopts distinct goals, needs a strategy, and has a separate budget.

The task of the administration then is to determine which services should be given increased support (*build*), maintained at the present level (*hold*), phased down (*harvest*), and terminated (*divest*). The principle is that the organization's resources should be allocated in accordance with the "attractiveness" of each service, rather than equally to all services. The task is to identify appropriate criteria for evaluating the attractiveness of various services.

One of the earliest and most popular approaches was developed by the Boston Consulting Group (BCG), a management consulting group. Its scheme called for rating all the organization's products (services) along two dimensions—market growth and market share (see Figure 3–2). *Market growth* is the annual rate of growth of the relevant market in which the product is sold. Relative *market share* is the organization's sales as a percentage of the leading firm's sales.[12] By dividing market

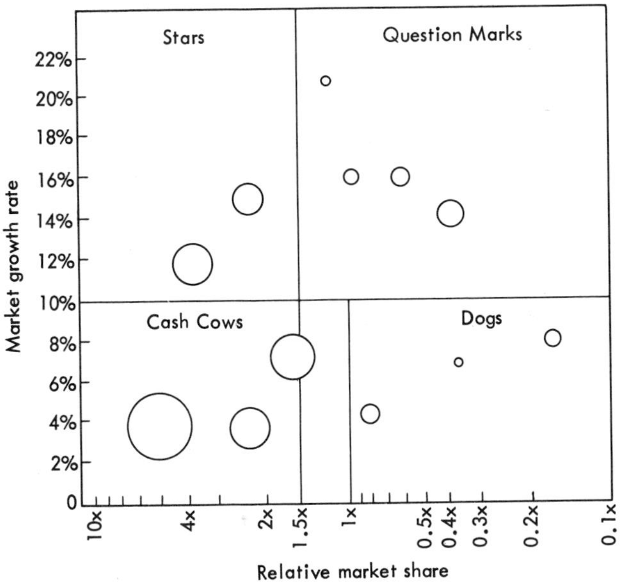

FIGURE 3–2 Boston Consulting Group Portfolio Approach
Adapted from: The Product Portfolio Matrix, © 1970, The Boston Consulting Group, Inc.

growth into high and low, four categories of products (businesses, services) emerge:

1. *Stars* are those products for which the organization enjoys high share in fast-growing markets. The organization will pour increasing resources into its stars in order to keep up with the market's growth and maintain share leadership.
2. *Cash cows* are those products for which the organization enjoys high share in slow-growth markets. Cash cows typically yield strong cash flows to an organization and pay the bill for other products that require investment. Without cash cows, an organization would need continuous subsidy.
3. *Question marks* are products for which the organization has only a small share in a fast-growing market. The organization faces the decision of whether to increase its investment in these products, hoping to make them stars, or to reduce or terminate its investment, on the grounds that the funds could be better used elsewhere in the organization.
4. *Dogs* are products that have a small market share in slow-growth or declining markets. Dogs produce little or no money for the organization. The organization will normally consider dropping them unless they are necessary for other reasons.

This scheme works well for traditional commercial businesses, but its value lessens in a field like health care, which does not necessarily seek rapid growth or high market share and often cannot control the "prices" it can charge. The BCG approach assumes that a high market share results in high-volume economies of scale. As the organization achieves greater economies of scale, its cost per unit of production is assumed to decline while its price per unit presumably stays the same, resulting in greater profitability per unit. But the health care field often profits less from high-volume economies of scale because it is so labor-intensive. As volume of services produced rises, so does the high variable-cost labor component associated with the production of the service, leaving little gain in profitability. Thus, the less labor-intensive, higher fixed-cost services, such as mechanized laboratory services, fit the BCG portfolio model better than highly labor-intensive services such as general medical care for the elderly.

In addition, the BCG portfolio approach assumes that "price" remains constant as cost per unit falls due to volume economies. Under traditional cost-based reimbursement, of course, this was not the case. The reimbursement rule of thumb, "cost or charges, whichever is less," meant that, if an organization's costs declined, its reimbursement also declined, resulting in no savings to the organization as a result of economies of scale. Moreover, in many cases the reimbursement per patient or per unit of service is set so low that it does not cover the organization's full costs; depending on the fixed costs/variable costs ratio, the organization may lose money for every additional patient served. At the very least, a service in which reimbursement does not cover full costs is not able to achieve a profit, and requires surplus revenues from other parts of the organization to subsidize it. In this situation, the high volume resulting from high market share brings financial difficulties rather than financial gain.

Consider, in a pre-DRG environment, a hospital, the majority of whose medical beds are filled by the elderly. The elderly constitute a rapidly growing health care market (high market growth). The hospital is serving more elderly than other hospitals nearby (high market share). By the BCG portfolio definition, the medical service should be a star. But the elderly require more nursing care than other patient segments.[13] Medicare does not reimburse for full costs. Thus, what would constitute a star in a normal commercial environment looks more like a dog in the health care field.

Under DRG reimbursement, the "price" remains constant, regardless of volume or costs, thus making the BCG portfolio more applicable. However, if the variable cost of the service is high and the fixed costs are low, the service still will not profit from a high market share and from the economies of scale a high volume can bring. Additionally, health care organizations anticipate that some DRG reimbursement rates will not cover full costs, particularly for the oldest and sickest patients. A high share of these patients, whether they be in high-growth markets or not, will not give the organization its cash cow.

Where the BCG approach does offer help is to the following: health care organizations that can set their own prices, such as medical group practices dealing with a self-pay market, and health care organizations that have less labor-intensive services. The BCG portfolio approach recognizes the value of one service, a cash cow, subsidizing another. In a hospital under cost-based reimbursement, laboratory and ancillary services often subsidized obstetrics and pediatrics. The former services produced a surplus; the latter services may not have been fully reimbursed and may have needed subsidization. Under prospective payment systems, certain DRGs will subsidize other DRGs. In order to make use of this cash producer/cash user scheme, health care organizations, particularly those that are nonprofit, must view profit-making not with alarm, but with the recognition that cash-using services can continue to be provided only if there are profitable cash-producing services to subsidize them.

An approach to portfolio evaluation with greater applicability to health care is General Electric's *strategic business planning grid* (see Figure 3–3). It uses two dimensions, market attractiveness and organizational strength. The best programs to offer are those that serve attrac-

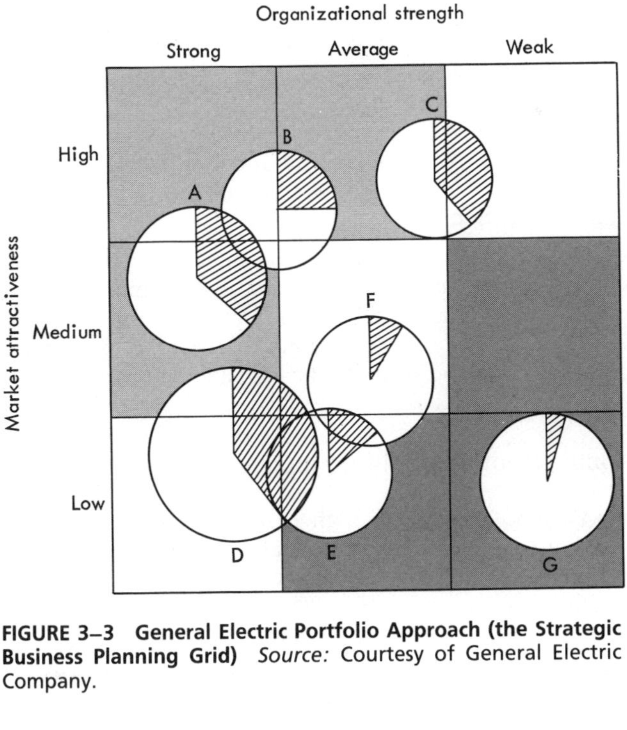

FIGURE 3–3 General Electric Portfolio Approach (the Strategic Business Planning Grid) *Source:* Courtesy of General Electric Company.

tive markets and for which the organization has high organizational strength.

In the original GE grid, the criteria for identifying market attractiveness were market size, market growth rate, profit margin, competitive intensity, cyclicality, seasonality, scale economies, and learning curve. Factors for measuring organizational strength were program quality, efficiency level, knowledge of the market, and marketing effectiveness.

To better fit the grid to the health care environment, we would modify the factors in the following ways. Market attractiveness would be a composite index composed of such factors as these:

Reimbursement mix and coverage. Markets primarily covered by private third-party insurance vs. government forms of insurance, for example, have traditionally been superior in terms of both amount of costs paid and speed of payment (cash flow), although this is now changing. These markets have also been more attractive due to fewer retroactive denials and less trouble needed to obtain payment. With prospective payment, reimbursement mix may become intimately tied to patient diagnosis mix.

Degree of regulation. The less regulated markets are more attractive than the highly regulated markets.

Competitive intensity. Markets with many strong competitors are less attractive than markets with fewer or weaker competitors.

Market size and market growth. Within the limits set by the existing and potential capacity of the organization to serve the market, larger markets and high-growth markets are more attractive than small and low-growth or declining markets.

Cyclicality and stability. Noncyclical and stable markets are more attractive than highly cyclical and unstable markets.

Scale economies and learning curve. Markets served by less labor-intensive services, where lower unit costs result in additional surplus (rather than lower reimbursement) for the organization are more attractive. Markets that offer high economies of scale and/or where unit costs fall as management accumulates experience are more attractive than markets with few economies of scale and/or that offer management little room to climb the learning curve.

Organizational strength would be judged by such factors as these:

Relative program quality. The higher the program quality (which could be composed of variables such as clinical strength, facilities, equipment, esthetics, and referral channels) relative to the competition, the greater its organizational strength.

Positioning and image. The greater the match between the position of a program and the overall image of the organization, the greater is the organizational strength. For example, a small rural hospital offering a highly sophisticated cardiac catheterization program would be a poor match.

Efficiency level. The more efficient the organization is at producing the program relative to competitors, the greater its organizational strength.

Market knowledge. The better the organization's knowledge of the customers (patients, clients) in a market, the greater its organizational strength.

The factors making up each dimension are scaled and weighted so that each current program achieves a number indicating its market attractiveness and organizational strength and therefore can be plotted in the grid. The grid is divided into three zones—green, yellow, and red. The meaning of the colors is the same as their meaning in a traffic light. The green zone consists of the three cells at the upper left, indicating programs that are located in attractive markets and for which there is organizational strength. The organization should invest in these programs and make them grow. The yellow zone consists of the diagonal cells stretching from the lower left to the upper right, indicating programs that are medium in overall attractiveness. The organization usually spends enough just to maintain these products. The red zone consists of the three cells on the lower right, indicating programs that are low in overall attractiveness. Here the organization gives serious consideration to harvesting or divesting.

As an example, consider program G in Figure 3–3. The graph indicates that program G is in an unattractive market and that the organization does not have substantial strengths to bring to it. It is a fairly large-volume product (indicated by the size of the circle), and the organization has only a small market share (indicated by the shaded wedge). The organization will want to consider phasing this product down or out.

The strategic business planning grid fits the health care field better than the BCG portfolio. However, the strategic business planning grid presents an ethical problem with which few other industries have to deal: Who will serve the universally unattractive markets? The grid suggests that organizations not serve unattractive markets. This is reasonable in commercial environments, but may be unacceptable in an industry which views its services as a "right" of the marketplace. Most people believe that health care is a right, a necessity rather than a luxury. And some health care markets may be unattractive for all organizations. The most likely market to fit this description is the sick elderly market, which is viewed as being costly to serve and historically poorly reimbursed. Under DRG's, many categories of the sick elderly are likely to be a universally unattractive market from a financial viewpoint. They nonetheless have a right to reasonable health care.

Product/Market Expansion Strategy. A health care organization that examines its current portfolio may discover that it does not have enough stars or cash cows and that it must become more aggressive in searching for new products and markets. Given the low availability of money plus threats of ever lower reimbursement levels for a significant number of patients, it is not uncommon for health care organizations to find that they need new cash-generating programs. What they need is a systematic approach to opportunity identification. A useful device for doing this is known as the product/market opportunity matrix (see Figure 3–4). Originally a 2 by 2 matrix proposed by Ansoff,[14] it is changed slightly here in order to show that the difference between the cells may be more one of degree than of kind. Markets are listed at the left and products along the top. The gray area between the cells represents the distinctions between existing and new markets, and between existing and new products or services.

Each cell presents a different type of opportunity. Take the example of a medical rehabilitation center that provides physical, speech, and other types of aggressive treatment therapies to adult patients with problems such as stroke and paraplegia. If the center can attract more patients like the ones it currently serves to use existing services, it is pursuing a *market penetration* strategy. If the rehabilitation center starts accepting teenagers with problems similar to those of the adult patients, it is serving *new markets.* The center may decide to make a videotape of a physical therapist demonstrating exercises patients can do once they return home. If it sells those tapes to its patients when they are about to be discharged, the center is pursuing the strategy of *product innovation.* And the center may develop a whole set of videotapes that show people whose jobs entail heavy lifting how to lift and exercise to avoid back strain. The center may promote and sell these tape sets to

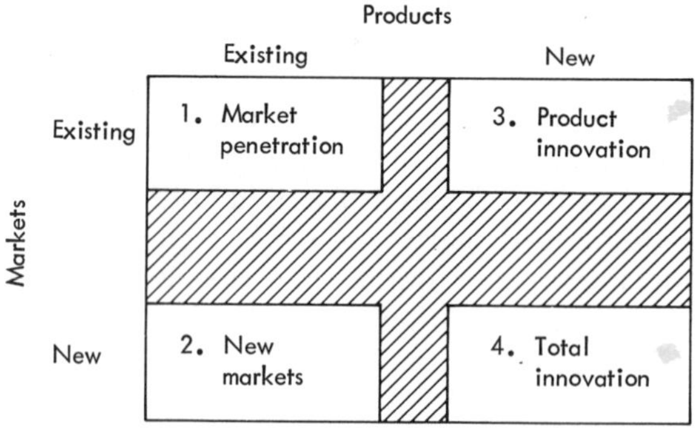

FIGURE 3–4 Product/Market Opportunity Matrix

companies which will show them to employees. This is a strategy of *total innovation.*

The strategic opportunity an organization pursues may fall into one of the four cells or it may fall into one of the gray areas between the cells. For example, the rehabilitation center may decide to serve children in need of aggressive therapy. This would constitute a new market (cell 2). However, in order to serve children adequately, the center would have to hire staff trained to deal with children; patient beds, wheelchairs and other equipment would have to be modified; play areas with appropriate toys would be necessary; and the center's general philosophy would probably have to be modified to reflect the very different needs of children. The center would have to modify its product in order to serve the new market. This strategy would fall in the gray area between cells 2 and 4 in the opportunity matrix.

One of the forms of new market opportunities (cell 2) an organization may pursue is *geographic expansion*—new geographic markets. Most health care organizations traditionally operated from one site. This generally limited them to the one geographic market defined by being within reasonable travel distance of the site. The option to expand to new geographic locations was historically pursued by only a few types of organizations, such as the religious hospital chains and the larger proprietary chains like Hospital Corporation of America and Homemakers Upjohn. In the newer, more competitive health care environment, we are seeing more geographic expansion through the use of multiple health care delivery sites. Chains of free-standing trauma centers, shopping mall dentist centers, nursing homes, hospitals, and the like are common in many parts of the country.

Organization Design

The purpose of strategy formulation is to develop strategies that will help the organization achieve its goals in the new environment. The existing organization must be capable of carrying out these strategies. It must have the *structure, people,* and *culture* to implement the strategy. For example, if a hospital wants to open an evening infertility clinic for working couples, it must have medical staff who are skilled in this area, as well as the clerical, security, and management staff to maintain this service during evening hours. Clearly, an organization's chosen strategies require appropriate skills and staff support to succeed. Most organization theorists believe that "structure should follow strategy," rather than the other way around.[15]

However, strategy may follow structure if inertia ("it's always been this way; why should we change?") and vested interests ("I'm not giving up any of my turf and control to someone else") take precedence over the need to respond to opportunities. In this case, the organization would be limiting itself to strategies that would be compatible with the existing organizational design. More important, in order to satisfy internal constraints, the organization would be limiting its adaptiveness.

In adopting a new strategic posture, the organization may also have to change the "culture" of the organization. The concept of corporate culture addresses the issue of what the organization thinks is important versus what is not in carrying out its mission. Health care organizations have generally stressed quality of clinical care, often to the exclusion of almost all other considerations. This medical or clinical culture has been critical of the business culture and of the marketing or survival culture. Health care managers who try to encourage the concept of personal caring—a kind bedside manner, pleasant delivery of nursing services, respecting the patient's requests to have full explanations about diagnosis and treatment—often encounter tremendous resistance: "My job is to diagnose and treat, not to sell. Your job is to attract patients." With the increasingly competitive health care environment, it is management's job to develop a culture where everyone sees his or her job as not just delivering clinical care, but also as sensing, serving, and satisfying the needs and the wants of the market. We will discuss organization design in more detail in Chapter 5.

Systems Design

The final step in strategic planning is to install the systems the organization needs to develop and carry out the strategies that will achieve its goals in the new environment. The three principal systems are the marketing information system, the marketing planning system, and the marketing control system.

Marketing Information System. The job of running an organization calls for continuous information about customers, marketing intermediaries, suppliers, competitors, publics, and the larger macroenvironment forces (demography, economy, politics, technology, and culture). This information can be obtained through planning, medical records and financial data, marketing intelligence, and marketing research. The information, if it is to be useful, must be accurate, timely, and comprehensive. The design of a modern marketing information system to support the organization's drive toward its goals is discussed in Chapter 6.

Marketing Planning System. Many health care organizations gather information in their planning process but fail to use this information in a disciplined way, particularly as it applies to marketing. Information, to be used effectively, requires a formal planning system in which annually developed long-term and short-term goals, strategies, marketing programs, and budgets are addressed from a marketing perspective. The planning discipline calls for a planning staff, planning resources, and a planning culture if it is to be successful. Luckily, many health care organizations have already developed the planning discipline and need only to give it a marketing perspective. The nature and design of an effective marketing planning system is discussed in Chapter 7.

Marketing Control System. Plans are useful only if they are implemented and monitored. The purpose of a marketing control system is to measure the results of a plan against the plan's goals and to take corrective action before it is too late. The corrective action may be to change the goals, plans, or implementation in the light of the new circumstances. The components of a marketing control system are also described in Chapter 7.

MARKETING STRATEGY

In this last section, we will examine the concept of marketing strategy and its relation to strategic planning. Strategic planning indicates the particular markets that represent the health care organization's best opportunities. The organization must develop a strategy for succeeding in each of these markets. Marketing strategy is the organization's adaptive strategy. We define it as follows:

> **Marketing strategy** is the selection of a target market(s), the choice of a competitive position, and the development of an effective marketing mix to reach and serve the chosen customers.

We examine the three major steps in marketing strategy: target market strategy, competitive positioning strategy, and marketing mix strategy. These basic ideas will be illustrated in terms of the following situation:

> Southwest Community Hospital is a full-service community hospital located in the suburbs 12 miles from the nearest city, which has two large teaching hospitals. In addition to the two teaching hospitals, there are at least eleven other community hospitals, most full-service, within a 12-mile radius of the city. Like most hospitals, Southwest Community finds it is having difficulty maintaining a comfortable census. Also, Southwest's fiscal officer has recently been heard issuing dire warnings about future financial problems due to low reimbursement rates and an unattractive patient diagnosis mix. The board wants Southwest's administrator to develop a marketing strategy for the late 1980s that will adapt the hospital to its best opportunities.

Target Market Strategy

The first step in preparing a marketing strategy is to understand the market.

> A **market** is the set of all people who have an actual or potential interest in a product or service.

The common definition of market in a commercial setting also includes the person's ability to pay for the product or service. A person who is interested in buying a car but has no money to pay for it is not considered part of the market. This aspect of the definition is not so clear in health care. Hospitals are mandated to serve people regardless of their ability to pay. While most hospitals do this, some will stabilize a nonpaying (not covered by reimbursement or able to self-pay) patient and then transfer that patient to a municipal hospital in order to avoid providing additional service to someone who cannot pay. On the other hand, many health care organizations run up significant bad debts each year by knowingly providing services to people who cannot pay. Some health care organizations choose not to serve patients who cannot pay. The Glenville Health Association, located in a poor neighborhood in Cleveland, considers itself a private group medical practice rather than a neighborhood health center. In spite of its choice of location, Glenville chooses to accept only those who can pay.

Whether to include "ability to pay" in the market definition is a choice; it is not a question answered by nonprofit or proprietary status. Some proprietary health care organizations provide services to those who cannot pay, while some nonprofit organizations do not. The choice to serve nonpaying patients is affected by the organization's ability to subsidize the bad debt by generating revenues elsewhere, by the organization's mission, and by the law.

Southwest Community Hospital might define its market as people residing or working in its community and in the eight surrounding communities. This is quite a large market, and Southwest would need only a small share to fill its beds and other services. But the administrator knows that not everyone wants to use Southwest Community, nor can Southwest serve every type of patient. Every market is heterogeneous; that is, it is made up of different types of customers or *market segments.* Therefore, the administrator would benefit from constructing a market segmentation scheme that outlines the major groups making up the market. Then the administrator could decide whether to try to serve all the segments (*mass marketing*) or concentrate on a few of the more promising ones (*target marketing*).

There are many ways to segment a market: by age, sex, income, life style, type of reimbursement, for example. Suppose the administrator

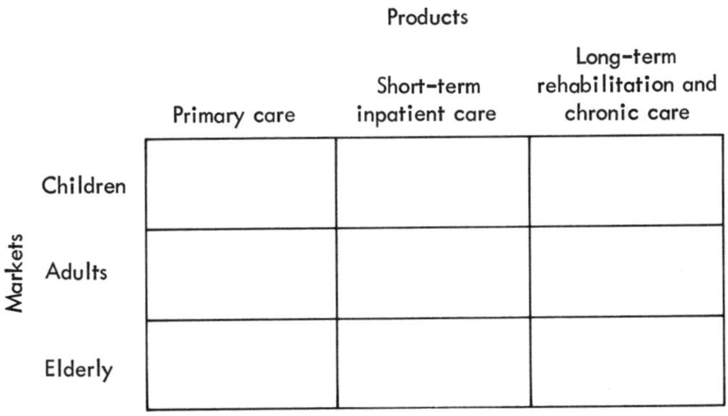

FIGURE 3–5 Segmentation of a Community Hospital Market

settles on the scheme shown in Figure 3–5. It shows three markets (children, adults, and elderly) and three products (primary care, short-term inpatient care, and long-term rehabilitation and chronic care.) The hospital is already providing primary care through its primary care evening and weekend clinic and has a small 12-bed rehabilitation unit, in addition to its main services of short-term intensive care. It is also serving all three markets. So it caters to all nine segments, but is not doing a distinguished job in any one. At the same time, competitors are beginning to concentrate on certain market segments and doing a first-class job. The administrator is wondering whether to pursue target marketing, and if so, what patterns to choose.

Five possible patterns of market coverage are shown in Figure 3–6 and described below:

1. *Product/market concentration* consists of an organization concentrating on only one product and one market segment—here, for example, providing chronic and rehabilitation care to the elderly.
2. *Product specialization* consists of the organization deciding to produce only one product (such as primary care) for all three markets.
3. *Market specialization* consists of the organization deciding to serve only one market segment (such as children) with all the products.
4. *Selective specialization* consists of the organization working in several product markets that have no relation to each other except that each provides an individually attractive opportunity.
5. *Full coverage* consists of an organization making the full range of products to serve all the market segments.

After researching these alternatives, the administrator decides the most attractive one for the hospital is product specialization—here,

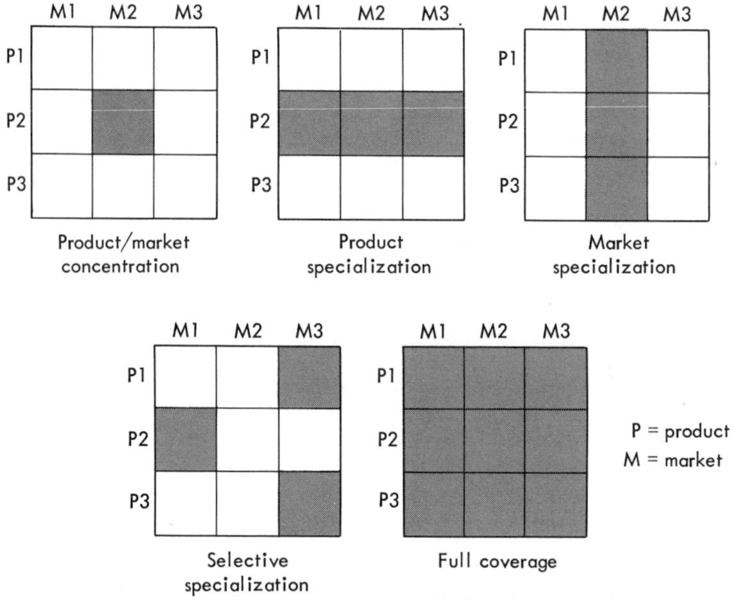

FIGURE 3–6 Five Patterns of Market Coverage *Source:* Adapted from Derek F. Abell, *Defining the Business: The Starting Point of Strategic Planning* (Englewood Cliffs, NJ: Prentice-Hall, Inc., 1980), chap. 8.

short-term inpatient care. This choice falls within the original mission of the hospital. However, the administrator also opts for a limited amount of market specialization as well by choosing to serve adults and the elderly, but not children.

The administrator's choice is dictated by the following conditions: (1) The provision of primary care is threatening to the medical staff and does not generate a surplus. (2) The current rehabilitation unit is too small to be financially viable. If it were to be expanded significantly, it would change the whole complexion of the hospital. Reimbursement rates for chronic and rehabilitation care are also not very attractive. (3) Three other hospitals have developed outstanding pediatric services, including one of the teaching hospitals, which provides 24-hour physician coverage of the pediatric service. It would be quite costly to develop a competitive service.

Having decided on short-term inpatient care for adults and the elderly, the administrator could choose to further refine or *subsegment* the market. This could be done, for example, geographically: the focus could be on the metropolitan market rather than the smaller nine-community service area. If the hospital is supported by a major religious organization, the market could be further segmented by religious affiliation.

Competitive Positioning Strategy

Having selected its target market, the hospital will now have to develop a competitive position strategy vis-à-vis other hospitals serving the same target market. Suppose there are three other hospitals within reasonable proximity of Southwest Community that provide good short-term inpatient care for adults. If the three hospitals are similar, then patients (and possibly physicians) would not have much basis for choice among the four. Their respective market shares would be left to chance. The antidote for this is competitive positioning, defined as follows:

> **Competitive positioning** is the act of developing and communicating meaningful differences between one's offer and those of competitors serving the same target market.

The key to competitive positioning is to ascertain the major attributes used by the target market to evaluate and choose among competitive organizations. Suppose the target market judges hospitals by their perceived medical quality (high versus low) and perceived personal care orientation (high versus low). Figure 3–7 shows the perceived competitive positions of the three competitive hospitals (A, B, C), and Southwest Community Hospital (D).

Hospitals A and B are perceived to give high-quality medical care,

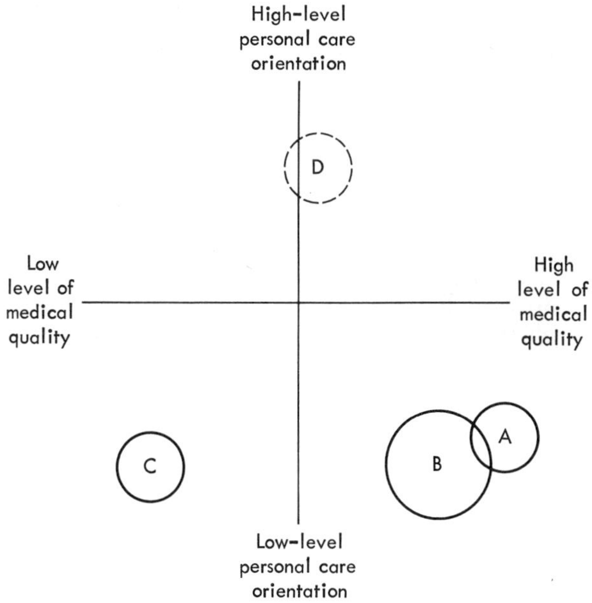

FIGURE 3–7 Competitive Positioning of Four Hospitals

but low personal care orientation, B being somewhat larger and of slightly lower quality than A. They are locked into competition for the same patients, since their differentiation is negligible. Hospital C is in trouble; it is viewed as providing poor medical care as well as poor personal care. Southwest Community Hospital, shown as D, is viewed as providing reasonable-quality medical care and higher than average personal care. Fortunately, there is no competition in this preference segment. The only question is whether there are enough patients seeking reasonable-quality medical care with a strong personal care component. If not, then D is not in a viable competitive position, and the administration has to think about repositioning the hospital toward a part of the market in which the demand is larger. (Note that the physician's role in the selection process is being understated here in order to illustrate a point.)

Marketing Mix Strategy

The next step is to develop a marketing mix that supports the hospital's ability to compete in its target market:

> **Marketing mix** is the particular blend of controllable marketing variables the firm uses to achieve its objective in the target market.

Although many variables make up the marketing mix, they can be classified into a few major groups. McCarthy formulated a popular classification called the four Ps: *product, price, place,* and *promotion.*[16] We discuss each of the four in detail in a later chapter.

The organization chooses a marketing mix that will support and reinforce its chosen competitive position. If the hospital wants to maintain and project a reputation as providing reasonable-quality medical care and high-quality personal care, it will attract to its medical staff reasonably well trained (but not nationally renowned) physicians. It will also develop personnel policies that will motivate nurses and other staff to provide warm and caring services to patients and to respond quickly to patients' needs. And it will invest in public relations and promotion to inform the public of its high level of personal care. In other words, the chosen competitive position dictates the elements of the marketing mix that will be emphasized.

This illustration shows that strategic planning must be supported by marketing strategy in order for the organization to adapt best to its market opportunities.

SUMMARY

A rapidly changing environment requires health care organizations to be adaptive. An adaptive health care organization operates systems for monitoring and interpreting environmental changes and shows a readiness to revise its mission, objectives, strategies, structure, and systems to keep up with its opportunities.

Strategic planning is a major tool for adapting to a changing environment, and it consists of several steps. The first is an environmental analysis. Major trends are identified, as are the implied opportunities and threats associated with them. The organization prepares plans for its most important opportunities and threats, and monitors others that might eventually have significance.

Following the environmental analysis, the organization proceeds to identify its major strengths and weaknesses in resources, such as staff, facilities, systems, and funds. It will favor those opportunities where it has distinctive competences and differential advantages in relation to competitors.

The next step is goal formulation. The organization establishes what it wants to achieve. It formulates its basic mission, its major objectives (qualitative variables to pursue), and its specific goals (quantified objectives with respect to magnitude, time, and who is responsible).

Strategy formulation is the effort to figure out a broad strategy for achieving goals. First, the organization analyzes its current product portfolio to determine which businesses (services, units) it should build, maintain, harvest, or terminate. Second, it seeks ideas for new or modified products and markets by using a product/market expansion matrix. The health care organization's strategy is likely to call for changes in structure, people, and culture. Strategy should dictate structure. Finally, the organization reviews its systems of information, planning, and control to be sure they are adequate to carry out the strategy successfully.

The strategic planning process needs marketing inputs. Following the choice of particular product/market targets, the organization proceeds to develop marketing strategies for each product market. Marketing strategy is the selection of a target market segment(s), the choice of a competitive position, and the development of an effective marketing mix to reach and serve the chosen target markets. A marketing mix consists of the particular blend of product, price, place, and promotion the organization uses to achieve its objectives in the target market.

NOTES

1. Peter Drucker, *Age of Discontinuity* (New York: Harper & Row, 1969).

2. Alvin Toffler, *Future Shock* (New York: Bantam, 1970).

3. Pfeffer and Salancik argue that environment is more critical than management quality in determining an organization's longevity.

See Jeffrey Pfeffer and Gerald R. Salancik, *The External Control of Organizations: A Resource Dependence Perspective* (New York: Harper & Row, 1978).

4. Environments have been classified in many ways. Among the dimensions used are the rapidity of change, the environment's simplicity or complexity, and so on. For a well-known classification see F. E. Emery and E. L. Trist, "The Causal Texture of Organizational Environments," *Human Relations* (February 1965), pp. 21–32.

5. Pfeffer and Salancik, *The External Control of Organizations,* chaps. 6–8.

6. For an in-depth discussion of both horizontal and vertical integration in the health care field, see chaps. 6 and 7 of Jeff Charles Goldsmith, *Can Hospitals Survive?: The New Competitive Health Care Market* (Homewood, Ill.: Dow Jones-Irwin, 1981).

7. For an excellent discussion of strategic planning, see Derek F. Abell and John S. Hammond, *Strategic Market Planning* (Englewood Cliffs, NJ: Prentice-Hall, 1979).

8. Terrence J. Rynne, "The Third Stage of Hospital Long-Range Planning: The Marketing Approach," *Health Care Management Review* (Summer 1980), pp. 7–15.

9. See Derek F. Abell, "Strategic Windows," *Journal of Marketing* (July 1978), pp. 21–26.

10. Those interested in pursuing the topic of strategic planning should see Abell and Hammond, *Strategic Market Planning;* M. E. Porter, *Competitive Strategy* (New York: Free Press, 1980); C. D. Burnett, D. P. Yeskey, and D. Richardson, "New Roles for Corporate Planners in the 1980s," *Journal of Business Strategy* (Fall 1983), pp. 64–68; and the *Strategic Management Journal* (any issue).

11. Richard Crater and Roberta N. Clarke, "Southern Jamaica Plain Health Center," Harvard Business School Case Services, #9-576-738, 1976.

12. This definition of market share is called *relative market share.* A relative market share of 10 means that the organization sells 10 times as much as the next largest organization. It should not be confused with *absolute market share,* which measures the organization's sales as a percentage of the total market size.

13. A summary of a research effort on the cost of serving different payer categories, performed by Lewin and Associates, can be found in "The Nursing Differential: New Study Finds Medicare Should Pay More," *Human-Size Hospital Newsletter* (February 1982), pp. 3–4.

14. H. Igor Ansoff, "Strategies for Diversification," *Harvard Business Review* (September–October 1957), pp. 113–24.

15. See Jay R. Galbraith and Daniel A. Nathanson, *Strategy Implementation: The Role of Structure and Progress* (St. Paul, MN: West Publishing, 1978). The authors elaborate on the thesis first proposed in Alfred D. Chandler, *Strategy and Structure* (Cambridge, MA: MIT Press, 1962).

16. E. Jerome McCarthy, *Basic Marketing: A Managerial Approach,* 6th ed. (Homewood, IL: Irwin, 1978), p. 39.

4

THE ENTREPRENEURIAL ORGANIZATION

The Elliot Hospital in Manchester, New Hampshire, is an entrepreneurial organization. Like other community hospitals around the country in the 1980s, Elliot faced increased competition in attracting patients and in staying financially healthy.

Frank Cronin, president of Elliot, sought to deal with the competitive and financial threats to the hospital by addressing the opportunities present in the marketplace. With his top management, he decided upon four particular issues to which the hospital could respond. First, the fastest growing part of his service area was a very attractive high-tech segment to the south of the hospital. The segment consisted of better-educated, higher-income white-collar singles and young families with one or more adults working in the high-tech companies that were rapidly expanding into southern New Hampshire. Second, Elliot had just been given approval to renovate its obstetric unit. Elliot already had more obstetric beds than its major competitor, the Catholic Medical Center, also in Manchester. Third, Elliot's Emergency Service (ES) had experienced a three-year decline in visits. Market research showed that the high-tech segment had a clear inpatient preference for Elliot, yet they did not tend to use its emergency service. And fourth, HMOs were just beginning to move into the area.

Recognizing that the four issues presented interrelated opportunities, Cronin and his management team developed a set of entrepreneurial strategies. The hospital sought successfully to develop a relationship with the major HMO entering the area. The market research on the high-tech segment indicated a great interest on their part in enrolling in HMOs, since many of them had no regular primary care physician.

Second, the same lack of a regular primary care physician resulted in many high-tech segment members using emergency services for primary care. An objective evaluation of Elliot's emergency service made it quite clear that the whole service needed modification. The waiting area, which consisted of a four-sided windowed area, gave the feeling of a fishbowl and offered no privacy. The hospital developed plans to expand the space, building in with plants and furniture psychological divisions providing a sense of privacy while still allowing the staff visually to monitor the waiting patients. A system was developed whereby waiting patients would be spoken with by staff every 15 minutes if, in fact, the patient had to wait that long. A dedicated children's area was being built into the waiting area, with smaller chairs, children's books, and toys. A stationary videoplayback monitor was to be built in, with videotapes on Elliot Hospital and health-related issues, as well as a few tapes to keep children entertained while they waited for themselves or a relative to be treated. A portable video monitor would be available in the exam rooms to show tapes relevant to a patient's diagnosis or discharge orders.

A new service called The Book Store would be opened adjacent to the emergency service waiting area. It would provide something for patients to do while waiting to be seen. It would also serve as a place for physicians to send patients when the physician wanted the patient to read up on a specific medical issue, and as a place the public would identify as a source of medical information. Recognizing that the high-tech segment was highly mobile and was not likely to know where Elliot Hospital was located, given its location away from any main roads in a suburban neighborhood, the management team planned to give a coupon for 35 percent off any book purchase up to $20, offered through Welcome Wagon, as a way to attract new residents to the hospital.

In addition to The Book Store, the Elliot decided to open a drugstore on the hospital's grounds as a way to serve patients using the emergency service and patients seeing hospital physicians whose offices were located on or near the hospital grounds. To serve the needs of the whole community, Elliot was developing plans for a fitness store, a store on the grounds that would carry fitness, exercise, and durable medical equipment. Included would be a back center carrying products such as the Balans chair and back support pillows for people with benign low back pain. This was viewed as being particularly attractive to the high-tech segment, which was very interested in health and fitness activities but was also very prone to back problems because their work entailed sitting all day. The hospital would periodically offer Back Clinics to teach people with back problems about appropriate exercise, life style, and rehabilitation activities to maintain their backs in good condition.

In order to make the renovated maternity unit attractive not only to the local conservative French Catholic population, but also to the more progressive high-tech segment, Elliot increased the number of birthing rooms to four, and outfitted them with curtains, pictures, radios with cassette players, and fresh flowers daily. It built a Jacuzzi and a winterized greenhouse into the maternity unit; it liberalized its policies regarding who could attend the labor, the birth, and anesthesia. In addition, it expanded and repackaged other services to women, including infertility, breast cancer, premenstrual syndrome, rape treatment and counseling, eating disorders, osteoporosis and miscarriage support groups.

An entrepreneurial organization goes one step further than an adaptive organization; it is not only willing but eager to change with the times. It does not simply watch things happen or wonder what happened; it makes things happen. It has developed a capacity to produce successful change. We define it as follows:

> An **entrepreneurial organization** is one with a high motivation and capability to identify and exploit new opportunities and convert them into successful enterprises.

In the past, health care organizations typically did not have an entrepreneurial view of themselves. Hospitals of all types, nursing homes, physicians' private practices, social service organizations, government and health education agencies were comfortable operating the same way year after year. The availability of federal and external funding in the 1960s brought with it the expansion of existing health care services, plus the division of existing services into subspecialty services (such as the development of separate oncology services for cancer patients, who in the 1950s would have been treated with other patients in the medical services of hospitals). This behavior addressed new opportunities—the newly available funds for expansion—but was not truly entrepreneurial because it allowed the organizations to continue to operate essentially as they had in the past.

Increasing competition, the cutbacks in reimbursement and charitable support, as well as the public outcry against increasing health care costs in the last decade, has caused many health care organizations to respond more entrepreneurially. The Brockton (MA) Visiting Nurse Association, for example, performs routine hypertension testing at area businesses, makes visits to all new mothers in the community within the first days after the mother and infant are home, and provides certified adult and pediatric hospice care, as well as offering the traditional home health services. The Lutheran General Hospital offers Tel-Med (phone-in information) services, an Older Adult Day Service Center, an Alcoholic Treatment Center, and a primary care health center in addition to routine hospital services. Other health care organizations have responded entrepreneurially by diversifying into totally new services and markets.

TYPES OF HEALTH CARE ENTREPRENEURSHIP

In health care, entrepreneurship has taken some particular forms. First, *joint ventures,* particularly between hospitals and physicians, have become popular. These ventures often focus on HMOs, PPOs, urgicenters, surgicenters, and free-standing laboratory and radiology centers. Under prospective payment systems the hospital is held responsible for costs, but the hospital's medical staff controls a large share of that cost. A joint venture in the form of an HMO or PPO gives the medical staff the same set of economic incentives as the hospital to hold costs down. This may also save the hospital from the arduous and sensitive task of having to police its own medical staff, since some mechanism is usually designed into the joint venture to perform that task.

Prospective pricing and other pressures also are causing hospitals to seek to *unbundle services.* The hospital sets up separate corporations to manage the affairs of the unbundled service, often in a for-profit corporation that is related to but is not a part of the hospital. The separate corporation may offer its services to the hospital at a predetermined favorable transfer price, but offer its services elsewhere at going market prices. Laboratory, radiology, laundry, wheelchair, and other apparatus maintenance and management consulting services are some of the services hospitals have unbundled.

The *retailing of medical services* is a third type of entrepreneurial venture now common. It may or may not involve a hospital, with or without its medical staff. Retailing efforts, such as walk-in medical clinics and shopping mall dental centers, are often the work of entrepreneurially oriented physicians or dentists who modify traditional private practice into a service that is more convenient for the consumer. More will be said about retailing in Chapter 14.

As noted above, entrepreneurship can be a positive force, when gone about correctly. At the base of every entrepreneurial venture should be a market opportunity which is systematically studied and then systematically planned and implemented. Entrepreneurial efforts entered into hurriedly, without the proper focus and planning, are likely to fail. An organization that wishes to be entrepreneurial must set up systems that will lead to successful new product launches. There is a proper way to introduce new products that usually raises the probability of success. Figure 4–1 shows the steps involved in new product development. Let us look at each step in detail.

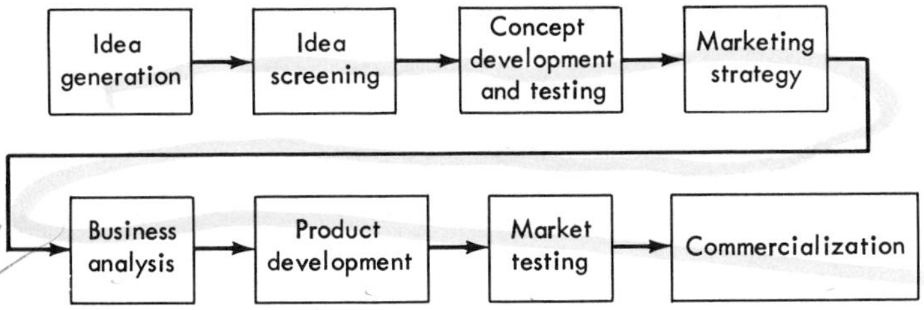

FIGURE 4–1 Major Stages in New Product Development

IDEA GENERATION

Health care organizations differ in their need for new product ideas. Some organizations do not have to find new things to do. A rate-setting commission, for example, is mandated to carry out certain procedures and is not interested, or even legally able, to consider undertaking new ventures not related to its main business. Other organizations are more in need of new product ideas because their main business is taking a turn for the worse. A drug abuse center may want to add new services such as soft drug addiction clinics and alcoholic abuse programs if fewer hard drug abusers are coming for treatment. A pediatric medical center may develop new services or expand to the older adolescent market in order to address a declining demand for traditional pediatric inpatient services. And many hospitals, foreseeing greater restrictions and declining reimbursement for inpatient services, are increasingly expanding into out-of-hospital services.

There are many excellent sources of new product ideas. Clients are a logical starting point. Their needs and wants can be monitored through direct surveys, projective tests, focus group discussions, and the letters and complaints they generate. Competitors should also be watched for the successful new activities they launch. The health care organization's manager and employees are another good source of ideas, as are management consultants, advertising agencies, trade associations, and marketing research firms.

Whatever the source of an idea, at least one of four general processes is responsible for producing it—inspiration, serendipity, client request, or formal creativity techniques. Other than maintaining as creative an atmosphere as possible and being alert to the occasional lucky accident, health care organizations have little control over the first two processes. Moreover, they seldom have significant input into what a client might request. Organizations, however, can train their executives to use certain creativity techniques. There are dozens of such techniques; we describe three below.[1]

1. *Client problem analysis.* This calls for interviewing clients and asking them to identify problems they have with the current services. A psychological counseling center may learn that patients are afraid of being seen in the waiting room by people who know them. This problem can be solved by developing an extra waiting room and separate exit for the patients.
2. *Product modification analysis.* This calls for looking at the various attributes of the current service and thinking about ways to modify, magnify, substitute, rearrange, reverse, or combine one or more features.[2] For example, psychological counseling originally called for a one-hour session with a single patient one or a few times a week. Over the years, it has spawned such modifications as family therapy, group therapy, and thera-

py for several hundred people gathered in one room. There has also been modification of the role of the therapist from authority figure to listener to facilitator.

3. *Brainstorming.* This calls for a group of six to ten people to be given a specific problem, such as "Think of new ways to deliver psychological counseling to more people." People are encouraged to come up with ideas—the wilder, the better. The participants agree not to criticize any ideas until the group runs out of further ideas.[3]

IDEA SCREENING

The purpose of idea screening is to take a look at the new product ideas and eliminate those that do not warrant further attention. The screening might result in an excellent idea being prematurely dropped. A worse possibility is that a bad idea might be accepted for further development. Each idea that is developed takes substantial management time and money. The purpose of screening is therefore to eliminate all but the most promising ideas.

Health care organizations should require each idea to be written up in a standard form for review by an objective group of people who are assigned the idea screening task. The form should describe the new service, the target market, the competition, and give a rough guess as to market size, price, development time, costs, and probable success.

The requirement that all new product ideas must be written up in standard form serves two useful purposes. First, it allows the review group to compare and contrast new product ideas more easily by providing the same information on each idea. Second, it forces the advocates of each new idea to think through the requirements necessary to make it successful. Hospital administrators are all too aware of the tendency of physicians to march in to their offices and say something like: "I have this great idea. We should start an internationally known pediatric diagnostic center." If forced to go through the discipline of writing up their ideas in a standardized format, many of these advocates would reevaluate the product idea and their support of it on a more realistic basis.

A screening procedure for evaluating new product proposals is shown in Figure 4–2. The first task is to determine whether the idea is attractive independent of the organization. A new product idea is attractive when it meets a real need or want (as defined by the marketplace, not the producer), and there is a sufficient number of people who would adopt it. Otherwise, the idea should be dropped. The second task is to determine whether the product is compatible with the organization's objectives. Four possible objectives are mentioned—health care image, a less highly regulated market, growth potential, and at-

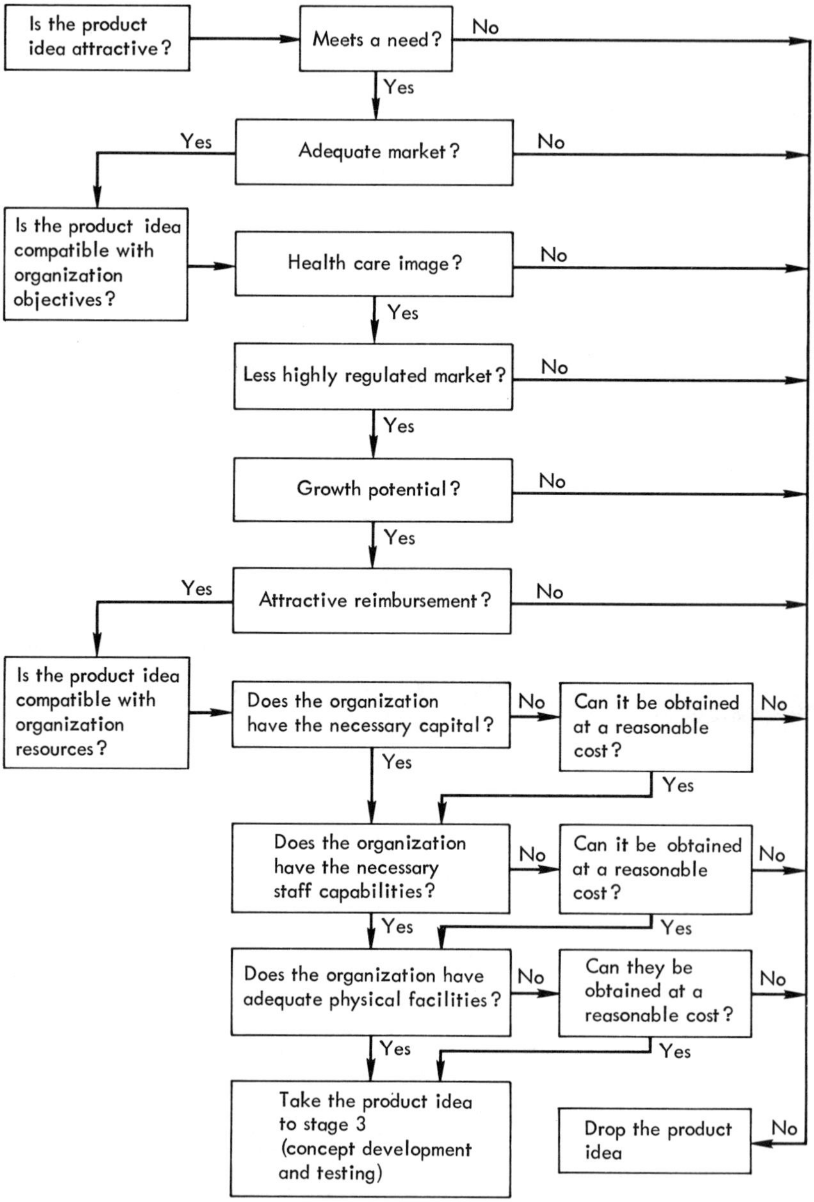

FIGURE 4–2 A Screening Procedure

tractive in terms of reimbursement. Others could be added. A strong negative answer to any one of these questions can disqualify the product idea from further consideration. The third task is to determine whether the product idea is compatible with the organization's resources; in the illustration, capital, staff capabilities, and facilities are used. If any of these resources is lacking, the question of obtaining it at a reasonable cost must be asked. A strong negative answer to any of these questions will also disqualify the idea from further consideration. Product ideas that pass all these tests move on to the third stage, that of concept development and testing.

CONCEPT DEVELOPMENT AND TESTING

Those ideas that survive screening must undergo further development into full product concepts. It is important to distinguish between a product idea, a product concept, and a product image. A *product idea* is a possible product, described in objective and functional terms, that the health care organization can see itself offering to the market. *A product concept* is a particular subjective consumer meaning that the organization tries to build into the product idea. A *product image* is the particular subjective picture consumers actually acquire of the product.

Concept Development

Suppose, as a result of screening a variety of new product ideas, such as a bedwetting clinic for children, a hypertension testing program, and a headache clinic, a community hospital decides the headache clinic is the most attractive. The next entrepreneurial task is to turn this product idea into an appealing product concept. Every product idea can be turned into several product concepts, such as these:

> Concept 1. A headache clinic which, after eliminating obvious physiological causes of headaches, treats the headaches through the use of biofeedback.
>
> Concept 2. A headache clinic that performs a complete physical examination and, if no physiological causes are found, treats the patient with individual counseling and therapy.
>
> Concept 3. A headache clinic that takes patients only after their headaches have been found to have no physiological cause, and treats headaches through alteration of diet, life style, and exercise.

Clearly, one product idea can give rise to a number of alternative product concepts.

Concept Testing

Concept testing calls for taking these concepts to the appropriate target consumers and getting their reactions. Each concept should be presented in written form in enough detail to allow the respondent to understand it and express his or her level of interest. Here is an example of concept 3 in more elaborate form:

> A headache clinic, called the Headache Treatment Center, which would take only those patients who had already been diagnosed as

> being medically sound (no brain tumors, etc.). The program would be self-pay or reimbursed if prescribed by a physician; would eliminate such foods as cheeses, chocolate, and red wine from patient's diet, since they are known to cause cluster headaches; would seek to identify and eliminate stressful elements in the patient's life style, and would place the patient on an exercise program, since exercise is known to alleviate depression.

Target consumers and referral sources (presumably physicians) are identified and interviewed about their reaction to this concept. One of the questions usually asked concerns intention to buy: "Would you definitely, probably, probably not, or definitely not use (or refer to) this headache center?" Suppose 10 percent of the target consumers said "definitely" and another 5 percent said "probably." The hospital would project these figures to the corresponding size of the target audience to decide whether the estimated number of patients would be sufficient. Even then, the estimate is tentative because people do not always carry out their stated intentions. By testing the alternative concepts with target consumers in this way, the hospital will learn which product concept has the best market potential.

MARKETING STRATEGY

At this point, the organization should develop a preliminary concept of the marketing strategy it will use to introduce the new program. This is necessary in order that the full revenue and cost implications of the new program can be evaluated. The marketing strategy should be spelled out in a statement consisting of three parts. The first describes the size, structure, and behavior of the target market, the intended positioning of the new product in this market, and the utilization and revenue goals in the first few years. Thus, for the headache treatment center:

> The target market is teenagers and adults living in the general metropolitan area of the community hospital who suffer from consistent, recurring, undiagnosed benign headaches. Because the target market presumably first sought medical diagnosis and treatment elsewhere with little success, many patients may be referred by those medical sources initially seen. This program will be differentiated from other sources of headache treatment by providing life style counseling as opposed to psychiatric treatment and by the use of no drugs or equipment for headache relief. The hospital will seek to treat 100 patients the first year with a net loss not to exceed $10,000. The second year will aim for utilization by 250 patients, including some patients from the first year. Further, the hospital would aim for 50 percent of the patients to be self-paying, resulting in a net surplus of $30,000.

The second part of the marketing strategy statement outlines the new product's intended price, distribution strategy, promotion strategy, and marketing budget for the first year:

> The new program will be offered in the ambulatory care wing of the hospital on Mondays, Thursdays, and Saturdays, from 9 A.M. to 5 P.M. Each patient will have four one-hour sessions the first month at $20 per session. It is then recommended that each patient return for one session every other month, for a total of four additional sessions. The first year's promotional budget will be $17,000, $9,000 of which will be spent on local advertising media, $4,000 on developing and printing promotional materials, and the remainder on the development of medical referrals. Another $10,000 will be spent on followup and monitoring the program.

The third part of the marketing strategy statement describes the intended long-run revenue and profit (surplus) goals and marketing mix strategy over time:

> The hospital ultimately hopes to achieve a steady utilization of this program by 300 patients a year. By the second year, if utilization projections are reached, a permanent program administrator will be assigned. Fees will be adjusted for inflation each year. The promotional budget will fluctuate between $15,000 and $24,000 yearly, depending upon utilization rates. Market research and followup will be budgeted at $10,000 annually. The program is expected to produce a yearly surplus of $30,000 to $35,000, and the surplus will be used to support other programs that are not self-paying.

BUSINESS ANALYSIS

As soon as a satisfactory product concept and marketing strategy have been developed, the organization is in a position to do a hard-headed analysis of the business attractiveness of the proposal. It must estimate possible revenues and costs for different possible utilization levels. *Breakeven analysis* is the most frequently used tool in this connection (see Chapter 13). Suppose the hospital learns it needs 140 patients to break even. If the hospital manages to attract more than 140 patients, this program will produce a net income that could be used to support other programs; if there is a patient shortfall, the hospital will lose money on this new program.

PRODUCT DEVELOPMENT AND MARKET TESTING

If the organization is satisfied that the product concept is financially viable, it can move toward turning the concept into concrete form. Here there is a major difference between physical products and services.

Products that take a physical, tangible form can be produced and tested in small numbers without setting up a whole new business. For example, a medical equipment company might have progressed through the business analysis stage with the product concept of a sleep apnea (suspension of breathing) alarm for babies. At this point, the company can develop a prototype of the alarm and then put it through a series of functional and consumer tests to ensure that the product performs well and is used as it should be. If it works, the equipment company can then proceed to market testing.

Market testing is the stage where the product and marketing program are introduced into more authentic consumer settings to learn how well the product will do before making a final decision to launch it in the marketplace. The equipment company might select a group of potential customers who agree to use the apnea alarm for a limited period of time. This test would expose unanticipated problems of safety, servicing, and misuse. After the test, the customer is given an opportunity to express purchase intent and other reactions.

The equipment company might also employ the ultimate form of testing a new product, test marketing. Test marketing can be viewed as a dress rehearsal for the total marketing strategy for the new product. The durable medical equipment company could develop a full promotional program and, using its intended pricing and distribution strategies, test the apnea alarm marketing strategy by targeting it to a small geographic area. Or it could test two or more marketing strategies by testing the product in two or more geographic areas, using a different marketing strategy in each.

Services do not have the same risk reduction options. The hospital wishing to develop the headache treatment center cannot develop a prototype of the service without actually setting up the whole service and incurring all the related costs (hiring staff, setting up scheduling, treatment, billing and other systems, and so on). Whereas the hospital plans to produce only one headache clinic, the durable medical equipment company plans to produce and sell many apnea alarms. This allows the equipment company to produce and test a few alarms before incurring the full costs of a market launch.

Furthermore, services are generally geographically limited in the target market they can serve. Hospitals have service areas outside of which they cannot typically expect to draw many patients. Home health agencies are limited to serving those communities to which their nurses, aides, and other staff can drive within a reasonable time period. Since most health care organizations service only one limited area, it is usually impossible to perform a test without affecting much of the ultimate target market. Test markets can be used by service organizations with two or more sites if the organization wants to measure the viability of the new program without installing it throughout the system. For example, the Adventist System, which includes a chain of hospitals in different states, introduced an occupational health program at the site of its Stoneham, Massachusetts, hospital. If the program proved successful there, the system would anticipate introducing the same program into many of its other hospitals. The Massachusetts program could be viewed as a test market.

Since the majority of health care organizations produce services and not tangible products, it is even more important for these organizations to do a good job on idea screening, concept development and testing, marketing strategy development, and business analysis. Otherwise, they face greater risks of reaching the commercialization stage with a program that will fail (see Exhibit 4–1).

EXHIBIT 4–1

The Lincoln International Health Care Clinic: An Enterpreneurial Mistake

The Lincoln Memorial Hospital was a 300-bed community hospital in a wealthy area of Miami, Florida. Lincoln Memorial Hospital had been experiencing a slow decline in census during the early 1980s. At the prodding of one of Lincoln Memorial Hospital's most heavily admitting physicians, Lincoln Memorial Hospital hired a marketing consultant who was a friend of the heavy admitter. With the understanding that he would develop a report to address the declining census, the consultant returned a few months later with a plan which suggested the following:

> That Lincoln Memorial Hospital develop the Lincoln International Health Care Clinic (LIHCC), an internationally known, sophisticated diagnosis and treatment center to be affiliated with the hospital and that LIHCC be heavily promoted.
>
> That the LIHCC would attract wealthy South Americans who often came to Miami for shopping trips, who owned condominiums in Florida, or who made special trips to the United States for medical care.
>
> That, for a price of $1,000 to $2,000 a year, these South Americans would become members of LIHCC, entitling them to use LIHCC's facilities on a fee for service basis. Membership also entailed a necessary three day physical examination at LIHCC each year.
>
> That LIHCC would have a sophisticated computer system and satellite linkup which would allow LIHCC to maintain complete medical records on each member, and to transfer these records to anywhere in the world, as needed by its members, via satellite.
>
> That LIHCC members, although likely to be residing for a few months each year all over the state of Florida, would use LIHCC for emergency purposes when in Florida, and would be hospitalized at Lincoln Memorial Hospital whenever hospitalization was needed.

> That LIHCC would be promoted through the South Americans' physicians to their clientele. In return for recommending their patients to LIHCC, the physicians would be paid $50 for each patient who was recommended.
>
> That the consultant run a test market at the cost of $350,000 over the next two years.

The consultant hired by Lincoln Memorial Hospital had an entrepreneurial spirit: he recognized that the influx of wealthy South Americans in Florida represented an opportunity. He was particularly taken with the idea that, since most of the South Americans arrived by air, and since the Miami International Airport was only ten minutes from the hospital, the LIHCC would be able to attract almost all wealthy South Americans entering Florida.

Lincoln Memorial Hospital had no system in place to evaluate new product ideas. Upon receiving the consultant's report, the hospital did no screening, concept developing or testing, developing of marketing strategy, or business analysis. Instead, it found itself being pressured by many of its physicians, including the heavy admitter friend of the consultant, to proceed with the plan. Clearly, the medical staff found the idea of being on the staff of an internationally known diagnostic center an attractive one.

On the verge of committing an initial $100,000 for the proposed test market, the hospital administrator hired outside marketing expertise, which uncovered the following:

> That most wealthy South Americans had their own well-trained personal physicians at home, and that, if they went to the United States for medical care, they went to highly sophisticated, highly reputed medical centers like the Cleveland Clinic or Mayo Clinic, not to a community hospital.
>
> That proximity to an international airport was not important to South Americans in selecting their sources of medical care in the United States. After all, if they were willing to go to the Cleveland Clinic (Cleveland, Ohio) and Mayo Clinic (Rochester, Minnesota), how important could an "international" location be?
>
> That most wealthy South Americans who visited Florida lived (when in Florida) closer to hospitals other than Lincoln Memorial Hospital. In the case of an emergency, it was unlikely that they would drive by nearby hospitals in order to reach Lincoln Memorial Hospital, a community hospital with no particular expertise in emergency care.
>
> That membership in LIHCC bought the South American very little of value except for maintenance of medical records at the cost of $1,000 to $2,000 a year. The sophisticated diagnosis and treatment which the LIHCC was supposed to provide were already available at local teaching hospitals in Miami without a membership charge and without the requirement of an annual time-consuming physical. The satellite linkup would be useful only in those few health facilities around the world which could receive satellite transmission.
>
> That most South American physicians had an economic disincentive to recommend their patients to LIHCC since they would essentially be giving away their own patients to another medical provider.

That the consultant had confused reputation, such as that which the Cleveland Clinic had taken decades to develop, with visibility, which the consultant hoped to achieve virtually overnight with promotion.

That any reasonable business analysis, no semblance of which appeared in the consultant's proposal, would have indicated that LIHCC was an expensive business venture, costing well into the millions of dollars in capital investment, with little likelihood of producing significant income.

That a "test market," as proposed by the consultant, could not be run without actually setting up the whole LIHCC. Otherwise the consultant, in "test market," would be promoting a service which did not exist.

The final point which convinced even the medical staff of Lincoln Memorial Hospital to avoid this new venture was that the consultant's proposal did not really address the underlying problem which it was intended to address: the hospital's declining census.

SOURCE: Roberta N. Clarke, "The Lincoln International Health Care Clinic," case study, Boston University, Boston, MA, 1980.

COMMERCIALIZATION

The results of the previous stages should give management enough information to make a final decision on a full-scale launch of a new program with all its attendant costs. As a guide to successful commercialization, health care organizations should use the theory of consumer adoption behavior, which attempts to throw light on how consumers react when they learn about new products.

The Consumer Adoption Process

The consumer adoption process begins where the organization's innovation process leaves off. It deals with the process by which potential customers come to learn about the new product or service, try it, and eventually adopt or reject it. The organization must understand this process so that it can bring about early market awareness and trial use.

Marketing Approaches. The earliest approach used by new product marketers for launching a new product was a *mass market approach.* For example, a mental health center might try to attract everyone to its family counseling sessions. However, this approach has two drawbacks: (1) It requires heavy marketing expenditures; and (2) it involves a substantial number of wasted exposures to nonpotential and low-potential buyers. These drawbacks have led to a second approach, called *target marketing.* This involves directing the product or service to the group that is likely to be most interested. It makes sense, provided strong prospects are identifiable. But even within the strong prospect group, people differ in how much interest they show in new products and in how fast they can be drawn into trying them. Certain persons are earlier adopters than others. The new product marketer ought to direct marketing efforts to those most likely to adopt the product early. *Early adopter theory* holds that:

1. Persons within a target market will differ in the amount of time that passes between their exposure to a new product and their trial of the new product.
2. Early adopters are likely to share some traits in common that differentiate them from late adopters.
3. Efficient media exist for reaching early-adopter types.
4. Early-adopter types are likely to be high on opinion leadership and therefore helpful in "advertising" the new product to other potential buyers.

Innovation Diffusion and Adoption. The theory of innovation diffusion and adoption provides clues to identifying the best early prospects. The central concept is that of an *innovation,* any good, service, or idea perceived by someone as new. The idea may have had a long history, but it is still an innovation to the person who sees it as being new.

Innovations are assimilated into the social system over time. *Diffusion* is the name given to "the spread of a new idea from its source of invention or creation to its ultimate users or adopters."[4] *Adoption,* on the other hand, focuses on "the mental process through which an individual passes from first hearing about an innovation to final adoption." Adoption is the decision by an individual to use an innovation regularly.

The differences among individuals in their response to new ideas is called their *innovativeness.* Specifically, innovativeness is "the degree to which an individual is relatively earlier in adopting new ideas than the other members of his social system." On the basis of their innovativeness, individuals can be classified into different *adopter categories.* Younger people with no regular physicians are generally viewed as likely early adopters of HMOs, while the elderly and those with satisfactory relationships with regular physicians are anticipated to be late adopters. Individuals can also be classified in terms of their influence on others with respect to innovations. *Opinion leaders* are "those individuals from whom others seek information or advice." These may include community and religious leaders, for instance. Individuals or firms who actively seek to change other people's minds are called *change agents.*

Propositions about the Consumer-Adoption Process

We are now ready to examine the main generalizations drawn from hundreds of studies of how people accept new ideas.

The first proposition is that *the individual consumer goes through a series of stages of acceptance in the process of adopting a new product.* The stages are classified by Rogers as follows:

1. *Awareness.* The individual becomes cognizant of the innovation but lacks information about it.
2. *Interest.* The individual is stimulated to seek information about the innovation.
3. *Evaluation.* The individual considers whether it would make sense to try the innovation.
4. *Trial.* The individual tries the innovation on a small scale to improve his or her estimate of its utility.
5. *Adoption.* The individual decides to make full and regular use of the innovation.

The value of this model of the adoption process is that it requires the innovator to think carefully about new product acceptance. Headache sufferers hearing about the hospital's headache program for the first time are not going to sign up immediately. The hospital will have to take concrete steps to maintain their interest, help them evaluate whether the program meets their needs, and make it easy for prospects to attend a one-hour session in order to sample the new program.

The second proposition is that *people differ markedly in their penchant for trying new products.* In each product area, there are apt to be pioneers and early adopters. Some people are the first to adopt new appliances, some physicians are the first to prescribe new medicines,[5] and some farmers are the first to adopt new farming methods.[6]

Other individuals tend to adopt innovations much later. This has led to a classification of people into the categories shown in Figure 4–3. The process is represented as following a normal (or near normal) distribution when plotted over time. After a slow start, an increasing

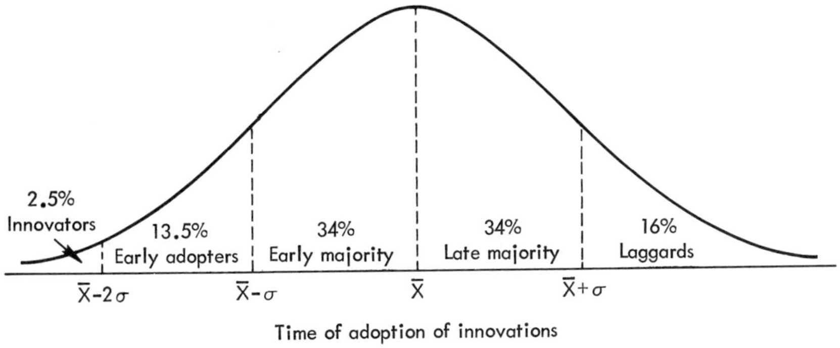

FIGURE 4–3 Adopter Categorization on the Basis of Relative Time of Adoption of Innovations *Source:* Redrawn fron Everett M. Rogers, *Diffusion of Innovations,* p. 162. By permission of The Free Press, a Division of Macmillan, Inc. Copyright © 1962 by The Free Press.

number of people adopt the innovation, the number reaches a peak, and then it diminishes as fewer people remain in the nonadopter category.

Convenient breaks in the distribution are used to establish categories. Thus, innovators are defined as the first 2.5 percent of the individuals to adopt a new idea; the early adopters are the next 13.5 percent who adopt the new idea, and so forth. Rogers has characterized the five groups in terms of ideational values. The dominant value of innovators is *venturesomeness;* they like to try new ideas, even at some risk, and are cosmopolitan in orientation. The dominant value of early adopters is *respect;* they enjoy a position in the community as opinion leaders and adopt new ideas early, but with discretion. The dominant value of the early majority is *deliberateness;* these people like to adopt new ideas before the average member of the social system, although they are rarely leaders. The dominant value of the late majority is *skepticism;* they do not adopt an innovation until the weight of majority opinion seems to legitimize its utility. Finally, the dominant value of the laggards is *tradition;* they are suspicious of any changes, mix with other tradition-bound people, and adopt the innovation only because it has now taken on a measure of tradition itself.

The marketing implication of the adopter classifications is that an innovating firm should direct its communications to those who are likely to be early adopters. Messages reaching late adopters and laggards are wasted. Drawing on several studies, Rogers offered the following hypothesis about early adopters:

> The relatively earlier adopters in a social system tend to be younger in age, have higher social status, a more favorable financial position, more specialized operations, and a different type of mental ability from later adopters. Earlier adopters utilize information sources that are more impersonal and cosmopolite than later adopters and that are in closer contact with the origin of new ideas. Earlier adopters utilize a greater number of different information sources than do later adopters. The social relationships of earlier adopters are more cosmopolite than for later adopters, and earlier adopters have more opinion leadership.[7]

Once the characteristics of early adopters are identified, a marketing communications program calculated to reach and interest these people can be developed for the new product. The known media habits of these people can be used to increase the effectiveness of the organization's advertising.

The third proposition is that *personal influence plays a very large role in the adoption of new products.* By personal influence is meant the effect of product statements made by one person on another's attitude or probability of purchase.[8] The significance of personal influence is greater in some situations and for some individuals than for others.

Personal influence seems to be more important in the evaluation stage of the adoption process. It seems to have more influence on the later adopters. And it appears to be more important in risky situations.

The fourth proposition is that *the character of the innovation itself affects the rate of adoption.* Five characteristics seem to have an especially important influence on the adoption rate.

1. The innovation's *relative advantage,* or the degree to which it appears superior to previous ideas. The greater the perceived relative advantage, whether in terms of higher quality, lower cost, and so on, the more quickly the innovation will be adopted.
2. The innovation's *compatibility,* or the degree to which it is consistent with the values and experiences of the individuals in the social system.
3. The innovation's *complexity,* or the degree to which it is relatively difficult to understand or use. The more complex innovations are likely to take a longer time to diffuse, other things being equal.
4. The innovation's *divisibility,* or the degree to which it can be tried on a limited basis. The evidence of many studies indicates that divisibility helps to increase the rate of adoption.
5. The innovation's *communicability,* or the degree to which the results are observable or describable to others. Innovations that lend themselves to better demonstration or description of advantage will diffuse faster in the social system.

Other characteristics have also been found to influence the rate of adoption—initial cost, continuing cost, risk and uncertainty, scientific credibility, and social approval. The new product marketer has to research the role of all these factors and give the key ones maximum attention in developing the new product marketing program.

SUMMARY

Health care organizations are more viable when they are entrepreneurial. Entrepreneurial organizations identify new opportunities and convert them into successful businesses. An organization that wants to be entrepreneurial must set up systems that will eliminate likely new product or service failures. In order to maximize the chances of successful new ventures, each stage in the new product development process must be carefully conducted.

The first stage, idea generation, involves a search for new product and service ideas through talking with various parties and applying idea-generating techniques. The second stage, idea screening, seeks to eliminate ideas that are unattractive or not viable for the organization. The third stage, concept development and testing, involves the effort to develop the idea into a sound concept and to estimate the number of target consumers who might be interested. The fourth stage, marketing strategy, involves developing a tentative plan for marketing the product. The fifth stage, business analysis, uses all the estimates of demand and cost to determine whether the product idea should be pursued. If the answer is yes, the organization considering introducing a new tangible product may proceed to product development and to market testing. A service organization with multiple locations may proceed to market testing in one of its many locations. A single-location service usually does not have the benefit of either of these stages (product development or market testing). The eighth stage, commercialization, involves the decision actually to launch the product or service. Commercialization strategy benefits greatly when it is based on the theory of innovation diffusion and consumer adoption processes.

NOTES

1. For a useful discussion of creativity techniques, see Sidney J. Parnes and Harold F. Harding, eds., *Source Book for Creative Thinking* (New York: Scribner's, 1962).

2. See Alex F. Osborne, *Applied Imagination,* 3rd ed. (New York: Scribner's, 1963), pp. 286–87.

3. Ibid., p. 156.

4. The discussion leans heavily on Everett M. Rogers, *Diffusion of Innovation* (New York: Free Press, 1962).

5. See James Coleman, Elihu Katz, and Herbert Menzel, "The Diffusion of an Innovation among Physicians," *Sociometry* (December 1957), pp. 253–70.

6. See J. Bohlen and G. Beal, *How Farm People Accept New Ideas,* Special Report No. 15 (Ames: Iowa State College Agricultural Extension Service, November 1955).

7. Everett M. Rogers, *Diffusion of Innovations* (New York: Free Press, 1962), p. 192.

8. See Elihu Katz and Paul F. Lazarsfeld, *Personal Influence* (New York: Free Press, 1955), p. 234.

PART II
Organizing Marketing

5

MARKETING ORGANIZATION

The Sisters of St. Mary run fourteen hospitals, one residential facility for the handicapped and disabled, and a small number of health clinics and family care centers. The corporate board of the Sisters of St. Mary has spent the past two years determining the role of planning in these institutions. Each institution now has a planning committee responsible for producing a long-range plan. A few of the larger institutions have hired their own planners.

Now the Sisters of St. Mary are considering whether to attempt to incorporate marketing into the overall organization and its institutions, and if so how. Three hospitals have merged marketing with planning by hiring a planner/marketer or by asking the planner to assume marketing duties as well. But these hospitals as well as some of the others wonder if, to carry out good marketing, they need to hire someone whose sole function is marketing. No hospital has yet taken this step.

Another possibility is hiring a marketer on the corporate level. This individual would answer to the corporate board or to the hospital board. This option leads to a new set of questions: Does a corporate marketer play a policy-setting role, a consulting or advisory role, or a marketing data collection and analysis role? Would a corporate marketer be a staff position, or would this individual have line responsibility as well? If the central office of the Sisters of St. Mary began to offer a variety of health care management services to other nonprofit health care organizations, would the marketer's role be expanded to include providing marketing services to these outside organizations?

From a brief examination of the marketing function, the Sisters of St. Mary have already concluded that it is wiser to associate marketing with planning than with public relations. They also have rejected the hiring of a marketing firm as a long-term solution to the need for organizational marketing. But like hundreds of other health care organizations examining this issue, they have not yet arrived at a solution about how to incorporate marketing into their organization.

All health care organizations engage in marketing. They may not call it marketing or even recognize it is marketing that they are doing. By offering products or services—including services such as health promotion and education; social, regulatory, policy-setting and reimbursement services; as well as primary and specialty medical services—a health care organization is engaged in marketing.

Prior to the mid-1970s, it was common for health care organizations to believe they did no marketing at all. Then, as the marketing function moved from being considered inappropriate to being recognized as necessary and useful, many health care organizations changed their tune, saying "Oh, yes, we do marketing," and would point to their directors of public relations, community affairs, development or planning. While, in fact, each of these positions is responsible for a part of the marketing process, none of them has the full range of responsibilities and the broad overview necessary for a complete marketing management function.

There has been a strong tendency among health care organizations to pursue one of two alternatives: (1) to assign the title of marketing to an existing administration function, such as public relations or planning; or (2) to avoid assigning the responsibility for marketing to any specific individual or group of administrators. We will examine these alternatives and other options which are now appearing in health care organizational structures as ways for the organization to adopt marketing.

MERGING MARKETING WITH AN EXISTING FUNCTION

A few years ago, the chief executive officer of a major urban teaching hospital decided his hospital needed marketing. However, he had not budgeted for a marketing position nor did he know where in the organization he would place the position. As he walked by a set of administrative offices, he passed a door with the sign "Director of Public Relations" on it. "That's it," he thought, "I'll make my public relations director the marketing director as well." Within two days, the sign on that same door said "Director of Public Relations and Marketing."

This apocryphal tale is unfortunately true, and also one that has been repeated with minor modifications in hundreds of health care organizations across the country. While public relations or community relations appear to be the functions most often assigned the additional marketing responsibility, development, planning, and medical affairs departments have also been placed in this position. The approach does have the value of saving the organization from having to hire an additional administrative-level person and does not require the organizational structure be changed in order to include this new position. However, its drawbacks far outweigh its advantages.

The greatest drawback is that the organization is no better prepared to market itself after the marketing function has been assigned to an existing position than it was before. The same people are still performing essentially the same jobs with the same expertise they had before. No additional marketing expertise has been gained by adding a title to someone's job. The only real change is that the sign on someone's door has been lengthened to read Director of (Public Relations, Community Relations, Public Affairs, Planning) and Marketing.

However, greater harm may come to the organization that takes this approach because the organization may now assume that it has, in assigning the marketing title, addressed its need. No purposeful, planned marketing analysis and strategic activities may follow. The person suddenly saddled with responsibility for marketing is usually not given the significant budget increases the additional responsibility implies. Therefore, even if the individual recognizes the appropriate tasks to pursue, it is unlikely that the budget will be there to pursue them. Nor is it likely that the newly titled marketer will have the authority to make marketing decisions (such as closing or opening a service, recruiting new practitioners, or renovating a facility). The assignment of the marketing function to an existing position may be a classic example of responsibility without the appropriate authority.

One other disadvantage associated with this approach is that the nature of the marketing activities will depend largely upon the background and inclincations of the individual assigned the marketing responsibility. If the public relations director's function is expanded to include marketing, the organization's marketing activities are likely to rely heavily on communications and promotion, to the detriment of the analysis of marketing information and marketing research, and the development of marketing strategies. If the marketing function lies within the planning office, as a number of articles recommend,[1,2] more of the necessary marketing analysis and strategy development are likely to happen, but implementation and followup are generally weak. Development officers are likely to view marketing with an eye to fundraising, and medical affairs directors stress the medical staff in the organization's marketing efforts.

The health care field remains confused about marketing because these different functions—public relations, community relations, planning, development medical affairs—each define marketing according to a particular area of interest. The organization that assigns marketing to a preexisting function at the very least should support substantial educational activities for the new "marketer" to guarantee that this individual has some knowledge of marketing. However, a public relations director with one marketing course is still primarily a public relations director, a medical affairs director with three short marketing seminars is still a medical affairs director. While this approach may be easy on the budget and cause little organizational disruption, it may introduce little or no marketing expertise into the organization.

But if the organization is committed to this approach, then the selection of which function should receive the added responsibility of marketing remains. This depends to a great extent on the existing organizational structure and the way it operates.

The strongest argument can be made for linking marketing with the planning function, if there is one. The two functions are very similar in their objectives and methodologies, and each has a significant focus on data collection and analysis. Public and community relations departments are less appropriate as homes for the marketing function. They tend to focus on the promotional tools used within a marketing strategy, without addressing the development of strategy itself.

Moreover, planning is usually found at a management level that could support the marketing function. Public and community relations are generally placed at too low a level in the organization to provide such support. A *Hospitals* magazine survey of salaries[3] supports this viewpoint; it notes that directors of community relations are paid on average 22 percent less than directors of planning—and salary is a reasonable reflection of status and authority. Kroger and Perry stated it more bluntly: "There is still a debate about where marketing should fall in the hospital organization chart—near the top or buried in the public relations department."[4]

The battle over "who owns marketing" has yet to be decided as of the mid-1980s. Two major arms of the American Hospital Association—the Society for Hospital Planning and the American Society for Hospital Public Relations—have both added the title "Marketing" to their names. Both believe they should "own" marketing. Their actions reflect the battles taking place at a lower level between planners and public relations directors in health care organizations around the country. While the argument can be made more strongly for linking planning with marketing and letting public relations handle marketing communications, there are health care organizations where directors of public or community relations have successfully taken on marketing, as have other existing positions.

When this happens, the approach of merging marketing with an existing function is likely to succeed if the new "marketer" (1) becomes trained in marketing management, (2) receives an adequate budget to support the organization's marketing efforts, and (3) is placed at a sufficiently high level within the organization to have the authority to carry out all relevant marketing activities. Without any one of these three, the new "marketer" is a marketer in name only.

ASSIGNING MARKETING TO NO ONE

Some health care organizations have avoided any discussion of marketing and its place in the organization. Others have actually chosen not to formally recognize the marketing function or not to assign it to a specific person or department. This reluctance can arise for a variety of reasons:

Influential members in the organization may believe that marketing is inappropriate and unethical in a health care setting. Therefore, no one should be expected to pursue marketing activities in the organization.

Some organizations believe that marketing is everyone's job. They fear that appointing a marketing director will lead employees to think that marketing is something done by the marketing director, rather than by everyone in the organization.

Administrators in some organizations think their directors of public relations, development, planning, and other related departments are doing enough marketing already.

Some organizations would prefer to hire marketing expertise in the form of marketing consultants, advertising agencies, and market research firms as needed, rather than assigning marketing full time to one individual or department.

Many health care organizations view marketing as an expense, not recognizing that successful marketing efforts pay for themselves. This view is exacerbated by the fact that marketing activities have not been reimbursable by most third parties under cost-based reimbursement.

Some health care organizations have assigned the marketing function to no one because, no matter to whom they assign it, whether to a new or an existing person or position, someone else in the organization will be unhappy. For example, if a new director of marketing position is created, the director of planning may fear losing some amount of authority and responsibility. And the public relations staff may argue against having to report to the administrator through the marketing director, where previously the public relations staff reported directly to the administrator.

Health care organizations that want to incorporate marketing into the organization without assigning it to a specific person might wish to consider the following:

1. Appointing marketing executives or marketing professors to the board of trustees in order to obtain their advice.
2. Inviting help from the marketing faculty of a business school, such as using a market research class to research a problem facing the organization.
3. Hiring a marketing consulting firm, a marketing research firm, or an advertising agency to do specific projects.
4. Sending key staff to marketing seminars, workshops, and courses to learn marketing.
5. Appointing a marketing committee comprised of people interested in—although not necessarily knowledgeable about—marketing.

But although these alternatives may each produce short-term value, they all have their drawbacks. Let us look more closely at each.

Appointing a Marketing Executive to the Board. An active marketing board member can be very useful in providing advice on specific issues, as well as in educating other board members about marketing. However, most board members are too involved with their own work and activities to devote sufficient attention to the time-consuming activities of marketing analysis and strategy development. Furthermore, these marketing board members will usually be offering advice without the benefit of aggregate marketing information and market research data.

In addition, they are likely to be heavily influenced by their industry background. A Procter & Gamble laundry detergent executive may put heavy emphasis on advertising spending because this is the key to success in the detergent industry. An IBM executive will emphasize personal selling because this is what succeeds in the computer industry. One further problem is that many board members are not knowledgeable about the health care industry. A marketing board member with little knowledge of the health care field may be of only limited help in developing successful marketing strategies.

Inviting Help from Marketing Faculty and Students. Like board members, most marketing faculty and students have limited knowledge of the health care field. The students may have limited knowledge of marketing as well. However, if directed and guided by a marketing professor, the students may produce useful results from a research project.

Health care managers should recognize that student projects must fit within the dictates of an academic schedule. This limits the projects to which students can address themselves to smaller issues that can be explored fully in a short time period. Larger issues of marketing strategy for the whole organization or even for a major service within the organization deserve more time and expertise than students can devote to them.

Hiring Outside Expertise for Specific Projects. The value of this approach largely depends on the quality of the outside expertise. This is particularly true in health care marketing, where much expertise is self-proclaimed, with little training or experience to support the claim. When the outside marketing firm is highly qualified, the health care organization may get valuable marketing help.

Health care organizations that rely on outside expertise face one of two problems: (1) The outside expertise addresses not only a series of unrelated small marketing issues, but also major strategic marketing issues affecting the organization over the long term. The problem is that the cost of such an effort, when provided by outside expertise, can be astronomical. (2) If outside expertise is brought in to address only a series of smaller, unrelated marketing problems, no one is addressing the larger issues that have long-term implications for the organization. This piecemeal approach is likely to leave the organization with either an inconsistent or no marketing strategy.

Sending Staff to Marketing Seminars. Until the time in the future when most health care managers will have had marketing as part of their academic training, the strategy of educating current staff is a good one. The drawbacks are that few good marketing seminars exist. Large numbers of marketing seminars take on a "show-and-tell" tone, a "this is how we filled our beds" approach. But these seminars often lack the conceptual underpinnings necessary to make the knowledge transferable. Also, most seminars are too short and at too elementary a level to provide sufficient training in marketing. In addition, many health care executives report that, while the marketing seminars they attended were interesting and potentially useful, their job descriptions remained the same as they were prior to the seminars. Since they had not done marketing prior to the seminar, they were not expected (or budgeted) to do it after attending the seminar either. What they had learned in the marketing seminars they were not able to put to good use.

Appointing a Marketing Committee. The appointing of a marketing committee is often the first step toward the formal recognition of a marketing function within a health care organization. The form and functions of marketing committees vary significantly from one health care organization to another. Some committees include only board members, while others involve administrators, clinicians, department heads, and community representatives and former patients. Sometimes marketing committees engage outside experts to help guide the committee's deliberations.

Some marketing committees function solely to recommend whether the organization should establish a formal marketing position. Others decide whether outside consultants or marketing firms should be hired and for what purposes. The most aggressive posture a marketing committee takes is that of engaging in marketing analysis and strategy development, identifying marketing problems and opportunities facing the organization. This requires collecting and analyzing significant amounts of information, and developing recommendations for short-term and long-term actions. The report of these marketing findings and recommendations is called a marketing audit (see Chapter 7).

A drawback to having a marketing committee is that no one on the committee may have any marketing expertise. In addition, the more aggressive the posture of the committee, the more time its activities will require and the more difficult it will be to maintain the participation of those who already have other commitments and demanding work schedules.

Some health care organizations that do not wish to assign the marketing function to just one individual pursue some combination of these alternatives while simultaneously assigning some marketing responsibility to all managers. Under this arrangement, managers are each responsible for marketing their own departments, as well as for marketing the organization as a whole. This arrangement can work quite well if the CEO is truly committeed to marketing and effectively communicates not only commitment, but the expectations that each manager, clinician, and staff member will assume some marketing responsibility. Without the commitment and active involvement in this effort, the likelihood of significant marketing activity decreases dramatically.

For an example of the consumer's viewpoint of the value of a marketing director vs. a marketing-oriented management, clinician, and staff team, see Exhibit 5–1.

HIRING A MARKETER

A more recent phenomenon among health care organizations is the hiring of an individual whose primary function is marketing.[5] As the advertisements in Figure 5–1 indicate, the nature of marketing positions in health care may vary significantly from one organization to another. If a health care organization does choose this route, it must address a number of considerations before it can even place an advertisement to attract candidates for the position.

EXHIBIT 5–1 Consumer's Viewpoint of the Value of a Marketing Director

Beth Israel Hospital

330 Brookline Avenue
Boston, MA 02215

NEWSLETTER FOR EMPLOYEES

from the office of the President, Mitchell T. Rabkin, MD

29 March 1984

Typically, I reprint one of the letters sent to me but this one, from the Washington Post of 19 March 1984, simply has to be shared in Boston. It responds to an article in the Post about hospitals using marketing departments to get patients.

> "I read -- with an attitude of "what next?" -- "Hospitals Are Competing for Patients" (front page, March 11). Why don't hospitals hire knowledgeable, caring and competent doctors, nurses and staff instead of marketing directors? Then patients would flock to their doors.
>
> If I sound a bit cynical, I am. A couple of years ago I had a health problem. After nine months, seven doctors (some referrals, some working together), thousands of dollars for tests, many hours lost from work and much mental duress with no positive results, I went to Boston's Beth Israel Hospital. There, with about one day's time investment, I found the answers and in less than 10 days was on the road to recovery.
>
> I found it interesting that the doctors who attended me at Beth Israel were not Personal Corporations (PCs), but then who would want to sue a competent doctor? The rates were 10 percent to 25 percent less, there were no problems with the billing department, and my records were mailed to my home within a week of my visit.
>
> This was quite impressive, since the Washington hospital I used lost my CAT scan and sonogram pictures. It sent bills to my company mail room instead of the insurance company, and sent me bills for services already paid for -- and then threatened me with legal action for non-payment. The only way I stopped all this was to call the hospital administrator and threaten a legal suit.
>
> Marketing director -- just what the patient needs!
>
> Amelia Wright
> Sumner, Maryland

* * *

Mitchell T. Rabkin, M.D.
President

Courtesy of Beth Israel Hospital, 330 Brookline Avenue, Boston, MA 02215.

Level of the Position within the Organization

Headhunting firms hired to locate health care marketers report that the positions they are seeking to fill generally fall into two categories: (1) marketing analysts, assistants, or directors, to be paid $25,000 to $35,000; and (2) marketing vice-presidents and managers, to be paid $60,000 or more. This typifies the choice health care organizations make when they create a marketing position.[6]

Because the position is new and its functions are uncertain, many organizations prefer to place the marketing position at a middle man-

MARKET ANALYST

The Cleveland Clinic Foundation, an internationally recognized, specialty medical care institution, currently seeks an individual experienced in marketing research. Our 1,000 bed hospital, outpatient clinic, research and education division comprise one of the largest medical centers in the world.

The Market Analyst will be responsible for gathering and analyzing data on the demographic, economic, and health characteristics of the Cleveland Clinic Foundation's primary service area. From data gathered, the analyst will participate in the identification of areas for new marketing activities, evaluate existing programs, and participate in long range planning.

Interested candidates must have knowledge of market research and survey research principles sufficient to carry out functions with relative independence. Experience in design of questionnaires, interviewing techniques and computer programming skills essential. Three years experience conducting surveys and implementing research studies in marketing, sociological, epidemiological, health education, or other research related setting required. Master's degree in related area can be substituted for experience.

The Cleveland Clinic Foundation offers an excellent salary and benefits package including 33 days paid time off per year. Applicants may send resume to:

Loren P. Obert
Professional Recruiter
CLEVELAND CLINIC FOUNDATION
9500 Euclid Ave.
Cleveland, Ohio 44106

EOE M/F/H

MARKETING OPERATIONS MANAGER

Institute of Health Maintenance

Develop new marketing tools, communications plans and conduct continuing market research to expand the reach of our already growing outpatient risk factor obesity treatment centers. Market our services to employers, associations and insurance carriers in this challenging management position.

You will need a college degree (MBA preferred) plus at least four years of closely related experience including a solid track record in analysis of nationwide trends, systems planning, and project management responsibility.

This highly visible position will offer you a competitive salary, a complete benefit program and significant opportunity for advancement. For a prompt and confidential review, please send your resume and salary requirements to

nmc

An Equal Opportunity Employer M/F

Personnel Manager
Institute of Health Maintenance
A Division of
NATIONAL MEDICAL CARE, INC.
John Hancock Tower
Boston, MA 02116

DIRECTOR OF MARKETING

Outstanding opportunity to advance your career in a position with a progressive 442 bed teaching hospital.

Successful candidate will develop and carry out effective marketing programs.

Degree('s) in Marketing or related field required. Proven experience in developing and constructing marketing programs necessary.

We provide an attractive compensation package and excellent salary. Interested and qualified candidates should submit resumes with salary requirements to:

David D'Eramo, Ph.D.
President and Chief Executive Officer
Saint Vincent Charity Hospital
and Health Center
2351 East 22nd Street
Cleveland, OH 44115

Equal Opportunity Employer M/F/H

FIGURE 5–1 Advertisements for Marketing Positions in Health Care Organizations *Source:* Courtesy of Cleveland Clinic Foundation, National Medical Care, Inc., and Saint Vincent Charity Hospital and Health Center.

agement or staff level in order to try it out. This alternative has lower direct costs (a lower salary level) and causes less trauma in the organization than creating a new position near the top of the management structure. But there are significant disadvantages to placing the marketing position at the lower management level;[7] see Exhibit 5–2 for an example. Few people who already have significant experience in marketing are willing to take a lower-level position. The lower-level position is typically filled by a new MBA, since that is what a $25,000 salary will buy. While able to collect and analyze marketing information, this person is rarely given the authority to do anything significant with the information. At that level, the marketer would be unlikely to have the ear of the president or to participate in strategy formulation. The marketer might also not have power to implement marketing strategies across the organization. Imagine a young recent graduate, in this position six months in a hospital, approaching the head of obstetrics and saying: "I'm sorry, doctor, but I think we're going to have to close six of your beds."

EXHIBIT 5–2

The Disadvantages of a Lower-Level Marketing Position

An illustration of the failure to position the marketing function properly within the organization is that of a large city hospital which made the mistake of assigning the organization's marketing to a mid-level supervisor already overloaded with administrative tasks. Not only was the supervisor unable to spend adequate time analyzing the hospital's major markets and competitive stance, but the supervisor also found that he was unable to obtain support for the few quite reasonable marketing actions he recommended. Because no one in top management had initiated the analysis from which the recommendation came and no top level manager was responsible for the marketing function, no one with the power to implement the recommended marketing actions would support them. The result was a frustrated supervisor who spent a good deal of his overallocated time on a nonproductive task and a hospital which missed out on two substantial market opportunities.

SOURCE: Roberta N. Clarke, "Marketing Health Care: Problems in Implementation," *Health Care Management Review* (Winter 1978), p. 24. Reprinted with permission of Aspen Systems Corporation, © 1978.

In contrast, the vice-president level position is not subject to these problems. It is preferable to put the position here because part of the marketer's job is to transform the thinking of top management, and this can be done only by an individual closely involved with top management.[8] Royce Diener, board chairman of American Medical International, also views marketing as a top management function; he says the two functions that should report directly to the CEO are strategic planning and marketing.[9]

One difficulty with establishing a vice-president of marketing position is filling it with the right person. While there are many people who are experienced and trained in marketing, few of them also have experience with the health care or social welfare fields. Some organizations have chosen to hire people with recognized marketing expertise in other services such as banking or airline transportation and then to educate them about the health care field on the job. Others have hired people at the lower-level position in anticipation of promoting them to vice-president in time.

Reporting and Working Relationships

One problem with establishing the position of vice-president of marketing is the disruption and trauma it may cause in the organization. It is possible that the directors of development and public relations would answer to the marketing vice-president, thus moving the directors one level further away from the top of the organization. This is indeed likely to cause resentment.[10] Or the planning office might be on equal footing with the marketing office. Resentment might occur because the planner must now share with the marketer some responsibility and authority which previously rested only with the planning office.

Deciding to whom the marketer answers and with whom the marketer works is not easy. There are no organizational models in the health care field into which marketing has been incorporated that have a sufficient history to be proven effective. Figure 5–2 shows some possible positions a community hospital might envision for marketing.

Responsibilities and Authority of the Marketing Position

The responsibility and authority of the position will vary according to where the position is placed in the organization and to whom the person reports. The lower the position is in the organizational structure, the more it becomes a staff position. This generally implies significant information collecting and analysis responsibility, but little authority to select and implement strategies. A vice-president of marketing, in contrast, has substantial authority to go beyond analysis to make, in conjunction with other top administrators and the board of trustees, major strategic decisions.

Credentials

Few individuals have academic training in the area of health care marketing; only a few more have credible experience in the area. This makes recruiting the right person for a health care marketing position difficult. Even for a lower-level position, the health care organization would ideally like to recruit someone with academic training in marketing. This usually means a recent MBA or an undergraduate with a marketing major.

At the vice-presidential level, most organizations would like to require credentials indicating substantial work experience in marketing. Previous academic training is an advantage, but it can be replaced

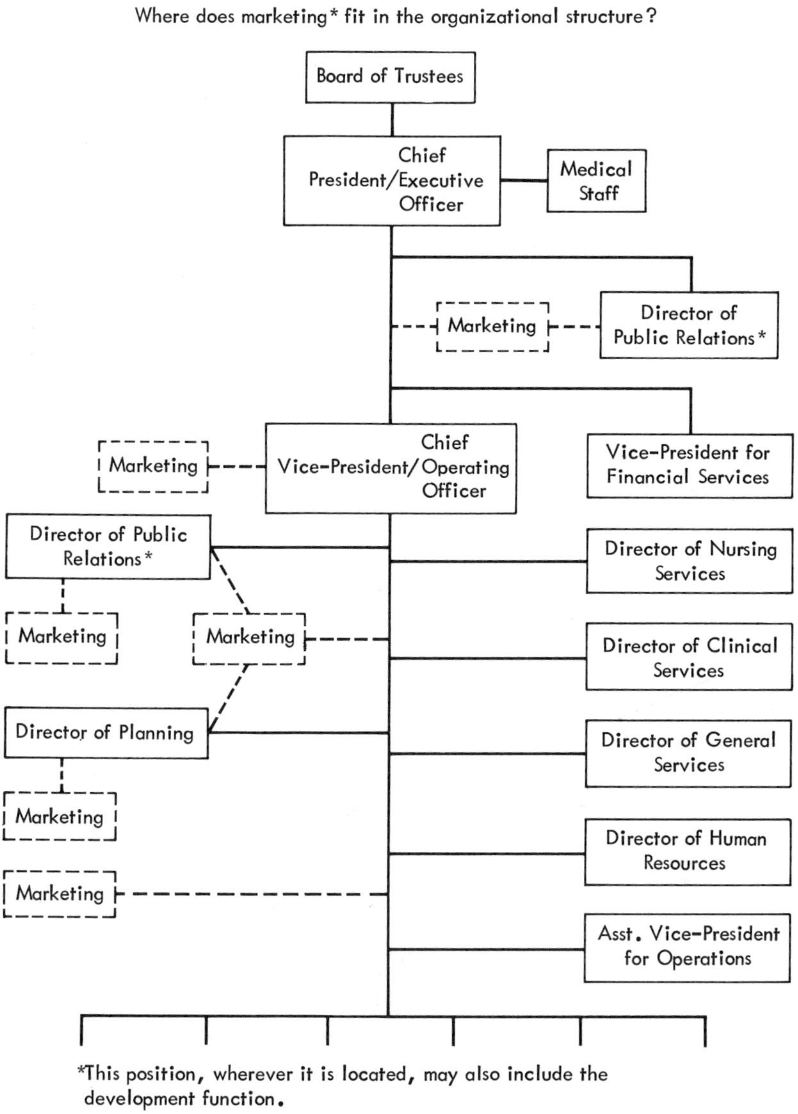

FIGURE 5–2 Community Hospital Organizational Structure

by significant experience. Yet the number of individuals with significant work experience in health care marketing (not just in promotion or planning) is so small that this recruitment criterion is not meaningful. So organizations turn to other criteria, such as familiarity with the field and with the organization, and a willingness to learn marketing.

One recent trend has been to take a middle- to upper-level manager in the organization, provide that individual with in-depth marketing training, and then make that person the marketing director or vice-president. This approach can be very attractive, since it introduces no new people into the top management structure (although it does introduce a new position), and thus may be less traumatic than bringing in someone from outside. If a marketer from outside the organization is hired, self-styled marketers—those who claim expertise when nothing in their background supports their claims—should be avoided. Since it is unlikely that other managers in the organization have marketing expertise, the organization can ill afford to hire someone with no expertise for their one and only marketing position. That still leaves the organization without anyone who can intelligently address marketing issues.

Dual Hierarchy

One credential a number of health care organizations have required of their marketers is a medical or clinical degree. They believe a clinical degree legitimizes the marketing person in the eyes of the clinical staff. Acceptance of the marketer by clinical staff is important because of the dual hierarchy of power.[11,12] This dual hierarchy is created by the health care organization's reliance on clinical and medical expertise to achieve its mission. Organizations with such a hierarchy of power have two management structures. One is the traditional management structure found in all substantial for-profit organizations; the other is a hierarchy structured around the medical professionals. The existence of two independent management structures in one organization can create substantial marketing management problems.

Medical staffs have often stood in the way of marketing efforts. Hospitals that have wanted to open primary care centers on evenings and weekends to better serve the community have sometimes been prevented from doing so by medical staffs that view hospital-based primary care as direct competition to their own private practices. Clinical staffs have sometimes also prevented hospitals from pursuing aggressive promotional strategies. One southwestern hospital's medical staff, in response to the hospital's advertising campaign, took out a counter-advertising campaign stating their refusal to support the hospital's advertising efforts. The hospital was ultimately forced to withdraw its advertising campaign.

The same dual hierarchy can affect other organizations as well. A home health agency that wanted to develop a self-pay patient segment found that its nurses refused to serve patients who did not clinically "need" nursing care, but wanted it and were willing to pay for it. By appointing a medical professional as marketer, an organization may be hoping to head off these types of problems. A medical professional will be more aware of the clinical staff's sensitivities regarding various marketing tactics, and will be better able to deal with these tactics. On the other hand, a medical professional who takes an administrative position (especially a marketing position) is often viewed as having "sold out" to the interests of administration. Even if the professional's title is director of medical affairs or vice-president of clinical relations, the clinician who assumes the position is often viewed as "not a real doctor/nurse/psychologist/social worker." The value of their clinical degree may not follow them into a marketing position.

The Corporate Marketing Position

The multi-unit health care organization has an additional option that alleviates some of the previously mentioned problems: It can hire a corporate marketer. The organizational structures in corporate offices of health care organizations are quite varied and not subject to the relatively rigid job definitions found in direct provider organizations. A corporate marketer can be hired at a significant corporate management level without causing the disruption that hiring a high-level marketer would cause in a direct provider organization. In addition, whereas a single organization might not be able to afford the high-level experienced marketer it would want, a corporate office servicing many provider organizations could allocate the cost of an expensive but experienced marketer across many organizations. This provides each organization with the marketing expertise it might want but otherwise not be able to afford.

The option of hiring a corporate marketer has other advantages as well. It allows marketing into the single-provider organization without requiring that the organization commit itself to a full-time marketer. Existing departments in direct provider organizations, such as planning and public relations, do not resent marketing from the corporate level because it poses no threats to their authority or reporting relationships within their own organizations. In essence, the corporate marketer, working out of a centralized corporate office, is a good way to introduce the marketing function into the single-unit organization.

The corporate marketer usually plays either a policymaking or marketing consulting role. As a policymaker, the corporate marketer may require or recommend that each single-unit organization implement certain policies which constitute good marketing. In one hospital chain, for example, most hospitals adopted a "quick triage" policy for emergency rooms; patients entering the emergency rooms were guaranteed to be seen by a medical professional within two minutes of arrival. The corporate marketer of a nursing home chain set a policy dictating that all member nursing homes provide waitress service on china or stoneware in the dining room as part of a campaign to attract more private paying patients.

The corporate marketer is very much like a regular marketing consultant, but may have a few advantages over outside consultants. The corporate marketing consultant has access to inside information. Also, the corporate marketing consultant is already familiar with the industry and corporate organization, if not the particular single-unit provider.

The option of hiring a corporate marketer is not limited to organizations that are members of a corporate chain. Regional or industry groups (trade associations) may hire corporate marketers, as may organizations that share services. A group of VNA (Visiting Nurse Association) administrators discussed the possibility of hiring a corporate marketer to examine marketing opportunities for VNAs across the country. Although the VNAs are relatively independent of each other, their common interests made hiring a corporate marketer a reasonable alternative.

The Miracle Worker

Assuming a competent individual is hired for a well-positioned marketing position, it is still possible for the organization to fail to reap the benefits of creating that position. The reason is that the organization views the marketer as the miracle worker: "Thank heavens we hired that marketer! Now we don't have to worry about census (utilization, image, patient mix, recruiting, etc.) any more. The marketer will take care of it for us."

The miracle worker syndrome afflicts organizations seeking easy solutions to difficult problems. These organizations hope that, by hiring a marketer (the easy solution), they will solve long-term complex problems with little pain or turmoil to the organization. This is not only unlikely, but also leads to the second stage of the miracle worker syndrome: the scapegoat syndrome: "What did I tell you? This marketing stuff is worthless. We brought in the marketing person to solve our census problem and what happens? The census gets worse."

These problems appear when the organization does not understand that the active involvement of the whole organization is necessary for success. The marketer may spearhead the analysis, strategy, and implementation of marketing, but these activities must be supported by the rest of the organization. Otherwise, the marketer might be like a general leading a military charge who turns around to discover no troops behind him.

EXPANDING THE MARKETING FUNCTION

Large-scale health care organizations, such as corporate hospital and nursing home chains, might initially think in terms of creating a whole marketing department. In 1984, Humana's corporate marketing department employed 22 people. Although most health care organizations will not need elaborate marketing departments in the near future, it is useful to consider the full range of job positions that might be found in a full-scale marketing department. Figure 5–3 shows a generic organization reflecting four dimensions of marketing: functions, products, markets, and territories. A detailed description of these job positions is presented in Table 5–1.

Of particular interest is the question of whether a health care organization should establish a product management system, a market management system, neither, or both. Normally, the first step in expanding a marketing department is to add some functional specialists, such as a marketing researcher and/or communication manager. The question of product and market managers arises later. Consider this question in connection with a multispecialty medical group practice. The group practice has many "products"—internal medicine, pediatrics, obstetrics/gynecology, psychiatry, and so on. A product management system would call for appointing a person to head each major service. Thus, the director of psychiatry would study people's needs and interests in mental health and would develop plans for expanding the offerings and attracting more mental health patients. The group practice also serves a variety of markets divided by sex, age, and other

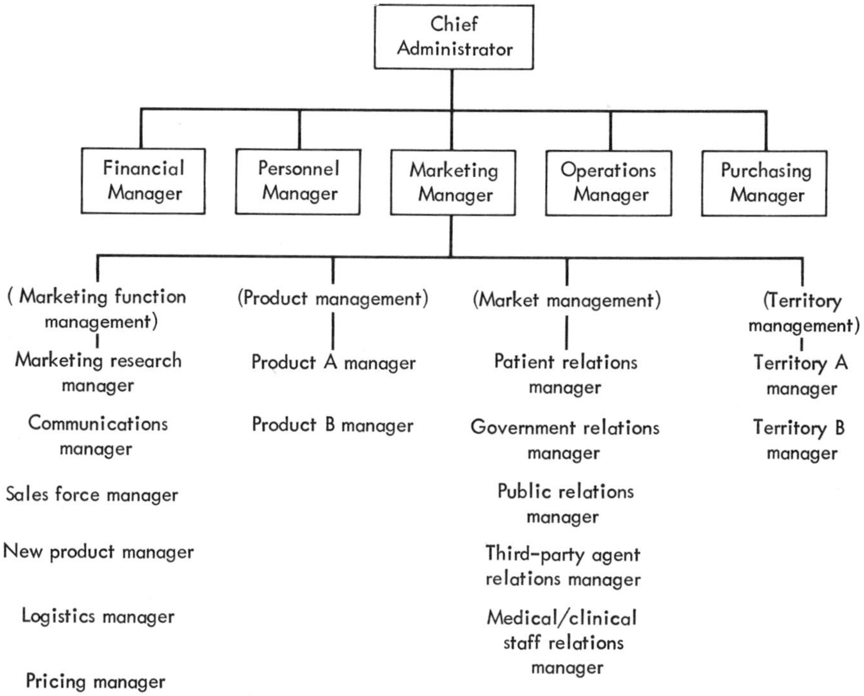

FIGURE 5–3 Generic Marketing Organization

TABLE 5–1 Generic Marketing Positions

Marketing manager
The marketing manager heads the health care organization's marketing activities. Tasks include providing a marketing point of view to the top administration; helping to formulate marketing plans for the organization; staffing, directing, and coordinating marketing activities; and proposing new products and services to meet emerging market needs.

Product manager
A product service manager is responsible for managing a particular product, service, or program of the health care organization. Tasks include proposing product objectives and goals, creating product strategies and plans, seeing that they are implemented, monitoring the results, and taking corrective action.

Marketing research manager
The marketing research manager has responsibility for developing and supervising research on the organization's markets and publics, and on the effectiveness of various marketing tools.

Communications manager
The communications manager provides expertise in the area of mass and selective communication and promotion. This person is knowledgeable about the design of commercial messages, media, and publicity.

Sales force manager
The sales force manager has responsibility for recruiting, training, assigning, directing, motivating, compensating, and evaluating salespeople, representatives and agents of the organization, and coordinating the work of the salespeople with the other marketing functions.

New product manager
The new product manager has responsibility for conceiving new products and services; screening and evaluating new product ideas; developing prototypes and testing them; and advising and helping to carry out introduction in the marketplace.

Logistics manager
The logistics manager has responsibility for planning and managing the distribution systems that make the organization's product and services available and accessible to potential users.

Pricing manager
The pricing manager is responsible for advising and/or setting prices for those services and programs for which the health care organization controls the price.

Patient relations manager
The patient relations manager has responsibility for managing patient services and handling patient complaints.

Government relations manager
The government relations manager provides the organization with intelligence on relevant developments in government and manages the organization's program of representation and presentation to government and regulatory organizations.

Public relations manager
The public relations manager has responsibility for communicating and dealing with various publics in matters involving the organization's image and activities.

Third-party agent relations manager
The third-party agent relations manager provides the organization with information on trends and new policies of third-party agents and manages the organization's program of representation and presentation to third parties.

Medical/clinical staff relations manager
The medical/clinical staff relations manager is responsible for managing medical/clinical staff services and handling medical/clinical staff complaints.

Territory manager
The territory manager has responsibility for managing the organization's products, services, and programs in a specific territory or service area.

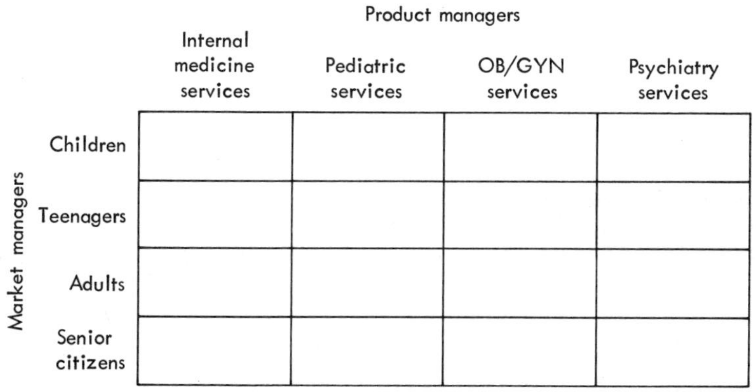

FIGURE 5–4 Matrix Organization

variables. A market management system would call for appointing a person to head each major market. Thus, the market manager for the elderly would study their needs and develop programs that satisfy their needs.

Clearly the group practice would be more effective by operating both a product and a market management system. This is called a matrix organization and is shown in Figure 5–4. However, the group practice would have to weigh the costs of these systems against the benefits. A good way to proceed is to install a few product and market managers in the major areas on a trial basis to see what the system produces and costs.

CREATING A MARKET-ORIENTED ORGANIZATION

Transforming a nonmarket-oriented organization into a fully responsive market-oriented organization is a long and difficult effort. Installing the marketing concept calls for major commitments and changes in the organization. As noted by Edward S. McKay, a well-known marketing consultant:

> It may require drastic and upsetting changes in organization. It usually demands new approaches to planning. It may set in motion a series of appraisals that will disclose surprising weakness in performance, distressing needs for modification of operating practices, and unexpected gaps, conflicts, or obsolescence in basic policies. Without doubt, it will call for a reorientation of business philosophy and for the reversal of some long-established attitudes. These changes will not be easy to implement. Objectives, obstacles, resistance, and deep-rooted habits will have to be overcome. Frequently, even difficult and painful restaffing programs are necessary before any real progress can be made in implementing the concept.[13]

An attempt to reorient an organization requires a plan based on sound principles for producing change. Achieving a marketing orientation calls for several measures beyond those of organizational design. The sum of these measures should work toward producing a market-oriented organization within a few years.

Top Management Support

A health care organization is not likely to develop a strong marketing orientation until its chief executive officer (CEO) believes in it, understands it, wants it, and wins the support of other high-level executives for building this function. The CEO is the organization's highest marketing executive, and must, through his or her own actions and words, create the climate for marketing. By setting a service-minded and responsive tone, the CEO sets in motion the acceptance of further marketing steps by those involved in the organization.

In-house Marketing Training

Prior to undertaking any marketing activities which would be noticeable to the marketplace, the organization must introduce marketing to its staff. Presumably, marketing training should start with top management (corporate and divisional management in a multi-institutional system) because their understanding and support is essential if the new marketing efforts are to work. Medical and clinical staffs should also be included in this educational process early on, especially in those organizations with a dual hierarchy. Otherwise, because of their significant power, these staffs could undo the good done by marketing activities undertaken by the rest of the organization. Marketing training for clinical staffs is also important because of their direct patient contact. See Exhibit 5–3 for an example of lack of marketing orientation among clinicians. Further training can then be provided to financial, operations, and other staff to enlist their understanding (see Exhibit 5–4).

EXHIBIT 5–3

The Knee

We are on attending rounds with the usual group: attending, senior resident, junior residents, and medical students. There are eight of us. Today we will learn how to examine the knee properly.

The door is open. The room is ordinary institutional yellow, a stained curtain between the beds. We enter in proper order behind our attending physician.

The knee is attached to a woman, perhaps 35 years old, dressed in her robe and nightgown. The attending physician asks the usual questions as he places his hand on the knee: "This knee bothers you?"

All eyes are on the knee; no one meets her eyes as she answers. The maneuvers begin—abduction, adduction, flexion, extension, rotation. She continues to tell her story, furtively pushing her clothing between her legs. Her endeavors are hopeless, for the full range of knee motion must be demonstrated. The door is open. Her embarrassment and helplessness are evident.

More maneuvers and a discussion of knee pathology ensue. She asks a question. No one notices.

More maneuvers. The door is open.

Now the uninvolved knee is examined—abduction, adduction, flexion, extension, rotation.

She gives up.

The door is open.

Now a discussion of surgical technique. Now review the knee examination. We file out through the open door.

She pulls the sheet up around her waist.

She is irrelevant.

SOURCE: "The Knee," by Constance J. Meyd, *Journal of the American Medical Association,* July 23/30, 1982. Copyright 1982, American Medical Association.

EXHIBIT 5–4 Hospital "Niceness" Training

Dose of Smiles Is Latest Prescription for Hospitals That Vie for Patients

Where do nice guys finish? First, say hospital administrators.

As competition increases in the health care industry, a growing number of hospitals are trying to give patients a better image of their personnel and facilities. To get smiling patients, administrators say, you first need smiling nurses, orderlies and doctors. The tool: "niceness" training.

"Formerly, the attitude was, 'They need us, we don't need them,'" says Mark Penkhus, executive vice president of St. Mary-Corwin Hospital in Pueblo, Colo. Now, he says, the watchwords are "patient relations."

OFFERS SEMINARS

Neu & Co., a Denver-based consulting firm, developed a patient-relations program called Pro-Med in 1980. Today, the program has 200 client hospitals. Neu offers seminars on communications and human-relations skills—and will even custom design a niceness-training program for a particular hospital.

"That doesn't mean (the hospital) didn't care before," says Carl Neu, president of the firm. But "we're in an age where we can't assume we have enough skills."

Northwestern Memorial Hospital in Chicago designed a five-hour seminar on niceness for its employees after a marketing survey showed that patients considered the hospital "impersonal." Telling health-care professionals that they needed a course on courtesy was touchy, says Curt Thompson, who is in charge of the hospital's patient relations. They had to feel that "they weren't being rapped over the knuckles," he says.

RESENT THE SUGGESTION

About 3,900 of Northwestern Memorial's 4,200 employees have taken the seminar, but only 100 of its 700 doctors have bothered. Many hospitals report that their doctors resent the implication that they need sensitivity training.

St. Mary-Corwin in Colorado has gone further than a half-day seminar. Officials redesigned the hospital to make it seem more like a hotel, including carpeting on every floor—a move that required buying new rollers for every piece of rolling equipment, Mr. Penkhus says.

The hospital now has volunteers serving as doormen, three-piece outfits for the cashiers and admitting personnel, sprigs of parsley and carnations on every dinner plate, and cable TV, Mr. Penkhus says. St. Mary-Corwin replaced its old mattresses with more comfortable ones and bought plush linens and towels, of which Mr. Penkhus seems especially proud. "You certainly can't see through them like most hospital towels," he says.

SOURCE: David Mills, *The Wall Street Journal,* September 24, 1984, p. 35.

Better Hiring Practices

Training can go only so far in inculcating the right attitudes in employees. If a nursing staff has grown accustomed to concentrating on clinical care at the expense of empathetic personal care, it will be hard to change attitudes. The organization can gradually rectify the imbalance by hiring nurses who are more people-oriented. The first principle in developing a caring staff is to hire caring people. Some people are more naturally service-minded than others, and this can be a criterion for hiring. Delta Airlines does most of its stewardess recruiting from the Deep South, where there is a tradition of hospitality; it avoids hiring in large northern cities, because people from these cities tend to be more abrupt with each other. Delta operates on the principle that it is easier to hire friendly people than to train unfriendly people to be friendly.

New employees should go through a training program that emphasizes the importance of creating consumer satisfaction. They can be taught to handle complaining and even abusive patients without getting upset or angry. Skills in listening and patient problem-solving would be part of the training. These skills are important in all businesses, as noted in Exhibit 5–5.

EXHIBIT 5–5

Disney—A Highly Responsive Organization

Service organizations—colleges, hospitals, social agencies, and others—are increasingly recognizing that their marketing mix consists not of four P's but five—product, price, place, promotion, and people. And people may be the most important P! The organization's employees come in continuous contact with consumers and create good or bad impressions about the organization as the case may be. Service organizations are eager to figure out how to produce a genuine customer-orientation and service-mindedness in their employees.

Not many organizations have really figured out how to "turn on" their inside people (employees) to serve their outside people (customers). Consider the following things that Disney does to market "positive customer relations" to its employees:

1. The personnel staff at Disney makes a special effort to welcome new job applicants and make a good impression on them. The initial impression is very important. Those who are hired are given clearly written instructions on what to expect—where to report, what to wear, and how long each training phase will take.
2. On the first day, new employees report to Disney University for an all-day orientation session. They sit four to a table, receive name tags, and enjoy coffee, juice, and a Danish. The four people at each table are asked to get to know each other and introduce each other, so that the new employee immediately knows three people and feels part of a group.
3. During the next eight hours, the employees are introduced to the Disney philosophy and operations, through the most modern audio-visual presentations. The new employees learn that they are in the entertainment business. They are "cast members" whose job it is to be enthusiastic, knowledgeable, and professional in serving Disney's "guests." Each division in the organization is described as to how these divisions relate to each other to produce the "show." They are then treated to a free lunch, and in the afternoon, the new employees are given a tour of the park and also shown the private recreational area set aside for the employees' exclusive use, namely a lake, recreation hall, picnic areas, boating and fishing, and a large library.

4. The next day, the new employees report to their assigned jobs, such as security hosts (policemen), transportation hosts (drivers), custodial hosts (street cleaners), or food and beverage hosts (restaurant workers). They will receive a few days of additional training before they go "onstage." When they really know their function, they receive their "theme costume" for that function and are ready to go onstage.
5. The new employees receive additional training on how to answer the scores of questions guests tend to ask about the park. And when they don't have the answer, they can dial a special number where a cadre of switchboard operators armed with thick factbooks stand ready to answer any question.
6. The employees regularly receive an eight-page 8 and half × 11 news paper called *Eyes and Ears* that features all sorts of activities, employment opportunities, special benefits, educational offerings, and so on. Each issue contains a generous number of employee pictures, all of them smiling.
7. Each Disney manager spends a week each year in "cross-utilization," namely giving up the desk and heading for the front line, such as taking tickets, selling popcorn, or loading or unloading rides. In this way, management stays in touch with the daily challenges of running the park and problems of maintaining quality to satisfy the millions of people who visit the theme park yearly. These managers also wear badges and every employee addresses other employees on a first-name basis, regardless of rank.
8. Every exiting employee receives a questionnaire to indicate how they felt about working for Disney, particularly any dissatisfactions they might have had. In this way, Disney's management can measure how good a job they are doing in producing employee satisfaction and ultimately customer relations.

No wonder Disney has had such huge success in satisfying their "guests." Their exchange with employees makes the latter feel important and personally responsible for the "show." The employees' sense of "owning this organization," of being worthwhile members of a worthwhile organization, results in their satisfaction spilling over to the millions of visitors with whom they come in contact.

SOURCE: Summary of major points in N. W. Pope, "Mickey Mouse Marketing," *American Banker,* July 25, 1979; and "More Mickey Mouse Marketing," *American Banker,* September 12, 1979.

Rewarding Market-Oriented Staff Members

One way for top management to convince everyone of the importance of marketing in the organization is to reward those who demonstrate good attitudes. The organization can make a point of citing employees who have done an outstanding job of serving patients. One nursing home gives a Sunshine Award of $100 each year to the patients' favorite employee. Some hospitals carry a picture in their employee magazine showing the employee of the month and describing how that person handled a difficult situation. By calling attention to examples of commendable customer-oriented performance, the organizations hope that other employees will be motivated to emulate this behavior.

Planning System Improvement

One of the most effective ways to build demand for stronger marketing is through improving the organization's strategic planning system. If the health care organization has neither strong marketing nor strong business or strategic planning, it might first design and install a strategic planning system. A strategic planning system goes beyond traditional health care planning. To make this system work, strong marketing data and analysis will be necessary, beginning with an analysis of the market. This will require strengthening the organization's marketing function. Strategic planning is largely an empty gesture without good marketing data and analysis.

SUMMARY

All organizations carry on marketing activities, whether or not they acknowledge it. To date, most health care organizations have pursued one of two options: assigning the marketing title to an existing administrative function, or not assigning it to anyone. While each option has advantages, the disadvantages of each may outweigh the advantages in the long run. A third option, which is newer to the health care field, is hiring a marketer. This raises issues of at what level within the organization the marketer should be positioned, the marketer's reporting and working relationships, responsibilities and authority, and the credentials a marketer should have. Each issue represents a potential problem for the organization if it is not addressed. For multi-institutional systems and other organizational groups, these problems can be bypassed by hiring a corporate marketer. One common problem with hiring a marketer is the miracle worker/scapegoat syndrome. Here the organization incorrectly lays total responsibility for marketing on the marketer without recognizing the need for total organizational involvement. Then, when the organization's marketing problems do not miraculously disappear, the marketer is made the scapegoat. As marketing expands, its organization will reflect four dimensions: functions, products, markets, and territories. To create a truly market-oriented organization requires several things: top management support, effective organizational design, in-house marketing training, better hiring practices, rewarding market-oriented employees, and improving the strategic planning system.

NOTES

1. Colleen Murphy Walter, "Academic Medical Center Features Image Analysis in Marketing Audit," *Hospital* (August 16, 1981), pp. 91–100.

2. "Hospitals Are Turning to Marketing Plans, Penn Report Says," *American Medical News* (October 9, 1981), p. 19.

3. Linda I. Collins, "A Survey of Hospital Salaries," *Hospital* (November 1, 1984), pp. 80–92.

4. Daniel A. Kroger and Frankie L. Perry, "Physician-Centered Marketing: A Practical Step to Hospital Survival," *Hospital and Health Services Administration* (May–June 1983), p. 43.

5. A September 11, 1979, article in the *Wall Street Journal* (page 11) reported that "no more than 10% of the nation's 7000 hospitals have set up formal programs or hired marketing directors. But the number of such hospitals is growing rapidly." Newer estimates of the proportion of hospitals with marketing directors or vice-presidents vary around 40 to 50 percent.

6. Douglass Marshall, "Setting Up a Marketing Department: Why? How?" *Hospital Progress* (June 1980), pp. 60–62.

7. Roberta N. Clarke, "Marketing Health Care: Problems in Implementation," *Health Care Management Review* (Winter 1978).

8. Richard D. O'Hallaron, Jeffry Staples, Paul Chiampa, "Marketing Your Hospital," *Hospital Progress* (December 1976), pp. 68–71.

9. Bruce Keppel, "Hospitals Look to Marketing as Remedy for Fiscal Ills," The *Hartford Courant,* March 22, 1872, p. C2.

10. Report and Recommendations of the ASHPR Marketing Task Force, American Society of Hospital Public Relations, September 1982.

11. Roberta Clarke, "Moving from Concept to Action: Strategic Barriers in Health Care Marketing," in *Marketing of Services,* J. H. Donnelly and W. R. George, eds., American Marketing Association Proceedings Series, 1981.

12. Roberta N. Clarke, "The Dual Hierarchy of Power," paper presented at Non-Profit Marketing Conference, American Marketing Association, Columbia, South Carolina, April 1982.

13. Edwards, S. McKay, *The Marketing Mystique* (New York: American Management Association, 1972), p. 22. Reprinted by permission of the publisher. © 1972 American Management Association, Inc. All rights reserved.

6

MARKETING INFORMATION AND RESEARCH

The Boston Visiting Nurse Association was the largest VNA in New England, providing the full range of home health services. While the Boston VNA used to be viewed as one of the "grand old ladies" of home health care, it had run into difficult times in the 1980s. Many proprietary home health agencies entered the market. Some of these were units of well-funded national home health chains with sophisticated marketing packages. Hospitals, which were the VNA's primary source of patients, had also begun to consider diversifying into home health care. A few, including one of the Boston VNA's major referral sources, had actually set up their own home health services.

A perusal of the Boston VNA's payor (third-party reimbursement) mix indicated that, over the course of five years, the agency's proportion of Medicaid and Medicare patients had grown. Simultaneously, the proportion of the more lucrative private pay and private insurance patients had declined. Already burdened by delayed payments by the state as well as by retroactive denials of payment, the agency felt it must pursue a strategy which would assure it greater financial viability.

The demand for the Boston VNA's home health aides and homemakers overwhelmed the demand for its highly skilled nurses and therapists. Third-party coverage for home health aides was very limited, and for homemakers, nonexistent. Therefore, the agency set out to develop a "personal care" service, staffed by aides and homemakers, to be directed to the self-pay market.

The Boston VNA management did not know how to proceed. Management felt it must have certain information before it could develop a marketing plan. Thus, the management requested a credible management consulting firm to propose a research study that would help the managers in their deliberations.

The marketing research firm proposed the following four objectives for the project:

1. To identify and describe the characteristics of potential purchasers of the proposed "personal care service" (such as age, position in the family, income level, etc.).
2. To describe the characteristics of the "personal care service" offering which will make it attractive to potential purchasers and give it a competitive advantage compared to similar offerings by other organizations. Possible advantageous characteristics include affiliation with the VNA name, quick availability of homemaker services, and guarantee of low homemaker turnover. This stage includes testing price points.
3. To estimate the number of potential purchasers in two or three areas to be selected. This should be viewed as a very rough estimate, primarily designed to allow the VNA to make a go/no-go decision. Actual market demand will be a function primarily of the VNA's market strategy for the service.
4. To develop a marketing strategy for launching the service in two or three test market areas. In addition to determining the issues suggested above, this objective would include aiding in the development of a promotional plan.

To address these issues, the marketing research firm would carry out five steps: (1) interviews with potential referral sources, (2) exploratory research among potential purchasers, (3) development of a competitive profile, (4) survey research on selected geographic areas, and (5) analysis, recommendations, and strategy development. The cost of this project was $60,000. The Boston VNA now had to decide whether to (1) authorize this research, (2) ask for a lower-cost study that would yield some but not all of the indicated information, or (3) drop the idea of marketing research and simply try out a number of tactics that might effectively market the "personal care" service.

SOURCE: Based on a proposal by Thomas E. Wilson, Director, Cambridge Research Institute, 1982; reprinted with permission.

Health care managers need timely, accurate and adequate information as a basis for making sound marketing decisions. We will use the term *marketing information system* (*MIS*) to describe the organization's system for gathering, analyzing, storing, and disseminating relevant marketing information. More formally:

> A **marketing information system** is a continuing and interacting structure of people, equipment, technology, and procedures designed to gather, sort, analyze, evaluate, and distribute pertinent, timely, and accurate information for use by marketing decision makers to improve their marketing planning, execution, and control.[1]

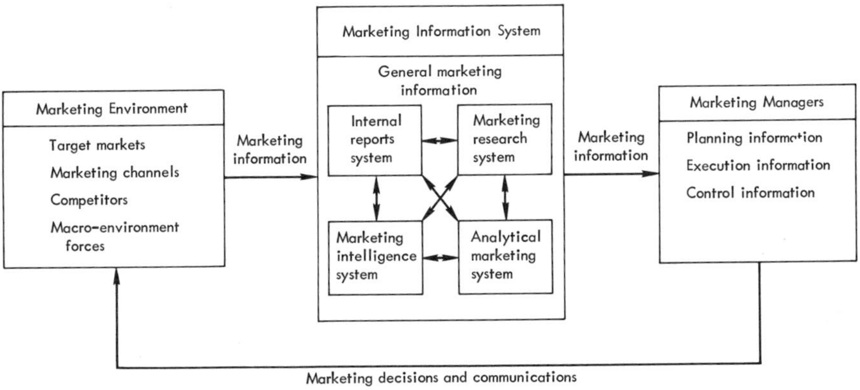

FIGURE 6–1 The Marketing Information System

The role and major subsystems of an MIS are illustrated in Figure 6–1. At the left is the marketing environment marketing managers must monitor—target markets, marketing channels, competitors, publics, and macro-envrionmental forces. Developments and trends in the marketing environment are picked up in the organization through one of four subsystems making up the marketing information system—the internal reports system, the marketing intelligence system, the marketing research system, and the analytical marketing system. The information then flows to the appropriate marketing managers (managers assigned marketing responsibility) to help them in planning, execution, and control. The resulting decisions and communications then flow back to the marketing environment.

INTERNAL RECORDS SYSTEM

The oldest and most basic information system used by managers is the internal records system. Every organization compiles information in the course of its operations.

A hospital will keep records on its patients, including names, addresses, ages, diagnosis, length of stay, supplies, ancillary and room charges, attending physician, and so on. From these records, the hospital can develop statistics on the number of daily admissions, average length of patient stay, average patient charge, frequency distribution of different illnesses, and other useful statistics. The hospital will also have records on physicians, nurses, costs, billings, assets and liabilities, all of which is indispensable information for making management decisions.

Every internal records system can be improved. Some need improvement only in speed and accuracy. Most health care organizations' internal records systems, however, also need greater comprehensiveness and the ability to consolidate all marketing data within one record system. Most commonly, a health care organization has two internal systems, the medical records and the financial records. Historically, data from one system could rarely be used by the other. Thus, the organization would be unable to generate such information as cost by diagnosis, profitability or loss by age of patient, and so on. This was because age and diagnostic information was in medical records, whereas cost and revenue information was in financial records. Under DRG and similar flat-fee reimbursement schemes, it becomes imperative to have financial and medical records interact in the information system. Many hospitals now have this capability, although other types of health care organizations generally do not.

When organizations seek to improve their internal records systems, the goal should be to design not the most elegant system, but the one that is cost effective in meeting managers' needs for information, planning, and control. A cross section of managers should be queried for their information needs. Exhibit 6–1 shows the major questions one might ask. Once their opinions are gathered, the system designers can set up an internal records system that reconciles (1) what managers

EXHIBIT 6–1

Determining Marketing Information Needs of Managers

1. What types of decisions are you regularly called upon to make?
2. What types of information do you need to make these decisions?
3. What types of information do you regularly get?
4. What types of special studies do you periodically request?
5. What types of information would you like to get that you are not now getting?
6. What information would you want daily? weekly? monthly? yearly?
7. What magazines and reports would you like to see routed to you on a regular basis?
8. What specific topics would you like to be kept informed of?
9. What types of data analysis programs would you like to see made available?
10. What do you think would be the four most helpful improvements that could be made in the present marketing information system?

think they need, (2) what managers really need, and (3) what is economically feasible.

In developing improved internal records systems, health care managers cannot afford to ignore the value of computers. Many computer software developers who serve the health care market as well as health care consultants dealing in information systems are now equally well or better versed in the internal records of health care organizations than are organization managers. With the advent of DRGs, software packages such as those offered by SMS, HBO & Co., Compucare, and Mediflex Systems have become available. They mesh medical records, financial records, and certain planning or demographic data into one program. Most of these software programs include internal information, such as ancillary charges per patient admitted by Dr. X, which the health care manager would like to have but never had access to before. The sophistication of the records system is likely to increase dramatically in the future as health care organizations recognize the ability of computers to enhance the collection and management of information.

MARKETING INTELLIGENCE SYSTEM

Whereas the internal reports system supplies managers with results data, the marketing intelligence system supplies managers with happenings data.

> The **marketing intelligence system** is the set of sources and procedures by which marketing executives obtain their everyday information about developments in the external marketing environment.

Most health care managers take a casual approach to marketing intelligence. They read newspapers and journals, and talk to various people who might pass on relevant information. While this approach will help them spot some important developments, it may also result in their missing or learning too late of others.

Health care organizations can take concrete steps to improve the quality of the marketing intelligence available to their managers. They can employ a clipping service that methodically scans a predetermined set of magazines and journals for relevant articles. They can encourage outside parties with whom they deal—suppliers, professional associations, alternative delivery systems, regulatory agencies, lawyers, and accountants—to pass on useful information. For example, a medical supplies salesman alerted a midwestern hospital to the competing hospital's plans to operate a free-standing ambulatory surgery center.

However, to guarantee that marketing intelligence is consistently collected and examined, the organization should assign the responsibility for gathering and disseminating marketing information to a specific office or person. In many hospitals, this responsibility would fall on the planning office, which already collects and analyzes some marketing information as planning data. In organizations with no planning office, an administrative or staff person would be assigned this function.

Responsibilities for managing marketing intelligence include developing a master index or software program of past and current information for storage and retrieval, evaluation of the reliability of information, the installation of suggestion and compliant systems, and the ongoing dissemination of relevant information to management. Those responsible for the marketing intelligence system might even hire people to carry on specialized intelligence-gathering activities.

They might use a commercial technique of hiring "mystery shoppers" to canvass their own organization and competitors' organizations. One hospital hired someone to join the volunteer groups of competing hospitals as well as their own. The "professional volunteer" reported widely differing levels of personal care and amenities provided to patients. One hospital, for example, gave the patient a choice of only two menus at every meal; another had an open menu of over a hundred items from which the patient could order any amount. Having a "mystery shopper" within one's own organization is an important way of learning whether the organization's own staff really has a customer orientation.

It is possible to combine the internal records system and the marketing intelligence system under the title of general marketing information, whether or not the actual collection and dissemination of the information is performed by the same office. Internal records provide internal marketing data, while marketing intelligence provides external marketing data. Table 6–1 provides a checklist of general marketing information for a community hospital.

MARKETING RESEARCH SYSTEM

From time to time health care managers need to commission specific marketing research studies in order to have adequate information to make decisions. Managers of health care organizations are increasingly finding that they need marketing research. Many studies could prove worthwhile to an organization, but in the face of limited budgets, health care organizations must know how to choose marketing research projects carefully, design them efficiently, and implement the results effectively. It is estimated that most health care organizations spend less than one and one-quarter percent of their budgets on recognized marketing activities,[2] compared to ten times that amount in many industries. But predictions are that this will change:

> Marketing research budgets will increase dramatically. As lifestyles change and competition increases, the need to develop new services

TABLE 6–1 General Marketing Information

INTERNAL	*EXTERNAL*	*INTERNAL*	*EXTERNAL*
Census—aggregate and by service Admissions/discharges: By service (medical, surgical, pediatric, etc.) By diagnosis within service by cost By physician By source of payment By patient origin by community By source of referral (medical staff, emergency room, outpatient department, etc.) By patient age By average length of stay Medical staff Aggregate number and department By credentials By specialty By age By practice plans By office location By use of ancillary services and operating room By admissions, by diagnosis By other hospital affiliations and percentage use of each other hospital affiliation	Characteristics of the hospital's service area Age distribution Income distribution Level of education By religion (if applicable) By culture or ethnic background (if applicable) By medical service Usage rates (inpatient, ambulatory, emergency room) Market size and growth rate Natality and mortality statistics Membership in HMOs (number of members in each HMO) Profile of MDs in hospital's market area Age Specialty Practice setting Office locations Admission rates Affiliations Patients' origins Credentials	Emergency department utilization Gross utilization By shift By time of year, day of week By source of payment By patient origin By community By type of diagnosis Time in waiting area until patient treated Percentage of EMS ambulance runs to emergency department Patient origin by incidence of emergency By source of referral (walk-in physician, fire, police, etc.) Percentage of emergency department patients admitted as inpatients Ambulatory medical services utilization Gross utilization By service By diagnosis By patient source By patient origin By community By source of referral By patient age Percentage of ambulatory pa-	Competitors Number of beds Occupancy by service Service configuration Characteristics of population served Service expansion or alteration plans, including major capital projects Medical staff makeup Prices Planning, regulatory and hospital reimbursement trends Medical (clinical) practice trends (i.e., decreasing tendency to hospitalize children, increasing use of home health care, etc.)

(continued)

TABLE 6–1 (continued)

INTERNAL	*EXTERNAL*	*INTERNAL*	*EXTERNAL*
By total hospital revenue generated		tients admitted as inpatients Financial information Revenues by department Expenditures by department Gross index of patient satisfaction with all services From patient cards From hospital ombudsmen	

Source: Roberta N. Clarke and Linda Shyavitz, "Marketing Information and Market Research—Valuable Tools for Managers," *Health Care Management Review* (Winter 1981), p. 74. Reprinted with permission of Aspen Systems Corporation © 1981.

or to modify those in existence also will occur. Marketing research activities will become a regular process in the development of new services. Recent research indicates that market research services and consultation are the No. 1 priority for executives currently involved with marketing activities within the hospital.[3]

Using Marketing Research Effectively

We define marketing research as follows:

> **Marketing research** is the systematic design, collection, analysis, and reporting of data and findings relevant to a specific marketing situation or problem facing an organization.

The key idea is that management initiates or commissions a study to develop information on a subject by a certain date. Numerous types of studies qualify as marketing research projects. Table 6–2 lists 33 different marketing research activities and the percentage of American companies carrying on each. The 10 most common activities are determination of market characteristics, measurement of market potentials, market share analysis, sales analysis, studies of business trends, competitive product studies, short-range forecasting, new product acceptance and potential, long-range forecasting, and pricing studies.

Who does these studies for an organization? Large commercial

TABLE 6–2 Major Marketing Research Activities

TYPE OF RESEARCH	*PERCENT DOING IT*
Advertising Research	
Motivation research	47%
Copy research	61
Media research	68
Studies of ad effectiveness	76
Studies of competitive advertising	67
Business Economics and Corporate Research	
Short-range forecasting (up to 1 year)	89
Long-range forecasting (over 1 year)	87
Studies of business trends	91
Pricing studies	83
Plant and warehouse location studies	68
Acquisition studies	73
Export and international studies	49
MIS (Management Information System)	80
Operations Research	65
Internal company employees	76
Corporate Responsibility Research	
Consumer "right to know" studies	18
Ecological impact studies	23
Studies of legal constraints on advertising and promotion	46
Social values and policies studies	39
Product Research	
New product acceptance and potential	76
Competitive product studies	87
Testing of existing products	80
Packaging research: design or physical characteristics	65
Sales and Market Research	
Measurement of market potentials	97
Market share analysis	97
Determination of market characteristics	97
Sales analysis	92
Establishment of sales quotas, territories	78
Distribution channel studies	71
Test markets, store audits	59
Consumer panel operations	63
Sales compensation studies	60
Promotional studies of premiums, coupons, sampling, deals, etc.	58

Source: Dik Warren Twedt, ed., *1983 Survey of Marketing Research* (Chicago: American Marketing Association, 1983), p. 41. Based on a sample of 599 companies.

organizations, in fact over 73 percent of all large business firms, have their own marketing research directors or departments. Even they, however, allocate as much as half of the market research department's budget to purchasing the services of outside marketing research companies. Smaller organizations, in which category most health care organizations fall, are not likely to employ a marketing research director and will typically buy outside marketing research when needed. *Brad-*

ford's Directory lists over 350 outside marketing research companies. They fall into three major categories.[4]

1. *Syndicated-service research firms.* These firms specialize in gathering continuous consumer and trade information which they sell in the form of standardized product reports on a fee-subscription basis to all clients. Marketing management can purchase syndicated reports on television audiences from Nielsen or the American Research Bureau (ARB); on radio audiences from ARB; on magazine audiences from Simmons or Target Group Index (TGI): and so on. The largest of these firms, the A. C. Nielsen Company, had estimated billings of $211 million in 1975. Until health care organizations begin engaging in substantial advertising efforts, syndicated service research firms will be of little value to them.
2. *Custom marketing research firms.* These firms can be hired to carry out one-of a-kind research projects to provide data needed by a particular client. They participate with the client in designing the study, and the report becomes the client's property. One of the leading custom marketing research firms is Market Facts, with annual billings of approximately $15 million.
3. *Specialty-line marketing research firms.* These firms provide specialized services to other marketing research firms and to organizations' marketing research departments. The best example is the field service firm, which sells field interviewing services to other firms.

Marketing researchers have also been steadily expanding and improving their techniques. Table 6–3 shows the approximate decade when various techniques began to be used in marketing research. All the techniques listed have been accepted by market researchers.

The challenge facing managers who need marketing research is to know enough about its potential and limitations so that they can get the right information at a reasonable cost and use it intelligently. If they know nothing about marketing research, they might allow the wrong information to be collected, or collected too expensively, or interpreted incorrectly. One protection against this is to work only with experienced, trained, and credible market researchers and agencies. The health care field has recently been plagued by large numbers of "marketing" consultants claiming market research capabilities. In fact, the backgrounds and experience of many of them indicate training in areas like public relations, graphics and design, and advertising and planning, but not marketing research. A hospital construction firm, for example, hired a former hospital public relations officer and a former nursing home administrator. They then mailed out brochures to hundreds of hospitals offering marketing research services performed by these two individuals, who in fact had never done *any* marketing research.

An equally important protection is that health care managers

TABLE 6–3 Evolving Techniques in Marketing Research

DECADE	*TECHNIQUE*
Prior to 1910	First-hand observation
	Elementary surveys
1910–20	Sales analysis
	Operating cost analysis
1920–30	Questionnaire construction
	Survey
1930–40	Quota sampling
	Simple correlation analysis
	Distribution cost analysis
	Store auditing techniques
1940–50	Probability sampling
	Regression methods
	Advanced statistical inference
	Consumer and store panels
1950–60	Motivation research
	Operations research
	Multiple regression and correlation
	Experimental design
	Attitude-measuring instruments
1960–70	Factor analysis and discriminant analysis
	Mathematical models
	Bayesian statistical analysis and decision theory
	Scaling theory
	Computer data processing and analysis
	Marketing simulation
	Information storage and retrieval
1970–80	Nonmetric multidimensional scaling
	Econometric models
	Comprehensive marketing planning models
	Test marketing laboratories

know enough about marketing research to assist in its planning and in the interpretation of results. Involvement of the health care organization's management in the process is also necessitated by the researchers' likely lack of knowledge of the health care field. Health care, as an industry, became interested in marketing and market research only recently. Consequently, there is no large group of market research consultants with substantial experience in health care market research. Most organizations looking for a market research consultant will find themselves talking to market researchers with little or no experience in health care management or to health care consultants with little or no expertise in marketing.

Since market research requires very specific technical skills, a health care organization faced with the choice between market researchers with no health care experience and health systems consul-

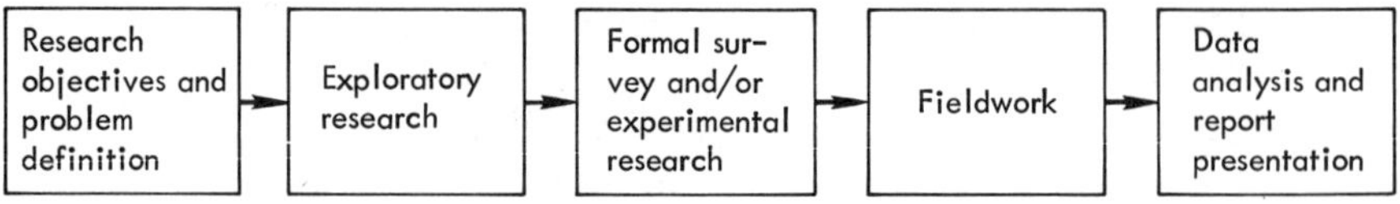

FIGURE 6–2 The Marketing Research Process

tants with no expertise in market research would be better off selecting the market research consultant. The health care organization can supplement the researcher's skills with its own knowledge of the health care field. If the health care organization selects a consultant with a similar lack of marketing research knowledge, who will provide the market research skills and experience?[5]

Figure 6–2 shows the five basic steps in good marketing research. We will illustrate these steps in connection with the following situation:

> The Coppleman Community Hospital was a medium-sized hospital in the suburbs of Atlanta. The hospital, while maintaining a high census, felt that the average age of its patients was increasing, resulting in greater Medicare billings, longer average length of stay by patients, and a growing tendency to be viewed as a facility for the chronically ill, all of which were disturbing. The hospital administrator did not know if the patient age increase was due to a general aging of the hospital's total service area (a market phenomenon) or was specific to the patient population using Coppleman Community Hospital (a market share and market segment phenomenon). Not knowing the causes, the administrator was unsure what actions to take. Recognizing the need for market research, the administrator engaged a recognized marketing consulting and research firm to carry out a study that would yield useful findings and recommendations.

Research Objectives and Problem Definition

The first step in research is to define the research objectives. The objective may be to learn more about a market, to find a practical idea for increasing the demand for a product or service, or to measure the impact of a marketing tool. The need to define research objectives requires the organization to have arrived at a useful definition of the problem. If the problem is stated vaguely, if the wrong problem is defined, or if the uses of the research are not made clear, then the results may prove useless or even misleading.

The marketing researchers in the Coppleman Community Hospital study defined the overall research objective as that of discovering the main factors that affected patients' and physicians' choice of hospital, how these factors varied by the age of the patient, and on the basis of these factors, recommending specific marketing actions available to Coppleman to attract a younger mix of patients. To accomplish this objective, the researchers identified the following main elements as influencing "hospital choice behavior":

1. The relative influence of physicians vs. consumers in the hospital selection decision process
2. The community's images of Coppleman Community Hospital and of competing hospitals
3. What people look for in a hospital, and whether this varies by age or diagnosis of the patient
4. Physicians' admitting patterns and whether these varied by age of the patient or by other significant characteristics
5. The role and effectiveness of different marketing tools

Exploratory Research

This step calls for carrying out preliminary research to learn more about the market before any formal research survey is undertaken. The major procedures at this stage include collecting secondary data, doing observational research, and carrying out informal interviewing with individuals and groups.

Secondary Data Research. In seeking information, a researcher should initially gather and review any secondary data that exist. *Secondary data* are relevant data that have been collected for another purpose (see Exhibit 6–2). Secondary data are normally quicker and less expensive to obtain and will give the researcher a start on the problem. Afterward, the researcher can gather *primary data,* original data to meet the problem at hand.

These secondary data are likely to provide many useful ideas and findings. The researchers must be careful in making inferences, however, because the secondary data were collected for a variety of purposes and under a variety of conditions that might limit their usefulness. Marketing researchers should check these data for relevance, impartiality, validity, and reliability. The researchers are also likely to find that the secondary data still leave many questions unanswered. They may need to collect primary data, either through observation or interviewing.

Observational Research. One major way to collect primary data is to carry out personal observation in various situations. The researchers could visit competing hospitals to see if they too had an aging patient mix. They could visit the waiting rooms of physicians' offices to see if Coppleman's physicians had older patient practices than the prac-

EXHIBIT 6–2

Major Sources of Secondary Data

In looking for secondary data, the Coppleman Community Hospital researchers can consult the following seven major sources of secondary data:[6]

1. *Internal organization records.* Researchers should check the hospital files for past figures on admissions and discharges, admission mix by physician and DRG, average length of stay by service and physician, and other data that might be relevant.
2. *Government.* The federal government publishes more marketing data than any other source in the country. Many organizations depend on data found in the *Census of Population, Census of Housing,* and *Census of Business,* as well as other Bureau of the Census documents. Local health regulatory agencies and public health departments also are sources of current and public information. Health care marketing researchers may discover valuable information from filed Certificate of Need applications, long-range plans (in those states where they are required), and hospital bond market prospectuses. The Coppleman Community Hospital researchers can use local census data to determine whether the hospital's whole service area is aging, and which communities in that area have younger residents.
3. *Trade, professional, and business associations.* The Coppleman Community Hospital is a member of the Georgia Hospital Association, which provides some information on hospital census and patient data for hospitals throughout the state. The researchers can ascertain whether Coppleman's aging patient population is mirrored by other hospitals' experiences or is exceptional.
4. *Competitors and other private organizations.* The researchers could see whether any useful secondary data can be obtained directly from other hospitals in the area or from nursing homes and home health agencies that take care of elderly patients once they leave the hospitals.
5. *Marketing firms.* Marketing research firms and consulting firms may possess some useful past studies of the hospital market.
6. *Universities, research organizations, and foundations.* These organizations may have reports or studies on the hospital industry.
7. *Published sources.* Researchers should examine published material in libraries on the subject of hospitals, hospital use, and the aging of the population. Among the marketing journals, marketers tend to consult the *Journal of Marketing, Journal of Marketing Research,* and *Journal of Consumer Research.* Useful general business magazines include *Business Week, Fortune, Forbes,* and *Harvard Business Review.* Some newspapers may be useful. The *Wall Street Journal* has been particularly quick to note marketing-related trends in health care. Two recent additions to published sources in marketing which are especially pertinent to health care organizations are the *Healthcare Marketing Report* and the *Journal of Health Care Marketing.*

tices of physicians who had privileges at competing hospitals. The researchers should also study the location of physician's offices to determine if Coppleman's physicians are located in aging areas.

Qualitative Interviewing. In addition to gathering data through observation, the researchers need to conduct some interviews during the exploratory stage of a marketing research project. The purpose of the interviewing is to collect and refine ideas on the factors that play a role in the problem being investigated. In the exploratory stage, the interviewing should be qualitatively rather than quantitatively oriented. Qualitative interviewing is largely open-ended. People are asked leading questions as a means of stimulating them to share their feelings and thoughts regarding hospital choice or other relevant topics. The distinct purposes of this research are to: (1) probe deeply into consumers' underlying needs, perceptions, preferences, and satisfactions, (2) gain greater familiarity and understanding of marketing problems whose causes are not known; and (3) develop ideas that can be investigated further through quantitative research.

Qualitative research is not only a desirable first step, it is sometimes the only step permitted by the budget of many health care organizations. For the Coppleman project, the researchers decided to interview younger residents of the hospital's service area (potential and past patients), as well as physicians with admitting privileges at Coppleman. In addition, the researchers interviewed members of the hospital's nursing staff and discharge planning department to see if they could add new perspectives to the problem. Two methods would be used: individual interviewing and group interviewing.

> **Individual interviewing** consists of interviewing one person at a time, either in person, over the telephone, or through the mail.
> **Group interviewing** consists of inviting from six to ten persons to gather for a few hours with a trained interviewer to discuss a product, service, organization, or other marketing entity.

An interviewer for a group needs good qualifications, including objectivity, knowledge of the subject matter and industry to be discussed, and some understanding of group dynamics and consumer behavior. The participants are normally paid a small sum for attending; the meeting is typically held in pleasant surroundings and refreshments are served to increase the informality. The group interviewer, in a group of younger community residents, starts with a broad question, such as "What health care services in the community have you used recently?" Questions would then move to the subject of hospitals and physicians, the hospital choice process, and Coppleman versus other hospitals. The interviewer encourages free discussion among the participants. At the same time, the interviewer "focuses" the discussion—

hence the name "focus group interviewing." Comments are recorded, preferably through video or tape-recording, and subsequently examined for clues to the consumer decision process. Focus group interviewing is becoming a major marketing research tool for gaining insight into consumers' thoughts and feelings.[7]

Formal Research

After defining the problem and doing exploratory research, the researchers may wish to carry out more formal research to measure magnitudes or test hypotheses. Suppose the Coppleman researchers noticed through exploratory research that some of the younger families belonged to a health maintenance organization (HMO) which used a competing hospital for inpatient care. The researchers, however, were not sure how extensive HMO enrollment was among younger families in the hospital's service area. They also learned that some physicians tended to admit younger patients to the in-town teaching hospitals, ostensibly because this was what the patients requested. Again, the researchers did not know how extensive this practice was. The hospital administrator agreed that it would be desirable to quantify these factors.

At this point, the researcher can proceed to design a formal survey or a marketing experiment.

Survey Research. Many managers take an overly simplistic view of survey work. They think that it consists of writing a few obvious questions and finding an adequate number of people in the target market to answer them. The fact is that amateur research is liable to many errors that can waste organization funds, management resources, and goodwill (see Exhibit 6–3 for an example). Designing a reliable survey is a job for a professional. Here we will describe what users of marketing research should know about developing the research instrument, making the sampling plan, and doing the fieldwork.

Research Instrument. The main survey research instrument is the questionnaire. Every questionnaire should be pretested on a pilot sample before being used on a large scale. A professional marketing researcher can usually spot several errors in a casually prepared questionnaire (see Exhibit 6–4).

One common type of error occurs in the types of questions asked—the inclusion of questions that cannot be answered, or would not be answered, or need not be answered. Each question should be checked to determine whether it is necessary in terms of the research objectives. Questions that are just interesting (except for one or two to start the interview) should be dropped because they lengthen the time required and try the respondent's patience.

The form of questions can make a substantial difference to the

EXHIBIT 6–3

An Example of Amateur Marketing Research

One example of this approach, of attempting to produce good, extensive market research cheaply with typically unsatisfactory results, is a community hospital which intended to do a survey of its service area. In the hopes of saving money, the hospital enlisted the aid of an undergraduate work-study student with little training in the market research area to direct community volunteers in the performance of the survey. Fewer volunteers than had originally voiced interest actually became involved in the survey, which thus lost momentum not only because of an inadequate number of volunteer surveyors to cover the neighborhood, but also because the work-study student spent little time on the project, recognizing that his commitment was over at the end of the semester, regardless of the state of the completion of the project.

An effort to complete the survey the following year, using teenagers sponsored by a federally-funded anti-poverty program as surveyors, also produced dismal results due to lack of commitment, training, and ability of the teenagers. The newest plan of the hospital is to send a survey force of nuns into the neighborhood to administer the research questionnaire on a door-to-door basis. Such a survey force will eliminate some of the problems (commitment, interest) of the earlier volunteer groups, but will necessarily introduce bias into areas of the questionnaire dealing with alcoholism, venereal disease, abortion and birth control, at the very least.

The survey which this hospital wanted done could have been performed well and quickly by a consulting or market research firm experienced in this type of research.

SOURCE: Roberta N. Clarke, "Marketing Health Care: Problems in Implementation," *Health Care Management Review* (Winter 1978), pp. 25–26. Reprinted with permission of Aspen Systems Corporation © 1978.

response. An *open-end question* is one in which the respondent is free to answer in his or her own words. A *close-end question* is one in which the possible answers are supplied. Each type of question can take several forms:

Dichotomous question: Have you ever been a patient at Coppleman Community Hospital before (excluding the emergency room)? Yes ( ) No ( )

Multiple choice question: At which hospital were you last hospitalized? (a) Atlanta General, (b) Georgia Medical Center, (c) Mercy Hospital, (d) Mitchell Hospital, (e) other.

Semantic differential questions: Copplemen Community Hospital is (a)

EXHIBIT 6–4

A "Questionable" Questionnaire

The following questionnaire contains questions prepared by a hospital administrator to be used in interviewing residents of the hospital's service area (potential patients). How do you feel about each question?

1. What is your income to the nearest hundred dollars?
2. Have you been sick in the last year?
3. Do you dislike going to hospitals? Yes ( ) No ( )
4. How many times in the past year have you seen advertisements for hospitals?
5. What are the most salient and determinant attributes in your selection of a hospital?
6. Don't you think people ought to support their community hospital so that they know it will be there in case of an emergency?

COMMENTS:

1. People don't necessarily know their income to the nearest hundred dollars, nor do they want to reveal their income that closely. Furthermore, a questionnaire should never open with such a personal question.
2. What does "sick" mean? Sick with a cold? Immobilized by a stroke? Hospitalized? One can be hospitalized without being sick, such as when a woman delivers a baby. Anyway, of what use are the answers to this question to the hospital?
3. "Dislike" is a relative term. Furthermore, is "yes" and "no," with no other qualifications, the best way to allow a response to the question? Why is the question being asked in the first place?
4. Who can remember this?
5. What is "salience" and "determinant attributes?" Don't use big words on me.
6. Loaded question. How can one answer "no," given the bias?

very friendly, (b) somewhat friendly, (c) neither friendly nor impersonal, (d) somewhat impersonal, (e) very impersonal.

Likert scale question: Consider the statement "Community hospitals provide lower quality medical care than teaching hospitals." Do you (a) strongly agree, (b) somewhat agree, (c) neither agree nor disagree, (d) somewhat disagree, (e) strongly disagree.

The choice of words also calls for considerable care. The researcher should strive for simple, direct, unambiguous, and unbiased wording.

Other dos and don'ts arise in connection with the sequencing of questions in the questionnaire. The lead questions should create interest, if possible. Open questions are usually better here. Difficult or personal questions should be introduced toward the end of the interview, in order not to create an emotional reaction that may affect subsequent answers or cause the respondent to break off the interview. The questions should be asked in as logical an order as possible in order to avoid confusing the respondent. Classificatory data on the respondent (age, income, occupation) are usually asked for last, because they tend to be less interesting and are on the personal side.

Sampling Plan. The other element of research design is a sampling plan, and it calls for four decisions.

1. *Sampling Unit.* This answers the question, who is to be surveyed? The proper sampling unit is not always obvious from the nature of the information sought. In the Coppleman survey, should the sampling unit be physicians, young families in the community, or only those young families who have already used Coppleman? Who is the usual instigator, influencer, decider, user, and/or purchaser?
2. *Sample size.* This answers the question, how many people should be surveyed? Large samples obviously give more reliable results. However, it is not necessary to sample the entire target market or even a substantial part of it to achieve satisfactory precision. Samples amounting to less than a fraction of 1 percent of a population can often provide good reliability, given a reasonable sampling procedure.
3. *Sampling procedure.* This answers the question, how should respondents be chosen? To draw valid and reliable inferences about the target market, a random probability sample of the population should be drawn. Random sampling allows the calculation of confidence limits for sampling error. But random sampling is almost always more costly than nonrandom sampling. Some marketing researchers feel that the extra expenditure for probability sampling could be put to better use. Specifically, more of the money of a fixed research budget could be spent in designing better questionnaires and hiring better interviewers to reduce response errors (biases created by patterns differentiating those who do respond from those who do not respond) and nonsampling errors, many of which have already been mentioned, which can be just as fatal as sampling errors. This is a real issue, one that the marketing researcher and marketing manager must weigh carefully (see Table 6–4).
4. *Means of contact.* This answers the question, how should the subjects be contacted? The choices are telephone, mail, or personal interview. Telephone interviewing is the best method for gathering information quickly. It also permits the interviewer to clarify questions. The two main drawbacks are that only people with telephones can be interviewed, and only short interviews can be done. The mail questionnaire may be the best way to reach those who will not give personal interviews or who might be

TABLE 6–4 Types of Probability and Nonprobability Samples

Probability sample	
Simple random sample	Every member of the population has a known and equal chance of selection.
Stratified random sample	The population is divided into mutually exclusive groups (such as age groups), and random samples are drawn from each group.
Cluster (area) sample	The population is divided into mutually exclusive groups (such as blocks), and the researcher draws a sample of the groups to interview.
Nonprobability sample	
Convenience sample	The researcher selects the easiest population members from which to obtain information.
Judgment sample	The researcher uses his/her judgment to select population members who are good prospects for accurate information.
Quota sample	The researcher finds and interviews a prescribed number of people in each of several categories.

biased by interviewers. On the other hand, mail questionnaires require simple and clearly worded questions, draw a lower return rate from the less well educated segments, and have a return rate that is usually low and/or slow. Personal interviewing is the most versatile of the three methods. The interviewer can ask more questions and can supplement the interview with personal observations. Personal interviewing is the most expensive method and requires more technical and managerial planning and supervision.

Experimental Research. We talked about formal research in its most common form, that of designing a survey. An increasing number of market researchers are eager to go beyond measuring the perceptions, preferences, and intentions of a target market and are seeking to measure actual cause and effect relationships. For example, the Coppleman Community Hospital researchers might like to know the answers to such questions as these:

> Would offering a set of health promotion programs addressing younger adults (stress management, parenting, how to treat sport injuries) attract more young adults to use the inpatient services of the hospital?
>
> Would the hospital attract more younger patients if it promoted the quality of its medical staff or the quality of personal care delivered by the nursing staff?

Each of these questions could be answered by the survey method. However, people may not give their true opinions or carry them out. Experimental research is more rigorous. Situations are created where the actual behavior of the target market can be observed and its causes identified.

Let us apply the experimental method to the second question. The hospital would have to draw up two promotional campaigns, one stressing the quality of its medical staff, the other focusing on the quality of the personal care delivered by its nursing staff. The researcher would have to select two subsamples, presumably from different communities within the hospital's service area. One subsample would be targeted with the "quality medical staff" campaign, the other with the "quality personal care" campaign. This would have to be a long-term effort, since people, especially younger people, are not hospitalized frequently. Over time, the hospital could keep track of how many younger people from each of the two communities used the hospital compared to a third community, called a control group, which received neither promotion campaign. Utilization rates would also have to be adjusted to take into account prior utilization of the hospital by younger members of the community. If utilization by younger people in one of the two communities did increase noticeably over time and the hospital administrator could think of no other factor to explain the increase, the administrator could feel comfortable in using that promotional campaign for the hospital's whole service area.

The experimental method is being increasingly recognized in marketing circles as the most rigorous and conclusive one to use if the proper controls can be exercised and the cost afforded. The method requires selecting matched groups of subjects, giving them different treatments, controlling extraneous variables, and checking on whether observed differences are statistically significant. To the extent that the design and execution of the experiment eliminates alternative hypotheses that might explain the same results, the research and marketing manager can have confidence in the conclusions.[8]

Fieldwork. The fieldwork phase of survey or experimental research follows after the research design has been finished and pretested. Some organizations will use volunteers; others will hire professional interviewers. Marketing research firms work hard to select and train interviewers who can be trusted, are personable, and are able to do their work in a reasonably short time. The fieldwork phase could be the most expensive and the most liable to error. Four major problems have to be dealt with in this phase:

1. *Not present.* When randomly selected respondents are not reached on the first call, the interviewer must call back later or substitute another respondent. Otherwise, nonresponse bias may be introduced.
2. *Refusal to cooperate.* After reaching the subjects, the interviewer must interest them in cooperating. Otherwise, nonresponse bias again may be introduced.
3. *Respondent bias.* The interviewer must encourage accurate and thoughtful answers.

4. *Interviewer bias.* Interviewers are capable of introducing a variety of biases into the interviewing process through the mere fact of their age, sex, manner, or intonation. In addition, there is the problem of conscious interviewer bias or dishonesty.

Data Analysis and Report Presentation

The final step in the marketing research process is to develop information and findings to present to the manager. The researcher will tabulate the data and develop one-way and two-way frequency distributions. Averages and measures of dispersion will be computed for the major variables. The researcher might attempt to apply some advanced statistical techniques and decision models in the hope of discovering additional findings. But the researcher's purpose is not to overwhelm management with numbers and fancy statistical procedures. It is to present major findings that will help the manager make better marketing decisions.

ANALYTICAL MARKETING SYSTEM

The marketing information system contains a fourth subsystem called the *analytical marketing system,* which consists of a set of advanced techniques for analyzing data and problems. These systems are able to produce more findings and conclusions than can be gained by just commonsense manipulation of the data. Large organizations tend to make extensive use of analytical marketing systems. In smaller organizations, managers often resist these approaches as too technical or expensive.

An analytical marketing system consists of two sets of tools known as the statistical bank and the model bank (see Figure 6–3). The *statistical bank* is a collection of advanced procedures for learning more about the relationships within a set of data and their statistical reliability. They allow management to go beyond the frequency distributions, means, and standard deviations in the data, and permit health care managers to get answers to such questions as these:

> What are the most important variables affecting my patient volume, and how important is each one?
>
> If I recruited three new internists and placed them in nearby communities, what would happen to patient volume?
>
> What are the most discriminating predictors of persons who are likely to "buy" my service versus my competitor's service?
>
> What are the best variables for segmenting my market, and how many segments will be created?

The statistical techniques are somewhat technical, and you are advised to consult other sources for understanding and using them.[9]

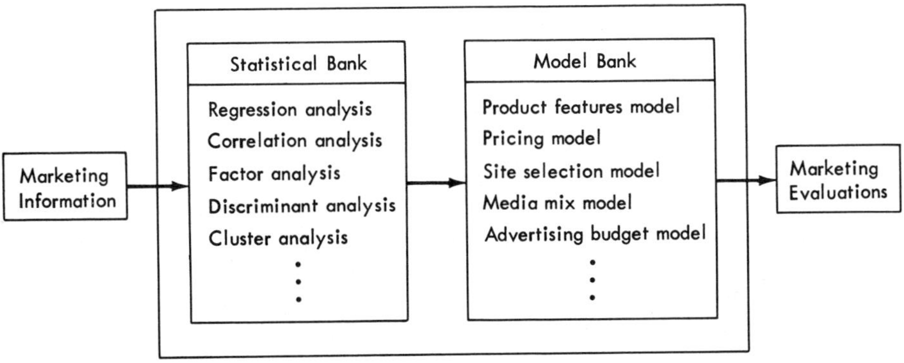

FIGURE 6–3 An Analytical Marketing System

The *model bank* is a collection of models that will help marketers make better decisions. Each model consists of a set of interrelated variables that represent some real system, process, or outcome. These models can help answer "what if?" and "which is best?" questions. In the last twenty years, scientists have developed a great number of models to help marketing executives do a better job of pricing, designing sales territories and sales call plans, selecting sites for outlets, developing optimal advertising media mixes, developing optimal advertising budgets, and forecasting new product sales.[10] Much of this information is readily translatable to the health care field.

SUMMARY

To carry out effective marketing, the health care organization needs timely, adequate, and accurate information that can be consolidated to provide maximum value. Four systems make up the organization's marketing information system.

The first, the internal records system, consists of all the information the organization gathers in the regular course of operations. It includes medical records and financial information, as well as information on other aspects of the organization's operations. In the future, it will also include DRG information. Many useful questions can be answered by analyzing the information in the internal records system.

The second, the marketing intelligence system, describes the set of sources and procedures by which administrators obtain their everyday information about developments in the marketplace. A health care organization can improve the quality of its marketing intelligence by assigning the responsibility for gathering and disseminating marketing information to one individual.

The third, the marketing research system, consists of the systematic design, collection, analysis, and reporting of data and findings relevant to a specific situation facing an organization. The marketing research process consists of five steps: developing the research objectives and problem definition; exploratory research; formal survey and/or experimental research; fieldwork; and data analysis and report presentation.

The fourth, the analytical marketing system, consists of two sets of advanced tools for analyzing marketing data and marketing problems. One set of tools is the statistical bank, which is a collection of statistical procedures for analyzing the relationships within a set of data and their statistical reliability. The other is the model bank, which is a collection of mathematical models that will help marketers make better decisions.

NOTES

1. The definition is adapted from Samuel V. Smith, Richard H. Brien, and James E. Stafford, "Marketing Information Systems: An Introductory Overview," in their *Readings in Marketing Information Systems* (Boston: Houghton Mifflin, 1968), p. 7.

2. Roberta N. Clarke and Linda J. Shyavitz, "Market Research: When, Why and How," *Health Care Management Review* (Winter 1982), p. 33.

3. Steven G. Hillestad and Eric N. Berkowitz, "Hospital Executives Need Marketing Tools to Meet Competition Challenges," *Modern Healthcare* (January 1982), p. 84. Reprinted with permission from the January 1982 issue of *Modern Healthcare Magazine.* Copyright Crain Communications, Inc., 740 N. Rush, Chicago, IL 60611. All rights reserved.

4. Ernest S. Bradford, *Bradford's Directory of Marketing Research Agencies and Management Consultants in the United States and the World,* 15th ed., 1973–1974 (Middlebury, VT: Bradford).

5. See Clarke and Shyavitz, "Market Research: Why, When and How," for a more detailed discussion of this subject.

6. For an excellent annotated reference to major secondary sources of business and marketing data, see Thomas C. Kinnear and James R. Taylor, *Marketing Research: An Applied Approach* (New York: McGraw-Hill, 1979), pp. 128–31, 138–71.

7. See Keith K. Cox et al., "Applications of Focus Group Interviews in Marketing," *Journal of Marketing* (January 1976), pp. 77–80; and Bobby J. Calder, "Focus Groups and the Nature of Qualitative Marketing Research," *Journal of Marketing Research* (August 1977), pp. 353–54. For discussion on focus group interviews in the health care environment, see William A. Flexner et al., "Discovering What the Health Consumer Really Wants," *Health Care Management Review* (Fall 1974).

8. For more reading on experimental research, see Seymour Banks, *Experimentation in Marketing* (New York: McGraw-Hill, 1965).

9. See David A. Acker, ed., *Multivariate Analysis in Marketing: Theory and Applications* (Belmont, CA: Wadsworth, 1971).

10. Various models are described in Gary Lilien and Philip Kotler, *Marketing Decision Making—A Model Building Approach* (New York: Harper and Row, 1983).

7

MARKETING PLANNING AND CONTROL

The Community Health Education Department of the Mt. Sinai Hospital in Cincinnati, with a national reputation for innovativeness, offered a wide array of health education programs. These included community health workshops, a health education computer network distributing health information through computer terminals in local libraries, screening and health education clinics, and a variety of health promotion sessions dealing with topics like smoking, CPR, eating disorders, and weight loss. The department had received a $25,000 two-year grant to set up a series of health education programs called Monday P.M., because they were held Monday evenings from 7:30 to 10 P.M. The series were intended to be self-supporting by the third year, when the grant ran out.

The health promotion department, which employed seven people, was directed by Sarah Smith, who reported directly to the chief executive officer of the hospital. The department was responsible for developing and offering health promotion programs and managing its own budget. The stated goals of its programs were "to augment the community health status" and "to fulfill societal goals."

The Monday P.M. series was made up of eight courses, each course running six Monday evenings in a row. Each course focused on a different subject area, such as nutrition, parenting, women's health issues, alcohol and chemical dependency. In addition, each of the six sessions within each course addressed a different aspect of the subject. For example, the titles of the six sessions of the nutrition course, called "You Are What You Eat," were:

Session 1: Nutrition Facts and Myths
Session 2: Alternative Eating Styles

Session 3: Eating Problems and Disorders

Session 4: Eating during Pregnancy

Session 5: Nutritional Guidelines for Older Americans

Session 6: Avoiding Excess Salt and Sugar

Each series' choice of health topics was decided upon by members of the health education department, with input from other staff in the hospital. There was no market research conducted into the interests and preferences of the communities the hospital wanted to serve. Pricing was established without testing the strength of price sensitivity and market demand. The annual promotion budget was arbitrarily set at $12,000, and further arbitrarily divided into funds for brochures, posters, direct mail, and radio and newspaper advertisements, without any measurement of the cost effectiveness of different media.

The lack of a systematic marketing planning approach was partly responsible for the following less than satisfactory results:

1. On average, each Monday P.M. series had only 40 people in the audience (27 percent of the 150-person capacity of the hospital auditorium, where the sessions were held). Generally, 30 preregistrants plus another 50 people who had not preregistered showed up at the beginning of each new series, but this dropped with each subsequent session. The last session of many of the series had a total audience of 20 or less.
2. The health education department felt, although it had done no research to prove it, that they were getting different people for each Monday P.M. series. Although they wanted to build a loyal, committed audience, they did not know if this audience turnover was good or bad.
3. The health education department had hoped for at least 100 people to attend each session. Instead, the sessions ran 13 to 55 percent of capacity.
4. Admission fees to the series for the year, anticipated to be $30,000 to $36,000, were only $17,000. While the grant paid the additional cost for the year, in the following year the program was expected to be self-sufficient.

To solve these problems, the Community Health Education Department invited MBA students from a local university to perform a marketing audit for the Monday P.M. series. The students researched the series and produced an audit containing a number of useful recommendations, including the following:

1. The whole health education department should install a marketing planning system which each year produces annual and long-range plans with clearly stated objectives, strategies, actions, budgets, and responsibility for each part of the plan assigned to specific people. As part of the department's activities, Monday P.M. would then be evaluated under this framework.
2. The Monday P.M. series addresses a different target market with each series. Those interested in women's health issues may have no interest in cardiovascular health, for example. More important, the target market of each session *within* a series varies. In the nutrition series alone, it would appear that the sessions are appealing to vegetarians (session 2), anorexics, bulemics and their families (session 3), pregnant women (session 4), the elderly (session 5), diabetics (session 6), and people with hypertension (session 6). The marketing mix strategy needed to address these differing target markets must also differ. For example, the elderly are fearful of going out

at night for safety reasons. The Monday P.M. sessions ought to be changed to Monday A.M. for them. The elderly are also more price conscious and might react positively to a lower price. In contrast, the parenting series should be targeted to young families, most of whom live twenty minutes or more away in the suburbs and are less likely to be price sensitive. The health education department should find a location closer to the target market at which to offer the series. We suggest that the offering of the health education department be redesigned around target markets (the elderly, young families, etc.). A whole series offered to one target market would be far more efficient and would allow the opportunity to develop "brand loyalty."

3. Marketing communications need to be strengthened. There is no continuity of design or logo to set the Mt. Sinai health education advertisements and publications apart from the large volume of promotional literature blitzing the potential market daily. Promotional posters are pinned up wherever the health education department staff happen to be after they've received a stack of posters to distribute. What, for example, is a "Staying Healthy over 60" poster doing in a record store catering to college students? Monday P.M. newspaper advertisements are neither informative nor eye-catching, and they appear only prior to the start of the series, with no reinforcing advertisements after the series has begun.

The health education department received the students' marketing audit and began to study the proposals for improving the marketing planning and control system.

The sophistication of the marketing planning and control systems operated by health care organizations varies significantly. What some organizations call a planning-control system turns out to be a budgeting system, designed to make sure expenses do not get out of hand. Other organizations with formal planning departments may do significant institutional planning; they examine the external environment on an aggregate level (general community needs, regional demographics, and federal guidelines), and compile a list of internal strengths and weaknesses.

Marketing planning takes this type of information and expands it. It also examines competitive behaviors, strengths, and weaknesses. It looks not only at aggregate market data, but at smaller consumer groups and segments. It includes a variety of publics that may have an impact on the organization under its scrutiny. And its underlying philosophy orients the health care organization toward its market's needs, rather than its own needs.

The overlap between marketing planning and traditional health planning cannot be strictly determined here. Some organizations, usually the smaller ones, do a minimal amount of planning. In contrast, the planning departments of a few larger health care organizations engage in a wide array of planning activities: financial planning, marketing planning, facilities and equipment planning, and human resource planning. Clearly, there is and should be some joint territory between traditional health planning and marketing planning. Just as clearly, there are differences between the two. Rather than trying to determine the overlap, particularly in view of the fact that the practice of marketing and planning in health care are both changing, in this chapter we will examine marketing planning and control as it should be performed. This leaves each health care organization with the responsibility for determining what aspects of marketing planning fall in the traditional health planner's lap and what aspects fall elsewhere.

Some administrators, especially those whose organizations are not yet engaged in a formal planning process, resist establishing the process, feeling it does not "fit" their organization:

> The department heads don't have time to write out annual plans, and I don't have time to read them.
>
> My service chiefs couldn't write a plan even if I asked them. They were selected because they are outstanding physicians, not outstanding managers. And as long as they perform well clinically, I would have to tolerate poor planning from them.
>
> My administrative staff would never use their plans. The plans would be nothing more than window dressing, used for political purposes and then filed away in a back drawer.
>
> How can you plan in an environment that can change overnight? With the stroke of a political pen, millions of dollars of medical benefits are wiped away in an instant. New people are elected to office and, all of a sudden, health care organizations are required to compete, not cooperate. How do you plan for that?

Without denying the validity of these arguments, we will argue that formal planning and control systems are beneficial and needed for the improvement of organizational performance. Melville C. Branch has perceptively summarized the main benefits of a formal planning system:

1. Encourages systematic thinking ahead by management
2. Leads to better coordination of organizational efforts
3. Leads to the development of performance standards for control
4. Causes the organization to sharpen its guiding objectives and policies
5. Results in better preparedness for sudden developments
6. Brings about a more vivid sense in the participating managers of their interacting responsibilities.[1]

The relationship between marketing planning and control is shown in Figure 7–1 and is a three-step process. The first step calls upon the organization to identify attractive target markets, to develop effec-

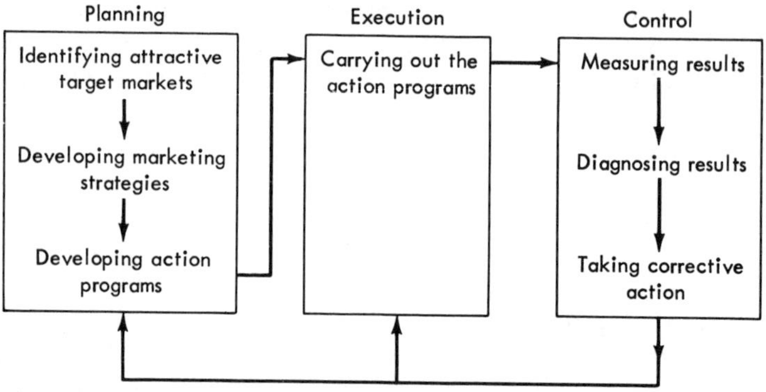

FIGURE 7–1 The Marketing Planning and Control System

tive marketing strategies, and to develop detailed action programs. The second step involves executing the action programs. The third step calls for marketing control to ensure that the objectives are being achieved. Marketing control requires measuring results, analyzing the causes of poor results, and taking corrective action. Corrective action consists of adjustments in the plan, its execution, or both.

MARKETING PLANNING

When an organization establishes a marketing planning system, it faces three questions: (1) How sophisticated should the planning system be? (2) What procedures should be used to carry on the planning process? (3) What should the contents of a marketing plan be?

Degree of Sophistication

Organizational planning systems tend to evolve through the following stages on their way to greater sophistication.

Unplanned Stage. When organizations are first established, management is engrossed in making the day-to-day decisions required for survival. There is usually no planning staff and hardly any time to plan. This particularly characterizes small organizations with very limited resources.

Budget System Stage. Management eventually recognizes the desirability of installing a budget system to improve the management of cash flow. Top management estimates the expected income and costs for the coming year, as do department managers. These budgets are financially, not strategically, oriented. Budgets are not the same as plans.

Project Planning Stage. Many organizations find that they need to develop plans for specific projects. Most health care planning offices developed for this purpose. A hospital's planning office will plan the development of the hospital's physical plant, the renovation of a hospital wing or floor.

Annual Planning Stage. Management eventually recognizes the need to develop an annual planning system based on *management by objectives*.[2] It has three options.

The first is *top-down planning*, so called because top management sets goals and plans for all the lower levels of management. This model is taken from military organizations, where generals prepare the plans and troops carry them out. Top-down planning is most prevalent in government agencies such as state Medicaid offices, where each level establishes the plans for the next lower level.

The second system is *bottom-up planning*, so called because the various units of the organization prepare their own goals and plans based on the best they think they can do, and send them to upper management for approval. Bottom-up planning is most often found in professionally oriented organizations and smaller organizations such as home health agencies.

Most organizations use a third system known as *goals down–plans up planning*. Here top management takes a broad look at the organization's opportunities and requirements and sets organizational goals for the year. The various units are then responsible for developing plans designed to help the organization reach these goals. These plans, when approved by top management, become the official annual plan.

Long-range Planning Stage. In this stage, the health care organization refines the planning system to improve its overall effectiveness, primarily through the addition of *long-range planning*. Management realizes that annual plans make sense only in the context of a long-range plan. In fact, the long-range plan should precede the annual plan, which should be a detailed version of the first year of the long-range plan. The long-range plan is reworked each year because the health care environment changes rapidly and requires an annual review of the organization's long-run assumptions.

Some health care organizations have skipped annual planning and possibly other stages because government agencies required the submission of long-range plans. As a result, many such organizations produce long-range plans, but no annual plans. And the long-range plans, produced purely for political or regulatory reasons, are of little practical help to management.

A further development is that the various plans begin to take on a more strategic character. When an organization first turns to long-range planning, it usually assumes that the future will be an extension of the present and that past strategies, organizational forms, and tactics will remain appropriate. Eventually management recognizes that the environment is full of probabilities, not certainties, and broader strategic thinking is required. The planning format is redesigned to stimulate managers to contemplate and evaluate alternative strategies that will leave the organization as well off as possible under different environmental conditions. Also, as the organization gains experience with planning, an effort is made to standardize the plan formats so that higher management can make better comparisons among similar units.

As the planning culture takes hold in the organization, further improvements are introduced. Managers receive more training in the use of financial analysis and are required to justify their recommendations not only in terms of patient volume or census, HMO member enrollment, and so on, but also in terms of financial measures such as cost-benefit or the cost effectiveness of an activity. Computer software programs help managers examine the impact of alternative marketing plans and environments on "sales" and "profit." Managers might also be asked to develop contingency plans showing how they would respond to specific threats and opportunities that might arise. These and other developments mark the emergence of a true strategic planning culture in the organization.

Designing the Planning Process

A planning system does not just happen; an appropriate system must be designed. It must be acceptable to the managers and compatible with the level of information and skill at their disposal. Often the initial system will be simple so that managers get used to writing plans. As they gain experience, changes and improvements will be made in the system to increase its effectiveness. Eventually managers will accept planning not as a chore, but as a tool to increase their own effectiveness.

Someone has to be responsible for designing the planning system. Many health care organizations are hiring a planner, if they don't have one already. The planning director may take responsibility for designing the planning system, or the responsibility may be assigned to a manager who has some background in marketing planning.

The planning director's job should not be to write the plans, but to educate and assist the managers in writing their plans. A maxim of planning is that it should be done by those who must carry out the plans. Line managers involved in planning their operations are (1) stimulated to think out their management objectives and strategies, and (2) motivated to achieve their goals.

One major task of the planning director is to develop a calendar for the planning process. The normal calendar steps are these:

1. Develop a set of relevant environmental facts and trends to distribute to managers in preparation for their planning.
2. Work with top management to develop a set of overall organizational objectives for the coming year to pass on to managers in preparation for their planning.
3. Work with individual managers to complete their marketing plans by a certain date.
4. Work with top management to review and approve (or modify) the various plans.
5. Develop a consolidated official plan for the organization for the coming period.

This sequence underscores the critical role of marketing planning in the overall management planning process. Individual managers start the process by setting marketing goals (such as census, enrollment, patient volume) for their programs for the coming period, along with proposed strategies and marketing budgets. Once top management approves these goals and strategies, decisions can be made on how much personnel to hire, how much supplies to order, how much money to borrow. Thus a commitment to a set of marketing goals precedes decisions on personnel, operations, and financial requirements.

The Format of a Marketing Plan

The appropriate standard format managers use in preparing their marketing plans, the topics and their sequence, can make a difference in the quality of planning results. A marketing plan should contain the following major sections: executive summary, situation analysis, objectives and goals, marketing strategy, action programs, budgets and controls (see Figure 7–2). We discuss the sections in the context of the following situation:

> The director of the Mt. Sinai Community Health Education Department asked each staff member to take responsibility for and develop a plan for a specific department program. One of them was Ann Buckley, who was assigned responsibility for building up the attendance at the Monday P.M. series.

Executive Summary. The planning document should open with a summary of the main goals and recommendations presented in the plan. Here is an abbreviated example:

> The 1986 Marketing Plan for increasing the attendance at the Monday P.M. series seeks to attract a total audience of 4,800 people across all sessions. With 48 sessions for the year, this averages out to

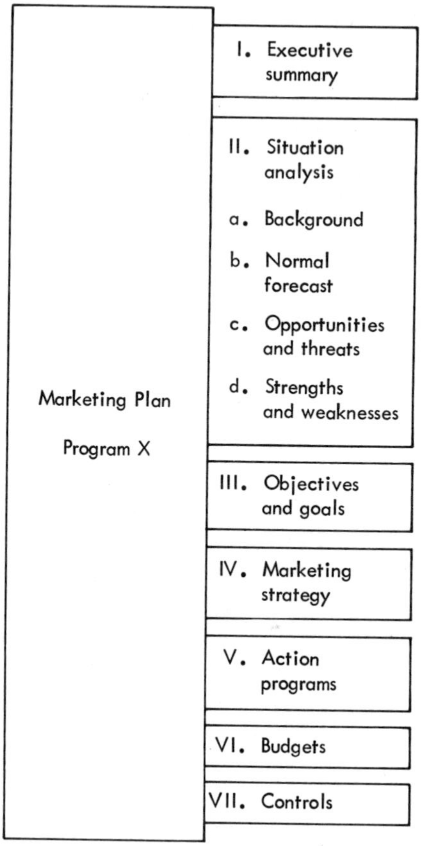

FIGURE 7–2 Content of a Marketing Plan

> 100 persons per session or 66 percent capacity if we remain in our present location. Assuming a preregistration fee of $30 for the series ($5 per session) and $7 per session for nonregistered walk-ins, and an audience breakdown of half preregistered, half walk-in, this would produce $28,800 in revenues for the department, bringing the series closer to its goal of self-sufficiency. To accomplish this, the plan calls for a marketing expenditure of $14,000. Of this, $4,000 will be spent on qualitative market research to determine areas of health interest in our community; $5,000 will be spent on developing a set of brochures which will be mailed at a cost of $800 to our target markets; $3,600 will be spent on local newspaper and radio advertising; and the remaining $600 will be spent on posters and handouts to be used as reminders of ongoing series.

The purpose of the executive summary is to permit higher management to preview the major thrust of each plan and to have the information

TABLE 7–1 Background Data

	1984 JUNE–DECEMBER	1985 JANUARY–MAY	1985 JUNE–DECEMBER
1. Number of series	3	3	3
2. Number of sessions	24	24	24
3. Capacity of auditorium	150	150	150
4. Average audience size per session	35	38	40
5. Audience as percent of capacity	23%	25%	27%
6. Average revenue* per session	$ 315	$ 342	$ 360
7. Total revenue	$ 7,560	$ 8,208	$ 8,640
8. Marketing cost	$ 5,500	$ 6,000	$ 6,000
9. Presentation costs†	$ 3,700	$ 3,200	$ 3,800
10. Administrative cost	$ 5,500	$ 6,100	$ 6,500
11. Total cost	$14,700	$15,300	$16,300
12. Net operating loss	$ 7,140	$ 7,092	$ 7,660

*Because preregistrants paid $30 in advance for the series, but often dropped out during the series, the revenue per audience member per session is higher than the ticket prices of $5 for preregistrants, $7 for walk-ins.

†Fees paid to those running or presenting a session.

that is critical in evaluating the plan. To facilitate this, a table of contents should follow the executive summary.

Situation Analysis. The first major section of the plan is the situation analysis, in which the manager describes the major features of the situation facing his or her operation. The situation analysis consists of four subsections—background, normal forecast, opportunities and threats, and strengths and weaknesses.

The *background* section starts with a summary of key performance indicators for the last few years. An example is shown in Table 7–1 for the Mt. Sinai Community Health Education Department's Monday P.M. series. Rows 1, 2, and 3 show that the number of series and sessions as well as audience capacity has remained constant over the three half-year periods since the series began. Rows 4 and 5 show that the audience size has grown slightly, as have revenues (rows 6 and 7). However, rows 8, 9, 10, and 11 indicate that marketing, presentation, and management costs in each case have been greater than revenues.

The Monday P.M. idea is making slow progress in terms of audience and "sales," but not improving financially. These data should be followed by a description of major developments in the marketplace, such as new competition, changes in community health interests, and other factors that would throw light on the marketplace.

The background information should be followed by a *forecast* of volume or audience size under "normal conditions"—that is, assuming no major changes in the marketing environment or marketing strategies. This forecast can be obtained in a number of ways. The assumption could be made that audience size would stay constant, or grow at the most recent rate of growth, or even decline. The basis of the forecast could be statistical curve fitting, surveying a sample of people who attended last year, and so on. The forecast will have to be revised if different environmental conditions are expected or different strategies are planned. If the forecast does not satisfy higher management, the planner will have to consider new strategies.

The normal forecast should be followed by a section in which the manager identifies the main *opportunities and threats* facing the organizational unit. Higher management can then review this list and raise any questions about what is or is not listed. The following year, management can see how many opportunities were acted on and what threats really occurred.

Exhibit 7–1 shows the opportunities and threats listed by Ann Buckley, manager of the Monday P.M. series. The opportunities and threats describe *outside* factors facing the organization. They are written to suggest some actions that might be warranted. The manager may be asked to rate the opportunities and threats for their potential impact and probability as an indicator of which deserve the most planning attention.

The manager should next list the main internal *strengths and weaknesses* of the organization (see Exhibit 7–1). The list of strengths has implications for strategy formulation, while the list of weaknesses has implications for investments to correct those weaknesses. Higher management can raise critical questions about the strengths and weaknesses identified by each manager.

Objectives and Goals. The situation analysis describes where the organization stands and where it might go. Now management must propose where that organization should go. Specific objectives and goals have to be set. Top management typically promulgates overall goals for the coming period for the organization as a whole. The director of the community health education department might state that the department wants to achieve (1) a 15 percent growth in people participating in the department's programs and (2) an operating loss not to exceed $25,000.

Each manager develops goals for his or her department within the context of these overall goals. Thus the Monday P.M. manager, reviewing top management's goals, decided on the following specific goals: (1) to attract 4,800 people, up from 1,900 people in the previous year; and

EXHIBIT 7–1

**Opportunities and Threats, Strengths and Weaknesses:
The Monday P.M. Series**

OPPORTUNITIES

1. There is a large potential audience in the nearby suburb of Cameron which is unaware of the Monday P.M. series, but which could be attracted to the series.
2. Some of Cincinnati's large corporations might sponsor one or two of the series if they could be effectively reached.
3. The local college community presents a large untapped market for the series.

THREATS

1. Poor local economic conditions may reduce the attendance rate.
2. The increasing parking problem is producing a lot of disgruntled series participants.
3. Two new proprietary competitors are coming on the scene. A weight loss clinic will be offering nutrition and weight loss classes to the public. A sports and health club will be offering classes to the public in cardiovascular health.

STRENGTHS

1. The audience has been satisfied with most of the past presenters, according to the evaluations.
2. No other hospital in the area offers such a broad range of health education programs.
3. The hospital, given its excellent reputation, lends credibility to the series.

WEAKNESSES

1. The staff, though enthusiastic, is not well trained in handling the various tasks that have to be done.
2. The access roads to the hospital are very busy and discourage people at greater distances from coming.
3. The health education department has mishandled some preregistration in the past, losing forms, payments and names, thereby creating some ill-will.

(2) to spend $14,000 to accomplish this. Other goals would also be listed here.

Marketing Strategy. The manager next outlines a marketing strategy for attaining the objectives. The marketing strategy describes the game plan by which the manager hopes to "win."

> **Marketing strategy** is the fundamental logic by which an organization unit tends to achieve its marketing objectives. Marketing strategy consists of a coordinated set of decisions on (1) target markets, (2) marketing mix, and (3) marketing expenditure level.

Management should introduce criteria to identify the most attractive markets, defined in terms of age, income, medical coverage, diagnosis, education, employment status, or other relevant criteria. Various markets should be rated on these criteria and markets with the greatest probable response to a unit of marketing effort selected as targets. Thus the Monday P.M. manager might conclude that the distant suburbs are too difficult to attract, and choose to focus on nearer suburbs and the city population.

The organization should develop a *strategic marketing mix* that answers such basic questions as whether to emphasize preregistration versus walk-in options. It should also develop a *tactical marketing mix*. The Monday P.M. manager may decide on mailing brochures to people living in the suburbs, and on heavy newspaper advertising to the urban residents who live close to the hospital.

Marketing strategy also calls for deciding on the *marketing expenditure level*. Organizations typically establish their marketing budget at some percentage of the "sales" revenue. For example, the health education department director might be willing to spend 20 percent of program "sales" revenue on marketing. Clearly, the more spent on marketing, the larger the audience sales should be. What an organization needs to know is the point at which increased sales or volume no longer bring increased profits, and in fact cut into profits. Most health care organizations do not allocate nearly enough to marketing. While businesses in the traditional commercial arena may spend 15 to 25 percent of sales on all forms of marketing, many health care organizations allocate less than 1 percent to it.

Action Programs. The marketing strategy needs to be turned into a specific set of actions for accomplishing the marketing goals. Each strategy element should be elaborated into appropriate actions. For example, the strategy element "decrease the parking problems associated with attending the Monday P.M. series" could lead to the following actions: "increase the parking spaces available to Monday P.M. attenders," "improve parking lot traffic management for incoming and outgoing traffic," and "arrange for signs in the hospital parking lot telling people where the series is being held." The actions that appear most cost effective should then be assigned to specific individuals with specific completion times.

The overall action plan can take the form of a table, with the 12 months (or 52 weeks) of the year serving as columns and various marketing activities serving as rows. Dates can be entered when various activities or expenditures will be started, reviewed, and completed. This action plan can be changed during the year as new problems and opportunities arise.

Budgets. The goals, strategies, and planned actions allow the manager to build a budget that is essentially a projected profit-and-loss statement. On the revenue side, it shows the forecasted unit sales and the expected net realized price. On the expense side, it shows the costs of production, marketing, and administration. The difference is the projected profit or loss. Management reviews the budget and either approves or modifies it. Once approved, the budget is the basis for marketing operations, financial planning, and personnel recruitment.

Controls. The last section of the plan describes the controls that will be applied to monitor the plan's progress. Normally the goals and budgets are spelled out for each month, quarter, or appropriate time period. This means that higher management can review the results each period and spot managers who are not attaining their goals. These managers will be asked to indicate what actions they will take to improve the results. This completes our description of the marketing plan; now we turn to the problem of marketing control.

MARKETING CONTROL

The purpose of marketing control is to maximize the probability that the organization will achieve its short-run and long-run objectives. Many surprises are likely to occur during the plan's execution that will call for new responses or adjustments. So control systems are an intrinsic part of the marketing planning process.

Marketing control is not a single process: there are three types of marketing control. *Annual plan control* refers to the steps taken during the year to monitor and correct deviations from the plan. *Profitability control* consists of efforts to determine the actual profit or loss of different services or products, territories, market segments, and distribution channels. *Strategic control* consists of a systematic evaluation of the organization's market performance in relation to its market opportunities.

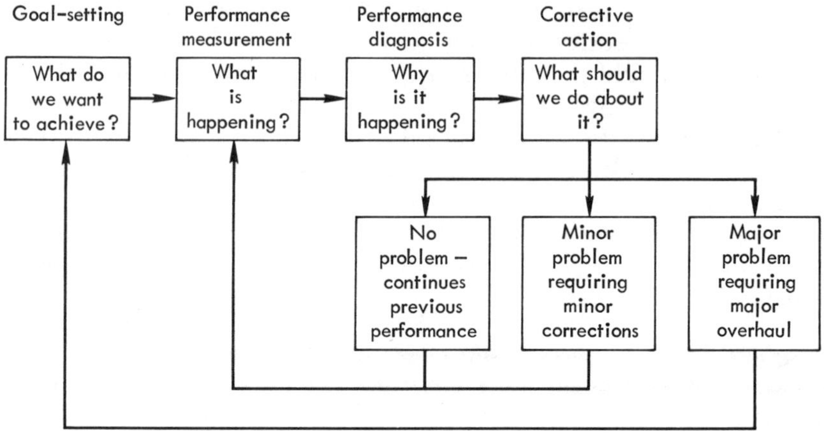

FIGURE 7–3 The Control Process

Annual Plan Control

The purpose of annual plan control is to make sure during the course of the year that the organization is achieving the results it established in its annual plan. This calls for the four steps shown in Figure 7–3. First, the various managers set and accept well-defined goals for each month, quarter, or other period during the plan year. Second, steps are taken to monitor results and developments during the year. Third, managers seek to diagnose the causes of any serious deviations in performance. Fourth, managers choose corrective actions that will close the gap between goals and performance.

This system is called *management by objectives.* Top management starts the process by developing the "volume," "census," "profit," and other aggregate goals for the planning period. These goals are broken down into subgoals for lower levels of management. During the period, managers receive reports that allow them to follow whether their subordinates are reaching their goals, and if not, to take the necessary corrective action.

What control tools are used by management to check on the progress of subordinates in reaching goals? The four main ones are sales analysis, market share analysis, marketing expense-to-sales analysis, and market attitude tracking.

Sales analysis is the effort to measure and evaluate the actual sales being achieved in relation to the goals set for different managers. Thus, the management of the Monday P.M. series would compare actual to expected attendance at the sessions by topic being covered, season, and so on to understand market behavior and preferences. If too few suburbanites are attending the series, or if certain series are being poorly attended, the reasons should be sought. Management can then identify the causes of the problem and take corrective action.

Organizations should periodically review whether they are gaining or losing ground relative to their competition. For example, the Chicago Lung Association continues to raise more money each year, but is slipping in its share of the total medical charity dollar and also in relation to specific competitors such as the American Heart Association and the American Cancer Association. *Market share* is a much better indicator of marketing effectiveness than total sales. It must, however, be used cautiously, because a poor definition of the market will produce misleading market share figures. The Humana Heart Institute in Kentucky, for example, should not measure its visibility in the marketplace against local community hospitals. Instead, it should measure it against other internationally known cardiac services.

Annual plan control also requires checking on various marketing expenses as a ratio of sales to make sure the organization is not overspending to achieve its goals. The ratios to watch are total *marketing expense to sales, sales force (usually called by other titles in health care) expense to sales, advertising to sales, sales promotion to sales, marketing research to sales,* and *sales management to sales.* The organization should check continuously on whether these ratios are appropriate, and whether shifting from one marketing tool to another could bring down total cost of sales. Management has to keep an eye on other performance ratios that say something about the efficiency of the marketing effort. An experienced fundraising director, for example, periodically checks the following ratios: revenue per fundraiser, number of prospects contacted per fundraiser per day, number of minutes per contact, revenue per contact hour, percentage of closure per contact, percentage of potential contributors covered, and number of lost contributors.

Organizations should also check periodically on consumer attitudes toward the organization. If market attitudes start eroding, they can lead to later declines in sales. Knowing this early can lead to preventive actions. Market attitude can be measured through well-established control systems such as complaint and suggestion boxes, client or patient panels, and patient or client satisfaction surveys.

Profitability Control

Besides annual plan control, organizations need to do periodic research to determine the actual profit or loss on their various services, patients groups, territories, and distribution channels. Consider hospitals. Hospitals are under great pressure for cost containment. Even prior to DRG reimbursement, an increasing number were driven to examine the costs of their various departments and activities. They discovered a great deal of variation in the financial results of different services. For example, hernia operations generally yielded a profit to the hospital, while inpatient psychiatric services sometimes represented a loss, at least under the traditional pricing and reimbursement programs. Hospitals are now examining the profitability or loss generated by each of the diagnosis-related groups. Hospitals need some cash-generating services and diagnoses to pay for the cash-losing services and diagnoses, and some hospitals have been dropping those services and diagnoses whose losses are too great.

Marketing profitability analysis requires a procedure for identifying all revenues generated by a particular unit or service and all costs associated with it. Sometimes this is fairly easy to do. A hospital can evaluate the cost of running a satellite branch because costs like rent, salaries, and utilities can be assigned to it. It is more difficult to isolate the revenues and costs of, say, an obstetrics department, because its presence also generates gynecological and pediatric business. In addition, assignment of overhead charges (a portion of the hospital's heat and maintenance costs) is somewhat arbitrary. Smaller organizations, such as a physician's private practice, a small mental health center, or an independent homemaking service may have even more difficulty doing a marketing profitability analysis because they may not have the systems to track their costs. However, given their size, they have fewer problems associated with the assignment of overhead charges.

Marketing profitability analysis provides information on the relative profitability of different services, programs, diagnoses, market segments, and other marketing entities. It does not imply that the best course of action is to drop the unprofitable marketing entities. Nor does it actually measure the likely profit improvement if these marginal entities are dropped. However, given the increasingly difficult fiscal challenges facing health care organizations today, managements must give thought to ways of improving revenues or reducing costs of all services, departments, and units of operation.

Strategic Control

From time to time, health care organizations need to take a critical look at their overall marketing performance. Marketing is an area where rapid obsolescence of objectives, policies, strategies, and programs is a constant possibility.

A major tool in this connection is the *marketing audit*. Organizations are increasingly turning to marketing audits to assess opportunities and operations. A marketing audit is defined as follows:[3]

> A **marketing audit** is a comprehensive, systematic, independent, and periodic examination of an organization's or, within an organization, a specific service's marketing environment, objectives, strategies, and activities with a view to determining problem areas and

opportunities and recommending a plan of action to improve the organization's marketing performance.

The four characteristics of a marketing audit are these:

1. *Comprehensive.* The marketing audit covers all the major marketing issues facing an organization or service, and not just troublespots.
2. *Systematic.* The marketing audit involves an orderly sequence of diagnostic steps covering the health care organization's marketing environment, internal marketing system, and specific marketing activities. The diagnosis is followed by a corrective action plan involving both short-run and long-run proposals to improve overall marketing effectiveness.
3. *Independent.* The marketing audit is normally conducted by an inside or outside party who has sufficient independence from the marketing department (if there is one) to have top management's confidence and the needed objectivity.
4. *Periodic.* The marketing audit should normally be carried out periodically instead of only when there is a crisis. It has benefits for the health care organization that is seemingly successful, as well as the one that is in deep trouble.

A marketing audit is carried out by an auditor who gathers information critical to evaluating the organization's performance. The auditor collects secondary data and also interviews managers, patients, staff, physicians and other clinicians, outreach workers, and others who might throw light on the organization's marketing performance. The auditor cannot rely only on internal management opinion, and must seek the opinions and evaluations of outsiders. Often the findings are a surprise, and sometimes a shock, to management.

Exhibit 7–2 is a guide to the kinds of questions the marketing auditor would raise for health care organizations. Not all the questions are important in every situation. The instrument will be modified depending on whether the organization is an inpatient facility, an ambulatory care organization, a clinician's private practice, a social service agency, a government agency, and so on.[4] However, all the topics covered in the marketing audit are relevant for consideration by all health care organizations.

The purpose of the marketing audit is to judge whether the organization is performing optimally from a marketing point of view. The auditor will produce some short-run and long-run recommendations for actions the organization could take to improve performance. Management must carefully consider these recommendations and implement those it feels would contribute to improved marketing performance. The marketing audit is not a marketing plan, but an independent appraisal by a competent consultant of the main problems and opportunities facing the organization and what it can do about them.

EXHIBIT 7–2

Marketing Audit Guide

THE MARKET AND MARKET SEGMENTS

How large is the territory covered by your market?

How have you determined this?

How is your market grouped?

___ Is it scattered?

___ How many important segments are there?

___ How are these segments determined (demographics, service usage, attitudinally)?

Is the market entirely urban, or is a fair proportion of it rural?

What percentage of your market uses third-party payment?

___ What are the attitudes and operations of third parties?

___ Are they all equally profitable?

What are the effects of the following factors on your market?

___ Age

___ Income

___ Occupation

___ Increasing population

___ Demographic shifting

___ Decreasing birthrate

What proportion of potential customers are familiar with your organization, services, programs?

___ What is your image in the marketplace?

___ What are the important components of your image?

THE ORGANIZATION

Short history of your organization:

___ When and how was it organized?

___ What has been the nature of its growth?

___ How fast and far have its markets expanded? Where do your patients come from geographically?

___ What is the basic policy of the organization? Is its focus on "health care?" "profit"?

___ What has been the financial history of the organization?

___ How has it been capitalized?

___ Have there been any account receivable problems?

___ What is inventory investment?

____ What has been the organization's success with the various services promoted?

How does your organization compare with the health care industry and the relevant subset of the health care industry?

____ Is the total volume (gross revenue, utilization) and/or profitability increasing, decreasing?

____ Have there been any fluctuations in revenue? If so, what were they due to?

What are the objectives and goals of the organization? How can they be expressed beyond the provision of "good health care"?

What are the organization's present strengths and weaknesses in:

____ Medical facilities

____ Management capabilities

____ Medical staff

____ Technical facilities

____ Reputation

____ Financial capabilities

____ Image

____ Interorganizational linkages

What is the labor environment for your organization?

____ For medical staff (nurses, physicians, etc.)?

____ For support personnel?

How dependent is your organization upon conditions of other industries (third party payers)? upon other health care delivery systems (HMOs, PPOs)?

Are weaknesses being compensated for and strengths being used? How?

How are the following areas of your marketing function organized?

____ Structure

____ Manpower

____ Reporting relationships

____ Decision-making power

What kind of external controls affect your organization?

____ Local?

____ State?

____ Federal?

____ Self-regulatory?

What are the trends in recent regulatory rulings?

COMPETITORS

How many competitors are in your industry?

____ How do you define your competitors?

____ Has this number increased or decreased in the last four years?

Is competition on a price or nonprice basis?

What are the choices afforded patients?

____ In services?

____ In payment?

What is your position in the market—size and strength—relative to competitors?

PRODUCTS AND SERVICES

Complete a list of your organization's products and services, both present and proposed

What are the general outstanding characteristics of each product or service?

What superiority or distinctiveness of products or services do you have as compared with competing organizations?

What is the total cost per service (in-use)? Is service over/under utilized?

What services are most heavily used? Why?

____ What is the profile of patients/physicians who use the services?

____ Are there distinct groups of users?

What are your organization's policies regarding:

____ Number and types of services to offer?

____ Assessing needs for service addition/deletion?

History or products and services (complete for major products and services):

____ How many did the organization originally have?

____ How many have been added or dropped?

____ What important changes have taken place in services during the last ten years?

____ Has demand for the services increased or decreased?

____ What are the common complaints against the service?

____ What services could be added to your organization that would make it more attractive to patients, medical staff, nonmedical personnel?

____ What are the strongest points of your services to patients, medical staff, nonmedical personnel?

____ Have you any other features that individualize your service or give you an advantage over competitors?

PRICE

What is the pricing strategy of the organization?

____ Cost-plus

____ Return on investment

____ Stabilization

____ Competitive pricing

How are prices for services determined?

____ How often are prices reviewed?

____ What factors contribute to price increase/decrease?

What have been the price trends for the past five years?

How are your pricing policies viewed by:

____ Patients

____ Physicians

____ Third-party payers

____ Competitors

____ Regulators

____ Employer groups

____ Alternative delivery systems

PROMOTION

What is the purpose of the organization's present promotional activities (including advertising)?

____ Protective

____ Educational

____ Search out new markets

____ Develop all markets

____ Establish a new service

Has this purpose undergone any change in recent years?

To whom has advertising appeal been largely directed?

____ Donors

____ Patients

  ____ Former or current

  ____ Prospective

____ Physicians

  ____ On staff

  ____ Potential

What media have been used?

Are the media still effective in reaching the intended audience?

What copy appeals have been notable in terms of response?

What methods have been used for measuring advertising effectiveness?

What is the role of public relations?

____ Is it a separate function/department?

____ What is the scope of responsibilities?

CHANNELS OF DISTRIBUTION

What are the trends in distribution in the industry?

____ What services are being performed on an ambulatory basis?

____ What services are being provided on an at-home basis?

____ Are satellite facilities being used?

What factors are considered in location decisions?

When did you last evaluate present location?

What distributors do you deal with? (e.g., medical supply houses, etc.)

How large an inventory must you carry?

SOURCE: Eric N. Berkowitz and William A. Flexner, "The Marketing Audit: A Tool for Health Service Organizations," *Health Care Management Review* (Fall 1978), pp. 55–56. Reprinted with permission of Aspen Systems Corporation. Copyright 1978, Aspen Systems Corporation.

Unfortunately, as uncommon as marketing planning is in health care organizations, marketing control is even less common. If health care organizations do bother to evaluate performance, it is usually limited to clinical evaluation: "We provided a (clinically) good service." In the process of providing these services, however, health care organiza-

EXHIBIT 7–3 Two Examples of Poor Marketing Control

Every year prior to National Nursing Home Week, newspapers and broadcasters call up local nursing homes, asking if they would like to place advertisements during that week in the local media. The majority of nursing homes do. Very few have ever tried to evaluate the effect of placing these advertisements. One nursing home administrator who did evaluate the expenditure said: "Never again. There are so many nursing home advertisements during that one week that all the ads get lost in the crowd. I don't think I've ever attracted one patient or received one comment due to placing ads during National Nursing Home Week."

A state Medicaid office sent out one-page letters—all black and white, small print, nonpersonalized "Dear Doctor" letters—to physicians every time the Medicaid pharmacological group identified a nonefficacious drug. The letters asked the physicians not to prescribe these drugs to their Medicaid patients, since the Medicaid office did not wish to pay for ineffective medications. (Because the efficacy of some of these drugs was still in dispute, Medicaid continued to pay for them if they were prescribed.) One Medicaid staff member estimated that 80,000 of these letters were sent out every year, but was unable to indicate how effective they were. A subsequent analysis indicated no significant change in physician prescribing behavior after the letters had been sent, and market research later suggested that most physicians threw the letters away without reading them.

tions are often squandering scarce resources, unaware of which resources are being productively used and which are being wasted. See Exhibit 7–3 for examples. It appears that the financial situation now facing health care organizations will no longer allow this extravagance.

SUMMARY

The marketing planning and control system guides the health care organization's operation in the marketplace. Health care organizations operate planning systems of various degrees of sophistication from simple budgeting systems, to annual planning systems, to long-range planning systems. The process starts with marketing forecasting and planning, followed by the development of a detailed business plan. The marketing plan contains the following sections: executive summary, situation analysis, objective and goals, marketing strategy, action program, budgets, and controls. The marketing strategy section of the plan defines the target markets, marketing mix, and marketing expenditure level that will be used to achieve the marketing objectives.

Marketing control is an intrinsic part of marketing planning. Organizations exercise at least three types of marketing control. Annual plan control consists of monitoring the current marketing performance to be sure that the annual sales and profit goals are being achieved. The main tools are sales analysis, market-share analysis, marketing expense-to-sales analysis. and market attitude tracking. If underperformance is detected, the organization can implement a variety of corrective measures. Profitability control consists of determining the actual profitability of different marketing entities, such as the organization's services and programs, market segments, and distribution channels. Marketing profitability analysis reveals the weaker marketing entities, although it does not indicate whether the weaker units should be bolstered or phased out. Strategic control consists of making sure that the organization's marketing objectives, strategies, and systems are optimally adapted to the current and forecasted marketing environment. It uses the tool known as the marketing audit, which is a comprehensive, systematic, independent, and periodic examination of the organization's marketing environment, objectives, strategies, and activities. The purpose of the marketing audit is to determine problem areas and recommend corrective short-run and long-run actions to improve the organization's overall marketing effectiveness.

NOTES

1. Melville C. Branch, *The Corporate Planning Process* (New York: American Management Association, 1962), pp. 48–49.

2. See D. D. McConkey, *MBO for Nonprofit Organizations* (New York: AMA-COM, 1975).

3. For details, see Philip Kotler, William Gregor, and William Rodgers, "The Marketing Audit Comes of Age," *Sloan Management Review* (Winter 1977), pp. 25–43. A preliminary marketing audit tool is described in Philip Kotler, "From Sales Obsession to Marketing Effectiveness," *Harvard Business Review* (November–December 1977), pp. 67–75.

4. For a marketing audit guide for social service organizations, see Douglas B. Herron, "Developing a Marketing Audit for Social Service Organizations," in Christopher H. Lovelock and Charles B. Weinberg, eds., *Readings in Public and Nonprofit Marketing* (Palo Alto, CA: The Scientific Press, 1978), pp. 269–71.

PART III
Analyzing Marketing Opportunities

8

MARKET MEASUREMENT AND FORECASTING

Grant Hospital is a 500-bed community hospital located a few miles north of downtown Chicago in an area peopled by varied ethnic groups. One of its major services is an alcoholism program designed to help employed alcoholics. The program, which was launched in 1968, has a 45-person staff that manages three distinct programs: (1) *inpatient treatment,* consisting of a 21-bed, hospital-based program; (2) *outpatient treatment,* offering counseling to about 170 patients per week; and (3) *training and consultation* direction to professionals and employers.

The program director became interested in adding a new service to treat the adolescent alcoholic, a segment Grant Hospital was not serving. The National Institute on Alcohol Abuse and Alcoholism estimates that 3.3 million teenagers—almost one in five—are "problem drinkers" who lose control at least once a year. Teenage alcoholism appears to have increased in recent years as a result of many states lowering the legal drinking age in the early seventies. The Insurance Institute of Highway Safety links the lowering of drinking ages to increases in teenage auto accidents and juvenile crime such as rowdyism and vandalism. For example, the under-20 group, although only 8.6 percent of the driving population in 1978, accounted for 18 percent of all traffic accident fatalities, and 25 percent were alcohol-related. Teenage drinking has become such a problem that the federal government now is denying major federal funds to states that do not raise the legal drinking age back to 21.

The director wanted to launch an inpatient program to treat male teenage alcoholics that would involve 15 beds and a 21-day stay. The viability of this program would depend upon Grant Hospital being able to attract about 255 patients each year (15 patients for 17 program cycles during the year). The director proceeded to make some rough calculations of the market size. The relevant area of Chicago was estimated to have about 100,000 alcoholics. About 10 percent, or 10,000, were estimated to be teenagers. Four-fifths of all alcoholics are male, and therefore she estimated that 8,000 male teenager alcoholics would be in the relevant area of Chicago. She estimated that only about half of them, or 4,000, would accept formal treatment. Of these, about 20 percent, or 800, would be willing to enter an inpatient program as opposed to an outpatient program. Since three other Chicago hospitals also ran male inpatient teenage alcoholism programs, the director figured that Grant could attract about one in four of these teenagers, or 250. If these estimates were correct, Grant could attract roughly the number of alcoholic teenagers it needs to run at 100 percent capacity. Since it could afford to run even at 80 percent capacity, the director felt that the market was probably large enough to enter and serve. Still, the director had some misgivings and decided that the next step would be to refine these estimates and get a better measure of how many male teenage alcoholics might be attracted to the inpatient program.

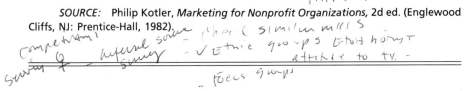

SOURCE: Philip Kotler, *Marketing for Nonprofit Organizations,* 2d ed. (Englewood Cliffs, NJ: Prentice-Hall, 1982).

We are now ready to turn our attention to the marketplace and seek ways to understand and measure it. The market is the organization's source of opportunities. The job of analyzing the marketplace breaks down into three major tasks:

1. *Market measurement and forecasting.* Determining the current and future size of the available market for the health care organization's products and services.
2. *Market segmentation.* Determining the main groups making up a market with a view to choosing the best target groups.
3. *Consumer analysis.* Determining consumer characteristics, specifically their needs, perceptions, preferences, and behavior, with a view toward adapting the offer to these characteristics.

All these steps make up what we call *market analysis.* In this chapter we deal with market measurement and forecasting; Chapter 9 will deal with market segmentation analysis, and Chapter 10 will deal with consumer analysis. Because the use of many health care services depends upon someone other than the ultimate consumer, market analyses in health care can be both complex and confusing. If the decision maker for inpatient hospitalization is the physician and not the patient, which should the hospital consider to be its market? Which does it measure? Does an HMO measure the market of local businesses to which it must initially sell, or the market of employed individuals and their families—potential HMO members—living within its service area?

The answer, of course, is not simple. An organization that has two or more markets which directly influence the decision to use its services cannot consider only one market to the exclusion of the others. This interactive or complex decision-making process will be examined in Chapter 10. Since volume, revenue, and usage are measured by the ultimate market or final user of the service (the patient being the final user in the case of most health care providers), that will be the market we will address in this chapter. However, the principles and tools we apply to the final user market can be equally well applied to other markets.

Market measurement and forecasting require that the health care organization research three questions:

1. Who is the market? (*market definition*)
2. How large is the current market? (*current market size measurement*)
3. What is the likely future size of the market? (*market forecasting*)

DEFINING THE MARKET

Every organization faces the task of defining who is in its market. Not everyone is a potential customer; not everyone is in the market for open heart surgery, 100 percent concurrent medical review services, osteopathic manipulation, or a shared services program. Organizations must distinguish between customers and noncustomers.

To define the market, the health care organization must carefully define the market offer. We can talk about the market for a private psychiatric hospital, or for its outpatient counseling services, or for its outpatient Troubled Teenager Program. Market definition and size would vary for each case. The more specifically we can define the product or service, the more carefully we can determine the market's boundaries and size. We define the market as follows:

> A **market** is the set of actual and potential consumers of a market offer.

Two comments are in order. The term "consumers" is shorthand for a number of other possible terms, such as patients, buyers, clients, customers, users, and audience. Furthermore, the consumers can be individuals, families, groups, or organizations. The term "market offer" is also shorthand for a tangible good, service, program, idea, or anything that might be offered to a group of responders.

Traditionally, those in the market for something are viewed as having three characteristics: interest, income or source of payment, and access. To illustrate this, consider the following:

> The head of the counseling program for troubled teenagers is concerned because the program is underutilized, generating insufficient revenue to break even, and therefore draining funds away from other programs in the hospital. He is interested in estimating whether there are enough teenagers in the hospital's service area who would be in the market for this program to justify keeping it going.

First, the program director must estimate the number of troubled teenagers in the hospital's service area whose families want counseling for them. He could do this by calling competing programs and finding out how many teenagers they serve. A more direct approach would be to phone a sample of families with teenagers and ask them about their level of interest in counseling services. Given the nature of the services, this would have to be handled sensitively. If 10 out of 100 families say they would be interested and the remainder would not, then it would appear that 10 percent have an interest in the program. This percentage can be multiplied by the population of families with teenagers in the community to estimate the potential market for this program. We define potential market as follows:

> The **potential market** is the set of consumers who profess some level of interest in a defined market offer.

Consumer interest is not enough to define a market. Health care services or programs that must be self-sufficient or produce a specified level of revenue or profit must also consider health insurance coverage and/or income—that is, ability of the market to pay for the purchase. In a self-pay market, the size of the market is a function not only of interest level, but also of income level. For health care services covered by insurance, consumer income is not as important as the extent and nature of the insurance coverage. Of course, even those with little income and no health insurance are entitled to necessary medical care and may simply be viewed as a less financially attractive segment of the potential market. And there are organizations and services for which income or health insurance coverage is not a defining variable because consumer use is not intended to generate revenue. Thus, in such cases as Alcoholics Anonymous, federally funded well-baby visits, and many social services for the poor, income or insurance coverage is not a factor in market size.

Market size may be cut down further by personal access barriers. Families interested in counseling for their teenagers may find the time or place at which the Troubled Teenager Program is offered inconvenient. Access factors will make the market smaller. The market that remains is called the available market:

> The **available market** is the set of consumers who have interest, income, or health insurance coverage, where necessary, and access to a particular market offer.

In the case of some offers, the organization will establish restrictions. The Troubled Teenager Program will not take anyone with a long history of criminal acts or delinquency. The program chooses to accept only those teenagers facing short-term difficulties. These teenagers constitute the qualified available market:

> The **qualified available market** is the set of consumers who have interest, income or health insurance coverage, where necessary, access, and qualification for the particular market offer.

Now the Troubled Teenager Program has the choice of going after the whole qualified available market or of concentrating its efforts on certain segments. In the latter case, we need the concept of the served market:

> The **served market** is the part of the qualified available market the organization puts effort into attracting and serving.

Suppose the hospital prefers to attract primarily younger teenagers (15 and younger) to its program and as a result promotes the program primarily to junior high schools. Here the served market is somewhat smaller than the qualified available market.

Once the program is advertised, it will attract an actual number of teenagers who will represent some fraction of the served market. The number who join the program is called the penetrated market:

> The **penetrated market** is the set of consumers who are actually consuming the product.

Figure 8–1 brings all these concepts together. The bar at the left illustrates the ratio of the potential market—all interested teenagers or their families—to the total population of families with teenagers, here 10 percent. The figure on the right illustrates several breakdowns of the potential market. The available market—those who have interest, income or insurance coverage, and access—are 40 percent of the potential consumers. The qualified available market—those who would meet the hospital's short-term treatment criteria—are 20 percent of the potential market, or 50 percent of the available market. The hospital is actively trying to attract half of these, or 10 percent of the potential market. Finally, the hospital is shown as actually enrolling 5 percent of the potential market in the program.

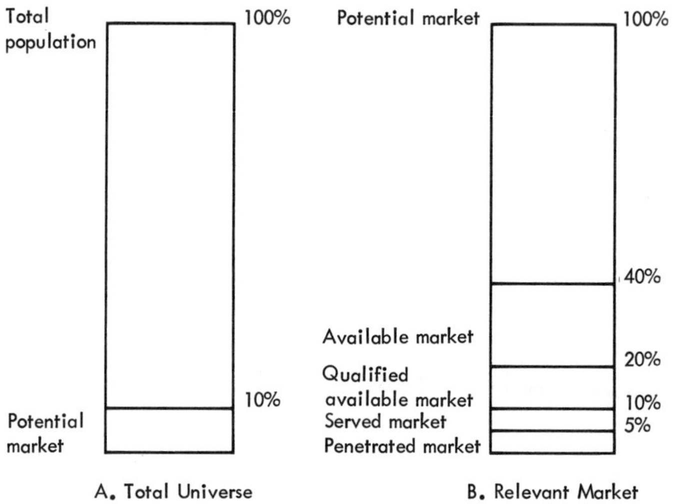

FIGURE 8–1 Levels of Market Definition

These definitions are a useful tool for marketing planning. If the organization is not satisfied with the size of its penetrated market, it can consider a number of actions. It can try to attract a larger percentage of people from its served market. If it finds that the nonenrolling part of the served market has chosen to receive counseling at a competing facility, the hospital might try to widen its served market by promoting the course in other suburbs. The hospital could also relax the qualifications for treatment, thus expanding the qualified available market by lowering the fee, improving the location and time at which the service is offered, and doing other things to reduce cost and access. Ultimately, the hospital could try to expand the potential market by launching a campaign to convert uninterested consumers into interested consumers.

MEASURING CURRENT MARKET DEMAND

We are now ready to examine some practical methods of estimating current market demand for a market offer. A health care organization will want to make four types of estimates: total market demand, area market demand, total market sales, and organization market share.

Estimating Total Market Demand

We define total market demand as follows:

Total market demand for a product or service is the total volume that would be bought by a defined consumer group in a defined

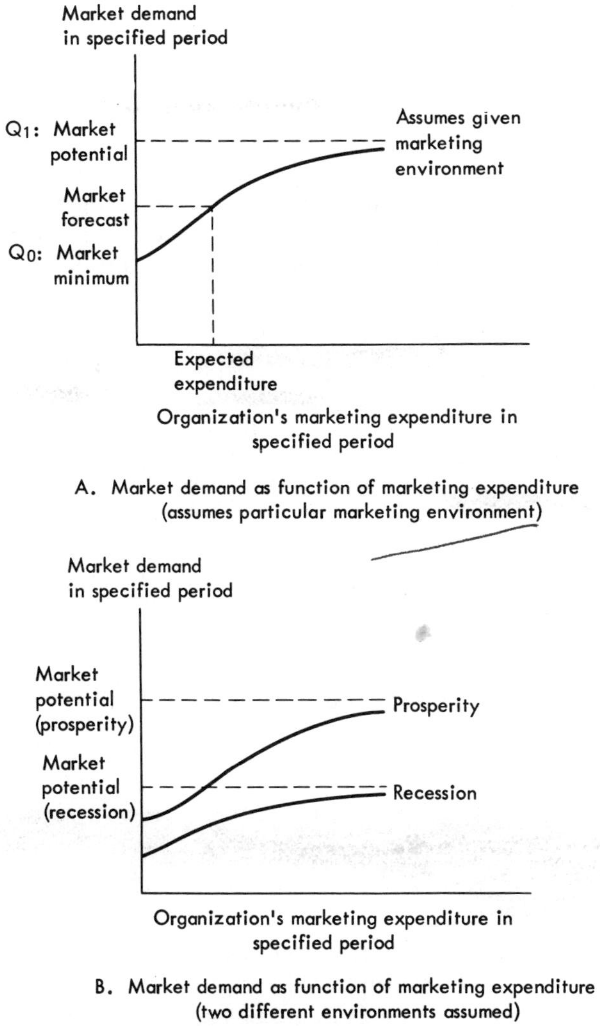

FIGURE 8–2 Market Demand

geographic area in a defined time period in a defined marketing environment under a defined marketing program.

The most important thing to realize about total market demand is that it is not a fixed number, but a function of the specified conditions. One of these conditions, for example, is the marketing program (product features, price, promotional expenditure level), and another is the state of the economy. The dependence of total market demand on these conditions is illustrated in Figure 8–2. The horizontal axis shows different possible levels of marketing expenditures by the organization in a given time period. The vertical axis shows the resulting demand level. The curve represents the estimated level of market demand associated with different marketing expenditure levels by the organization. We see that some base sales (called the *market minimum*) would take place without any demand-stimulating expenditures by the organization. Positive marketing expenditures would yield higher levels of demand, first at an increasing rate and then at a decreasing rate. Marketing expenditures higher than a certain level would not stimulate much further demand, suggesting an upper limit to market demand called the *market potential.*

The distance between the market minimum and the market potential shows the overall *marketing sensitivity of demand.* We can think of two extreme types of markets, the *expansible* and the *nonexpansible.* An expansible market, such as a market for nonsymptomatic health care, like CPR classes, is affected by the level of marketing expenditures. In terms of Figure 8–2(a) the distance between Q_0 and Q_1 is relatively large. A nonexpansible market, such as the market for kidney transplant surgery, is not much affected by level of marketing expenditures; the distance between Q_0 and Q_1 is relatively small. The organization selling in a nonexpansible market can take the market's size (the level of *primary demand*) for granted and concentrate its resources on getting a desired market share (the level of *selective demand*).

Only one of the many possible levels of marketing expenditure will actually be chosen by the organization. The market demand corresponding to this expenditure level is called the market forecast.

> The **market forecast** shows the expected level of market demand for the expected level of organizational marketing expenditure in the given environment.

If a different environment is assumed, the market demand function would have to be estimated again. Consider the economic environment. Even the market for health care is higher during prosperity than recession because market demand is income- and health-insurance-elastic, as Exhibit 8–1 describes. The dependence of market demand on the environment is illustrated in Figure 8–2(b).

The main point is that the marketer should carefully define the situation for which market demand is being estimated. The marketer can use what is known as the *chain ratio method* to make the estimate. This method involves multiplying a base number by a succession of percentages that lead to the defined consumer set. Here is an example:

> A national health care association estimates the demand for full-time registered nurses working in hospitals will be 550,000 in the following year. The question is whether this is a high or low figure in

EXHIBIT 8–1 Detroit Syndrome

Many Autoworkers Forgo Health Coverage after Being Laid Off

As They Defer Medical Care, Experts Fear the Effects; Will Taxpayers Get Bill? Even Doctors Are Suffering

Detroit—Margie Wilde, who had a kidney removed back in 1950, has stopped having the recommended regular blood and urine tests since her husband was laid off as an auto-supply worker two years ago.

Thomas Arnold, laid off by Chrysler Corp. two years ago, is putting off a needed hernia operation. His wife, Karen, says the Arnolds are putting off something else as well. "We would probably have tried to have children by now," she says, "but the hospital bill would be sky-high."

The problem in each case is health insurance. The Wildes and the Arnolds, like a lot of other people in this depressed area, don't have any. Since 1979, at least 355,000 laid-off people in Michigan have lost their company-paid insurance. Nationally, according to Battelle Human Affairs Research Centers of Seattle, up to 91% of all laid-off people lost their company-paid health insurance for some period of time.

As the unemployment rate climbs—to 9% nationally in March and 17% in Michigan—many of the jobless find they can't afford to maintain health insurance with their slim resources. Some can qualify for government-run Medicaid, but many others simply hope to remain healthy.

DEFERRAL SYNDROME

The United Auto Workers figures that about 270,000 former Big Three auto workers and their families haven't any insurance. Without income or insurance, "people are deferring all activities except the most necessary ones," says Stephen Blount, a medical consultant with the Detroit Health Department. Detroit-area doctors say visits have declined as much as 30% as people dose themselves with home remedies, phone to wheedle prescriptions from reluctant physicians or simply tough out illnesses they once would have had checked.

Mr. and Mrs. Wilde can't afford any coverage on their income of about $400 a month. So Mrs. Wilde cares for herself with antibiotics for her kidney condition, ordered at a discount through a retired persons' association.

Patients are visiting doctors less often, say Baha Onder, a physician in suburban Farmington Hills, Mich. When they do come in for the $20 visit, he says they are increasingly "declining lab work and X-rays." The insurance wouldn't usually have paid his office fees, but it would have covered the additional procedures.

Delores Baker, a gynecologist in Detroit, says that patients who used to come in for Pap smear cancer-detection tests "don't come in anymore." She feels that annual gynecological checkups, which were covered by some insurance plans, were the only chance some women had for the early detection of other serious health problems, such as high blood pressure or breast lumps.

SOURCE: Amanda Bennett, "Detroit Syndrome," *Wall Street Journal,* April 6, 1982, p. 1. Reprinted by permission of *The Wall Street Journal,*

relation to the market potential. The market potential has been estimated by the chain ratio method as follows:

Total number of registered nurses	1,500,000
Percentage who are practicing	× .75
Percentage of those practicing who work full-time	× .67
Percentage of those who are practicing and work full-time who are working in hospitals	× .60

This chain of numbers shows the market potential to be about 450,000 nurses. Since it is estimated that, nationally, hospitals will need 550,000 full-time nurses, this suggests a shortfall of 100,000 nurses.

Estimating Area Market Demand

The market demand for a product or service may vary geographically. So the organization must decide where to focus its marketing effort. It might focus on the area exhibiting the greatest market demand, since it would appear to be the area most positively disposed toward the organization. On the other hand, it might direct its attention to an area that has received insufficient marketing attention from the organization.

There are a number of ways of estimating the market demand of different geographic areas. We will illustrate them in connection with the following situation:

> The Maxwell Hospital attracts most of its patients from Canton, the community in which it is situated, and from three suburbs to the west of Canton. The hospital CEO feels that additional patients can be attracted from the suburbs to the south of Canton, such as Beechwood, Babylon, Barrington, and Coe. However, the hospital cannot adequately market to all these suburbs and wants to identify those with the highest potential.

We will consider some methods for estimating area market potential.

Area Analysis of Current Sales. One common approach is to study the areas current patients are coming from. One can prepare a dot map showing the number of patients from different areas. Suppose the CEO finds that 8 percent of the hospital's patients come from Babylon and 4 percent from Coe. The administrator may conclude that Babylon is a better "market" than Coe, in that it might have more people who are apt to use Maxwell. A further implication is that Babylon might deserve twice the marketing effort as Coe.

Although this is a common way to estimate area market potential, it can be misleading. Current area "sales" or patient volume reflect not only differences in market potential, but also differences in market cultivation. Suppose that in Babylon there are 10 physicians in practice who admit to Maxwell, while in Coe there are none. We might conclude that Coe could have substantially more potential, since 4 percent of the patients came from Coe in spite of the inconvenience of having to go out of their community to see their Maxwell-affiliated physician. Furthermore, even if we believe that Babylon has twice as much market potential as Coe, it does not follow that Babylon deserves twice the effort. It may deserve four times the effort, three times the effort, or the same effort. We would have to estimate the marginal response to additional marketing effort, such as the recruiting of a new physician to the community, that would occur in each community.

Single-Factor and Multiple-Factor Indicators. Here management tries to discover a single factor or multiple factors that would reflect the market potential of different communities. The number of people over the age of 55 in a community is probably a good single-factor indicator of the community's market potential for a cardiac intensive care unit. One study of dental utilization produced a multiple-factor indicator identifying high market potential among families that resided in urban areas, had lived there for 3 to 5 years, were white, Jewish, upper middle class, and with annual household incomes of $10,000 or more.[1]

The health care field is accustomed to thinking of estimating demand using morbidity statistics. While these data are directly related to demand in many cases, they present a problem: Except for an occasional research project by a local university or the federal government, morbidity data are not locally collected and therefore cannot be used. Luckily, inpatient demand is somewhat related to demographic data such as age and sex that can be used as demand estimation factors. Ambulatory demand is not as closely related to the easily available demographic and census data and is therefore more difficult to estimate.

For decades, health care research has noted a set of demand-influencing factors that do not by themselves influence demand in other industries: supply factors. If the automobile industry produces a supply of cars in excess of demand but does not lower sales prices in order to sell more cars, the demand for cars is not influenced upward—or downward—by the excess supply. In contrast, Milt Roemer noted in the 1950s[2] that the demand for hospital beds in a community expands to meet the supply. Subsequent studies have noted the impact of supply factors in a community (number and specialty of physicians, number of hospital beds) on market demand (see Exhibit 8–2). Thus, in addition to market factor indicators, health care marketers must consider supply factor indicators in estimating demand. (For more discussion on the factors affecting supply, see Chapter 13.)

Distance-adjusted Index. One more factor should be taken into consideration in developing the market potential of different communities. Studies show that market potential drops with distance from the site of the offer, because people view travel as a cost and prefer to patronize services closer to their residences. In fact, some early studies indicated that market attractiveness falls off with the square of the distance of the market from the location of the service. Market potential figures must be adjusted according to the nature of the service. Patients are willing to travel much farther to see a specialist for sophisticated diagnosis than to see a pediatrician for a well-baby visit. Market potential is considered positively correlated with the size of the target population and inversely correlated with the squared distance of the target population from the location of the service.[3]

Estimating Total Market Sales

Besides measuring potential demand, a health care organization will want to know the actual total "sales" (patient volume, laboratory services utilization, and so on) in its market. This requires identifying the other organizations serving the same market. This is not always as simple as it sounds, because of the many definitions of a market. Should a hospital with an urgent-care ambulatory clinic identify the emergency rooms of other hospitals as serving the same market? What about a local medical group practice? Or a nearby neighborhood health center?

The identification of competing organizations serving the same market is also being made more difficult by the diversification of some health care organizations into new markets and by the appearance of new forms of health care delivery. Whereas ten years ago a hospital inpatient surgical service could easily identify all its competition by looking at other hospital inpatient surgical services, today it must also identify the ambulatory surgery centers housed in its own and other hospitals, as well as the free-standing one-day surgery clinics. Home health agencies can no longer identify their competition for the market solely as other home health agencies. They must also recognize that community hospitals, rehabilitation hospitals, large medical group practices, and national home health care chains may be providing home health care to their market. The health care organization must carefully

EXHIBIT 8–2 The Impact of Supply Factors on Market Demand

The Health Planning Council for Greater Boston released a study revealing that rates of 22 common surgical procedures vary widely across the face of Massachusetts. Overall surgery rates in Massachusetts differ from one community to another almost by a factor of three, the study found. Individual types of surgery are far more available. Tonsillectomies, for example, are performed 15 times more often in some Massachusetts communities than in others.

Similar studies in Vermont, Rhode Island, Iowa, England and Scandinavia have been remarkably consistent. They all demonstrate that there is very little agreement among doctors about when to hospitalize and when to operate.

The disparities are by no means limited to surgery. . . . The residents of Ellsworth, Maine, are hospitalized for atherosclerosis (hardening of the arteries) 12 times more often than people living in Norway, Maine.

The newly appreciated disparities in hospital use "cannot be explained on the basis of differences in the age or distribution of disease among populations," comments Dr. Philip Caper of Harvard University.

Traditionally, health planners and policy analysts have had to rely on hospital-based data. If a hospital's occupancy rate is high, for instance, the assumption has been made that this demonstrates a need for its services—or even its expansion. By contrast, the above analysis often suggests that the doctors at that hospital are simply much more liberal in their "practice styles."

SOURCE: Richard A. Knox, "The Many Faces of Health Care," *The Boston Globe,* August 20, 1984, p. 41. Reprinted courtesy of *The Boston Globe.*

Study Finds Community Health Needs Don't Dictate Hospital Use, Cost

The quantity and cost of hospital care are linked more directly to the number of physicians, their specialties, and the number of available hospital beds in a community than they are to the health needs of a community's residents, according to a study of variations in health care among 193 New England communities. "Where there are many hospital beds per capita and many physicians whose specialty or style of practice requires frequent hospitalization, there is more treatment in hospitals and greater expenditure per capita for hospital care," according to a report in the April issue of *Scientific American.* The report also found that a hospital's expansion rate is determined more by the facility's priorities than by the medical needs of the population it serves. The more physicians a hospital recruits, the more beds it fills, and the more beds it will attempt to add, the researchers found. Emphasizing that "more medical treatment is not necessarily better treatment," the report concluded that "informed patients may therefore be the most important factor in making rates of treatment reflect health needs and eliminating unnecessary medicine."

SOURCE: Reprinted by permission from *Hospital Week,* Vol. 18, No. 16, April 23, 1982. Copyright 1982, American Hospital Publishing, Inc.

define its real competition as the first step in developing an estimate of total market size and its share of that market.

Then the organization has to estimate the "sales" (patient volume, utilization, visits, and so on) of each competitor. How can this information be obtained? The easiest way is to contact each competitor and offer to exchange information. In this way, each organization can measure its performance against every other organization and against the total sales for the market. In some states, the state hospital association performs this task for hospitals, collecting data on inpatient and ambulatory usage. Private health data consortium organizations and others, such as S.V.P./Find, may also play this role, again primarily for hospitals, leaving medical practices, nursing homes, and other health care organizations with no easy way to obtain market size information. And exchanging sales information is not always possible. Certain competitors may not be willing to divulge this information. In this case, the organization can still compare its sales to the sales of cooperating organizations.

If collecting data on the competition through a trade association or direct exchange is not available, the organization will have to estimate the sales of one or more competitors through indirect methods. For example, a nursing home might infer the number of patients at a competing nursing home from the number of beds, the size of the staff, or other clues. In the industrial world, a company estimates the sales of another company by finding out how many shifts the factory is operating or how much raw material it is ordering from suppliers.

Estimating Organization Market Share

The organization's own "sales" do not tell the whole story of how well it is doing. Suppose a pediatric group practice is growing at 5 percent a year while competing pediatric practices are growing at 10 percent. The first practice is actually losing its relative standing in the marketplace. Health care organizations will therefore want to compare their "sales" with those of competitors.

Organizations should try to estimate at least three market share figures. Ideally, the organization should know its: (1) share of the total market, (2) share of the served market, and (3) share relative to the leading competitor or leading three competitors. Each of these measures yields useful information about the organization's market performance and potential.

FORECASTING FUTURE DEMAND

Having looked at ways to estimate current demand, we are now ready to examine the problem of forecasting demand. Very few products or services lend themselves to easy forecasting. The few cases generally involve a product whose absolute level or trend is fairly constant and where competition is nonexistent or stable. This situation does not often exist in health care. In the vast majority of health care and social service markets, total market demand and specific organization demands are not stable from one year to the next, and good forecasting becomes a key factor in effective performance. Poor forecasting can lead to excess or insufficient personnel, supplies, equipment, and facilities. This is particularly true for inpatient facilities, which carry high fixed costs that cannot be significantly lowered if volume declines. The more unstable the demand, the more critical is accurate forecasting and the more elaborate the forecasting procedure.

In approaching forecasting, one should list all the factors that might affect future demand and predict each factor's likely future level and effect on demand. The factors affecting demand might be classified into three categories: (1) *noncontrollable macro environment factors* such as the state of the economy, new technologies, and new reimbursement policies; (2) *competitive factors* such as competitors' new facilities, new services, and promotional expenditures; and (3) *organizational factors* such as the organization's facilities, new services, and promotional expenditures.

Organizations use various methods to forecast future demand. The five major methods discussed here arise out of three information bases for building a forecast. A forecast can be based on what people say, what people do, or what people have done. The first basis—what people say—involves systematic determination of the opinions of buyers or of those close to them, such as patients' families and physicians. It encompasses two methods: (1) buyer intention surveys, and (2) middleman estimates. Building a forecast on what people do involves another method: (3) market testing. The final basis—what people have done—involves using statistical tools to analyze records of past behavior, using either (4) time-series analysis or (5) statistical demand analysis.

Buyer Intention Surveys

One way to form an estimate of future demand is to ask a sample of target buyers to state their intentions for the forthcoming period. Suppose a health maintenance organization (HMO) is trying to estimate the number of enrolled members who will enroll again the following year. Added to the estimates of the following year's growth in new members, this gives the HMO an estimate of total enrollment. The purpose is to hire enough staff to service the level of demand. A small number of enrolled members can be asked to indicate if they intend to re-enroll. If 90 percent say they do intend to, the HMO can multiply this against the number of currently enrolled members and infer the number who plan to re-enroll.

The reliability of buyer intention forecasts depends on (1) buyers having clear intentions, (2) buyers being likely to carry out their stated intentions, and (3) buyers being willing to describe their intentions to interviewers. To the extent that these assumptions are weak, then the results must be used with caution. Much health care use arises from unanticipated illness or accidents. Therefore, potential patients, when questioned, are unlikely to have clear intentions. Physicians are a little better able to predict their mix of patients, given historical experience, and might be somewhat better able to provide buyer intention forecasts.

Buyer intentions could be asked in a number of ways. Take the HMO trying to estimate re-enrollment. A "yes or no" form of the question would be: "Do you intend to re-enroll in the HMO next year?" This requires the respondent to make a definite choice. Some researchers prefer this question: "Will you (a) definitely re-enroll, (b) probably re-enroll, (c) probably not re-enroll, or (d) definitely not re-enroll in the HMO next year?" These researchers feel that the "definitely re-enrolls" would be fairly dependable as a minimum estimate and some fraction of the "probably re-enrolls" could be added to arrive at a forecast. More recently, some researchers have recommended using a full purchase probability scale:

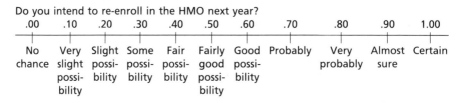

Do you intend to re-enroll in the HMO next year?

.00	.10	.20	.30	.40	.50	.60	.70	.80	.90	1.00
No chance	Very slight possibility	Slight possibility	Some possibility	Fair possibility	Fairly good possibility	Good possibility	Probably	Very probably	Almost sure	Certain

Here the researcher uses various fractions of the positive responders to form an estimate. The researcher can improve the system over time by checking the forecasts against actual behavior and seeing what weights would have improved the forecast.

Middleman Estimates

Another way of developing a forecast is to ask people who are close to the buyers what those buyers are likely to do. For example, a hospital that is trying to anticipate utilization of its services might ask each physician on its staff, or at least the chiefs of each of its services, to estimate admissions. The service chiefs will examine past data plus what they have heard recently and prepare a forecast. Some service chiefs will overestimate (the optimists), and some will underestimate (the pessimists). If individual chiefs are fairly consistent overestimators or underestimators, their forecasts can be adjusted by management for known bias before those forecasts are used for planning purposes. (The greater likelihood is that they will all be optimists in fighting for their share of the hospital's beds!)

When business firms use this method, they ask for estimates from their sales force, distributors, and dealers, since all of these are presumably closer to the customers and can give an opinion about likely demand. Health care organizations can also find similar "experts." A national fundraising organization can ask its regional chairpersons to make estimates, and they in turn can ask their individual fundraisers for estimates. Nursing home administrators can turn to hospital discharge planners as "experts." Asking people who come in contact with the buyers for their estimates is called *grassroots forecasting*. Grassroots forecasters should be given a set of basic assumptions about the coming year, such as the state of the economy, the organization's tentative marketing plans, and so on. This is preferable to allowing each expert to make personal assumptions about major demand influences that will operate next year.

Grassroots forecasting has two major advantages. In the case where the people involved in the marketing process submit the grassroots forecasts, the same people will have more confidence in the derived "sales" quotas they get back and will have more incentive to achieve them. Grassroots forecasting also results in estimates broken down by product or service, territory, customer, and estimator, which makes the setting of individual quotas easier. Its major disadvantage is that, as with buyer intention surveys, it is difficult to predict health care purchases that are motivated by unanticipated, usually unpredictable illnesses and accidents. The more chronic or predictable the disease, the easier it is to forecast. It is also difficult to predict health care purchases that are affected by reimbursement when, as of the mid-1980s, reimbursement policies are changing so dramatically and so rapidly.

Market Tests

In those cases where the buyers do not plan their purchases carefully, are very erratic in carrying out their intentions, or where experts are not very good guessers, a more direct market test of likely behavior is desirable. A direct market test is especially desirable in forecasting the sales of a new service or the likely sales of an established service (or product) in a new geographic area. However, as we noted in the discussion of market tests in Chapter 4, the option of market testing is available only to service operations with multiple locations or to organizations producing a tangible product for a geographically segmentable market.

Time Series Analysis

As an alternative to costly surveys or market tests, many health care organizations can prepare forecasts on the basis of a statistical analysis of past data. The underlying logic is that past time series reflect causal relations that can be uncovered through statistical analysis. The findings can be used to predict future "sales."

A time series of past utilization or sales of a product or service can be analyzed into four major components.

1. The first component, *trend* (*T*), reflects the basic level and rate of change in the size of the market. It is found by fitting a straight or curved line through the time series data. The past trend can be extrapolated to estimate next year's trend level.
2. A second component, *cycle* (*C*), might also be observed in a time series. Health care utilization may be affected by periodic swings in general economic activity. If the stage of the business cycle can be predicted for the next period, this can be used to adjust the trend value up or down.
3. A third component, *season* (*S*), would capture any consistent pattern of utilization and sales movements within the year. The term season is used to describe any recurrent hourly, daily, weekly, monthly, or quarterly sales pattern. The seasonal component may be related to weather factors that influence, for example, whether an internist sees many flu cases versus many sun poisoning cases. The seasonal component can also relate to holidays, to the skiing season, and so on. The researcher would adjust the estimate for, say, a particular month by the known seasonal level for that month.
4. The fourth component, *erratic events* (*E*), includes strikes, blizzards, fads, riots, fires, war scares, dramatic politically motivated health coverage cuts, and other disturbances. This erratic component has the effect of obscuring the more systematic components. It represents everything that remains unanalyzed in the time series and cannot be predicted in the future. It shows the average size of the error that is likely to characterize time series forecasting.

Here is an example of how time series forecasting works:

A pediatric group practice had 9,000 visits this year. It wants to predict next year's July visits in order to schedule vacations for the nursing staff. The long-term trend shows a 5 percent visit growth rate per year. This implies visits next year of 9,450 (9,000 × 1.05). However, a business recession is expected next year, and this generally depresses pediatric nonsymptomatic visits to 90 percent of the expected trend level. This means visits next year will more likely be 8,505 (9,450 × .90). If attendance is the same each month, this would mean monthly attendance of 709 (8,505/12). However, July is a below-average month, with a seasonal index of .80. Therefore, July visits may be as low as 567 (709 × .8). No erratic events, such as a chicken pox epidemic or new competitive pediatric practice, are expected. Therefore, the best estimate of next July's visits is 567.

Statistical Demand Analysis

Numerous real factors affect the "sales" of any product or service:

> **Statistical demand analysis** is a set of statistical procedures designed to discover the most important real factors affecting sales and their relative influence.

The factors most commonly analyzed are prices and income or health insurance coverage where relevant, population, and promotion.

Statistical demand analysis consists of expressing sales (Q) as a dependent variable and trying to explain sales variation as a result of variation in a number of independent demand variables $X_1, X_2, \ldots, X_n$; that is:

$$Q = f(X_1, X_2, \ldots, X_n) \tag{8–1}$$

This says that the level of sales, Q, is a function of the levels of the independent factors $X_1, X_2, \ldots, X_n$. Using a technique called multiple regression analysis, various equation forms can be statistically fitted to the data in the search for the best predicting factors and equations.[4]

Here is an example:

> A regional chain of health promotion and exercise centers sought to forecast enrollment in the next year at each of its centers. The following equation was fitted to past data:
>
> $$Q = 350 + 40\ S_1 - 75\ S_2 \tag{8–2}$$
>
> when S_1 = average education level in the center's community
> S_2 = age of the center
>
> For example, the Denver health and exercise center will be four years old next year and is located in a community whose residents average 13 years of formal education. Using Equation 8–2, we would predict that the center's enrollment would be:
>
> $$Q = 350 + 40\ (13) - 75\ (4) = 570$$
>
> If this equation predicts center enrollment satisfactorily for the various centers, then the regional chain can assume it has identified two key factors influencing enrollment. It may want to explore the exact influence of these factors as well as other factors that might be added to improve the equation's forecasting accuracy.

Marketing researchers are constantly improving the tools for producing reliable market size estimates and sales forecasts. The great demand by marketers for measures and forecasts on which to base their marketing decisions is being matched on the supply side by an encouraging increase in health care data and tools to aid marketers in planning, execution, and control.

SUMMARY

In order to carry out their responsibilities for marketing planning, execution, and control, marketing managers need measures of current and future market size. We define a market as the set of actual and potential consumers of a market offer. Being in the market means having interest, income or health insurance coverage where necessary, and access to the market offer. The marketer's task is to distinguish between various levels of the market that is being investigated, such as the potential market, available market, qualified available market, served market, and penetrated market.

The next step is to estimate the size of current demand. Total current demand can be estimated through the chain ratio method, which involves multiplying a base number by a succession of appropriate percentages to arrive at the defined market. Area market demand can be estimated in three ways: area analysis of current sales, single-factor and multiple-factor indicators, or distance-adjusted indicators. Actual market size requires identifying the relevant competitors and using some method of estimating the sales of each. Finally, the organization should compare its sales or patient volume to the total relevant market size to find whether its market share is improving or declining.

For estimating future demand, an organization may use one or any combination of five forecasting methods: buyer intention surveys, middleman estimates, market tests, time series analysis, or statistical demand analysis. These methods vary in their appropriateness with the purpose of the forecast, the type of product or service, and the availability and reliability of data.

NOTES

1. See Thomas T. H. Wan and Ann Stromberg Yates, "Prediction of Dental Services Utilization: A Multivariate Approach," in *Systems Analysis in Health Care* (New York: Praeger, 1979), p. 172.

2. Milton I. Roemer, M. D., "Bed Supply and Hospital Utilization," *Hospitals* (November 1, 1961), pp. 36–42.

3. See George Schwartz, *Development of Marketing Theory* (Cincinnati: Southwestern Publishing 1963), pp. 9–36.

4. See William F. Massy, "Statistical Analysis of Relations between Variables," in *Multivariate Analysis in Marketing: Theory and Applications,* ed. David A. Aaker (Belmont, CA: Wadsworth, 1971), pp. 5–35.

9

MARKET SEGMENTATION AND TARGETING

The American Occupational Therapy Association (AOTA) recognized that it suffered an awareness problem: Many people, including health care professionals, had only a vague idea of what an occupational therapist does. Health professionals were not referring patients to occupational therapists as often as they might. Insurance companies and legislators also did not understand the role of occupational therapists in restoring patients to the fullest recovery possible. As a result, coverage for occupational therapy services was limited. And AOTA was concerned that not enough high school students were turning to occupational therapy as a career.

To combat these problems, in early 1981 AOTA hired a top-notch public relations firm. The firm was charged with increasing awareness of occupational therapy and of AOTA. In late 1981, the firm sent a progress report to AOTA, from which the following excerpt is taken:

> The primary objective of the public relations campaign is to highlight the many ways in which occupational therapy programs and services fill important social and community needs and to elevate the reputation of the profession through greater public awareness.
>
> Accordingly, the program that has been developed and implemented during 1981 has focused on developing exposure on occupational therapy in the mass media. We have concentrated on reaching the largest numbers of people, working with a wide range of media including national magazines, publications reaching specialty audiences and major daily newspapers. We have also worked with broadcast media, including local and national radio and television talk programs. . . . We structured this campaign with the aim of producing at least 57 articles or broadcasts in order to meet the suggested goals. We are pleased that we were able to exceed these goals.

The progress report went on to list published and pending articles on occupational therapy from a large number of publications, including:

U.S. News & World Report
Grit
Women's Day
Popular Science
Baby Talk
Ebony
Technology Magazine
Senior World
Mechanix Illustrated

AOTA management was pleased to find the goals for numbers of articles placed had been surpassed. However, as it looked down the list of publications carrying these articles, it began to question whether their strategy to address the awareness problem needed to be more sophisticated. The magazines in which articles had been placed addressed a wide variety of audiences, such as women, blacks, parents of babies, the elderly, mechanics, and people interested in technology, science, or current news reports. Yet the people whose attention AOTA really needed to attract were physicians, other health professionals and managers, health insurance companies, legislators, high school guidance counselors, and their students.

Subsequent discussions led AOTA to recognize the need to segment the market. Given the organization's limited resources, AOTA management recognized it could not educate everyone about occupational therapy. Therefore, it wisely chose to target further awareness-raising efforts toward those groups who could directly affect the acceptance, education, or employment of occupational therapists.

SOURCE: The American Occupational Therapy Association, Inc., Rockville, MD.

All organizations sooner or later recognize that they cannot reach and appeal to all consumers. The consumers may be too numerous, widely scattered, and varied in their needs. Competing organizations may be better able to attract certain segments of the market. Each organization should therefore identify the most attractive parts of the market that it could effectively serve. This philosophy has not often been practiced by health care organizations, most of which are divided in their thinking about how to operate in a market. They look upon it in three ways:

1. *Mass marketing.* Mass marketing is a style of marketing where the organization mass-produces and mass-distributes one market offer and attempts to attract every eligible person to its use. The Prudential Insurance Com-

pany could conceivably offer only one form of health insurance and try to attract all customers to buy this one form of insurance. The argument for mass marketing is that it results in the lowest costs and prices, and therefore creates the largest potential market. The mass marketer pays little or no attention to differences in consumer preferences.

2. *Service-differentiated marketing.* Service differentiation is a style of marketing where the organization prepares two or more offers for the market as a whole. The market offers may exhibit different features, styles, quality, and so on. The Prudential Insurance Company could offer full and partial coverage insurance programs and leave it to the customer to make the choice. The offers are not designed for different groups so much as to offer alternatives to everyone in the market.
3. *Target marketing.* In target marketing the organization distinguishes between different segments making up the market, chooses one or more of these segments to focus on, and develops market offers and marketing mixes tailored to meet the needs of each target market. For example, the Prudential Insurance Company could develop a health insurance package for top management that provides maximum coverage for all types of health care services, albeit at a high price.

Health care organizations today practice all these styles of marketing. However, there is strong movement away from mass and service-differentiated marketing toward target marketing, which has at least three particular benefits:

1. *Organizations using it are in a better position to spot market opportunities.* They are able to notice market segments whose needs are not being met by current product or service offers.
2. *Organizations using it can make finer adjustments of products and services to match the desires of the market.* They are able to interview members of the target market and get a good picture of their specific needs and desires.
3. *Organizations using it can make finer adjustments in their prices, distribution channels, and promotional mix.* Instead of trying to draw in all potential buyers with a shotgun approach, sellers can create separate marketing programs aimed at each target market (a rifle approach).

In order to practice target marketing, the organization must complete two major steps (see Figure 9–1). The first is *market segmentation,* the act of dividing a market into distinct and meaningful groups of consumers who might merit separate products and/or marketing mixes. Market segmentation requires identifying the different bases for segmenting the market, developing profiles of the resulting segments, and developing measures of each segment's attractiveness. The second step is *target marketing,* the act of selecting one or more of the market segments and developing a positioning and marketing mix strategy for each. In this chapter we describe the major concepts and tools for market segmentation and targeting.

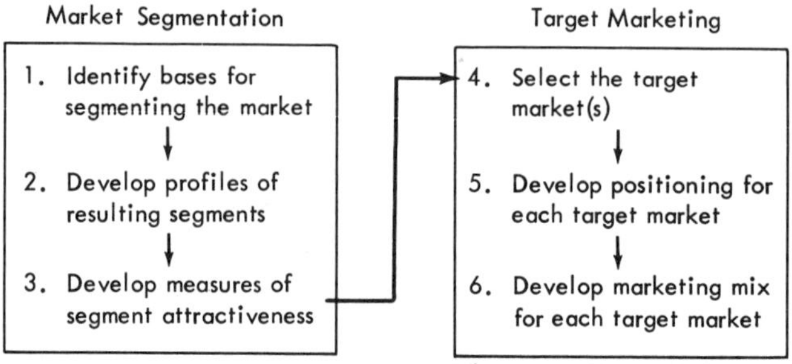

FIGURE 9–1 Steps in Market Segmentation and Target Marketing

MARKET SEGMENTATION

Markets consist of buyers, and buyers are likely to differ in one or more respects. They may differ in desires, resources, geographical location, buying attitudes, buying practices, and so on, and any of these variables can be used to segment a market. Before we look at some of these, we first illustrate the general approach to segmenting a market.

The General Approach to Segmenting a Market

Figure 9–2(a) shows a market consisting of six buyers. The maximum number of segments a market can contain is the total number of buyers making up that market. Each buyer is potentially a separate market. Ideally, a seller might study each buyer in order to tailor the marketing program to that buyer's needs. Where there are only a few buyers, this may be feasible. For example, a therapist tailors the treatment to each patient, depending on what the patient needs. At one level all medical care is customized, depending on diagnosis and required treatment. But health care programs and services are not. This ultimate degree of market segmentation is illustrated in Figure 9–2(b).

Most sellers will not find it worthwhile to customize a product to satisfy each buyer's specific requirements. Instead, the seller identifies broad classes of buyers who differ in their product requirements and marketing responses. For example, the seller may discover that income groups differ in their service requirements and marketing responses. In Figure 9–2(c), a number (1, 2, or 3) is used to identify income class. Lines are drawn around buyers in the same income class. Segmentation by income class results in three segments. Or the seller may find pronounced differences in buyer behavior between younger and older buyers. In Figure 9–2(d), a letter is used to indicate the buyer's age class. Segmentation of the market by age class results in two segments, both equally numerous.

It may turn out that income and age both count heavily in differ-

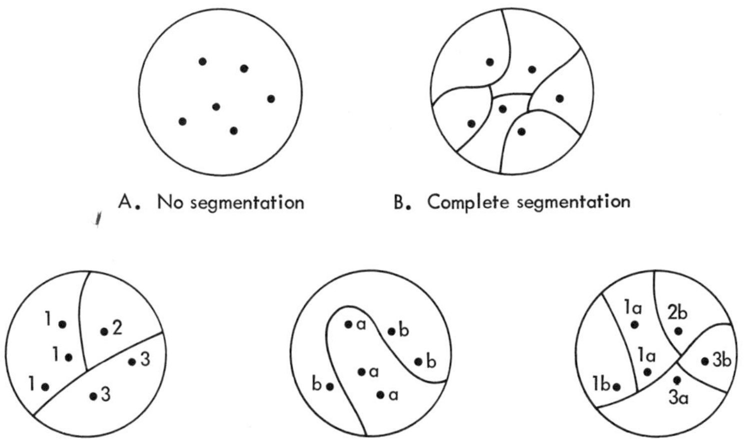

A. No segmentation

B. Complete segmentation

C. Segmentation by income classes 1, 2, and 3

D. Segmentation by age classes a and b

E. Segmentation by income and age

FIGURE 9–2 Different Approaches to Segmentation of a Market

entiating buyer behavior, and the seller may find it desirable to partition the market according to those joint characteristics. Figure 9–2(e) shows that segment 1a contains two buyers, segment 2a contains no buyers (a null segment), and each of the other segments contains one buyer. In general, as the market is segmented on the basis of a larger set of joint characteristics, the seller achieves finer precision, but at the price of multiplying the number of segments and reducing the population in each. If the seller segmented the market using all conceivable characteristics, the market would again look like that in Figure 9–2(b), where each buyer would be a separate segment.

In the illustration, the market was segmented by income and age. This resulted in different demographic segments. Suppose instead that buyers are asked how much they want of each of two product attributes (say medical sophistication and nursing care in the case of a hospital). Now the results identify different *preference segments* in the market. Three different patterns can emerge:

1. *Homogeneous preferences.* Figure 9–3(a) reveals a market where all patients have roughly the same preference. The market shows no natural segments, at least as far as the two attributes are concerned. We would predict that hospitals would highly resemble each other because all have to please the same kind of patient.
2. *Diffused preferences.* At the other extreme, patient preferences may be scattered fairly evenly, with no concentration, as in Figure 9–3(b). We would predict that different types of hospitals would appear to satisfy different parts of the market.

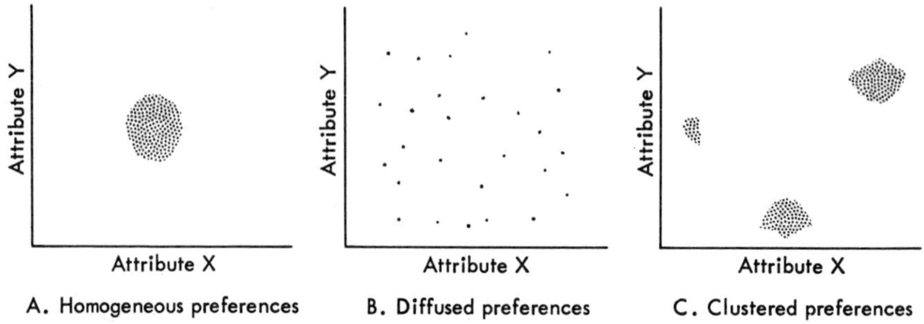

FIGURE 9–3 Basic Market Preference Patterns

3. *Clustered preferences.* An intermediate possibility is the appearance of distinct preference clusters called *natural market segments,* as in Figure 9–3(c). We would predict that hospitals would cluster into three basic groups catering to the three types of patients.

So segmentation could indicate the existence of natural market segments, or it could be used to construct artificial market segments, or it could reveal the lack of any segments. Let us look now at specific variables that can be used to segment markets.

BASES FOR SEGMENTING MARKETS

There is no one, or right, way to segment a market. A market can be segmented in a number of ways by introducing different variables and seeing which reveal the most in the way of market opportunities. Sometimes the marketer has to try out various segmentation variables, singly and in combination, before hitting on a useful way to look at the market structure. The major geographic, demographic, psychographic, and behavioristic variables used in segmenting consumer markets are shown in Table 9–1. We will examine each in detail.

Geographic Segmentation

In geographic segmentation, the market is divided into different geographical entities, such as nations, states, regions, service areas, cities, or neighborhoods, based on the notion that consumer needs or responses vary geographically. Most health care organizations operate in a specific and limited geographic area called a *service area,* presumably specializing in meeting that area's health needs. Other health care organizations offer services in a diverse set of geographic areas, attending to variations in geographic needs and preferences. For example, Hospital Corporation of America operates many hospitals, each with programs adapted partly to the needs and interests of the local inhabi-

TABLE 9–1 Major Segmentation Variables for Consumer Markets

VARIABLE	TYPICAL BREAKDOWNS
Geographical	
Region	Pacific, Mountain, West North Central, West South Central, East North Central, East South Central, South Atlantic, Middle Atlantic, New England
County size	A, B, C, D
City of SMSA size	Under 5,000, 5,000–20,000, 20,000–50,000, 50,000–100,000, 100,000–250,000, 250,000–500,000, 500,000–1,000,000, 1,000,000–4,000,000, over 4,000,000
Density	Urban, suburban, rural
Climate	Northern, southern
Demographic	
Age	Under 6, 6–11, 12–19, 20–34, 35–49, 50–64, 65+
Sex	Male, female
Family size	1–2, 3–4, 5+
Family life cycle	Young, single; young, married, no children; young, married, youngest child under 6; young, married, youngest child 6 or over; older, married, with children; older, married, no children under 18; older, single; other
Income	Under $2,500, $2,500–$5,000, $5,000–$7,500, $7,500–$10,000, $10,000–$15,000, $15,000–$20,000, $20,000–$30,000, $30,000–$50,000, over $50,000
Occupation	Professional and technical; managers, officials, and proprietors; clerical, sales; craftsmen, foremen; operatives; farmers; retired; students; housewives; unemployed
Education	Grade school or less, some high school, graduated high school, some college, graduated college
Religion	Catholic, Protestant, Jewish, other
Race	White, black, Oriental
Nationality	American, British, French, German, Scandinavian, Italian, Latin American, Middle Eastern, Japanese
Psychographic	
Social class	Lower lower, upper lower, lower middle, upper middle, lower upper, upper upper
Life style	Straight, swinger, longhair, yuppie
Personality	Compulsive, gregarious, authoritarian, ambitious
Behavioristic	
Purchase occasion	Regular occasion, special occasion
Benefits sought	Quality, service, economy
User status	Nonuser, ex-user, potential user, first-time user, regular user
Usage rate	Light user, medium user, heavy user
Loyalty status	None, medium, strong, absolute
Readiness stage	Unaware, aware, informed, interested, desirous, intending to buy
Attitude toward product	Enthusiastic, positive, indifferent, negative, hostile

tants. In contrast, sometimes many hospitals in a chain all offer exactly the same service configuration, and all do the same thing.

Demographic Segmentation

In demographic segmentation, the market is divided into different groups on the basis of demographic variables such as age, sex, family size, employment status, income, occupation, type of health care insurance education, religion, race, and nationality. Demographic variables have long been the most popular bases for distinguishing consumer groups in the health care field. One reason is that health care use is often highly associated with demographic variables: Obstetric services are used by women; the majority of chronic care services are provided to the elderly; sickle cell anemia affects blacks and Tay-Sachs affects Jews, and so on. Demographic variables are also easier to measure than most other types of variables. Even when the target market is described in nondemographic terms (say a personality type), the link to demographic characteristics is necessary in order to identify the size of the target market and how to reach it efficiently.

Age and Life Cycle Stage. Consumer wants and health needs change with age and life cycle. Medical specialties reflect this: Pediatricians treat children, dermatologists treat many teenagers, obstetricians see women between the ages of 15 and 50, cardiologists tend to treat people over 50, and a new specialty of geriatricians is developing to treat the elderly.

Disease or Diagnostic Category. Clearly, most health care providers segment their markets first according to the disease or diagnosis of the patient. This is particularly true now that much reimbursement may be dependent upon DRGs (diagnosis-related groups). Some health care organizations are set up specifically to serve a certain diagnostic segment. Psychiatric hospitals, bone and joint disease hospitals, and maternity hospitals all fall into this group. Within health care organizations, patients are often grouped according to their diagnoses. Thus, hospitals may have cardiac intensive care units, burn units, maternity services, psychiatric services, and so on.

Sex. Health care providers operating within a facility have recognized the need for sex segmentation in providing treatment. Women and men being served on an inpatient basis are rarely housed in the same rooms. New opportunities in sex segmentation are arising as a result of the women's movement. Sensitivity to women's demands regarding health care services have resulted in organizations seeking more women physicians, in more medical research related to infertility, menopause, and osteoporosis, and in the development of less disfiguring treatments for breast cancer.

Health Insurance. As the fiscal officers of every health care provider organization know, health insurance is an important segmentation variable. A major goal of many health care providers is to lessen utilization of their services by the uninsured and by government-insured segments, while simultaneously increasing utilization by the privately insured (see Exhibit 9–1). Changing reimbursement policies could drastically affect the importance of health insurance as a segmentation variable.

Income. Income segmentation is another old practice in the health care sector. Many hospitals offer patients a choice of rooms with three or more people, double occupancy (euphemistically known as semi-private), and single-occupancy rooms, the latter often not being covered by health insurance, to cater to the preferences of the higher-income groups. Massachusetts General Hospital in Boston has the Phillips House, an entire building designed to serve more affluent patients. Because psychiatric health insurance coverage is not adequate to deal with many long-term psychiatric cases, income of the patient's family often determines whether the person is treated in a private or a public facility.

Multivariable Segmentation

Often health care organizations will segment a market by combining two or more variables. For example, the Charles Home for the Blind in the past accepted all blind people who needed residential care, psychological counseling, or vocational training. However, it will not be able to serve all the blind in the future because of limited facilities and funds, and because other institutions are serving certain groups as well. Management is trying to assess which segments deserve priority. To aid in this decision, it segmented the blind into twenty groups through the use of four segmentation variables (see Figure 9–4). Management felt that the needs and required treatments of these segments differed, and undertook to study which groups it could best serve, with the intention of concentrating on these groups.[1]

Multivariable segmentation is prevalent in health care. The Shriners, for example, support hospitals that serve a combination of age and diagnostic segments: the Shriners Hospitals for Crippled Children (the child age segment) treat children with orthopedic problems and with burns (diagnostic segments). The identification of people who are at risk for certain medical problems often takes the form of multivariable segmentation. Very often, this segmentation is made possible through the

EXHIBIT 9–1

Segmentation by Health Insurance and Income

Foreign patients have long sought medical care in sophisticated U.S. hospitals. But now, some U.S. hospitals, facing tighter health care budgets and dwindling occupancy rates, have started seeking foreign patients. . . .

Even when foreign patients make up only 3% to 5% of a hospital's admissions, the additional revenue can make a significant difference. Often patients make the trip to the U.S. for major procedures like coronary bypass surgery, which can cost $20,000. The people who can afford such a trip typically come with dollars in hand, and they pay all the charges. By contrast, the Medicare and Medicaid Programs in the U.S. pay less than full charge. . . .

Some hospitals are trying to broaden the market beyond the wealthy classes by arranging payment plans with the health programs established by foreign governments. Miami's Mercy Hospital says it has agreements with some Latin American governments that are willing to pay full charge. . . .

SOURCE: Richard Koenig, "Hospitals Woo Rich Patients from Abroad, *Wall Street Journal,* November 6, 1984, p. 31. Reprinted by permission of the *Wall Street Journal* © Dow Jones & Company, Inc. 1984. All rights reserved.

. . . Humana and other proprietary hospitals have been accused of geographic discrimination and cream skimming. They attract patients who have private insurance or simple medical problems, leaving the poor and difficult cases to financially strapped teaching or public hospitals. Even some tax-exempt hospitals in Chicago are transferring Medicaid patients to Cook County Hospital because these private hospitals say they cannot afford to treat public assistance patients.

Says Dick Rand, health care educator with the American College of Hospital Administrators:

> Every hospital would love to treat only privately insured patients. Given the choice of the privately insured patient who pays full charges and the public assistance patient whose case is only partially reimbursed by the government, of course, hospitals, whether for-profit or nonprofit, will market to the carriage trade. It's prudent business.

SOURCE: Fern Schumer, "Hospitals in the Market for 'Clients,' Not 'Patients'," *Chicago Tribune,* October 19, 1981, p. 11. Reprinted with permission.

		Single Handicapped		Multiple Handicapped	
		Partially sighted	Totally blind	Partially sighted	Totally blind
Congenital	Elderly				
	Working-age adult				
	Child				
Adventitious	Elderly				
	Working-age adult				
	Child				

FIGURE 9–4 Segmentation of the Blind Market *SOURCE:* Adapted from teaching note 5–573–074, The Richardson Center for the Blind, prepared by Roberta N. Clarke under the supervision of Benson P. Shapiro, Harvard Business School, 1973.

use of epidemiological data. Epidemiologists generate an enormous amount of data that link certain demographic or life style characteristics to disease (see Exhibit 9–2). The use of a single segmentation variable is easier, but often less exact.

Psychographic Segmentation

People within the same demographic group can exhibit very different psychographic profiles. Demographics do not necessarily reveal anything about attitudes, life styles, or even health care service utilization. Marketers therefore moved to psychographic segmentation. In psychographic segmentation, buyers are divided into groups on the basis of social class, life style, or personality characteristics.

Social Class. Social classes are relatively homogeneous and enduring divisions in a society that are hierarchically ordered and whose members share similar values, interests, and behaviors. Social scientists have distinguished six social classes: (1) upper upper (less than 1 percent); (2) lower upper (about 2 percent); (3) upper middle (12 percent); (4) lower middle (30 percent); (5) upper lower (35 percent); and (6) lower lower (20 percent), using variables such as income, occupation, education, and type of residence.[2] Social classes may show distinct health behaviors and health care consumption patterns. Certain types of sport injuries—tennis elbow, for example—are found primarily in the upper and upper middle classes. Heroin addiction, on the other hand, is found primarily in the lower classes, as is lead paint poisoning in children.

EXHIBIT 9–2

Who Is at Risk for Breast Cancer?

Compared to women in general:

If you are the daughter of a breast cancer victim, you have twice the risk.

If you are a sister, you have two and a half times the risk.

If you have never had any children, you have one and a half times the risk (of a woman who has had children).

If your first full-term pregnancy came after age 25, you have twice the risk (of women who got pregnant sooner); after 31, three times the risk of the women pregnant before 21.

If you began menstruating before the age of 13 (in the U.S.) and had a late menopause (about age 50 in the U.S.), you have twice the risk.

If you have a history of benign breast disease, there may be an increased risk. (Doctors disagree strongly on this point, since the apparent link may be only statistical.)

Some experts believe that your risks are also somewhat greater if you eat large amounts of fat, have earwax that is wet rather than dry, have a hypothyroid (underfunction thyroid) condition, live in a cold climate, or have a relatively high socio-economic status. Certain types of obesity, limited to fat intake, and Jewish background are also likely factors. One woman in thirteen will develop breast cancer, and this rate may be rising. The risk is lowest under the age of 30 (10 per 100,000), rising as we get older (e.g., at age 70 it is 200 per 100,000). The earlier menopause, whether artificial (via surgery) or natural, the lower the risk.

SOURCE: *Breast Cancer Resource Guide,* published by the National Women's Health Network, Washington, D.C., 1981, p. 22. Adapted from Dr. H. P. Leis, Jr., New York Medical College, in a report to the International College of Surgeons, San Diego Meeting, 1974.

Life Style. Different consumer life styles are found within and even between social classes. Researchers have found that they can identify life styles by interviewing people about their activities, interests, and opinions and clustering similar groups. This type of segmentation is also useful in the health care field. Life style is clearly a predictive factor in health care consumption. People whose life style supports excessive drinking are more prone to alcoholism, liver and nutritional diseases, and automobile accidents. Eating habits, also a life style factor, are related to hypertension, heart attacks, obesity, back problems, and a host of other illnesses. The same types of health problems can be

EXHIBIT 9–3

Life Style Segmentation

Health Services Designed for International Travelers and Visiting Travelers

HERE'S TO YOUR HEALTH: The medical staff of the International Health Care Service (IHCS) at the New York Hospital-Cornell Medical Center has put together a health-care handbook for the international traveler. The pocket-sized pamphlet goes into the food and water questions, immunizations and more. The booklet costs $1.00—though it is free to travelers who utilize IHCS services. For the "International Health Care Traveler's Guide," and/or more information on ICHS, write to the International Health Care Service, New York Hospital-Cornell Medical Center, Box 210, 525 East 68th Street, New York, NY 10021; or call (212) 472-4284. . . . A Traveler's Clinic has been set up at the University of Virginia Medical Center. The hours are 2:00 to 5:00 P.M. on Thursdays, but patients also are seen on an emergency basis. Services include immunizations and medical counseling before a trip; consultations and care, if necessary, afterward. For more information, call (804) 924-5241.

SOURCE: "Executive Travel File," *Frequent Flyer,* January 1982, p. 16.

related to sedentary and to active life styles (see Exhibit 9–3 for a brief description of health services developed for another life style segment).

Some researchers prefer more product-specific life style studies. Ruth Ziff has studied life styles related to drug purchase that would be of interest to hospitals and physicians. She identified the following four drug life styles (percentage of each shown in parenthesis):

Realists (35%) are not health fatalists, nor excessively concerned with protection or germs. They view remedies positively, want something that is convenient and works, and do not feel the need of a doctor-recommended medicine.

Authority seekers (31%) are doctor-and-prescription oriented, are neither fatalists nor stoics concerning health, but they prefer the stamp of authority on what they do take.

Skeptics (23%) have a low health concern, are least likely to resort to medication, and are highly skeptical of cold remedies.

Hypochondriacs (11%) have high health concern, regard themselves as prone to any bug going around and tend to take medication at the first symptom. They do not look for strength in what they take, but need some mild authority reassurance.[3]

Personality. Marketers have also used personality variables to segment markets. They try to endow their products or services with *brand personalities* (self-images or self-concepts). The government's antismoking campaign is trying to attract and persuade teenage girls not to smoke. It enlisted Brooke Shields, an attractive personality to teenager girls, to carry the message. Professional Research Associates, a market research firm in Chicago, has developed personality profiles of different physician specialties, noting that the various specialties respond differently to marketing tools and promotional messages. See Exhibit 9–4 for a discussion of personality segmentation of the physician market.

Behavioristic Segmentation

In behavioristic segmentation, buyers are divided into groups on the basis of their knowledge, attitude, use, or response to an actual service or its attributes. Many marketers believe that behavioristic variables are the best starting point for constructing market segments.

Purchase Occasion. Buyers can be distinguished according to occasions when they purchase a product or service. For example, patients who make appointments with physicians include those who have symptoms, those who have no symptoms but want a checkup, those who are seeking preventive care such as immunizations, and those who are seeking medical advice. Some medical group practices have launched campaigns to encourage the preventive care segment to make appointments with their nurse practitioners instead of the physicians, and have even considered charging lower fees as an incentive.

Benefits Sought. Buyers can be segmented according to the particular benefit(s) they are seeking through the consumption of the product or service. Some consumers look for one dominant benefit from the product, and others seek a particular *benefit bundle*.[4] Many markets are made up of four core benefit segments: quality buyers, service buyers, value buyers, and economy buyers. *Quality* buyers seek out the best product and are not concerned with cost. A quality seeker in the hospital market might consider only teaching hospitals or the best medical center. *Service* buyers look for the best personal and nursing care, and assume that all medical care is adequate. A service seeker might choose a community hospital with nice amenities and an empathetic nursing staff. *Value* buyers look for the best value for the money and expect the service to match the price. A value buyer might go to a dentist who is reasonably priced and who has a reasonable reputation. *Economy* buyers are primarily interested in minimizing cost and favor the least expensive market offer. Many retail dental chains, offering dental cleanings for $9 each, are appealing to this segment.

EXHIBIT 9–4

Personality Segmentation of the Physician Market

> An internist is someone who knows everything and does nothing. A surgeon is someone who does everything and knows nothing. A psychiatrist is someone who knows nothing and does nothing. A pathologist is someone who knows everything and does everything too late.
>
> —Anonymous

Blame it on Hippocrates, this penchant for pigeonholing doctors' personalities according to their specialty.

Back in the fifth century before Christ, the Greek healer known as the "Father of Medicine" exhorted young men: "He who wishes to be a surgeon should go to war." Naturally the battlefield provided those early surgeons with more patients than if they simply hung out a shingle. But it also gave them a taste for the active life, and a reputation for having that taste still clings to them.

Doctors down through the ages have embraced and embellished such stereotypes—even while publicly pooh-poohing them—until every medical specialty now has its myth. Hence we have such species as the intellectual internist, the childlike pediatrician and the womanizing (or woman-hating) obstetrician-gynecologist.

So fine a science has this become that some doctors boast they can spot specialists across a crowded room.

YOU ARE WHAT YOU TREAT

"You can walk into a party and immediately tell who's a surgeon and who's an internist," says Dr. Harwell Whisennand, a Houston cardiac surgeon and assistant professor at Baylor College of Medicine. "The surgeons are all carrying on and having a good time. The internists are smoking pipes and discussing great books."

If you follow this school of character analysis, it will come as no surprise that Dr. Whisennand's curriculum vitae includes college football, fraternity life, a long Army stint, and a close personal relationship with his midnight-blue Porsche, which he asserts can do 147 miles an hour. Old Hippocrates would smile.

Internist Richard G. Williams of Pinole, California, doesn't smoke a pipe but has a passing acquaintance with great books. He confesses to having spent a whole weekend at a Herman Melville seminar. . . .

SAID NORMAN BLANK, PROFESSOR OF
RADIOLOGY AT STANFORD UNIVERSITY MEDICAL
SCHOOL:

"I never tell doctor jokes to my laymen friends. I don't want them to worry when they're sitting in the waiting room.

WHAT WILL WIFE THINK?

Other doctors worry more about what their spouses think of these stereotypes. Obstetrician-gynecologists, many long-married family men, protest that they are neither roues nor misogynists.

A woman obstetrician-gynecologist, Maida Taylor of San Francisco, vouches for her male colleagues, sort of. They aren't all rakes, she says, but she adds that some are inclined toward gross anatomical humor. "One guy I know will say 'At your cervix' and 'Dilated to meet you,'" she groans. "He's a real scream."

Other practitioners with sunnier stereotypes actually endorse them. Pediatricians, for example, are reputed to be warm, candid, open. "I believe it implicitly," says Dr. William Solomon, a boyish-looking child specialist whose San Francisco office is outfitted with pint-sized plastic furniture. He wears ties bedecked with whales and dinosaurs to divert his patients.

"Pediatricians tend to be warm, casual people who aren't interested in quoting the journals or preserving the cult of the physician," he says. "That's because kids don't buy pomp. And it's hard to be pompous anyway when a kid urinates on you or bites your hand."

HONORABLE NEUROSES

Most maligned are the psychiatrists, who are reputed to need therapy as much as their patients. Discounting the hyperbole, some psychiatrists concede there is a kernel of truth to this.

"The stereotype of the psychiatrist as someone seeking to resolve his own conflicts is partly true," says Dr. Samuel Ritvo, clinical professor of psychiatry at Yale and a past president of the American Psychoanalytic Association. "Of course, you can't be very sick and be a very good psychiatrist. But to have some neurosis is an honorable thing."

"The maxim 'Physician, heal thyself,'" Dr. Ritvo says, "is the reason some psychiatrists enter the field."

Of doctor stereotypes in general, he says: "My hunch is that they're partly true, partly received folk wisdom." He even tells of a friend so shy and taciturn, that he found a perfect niche as an anesthesiologist, putting patients to sleep so that he wouldn't have to make conversation.

"As my mother used to say, God has something for everyone," he says.

SOURCE: Marilyn Chase, "A Radiologist's Dog and Other Old Jokes about the Specialists," *Wall Street Journal,* May 15, 1984, p. 1. Reprinted by permission of the *Wall Street Journal,*

Benefit segmentation works best when the benefits people seek can be correlated with demographics or other identifiable segmentation variables, making it easier to reach the benefit segments efficiently. But note that ultimately the health care system fails to provide the primary benefit people seek from the system: prevention of death. However, people *want* to believe that the health care system can protect them from illness and death. Therefore, in their minds they imbue the professionals, the organizations, and the technologies with the ability to deliver these benefits, not realizing the limitations of medical care. This led Duncan Neuhauser, a recognized health care policy expert, to comment: "The more ignorant a person is of the health care system, the more benefit he derives from it."

In addition to wanting the benefits of protection from illness and death, consumers want other benefits: alleviation of pain (both psychological and emotional), reassurance, attention, advice, training (such as CPR), and comfort. In the effort to provide the best clinical care, health care providers should not forget that these other benefits are sought as well.

User Status. Many markets can be segmented into nonusers, ex-users, potential users, first-time users, and regular users of a product. This segmentation variable is helpful to antidrug agencies planning education programs and campaigns. They direct much of their effort at identifying potential users of hard drugs and discouraging them through information and persuasive campaigns. They also sponsor rehabilitation programs to help regular users who want to quit their habit. They utilize ex-users in various programs to add credibility to their effort.

Usage Rate. Many markets can be segmented into light-, medium-, and heavy-user groups (volume segmentation). Heavy users may constitute only a small percentage of the numerical size of the market, but a major percentage of the unit volume consumed. The rule of thumb is that 20 percent of the market generates 80 percent of the volume. Hospital administrators are familiar with this heavy user phenomenon, even if they do not recognize it as such. Physician admitting patterns traditionally fit this segmentation style; that is, a small number of physicians usually admit the vast majority of a hospital's patients (see Figure 9–5).

Because they rely on heavy users for so much of their volume, health care provider organizations should make a great effort to determine identifying characteristics (which are usually demographic factors) and ways to promote to heavy users. For provider organizations, the heavy users are often referral sources. These are easily identified if

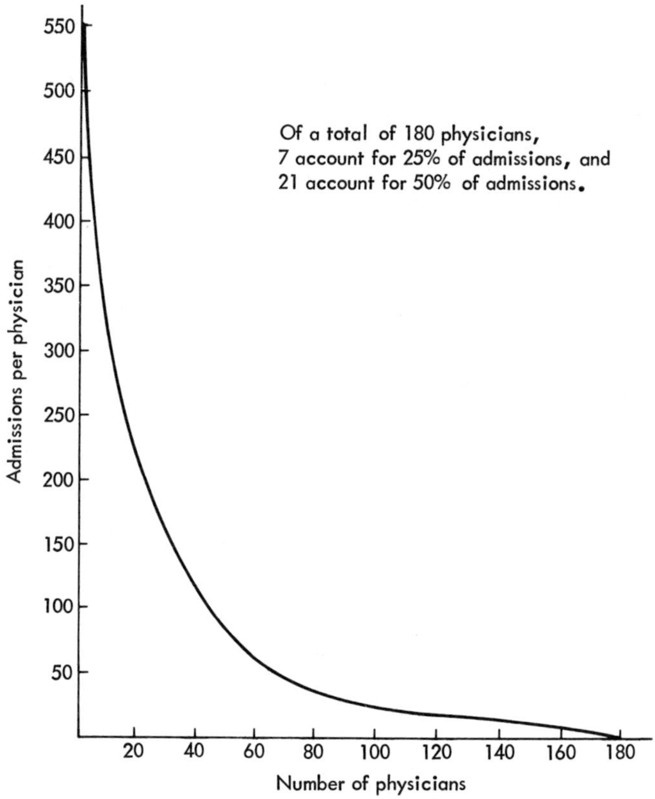

FIGURE 9–5 A Hospital's Heavy User Segment: Frequency Distribution of Physicians Admissions to the Department of Medicine

the health care organization keeps reasonable records, and are most often reached through personal contact.

Other health care organizations might use volume segmentation differently. Antismoking campaigns, instead of aiming at the heaviest smokers, whose habits may be too ingrained to change, are seeking to address new smokers and those who are not yet smokers. Social marketing agencies like these must consider whether to use their limited budgets to go after a few heavy users who may be highly resistant to the desired change of behavior, or many light users who are less resistant.

Loyalty Status. Loyalty status describes the strength of a consumer's preference. The amount of loyalty can range from zero to absolute. A health care organization should study its present customers and analyze their degree of loyalty. Four groups can be distinguished: (1) *hard-core loyals,* who are devoted to the organization; (2) *soft-core loyals,* who are devoted to two or three organizations; (3) *shifting loyals,* who are moving from favoring one organization to favoring another; and (4) *switchers,* who show no loyalty to any organization. If most of the organization's customers are hard-core loyals, or even soft-core loyals, the organization is basically healthy. It might study its loyals to discover what satisfactions they derive from affiliation, and then attempt to attract others who are seeking the same satisfactions.

Physicians who admit to only one hospital and discharge planners who refer to only one home health agency are hard-core loyals. In contrast, Flexner and Berkowitz have identified a switcher group they call the "Have no physician segment." This segment, which constitutes 20 percent of the population and cuts across social classes, has no physicians and does not want any. The segment is described as being young males, usually single, who tend to rent rather than own their homes, to have lived at their present address for less than three years, and who are skeptical about physicians and the whole health care system. As opposed to being loyal to one physician, this segment resorts to hospital emergency rooms when sick.[5]

Stages of Buyer Readiness. At any point in time, people are in various stages of readiness for buying a product; some are *aware;* some are *informed;* some are *interested;* some are *desirous;* and some *intend to buy.* The distribution of people over stages of readiness makes a big difference in designing a marketing program. Suppose a health agency wants to attract women to take a regular Pap test to detect cervical cancer. At the beginning, most of the potential market is unaware of the concept—see Figure 9–6(a). The marketing effort should go into high-reach advertising and publicity using a simple message. If successful, more of the market will be aware of the Pap test but need more knowl-

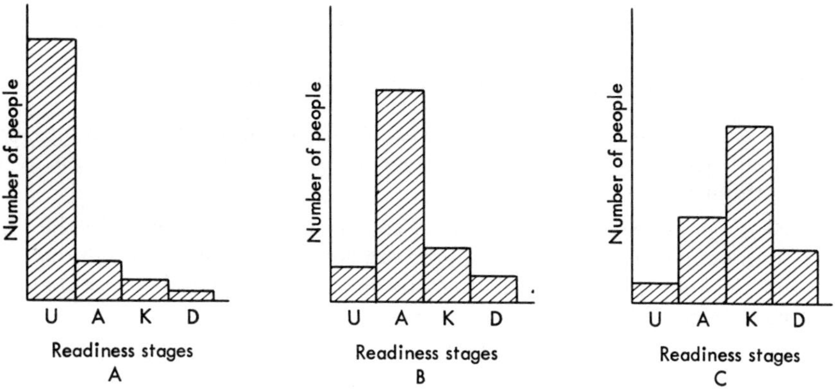

Note: U = unaware; A = aware only; K = knowledgeable; D = desirous.

FIGURE 9–6 Stages of Market Readiness

edge—see Figure 9–6(b). After knowledge is built up, the advertising should be changed to dramatize the benefits of taking a regular examination and the risks of not taking it, to move more people into a stage of desire—see Figure 9–6(c). Facilities should also be readied for handling the large number of women who may be motivated to take the examination. In general, the marketing program must be adjusted to the changing distribution of buyer readiness.

Attitude. Markets can be segmented according to consumer attitudes toward a product. For example, a new hospice in a midwestern city wanted to know what level of support and referrals it would receive from local physicians. It polled all the local physicians who might be treating terminally ill patients and found that 20 percent were *enthusiasts,* 25 percent were *positives,* 10 percent were *indifferents,* 35 percent were *negatives,* and 10 percent were *hostiles.* Each segment has a distinct profile. The enthusiasts tended to be general practice physicians with an older clientele; the hostiles were generally older specialists whose practices were hospital-oriented.

Segmenting Organizational Markets

Health care organizations market not only to individual consumers, but also to organizations. A mental health center wants to promote an employee assistance program to local businesses. A state community service agency association wants to motivate its local chapters to improve their member services. A local hospital wants to convince adjacent hospitals to use its blood bank services. In all these cases, the organization is seeking to get other organizations to buy something. We will discuss how organizations buy in the next chapter; here we want to examine how a market of organizations might be segmented.

We will use the example of an industrial medical clinic trying to identify appropriate businesses to which to sell its industrial health program. Here are some of the major ways to segment organizations, as applied to businesses purchasing industrial health care:

1. By *organization size.* Businesses can be divided into large, medium, and small. The industrial medical clinic could decide that its best chances lie with medium-size businesses.
2. By *geographical location.* Businesses can be divided as to whether they are in the same city as the clinic, in the same state, or far away. The industrial medical clinic might decide to focus on local businesses because they are more accessible and therefore easier to serve.
3. By *interest profile.* Businesses have different interest profiles. The clinic could identify those businesses that have demonstrated some interest in employee health care.

4. By *resource level.* Businesses differ in the amount of resources they have and are willing to devote to particular programs. The clinic would want to approach only businesses with sufficient income to purchase industrial health services.
5. By *buying criteria.* Businesses differ in the qualities they look for in personnel and benefits decisions. Some businesses emphasize programs that are attractive to their unions. Others stress lowered absenteeism or lower compensation premiums. The clinic should focus on those businesses whose buying criteria match the clinic's strengths.
6. By *buying process.* Businesses differ in how much documentation they require and the length of their review and decision process. The clinic may want to work only with businesses that require little documentation and make decisions quickly.

Requirements for Effective Segmentation

There are many ways to segment a market, and not all segments are meaningful from a marketing point of view. To be maximally useful, market segments should exhibit the following characteristics:

1. *Measurability.* This is the degree to which the size, purchasing power, and profile of the resulting segments can be easily measured. Certain segments are hard to measure—for example, the number of white upper-income teenage female drug addicts, since this segment is engaged in secretive and hidden behavior.
2. *Accessibility.* This is the degree to which the segments can be reached and served effectively. It would be hard for a drug treatment center to develop efficient media to locate and communicate with white female drug addicts.
3. *Substantiality.* This is the degree to which the segments are large enough to be worth pursuing. The drug treatment center is likely to decide that white, affluent female drug addicts are too few to be worth the development of a special marketing program.

TARGET MARKETING

Market segmentation reveals the market segment opportunities facing the organization. At this point, the organization has to decide among three broad selection strategies (see Figure 9–7):

1. *Undifferentiated marketing.* The organization can decide to go after the whole market with one offer and marketing mix, to attract as many consumers as possible (this is another name for mass marketing).
2. *Differentiated marketing.* The organization can decide to go after several market segments, and develop an effective offer and marketing mix for each.

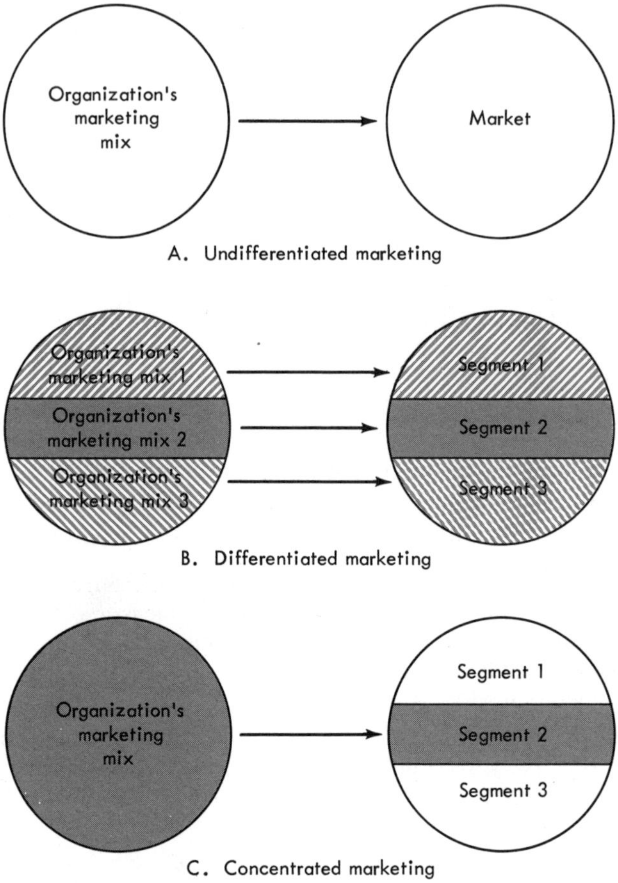

FIGURE 9–7 Three Alternative Market Selection Strategies

3. *Concentrated marketing.* The organization can decide to go after one market segment and develop one offer and marketing mix.

Undifferentiated Marketing

In undifferentiated marketing,[6] the organization chooses not to recognize the different segments making up the market. It treats the market as an aggregate, and focuses on what is common in the needs of consumers rather than on what is different. It tries to design a product and a program that appeal to the broadest number of buyers. It would be exemplified by a cancer center that offers only chemotherapy as treatment, and a family planning organization that tries to promote the same birth control method for everyone.

Undifferentiated marketing is typically defended on the grounds of cost economies. It is "the marketing counterpart to standardization and mass production in manufacturing."[7] Product costs, research costs, media costs, and training costs are all kept low through promoting only one product. The lower cost, however, is accompanied by reduced consumer satisfaction because of failure to meet individual needs. Competitors have an incentive to reach and serve the relatively neglected segments, and to become more strongly entrenched in this market.

Differentiated Marketing

With differentiated marketing, an organization decides to operate in two or more segments of the market, but designs separate product and/or programs for each. By offering product and marketing variations, it hopes to attain higher volume and establish a deeper position within each segment. It hopes that a deep position in several segments will strengthen overall identification of the organization within the product field. Furthermore, it hopes for greater loyalty and repeat purchasing, because the organization's offerings have been bent to the customer's desire, rather than the other way around.

The net effect of differentiated marketing is to create more total volume for the organization than undifferentiated marketing. However, it also tends to create higher costs of doing business. The organization has to spend more on product management, marketing research, communication materials, advertising, and sales training. Since differentiated marketing leads to higher volume and higher costs, nothing can be predicted about the wisdom of this strategy. Some organizations push differentiated marketing too far; they run more segmented programs than are economically feasible. Community hospitals with limited resources that try to serve all segments of the community with a wide variety of services might fall into this trap.

Concentrated Marketing

Concentrated marketing occurs when an organization decides to divide the market into meaningful segments and devote its major effort to one segment. Instead of spreading itself thin in many parts of the market, it concentrates on serving a particular segment well. Through concentrated marketing, the organization usually achieves a strong following and standing in a particular segment. It enjoys greater knowledge of the segment's needs and behavior, and it also achieves operating economies through specialization in production, distribution, and promotion. This type of marketing is done by a social marketing group that decides to focus on alcoholism, or a nursing home that accepts only stroke patients.

Concentrated marketing does involve higher than normal risk, because the market may suddenly decline or disappear. The National

Foundation for Infantile Paralysis almost folded when the Salk vaccine was developed. Fortunately, the foundation was able to turn its huge fundraising apparatus over to another medical cause.

Choosing among Market Selection Strategies

The actual choice of a marketing strategy depends on the specific situation facing the organization. If it has limited resources, it will probably choose concentrated marketing because it does not have enough resources to relate to the whole market and/or to tailor special services for each segment. If the market is fairly homogeneous in its needs and desires, the organization will probably choose undifferentiated marketing because little would be gained by differentiated offerings. If the organization aspires to be a leader in several segments of the market, it will choose differentiated marketing. If competitors have already established dominance in all but a few segments of the market, the organization might try to concentrate on one of the remaining segments. Many organizations start out with a strategy of undifferentiated or concentrated marketing, and if they are successful, evolve into a strategy of differentiated marketing.

If the organization elects to use a concentrated or differentiated marketing strategy, it has to evaluate carefully the best segment(s) to serve. The best way to do this is to apply the General Electric strategic business planning grid discussed in Chapter 3. Each segment should be rated on market attractiveness and the organization's strengths. The organization should focus on those segments that have intrinsic attractiveness and that it has a differential advantage in serving.

SUMMARY

Health care organizations can take three different approaches to a market. Mass marketing is the decision to mass-produce and distribute one product or service and attempt to attract eveyone. Product or service differentiation is the decision to produce two or more products differentiated in terms of access, features, quality, and so on, so as to offer variety to the market and distinguish the organization's products from those of competitors. Target marketing is the decision to distinguish the different groups that make up a market and to develop appropriate products and marketing mixes for each market. Health care organizations today are moving away from mass marketing and product differentiation toward target marketing, because the latter is more helpful in spotting market opportunities and developing more attractive products and marketing mixes.

The key step in target marketing is segmentation, which is the act of dividing a market into distinct groups of buyers who might merit separate products and/or marketing mixes. Market segmentation is a creative act. The investigator tries different variables to see which reveal the best opportunities. For consumer marketing, the major segmentation variables are broadly classified as geographic, demographic, psychographic, and behavioristic. Organizational markets can be segmented by such variables as organization size, geographic location, interest profile, resource level, buying criteria, and buying process. The effectiveness of the segmentation exercise depends upon arriving at segments that are measurable, accessible, and substantial.

The organization then has to choose a market selection strategy, either ignoring segment differences (undifferentiated marketing), developing differentiated products and marketing programs for several segments (differentiated marketing), or going after only one or a few segments (concentrated marketing). No particular strategy is superior in all circumstances; much depends on organizational resources, product homogeneity, market homogeneity, and competitive marketing strategies. The organization should focus on those segments that are intrinsically attractive and that it can serve with distinctive competence.

NOTES

1. For an interesting case, see "The Richardson Center for the Blind," in Christopher H. Lovelock and Charles B. Weinberg, *Cases in Public and Nonprofit Marketing* (Palo Alto, CA: The Scientific Press, 1977), pp. 61–72.

2. See James F. Engel, Roger D. Blackwell, and David T. Kollat, *Consumer Behavior,* 3d ed. (New York: Holt, Rinehart and Winston, 1978), pp. 127–28.

3. Ruth Ziff, "Psychographics for Market Segmentation," *Journal of Advertising Research* (April 1971), pp. 3–9.

4. See Paul E. Green, Yoram Wind, and Arun K. Jain, "Benefit Bundle Analysis," *Journal of Advertising Research* (April 1972), pp. 31–36.

5. William A. Flexner and Eric N. Berkowitz, "In Search of New Hospital Markets: An Analysis of the 'Have No Physician' Segment," *1979 AMA Educators' Conference Proceedings* (Chicago: American Marketing Association).

6. See Wendell R. Smith, "Product Differentiation and Market Segmentation As Alternative Marketing Strategies," *Journal of Marketing* (July 1956), pp. 3–8; and Alan A. Roberts, "Applying the Strategy of Market Segmentation," *Business Horizons* (Fall 1961), pp. 65–72.

7. Smith, "Product Differentiation," p. 4.

10

CONSUMER ANALYSIS

The Preventive Care Health Plan, a four-year-old health maintenance organization (HMO) in a major metropolitan area, had previously been the only HMO in its area. In 1985 it found that two new HMOs, one being offered by a large health insurance organization, the other by a hospital, were to be opened within the year. Growth had been slow but steady for the Preventive Health Care Plan; at the end of four years of operation, it had more than 20,000 members. The local business community had been very supportive, since PCHP provided a comprehensive but lower-cost health care option than the traditional health insurance packages. Initially, in order to assure its success, the top management of many local businesses had met personally with the PCHP marketing staff. This support generated positive feelings for PCHP within the businesses, easy access by PCHP marketing staff to the businesses' employees for promotional purposes, and significant enrollments from the day it opened.

Now, with new competition coming on the scene, it seemed the Preventive Care Health Plan would have to reassess its marketing strategy. PCHP's marketing director, in her recent contacts with the business community, had received clear signals that top management no longer wanted to deal directly with PCHP's marketing staff. While they had been willing to get personally involved in handling their businesses' relationship with one HMO, they were not willing to do so with three. The message the marketing director kept hearing was that she should go through "appropriate channels."

As she sat at her desk wondering exactly what the "appropriate channels" were, other questions presented themselves. She drew up a list of them to discuss with the president:

1. Now that we can no longer meet with the presidents and CEOs of the business community to promote PCHP, with whom should we be meeting? The personnel director? The benefits office? The company nurse or physician? The union leadership, if there is a union?
2. How many of these people do we need to see? Is one enough? Will that one communicate the necessary information to all the other relevant people within the client business?
3. The benefits clerk is often the person who has the most input into the individual reenrollment decisions of existing employees and enrollment decisions for new employees. In companies where PCHP is already offered as an option, is this the person we should be targeting?
4. What do these people want to know about us versus the two new competitors? What will make them prefer us to the competition? What do they dislike about us? What do they like about us? Is cost the only important issue?

The marketing director also realized that there was another whole set of questions to which she did not have any answers. She added them to her list:

1. Who are our enrolled members? We know where they live and work, but we don't know why they joined. What did they expect when they enrolled?
2. How are people who enrolled different from people who did not enroll?
3. Since the employed person who enrolls in PCHP enrolls the whole family, who in the family is most important in making the decision to join? The wife? The husband? Do they each want the same benefits from PCHP?
4. What can we do to keep an enrolled family or individual from switching to one of our competitors? When they do disenroll, to which competitors do they go? Do they go because of cost, choice of hospitals, choice of physicians, or for other reasons?
5. What do we know about people who did not renew? Why did they drop out?

Health care organizations vary in the amount of information they systematically gather about their target markets. Among health care providers, hospitals do a fair job of collecting information. Smaller organizations, like hospices and nursing homes, do a poor to fair job, and most private group practices collect no information at all. Local regulatory agencies collect a lot of information on their communities, but some would argue that these communities are not the regulatory agencies' market; that government and the business community is. And other nonprovider health organizations, such as state Medicaid offices and health promotion agencies, do not collect a significant amount of market data.

Whatever data are collected in all these organizations tends to be demographic, which is the type of data health planners and economists

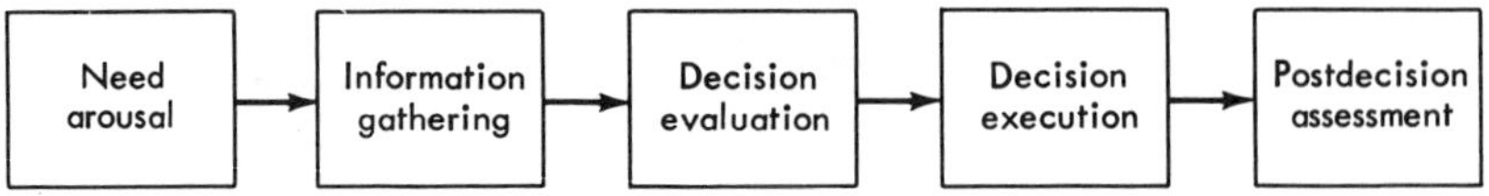

FIGURE 10–1 Five-stage Model of the Consumer Buying Process

are trained to manipulate. Rarely does one see awareness, perception, or preference data, and usage information is available only on a gross level.[1]

Health care organizations must go beyond measuring total market size and market segment characteristics to understanding how individual consumers see, think, feel, and act. This is what it means to be consumer-minded. Knowing the consumer is the basis for effective product or service development, pricing, distribution, and promotion.

When we say "consumer," we mean the person or organization that is the target of the marketing effort. We will deal with individual buyers in the first part of the chapter and organizational buyers in the second part. In both cases we will seek to understand the buying process through which the consumer goes. We see this process as consisting of the five stages shown in Figure 10–1. The stages answer the following questions:

1. What needs and wants give rise to interest in buying or consuming the product? (Need arousal)
2. What does the consumer do to gather information relevant to the felt need? (Information gathering)
3. How does the consumer evaluate the alternatives? (Decision evaluation)
4. How does the consumer carry out the purchase? (Decision execution)
5. How does the consumer's postpurchase experience with the product affect his or her subsequent attitude and behavior toward the product? (Postdecision assessment)

This model emphasizes that the buying process starts long before the actual purchase and has consequences long after. It encourages the marketer to focus on the whole process, rather than on the purchase decision.[2]

INDIVIDUAL BUYER BEHAVIOR

We will examine the buying behavior of individuals seeking to satisfy their own wants. We want to understand how consumers make choices among health and social services they may need or want. We will choose one "buying" situation—that of a woman selecting an obstetrician—and examine it carefully. Many obstetricians are eager to understand this process because the pool of women who will be having babies is predicted to shrink again, as it did in the early 1970s. We will look at a hypothetical woman named Rhoda Smith who is beginning to think about finding an obstetrician.

Need Arousal

The first task is to understand how consumers develop their initial interest in the product class and what needs and wants become involved in their decision making. Need arousal breaks down into three issues:

1. What factors initially trigger an interest in a product class? (Triggering factors)
2. What deeper needs and values come into play when the consumer considers the product class? (Basic needs)
3. What specific wants usually become activated by these needs? (Specific needs)

Triggering Factors. A person's interest in a product class can be stimulated by internal or external cues. An *internal* cue consists of the person beginning to feel a need for, or readiness to do, something. The cue might take the form of a physiological stimulus, such as hunger or pain, or a psychological stimulus, such as boredom or anxiety. An *external* cue consists of something from the outside coming to the person's attention and stimulating interest in the product class. The external cue can be personal (a friend, a spouse, or salesperson) or nonpersonal (a magazine article, store display, or ad). Furthermore, the external cues can be either marketer-controlled (such as ads and salespeople) or nonmarketer controlled (such as friends and natural settings).

One important marketing task is to survey consumers to learn the major types of triggering cues that stimulate their interest in the particular product class. They can be asked: "Recall what set your interest in motion in this object or activity." Women who start to think about selecting an obstetrician may be stimulated by a number of cues. They may be pregnant, they may be thinking about getting pregnant, or they may be wondering why they are not getting pregnant. If Rhoda Smith is thinking about getting pregnant, her triggering cues may include:

1. Reaching age 30 and feeling it is time to become pregnant (Internal cue)
2. Having a close friend become pregnant (External personal cue)
3. Seeing a newspaper interview with a local obstetrician on the difficulties of getting pregnant as a woman grows older (External nonpersonal marketer-controlled cue)
4. Her husband's frequent remarks about wanting a family (External personal nonmarketer controlled cue)

Triggering cues under marketer control can be directed to the target market to stimulate interest in the product category. Antismoking health promotion groups, for example, post signs, engage in public relations activities, and run advertisements to stimulate interest in stopping smoking.

Basic Needs. The triggering cues have the capacity to arouse a set of needs in the person. They do not *create* the needs, but only activate existing ones. The marketer's task is to understand which of the individual's basic needs might be served by the product class.

One of the most useful typologies is Maslow's hierarchy of needs,[3] shown in Figure 10–2. Maslow believed that people act to satisfy the lower needs first. For example, a starving man first devotes his energy to finding food. If this basic need is satisfied, he can spend more time on his safety needs, such as eating the right foods and breathing good air. When he feels safe, he can take the time to deepen his social affiliations and friendships. Still later, he can develop pursuits that will meet his need for self-esteem and the esteem of others. Once these needs are satisfied, he is free to actualize his potential in other ways. As each lower-level need is satisfied it ceases to be a motivator, and a higher need starts defining the person's motivational orientation.

It is easy to see Maslow's hierarchy of needs at work in the health care field. The very poor, for example, will not undertake self-actualizing health activities, like jogging or exercise, until their basic needs for

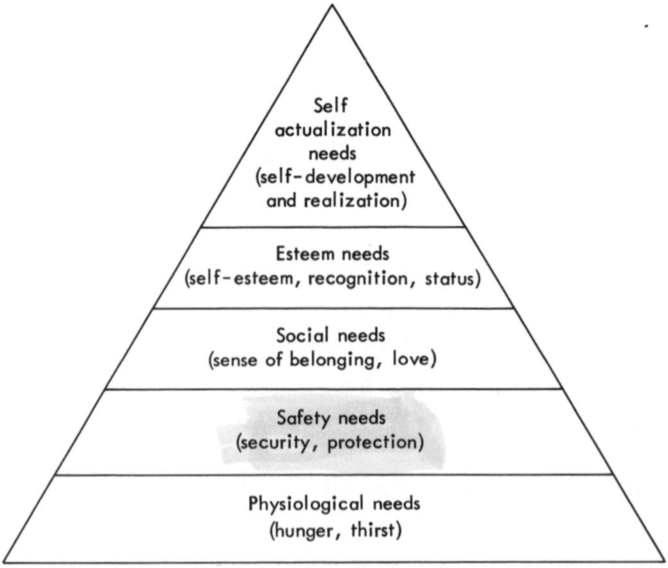

FIGURE 10–2 Maslow's Hierarchy of Needs

food and shelter are met. We see that certain health care and social services cater to physiological needs, like the Meals on Wheels programs for the elderly, while others, like sports medicine clinics and psychological counseling, appeal to the higher social, esteem, and self-actualization needs.

A person's needs may be in conflict. Rhoda Smith, for example, may have both high social needs and high self-actualizing needs. The social need may lead her to want to have a baby, while her self-actualizing need may cause her to not want a baby for fear it would hurt her career. This can create mental conflict, which can be resolved either by treating one need as more important or by fluctuating between the two needs at different times. Here is where *values*—the principles the person employs to choose among competing ends—come into play. Marketers should study people's value systems as well as their need systems to understand behavior.

Specific Wants. People who develop an interest in a specific product class are usually able to identify specific wants they would like the product class to satisfy. Wants are product-specific. These wants can be discovered, in the case of a woman seeking an obstetrician, by asking women what *product attributes* they look for in an obstetrician. Some frequently mentioned by women are these: (1) clinical competence; (2) an empathetic or good bedside manner; (3) willingness to spend time with the patient and to answer the patient's questions; (4) flexibility to meet the patient's requests for such things as a natural childbirth and sibling attendance at the birth; and (5) women obstetricians. Women vary in what they want of each product attribute and in the relative importance of the product attributes. We can imagine Rhoda Smith, for example, wanting an obstetrician who is flexible and willing to answer questions and who has a reasonable bedside manner. Ms. Smith assumes that all obstetricians are competent to deliver babies, and does not care if the obstetrician is male or female.

No obstetric practice can satisfy every woman's *hierarchy of wants.* Each obstetric practice, whether purposefully or otherwise, shapes itself to meet the want hierarchy of some segments of women better than others. Each obstetrician should periodically review whether women's want patterns are shifting in a way that favors or disfavors the practice's "brand" of obstetrics. Exhibit 6–4 (Chapter 6) explains and provides examples of how to measure consumer needs and wants.

It should be noted that, particularly in health care, the assessing of wants must be done carefully and sensitively. There are many health care issues on which people may not know or want to share their true feelings. For example, women who have never given birth before may believe that they want no drugs during the childbirth process, and yet find that they do want them when they are actually in labor. Husbands who are ambivalent about accompanying their wives through labor and delivery may be afraid to say so, given their wives' expectations and current norms.

Information Gathering

Consumers facing a buying decision will do varying degrees of information gathering, depending on the product class and their own level of need for information. The marketer is interested in the following two questions at this stage:

1. How much information are consumers likely to gather before making a decision in this product class? (Information neediness)
2. What information sources will consumers use, and what will be their relative influence? (Information sources)

Information Neediness. Buyers vary greatly in the amount of their information gathering. (1) some individuals collect more information regarding their purchases across many product classes, and (2) certain product class categories generate more information-gathering behavior across all types of individuals. For example, some people will check *Consumer Reports* on all household purchases, and most people will collect a substantial amount of information on cars before buying one.

We can distinguish between two broad levels of information gathering. The milder level is called *heightened attention.* Thus, Rhoda Smith may simply become more attentive to information about obstetrics by noticing newspaper articles about it and listening to friends discuss it. On the other hand, she may undertake an active *information search:* she looks for books on the subject, discusses it with friends, and consults her internist. How much she undertakes depends upon the strength of her drive, the amount of information she initially has, the ease of obtaining additional information, the value she places on additional information, and the satisfaction she gets from the search.

Normally, the amount of consumer information gathering increases as the consumer moves to more complex, high-risk, and important buying decisions. For example, consumers will gather relatively little information on where to have their blood pressure checked. They view this as a low-risk, relatively unimportant "purchase" that can be performed adequately by anyone offering the service. On the other hand, they will ask many questions about where to have elective surgery, about who will perform it, and so on. This is because surgery is a higher-risk, more complex procedure which, by its nature, presents more issues for the consumer to consider.

TABLE 10–1 Three Models of Purchase Behavior

	LOW-INVOLVEMENT MODEL	*LEARNING MODEL*	*DISSONANCE-ATTRIBUTION MODEL*
Information neediness	Low	High	High
Perceived information availability	Low	High	Low

Perceived Information Availability. People's purchase behaviors are determined by a combination of information neediness and the perceived availability of information. Ray et al. identified three models of purchase behavior based on these factors[4] (see Table 10–1). In the *low-involvement model,* buyers who face low risk and simple purchase decisions gather little information. They perceive there to be little information of value available on the purchase alternatives and little information that will differentiate between the alternatives. Therefore, they see no reason to seek information, since it is not likely to change their purchase behavior. A good example of low-involvement behavior is a new employee who is going for a tuberculosis test because it is required by the employer. The employee neither needs nor looks for information on alternative providers of the test, does not believe much information is available on the subject, and believes that all providers will perform similarly anyway. Much preventive care and some early disease diagnosis falls into this category.

Most people assume that buyers act according to the *learning model.* People gather information, analyze it, form attitudes about the purchase alternatives based on their analysis, and then make a decision about which alternative to buy. Economists refer to this as the "rational man hypothesis" because anyone exhibiting this behavior appears to be acting rationally.

Rhoda Smith might behave this way. She might set up appointments to interview a few obstetricians recommended to her. She might call up local hospitals and ask for their recommendations regarding obstetricians, and she might ask friends who have had babies recently for their advice. Similarly, a family looking for a nursing home for an elderly relative might visit a variety of nursing homes, speak with the family physician and friends about area nursing homes, and contact the local hospital's discharge planner for his or her opinions. This would produce a lot of information that would presumably allow the family to differentiate among the nursing homes, and then to decide which is the best for their elderly relative. The learning model assumes (1) that the purchase decision is important, high-risk, and/or complex, so that the buyer wants information; (2) that the buyer perceives information is readily available; and (3) that the buyer believes the information will allow the buyer to distinguish among purchase alternatives.

The *dissonance-attribution model* is similar to the learning model in that the purchaser views the buying decision as high-risk or important, but does not perceive information to be available that can be used to distinguish among alternatives. The resulting behavior sometimes appears to be irrational or irresponsible. The purchaser, faced with an important decision and no usable information on which to base that decision, arbitrarily decides on a purchase. After the fact of the purchase, the consumer may decide the purchase was a wise or unwise decision and may even seek information on the purchase choice.

Many people, for example, pick a primary care physician out of the Yellow Pages, even though the Yellow Pages listing gives no information other than the physician's specialty, address, and telephone number. Given the importance of having a competent physician with whom one can have a trusting, comfortable patient-physician relationship, this decision process seems irrational. However, it is based on two factors: (1) There is very little information available on physicians. With a few exceptions, such as *The Dictionary of Medical Specialists,* which may be found in some public libraries, there are no *Consumer Reports* type publications rating physicians, and aside from the Yellow Pages, there are not generally any easily available listings of local physicians; (2) the information that is available does not allow meaningful distinctions between physicians. When there is information available outside the Yellow Page listings such as is sometimes provided by hospitals about their medical staffs or by local medical societies, it is often no more than what can be found in the telephone book. A few local consumer groups have recently tried to provide better information by listing parking availability, languages spoken, and the like about local physicians.

Some people try to gather information that will distinguish among physicians by speaking to friends and neighbors. Assuming these information sources are not themselves medical professionals, they will be unable to judge the medical competence of various physicians. In addition, they are likely to be able to provide information only on their own primary care physician. The information seeker still cannot compare the purchase alternatives (different physicians). And the nature of the information a friend or neighbor is able to provide is very personal—"I like my doctor," or "She's the best doctor I've ever had"—and not necessarily translatable to the personal reaction the potential purchaser will have to that physician.

The primary argument for allowing physicians, hospitals, and other medical providers to advertise is to allow consumers to make more intelligent and reasoned decisions in their selections of providers. The proponents of medical advertising believe that the provision of adequate information would transform what are currently dissonance-attribution model purchase decisions into learning model decisions. Whether or not this is true would depend upon the type of information included in medical advertising and whether this information would allow consumers to draw meaningful distinctions among medical providers, whether they be individual or organizational providers.

Information Sources. Of key interest to the marketer are the major information sources to which the consumer will turn and the relative influences each will have. Earlier we classified consumer information sources into four groups: (1) *personal nonmarketer controlled* (family, friends, one's personal physician); (2) *personal marketer controlled* (sales representatives); (3) *nonpersonal nonmarketer controlled* (mass media, natural settings); and (4) *nonpersonal marketer controlled* (ads, catalogs). A consumer may be exposed to all these sources. The marketer's task is to interview consumers and ask what sources of information they sought or received in the course of the buying process. On this basis, a map can be drawn showing the most frequent sources. Figure 10–3 identifies the major sources a lucid, terminally ill person

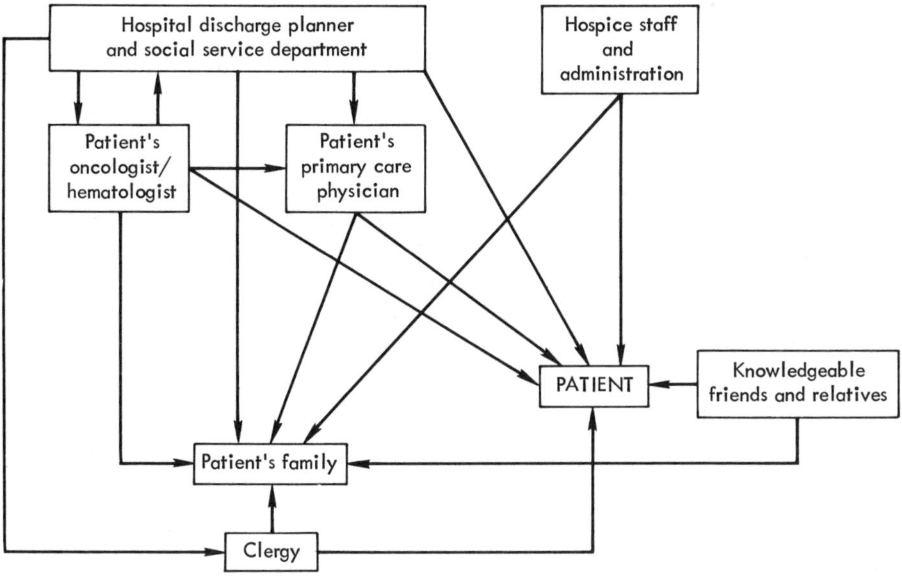

FIGURE 10–3 Information Sources Influencing a Terminally Ill Patient's Hospice Selection

might rely on in gathering information about hospices. The diagram is limited to personal sources.

Clearly, this can be a very complex process. The buyer not only receives information from different sources, but also places different values on the information from each source. For example, the patient may like and respect the primary care physician, but may place greater value on the advice of the discharge planner because she has more frequent contact with the area hospices. Consciously or unconsciously, the buyer gives weight to the source's credibility in deciding how to use the information. An information source is more credible when the source is trustworthy, expert, and likable. In addition, the more the purchaser respects the information source, the more the motivation to comply with the source's advice.

Marketers will find it worthwhile to study consumers' information sources whenever (1) a substantial percentage of consumers engage in active search, and (2) consumers show some stable patterns of using the respective information sources. Identifying the information sources and their respective influence calls for interviewing consumers and asking them how they happened to hear about the product or service, what sources of information they turned to, what type of information came from each source, what credence they put in each source, and what influence each source of information had on the final decision. Marketers can use the findings to plan effective communications and stimulate favorable word of mouth.

Decision Evaluation

A consumer who follows the learning model arrives at an increasingly clear picture of the major available choices. He or she eliminates certain alternatives and moves toward making a choice among the few remaining ones. This process of *choice narrowing* can be illustrated for Rhoda Smith as she faces the obstetrician selection decision. Figure 10–4 shows her hypothetical movement from a broad set of generic alternatives to a narrow set of brand alternatives. At the beginning, Rhoda Smith considers trying to get pregnant right away, not having a baby in the foreseeable future, and delaying the decision for a year. The last two alternatives would allow her to continue seeing her internist for gynecological care, but the first alternative would require her to find an obstetrician soon. Rhoda Smith considers her needs and values. This clarifies what she really wants, which is to have a baby soon. Now she must find an obstetrician. This raises the next question: What type of obstetric practice? She can distinguish (on one dimension among many) among three alternative types in her community: a solo practice, a group practice, and an obstetrician in practice with a nurse-midwife. Again, she considers her needs and values and concludes she

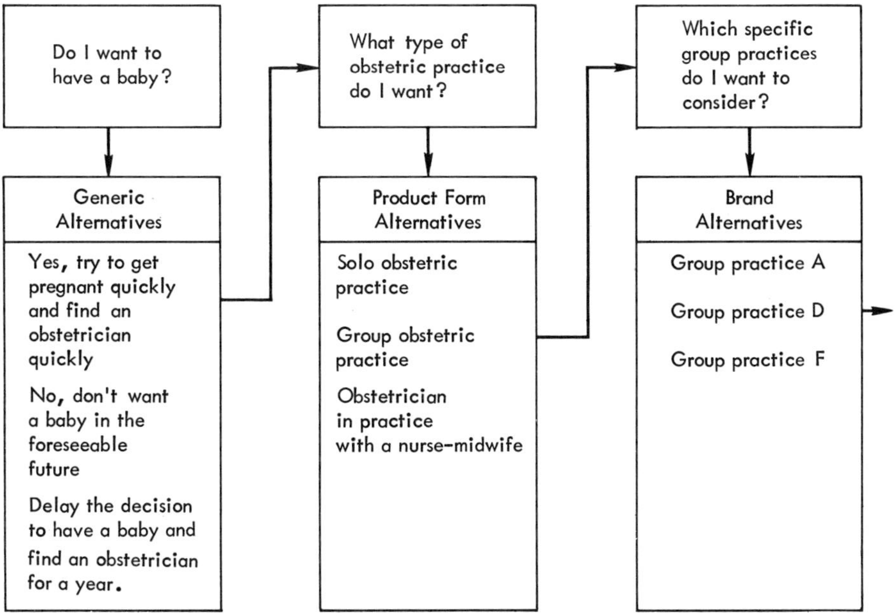

Do I want to have a baby?
Generic Alternatives
Yes, try to get pregnant quickly and find an obstetrician quickly
No, don't want a baby in the foreseeable future
Delay the decision to have a baby and find an obstetrician for a year.
What type of obstetric practice do I want?
Product Form Alternatives
Solo obstetric practice
Group obstetric practice
Obstetrician in practice with a nurse-midwife
Which specific group practices do I want to consider?
Brand Alternatives
Group practice A
Group practice D
Group practice F

FIGURE 10–4 Narrowing the Choice Process

wants a group practice. The next move is to narrow the choice to some specific group practices from which she makes her selection, in this case, group practice D.

We can now look more closely at how Rhoda Smith narrowed her choice to these three obstetric practices. Figure 10–5 shows a succession of sets involved in this decision process. The *total set* represents all obstetric practices that exist within reasonable distance of Rhoda Smith, whether or not she knows of them. The total set can be divided into the consumer's *awareness set* (those practices she has heard of) and the *unawareness set.* Of those she is aware of, she will want to consider only a limited number. They constitute her *consideration set,* and the others are relegated to an *infeasible set.* As she gathers additional information, a few practices remain strong and they constitute her *choice set.* The others are relegated to a *nonchoice set.*

The implication of this narrowing process is that a product competes with a large number of other products for the consumer's attention. If a product is not in the *evoked set*—that is, the set of alternatives the buyer considers at the relevant stage of the decision process, then that product will not be purchased. It is quite common for certain types of health care and social service organizations, such as nursing homes and mental health facilities, to remain in the unawareness set of most individuals, since they do not anticipate needing the services of these

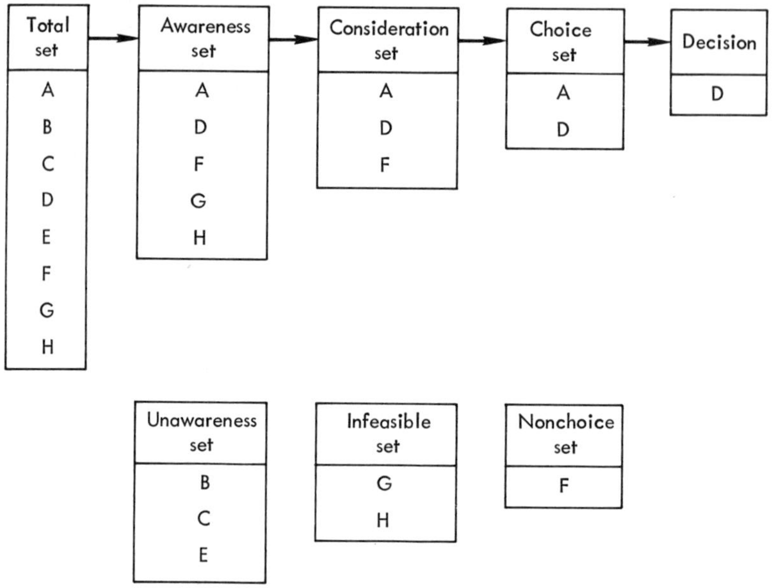

Note: Each letter represents an obstetric practice.

FIGURE 10–5 Successive Sets in Consumer Decision Making

organizations. All health care organizations at times fall into infeasible sets or nonchoice sets. The health care marketer, then, must aim to get the product into the evoked set of the target buyers. In the final step of this decision-making process, Rhoda Smith evaluates the obstetric practices in the evoked set and then makes a final choice, in this case obstetric practice D.

How does the consumer make a choice among the final objects in the choice set? He or she forms a set of preferences and chooses the most preferable alternative. Three standard methods of measuring consumer preferences are described in Exhibit 10–1.

Sophisticated market researchers are able to break down preference formation into these issues:

1. *Product attributes.* Consumers see a given product as consisting of one or more attributes. Rhoda Smith named clinical competence, an empathetic manner, willingness to answer questions, and flexibility in clinical practices as the product attributes of obstetric practices.
2. *Brand perceptions.* Consumers are assumed to have a perception about where each brand stands on each attribute. The set of perceptions about a particular brand is known as the *brand image.*
3. *Utility function.* The utility function is the consumer's varying level of satisfaction with varying levels of an attribute. If we combine the at-

EXHIBIT 10–1

How Can Consumer Preferences Be Measured?

Suppose a specific individual is asked to consider a set of three objects—A, B, and C. They might be three alternative advertisements for a charity drive, three different medical plans offered by a health maintenance organization, or three different CPR programs. There are three methods—simple rank ordering, paired comparison, and monadic rating—for measuring an individual's preference.

The simplest method is to ask the individual to rank the three objects in order of preference. The individual may respond with A B C. This method does not reveal how intensely the individual feels about each object. He may not like any one of them very much. Nor does this indicate how much he prefers one object to another. The method is also difficult to use when the set of objects is large.

A second method is to present a set of objects to the individual, two at a time, asking which is preferred in each pair. Thus, the individual could be presented with the pairs AB, AC, and BC. Say that he prefers A to B, A to C, and B to C. Then we could conclude the A B C. Many organizations use paired comparison because of two major advantages. First, people find it easy to state their preference between two objects at a time. The second advantage is that the paired comparison method allows the individual to concentrate intensely on the two objects, noting their differences and similarities.

The third method is to ask the individual to rate his liking of each product on a scale. Suppose the following 7-point scale is used:

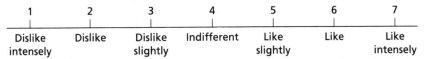

1	2	3	4	5	6	7
Dislike intensely	Dislike	Dislike slightly	Indifferent	Like slightly	Like	Like intensely

Suppose the individuals return the following ratings: A = 6, B = 5, and C = 3. This yields more information than the previous rating methods. We can readily derive the individual's preference order (A B C) and even know the qualitative levels of his preference for each and the rough distance between preferences. This method is also easier for respondents to use than the previous methods, especially when there is a large set of objects to evaluate.

tribute levels where Rhoda Smith's utilities are highest, they would make up Rhoda Smith's ideal obstetric practice.

4. *Important weights.* The consumer is likely to attach different levels of importance to various attributes. For example, Rhoda Smith may think that an empathetic manner is more important than flexibility with regard to clinical practice.
5. *Evaluation procedures.* This is the process by which the consumer arrives at attitudes (judgments, preferences) toward the brand alternatives. Unfortunately no one specific evaluation process is used by all consumers, or even by one consumer in all situations.[5] In some evaluations, the consumer sets minimum attribute levels and drops from consideration those products or services that fall short on any one attribute. In others, the consumer considers only the most important attribute or only those attributes along which the alternatives differ significantly.

Suppose an organization wants to strengthen its chances of attracting a particular consumer segment. Again, take an obstetric practice. It can consider at least six alternatives:[6]

1. *Modifying the product.* The obstetric practice could alter its attributes to bring it closer to this segment's ideal practice. For example, obstetric practice B could increase its progressive orientation if that is an attribute highly valued by the segment. This is called *real repositioning.*
2. *Altering perceptions of the product.* The obstetric practice could try to alter women's perceptions of where it actually stands on key attributes. Thus, Rhoda Smith may believe that the obstetricians are more distant than they actually are. Marketing communications can be used to correct this. This is called *psychological repositioning.*
3. *Altering perceptions of competitors' brands.* The obstetric practice could try to alter women's perceptions of where a popular competing practice stands on different attributes. This is called *competitive depositioning.* This was the task taken by Bay State Health Care Foundation, an HMO, which attempted to alter perceptions of Blue Cross/Blue Shield using advertisements showing a patient trying to choose between a health plan "run by people who bill you" (Blue Cross/Blue Shield) and another "run by people who cure you" (Bay State).[7]
4. *Altering the attribute importance weights.* The obstetric practice could try to persuade women to attach more importance to those attributes in which the practice happens to excel. For example, the all-female physician obstetric practice can attempt to persuade women that having female obstetricians guarantees the best and most empathetic obstetric care.
5. *Calling attention to neglected attributes.* The obstetric practice could try to convince women to pay attention to an attribute they are normally unaware of or indifferent to. If obstetric practice B offers free Lamaze classes, it might promote the classes as a fringe benefit.
6. *Shifting the ideal product.* The obstetric practice could try to persuade women to change their ideal levels for one or more attributes. Since the

obstetricians in obstetric practice B are not willing to modify their practice styles, believing this will sacrifice clinical quality in order to attract more business, obstetric practice B might try to convince women that less flexible clinical practices are ideal.

Health care organizations need to evaluate these alternative strategies according to their feasibility and costs. The difficulty of implementing each strategy, such as repositioning the obstetric practice, shifting importance weights, or shifting the ideal product, should not be underestimated.

Decision Execution

The evaluation stage leads the consumer to form a ranked set of preferences among the alternative products in the choice set. Normally, the consumer will move toward the purchase of the most preferred product. He or she will form a purchase intention. However, at least three factors can intervene between a purchase intention and a purchase decision.[8]

The first is the *attitude of others.* Suppose Rhoda Smith prefers obstetric practice D, but her closest friends strongly recommend a different practice. Rhoda Smith's purchase probability for obstetric practice D will be somewhat reduced. The extent to which the attitude of another buying participant will reduce one's preferred alternative depends upon two things: (1) the intensity of the other person's negative attitude toward the consumer's preferred alternative, and (2) the consumer's motivation to comply with the other person's wishes. The more intense the other person's negativism and the closer the other person is to the consumer, the more the consumer will revise downward his or her purchase intention.[9]

Purchase intention is also influenced by *anticipated situational factors.* The consumer forms a purchase intention on the basis of such factors as expected family income, expected total cost of the product, and expected benefits of the product. When the consumer is about to act, *unanticipated situational factors* may prevent carrying out the purchase intention. Rhoda Smith's husband may lose his job, causing the couple to postpone having a baby until he finds new employment. Rhoda Smith may decide, upon meeting the physicians in the group practice, that she doesn't like their personalities. Marketers believe that unanticipated factors in the *critical contact situation* can have a great influence on the final decision.

Thus, preferences, and even purchase intentions, are not completely reliable predictors of actual buying behavior. They give direction to purchase behavior, but they fail to include a number of additional factors that may intervene.

The decision of an individual to modify, postpone, or avoid a purchase decision is heavily influenced by perceived risk. Marketers have devoted a lot of effort to understanding buying behavior as *risk taking.*[10] The amount of perceived risk varies with the importance the consumer attaches to the purchase, the amount of attribute uncertainty, and the amount of consumer self-confidence. A kidney transplant would be considered a high perceived risk "purchase," given the expense, the possibility of rejection of the kidney, the attendant complications, as well as the pain. In contrast, going to an allergist for a monthly shot has relatively low perceived risk, since it is a low-cost purchase with little pain and fairly certain outcome.

Consumers develop certain routines for risk reduction, such as decision avoidance, information gathering from friends and relevant professionals, and preference for recognized names. This last factor, preference for recognized names, plays a key role in many health care decisions. Because many health care purchases have high perceived risk, consumers are driven to try to lessen that risk. A simple way is to buy the "recognized brand"—that is, the good teaching hospital, the most recognizable health insurer, the well-known physician, or the family planning center with the well-advertised name. The marketer must understand the factors that provoke a feeling of risk in the consumer and attempt to provide information and support that will help reduce this risk.

Postdecision Assessment

After purchasing and trying the product, the consumer will experience some level of satisfaction or dissatisfaction. Based on this, the consumer will engage in postpurchase actions that will have implications for the marketer. Here we want to look at the marketing implications of postpurchase satisfaction and actions.

Postpurchase Satisfaction. What determines whether the consumer is highly satisfied, somewhat satisfied, somewhat unsatisfied, or highly unsatisfied with a purchase? There are two major theories. One called *expectations-performance theory,* holds that satisfaction is a function of the consumer's product *expectations* and the product's *perceived performance.*[11] If the product matches expectations, the consumer is satisfied; if it exceeds them, he or she is highly satisfied; if it falls short, he or she is dissatisfied.

Consumers form their expectations on the basis of messages and claims sent out by the seller and other communication sources. If these sources make exaggerated claims for the product, consumers who buy will experience *disconfirmed expectations* that lead to dissatisfaction. If obstetric practice D does not live up to Rhoda Smith's expectations, she will lessen her positive attitude toward the practice. She may switch to another practice or speak negatively of obstetric practice D. On the other hand, if the obstetric practice meets her expectations, she will tend to be a satisfied patient.

The consumer's satisfaction or dissatisfaction will be greater the larger the gap between expectations and performance. Here the consumer's coping style also plays a role. Some consumers will tend to magnify the gap when the product is not perfect, and they will be highly dissatisfied. Other consumers will tend to minimize the gap, and they will feel less dissatisfied.[12]

This theory suggests that the seller should make product claims which faithfully represent the product's likely performance so that buyers experience satisfaction. Some sellers might even understate performance levels slightly so that consumers experience higher than expected satisfaction with the product.

The other theory of postpurchase satisfaction is called *cognitive dissonance theory*. It holds that almost every purchase is likely to lead to some postpurchase discomfort, and the issues are how much discomfort and what the consumer will do about it. As Festinger states:

> When a person chooses between two or more alternatives, discomfort or dissonance will almost inevitably arise because of the person's knowledge that, while the decision he has made has certain advantages, it also has some disadvantages. Dissonance arises after almost every decision, and further, the individual will invariably take steps to reduce this dissonance.[13]

Under this theory, we can expect Rhoda Smith to feel some postpurchase dissonance about her obstetric practice choice. Problems with physicians, long delays in the practice's waiting area to see the physician, or a difficult parking situation are likely to stir doubts in her mind as to whether she made the right choice. She will undertake certain actions to reduce this dissonance.

Postpurchase Actions. The consumer's satisfaction or dissatisfaction with the purchase choice will feed back on subsequent behavior. If the consumer is satisfied, then he or she will exhibit a higher probability of purchasing the product on the next occasion. The satisfied consumer will also tend to say good things about the product to others. According to marketers, "Our best advertisement is a satisfied customer."

A dissatisfied consumer will respond differently. The dissonant consumer will seek ways to reduce the dissonance because of a drive in the human organism "to establish internal harmony, consistency, or congruity among his opinions, knowledge, and values."[14] Dissonant consumers will resort to one of two courses of action. They may try to reduce the dissonance by *abandoning or returning* the product, or they may try to reduce the dissonance by seeking information that will *con-*

firm its high value (or avoiding information that might disconfirm its high value). Rhoda Smith might switch to a different obstetric practice, or she might seek information that would lead her to feel better about the practice she currently uses.

Organizations can take positive steps to help buyers feel good about their choices. An obstetric practice can send "welcome" letters to new patients. It can survey them after they have had a few physician visits for suggestions and complaints. It can hand out "Helpful Hints in Pregnancy" and other useful information that will reinforce positive attitudes toward the practice. It can send flowers to patients upon the birth of their babies. Postpurchase communications to buyers have been shown to cut the rate of consumer postpurchase dissatisfaction.[15]

Specialized Models of Individual Buyer Behavior

The differences in consumer behavior that differentiate preventive health care and early disease diagnosis from symptomatic care are due to varying emphases on the different buying process stages. Preventive care and early disease diagnosis tend to focus on the early stages of the consumer buying process. Consider the health belief model shown in Figure 10–6, the classic model of consumer preventive health behavior. According to this model, the probability that a consumer will engage in preventive health behavior is a function of four factors:

1. *Perceived susceptibility* to a disease and *perceived seriousness* of the disease—in marketing terms, perceived risk
2. A variety of *patient-specific modifying factors* that influence the motivation to seek care—in marketing terms, need arousal
3. The *perceived benefits of* engaging in the health behavior—in marketing terms, the perceived information availability which can or cannot differentiate between engaging vs. not engaging in the behavior
4. *Cues to action*—in marketing terms, marketer- and nonmarketer-controlled personal and nonpersonal cues

The health belief model also considers barriers to action. But this is more a distribution or access issue (see Chapter 14). The health belief model focuses on the generation of *primary demand* ("Should I get a Pap smear?" "Do I need to keep taking my blood pressure medication?") instead of *selective demand* ("Which doctor should I go to for a Pap smear?" "Which brand of blood pressure medication should I buy?"). Symptomatic health care consumer behavior focuses on selective demand. If a consumer is in pain and the physician suggests hospitalization, the question the consumer has traditionally asked is "Which hospital should I go to?" not "Should I be hospitalized?" Nowadays, due to health insurance packages and provider programs that seek to lessen hospitalization, the consumer is more likely to ask the latter question.

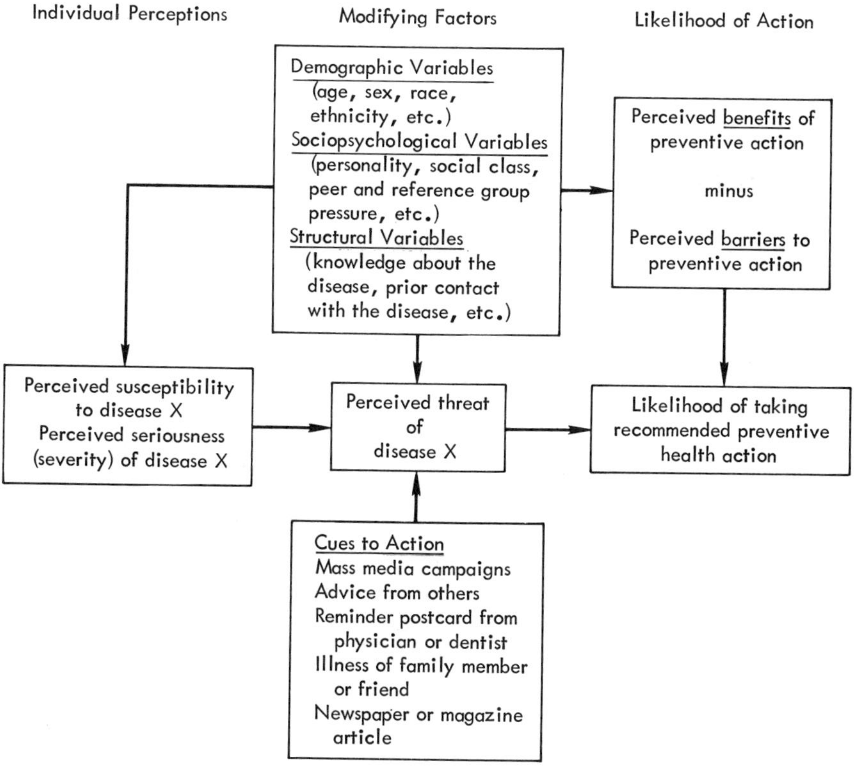

FIGURE 10–6 The Health Belief Model *Source:* Irwin M. Rosenstock, "Historical Origins of the Health Belief Model," in *The Health Belief Model and Personal Health Behavior,* Marshall H. Becker, ed. (Thorofare, NJ: Charles B. Slack, Inc., 1974), p. 7. By permission.

To answer the selective demand question, the consumer must pass through the early stages of consumer buying process, but also put equal weight on the later stages of decision evaluation, decision execution, and postdecision assessment.

We might categorize preventive and most early disease diagnosis health care behavior as typically low involvement; symptomatic care is high involvement. Pain, fear, or discomfort, the ways in which symptoms manifest themselves, are very involving.

It is important for health care marketers to understand the nature of what they are marketing and to recognize that the consumer buying process will vary according to the nature of the service.

Decision-Making Unit

All marketers must consider the *decision-making unit* in their consumer analyses. While some purchases involve only one consumer from start to finish of the process, many purchases rely upon a number of people filling five roles:

1. *Initiator.* The initiator is the person who first suggests or thinks of the idea of buying the particular product or service.
2. *Influencer.* An influencer is a person whose views or advice carries some influence on the final decision.
3. *Decider.* The decider is a person who ultimately determines any part or the whole of the buying decision: whether to buy, what to buy, how to buy, when to buy, or where to buy.
4. *Buyer.* The buyer is the person who pays for purchase.
5. *User.* The user is the person(s) who consumes or uses the product or service.

The health care field is particularly prone to having many people involved in the decision-making unit. Figure 10–7 gives three examples of possible decision-making units involving the health care purchases of Joel Jones. The first decision is whether Joel Jones should see his family physician due to fatigue and discomfort in his chest. Joel suggests the idea initially. His wife agrees he should see his physician, as do visiting friends. Joel decides to go, makes the visit, which he pays for out of pocket, and uses the physician's services.

In the second purchase decision, Joel Jones is still the user of the services, but the rest of the decision-making unit changes considerably. The family physician examines Mr. Jones, suspects a major problem with his aorta, and calls in consulting cardiologists (physicians). They decide to run a series of tests, the net result of which is the decision by the consulting physicians that Joel needs open heart surgery. The surgery is covered by Blue Cross/Blue Shield, and the user of these services is Joel Jones.

The third purchase decision is a little more complex. The hospital discharge planner believes Joel Jones will need some additional nursing care once he is discharged. She recommends home health care services. Various people have input into that decision: Joel Jones' family physician, Joel Jones himself, Joel Jones' wife and friends, and a few of the nurses caring for him in the hospital. The decision seems to be largely controlled by the discharge planner because of the considerable influence the planner has over the family physician in these matters. But the family physician is also in a decision-making role because, without the physician's signature on a prescription for home health care, it will not be covered by Blue Cross/Blue Shield. Also, if Joel Jones decides he wants home health services beyond what is covered, he will have to pay out of pocket.

Health care marketers must recognize the complexity of the deci-

	Decision to See a Physician	Decision That Joel Needs an Operation	Decision That Joel Needs Home Health Care
Initiator	Joel Jones	Joel Jones' family physician	Hospital discharge planner
Influencer	Joel Jones' wife and friends	Consulting physicians in cardiology	Joel Jones' family physician, wife, ward nurses, friends
Decider	Joel Jones	Consulting physicians	Family physician Discharge planner
Purchaser	Joel Jones	Blue Cross/Blue Shield	Blue Cross/Blue Shield Self-pay
User	Joel Jones	Joel Jones	Joel Jones

FIGURE 10–7 Examples of Decision-making Units in Health Care Setting

sion-making units involved in purchasing their products or services in order to identify the appropriate target market. A home health agency, for example, may define its target markets as hospital discharge planners and admitting physicians, since it is they who often decide whether or not a patient will purchase home health services, not the patient. In many ways, third-party reimbursement agencies are also deciders because, in their role as purchasers, they may refuse to cover certain services. This takes away the option of the target deciders to decide on a purchase that will not be paid for. Chronologically, reimbursement agencies must first decide to "buy into" covering a health care service before physicians, social workers, patients, or other deciders decide to purchase the services, unless the patient is willing to pay.

One facet of the decision-making unit in health care settings has been receiving a lot of attention recently—the role the physician plays in deciding if the patient should get care and what type of care the patient should have. As the American public and business community have become more sensitive to the high cost of health care, they have recognized that the physician has played the deciding role in generating most health care costs. The patient may have been nothing more than the user of services. This has led to suggestions that physicians be held financially accountable for their clinical decisions. The California Medical Association has published a booklet called "Cost Containment for Medical Staffs," and medical schools are beginning to educate students about the costs of services and supplies. More important, new reimbursement packages embodied in preferred provider organizations and health maintenance organizations have put physician groups (not individual physicians) at financial risk for overuse of medical resources. These organizations and employers have also begun to examine physicians for expensive medical resource overuse.

Another aspect of the "physician as decider" role that is coming under scrutiny regards the paternalism inherent in one person (the physician) deciding what another person (the patient) will buy in the way of medical services and products. Consumerism has entered the health care field, creating a large group of consumers who want to ask more questions, get more answers, and make their own decisions about purchases of health care services. One manifestation is the People's Medical Society, a health care consumerism group started in 1983 which, only two years later, had a membership of 65,000. Also indicative of this growing consumer feeling is the following:

> If you have ever hired a lawyer, an architect, or an accountant, you've probably felt that they were working *for* you and therefore you had little hesitancy about dropping them if you weren't pleased. Contrast such feeling with those you have toward doctors. Even those among us who can afford to have (we never say "hire") private physicians don't assume that they are automatically working in our service. More likely, we feel hesitant to question their procedures, their fees, or their hours, and often we're simply grateful that we're able to see them at all, particularly if they're well recommended. Even if we don't like them, we worry about dropping them. Will we be able to find another? Will another have the right hospital affiliations? Suppose the new one is worse than the old? Because we feel so little control over doctors, we exempt them from the kind of judgment we exercise over other professionals for whose services we pay. Nevertheless, so long as we're paying, we retain an element of choice, albeit small. We can shop around, we can compare notes and we can drop one doctor and switch to another, even if we do so hesitantly.[16]

Even medical products marketers are beginning to take note of this trend. Traditionally, pharmaceutical manufacturers have promoted prescription drugs to physicians, because the consumer cannot purchase the drugs without a physician's prescription. That is, even though the consumer is the user (and usually the purchaser as well), the physician is the decider. In an effort to allow the consumer to play a greater role in the decision-making process, Merck, Sharp & Dohme has begun to advertise a prescription drug, Pneumovax, directly to the consumer. While the consumer movement heralds this as one more step (as well as the laws regarding consumer-requested substitution of generic drugs for brand name drugs) toward giving the consumer greater control in the decision-making unit affecting health care purchases, others worry that it will take away from the physician power that really belongs in the physician's hands (see Exhibit 10–2).

Health care organizations have sometimes overestimated the decision-making role of physicians in health care purchases as well. The Massachusetts State Medicaid Office, in a federally funded research project, was attempting to decrease physicians' prescribing of medically ineffective procedures. One of these procedures was at-home respiratory therapy following hospitalization, which was ineffective in about 80 percent of the cases for which it was prescribed. Figuring that physicians were the appropriate target because their prescription was necessary to get reimbursement for therapy, the state Medicaid office sent letters explaining what they wanted to every Massachusetts physician who had prescribed at-home respiratory therapy to a Medicaid patient within the three previous years. The research group watched physician prescribing behavior and, seeing no change after six months, wondered what went wrong.

What was wrong was a failure of the researchers to assess the decision-making unit roles correctly. Many of the therapists who provided therapy to hospitalized patients would say to the physician, "I think this patient should continue respiratory therapy at home." The physician, knowing little about respiratory therapy and assuming the therapist was the expert on the matter, would automatically say "Fine," and sign the prescription. It was really the respiratory therapist who should have been the Medicaid reseacher's target. The respiratory therapist was the decider; the physician could have been viewed as little more than a hand with a pen and a prescription blank.

There are, of course, thousands of other examples of failure to understand the decision-making unit in a health care purchase. Health care organizations must identify who plays what roles in the decision-making units relevant to their offering. They must decide who is truly the decider or the most important people influencing the outcome of the consumer choice process. It is those people who constitute the target market around whom the health care organization's marketing strategy is built.

ORGANIZATION BUYER BEHAVIOR

Health care and social services organizations market not only to individuals, but also to organizations. Here are some examples:

> An ambulatory mental health center wishes to expand its clientele by gaining referrals from the local school system and from the courts. It must determine what features to incorporate into its services in order to make itself attractive to these organizations.

EXHIBIT 10–2

It's Just What TV Ordered

The good news for hypochondriacs today is that the Food and Drug Administration has given permission to companies to advertise prescription drugs directly to the public.

There is no law on the books preventing pharmaceutical people from advertising prescription-type drugs to patients, but they refrained from doing it in the past, figuring the doctor might be a better judge of what the patient needed.

But business is business, and the companies now feel if a patient is educated in the efficacy of a certain prescription drug, sales will soar, and it will give doctors less work to do.

The only ones who are not thrilled by the pharmaceutical companies drumbeating their prescription drugs are doctors. The fear is that most people bombarded by commercials may believe the actors on TV, rather than their physicians.

There is no reason NOT to believe that this scene may soon be playing in your local doctor's office:

The M.D., after examining the patient: "You seem to have a chest infection. I'm going to give you a prescription. Take four a day, six hours apart."

"What are you giving me?"

"Dundemycin. I've had very good luck with it for chest infections."

"But eight out of ten doctors are prescribing Carraflex for people with chest problems."

"Where did you hear that?"

"Orsen Welles said it on television during a commercial last night. I think it was Orsen Wells—but it could have been Robert Young or Ricardo Montalban."

"With all due respect to those fine actors, I don't believe they know much about chest infections."

"Maybe so, but whoever it was held up a test tube of bronchial bacteria and then showed how Carraflex killed them twice as fast as Dundemycin."

"The reason I don't prescribe Carraflex is that it tends to have side effects such as nausea, palpitations of the heart, and can even cause severe kidney damage."

"They didn't say anything about that in the commercial."

"They wouldn't. If they had to read all the side effects of Carraflex, they couldn't afford the TV time. Please take the Dundemycin. I'm sure it will clear it up."

"I don't know, Doc. I respect you, but Orson Welles knows a lot about medicine. And Robert Young has played a doctor on TV for years. And as far as Ricardo Montalban goes, I'm not one of those people who think a guy is a lousy M.D. just because he speaks with an accent."

"You're going to have to get another doctor if you want a different prescription."

"That's what they said in the TV commercial. 'If your M.D. is not clued in on the miraculous medical benefits of Carraflex, find yourself a doctor who is!' No hard feelings, Doc?"

"Of course not. Miss Denna, send in the next patient. Ah, Mr. Rubin, what seems to be wrong?"

"You gave me a sleeping pill prescription for Lahdeedah."

"I remember. You said it was satisfactory."

"Yes, but that's before I heard about Blissnatabs. Apparently they're the only pills on the market that make you dream of Brooke Shields."

"Who told you that?"

"Brooke Shields. She did a commercial on it last night."

"Frankly, with your blood pressure I don't think you're up to dreaming about Brooke Shields. Besides, Blissnatabs are twice as expensive as Lahdeedah, because of this particular advertising campaign."

"You doctors are all alike. You resent your patients knowing as much about medicine as you do."

SOURCE: Art Buchwald, "It's just what TV ordered," *The Boston Globe,* March 16, 1982, p. 17.

A large hospital is trying to convince a group of small hospitals to share services, such as laundry and lab work, to bring down costs. The hospital is also trying to convince the local health system agency to approve its application to open a new burn unit to serve the area. And it is negotiating with the two largest employers in its service area to utilize its physicians and facilities in a preferred provider organization.

A national clinical professional association needs a strategy to convince its local chapters to take voluntarily a smaller share of the membership dues so that more money will be available to lobby in Washington for certain reforms.

The PSRO of Worcester, Massachusetts, wants to market potentially cost-saving "private review" services to area industry. The services consist of PSRO-employed physicians monitoring the volume and type of health services received by employees of the businesses.

Health care organizations need to understand the buying organization's needs, resources, policies, and buying procedures. They must take into account several considerations not normally found in consumer marketing:

1. Organizations buy goods, services, and ideas for such purposes as making profits, reducing costs, serving their internal clientele's needs, and meeting social, regulatory, and legal obligations.

2. More persons may participate in organizational buying decisions than in consumer buying decisions. The decision participants usually have varying responsibilities and apply varying criteria to the purchase decision.
3. The buyers operate under the shadow of formal policies, constraints, and requirements established by their organizations.
4. Selling to organizations involves more personal contact and negotiation than consumer marketing.

We are now ready to examine how organization buyers move through the buying process. As an illustration, we will assume that the Cleveland Clinic hopes to attract a large corporation to make a major grant toward building a new clinic wing.

Need Arousal

The first step calls for the marketer to identify corporate prospects and to gain their attention and interest in the proposal. The Cleveland Clinic would approach corporations that have made generous gifts to health care organizations and corporations whose employees rely heavily on the Cleveland Clinic for medical care. "Qualifying the prospect" can save the marketer much wasted time and effort.

The next step is to understand the basic needs and wants of target organizations. This is fairly straightforward in the case of corporations, whose main objectives are to make money, save money, and be good corporate citizens. The Cleveland Clinic can help corporations save money by offering health care at a lower cost to their employees or by mounting preventive care and early disease diagnosis programs that will keep their employees healthier, thereby lowering absenteeism, turnover, and health care costs. It can also appeal to the corporation's wish to be a good corporate citizen. Most corporations welcome favorable publicity about their "good deeds"; in this way, they build a fund of goodwill they can draw upon when adverse events take place. The Cleveland Clinic can meet this need by offering to name the new wing after the corporation or arrange other publicity showing the corporation's generosity.

The selling organization needs to analyze the objectives or mission, goals, plans, and criteria of each prospect organization so that it can develop appropriate products and appeals. A health care organization must develop its offerings and state its case in a way that meets the issues uppermost in the minds of the prospect buyer organizations.

Information Gathering

The buying organization will need to consider the selling organization's proposition and gather information. The amount of information needed will depend on the type of buying situation and on the buying organization's familiarity with the seller. Robinson et al. distinguish among three types of buying situations called *buy classes:*[17]

1. *Straight rebuy.* Here the buying organization is buying something similar to what it has bought before. For example, the local corporation may make a small donation to the Cleveland Clinic every year. In the absence of major new factors, it might donate the same amount as the previous year. It may also have purchased the services of a Cleveland-Clinic-sponsored stop-smoking program for the three previous years and will do so again the following year. This is analogous to "routinized response behavior" in the individual buying situation. In a straight rebuy, the buyer will not need much information because it knows the proposition and the seller from previous dealings.
2. *Modified rebuy.* The modified rebuy describes a situation where the buyer is considering modifying something it has purchased in the past. The task calls for "limited problem solving" and hence more information than in the case of a straight rebuy. The local corporation will want specific information to evaluate whether the Cleveland Clinic needs a new wing, whether the new wing will result in lower overall health care costs or broader health care capabilities for its employees, and what alternative financing is available.
3. *New task.* The new task faces an organizational buyer presented with a new offer of an unfamiliar kind from an unfamiliar seller. An example would be a Houston corporation, which has never had contact with the Cleveland Clinic, being asked to donate the new wing. The Houston corporation will face extensive problem solving and need to gather considerable information prior to making any decision.

Another issue deals with the likely sources of information to which the organizational buyer will turn. One source is the seller. The seller can be more effective by supplying relevant and credible information to the buying organization. The seller should also anticipate the other information sources the organization buyer is likely to tap in the information-gathering process.

Decision Evaluation

Each buying organization will have certain established ways of evaluating different types of "purchases." Straight rebuy decisions may be in the hands of a single officer who makes the decision in a fairly routine way. Modified rebuys may be in the hands of a small middle management committee, with the members coming from different business functions. New tasks may be in the hands of a high-level management committee, again with members representing different areas.

The seller must attempt to identify the people in the buying organization who are likely to be involved in the buying process. Webster and Wind call the decision-making unit of a buying organization the *buying center,* defined as "all those individuals and groups who participate in the purchasing decision-making process, who share some common goals and the risks arising from the decisions."[18] The buying center includes all members of the organization who play any of five roles in the buying process:[19]

1. *Users.* Users are the members of the organization who will use the product or service. In many cases, the users initiate the buying project and play an important role in defining the specifications.
2. *Influencers.* Influencers are those members of the organization who directly or indirectly influence the buying decision. They often help develop specifications and also provide information for evaluating alternatives. Expert personnel are particularly important as influencers.
3. *Buyers.* Buyers are organizational members with formal authority for selecting among competitive suppliers and negotiating terms. Buyers may help shape product specification, but they play their major role in selecting vendors and negotiating within the buying constraints.
4. *Deciders.* Deciders are organizational members who have formal or informal power to select or approve the final suppliers. In the routine buying of standard items, the buyers are often the deciders. In more complex buying, the officers of the buying organization are often the deciders.
5. *Gatekeepers.* Gatekeepers are members of the organization who control the flow of information to others. For example, a purchasing agent (for products) or benefits officer (for health services) can prevent sellers from seeing and influencing others in the organization.

The seller's task is to identify the members of the buying center and try to figure out (1) in what decisions they exercise influence, (2) their relative degree of influence, and (3) the evaluation criteria each decision participant uses. This knowledge can help the seller know the *key buying influencers* who must be reached personally (through multilevel, in-depth selling) or through nonpersonal communications.

Organization buyers are subject to many influences when they meet to make decisions. The process may be highly rational, in that the buyers rate proposals on such attributes as (1) seller credibility, (2) seller efficiency, (3) impact of the proposal on profits, costs, and other dimensions, (4) amount of goodwill created, and so on. To the extent that the process is a rational one, the seller will want to make the strongest case in rational terms.

For example, starting in fall 1982, California hospitals wishing to continue to be reimbursed for treating Medi-Cal (California Medicaid) patients were forced to arrange contracts with a special negotiator in the governor's office. This individual, called the Medi-Cal czar, was charged with negotiating purchase agreements (contracts) based primarily on competitive bids for per diem costs. In addition, other rational factors were considered:

> beneficiary access, utilization controls, ability to render quality services efficiently and economically, ability to provide or arrange needed specialized services, protection against fraud and abuse, other factors which would enhance the quality of care, capacity to provide a given tertiary service, such as specialized children's services, on a regional basis, and recognition of the variations in severity of illness and complexity of care.[20]

Sellers also recognize the role of personal motives in the organization buying process, such as buyers who respond to personal favors (self-aggrandizement), to attention (ego enhancement), or to personal risk containment (risk avoiders). A study of buyers in ten large organizations concluded:

> Corporate decision-makers remain human after they enter the office. They respond to "image"; they buy from companies to which they feel "close"; they favor suppliers who show them respect and personal considerations, and who do extra things "for them"; they "over-react" to real or imagined slights, tending to reject companies which fail to respond or delay in submitting requested bids.[21]

This suggests that sellers should also take into account the human and social factors in buying situations and address emotional and interpersonal as well as rational appeals.

Decision Execution

After the buying organization has decided to favor the offer, it must put the finishing touches on it. Buyer and seller have to negotiate the exact terms and timing of various steps. The corporation that agrees to make a gift to the Cleveland Clinic would need to decide on the exact amount, how to pay it, when to pay it, and what compliance conditions to establish. Any of these steps can involve further negotiation. The seller should anticipate these issues and be prepared to work them through smoothly.

Organization buyers have also been known to cancel or withdraw at the last minute, given new conditions or information. The buyer may have heard something negative about the seller or may have encountered a cash flow problem. The practical implication is that the seller's work is not done after receiving news of a favorable decision. The alert seller will want to keep in touch with the buyer to make sure that the agreement is enacted smoothly.

Postdecision Assessment

The buying organization will usually undertake a periodic performance audit to make sure that the seller is performing according to expectations. It is in the seller's interest to negotiate clear performance goals with the buying organization in the decision stage. Then the seller knows what is expected and can periodically supply the buyer with relevant information on performance. The Cleveland Clinic, for example, can keep a large corporate donor informed about the way the money is spent and the results achieved with the grant. By demonstrating responsible performance, the clinic will be able to go back to the same corporation and ask for another grant based on the satisfactory results it has produced.

SUMMARY

At the heart of marketing analysis is the understanding of human needs, wants, and buying behavior. We can distinguish between individual and organizational buying behavior. Because the individual's buying behavior in health care services is often a function of an extensive decision-making unit, the differences between individual and organizational buying behavior are more of degree than of kind.

Individual buyers tend to pass through five stages in connection with a purchase. The first stage is need arousal, which involves understanding what factors trigger interest in the product category, what basic needs become involved, and what specific wants are activated by these underlying needs. The second stage, information gathering, consists of the prospective buyer needing certain information and approaching certain sources for this information. The third stage, decision evaluation, consists of the buyer evaluating choices and developing a preference for one of them. The fourth stage, decision execution, describes additional factors (the attitudes of others, anticipated and unanticipated situational factors) that influence the final choice. The fifth stage, postdecision assessment, involves the buyer in reviewing the purchase, experiencing satisfaction or dissatisfaction, and taking postpurchase action. Preventive care, early disease diagnosis, and symptomatic care behavior can all be explained by these stages, although they vary in level of consumer involvement and in their focus on primary versus selective demand.

Organizations go through the same five stages in buying a good or service. The organization's buying center consists of individuals who participate in the purchasing decision-making process as users, influencers, buyers, deciders, or gatekeepers. The number and behavior of members of the buying center varies with the complexity, expensiveness, and riskiness of the purchase.

NOTES

1. For exceptions to this, see Irwin M. Rosenstock, "The Health Belief Model and Preventive Health Behavior," *Health Education Mono-*

graphs, 2, pp. 354–86. See also Richard L. Oliver and Philip K. Berger, "A Path Analysis of Preventive Health Care Decision Models," *Journal of Consumer Research,* (September 1979), pp. 113–22.

2. Several models of the consumer buying process have been developed by marketing scholars. The most prominent are: John A. Howard and Jagdish N. Sheth, *The Theory of Buyer Behavior* (New York: Wiley, 1969); Francesco M. Nicosia, *Consumer Decision Processes* (Englewood Cliffs, NJ: Prentice-Hall, 1966); and James F. Engel, Robert D. Blackwell, and David T. Kollat, *Consumer Behavior,* 3d ed. (New York: Holt, Rinehart and Winston, 1978).

3. Abraham H. Maslow, *Motivation and Personality* (New York: Harper & Row, 1954), pp. 80–106.

4. Michael L. Ray, *Marketing Communication and the Hierarchy of Effects* (Cambridge, MA: Marketing Science Institute, November 1973).

5. See Paul E. Green and Yoram Wind, *Multiattribute Decisions in Marketing: A Measurement Approach* (Hinsdale, IL: Dryden, 1973), chap. 2.

6. See Harper W. Boyd, Jr., Michael L. Ray, and Edward C. Strong, "An Attitudinal Framework for Advertising Strategy," *Journal of Marketing* (April 1972), pp. 27–33.

7. "The HMO Ad Campaign . . . It's Health, Hot and Heavy," *The Boston Globe,* May 17, 1985, p. 82.

8. See Jagdish N. Sheth, "An Investigation of Relationships Among Evaluative Beliefs, Affect, Behavioral Intention, and Behavior," in *Consumer Behavior: Theory and Application,* ed. John U. Farley, John A. Howard, and L. Winston Ring (Boston: Allyn & Bacon, 1974), pp. 89–114.

9. See Martin Fishbein, "Attitude and Prediction of Behavior," in *Readings in Attitude Theory and Measurement,* ed. Martin Fishbein (New York: Wiley, 1967), pp. 477–92.

10. See Raymond A. Bauer, "Consumer Behavior as Risk Taking," in Donald F. Cox, ed., *Risk Taking and Information Handling in Consumer Behavior* (Boston: Division of Research, Harvard Business School, 1967); and James W. Taylor, "The Role of Risk in Consumer Behavior," *Journal of Marketing* (April 1974), pp. 54–60.

11. See John E. Swan and Linda Jones Combs, "Product Performance and Consumer Satisfaction: A New Concept," *Journal of Marketing Research* (April 1976), pp. 25–33.

12. See Ralph E. Anderson, "Consumer Dissatisfaction: The Effect of Disconfirmed Expectancy on Perceived Product Performance," *Journal of Marketing Research* (February 1973), pp. 38–44.

13. Leon Festinger and Dana Bramel, "The Reactions of Humans to Cognitive Dissonance," in Arthur J. Bachrach, ed., *Experimental Foundations of Clinical Psychology* (New York: Basic Books, 1962), pp. 251–62. Copyright © 1962 by Basic Books, Inc. Publishers. Reprinted by permission of the publisher.

14. Leon Festinger, *A Theory of Cognitive Dissonance* (Stanford, CA: Stanford University Press, 1957), p. 260.

15. See James H. Donnelly, Jr., and John M. Ivancevich, "Post-Purchase Reinforcement and Back-Out Behavior," *Journal of Marketing Research* (August 1970), pp. 399–400.

16. Ellen Frankfort, *Vaginal Politics* (New York: Quandrangle Books, 1972), pp. 12–13.

17. Patrick J. Robinson, Charles W. Faris, and Yoram Wind, *Industrial Buying and Creative Marketing* (Boston: Allyn and Bacon, 1967).

18. Frederick E. Webster, Jr., and Yoram Wind, *Organizational Buying Behavior* (Englewood Cliffs, NJ: Prentice-Hall, 1972), p. 6.

19. Ibid., pp. 78–80.

20. An excerpt from "First Reading: A Report on Government Affairs," published by the California Hospital Association, Sacramento, July 1982.

21. See Murray Harding, "Who Really Makes the Purchasing Decision?" *Industrial Marketing* (September 1966), p. 76. This point of view is further developed in Ernest Dichter, "Industrial Buying Is Based on Same 'Only Human' Emotional Factors That Motivate Consumer Market's Housewife," *Industrial Marketing* (February 1973), pp. 14–16.

PART IV
Planning the Marketing Mix

11

MARKETING PROGRAMMING AND BUDGETING

The Office of Technology Assessment (OTA) is advocating the increasing use of cost-effectiveness analysis and cost-benefit analysis in the health care sector. The OTA staff studied the application of these techniques in a variety of settings, including health planning programs, reimbursement policies, HMOs, and the market approval process for drugs. While pointing out that the Food and Drug Administration (FDA) is responsible only for assessing a drug's efficacy and safety, OTA noted the the FDA could also perform a cost-effectiveness analysis to determine if a drug was economical compared to other alternatives.

The OTA provided a hypothetical model of a cost-effectiveness analysis for drug D, used to treat hypertension, which is seeking FDA approval. Drug D would be compared to approved drug A, to surgical procedure X, and to biofeedback. First, the FDA would have to assess in units the net health effect of each of the alternatives, based on efficacy, side effects, and other morbidity and mortality statistics associated with each treatment. Then the FDA would determine the net cost of each alternative, including the cost of the treatment itself, as well as the cost of other treatments necessitated by the use of the initial treatment.

With both net cost and units of net health effect figures for each of the alternatives, the FDA could then determine cost-effectiveness ratios for each:

$$\text{cost-effectiveness ratio} = \frac{\text{net cost}}{\text{units of net health effect}}$$

The OTA provided the following hypothetical cost-effectiveness ratio outcomes for the four alternatives:

HYPERTENSION TREATMENT	*COST-EFFECTIVENESS RATIO*
Drug D	400
Drug A	250
Surgical procedure X	3,000
Biofeedback	100

Assuming no other treatment forms were available, the FDA could conclude that biofeedback is the most cost-effective form of treatment and surgical procedure X the least. The FDA might also consider not approving drug D, since it is less cost effective than drug A.

However, the OTA suggests that cost-effectiveness analysis alone not be the deciding factor in FDA drug approval, since cost-effectiveness ratios are based on changeable assumptions. For example, the FDA neither controls nor influences the prices charged for drugs. Even if drug manufacturers in good faith estimate the prices they will charge for new drugs, these prices will change because of market forces, the economic environment and the company's financial status. Net cost estimates could therefore vary tremendously.

Second, the FDA would have to carefully and clinically segment the market, since a drug might be very cost-effective for one segment, such as young persons with uncontrollable hypertension, and not for other segments. Third, the differences in the cost-effectiveness ratios of 20 drugs all intended to treat the same problem may be so minimal as to make a cost-effectiveness analysis worthless. Fourth, the cost effectiveness of a drug may be strongly influenced by factors the FDA would not routinely consider, including failure to take the drug as prescribed due to taste, side effects, or complexity of the dosage regimen.

SOURCE: Summarized from Chapter 8, "Market Approval for Drugs and Medical Devices," in *The Implications of Cost-Effectiveness Analysis of Medical Technology,* Office of Technology Assessment, Washington, D.C., August 1980.

We are now ready to consider the technical aspects of developing and choosing cost-effective marketing programs. In this chapter we examine the planning and budgeting tools available to marketing managers in the health care and social service sectors. In the remaining chapters in this part we will examine specific marketing elements—product, price, place, and promotion variables.

An organization seeking marketing programming that is cost effective will have to face the following four issues:

1. How can the organization choose among competing programs? (Benefit-cost analysis)
2. What marketing/financial objective should be pursued? (Goal specification)

3. How much should the organization spend on marketing? (Optimal expenditure level)
4. How can the organization determine the optimal marketing mix? (Optimal marketing mix)

CHOOSING AMONG COMPETING PROGRAMS THROUGH BENEFIT-COST ANALYSIS

A common problem facing health care and social service organizations is choosing among programs that all fall within the scope of the organization's objectives. Consider the following situations:

> The American Cancer Society is trying to decide between sponsoring a national cervical cancer detection program or a national skin cancer detection program.
>
> A regional health planning technical assistance agency, finding its federally funded support decimated by budget cuts, is trying to decide between selling health planning services to hospitals or selling information and documentation services to state and local government, as a way to compensate for less federal support.
>
> A nursing school is trying to decide between maintaining and strengthening its three-year hospital-based certificate program or developing a four-year academic program that would grant a B.S. in nursing.
>
> A national clinical professional association is trying to decide between developing programs that will encourage greater participation among its existing members or developing a campaign to attract more new members.
>
> A psychiatric hospital is trying to decide between building a new inpatient building on its grounds or opening two new ambulatory mental health centers in the community.
>
> An agency for people suffering visual degeneration is trying to decide between allocating its limited funds to fundraising or to providing additional services to its members.

These examples involve organizations facing a choice between two programs. They can choose one of the programs, or they may be able to fund both on a smaller scale. However, resources in health care organizations are often so limited that the decision to provide two programs may result in neither receiving adequate funding. Health care organizations should attempt to measure the benefits and costs expected from each program in order to make a choice. The benefits are all the contributions a particular program will make to the organization's objectives.

The costs are all the deductions a particular program will take from alternative organization objectives. A particular program is considered worthwhile when its benefits exceed its costs.

The Theory of Benefit-Cost Analysis

Suppose a health care organization is considering three programs, X, Y, and Z. Each is estimated to cost about the same, say, 10 (in thousands of dollars). Each program, however, is estimated to yield a different level of benefits. The data on the three programs are shown in Table 11–1.

All three programs show a positive net benefit (B − C) as well as a benefit/cost ratio (B/C) greater than 1. On both criteria the best program is X, the next Y, and the last Z. If the organization has funds of only 10, it should invest in program X. If the organization has funds of 20, it should invest in programs X and Y. If the organization has funds of 30, it should invest in all three programs, because in all programs the benefits exceed the costs.

Now consider the data in Table 11–1 showing the three programs differing in costs as well as benefits. In this case, the net benefits and the benefit/cost ratios do not show the same rank order. Program X stands highest in net benefit but lowest in benefit/cost ratio. Which criteria should dominate? Generally, the benefit/cost ratio is more rational, because it shows the productivity of the funds. If funds of 5 were available, they should be spent on Z, because they will yield four times the benefit per dollar of cost. If funds of 15 are available, they should be spent on Y and Z. This will yield benefits of 50 altogether, which is an average benefit/cost ratio of 3 1/3 per dollar of cost. Notice that pro-

TABLE 11–1 Examples of Benefit-Cost Comparisons

		A. EQUAL COSTS		
PROGRAM	*B BENEFITS*	*C COSTS*	*B − C NET BENEFIT*	*B/C BENEFIT/COST RATIO*
X	60	10	50	6
Y	30	10	20	3
Z	20	10	10	2
		B. UNEQUAL COSTS		
PROGRAM	*B BENEFITS*	*C COSTS*	*B − C NET BENEFIT*	*B/C BENEFIT/COST RATIO*
X	60	30	30	2
Y	30	10	20	3
Z	20	5	15	4

gram X, although yielding net benefits of 30, shows a benefit/cost ratio of only 2. Program X would be preferred over programs Y and Z only if the three programs were mutually exclusive, funds of 30 were available, and the objective was to maximize the net benefit.

One might reasonably ask how these benefits and costs are quantified in the first place. The organization is usually in a position to quantify the dollar costs of a program. But if the program leads to some social costs, these are harder to estimate. A hospital, for example, typically looks at the cost of a new building in financial terms. But new buildings may negatively affect the local neighborhood and create community hostility. Harvard University experienced this problem when it was planning to build a new facility, the Brigham and Women's Hospital. The local community banded together to complain about the planned hospital's encroachment into a residential area, about the traffic and parking difficulties the hospital would bring, about the noise from ambulances, and about pollution from an associated energy plant. While difficult to quantify, these social costs provided to be quite high in terms of building delays, image problems, and negotiated settlements with the neighborhood.

Evaluating benefits poses many tough problems. Identified benefits tend to fall into three groups:

1. *Monetarily quantifiable benefits*—benefits whose total value can be expressed in dollars
2. *Nonmonetary quantifiable benefits*—benefits whose total value can be expressed in some specific nonmonetary measure, such as "lives saved"
3. *Nonquantifiable benefits*—benefits whose total value cannot be expressed quantitatively, such as amount of health created or beauty produced

Suppose a certain program is estimated to have several benefits, all of which can be measured in dollars. This is the easiest case to handle. Suppose all the benefits can be measured in terms of a common nonmonetary value, such as "lives saved." In this case, we sum up the lives saved as a result of each benefit of the program. A third possibility occurs when the various benefits do not all share a common value. Some analysts prefer to make a two-stage analysis, the first including only the quantifiable benefits and costs. If the benefit/cost ratio is less than 1, the program may nevertheless be good if the nonquantifiable benefits substantially exceed the costs.

The value of trying to quantify the benefits in dollars or some other common denominator is readily apparent, and has led to a number of ingenious ways to try to capture the dollar value of a benefit. One approach is to try to find an existing market price for the benefit. If a child abuse prevention program is expected to prevent a certain number of children from being injured, the present value of the medical and social services that would have been used to treat them can be used as a measure of the value of the program. If an antismoking program is expected to increase the life expectancy of its participants, the expected increased lifetime earnings, plus the medical costs that of treating their lung cancer, emphysema, and so on, could be used as the monetary value of this benefit. The second approach is used when there is no existing market price for the type of benefit being created by the program. In this approach, people can be asked how much they would be willing to pay for that benefit. If an arthritis clinic is being considered by a local hospital, potential users could be asked how much they would be willing to pay per visit, and how often they would visit.

Problems in Benefit/Cost Analysis

Some of the problems of putting benefit/cost analysis to practical use should now be apparent. Even if we manage to achieve dollar values for the various benefits and costs, the technique makes certain assumptions that should be stated clearly and that could affect the decision.

First, the technique assumes that the program, if adopted, would not yield outputs sufficient to change the market prices that were used to estimate the benefits of the program. For example, if successful antismoking programs are introduced throughout the country, they will increase the number of people who will live well into old age, and who will consume many geriatric-related medical services they would not have otherwise used. Therefore, the lifetime earnings and saved medical expenses overstate the benefits of the program.

Second, the technique makes no allowance for the redistributional benefits caused by the program. Some analysts believe the technique should give weight to positive redistribution effects. For example, measures such as "lives saved per thousand dollars" ignore whose lives are saved. If two programs would save an equal number of lives for the same cost, but one would save the lives of children (say leukemia research programs) and others would save the lives of octogenarians (say geriatric research programs), many analysts say preference should be given to the former program. This would imply using a measure of the weighted number of lives saved, with agreed-upon weights for factors such as age.

Third, the technique assumes that economic value should be given the main weight in program decisions. Critics resent the notion that everything worthwhile can be measured in dollars. They see the value of a child abuse prevention program not so much in saved medical and social service expenses, but in terms of happier, healthier children and families.

Finally, the technique assumes that the rank-ordering of projects is insensitive to the particular measure of benefit used, providing each is a highly respected measure. In a study of the net benefit of investing in different disease control programs, arthritis did not seem important when the criterion "lives saved" was used, because arthritis does not kill people. On the other hand, arthritis rates as a high-priority research problem when the criterion "dollars saved through avoiding medical treatment" was used.[1] So various programs may rank differently, depending on the benefit measure used.

The use of cost/benefit analysis and cost-effectiveness analysis in the health care and social service sectors has been limited, restricted primarily to a few public health programs and catastrophic illness treatment programs. The reimbursement policies of third parties like Blue Cross/Blue Shield and Medicare, which strongly influence the "cost" part of the cost/benefit analyses, are set without consideration of benefits, as evidenced by the fact that 28 percent of the Medicare budget in 1984 was spent on maintaining people in their last month of life. The Public Health Service, from which the Health Care Financing Administration sometimes seeks reimbursement recommendations, uses efficacy, safety, stage of the product/technology's development, and acceptance by the medical community as reimbursement policy criteria, but not cost or often quantified benefits.

The public policy and health policy issues to which cost/benefit analysis have been applied commonly quantify benefits in terms of years of life saved, days of disability avoided, or quality of life compounded with years of life saved. Critics claim that estimates of these measures are based on so many questionable assumptions as to render the estimates worthless. More important, the decision to establish or not establish a health care or social service program may involve ethical, moral, and political issues that can never be quantified—see Exhibit 11–1 for an example.

These difficulties are not created by the technique; they exist because the world is complex. The technique was never intended to replace judgment, but to systematize and quantify it where possible. Benefit/cost analysis suggests the important factors that should be considered, and the information that is needed. It adds relevant data to what otherwise would be a wholly subjective act of decision making. It rests on the premise that organized ignorance is to be preferred to disorganized ignorance in making decisions.

In addition, although cost/benefit studies usually take a societal perspective, the decision on selection of organizational versus public policy programs may be better suited to cost/benefit analysis. A large medical group practice, trying to decide between offering a How to Deal with Stress program series and a Soft Drug Addiction series, can quantify this decision by estimating how many people would attend at a specific price, how much it would cost to run each series, and how much benefit would accrue to the patients who attended (see Table 11–2).

From an organizational standpoint, the How to Deal with Stress

EXHIBIT 11–1

Health Care Rationing: The Ultimate Form of Health Care Cost/Benefit Analysis

Each new advance in high-technology medicine sharpens the debate over ethical questions—who should receive treatment with these expensive new technologies, who should pay, and who should decide. Increasingly, the critical decisions are being made not by government, doctors, insurers, or patients, but by those who pay as large a share of health care costs in America as the government does—corporate employers. . . .

"Corporations are being asked to play God with money," says an official at one Fortune 500 company. Should the company pay for controversial and extraordinarily expensive procedures that may prolong life only for a short time? Should it pay for a liver transplant that costs up to $240,000 but keeps most adult recipients alive for less than a year?

Insurance companies pass profound ethical decisions along to their corporate clients by having clients determine what treatment will be covered. . . . "Nothing could hurt an insurance company more than making the evening news with headlines that some huge insurance company won't pay for little Sally's liver transplant. The public relations stakes are too high.'"

The trouble is, no one has the authority or the inclination to set up guidelines on what ought to be covered by medical plans. The private sector might prefer to leave the issue to the government, but law makers recognize the political risk in overtly rationing health care and are unwilling to assume responsibility.

Says Dr. William Schwartz, professor of medicine at Tufts University and co-author of a book on rationing health care, (outside) agencies can identify useless technologies, but they can't do much about the moral dilemmas. "Consider a patient with an unusual type of chest pain that leads doctors in an emergency room to believe there's a 5% chance that he is having a heart attack. If hospitals placed all those patients in intensive care, it would cost $2 million to save one life. Is that too much? How far do you go to save a life?"

SOURCE: Fern Schumer Chapman, "Deciding Who Pays to Save Lives", *Fortune,* May 27, 1985, pp. 59–70.

series is more attractive because it produces a greater profit. From the patient's viewpoint, it is also a better program because the "profit" to the patient—the benefits minus the costs—($2,500 − [$60 − $120] = $2,320) is greater than for the Soft Drug Addiction series ($1,200 − $40 = $1,160). But suppose, for a moment, that the organizational profit is

TABLE 11–2 A Medical Group Practice Cost/Benefit Example

	HOW TO DEAL WITH STRESS	*SOFT DRUG ADDICTION*
Estimated price for series	$60	$40
How many would attend	100	50
Revenue for group practice	$6,000	$2,000
Cost of running series	$1,200	$450
Profit (or surplus) revenue minus costs, including marketing costs	$4,800	$1,550
Additional costs to patient	Possible add-on costs of biofeedback equipment (quantifiable cost: $120)	Psychic costs of recognizing addiction to soft drugs (nonquantifiable)
Benefits to patient	Prevention of stress-related health problems such as heart disease, headaches, sleeping disorders (quantifiable savings: $2,500)	Freedom from addiction and from addiction-related diseases, savings on soft drugs which need not be bought if addiction is broken (quantifiable savings: $1,200)

higher for the stress series, but the patient profit is higher for the soft drug series. A public health cost/benefit analysis would implicitly assume that the objective is to maximize the patient's "profit"; so the Soft Drug Addiction series would be selected. However, organizations tend to act in their own best interests. On that basis, the group practice would select the How to Deal with Stress series.

There is an implicit moral dilemma here, based on the objectives of the organization. The use of the cost/benefit analysis technique allows the organization to recognize this conflict of interest between itself and its market without making the choice for the organization. If the group practice's objective is to maximize profit, it would select the stress series. This could be ethically justified, since both series result in a net surplus for the patient. If the group practice's objective is to serve its patients best, it would select the soft drug series, which still results in a net profit for the group practice, although a lower one than for the other series.

We will assume that no health care organization will purposely establish a program for which the market's costs are greater than its benefits. Most organizations will also not willingly introduce programs that produce a negative profit (a loss) unless these programs are related to other profit-producing programs or are considered a necessity of the marketplace. But within these parameters, there are still many objectives an organization may pursue.

ESTABLISHING THE MARKETING/FINANCIAL OBJECTIVES

A major requirement in the marketing programming process is to clarify the organization's overall objective. We are now ready to contrast seven marketing/financial objectives that might be pursued by health care and social service organizations.

Some Possible Objectives

Profit Maximization. Some health care organizations adopt the profit-maximizing objective. In a self-pay market, this does not necessarily mean charging the highest possible fees, because this would presumably lower demand. In a self-pay program, managers would have to know if and how the quantity of service sold would be affected by price. In markets covered by cost-based reimbursement, health care organizations have often maximized stated costs and charges, since this has maximized revenues and therefore profit without affecting demand. This may change as the consumer is placed more at risk for health care costs; DRG and other prospective payment reimbursement also changes this behavior.

Profit maximization does not mean keeping marketing costs low; greater marketing effort can result in greater demand and greater revenue, although this is not true in situations where reimbursement is limited by revenue caps. Health care organizations will want to know how demand and donations are affected by the marketing expenditure level. Managers will want to find the price and marketing expenditure level that will maximize the organization's surplus.

Revenue Maximization. An alternative objective is to try to maximize total revenue, even though high costs might be incurred. Unlike other fields, in cost-based reimbursed markets in health care, revenue has been closely correlated with costs. High costs have meant high revenue without the organization's profit being penalized. Under cost-based reimbursement, most health care organizations have sought to maximize revenue.

Usage Maximization. Some health care organizations are primarily interested in maximizing the number of users of services. City and municipal hospitals may be eager to maximize the annual number of patients because this is taken as a sign that they are providing needed services to the community. Various city government groups look at census and usage to determine institution budgets for next year.

Usage Targeting. Organizations with fixed service capacities typically set price and marketing expenditures to produce a capacity audience. For example, HMOs experiencing less than capacity membership might lower their prices or increase their selling efforts to attract more members. If the potential members exceed capacity, the HMO might raise prices and temporarily discontinue selling efforts, thus increasing revenues while meeting capacity.

Full Cost Recovery. Some organizations are primarily interested in breaking even each year. They would like to provide as much service as they can as long as their sales revenue, plus donations if they are nonprofit, just cover their costs. Many public agencies have this objective; they spend any remaining funds toward the end of the year to avoid showing a profit that might lead to receiving a lower budget next year.

Partial Cost Recovery. Some organizations operate with a chronic deficit each year. Examples include municipal hospitals, state schools for the mentally retarded, and other publicly supported organizations. There is no reasonable price and marketing expenditure level that would bring these organizations close to breaking even. Instead, their aim is to keep the annual deficit from exceeding a certain amount. Public authorities then cover the annual deficit with public funds raised through taxes.

Producer Satisfaction Maximization. Many health care organizations are as eager to satisfy the wants of their own staff or governing bodies as those of the publics they serve. One often hears the criticism that hospitals place the needs of physicians before those of patients. And board members' pet projects sometimes turn into health care organizations' new programs, whether or not these programs are needed by the marketplace. According to Etgar and Ratchford:

> . . . the product is created mainly for the satisfaction of producers themselves. . . . The organization will modify its product away from the one which gives its own members the most satisfaction only insofar as is necessary to obtain enough revenue from these customer groups to survive financially.[2]

McKnight goes further and argues that most nonprofit organizations, including health care and social service organizations, and professionals are basically self-serving and oriented toward maximizing their own interests.[3]

Examples of Revenue Functions

In the preceding analysis, we used the simple sales revenue function; that is, total revenue (*R*) is average price (*P*) charged or received by the organization times quantity sold (Q): $R = PQ$. This function, when elaborated, reveals a larger number of marketing actions an organization can take to increase revenue. Consider, for example, a nonteaching hospital and a health care trade association.

Hospital Revenue Function. A hospital gets its sales revenue from operating a number of "businesses," including inpatient services, outpatient services, a gift shop, and so on. Each of these requires pricing and marketing expenditure planning. Consider inpatient services. Here the hospital is interested in filling its beds to capacity—that is, it seeks a high occupancy rate. Its revenue function, PQ, can be broken into the following elements:

inpatient revenue = average revenue per patient per day × annual number of admissions × average length of patient stay in days

Hospitals have recently been experiencing declining inpatient revenue because one or more of the three factors has changed. First, average revenue per patient per day has declined due to the dramatic growth of HMOs and PPOs, which negotiate for lower per diem hospital rates; the drop in hospital-based diagnostic tests due to cost containment measures; and new reimbursement policies such as Medicare's DRGs, which are less generous than historical cost-based reimbursement. Second, annual number of admissions may have declined due to changes in clinical practice; the growth of HMOs and PPOs, which minimize hospital usage; to corporate-supported measures to drive down hospitalization, such as required second opinions and the necessity of securing corporate approval prior to any hospital admission; and the declining size of certain market segments, such as obstetric and pediatric patients. Third, the average length of stay has been declining because of federal (and in some cases, corporate) initiatives that penalize hospitals for keeping patients in beyond statistically determined limits. If the hospital cannot fill the empty bed quickly, revenue is lost. On the other hand, the growing geriatric population tends to need longer, but due to DRGs less profitable, average lengths of stay.

Hospitals can attempt to offset each of these factors by taking positive marketing actions. Average revenue per patient can be increased by seeking a more profitable mix of patients. The annual number of admitted patients can be boosted by attracting more active physicians, improving patient care, and adding high-growth specialties. The average length of stay can be modified by the hospital by emphasizing specialties that produce short but higher revenue patient stays, assuming that the hospital can continue to maintain a high census of shorter-stay patients.

Trade Association Revenue Function. A professional or health care trade association collects sales revenue from three major sources:

membership dues, publications, and conferences. The sales revenue function can be modeled as follows:

$$\text{sales revenue} = \begin{bmatrix}\text{annual}\\ \text{dues}\end{bmatrix}\left[\begin{pmatrix}\text{number of}\\ \text{last year's}\\ \text{members}\end{pmatrix}\begin{pmatrix}\text{percentage}\\ \text{who}\\ \text{renew}\end{pmatrix} + \begin{matrix}\text{number of}\\ \text{new}\\ \text{members}\end{matrix}\right]$$
$$+ \begin{bmatrix}\text{price per}\\ \text{issue}\end{bmatrix}\begin{bmatrix}\text{number of}\\ \text{issues/yr}\end{bmatrix}\begin{bmatrix}\text{average number}\\ \text{of copies sold}\\ \text{per issue}\end{bmatrix}$$
$$+ \begin{bmatrix}\text{registration}\\ \text{fee}\end{bmatrix}\begin{bmatrix}\text{average number}\\ \text{of attendees per}\\ \text{conference}\end{bmatrix}\begin{bmatrix}\text{annual number}\\ \text{of conferences}\end{bmatrix} + [\text{other}]$$

This elaboration of the revenue function helps pinpoint positive marketing actions. First, the trade association can consider raising its annual dues, although it must take into account the impact of an increase on the renewal rate and number of new members attracted. The trade association can also improve the job it is doing to encourage membership renewal and attract new members. Second, the trade association can increase its publication revenue by raising the price per issue and/or increasing the number of issues per year and/or increasing the average number of copies sold per issue. Third, the association can increase conference revenue by raising the registration fee, attracting a larger average number of attendees per conference, and increasing the annual number of conferences. Each of these variables can be influenced by specific marketing actions. The organization can build its marketing plans by examining each revenue component and determining what it can accomplish.

DECIDING ON THE OPTIMAL LEVEL OF MARKETING EXPENDITURES

Many health care organizations that turn to formal marketing ask this question: "What is the proper amount to spend on marketing?" One nursing home administrator specifically asked: "How many marketing dollars should I budget to keep my beds filled with private pay patients?" Unfortunately, the answer is not simple. We will describe the five major approaches to establishing marketing budgets.

The Affordable Method

Many organizations set their marketing budget on the basis of what they think they can afford. A health care administrator will balance all the competing claims for funds and arrive at an arbitrary amount that can be spent on marketing. Setting budgets in this way is tantamount to saying that the relationship between marketing expenditure and sales is unknown and unknowable. As long as the organization can spare some funds for marketing, it will be done as a form of insurance. The basic weakness is that this approach leads to a changing level of marketing expenditure each year, making it difficult to attain long-run results. Also, since marketing costs are not formally covered by third-party reimbursement, many health care managers feel they cannot afford this "expense." They do not recognize that money spent on marketing is an investment.

Percentage of Sales Method

Many organizations prefer to set their marketing budget as a specified percent of revenue (either current or anticipated) or of the average "sales" price. A health promotion organization anticipating revenues of $250,000 for its health promotion seminars might decide to spend 5 percent, or $12,500, on marketing. The percentage of sales method was the approach used in an early book on hospital marketing. The author recommended that a hospital spend 0.6 percent of overall revenues on marketing planning, marketing audit, and consumer research activities, plus another 0.9 percent on promotional efforts.[4] This did not include the managerial costs involved in other marketing areas, such as new service development, pricing and channel management, sales force costs, and so on. The 1.5 percent of total revenues the author recommended be allocated to marketing is dramatically less than the range allocated in most other industries.

The main advantage of the method is that it leads to a predictable budget each year once the sales, utilization, or census goal is set. It also keeps marketing costs under reasonable control. Nevertheless, the method has little else to recommend it. It does not provide a logical basis for the choice of a specific percentage, except what has been done in the past, or what competitors are doing. It discourages experimentation and the development of budgets on an opportunity basis.

Competitive-Based Method

Some organizations set their marketing budgets specifically in relation to competitors' outlays. A health maintenance organization may decide on its marketing budget by investigating what its main competitor is spending. The HMO may decide to spend more, less, or the same. It would spend more if it wants to overtake or surpass the other HMO; it would spend less if it believes that it can achieve more impace and/or efficiency with the funds. It would spend the same if it believes that the competitor has figured out the proper amount to spend or if it believes that maintaining competitive parity will avoid an aggressive reaction by the competitor.

Knowing what the competition is spending is undoubtedly useful information. However, basing one's spending on this information alone is not warranted. Marketing objectives, resources, and opportunities are likely to differ so much among organizations that budgets are hardly a guide for other organizations to follow.

Objective and Task Method

The objective and task method calls on marketers to develop a budget by (1) defining their marketing objectives as specifically as possible, (2) determining the tasks that must be performed to achieve these objectives, and (3) estimating the costs of performing those tasks. The sum of these costs is the proposed marketing budget.

As an example, consider a Visiting Nurse Association (VNA) agency that seeks to attract 4,000 reimbursement-covered or self-pay patients. The administrator might estimate that the agency staff would have to visit 100 physicians or discharge planners in order to generate 5,000 referrals, 4,400 of whom would be covered by third-party reimbursement or would be self-pay, of which 4,000 would choose to be served by VNA. Each step requires a specific set of activities, the cost of each of which can be estimated. Table 11–3 shows the hypothetical estimate of costs involved in referral development and patient attraction aimed at the final objective of 4,000 "paying" patients. The VNA manager built up the marketing budget by defining the objectives, identifying the rquired tasks, and costing them.

TABLE 11–3 Hypothetical Budget for Referral Development and Patient Attraction for a Visiting Nurse Association

100 visits to physicians and discharge planners	Staff time to set up appointments, send letters confirming appointment times, and visit with physician or discharge planner	$18,000
	Promotional literature and gifts left with physician or discharge planner	420
	Travel expense for visiting staff member	380
5,000 referrals	Staff time to handle referral calls	6,000
4,400 referred self-pay or third party covered patients	Staff time spent on determining financial coverage of patient	1,200
4,000 covered or self-pay patients choosing to use the VNA	Staff time by liaison nurse spent with patients or patients' families reassuring them that the VNA is the right choice	2,000
		$28,000

Note: Cost per covered/self-pay patient attracted = $28,000/4,000 = $7.

This is a superior method of setting the marketing budget. It requires management to think through its objectives and marketing activities. Its major limitation is failure to consider alternative marketing objectives and budgets in the search for the optimal course of action. We now turn to a method that is theoretically the soundest for setting the marketing budget.

Sales Response Optimization Method

Sales response optimization requires that the manager estimate the relation between sales response and alternative levels of the marketing budget. The estimate is captured in the sales response function, which is defined as follows:

> A **sales response function** forecasts the likely sales volume during a specified time period associated with different possible levels of a marketing element.

The best-known sales response function is the demand function, illustrated in Figure 11–1. This function shows that sales are higher in any given period, the lower the price. In the illustration, a price of $24 leads to sales of 8,000 units in that period, but a price of $16 would have led to sales of 14,000 units. The demand curve is curvilinear, although other shapes are possible. This sales response function is applicable to certain self-pay exchanges in health care, but not to those where the customer is fully covered by third-party reimbursement.

Suppose that the marketing variable is not price, but total marketing dollars spent on sales force, advertising, and other marketing activities. In this case, the sales response function is likely to resemble

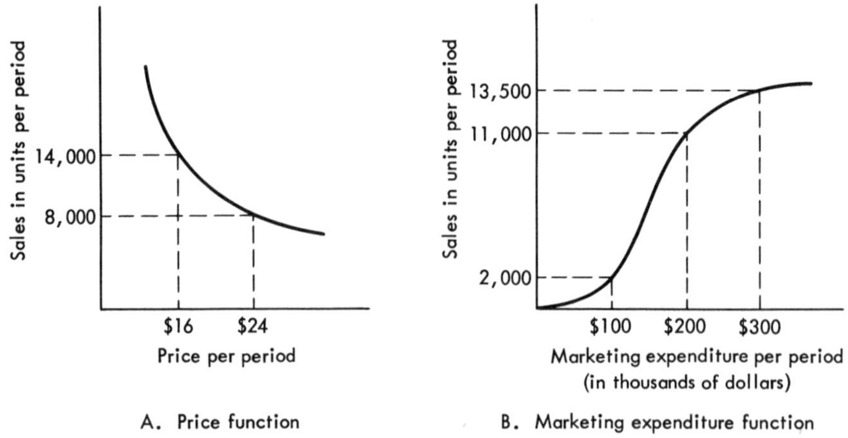

FIGURE 11–1 Sales Response Functions

Figure 11–1(b). This function states that the more the organization spends in a given period on its marketing effort, the higher sales are likely to be. The particular function is S-shaped, although other shapes are possible. The S-shaped function says that low levels of marketing expenditure are not likely to produce much sales. Too few buyers will be reached, or reached effectively. Higher levels of marketing expenditure per period will produce much higher levels of sales. Very high expenditures per period, however, may not add much more in sales and could represent "marketing overkill."

Eventually diminishing returns happen for a number of reasons. Even in health care, there is an upper limit to the total potential demand for any particular product or service. The easier sales prospects are sold first; the more resistant prospects remain. As the upper limit is approached, it becomes increasingly expensive to stimulate further sales. Also, as an organization steps up its marketing effort, its competitors are likely to do the same. The net result is that each organization experiences increasing sales resistance. In the third place, if sales were to continue to increase at an increasing rate, natural monopolies would result. A single organization would tend to take over in each industry because of the greater level of its marketing effort. Yet this is contrary to what we observe in industry. Health care organizations spend so little on marketing that at this point in time, the problem of "marketing overkill" need not concern them.

How can a marketing manager estimate the sales response function? Three methods are available. The first is the *statistical method.* The manager gathers data on past sales and levels of marketing mix variables and estimates the sales response functions using statistical estimation procedures.[5] The *experimental method* which calls for deliberately varying the marketing expenditure levels in matched samples of geographical or other units and noting the resulting sales volume.[6] In the *judgmental method,* experts are asked to estimate the probable sales response.[7]

Once the sales response function is estimated, it is used to set an optimal marketing budget. First, the organization's objective is defined. Suppose the organization wants to maximize profit. Graphically, we must introduce some further curves to find the point of optimal expenditure. The analysis is shown in Figure 11–2. The key function we start with is sales response. It resembles the S-shaped sales response function in Figure 11–1(b) except for two differences. First, sales response is expressed in terms of dollars instead of units, so that we can find the profit-maximizing marketing expenditure. Second, the sales response function is shown as starting above zero sales, on the argument that some sales might take place even in the absence of marketing expenditures.

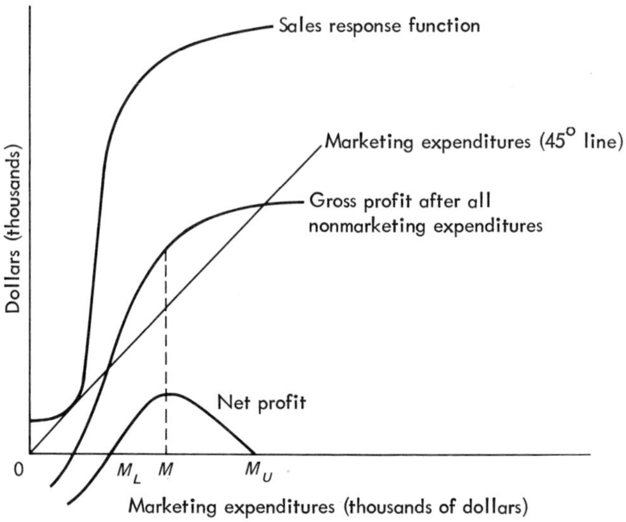

FIGURE 11–2 Relationship between Sales Volume, Marketing Expenditures, and Surplus

To find the optimal marketing expenditure, the marketing manager subtracts all nonmarketing costs from the sales-response function to derive the gross profit curve. Next, marketing expenditures are drawn in such a way that a dollar on one axis is projected as a dollar on the other axis. This amounts to a 45° line when the axes are scaled in identical dollar intervals. The marketing expenditures curve is then subtracted from the gross profit curve to derive the net profit curve. The net surplus curve shows positive net profit with marketing expenditures between M_L and M_U, which could be defined as the rational range of marketing expenditure. The net profit curve reaches a maximum at M. Therefore the marketing expenditure that would maximize net profit is $\$M$.

DEVELOPING A COST-EFFECTIVE MARKETING MIX

The impact of a given marketing budget on demand depends not only on the size of the budget, but also on how the budget is allocated to the various marketing activities. An organization has a lot of options in how to spend a given budget. For example, a health maintenance organization marketing director can spend the marketing budget on the following items: (1) sales staff/account representatives, (2) direct mail, (3) media advertising, (4) marketing research, (5) a hospitality training program for employees, (6) publicity. The key task is to decide, for any given marketing objective, on the most cost-effective marketing mix.

Before looking at how the marketing mix should be established, let us consider how it is established in practice. Most organizations develop rules of thumb to guide allocations to marketing activities. One HMO may find that sending out sales staff to participating member organizations produces the greatest gains in enrollment and thus decide to commit over 50 percent of its budget to supporting the sales staff. Another HMO may find that the name recognition achieved by broadcast advertising produces many new companies and employees interested in enrolling; it makes broadcast advertising the largest part of its budget.

After a certain division of the funds gets established, management tends to adhere to it year after year. Management gives thought to a drastic redeployment only if major changes occur in the known effectiveness or cost of different marketing tools. For example, the cost of travel in the past few years has increased so much that some HMOs are reducing the number of personal visits their sales staffs make to companies, and substituting increased use of mail and telephone selling. In principle, each marketing element can substitute for another to some extent. An HMO can seek more members by lowering its price, increasing the number of sales staff, or adding more services to the benefit package. The organization must constantly try to assess the relative productivity of these different tools. One reason to create a marketing department in an organization is to achieve this managed coordination over all the interrelated tools of marketing.

Theory of the Optimal Marketing Mix

Here we want to explore how the optimal marketing mix would be determined in principle. Consider an HMO marketing office that uses advertising and a salesforce as the two major elements of the marketing mix (in this case, the promotional mix). Clearly, there are an infinite number of combinations of spending on these two items, as shown in Figure 11–3(a). If there are no constraints on advertising and sales force expenditure, then every point in the A–S plane shown in Figure 11–3(a) is a possible marketing mix. An arbitrary line drawn from the origin, called a constant mix line, shows the set of all marketing mixes where the two tools are in a fixed ratio but where the budget varies. Another arbitrary line, called a constant budget line, shows a set of varying mixes that would be affordable with a fixed marketing budget.

Associated with every possible marketing mix is a resulting sales level. Three sales levels are shown in Figure 11–3(a). The marketing mix (A_1S_2)—calling for a small budget and a rough equality between advertising and salesforce—is expected to produce sales of Q_1. The marketing mix (A_2S_1) involves the same budget with more expenditure on advertising than on salesforce; this is expected to produce slightly higher sales, Q_2. The mix (A_3S_3) calls for a larger budget but a relatively equal

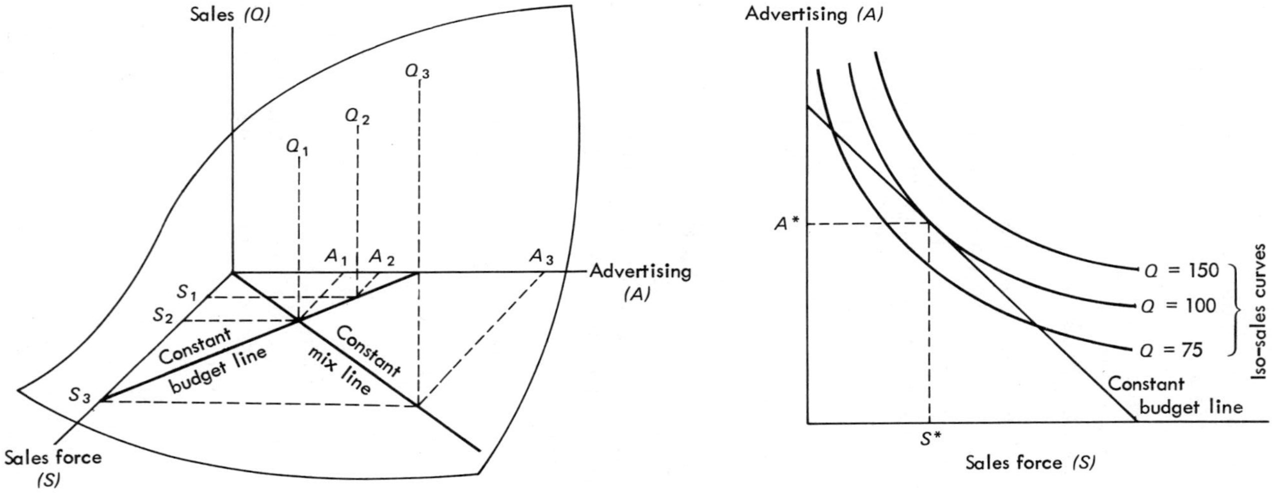

A. Relation of sales to different marketing mixes of advertising and sales force

B. Finding the optional marketing mix for a given marketing budget

FIGURE 11–3 The Sales Function Associated with Two Marketing-Mix Elements

split between advertising and sales force, with a sales estimate of Q_3. Given these and many other possible marketing mixes, the marketer's job is to find the sales equation that predicts the *Q*s.

For a given marketing budget, the money should be divided among the various tools in a way that gives the same marginal profit on the marginal dollar spent on each tool. A geometrical version of the solution is shown in Figure 11–3(b). Here we are looking down at the *A–S* plane shown in Figure 11–3(a). A constant budget line is shown, indicating all the alternative marketing mixes that could be achieved with this budget. The curved lines are called *iso-sales curves.* An iso-sales curve shows the different mixes of advertising and personal selling that would produce a given level of sales. It is a projection into the *A–S* plane of the set of points resulting from horizontal slicing of the sales function shown in Figure 11–3(a) at a given level of sales. Figure 11–3(b) shows iso-sales curves for three different sales levels: 75, 100, and 150 units. Given the budget line, it is not possible to attain sales of more than 100 units. The optimum marketing mix is shown at the point of tangency between the budget line and the last-touching iso-sales curve above it. Consequently, the marketing mix (A^*S^*), which calls for somewhat more advertising than sales force, is the sales-maximizing (and in this case profit-maximizing) marketing mix.[8]

Determining the Optimal Marketing Mix

The theory can be turned into a practical method for evaluating different marketing mixes. Consider the director of a mental health center that offers one-time counseling sessions for people who feel they need to think through a problem with a professional. Suppose the director, Ms. Smith, has three decisions to make with regard to marketing the program: the price per session (*P*), the amount to spend on local newspaper, cable television, and radio advertising (*A*), and the amount to spend on direct mail (*M*). Last year the mental health center charged $40 per session, and spent $10,000 on broadcast advertising and $3,000 on direct mail. The director now wants to consider departing from this low-price, low-promotion strategy, which attracted roughly 1,450 people.

She is considering raising the session price to $60, and possibly spending as much as $20,000 on local broadcast advertising and $7,000 on direct mail. Ms. Smith develops a set of alternative marketing mix strategies from which to make a choice. Suppose she generates the eight strategies shown in the first three columns of Table 11–4 (the first listed strategy is the one used last year). These strategies were formed by assuming a high and low level of each of the three marketing variables.

Her next step is to estimate the likely patient demand (*Q*) (number of patients seeking one-time counseling sessions) that would be attained with each alternative mix. These estimates cannot come out of statis-

TABLE 11–4 Marketing Mixes and Estimated Number of Inquiries

MARKETING MIX	*PRICE (P)*	*ADVERTISING (A)*	*DIRECT MAIL (M)*	*PATIENT DEMAND (Q)*	*PROFIT OR SURPLUS (S)*
1	$40	$10,000	$3,000	1,450	$3,250
2	40	20,000	3,000	1,600	−3,000
3	40	10,000	7,000	1,500	500
4	40	20,000	7,000	1,750	−3,250
5	60	10,000	3,000	825	4,125
6	60	20,000	3,000	900	−2,500
7	60	10,000	7,000	850	1,250
8	60	20,000	7,000	1,000	−2,000

tical analysis of past data because the center has never charged $60 for a one-time counseling session or ever spent more than approximately $13,000 on marketing the one-time sessions. She and her associates have to make educated guesses based on their "feel" for the market. The resulting estimates are shown in the next-to-last column of Table 11–4. The whole table represents Ms. Smith's picture of the sales response function $Q = f(P,A,S)$, where the number of inquiries is a function of price, broadcast advertising, and direct mail.

The optimal marketing mix strategy will depend on the organization's objective. If the center wants to maximize patient demand, the best strategy is marketing mix 4, consisting of a low session price of $40 and a high expenditure of $20,000 and $7,000 on advertising and direct mail, respectively. But the center should be aware of the cost—a loss of $3,250—of this strategy. Suppose the center's fixed costs for this service are $20,000, and per-session variable costs are $15 for each inquiry handled.

We may determine the surplus or loss for each of the marketing mix alternatives. We define surplus (S) or profit as being the difference between total revenue (R) and total cost (C); that is:

$$S = R - C \tag{11–1}$$

The total revenue (R) is the average price (P) charged by the organization times the quantity sold (Q), plus donations (D), if there are any:

$$R = PQ + D \tag{11–2}$$

The total cost (C) is made up of variable cost (V), fixed cost (F), and marketing cost (M). Variable cost (V) is the unit cost (c) times the quantity sold (Q); that is, $V = cQ$. Then total cost is

$$C = cQ + E + M \tag{11–3}$$

Substituting (11–2) and (11–3) into (11–1), the equation for surplus is:

$$S = PQ + D - cQ - F - M$$

or

$$S = (P - c)Q + D - F - M \quad \textbf{(11–4)}$$

Using the surplus equation, we can determine the surplus for marketing mix 4:

$$S = (40 - 15)1750 + 0 - 20{,}000 - 27{,}000 = -\$3{,}250$$

That is, the mental health center contracts a deficit of $3,250 by using this strategy. The surpluses (deficits) yielded by the other strategies are shown in the last column of Table 11–4.

Suppose the mental health center wanted to avoid a deficit for this program and in fact wanted to maximize the surplus to help cover the costs of other services. Then the optimal marketing mix strategy would be 5, consisting of a fee of $60 and a low budget of $10,000 and $3,000 spent on broadcast advertising and direct mail, respectively. Unfortunately, this will produce only 825 patients, far fewer than the number needed to keep the currently employed staff busy. The main point is that Ms. Smith should prepare these sales response estimates in order to determine the strategy that would produce the best balance among the competing objectives of patient demand and cost.

Using Cost-Effectiveness Analysis for Determining Marketing Mix

Once a marketing mix strategy is chosen, there are further decisions of a more tactical nature. Suppose the mental health center decided to use marketing mix 4 because it is anxious to produce the largest possible patient demand for this service, even though this will produce a deficit. In deciding to spend $20,000 on broadcast advertising, it must now allocate this to competing advertising media, such as cable television, newspaper, and radio ads. As an aid to determining the optimal media mix, the center can apply cost-effectiveness analysis. Cost-effectiveness analysis is the general name given to researching the effect of variations in cost on results.

Figure 11–4 shows Ms. Smith's estimates of how many patient visits would be produced by using different advertising media at different levels. She sees cable television producing a linear growth in patient demand. Newspaper advertising is seen to produce a low level of response if used at a low level, increasing returns if used at a medium level, and diminishing returns if used at a high level. Radio is seen to produce a high number of patient visits if used at a low level and rapidly diminishing incremental returns thereafter.

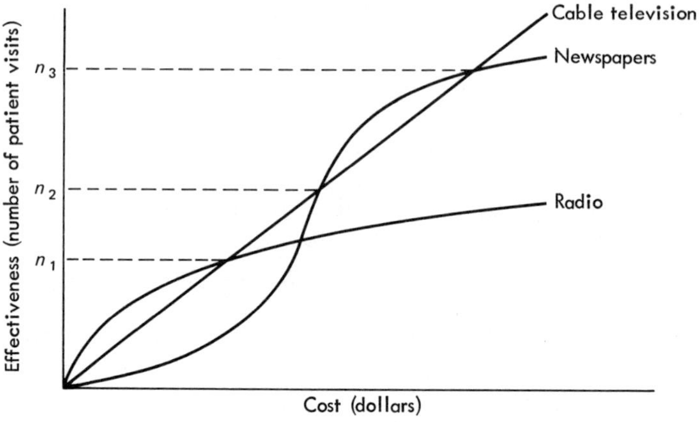

FIGURE 11–4 Cost Effectiveness Functions

Given the cost-effectiveness functions shown in Figure 11–4, which method is the most cost-effective to produce patient demand? The answer depends on how much patient demand the center is seeking. If the center would be satisfied to attract fewer than n_1 patients, then radio is the most cost-effective medium. If the center is trying to attract between n_1 and n_2 patients, then cable television is the most cost-effective medium. If the center is trying to attract between n_2 and n_3 inquiries, then newspaper advertising is the most cost-effective single method. If the center is trying to attract more than n_3 inquiries, cable television is once again the most cost-effective single medium.

If these media reach entirely different segments of the market, it would be better to use a combination of them to attract a given number of patients. Each medium would be used to a level at which all marginal productivities are equal.

Additional Factors Influencing Choice of Marketing Mix

We have examined the appropriate marketing mix in terms of sales response functions. Now we will see what real factors influence this mix: (1) the type of consumer—individual versus organizational; (2) the communications task to be accomplished; (3) the stage of the product life cycle; and (4) the economic outlook.

Type of Consumer. Historically, there has been a considerable difference in the marketing mixes used by organizations selling services to households versus other organizations. The differences are illustrated in Figure 11–5(a). Physicians and other clinical professionals may be viewed as "other organizations" for this discussion. Advertising is widely felt to be the most important tool in promoting to households and

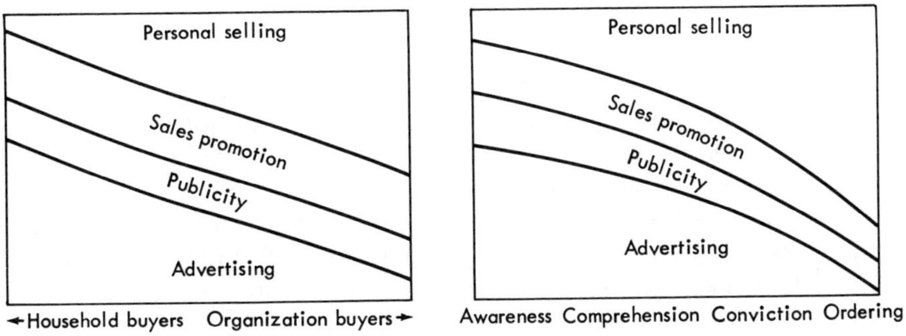

A. Normal marketing mix for household buyers versus organization buyers

B. Marketing mix cost effectiveness at different buyer readiness stages

FIGURE 11–5 Communications Mix as a Function of Type of Market and Buyer Readiness Stage

personal selling the most important tool in promoting to organizations. Sales promotion is considered of equal, though smaller, importance in both markets. And publicity is considered to have even smaller, but equal, importance in both markets. These proportions, however, are not to be taken as authoritative. Many cases exist where marketers adopted different proportions with good success.

The Communications Task. The optimal marketing mix also depends on the nature of the communications task or objective. Figure 11–5(b) shows the general findings that have come out of a number of studies.[9] Advertising, sales promotion, and publicity are the most cost-effective tools in building buyer awareness, more than "cold calls" from sales representatives. Advertising is highly cost effective in producing comprehension, with personal selling coming in second. Buyer conviction is influenced most by personal selling, followed by advertising. Finally, placing an order is predominantly a function of the sales call, with an assist from sales promotion.[10]

These findings have important practical implications. First, the organization could effect promotional economies by cutting back on the involvement of salespeople in the early stages of the selling job so that they can concentrate on the vital phase: closing the sale. Second, when advertising is relied on to do more of the job, it should take different forms, some addressed to building product awareness and some to producing comprehension.

Product Life Cycle Stage. The effectiveness of marketing expenditures varies at different stages of the product life cycle (see Chapter 12 for a detailed discussion of the product life cycle).

Advertising and promotion are important in the introduction stage because the market is not aware of the product. Sales promotion in particular stimulates interest and trial of the new product.

In the growth stage, word-of-mouth begins to work for the new product and partially replaces or supplements promotion efforts. If the organization wants to build its market share, it should continue to promote vigorously during the growth stage.

The maturity stage is marked by intensified promotional expenditures to meet competition and to advertise new product uses and features. There may be an increase in sales promotion effort relative to advertising effort.

In the decline stage, if there is one, many organizations reduce promotion expenditures to improve profit margins. Publicity is cut down; the salesforce gives the product only minimal attention; and advertising is cut to a reminder level. Sales promotion is probably the most used tool at this stage.

The Economic Outlook. Health care organizations would do well to revise their marketing mixes with shifts in the economic outlook. During recessions, for example, consumers become highly price conscious. They cut back on expensive discretionary health care expenditures. They look for value or low price. The organization can do at least three things to respond: (1) It can increase its sales promotion relative to advertising, since people are looking for deals; (2) it can emphasize value and price in its communications; and (3) it can develop messages that help customers know how and where to buy intelligently.

SUMMARY

There are four tasks in developing and choosing cost-effective programs. The first is to choose between alternative products or programs. Here cost-benefit analysis is helpful. Programs which have the highest benefit/cost ratio are preferred. To calculate benefits and costs, monetary and quantitative measures are preferred, although ultimately nonquantifiable benefits and moral or ethical issues should be taken into account.

The second task is to choose among alternative marketing objectives. The most common objectives of organizations are profit maximization, revenue maximization, usage maximization, usage targeting, full cost recovery, partial cost recovery, and producer satisfaction maximization. A health care organization's choice of objectives will vary according to whether or not it is primarily cost-reimbursed or prepaid, whether or not it is publicly financed, and whether it is for or not for profit.

The third task is to decide on the marketing expenditure level. Health care organizations decide on their expenditure level using one of five methods: affordable method, percentage of sales method, competitive-based method, objective-and-task method, and sales response optimization method. The fourth task is to develop an optimal marketing mix of product, price, place and promotion. The optimal marketing mix can be set if the sales response function for each separate element is known. The appropriate marketing mix varies with the type of buyer (individuals or organizations), the communication task, the stage of the product life cycle, and the economic outlook.

NOTES

1. "Benefit/Cost Analyses for Health Care Systems," *Annals of the American Academy of Political and Social Science* (January 1972), pp. 90–99, esp. p. 94.

2. Michael Etgar and Brian R. Ratchford, "Marketing Management and Marketing Concept: Their Conflict in Non-Profit Organizations," *1974 Proceedings* (Chicago: American Marketing Association, 1974).

3. John McKnight, "Professional Service Business," *Social Policy* (November–December 1977), pp. 110–16.

4. Norman H. McMillan, *Marketing Your Hospital* (Chicago: American Hospital Association, 1981), pp. 100–01.

5. For an example of this method, see David B. Montgomery and Alvin J. Silk, "Estimating Dynamic Effects of Market Communications Expenditures," *Management Science* (June 1972), pp. 485–501.

6. For an example, see Russell Ackoff and James R. Emshoff, "Advertising Research at Anheuser-Busch," *Sloan Management Review* (Winter 1975), pp. 1–15.

7. See Philip Kotler, "A Guide to Gathering Expert Estimates," *Business Horizons* (October 1970), pp. 79–87.

8. For additional theory, see Robert Dorfman and Peter O. Steiner, "Optimal Advertising and Optimal Quality," *American Economic Review* (December 1954), pp. 826–36; and Robert Ferber and P. J. Verdoorn, *Research Methods in Economics and Business* (New York: Macmillan, 1962), p. 535.

9. "What IBM Found about Ways to Influence Selling," *Business Week,* December 5, 1959, pp. 69–70; and Harold C. Cash and William J. Crissy, "Comparison of Advertising and Selling," *The Psychology of Selling,* vol. 12 (Flushing, NY: Personal Development Associates, 1965).

10. Research by Swinyard and Ray has challenged the finding that advertising is more effective when it precedes the sales call. They found that women household residents who were first contacted by a

Red Cross volunteer followed by some mailings expressed a higher intention to donate blood than a similar group who first received the mailings and then the sales call. See William R. Swinyard and Michael L. Ray, "Advertising-Selling Interactions: An Attribution Theory Experiment," *Journal of Marketing Research* (November 1977), pp. 509–16.

12

PRODUCT DECISIONS

A chiropractic clinic on the East Coast decided that it wanted to heighten interest and introduce more people to chiropractic medicine by holding free educational sessions that included an initial chiropractic examination. It chose to offer these sessions in midafternoon, since that was when it tended to be the least busy. In order to appear as up-to-date as possible and be able to cover a wide range of topics, the clinic purchased video playback equipment and a large set of "Introduction to Chiropractic" tapes. It then began extensive promotion of these educational sessions.

The problem was that no one came. The initial information the clinic received from helpful friends and relatives suggested that midafternoon was an inconvenient time; mothers who did not work had to be home for children arriving from school, and people who were working were still at their jobs.

In order not to lose the value of the investment in the video equipment and tapes, the chiropractic clinic attempted to offer the educational sessions again in the evening. Again, even with costly promotion, very few people came. A small market research effort which they subsequently commissioned showed that (1) people who weren't already using chiropractors had a negative view of them; (2) people who were having no back pain saw no advantage to attending the sessions; and (3) the point at which people chose to start seeing a chiropracter was when they had back pain. Thus, availability of educational sessions did not change attitudes or behavior.

Most products of the health care and social service systems are *services:* medical assessment, diagnostic and treatment services, medical rehabilitation services, preventive care services, health education, promotion and training services, industrial health services, health regulatory and policy-setting services, health research services, and a vast array of related social services. There are a variety of tangible health care *products* as well, all are intended to benefit people's health. Examples include Lactaid (a milk product that can be digested by many people who are otherwise milk intolerant), the Mt. Auburn Hospital Whole Health Calendar (a calendar produced by a Cambridge, Massachusetts, hospital containing daily, weekly , and quarterly health hints), a vast array of pharmaceutical products, and many health aids such as the Hoover cane for the visually impaired, hearing aids for the deaf, wheelchairs, walkers, and transcutaneous electrical nerve stimulators for those in acute chronic pain.

It has been common for people working in the health care field to associate tangible product marketing with commercial product marketing in such industries as ready-to-eat cereals and automobiles. In fact, the marketing of tangible health care products is not substantially different from the marketing of traditional commercial products.

MANAGING SERVICES

The differences that do exist between health care services marketing and tangible product marketing, whether health care products or otherwise, can be accounted for by the unique nature of services. A service can be defined as follows:

> A **service** is any activity or benefit that one party can offer to another that is essentially intangible and does not result in the ownership of anything. Its production may or may not be tied to a physical product.

The Nature and Characteristics of Services

Services have four distinctive characteristics that must be given special consideration when designing marketing strategies:[1] intangibility, inseparability, variability, perishability.

Intangibility. Services are intangible—that is, they cannot be seen tasted, felt, heard, or smelled before they are produced. A patient purchasing cosmetic surgery cannot see the results before the purchase; and a patient receiving chemotherapy cannot know the value of the service in advance. Under the circumstances, purchase requires confidence in the provider.

Service providers may try to increase the clients' confidence in them in four ways. First, they may try to increase the service's tangibility.[2] A plastic surgeon can make a drawing or clay model showing the patient's expected appearance after the surgery. A woman about to have a mastectomy may be visited at the physician's request by a woman who has already had a mastectomy to show the first woman that she can look the same after the operation as before. The physical facility in which a service is delivered can take on enormous importance because it may be the only part of the service which is tangible. Many health facilities pay great attention to layout, exterior and interior design, color, lighting, and general atmosphere.

Second, service providers can emphasize the benefits of the service rather than just describing its features. This is common in health care. Patients have often been told "This operation (medication, treatment) will allow you to walk (bend, chew, and so on) without pain." In fact, the features of medical services in the past were often not described, while the benefits were. Patients who had operations rarely were given descriptions of what would be done, the provider's attitude being: "Don't you worry—I'll take care of it." Only recently have physicians begun to educate consumers about the features of many of the services they receive. A balance between the descriptions of features and benefits is needed.

Third, service providers can put brand names on their services to increase confidence. There is not a significant amount of branding yet in health care because most health care organizations act as separate, independent entities. As centralized provider chains like Hospital Corporation of American and National Medical Enterprises grow, we expect to see greater branding of hospitals and other health facilities. We might eventually check into an HCA hospital, as we check into a Hyatt hotel. This is already the case with Humana hospitals, most of which carry the Humana name.

Fourth, service providers can use a highly regarded personality to add tangibility to the service, just as muscular dystrophy has done with its Jerry Lewis telethons, and Lou Gehrig's disease with Lou Gehrig. For this to be an effective strategy, the organization has to undertake significant promotion. Since there is still substantial ambivalence toward aggressive promotion in the health care field, this last strategy is not likely to be popular with many organizations in the near future.

Inseparability. A service is inseparable from the source that provides it. Its very act of being created requires the source, whether a person or machine, to be present. In other words, production and consumption occur simultaneously. This contrasts to a product, which exists whether or not its source is present. Consider going to a dentist's office. The dental services cannot be produced and delivered unless the dentist is there. And a patient cannot be X-rayed unless the X-ray machine is there.

Inseparability results in a limitation of the number of people who can receive a service. A dentist may work only eight hours a day, seeing on average two patients an hour, or sixteen patients a day.

Variability. A service can be highly variable, depending upon *who* is providing it, *when* it is being provided, and even *who else* is there as part of the service experience. An artificial heart operation by Dr. William DeVries is likely to be of higher quality than the same operation performed by a physician with little or no experience. And Dr. DeVrie's quality can vary depending on his energy and mental state at the time of the operation. The patient recuperating from this heart transplant will find his experience of the hospital's service will vary depending upon the patient with whom he shares a hospital room. If the patient needs rest and quiet and the roommate's sickness causes constant commotion and noise, the patient's hospital experience will be different from what it would be if he had a quiet, restful roommate or no roommate at all.

Purchasers of services, aware of variability, engage in risk-reducing behavior by talking to others to identify the "best" doctor, hospital, nursing home, and so on. Service firms should make an effort to provide not only high but consistent quality in their service offers, and to monitor the consistency of quality with customer satisfaction monitoring systems.

Perishability. Services cannot be stored. A car can be kept in inventory until it is sold, but the revenue on an unoccupied nursing home bed is lost forever. Some physicians charge patients for missed appointments because the appointment time with no patient to serve is lost revenue for the physician. The perishability of services is not a problem when demand is steady because it is easy to staff the services in advance. When demand fluctuates significantly, service organizations have problems. The emergency service of a hospital must be staffed and equipped to handle emergencies at all times. Most of the time there are no real emergencies, while many emergencies tend to come at emergency "rush hours," like Saturday nights.

Service organizations have several means available to try to better match demand and service capacity. Sasser has described several strategies for managing demand and supply.[3] On the demand side:

1. *Differential pricing* is a practice commonly used by mass transit organizations, but is infrequently seen in health care. The Harvard Community Health Plan, a Boston-based HMO, charges $1 for an appointment with the physician during business hours, but $3 for the same visit on evenings

and weekends. A health care organization reimbursed by a third party may not have this option available, given third-party constraints.

2. *Nonpeak demand can be developed* through marketing campaigns. For example, Sunrise Hospital in Las Vegas attempted to persuade people to use the hospital on weekends, when census was at its lowest for the week, by offering a lottery to weekend users of inpatient services.
3. *Reservation systems* are a way to presell service, know how much service is needed, and reduce customer waiting. For example, hospitals assign patient beds by requiring physicians to make reservations.

On the supply side:

1. *Part-time employees* can be used to serve peak demand. Many hospitals, for example, rely on hiring additional part-time nurses when census is unusually high. In addition, staffing levels on weekends are kept low due to low demand.
2. *Peak-time efficiency* routines can be introduced. For example, one private psychiatric hospital, recognizing that the Christmas–New Year holidays provide a peak of mental illness problems, runs daily sessions during these holidays staffed by psychiatric social workers and open to anyone in need of help.
3. *Increased consumer participation* in the tasks can be used. For example, new patients may be asked to fill out their own medical histories before seeing a physician.[4]
4. *Shared services* can be developed. For example, several hospitals can agree to share medical equipment based on demand. Or a hospital may have "swing" beds that can be used for one of two services, depending upon which service is busiest.
5. *Facilities with built-in expansion possibilities* can be developed. For example, some new nursing homes have been built in such a way that new floors can easily be added.

Classification of Services

Services are of many types, making it difficult to generalize about them. Services can be *people-based* or *equipment-based,* or a combination of both. A psychoanalyst can serve patients with little or no equipment, whereas a team of surgeons requires enormous support equipment to perform a kidney transplant. In people-based services, we can distinguish between those involving professionals (physicians, nurses, social workers) and those involving skilled and unskilled labor (aides, housekeepers, technicians). In equipment-based services, we can distinguish services involving automated equipment (blood analyzers, blood pressure testing machines in drugstores), equipment operated by relatively unskilled labor (telephone switchboards, nursing home stoves and kitchen equipment), and equipment operated by skilled labor (ultrasound, cardiac catheterization equipment).

Services also vary in the degree to which the client's presence is necessary to the service. Brain surgery involves the client's presence, but the repair of wheelchairs does not. To the extent that the client must be present, the service provider has to be considerate of the client's needs. Inpatient rooms, for example, need to be decorated and comfortable because they are part of the service for which the patient is present.

Marketing in the Service Sector

Service-based organizations typically lag behind product-based firms in their understanding and use of marketing. George and Barksdale surveyed four hundred service and manufacturing firms and concluded:

> In comparison to manufacturing firms, service firms appear to be: (1) generally less likely to have marketing mix activities carried out in the marketing department, (2) less likely to perform analysis in the offering area, (3) more likely to handle their advertising internally rather than go to outside agencies, (4) less likely to have an overall sales plan, (5) less likely to develop sales training programs, (6) less likely to use marketing research firms and marketing consultants, and (7) less likely to spend as much on marketing when expressed as a percentage of gross sales.[5]

Why have service firms neglected marketing? Many service organizations are small and do not use modern management techniques such as marketing, which they may not understand and which they view as expensive. Health care, social service, and nonprofit organizations in particular have historically been antagonistic to the idea of marketing, believing it is unprofessional or unethical. It is only within the past decade that these organizations have felt the need to compete for patients, funds, and other resources.

Service organizations that have begun to develop an expertise in marketing can profit by studying the few service industries that moved into marketing earlier. Airlines were one of the first such industries to study their customers and competition and take positive steps to make trips easier and more pleasant. They first had to build confidence in air travel and them compete in preflight, inflight, and postflight services to win customer loyalty. Banks represent a service industry that moved from hostility to marketing to aggressive marketing in a relatively short period of time. At first they saw marketing mainly as promotion and friendliness, but over time they have moved toward setting up marketing organization, information, planning, and control systems.[6] Many banks have redesigned their interiors so they look like living rooms instead of mausoleums; expanded their service hours; increased the number of service products; and so on.

One of the main needs in service marketing is to find ways to increase productivity. The service business is highly labor-intensive, causing costs to rise very fast, as exemplified by the soaring costs of hospital and other inpatient care. You may assume that little can be done to increase productivity in health care, but this is not true. Here are five broad approaches to improving productivity:

1. Service providers may be encouraged to work more efficiently or more skillfully. The Johns Hopkins Medical Center started an employee Idea Bank, offering any employee 10 percent of the savings for each idea that resulted in saving money.
2. The quantity of service can be increased by tolerating a small decline in quality. This approach is possible and has actually happened in health care organizations where budget cuts forced staff cuts, yet the organization has kept the same number of patients.
3. The service organization can add capital-intensive equipment to increase its delivery capabilities. Levitt has recommended that management adopt a "manufacturing attitude" toward the production of services, as represented by the assembly line principles McDonald's applied to fast food retailing, culminating in the "technological hamburger."[7] See Exhibit 12–1 for a health care example of the manufacturing attitude.
4. The need for a service may be reduced or eliminated by inventing a product solution. Consider how streptomycin reduced the need for tuberculosis sanitariums and the Salk vaccine, for schools for polio victims.
5. It is possible to design more effective services that eliminate or reduce the need for less effective services. Promoting exercise and modified diet may reduce the need for more expensive medical services later on.

The Product Is the Person

In health care more than in other services, the product is the person. When the patient thinks of medical care, he or she thinks of the physician. When the patient thinks of a hospital or a nursing home, he or she thinks of the nurses, the aides, the physical therapist, the housekeeper, and so on. The patient envisions medical care in terms of the people who deliver it. Thus the fifth P of marketing is the organization's people.

To control the product that is being produced, therefore, the health care organization must control the people who deliver it. This ties in with the concepts that services are inseparable from the sources that (or who) provide it and that service delivery is variable.

Service organizations in other industries, particularly the airline and hotel industries, devote significant management time and resources to this issue. They train the people they hire to provide uniform and friendly service, in addition to providing technically competent service. The airlines in particular are known to run all flight attendants,

EXHIBIT 12–1 The Manufacturing Attitude in Health Care

A Doctor's Drive-In: Pediatrician in Utah Isn't Kidding Around

He Cites Benefits of Bypassing Crowded Waiting Rooms: Is Personal Touch Missing?

BOUNTIFUL, Utah—Renate Allen drives through a swirling snowstorm, taking her daughter to an appointment with the pediatrician in this Salt Lake City suburb.

As they approach the low-slung, motel-like building, signs in the driveway point the way: "Appointments—Brown Doors. Accidents—Orange Doors. Business—Glass Doors."

Mrs. Allen stops near one of the six brown doors and leads her daughter, eight-year-old Michelle, through a door with a green light over it, directly into an examination room. The room looks like a motel room, with a divan, stuffed chairs and walnut-finish chest of drawers.

Inside, Mrs. Allen and Michelle hear a taped message that the doctor is on schedule and will see them shortly. The doctor's aides have noted their arrival with the help of closed-circuit cameras in the parking area and a computerized device that records their time of entering the examining room.

NEW IDEA

The doctor, Glen C. Griffin, has one of the nation's few such drive-in pediatrics offices. Olin Shivers in Atlanta claims to have the first, and he extols its benefits: "The usual medical waiting room is a hotbed of infection, not a nice place to take your child."

Dr. Griffin's office, moreover, is probably the most automated, at least for an individual practitioner. Glenn Austin of Los Altos, Calif., the president of the American Academy of Pediatrics, says of Dr. Griffin's facility here: "Nobody else has applied electronics the way Dr. Griffin has."

Dr. Austin suggests that the drive-in concept has a limited application, as it probably wouldn't be feasible in dense, high-overhead areas. And he adds, "The electronic drive-in office is fine as long as you don't lose the personal doctor-patient relationship in the process."

Bountiful's Dr. Griffin believes his facility enhances this relationship. "I want my patients to feel as relaxed as if they were at home," he says. "That can be part of the treatment."

INCREASED EFFICIENCY

Dr. Griffin designed the office himself in 1976 after concluding that his old office was inefficient for him as well as for his patients.

"I wondered if patients could be handled on the day the problem appears, through an efficient operation," he says. "If the appointment is four, five days in the future, it may not do the patient any good." So the office now normally handles same-day appointments, six days a week.

The examination rooms are joined at the rear to a long hall and an open area through which the doctor makes his rounds, accompanied by an aide. Lights at the doors indicate where the patients are waiting, and timers indicate how long the patients have been there.

The system allows Dr. Griffin to handle an average of 40 patients a day and peak periods of 50 patients a day, against the average pediatrician's patient quota of 30 a day. "Efficiency means eliminating wasted motion," he says. "It doesn't mean robbing the patient of needed attention."

Other efficiencies in the Griffin office are a laboratory for on-the-spot tests and a routine system to provide the parents with records of the child's diagnosis and treatment. Dr. Griffin, whose syndicated medical column appears in such papers as the *Houston Post* and *Salt Lake City Desert News,* also provides the parent with copies of articles he has written that are relevant to the patient's condition.

"He tells you everything," says Annette DeMille, who has brought her six-year-old son, Andy, to Dr. Griffin for treatment of an allergy. She also likes the privacy. "I don't have to worry about my children catching diseases from other kids waiting in a reception room."

Susan Evans and her two-year-old son, Alan, certainly find the Griffin office to their liking. Alan spends the time waiting for the doctor's arrival swinging on the curtains, and when the doctor arrives he shows off his Popeye sweatshirt.

Dr. Griffin reaches into the chest of drawers that serves as his medical-supplies cabinet and picks up a light to examine Alan's ear infection. Next, he pulls out a tongue depressor, examines Alan's throat and, without looking, tosses the depressor over his shoulder and hits the wastebasket dead center.

DUPLICATED ROOMS

"Every examining room is exactly the same," Dr. Griffin explains, and each is a fully equipped office. "So I don't have to search for anything, even the wastebasket."

Dr. Griffin, who sometimes talks of his operation in terms more appropriate to an efficiency expert, says he is currently looking into ways to use microprocessors to eliminate button-pushing for the eight tape recordings he uses to convey information to patients in the examining rooms.

First voice: "Please sit down and rest awhile. The doctor is delayed."

Second voice, interrupting: "But it's going to be more than a little while."

First voice: "I know. There's been an emergency."

Second voice: "What's an emergency?"

The conversation continues, giving the patients the feeling that they aren't being needlessly neglected. Meantime, the receptionist is phoning to tell patients with later appointments to delay their arrivals.

One Griffin son, Mark, 19, opens the office daily at 7 A.M. and answers the phone to schedule appointments starting at 8 A.M. The early opening of the office has reduced Dr. Griffin's house calls to a minimum, because parents can call starting at 7 A.M. for same-day appointments.

As Dr. Griffin makes his rounds of his look-alike examining rooms, he arrives on schedule at the room where Mrs. Allen and young Michelle are awaiting a report on Michelle's head injury, sustained in a fall.

"Everything is fine," he says without preliminaries on entering the room. "The X-rays show that nothing serious is behind those headaches."

SOURCE: Ray Vicker, "A Doctor's Drive-In: Pediatrician in Utah Isn't Kidding Around," *The Wall Street Journal,* January 27, 1982, p. 1. Reprinted by permission of *The Wall Street Journal,*

reservation sales agents, and other employees who have customer contact through "smile school." Employees are expected and trained to engage in pleasant customer interaction at all times; even passengers who have had too much to drink prior to getting on the plane are to be treated with courtesy and respect. Employees in these companies are evaluated and compensated based on the performance not only of technical duties, but also of customer interactions. This requires building a supervisory system that is responsible for this ongoing evaluation of employee-customer interaction. It also requires the leadership of the organization to place personal value on good service marketing. No supervisory system can produce courteous, friendly employees if the leadership itself is not courteous and friendly.[8]

It is rare today to see similar training and evaluation systems in health care or social service organizations. While clinical incompetence may be detected and addressed by the organization, service incompetence in the sense of frequent negative customer interactions is not. Consider the two letters to Ann Landers in Exhibit 12–2. They are speaking not about the failure to deliver adequate clinical care, but the failure of service providers to be empathetic, sensitive, and communicative to all their "customers." This includes visitors and relatives, as well as the patients themselves.

While the health care industry prides itself on being a service industry, on the whole it has done relatively little to ensure that it delivers the warm, compassionate service to which it lays claim. An organization truly wishing to deliver this kind of service must select, train, motivate, evaluate, and compensate employees to perform. Over time, this system evolves into an organizational culture that affects the behavior even of those providers who are involved with an organization but not employed by it, such as private practice physicians affiliated with a local hospital.

EXHIBIT 12–2 Examples of Service Incompetence

Dear Ann Landers:

Looking for a brand-new subject? Here's one: it's the way nurses treat visitors and family of the long-term patient.

My wife has suffered from a systemic sclerosis that is progressive and incurable throughout the 41 years of our marriage. She has been confined in at least eight hospitals from three days to five months, so I know what goes on within those walls.

Maybe those nurses are dedicated to the humane treatment of the ill and injured, but they show very little compassion for relatives who come to visit. The best I ever got was a staged smile and icy "Good morning"—on the run, to make sure there would be no further conversation.

Time after time I have been made to feel like a nuisance, something to be avoided or ignored like a piece of equipment left in the hallway.

I wonder why members of the nursing profession who are supposed to be dedicated to serving the sick have so little compassion for those who are suffering anxiety and heartache because someone dear to us is ill. We don't ask much—just a little smile and a few words.

—Resentful in Stockton

Dear Ann Landers:

Yesterday I had a complete physical that was required by a firm I started with recently. I am a healthy young woman (23), and this was my first thorough internal examination by a physician.

The doctor peered into every crevice with lights and poked with instruments. The exam lasted at least 20 minutes. He didn't say ONE word the whole time. After I put my clothes on, he said I was very healthy and the results of the blood test and urinalysis would arrive in the mail.

This doctor is extremely competent and highly respected, but on a scale of 1 to 10, I would give him a 6. Why? Because he didn't utter one word throughout the entire examination. If he had said just a few phrases . . . "Everything is fine here" or "No problem . . . looks excellent," he would have made me feel so much better. Silence during a physical examination can be terribly frightening to a patient.

Please print my letter, Ann. So many doctors need to know this, and it's something they don't teach in medical school.

—I live in Chicago

I hope every person who has an appointment for a physical will clip this column and hand it to the doctor BEFORE going into the examining room. It's amazing how many competent physicians are insensitive or unaware of this critical aspect of patient care. Thanks for all the good you did today.

SOURCE: Reprinted by permission of News America Syndicate, Ann Landers, and *The Boston Globe. The Boston Globe,* February 27, 1982, p. 16; October 9, 1981, p. 62.

Product/Service Policy

Although the primary products of the health care system are services, we will continue to use the term "product" generically to include products and services. We define product as follows:

> A **product** is anything that can be offered to a market to satisfy a need. It includes physical objects, services, persons, places, organizations, and ideas. Other names for a product include *offer, value, package,* or *benefit bundle.*

Organizations face a large number of decisions in the product area. We examine the following three questions:

1. How can the organization assess and improve its overall product mix? (Product mix decisions)
2. How can the organization assess and improve individual products in its mix? (Product item decisions)
3. How can the organization improve its handling of its products over their life cycles? (Product life cycle decision)

PRODUCT MIX DECISIONS

Most health care organizations are multiproduct or multiservice firms. Here are some examples:

> The Consultation and Guidance Center, Inc. in Silver Springs, Maryland, offers individual therapy, group therapy, family therapy, marriage counseling, and psychological testing.
>
> Teaching hospitals have three product lines, each with many specific products. They are (1) teaching, (2) research, and (3) patient care. Often, teaching hospitals are accused of ordering the product lines in importance as listed.
>
> The Hospital/Home Health Care Agency of Torrance, California, offers a wide product line including skilled nursing care, physical therapy, speech therapy, occupational therapy, medical social services, home health aide and homemaking services, hospice services, and the rental of durable medical equipment.

For clarity, we will use the following definitions:

Product mix is the set of all product lines and items that a particular organization makes available to consumers.

Product line is a group of products within a product mix that are closely related, either because they function in a similar manner, are made available to the same consumers, or are marketed through the same channels.

Product item is a distinct unit within a product line that is distinguishable by its purpose, its target market, its price, or some other attribute.

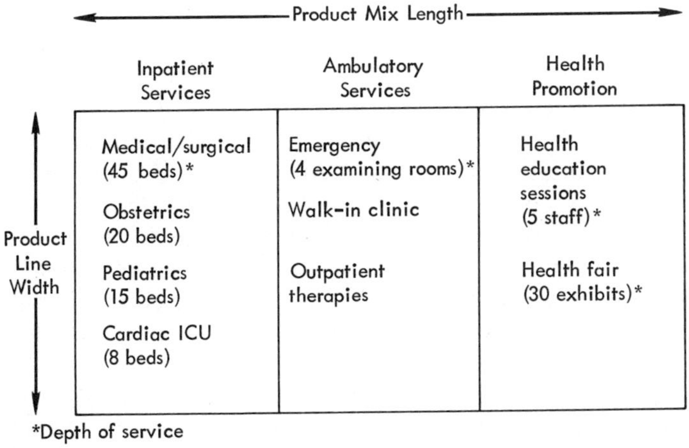

FIGURE 12–1 Length, Width, and Depth of a Rural Hospital's Product Mix

We can describe an organization's product mix in terms of its *length, width,* and *depth.* These concepts are illustrated in Figure 12–1 for the product mix of a hypothetical rural hospital. We see that the product mix, in terms of its length, consists of three product lines: inpatient services, ambulatory services, and health promotion. Each product line has a certain width: the inpatient services include medical/surgical, pediatric, obstetric, and cardiac intensive care. Finally, each product item has a certain depth: the hospital contains 15 pediatric beds, for example.

Suppose the hospital is thinking of expanding its product mix. This could be accomplished in any of three ways. It could lengthen its product mix by adding, say, a free-standing mental health clinic. Or the hospital could add another inpatient service, say, psychiatric; this extends the width of its inpatient service line. Or the hospital could add additional beds, assuming it has regulatory approval; this deepens its number of beds.

Suppose, on the other hand, that the hospital considered contracting its product mix either to bring down its costs or to attain a more specialized position in the marketplace. The hospital could drop health promotion and concentrate on direct provider services. It could eliminate certain inpatient services, such as obstetric and pediatrics, in a move to be an adult hospital. Or it could decide to carry fewer units of each bed type.

In considering the product mix, we should recognize that the various products will differ in their relative contribution to the organization. Some constitute the *core* products of that institution and others are *ancillary* products. Thus, inpatient services are the core product of the hospital and health promotion is an ancillary product (although this traditional focus on inpatient services is in the process of changing in many hospitals).

Furthermore, certain services will play a major role in attracting patients: they are called *product leaders* or *flagship products.* Most patients, for example, will use the emergency department at one point or another. The emergency service is often viewed as the selling arm of the hospital and may be viewed as a product leader. Some organizations also have *crown jewels* in their product mix which they promote aggressively as a symbol. Many hospitals promote their most sophisticated services as their crown jewels, hoping to convince the public that these services symbolize a general level of sophistication throughout the hospital.

Health care organizations should periodically reassess their product mix, since the mix establishes the organization's position vis-à-vis competitors and is the source of costs. This reassessment should result in the organization eliminating product items whose costs exceed their benefits. However, because of the importance of product line relationships, health care organizations should identify the impact the elimination of one product item will have on others. For example, a hospital that decided to eliminate obstetrics would probably also lose gynecology and pediatrics over time. So the decision to eliminate individual product items can be made only in the context of its effect on the whole organization.

PRODUCT ITEM DECISIONS

In developing a product to offer to a market, the product planner has to distinguish three levels of the concept of a product: core, tangible, and augmented.

Core Product

At the fundamental level stands the core product, which answers the questions: What is the consumer really seeking? What need is the product really satisfying? A hospital produces surgery, but patients are really buying alleviation of pain. A medical school produces knowledge, but many students are really buying marketability. A rehabilitation center produces rehabilitation services, but the patient may be buying hope and the potential of a return to work. The marketer's job is to uncover the essential needs hiding under every product so that product benefits, not just product features, can be described. The core product stands at the center of the total product, as shown in Figure 12–2.

Tangible Product

The core product is always made available to the buyer in some tangible form. Consider a mother in labor in a hospital. The core prod-

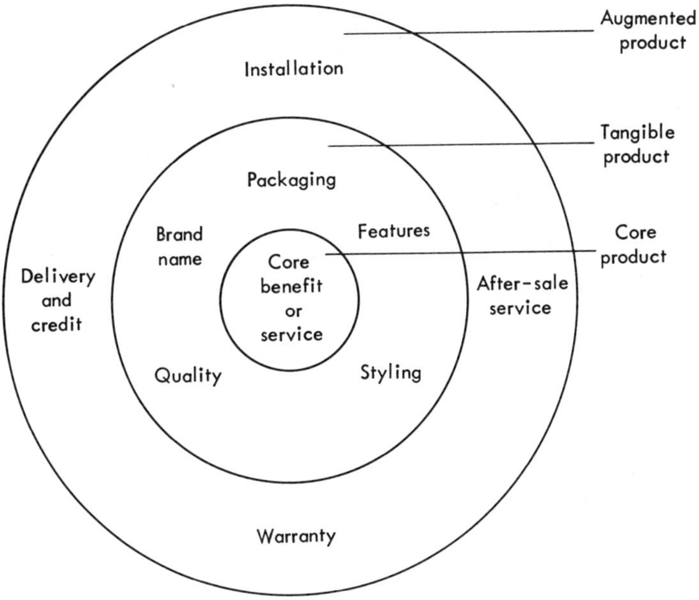

FIGURE 12–2 Three Levels of Product

uct the laboring mother wants is an easy and safe delivery. The normal tangible product had historically taken the form of a hospital delivery ward. The woman in labor was wheeled in, transferred to an examining table, and anesthetized. A physician and nurses aided her in delivery, and her husband was not allowed into the room. Clearly, this is not the only form the tangible product can take, as witnessed by the now popular form known as the alternative birthing center:

> Mickey Johnson . . . entered what might have been a cheery, yellow tinted bedroom in suburbia furnished with rocking chairs and an old-fashioned walnut armoire. Well-tended plants hung from the ceiling. There was even a stereo to play Mickey's favorite music. During the long, painful hours of labor, she was free to get up and pace the corridors. Her husband, Bruce, was at her side during the critical moment of delivery. Almost immediately afterward, the doctor handed him the squealing infant, and the awed father was allowed to cut the umbilical cord and give his 7-pound, 8-ounce son his first bath. The baby was not taken away but spent the night with his parents.[9]

A tangible product can be described as having up to five characteristics: First, it has a certain *styling,* as is apparent in the difference between a cold hospital delivery room and a warm "suburban-like" bedroom. Second, it has certain *features,* such as the fact that the mother is free to move around the room, allowed to have her husband and children with her, and so on. Third, the tangible product has a certain *quality level,* both in its physical materials and the care with which it is run. Fourth, the tangible product has a certain *packaging,* here represented by the larger hospital in which it is contained. Fifth, the tangible product may have a *brand* name; in this case, Illinois Masonic's Alternative Birthing Center. We will examine these five controllable characteristics of a tangible product in more detail.

Styling. Styling means giving a product or service a distinctive look or "feel." Much of the competition in durable goods—such as automobiles, and electronic products—is style competition. Style is also expressed in the design of physicians' offices, hospitals, HMOs, welfare offices, and other edifices where services are offered. Even the clinical aspects of medical services are styled: Medical providers differ in their styles of treating back pain. Some recommend rest, some prescribe drugs, others recommend exercise. A few prescribe acupuncture, chiropractice, or hypnosis.

An organization may find that its style is no longer appropriate or effective with its target audience. A hospital that sticks with the traditional labor and delivery room where fathers are not allowed may find itself drawing fewer deliveries relative to hospitals providing birthing rooms, birthing chairs, and so on. This hospital may want to consider modifying its style to meet changing market wants.

Features. Features represent individual components of the tangible product that could be easily added or subtracted without changing style or quality. Consider a health maintenance organization that is seeking to expand membership. There are many feature improvements it could offer:

1. Expanding its hours of operation to include weekday evenings
2. Adding dental service as an optional feature for a small additional fee
3. Offering a free ten-week smoker's clinic for members wishing to quit smoking

The use of features has many advantages. The organization can go after specific market segments by selecting those features that would appeal most to these segments. Features are a tool for achieving product differentiation vis-à-vis competitors. They have the advantage of being easy to add or drop quickly, or made optional at little expense. They may be newsworthy and useful in attracting free media publicity.[10]

Quality. Quality represents the perceived level of performance in a product or service. As previously pointed out, service products in particular are tremendously variable, depending upon who is providing them and how much control the organization exercises over its providers.

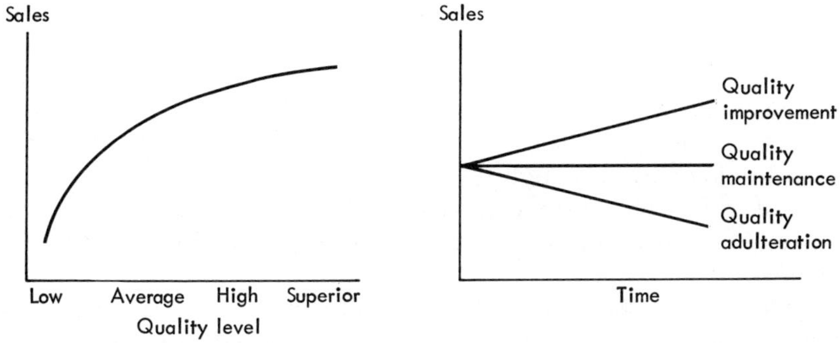

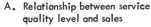

A. Relationship between service quality level and sales

B. Three strategies for service quality management through time

FIGURE 12–3 Quality Level Strategies

Given the preoccupation of the health care field with quality, particularly the quality of clinical care, an important question to ask is this: How does sales response vary with the level of perceived quality? Figure 12–3(a) shows a plausible relationship between sales and quality level. The curve says that higher perceived quality leads to higher sales. It also says that very high quality may not add much additional sales either because consumers cannot perceive very high quality, or because they do not value it that much. Health care managers and providers should note that this does not address quality in the sense that quality assurance activities do. Rather, it refers to the market's perception of quality. These perceptions may be incorrect from a clinical standpoint, but the market acts on the basis of what it perceives. The consumer market, because it is unable to judge clinical care, will often judge the service aspects of what is offered: the friendliness of the providers, the design and atmosphere of the facilities, the hours of service availability, and so on.

An organization must not only set an initial standard for quality, but must manage its quality level over time. It has three options; see Figure 12–3(b). It can attempt to improve its quality level over time through better selection, training, and rewarding of employees and through improving facilities. This strategy should lead to improved market interest and response. The second option is to maintain its present level of quality and emphasize other dimensions of the business. The third option is to allow quality to decline over time. This may be done deliberately when the institution wants to withdraw from the business. Otherwise, it indicates poor management, makes little strategic sense, and may lead the organization down the road to extinction.

Packaging. Packaging is the container or wrapper surrounding the specific product or service. We know that good packaging can add value beyond that perceived in the product itself; consider the fancy perfume bottle and its contribution to the "feeling" of the perfume. In the case of a service, the packaging represents the contribution of the larger context in which the product is found. A teaching hospital offers to all its services the image of medical sophistication and state-of-the-art technology, even though this may not be true across all services. In contrast, many of the same services, housed in a rural hospital, would be viewed as less sophisticated but more personable and more convenient.

Packaging also covers the bundling of individual products. Diabetes clinics, arthritis clinics, glaucoma clinics, general social services, hot lunches, podiatry services, and scheduled social activities may be offered individually by a nursing home or health center. Pulled together as one package, they become Elder Care or day care services for the elderly. Many health care organizations fail to recognize that repackaging of existing services may allow them to offer what is ostensibly a new product to a new marketplace. One home health agency was already providing 24-hour care to terminally ill patients at home, bereavement counseling for patients and family, and a physician if needed. It packaged these services together under the name Hospice at Home and directed the services toward the hospice market, to which it had previously not promoted.

Branding. The products and services of a seller can be branded—that is, given a name, term, sign, symbol, or design which identifies them as the seller's to differentiate them from competitor's offerings. Branding can add value to the seller's offer and more satisfaction for the buyer. As an example, there are thousands of mental health centers throughout the country. They have found that the term "mental health center" is offensive to many people, since it suggests mental illness. The whole industry is looking for another name that would create more positive feelings. The Rush Presbyterian Hospital of Chicago renamed its mental health center The Institute for Living, feeling that this brand name would work better.

In a similar vein, the social movement known as birth control came under sharp attack from certain religious, ethnic, and economic groups that viewed it as a government attempt to dictate who can and cannot have babies. Advocates of birth control changed the name to family planning, since this eliminated the suggestion of outside control and replaced it with the notion that the family makes the decision. This has worked well, but today in some countries the term family planning has fallen into disrepute. For example, family planning has acquired a bad name in India because the government pushed birth control measures too harshly, and a new brand name is needed to fit the new approach to India's population problem.

Many services and social movements carry brand names to distinguish them from one another. Thus, charitable organizations carry such names as Christmas Seal (lung association), Easter Seal (handicapped people), and March of Dimes (birth defects). Help-the-poor organizations carry such brand names as Salvation Army and Goodwill Industries. Mass therapy organizations carry such brand names as Scientology, Transcendental Meditation, Silva Mind Control, and Est. Medical and dental provider chains have begun to use branding. The most aggressive of these is Humana, which has used its name to brand most of its hospitals as well as its alternative delivery system, HumanaCare. We can anticipate increased branding of medical services as provider chains grow.

The creation of a brand name to symbolize the organization's product or service can contribute a number of values. An organization feels proprietary toward its brand name and therefore normally works hard to insure the quality and consistency of its service. It wants its brand name to create buyer confidence in its service and lead to brand preference and repeat purchase. Buyers benefit because they can identify the various brands, acquire a stock of information about their respective quality, choose the best brand, and stick with it as long as it satisfies them.

Augmented Product

The marketer can offer the target market additional services and benefits that go beyond the tangible product, resulting in an augmented product. The Illinois Masonic Hospital can, along with the birthing room, offer longer payment terms, a satisfaction guarantee, home visits to the new mother, and so on. Organizations augment their tangible product to meet additional consumer wants and/or to differentiate their product from competition. As more birthing rooms have appeared in America's hospitals, competition has increased not only between delivery wards and birthing rooms, but even more so among the new birthing rooms themselves. Final outcomes will depend not only on the tangible product characteristics, but upon what organizations add to their tangible products in the way of additional benefits. As Levitt states:

> The *new competition* is not between what companies produce in their factories, but between *what they add to their factory output in the form of packaging, services, advertising, customer advice, financing, delivery arrangements, warehousing, and other things that people value.*[11]

Thus we see that a product is not a simple thing, but a complex offer consisting of a core need-satisfying service, a set of tangible characteristics, and a set of augmented benefits. The health care organization should examine each of its products and design them in a way that will distinguish them from competitors' offers and carry the intended qualities to the intended target market. The more the product can be taken out of the commodity class and moved toward the branded class, the more control the organization will have over the level, timing, and composition of demand for its product.

PRODUCT LIFE CYCLE

It is not possible for a product's characteristics and marketing approach to remain optimal for all time. Broad changes in the macroenvironment (population, economy, politics, technology, and culture), as well as specific changes in the market environment (buyers, competitors, dealers, suppliers) will call for major adjustments at key points in the product's history. The nature of the appropriate adjustments can be conveyed through the concept of the *product life cycle.*

Product life cycle theory views products and services as having something like a biological life cycle. Products and services are viewed as being born, growing, living, and ultimately dying. One has to think only of the practices of bloodletting and phrenology to recognize clinical practices that have run the full course of the product life cycle. Health and social service provider organizations such as tuberculosis sanitoriums, public health service hospitals, and residential homes for unwed mothers have also run the same course, by and large. The product life cycle theory says that a typical product exhibits an S-shaped sales curve marked by the following four stages (see Figure 12–4).

1. *Introduction,* a period of slow sales growth as the product is introduced in the market.
2. *Growth,* a period of rapid market acceptance.
3. *Maturity,* a period of slowdown in sales growth because the product has achieved acceptance by most of the potential buyers.
4. *Decline,* the period when sales show a strong downward drift.

The product life cycle (PLC) concept can be defined further according to whether it describes a product class (mental health service), a product form (psychoanalysis), or a brand (Menninger Clinic). The PLC concept has a different degree of applicability in each case. *Product classes* have the longest life cycles. The sales of many product classes can be expected to continue in the mature stage for an indefinite duration. "Mental health service" began centuries ago with organized religion and can be expected to persist indefinitely. Product forms, on the other hand, tend to exhibit more standard PLC histories. Mental health services are dispensed in such forms as psychoanalysis, bioenergetics, group therapy, and so on, some of which are beginning to show signs of

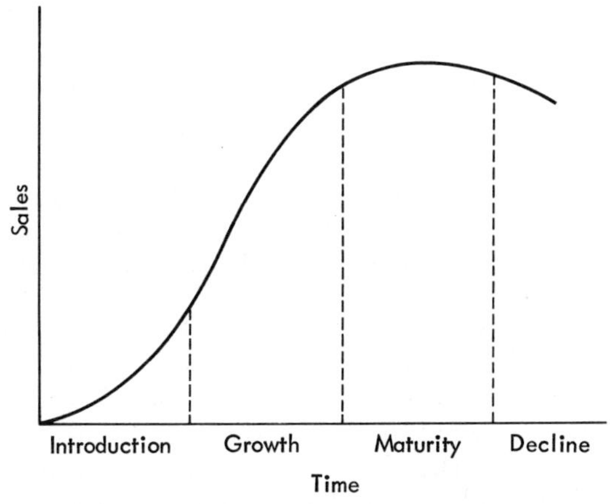

FIGURE 12–4 Typical S-Shaped Product Life Cycle

maturity. As for brands, they are the most likely to show finite histories. The Menninger Clinic is a well-known psychoanalytically oriented clinic that had a period of rapid growth and is now in maturity. It will pass out of existence eventually, like most brands and institutions.

Many products do not exhibit an S-shaped life cycle. Three other common patterns are these:

1. *Scalloped pattern,* Figure 12–5(a). In this case, product sales during the mature stage suddenly break into a new life cycle. The product's new life is triggered by product modifications, new uses, new users, changing tastes, or other factors. For example, the market for psychotherapy reached maturity at one point and then the emergence of group therapy gave it a whole new market. Heart transplant surgery has also followed this pattern.
2. *Cyclical pattern,* Figure 12–5(b). The sales of some products show a cyclical pattern. For example, inpatient hospital census goes through alternating periods of high and low census each year (high in the winter, low in the

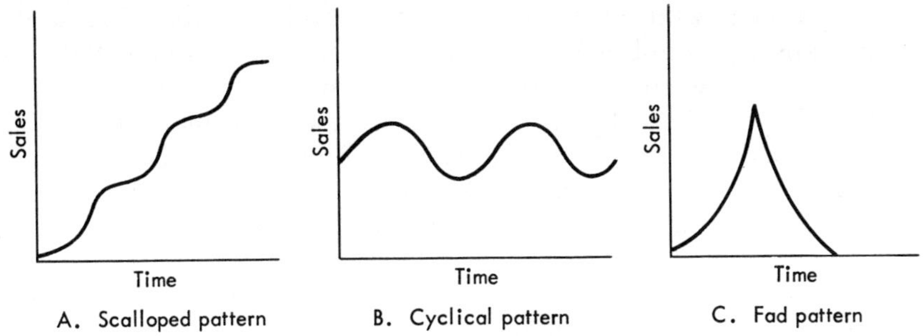

FIGURE 12–5 Three Anomalous Product Life Cycle Patterns

summer), reflecting changes in demand and supply due to seasonal changes. The decline stage is not time to eliminate the product but to maintain as much of it as possible, awaiting the next boom.

3. *Fad pattern,* Figure 12–5(c). Here a new product comes on the market, attracts attention, is adopted with great zeal, peaks early, and declines rapidly. The acceptance cycle is short, and the product tends to attract only a limited following of people who are looking for excitement or diversion. Some forms of therapy exhibit the pattern of a fad, as do fad diets.

While the product life cycle theory is generally accepted by marketers, there is significant debate about the latter part of the product life cycle. The adoption of innovation theory (see Chapter 4) explains the early stages of the product life cycle, from introduction through growth and into early maturity. However, there is little theoretical basis for the late maturity and decline stages. Some marketers believe that a product or service need never decline or die if it is well managed.[12] They suggest that the self-fulfilling prophecy is at work in the death of many products: If you believe the product is in the decline stage, you fail to support it properly, which results in its declining more, until ultimately it dies. The exceptions to this belief take place when there is major technological (or clinical) change. Buggy whips, for example, could not be saved from decline because of the advent of the automobile.

There is also some debate regarding the applicability of the product life cycle to service organizations. Inpatient institutions, for example, often seem to defy the life cycle. A major community hospital is not likely to die, because community demand for medical services will always exist. Nor will the product, "medical/surgical services," go into decline, because demand for these services are continuous. However, the method of delivering many of these services may be replaced by new technologies. The CAT scanner and ultrasound technologies replaced more invasive diagnostic techniques. The evolutionary replacement of one medical technology with another is essentially an example of the decline of one technology and the rise of another.

Health care and social service managers should recognize both the value and the limitations of the product life cycle. Because of regulatory restrictions and reimbursement policies, competitive forces that create product life cycles in other industries have not until recently been present in the health and welfare fields. In addition, many health care organizations will never show signs of decline because the need for the services they provide is endless. However, the specific products organizations offer to meet these needs will vary according to the available technologies, to what is reimbursed, and to what the political and regulatory environment will allow.

We will now return to the idealized S-shaped PLC to examine characteristics and appropriate marketing strategies at each stage.

Introduction Stage

The introduction stage takes place when the new product or service is first made available to the marketplace. Introduction into one or more markets takes time, and sales growth is apt to be slow. Consider how long it took for the "new math" to be accepted in America's public schools, or the fluoride treatment of water to be introduced in America's cities. Today, nutrition experts are trying to find faster ways to get malnourished populations to accept new foods that will contribute to their health.

Buzzell identified four causes for the slow growth during the introduction stage: (1) delays in the expansion of production capacity; (2) technical problems ("working out the bugs"); (3) delays in making the product available to customers through distribution outlets; and (4) customer reluctance to change established behavior patterns.[13] In the case of expensive new products for markets not covered by third-party reimbursement, growth is retarded by additional factors, such as the small number of buyers who are attuned to innovations and the high cost of the product. An example of this is in-vitro fertilization (test-tube babies); in spite of estimates of 20 percent of all married couples in the United States being infertile, relatively few can afford to pay roughly $5,000 out of pocket for each month they go through the program.

In the introductory stage, costs are high because of low adoption and heavy production, distribution, and promotion expenses. Promotional expenditures are at their highest ratio to sales "because of the need for a high level of promotional effort to (1) inform potential consumers of the new and unknown product, (2) induce trial of the product, and (3) secure distribution in retail outlets,"[14] or secure the involvement of referral channels. The organizations direct their selling effort to those buyers who are the readiest to buy—namely, early adopter types. Management should be guided by the findings in the field on innovation and diffusion theory in designing their introductory marketing plans (see Chapter 4).

Unfortunately, it is the norm in the health care environment to provide inadequate support to new products and services. As a result, insufficient demand is generated, leading managers to conclude the new product or service was not a good idea. A midwestern teaching hospital opened a headache clinic, placed three small advertisements in the city's newspaper, and waited for the onslaught of patients which never arrived. It closed the clinic within six months. Less than a year later, a neighboring community hospital opened a headache clinic. It promoted the clinic aggressively to local primary care practitioners, psychiatrists, and neurologists, invested heavily in advertising citywide, and sent out on request, as advertised, a self-assessment questionnaire which patients would bring with them on their first visit. The clinic was flooded with patients within six months.

Growth Stage

If the new product satisfies the market, sales will start climbing substantially. The early adopters will continue their purchasing and other consumers will follow their lead, especially if there is favorable word of mouth. New competitors may enter the market, attracted by the opportunity. They may introduce feature, style, and packaging variations, and this will expand the market. During this stage the organization tries to sustain rapid market growth as long as possible. This is accomplished in several ways:

1. The organization undertakes to improve product quality and add new features and models.
2. It vigorously searches out new market segments to enter.
3. It keeps its eyes open for new distribution channels to gain additional product exposure.
4. It shifts its promotion from building product awareness to trying to bring about product conviction and purchase.

Maturity Stage

At some point, a product's rate of sales growth will slow, and the product will enter a stage of relative maturity. This stage normally lasts much longer than the previous stages, and it poses some of the most formidable challenges to marketing management. *Most products are in the maturity stage of the life cycle, and therefore most of marketing management deals with the mature product.*

The beginning of a slowdown in the rate of sales growth has the effect of producing overcapacity in the industry. This overcapacity leads to intensified competition. In traditional commercial fields, this competition often leads some organizations to increase their research and development budgets to find better versions of the product, or takes the form of price cutting and increased promotion. In health care, it is more likely to consist of recruiting more referrers and adding more product features. Some organizations resort to modifying their customer or product mix. Increasingly, like commercial organizations, health care organizations are turning to price cutting and promotion. But these steps result in higher costs. Some of the weaker competitors start dropping out. The industry eventually consists of a set of well-entrenched competitors whose basic orientation is toward gaining competitive advantage.

Decline Stage

Many product forms and brands eventually enter a stage of sales decline. The decline may be slow or rapid. Sales may plunge to zero and the product may be withdrawn from the market, or they may petrify at a low level and continue there for many years. Many schools of social work have acknowledged a long-term decline in the size of their student body. The universities in which the schools are housed have wrestled with what to do with these weakening products.

Sales decline for a number of reasons. Technical advances may give birth to new product classes, forms, and brands, which become effective substitutes. Changes in fashion or tastes lead to buyer erosion. All of these factors have the effect of intensifying overcapacity and competition.

As sales decline, some organizations withdraw from the industry in order to invest their resources in more attractive markets. Those remaining tend to reduce the number of product offerings. They withdraw from smaller market segments and marginal distribution changes. The promotion budget is reduced.

Unless there are strong reasons, carrying a weak product is very costly to the organization. The cost of maintaining a weak product is not just the amount of uncovered cost; no financial accounting can adequately convey all the hidden costs. The weak product tends to consume a disporportionate amount of management's time; it may require frequent price adjustment if it is a self-pay service; it may require full staffing even if it is chronically under capacity; it requires promotional attention that might better be diverted to making the "healthy" products more profitable; and its very unfitness can cause customer misgivings and cast a shadow on the organization's image. The biggest cost imposed by carrying weak products may lie in the future. By not being eliminated at the proper time, these products delay the aggressive search for replacements; they create a lopsided product mix, long on "yesterday's breadwinners" and short on "tomorrow's breadwinners"; they depress current cash and weaken the organization's hold on the future.

An organization faces a number of tasks and decisions in handling its aging products.

Identifying the Weak Products. The first task is to establish a system that will identify those products that are in a declining stage. Six steps are involved:

1. A product review committee is appointed with the responsibility for developing a system for periodically reviewing weak products in the organization's mix.
2. This committee meets and develops a set of objectives and procedures for reviewing weak products.
3. The controller's office fills out data for each product showing trends in market size, market share, prices or reimbursement levels, and costs.

4. This information is run against a (usually computerized) management information program that identifies the most dubious products. The criteria include the number of years of sales decline, market share trends, cost trends, reimbursement trends, clinical practice trends, and business environment and regulatory trends.
5. Products put on the dubious list are then reported to those managers responsible for them. The managers fill out forms showing where they think sales and costs on dubious products will go with no change in the current marketing program and with their recommended changes in the current program.
6. The product review committee examines the product rating form for each dubious product and makes a recommendation to leave it alone, to modify its marketing strategy, or to drop it.[15]

While many organizations keep weak products too long, health care organizations seem particularly prone to do so. Often a weak product is kept around because of the ardent supporter syndrome: "We can't eliminate the industrial annual physical exam program. That's Dr. Smith's 'baby' and he admits a lot of patients here." If the ardent supporter is not also fiscally responsible for the program, the weak program is often apt to be kept too long. Weak programs are also kept because "the patients need this program." This is a difficult argument to combat. If, in fact, a sufficient number of people need a program, the organization might be able to strengthen utilization with sufficient promotion. Otherwise, not enough people may "need" the program to justify the cost of its existence.

Determining Marketing Strategies. In the face of declining sales, some organizations will abandon the market earlier than others. The organizations that remain enjoy a temporary increase in sales as they pick up the customers of the withdrawing organizations. Thus, any particular organization faces the issue of whether it should be the one to stay in the market until the end. Exhibit 12–3 describes a rehabilitation center that decided to drop an underutilized service rather than stay in the market.

If it decides to stay in the market, the organization faces further strategic choices. The organization could adopt a *continuation strategy,* in which case it continues its past marketing strategy—same market segments, channels, pricing, and promotion. Or it could follow a *concentration strategy,* in which case it concentrates its resources in the strongest markets while phasing out its efforts elsewhere. Finally, it could follow a *harvesting strategy,* in which case it sharply reduces its expenses to increase current cash, knowing that this will accelerate the rate of sales decline and ultimate demise of the product.

The Drop Decision. When a product has been singled out for elimination, the organization faces further decisions. First, if the prod-

EXHIBIT 12–3

A Consulting Team Reviews Whether an Underutilized Hospital Service Should Be Dropped

A medical rehabilitation center with a spinal cord injury unit found a long-term trend of underutilization of this unit. Therefore, the rehabilitation center called in an outside consulting team to make recommendations to increase the unit's utilization. The consulting team ascertained: (1) the number and nature of competitive spinal cord injury units in the same geographical area, and the number of patients served by these units; (2) the nature of the spinal cord injury services offered by the center, and satisfaction with these services on the part of former patients, referring physicians and third party payers with some influence on the patient's choice of service unit; (3) long-term trends in primary demand (total size) of the market; and (4) the referral mechanisms by which potential patients were or were not referred to the specific spinal cord injury unit.

The consulting team was able to discover declining primary demand, a large number of other spinal cord injury units which were also underutilized and a competitive service unit nearby with superior resources, equipment and facilities, a higher staff/patient ratio, and an excellent referral system. Therefore, the consulting team recommended an action which the center itself may not have seen as quickly, had the recommendation been generated internally: that the center close its spinal cord injury unit, since it would be unlikely to counteract its underutilization trend; and that the center focus its resources on other offered services which faced less competition and for which there was yet unmet demand.

SOURCE: Roberta N. Clarke, "Marketing Health Care: Problems in Implementation," *Health Care Management Review* (Winter 1978). Reprinted with permission Aspen Systems Corporation, © 1978.

uct is a tangible one, the organization has the option of selling or transferring the product to someone else or dropping it completely. Second, it has to decide whether the product should be dropped quickly or slowly. Third, it has to decide on the level of service to maintain to cover existing units.

Various government units have adopted sunset proposals for the review and termination of government programs on a regular cycle. Each federal program receives a review on a five- or six-year cycle. The reviewing committee determines whether the current program has met its objectives, whether it should be continued at the same budget level, or with higher or lower funding.

SUMMARY

Health care and social service organizations are primarily in the service business. Services can be defined as activities or benefits one party can offer to another that are essentially intangible and do not result in the ownership of anything. Services are intangible, inseparable, variable, and perishable. Services can be classified according to whether they are people- or equipment-based, and whether the client's presence is necessary. In health care, services are largely people-based, in spite of a growing reliance on medical technology. Service industries have lagged behind manufacturing firms in adopting and using marketing concepts. Yet rising costs and increased competition have forced service industries to search for new ways to increase productivity and responsiveness.

Most health care organizations are multiproduct or multiservice firms. They make decisions on the product mix, on each product item, and marketing mix strategies for each product at each stage of its life cycle. An organization's product mix can be described in terms of length, width, and depth. Some products constitute an organization's core products and others its ancillary products. Organizations may develop product leaders or crown jewels to advertise the organization.

A product itself can be defined as anything that can be offered to a market to satisfy a need. Three levels of the concept of a product can be distinguished. The core product answers the question: What need is the product really meeting? The tangible product is the form in which the product is seen or experienced: It includes the product's features, styling, quality, brand name, and packaging. The augmented product consists of the tangible product and additional services and benefits that differentiate the product from competitive offerings.

Products pass through a product life cycle consisting of four stages: introduction, growth, maturity, and decline. The S-shaped life cycle curve is the most common, but other patterns include a scalloped pattern, a cyclical pattern, and a fad pattern. There is some debate about whether the late maturity and decline stages are a result of a self-fulfilling expectation, where organizations cause the products to go into decline by providing inadequate support. Each stage of the life cycle presents new marketing challenges and requires adjustments in the target market and marketing mix.

NOTES

1. For further discussion of the marketing of professional services, see Doris Van Doren, Louise Smith, and Ronald Biglin, "The Challenges of Professional Services Marketing," *Journal of Consumers Marketing*, 2, 2 (Spring 1985), pp. 19–27.

2. Theodore Levitt, "Marketing Intangible Products and Product Intangibles," *Harvard Business Review* (May–June 1981), pp. 94–102.

3. See W. Earl Sasser, "Match Supply and Demand in Service Industries," *Harvard Business Review* (November–December 1976), pp. 133–40.

4. See Christopher H. Lovelock and Robert F. Young, "Look to Consumers to Increase Productivity," *Harvard Business Review* (May–June 1979), for a discussion of consumer involvement in the production of services.

5. William R. George and Hiran C. Barksdale, "Marketing Activities in the Service Industries," *Journal of Marketing* (October 1974), p. 65.

6. See Daniel T. Carroll, "Ten Commandments for Bank Marketing," *Bankers Magazine* (Autumn 1970), pp. 74–80.

7. Theodore Levitt, "Product-Line Approach to Service," *Harvard Business Review* (September–October 1972), pp. 41–52; see also his "The Industrialization of Service," *Harvard Business Review* (September–October 1976), pp. 63–74.

8. For an in-depth discussion of the recognition of people as service providers, see Tom Peters and Nancy Austin, *A Passion for Excellence* (New York: Random House, 1985), chap. 4, and chaps. 13–15.

9. "Special Delivery: With Even a Little Labor Music," *Time,* April 24, 1978, p. 60.

10. See John B. Stewart, "Functional Features in Product Strategy," *Harvard Business Review* (March–April 1959), pp. 65–78.

11. Theodore Levitt, *The Marketing Mode* (New York: McGraw-Hill, 1969), p. 2.

12. Nariman K. Dhalla and Sonia Yuspeh, "Forget the Product Life Cycle Concept," *Harvard Business Review* (January 1976).

13. Robert D. Buzzell, "Competitor Behavior and the Product Life Cycle," in *New Ideas for Successful Marketing,* John S. Wright and Jac L. Goldstucker, eds. (Chicago: American Marketing Association, 1966), pp. 46–68, p. 51.

14. Ibid., p. 51.

15. This system is spelled out in Philip Kotler, "Phasing Out Weak Products," *Harvard Business Review* (March–April 1965), pp. 107–18.

13

PRICE DECISIONS

Boston City Hospital is a municipal hospital which has the responsibility and reputation for service to the indigent. Historically the city reimbursed the hospital for deficits incurred in the course of providing free care to those who were presumed to be unable to pay. In 1979, however, the city, while acknowledging that deficit funding would continue, mandated that the deficit must be lessened, including the deficit for the Boston City Hospital Ambulatory Care Center (ACC).

The hospital estimated that roughly 40 percent of the annual 219,000 visits to the Ambulatory Care Center were made by self-pay clients (clients for whom there were no third-party payers.) A billing system mailed bills to both third-party and self-paying clients shortly after service delivery. In 1979, the fee for a single visit was $65, an amount considered unrealistically high for most of the self-pay population. The hospital has a sliding scale fee, but only 5 percent of the self-payers had been processed onto that system. It was not surprising, therefore, that the hospital collected less than 1 percent of all bills sent to self-pay clients of the outpatient department.

Faced with the prospect of lower deficit funding, the hospital sought to increase the amount of revenue collected from Ambulatory Care Center self-payers. One alternative was for the hospital to begin charging a modest fee to be paid in the ACC lobby before services were rendered. The reasoning behind this was that an immediate on-the-spot request for a small sum of money would generate greater revenues than a deferred bill for a large sum sent after the service has been rendered.

To obtain information on people's willingness to pay at the door, a survey was conducted. Interviewees were questioned about their willingness to pay a small sum at the door versus receiving a bill for $65 after the visit, about their awareness of the sliding fee scale, and about how much they would be willing to pay at the door. Three amounts were named: $6.50 and $13, representing 10 and 20 percent, respectively, of the $65 authorized charge, and $10, included to see if a round number would have more appeal.

The results suggested that most people preferred to pay a smaller amount at the door, but noted that they might not have the cash available at the time of service. (Preference for payment amount was relatively equally split between $6.50 and $13.) Therefore, a policy of payment at the door might not mean significantly increased collections, regardless of a change in price. The clients were also generally unaware of the sliding fee scale. And surprisingly, 20 percent of the respondents said that they had health insurance.

The hospital administration then began to consider other alternatives to increase Ambulatory Care Center revenues. These included promoting patient awareness of the sliding fee schedule and changing the patient financial mix by developing an intake mechanism that maximizes the identification of patients eligible for third-party insurance.

SOURCE: Based on material found in an unpublished class paper by Jane Carey, Jill McKinney, Mark Perkins, Richard Slusky, and Sarah Turner, "Marketing Survey—Boston City Hospital Ambulatory Care Center," December 14, 1979, Boston University Health Care Management Program.

One marketing tool that has presented persistent application problems in the health care arena is price. What *price* means and where and how it can be used as a strategic tool remains unclear because of third-party reimbursement, the constant threat of change in reimbursement policies, regulated pricing structures, apparent consumer price insensitivity, and characteristic lack of price awareness. Moreover, the role of price varies according to whether one is considering a reimbursed (insured) or nonreimbursed service, whether the focus of discussion is an individual medical service or a health insurance package to cover a collection of individual medical services, and whether the target market consists of patients, insurers, the government, or employers.

Prices go by various names. Health insurance companies and health maintenance organizations charge *premiums*. Individual clinicians require the payment of *fees*. Inpatient facilities have historically billed for *charges*. However, they are often reimbursed on the basis of *costs*, resulting in a constant confusion in the health care field between costs and prices. As one of many examples, an article entitled "Are Consumers Sensitive to Hospital Costs?"[1] used the terms "cost" and "price" interchangeably.

In addition, price includes subsidiary decision elements. *List* price is the stated price of the product or service. *Actual* price may be greater or smaller, depending upon the presence of a *premium* or *discount*. Discounts can be extended to special groups such as HMOs, PPOs, employer groups, and senior citizens. Sliding scale fees are examples of discounts to the poor.

Price is most often used to describe the actual charge made by an organization, yet it is not the only cost to the customer. Adam Smith noted long ago: "The real price of everything, what everything really costs to the man who wants to acquire it, is the toil and trouble of acquiring it." In addition to the price, customers face three other costs: effort costs, psychic costs, and waiting costs. Consider the problem of encouraging more middle-aged men to take a cardiovascular test. A prospect's resistance to doing this can be based on (1) an actual price of $100 for the test; (2) the time, cost, and trouble of traveling a long distance to the test center; (3) the fear of hearing bad news about one's heart; and (4) the waiting in the office for the test to begin. The cardiovascular center must recognize that its price of $100 is not the only deterrent, and that finding ways to reduce other customer costs may lead to more purchases.[2]

In the first part of this chapter, we will discuss classical pricing concepts and issues. In the second part we will address pricing issues specific to health care and social service organizations. These issues include the relationship of price, supply and demand, consumer awareness of and sensitivity to price, and the effect of reimbursement on pricing strategies.

In handling the complex issue of pricing, an organization should proceed through four stages. First, it should determine the *pricing objective*—to maximize surplus or profit, usage, or some other objective. Second, it should determine the *pricing strategy*—whether price should be cost-based, demand-based, or competition-based. Third, it should determine pricing in situations such as self-pay markets and reimbursed markets. Finally it should anticipate possible changes in reimbursement procedures in the future and how to respond to them.

SETTING PRICING OBJECTIVES

In spite of the complexity introduced by self-pay versus reimbursed markets, by charges versus costs versus negotiated prices, by no-pays, by retroactive denials of payment and the like, health care managers must still determine pricing objectives for their organizations. The term *price* must be redefined according to the specific situation. In self-pay markets *price* is the appropriate term, representing the amount consumers pay out-of-pocket to the organization. In some reimbursed markets, the relevant issue is revenue, whether revenue is determined by costs or charges ("prices"). Health care organizations often allocate fixed costs so as to maximize revenue when reimbursement is cost-based. In other reimbursement situations, *price* is the term used to describe a dictated charge based on costs or a negotiated charge based on competitive bids. An understanding of pricing objectives in health care must take these definitions of price into account. At least seven different pricing objectives can be distinguished: surplus maximization, net patient service revenue maximization, cost recovery, usage maximization, market disincentivization, public relations enhancement, and cross-subsidization.

Surplus or Profit Maximization

Surplus is the difference between net patient service revenue (total revenue minus discounts, bad debts, and contractual allowances, should there be any) and expenses. In most businesses, the term used for this difference is *profit.* Historically, most health care organizations were not-for-profit, meaning that they did not seek to make a profit and often operated at a loss. When their net revenues did by chance exceed expenses, it was called a surplus. When they operated at a loss, they anticipated that external funds from donors, grants, and other sources would compensate.

The dramatic decline in external funds to compensate for operating losses over the past decade has caused many nonprofit health care organizations to think and behave more like larger proprietary organizations. As a result, many more of them now use the term *profit.* Rather than assuming "it's wrong to make money serving the sick," many managers now recognize the need to make a surplus in order to build up reserves for future capital investments and to carry the organization through financially difficult periods (see Exhibit 13–1 for an example of this change in attitude).

But the objectives of *making* a surplus versus *maximizing* surplus are different. Most health care organizations dealing with reimbursed markets, particularly the not-for-profit, seek only to make a surplus sufficient to cover future anticipated operating and capital needs. They do not seek the largest possible surplus, but rather a surplus sufficient for near future needs. Initially it was thought that even proprietary health care chains, whose growth rates made them the darlings of Wall Street in the 1970s, did not attempt to maximize surplus. Their success in creating surplus was believed to come primarily from realizing savings in expenses through economies of scale and more effective centralized management. However, some studies have suggested that their earnings growth is a result of aggressive pricing and collection strategies rather than operating efficiency.[3]

Net Patient Service Revenue Maximization

The pricing or revenue objective of health care organizations when dealing primarily in cost-based reimbursed markets is to maximize net patient service revenue (total revenue minus discounts, bad debts, con-

EXHIBIT 13–1 Changing the Health Care Philosophy toward the Business Ethic

Survival Tactics

To Keep Doors Open, Nonprofit Hospitals Act Like Businesses

DAYTON, Ohio—L. R. "Rush" Jordan, a suave and gracious Southerner, is proud indeed of the turnaround in the business he came North to run some four years ago. "The corporation," as Mr. Jordan calls it, was barely breaking even then; but now, he says, it is generating a healthy profit, its market share is growing and its product line is expanding.

Mr. Jordan is the administrator of Miami Valley Hospital, a 772-bed, nonprofit medical center here. And if Mr. Jordan's business terminology (he also calls himself "chief executive officer") makes it sound as if he runs a corporate enterprise rather than a hospital, the usage is deliberate. He—and a growing number of other hospital officials—maintain that if hospitals don't become more businesslike, they won't survive.

What's more, says Mr. Jordan, "I'm not looking to just survive, I'm looking to thrive." He adds: "No matter how much do-goodism is in our hearts, we can't do good unless the bottom line is there. . . ."

The Valley's long-range strategy, its administrators say, is to develop profit-making businesses. Along those lines, it sells the services of its communications staff to outlying hospitals and has thereby brought in $60,000 this year.

The Valley is also selling other services, including its marketing, finance, speech therapy and pain-management programs. And to do so, Mr. Jordan says, the Valley's board of trustees last year formed a private, for-profit company that, like a bank holding company, owns the nonprofit hospital as well as several profit-making concerns. That action, he explains, was necessary because the current system of insurance reimbursement requires hospitals to use revenues from money-making activities to offset high prices of other services. "It's a system that discourages innovation and inhibits at the accumulation of needed capital," he says. . . .

Pondering the outlook for the Valley, Mr. Jordan says: "In the near future, very soon, businesses will be forcing us to compete for their employees (as patients) on the basis of price." Already, a group of corporate benefit managers in Dayton has formed its own coalition and is currently designing health-insurance plans that would encourage employees to use less-costly facilities. Under such plans, if the worker goes to a high priced hospital, he would get only part of his bill reimbursed; by going to a cheaper hospital, he would get all of his bill reimbursed.

Mr. Jordan believes that to keep the Valley's prices down, the hospital must spread its costs over a large number of programs. Already, servicing the debt for the hospital's recently completed construction project will account for nearly half the boost in 1983 room charges. (The Valley will charge $172 for a semiprivate room next year, up $15 from this year's $157.)

"Financially, hospitals are in a very hostile climate," Mr. Jordan says. "We have no choice but to diversify, to spread our costs into areas where we can accumulate capital."

SOURCE: Michael Waldholz, "To Keep Doors Open, Nonprofit Hospitals Act Like Businesses," *The Wall Street Journal,* December 29, 1982, p. 1. Reprinted by permission of *The Wall Street Journal,*

tractual allowances, retroactive denials, and disallowed expenses). Traditional cost-based reimbursement does not motivate an organization to cut cost, nor does it allow much opportunity to demand a higher percentage of surplus per unit of service. Therefore, most organizations operating under these conditions implicitly operate by the objective of maximizing net patient service revenue. One outcome is to seek to maximize the number of charge-based patients (usually commercially insured patients) served by the organization. Charge-based patients bring in both higher revenue and higher surplus per unit of service.

Success in maximizing net patient service revenue provides three advantages: (1) Where reimbursement does exceed cost (when reimbursement includes a surplus per unit payment), maximizing net patient service revenue maximizes absolute surplus dollars; (2) even when reimbursement covers costs only, greater net patient service revenue can result in better coverage of fixed costs; (3) if net patient service revenues are maximized, this should mean that the health care organization is being utilized at close to capacity, which positions it well politically for the purposes of future expansion, and in terms of public relations. It also means that the organization will not suffer the financial penalty built into some reimbursement formulas for underutilization.

From a marketing perspective, maximizing net patient service revenue can be achieved through attracting not just the highest possible volume of patients able to be served by the organization, but by drawing in the most financially attractive (usually commercially insured) patients. This objective must be meshed, nevertheless, with the ethical consideration of serving the poor or nonreimbursed patient. Maximizing net patient service revenue is also influenced by financial and accounting decisions regarding the allocation of costs. Health care organizations often allocate heavy fixed costs to the services that are most heavily utilized by cost-reimbursed patients. As a result, discussions of maximizing net patient service revenue extend well beyond marketing into finance and accounting.

Some health care organizations and efforts clearly seek to maximize surplus. They fall into two categories: fundraising efforts and self-pay markets. A charity organization will set the price for attending a major benefit dinner with the objective of maximizing its receipts over its costs. A retail dental chain serving a largely self-pay market may seek to maximize its profits in order to please its shareholders.

Surplus maximizing pricing requires the organization to estimate two functions, the demand function and the cost function. These two functions are sufficient for deriving the theoretically best price. The demand function describes the expected quantity demanded per period (Q) at various prices (P) that might be charged. Suppose the organization is able to determine through demand analysis that its demand equation is

$$Q = 1{,}000 - 4P \qquad \textbf{(13–1)}$$

This says that demand is forecasted to be at most 1,000 units; and for every $1 of price, there will be 4 fewer units sold. Thus the number of units purchased at a price of, say, $150 would be 400 units [$Q = 1{,}000 - 4(150)$].

The cost function describes the expected total cost (C) for various quantities per period (Q) that might be produced. Suppose the organization derived the following cost equation for its service:

$$C = 6{,}000 + 50\,Q \qquad \textbf{(13–2)}$$

With these demand and cost equations, the organization is in a position to determine the surplus-maximization price. Needed are two more equations, both definitional in nature. First, total revenue (R) is equal to price times quantity sold:

$$R = PQ \qquad \textbf{(13–3)}$$

Second, total surplus (S) is the difference between total revenue and total cost:

$$S = R - C \qquad \textbf{(13–4)}$$

With these four equations, the organization is in a position to find the surplus-maximizing price. The surplus equation (13–4) can be turned into a pure function of the price charged:

$$S = R - C$$

$$S = PQ - C$$

$$S = PQ - (6{,}000 + 50Q)$$

$$S = P\,(1{,}000 - 4P) - 6{,}000 - 50\,(1{,}000 - 4P)$$

$$S = 1{,}000P - 4P^2 - 6{,}000 - 50{,}000 + 200P$$

$$S = -56{,}000 + 1{,}200P - 4P^2 \qquad \textbf{(13–5)}$$

Equation 13–5 shows total surplus expressed as a function of the price that will be charged. The surplus-maximizing price can be found by using differential calculus or trial and error, trying out different prices to determine the shape of the surplus function and the location of the maximum price. The surplus function turns out to be a parabola or hatlike figure, and surplus reaches its highest point ($34,000) at a price of $150. At this price, the organization sells 400 units that produce a total revenue of $60,000.

This model for finding the surplus-maximizing price, in spite of its theoretical elegance, is subject to four practical limitations:

1. The model shows how to find the price that maximizes short-run rather than long-run surplus. There may be a tradeoff between short-run and long-run surplus maximization, as when buyers get angry at the high price and eventually switch to other sellers.
2. There are other parties to consider in setting a price, even in non-third-party reimbursement settings. The model considers only the ultimate consumers' response to alternative prices; but employers, insurers, competitors, suppliers, professional associations, government, and the general public also may respond. Employers and insurers who try to influence where employees receive health care may modify coverage away from high-priced providers, thereby lessening demand. A high price might lead competitors to raise or lower prices, in which case the demand would be different than suggested by the demand function if it assumed no competitive reaction. Various suppliers may take the price to reflect the organization's ability to pay and may raise their prices accordingly, in which case the cost function would be different than that assumed with no supplier reaction. Professional associations may have strong feelings or policies about appropriate prices. The government, acting in the public interest, might establish a price ceiling, and this may exclude the surplus-maximizing price. Finally, the general public might complain about the organization if its price appears to be too high.
3. This pricing model assumes that price can be set independently of the other elements in the marketing mix. But the other elements will affect demand and must be part of the demand function in searching for the optimal price. Thus, an optometry store can charge higher prices if it provides better than average service, a broader product line, or in some other way builds consumer interest and loyalty.
4. This pricing model assumes that the demand and cost function can be estimated accurately. In the case of a new service, there is no experience upon which to base these estimates. Unless data are available on a similar service, estimates are likely to be highly subjective. Even with established services, this model is difficult to implement. Demand may not be highly predictable or may not be closely related to price. For example, prospective parents seeking to take a Lamaze childbirth course rarely seek price comparisons in order to select the least expensive course; they rely instead on recommendation of experts or friends. This model is also difficult to utilize if cost functions are not known accurately. Many health care orga-

nizations are not yet financially sophisticated enough to be able to determine their own cost functions. A solo practitioner dental office rarely has financial talents available to it beyond bookkeeping and basic accounting, and even large inpatient facilities are only now developing information systems that allow them to assess accurately fully allocated costs and marginal costs.

Cost Recovery

Many health care organizations seek a price or effective revenue per unit of service that allows them to recover all or a reasonable part of their costs. Cost-based reimbursement was developed with this pricing (revenue) objective in mind. Blue Cross/Blue Shield, for example, has traditionally provided for *full cost recovery*. Some health care or social service organizations seek only *partial cost recovery* because they rely on external sources to compensate for unrecovered costs. Municipal health care organizations could conceivably charge higher prices and increase their revenue to break even, but this might result in denial of service to the segment without health care coverage which the municipal health care organizations were originally developed to serve. Medical schools often seek to recover their operating costs through tuition, relying on gifts, grants, bond issues, or other sources to raise needed capital.

Again, like the surplus maximization model, the cost recovery model requires the organization to know what its costs are—and are likely to be—in order to set prices. DRG reimbursement is intended to be based on a cost recovery objective, averaging costs across a large range of providers. In reimbursed settings, health care organizations, to determine costs, must be aware not only of general operating and capital costs, but also of retroactive denials, disallowed expenses, delayed payments, and resulting cash flow problems characteristic of organizations relying heavily on third-party reimbursement.

Usage Maximization

Health care and social service organizations may seek to maximize the total number of users of the service. The objective of maximizing net patient service revenue entails, among other activities, maximizing utilization. If variable costs are low, if there are no revenue caps, and if each user represents additional revenue to the organization, the health care organization may wish to maximize utilization. Health promotion programs often fit this model. Organizations which feel that users and society profit from their services sometimes lower their prices in order to maximize utilization. Exhibit 13–2 contains an example. In the belief that a low price attracts greater utilization, some organizations offer their products or services for free. Even here there can be exceptions. Consider the following situation:[4]

EXHIBIT 13–2 Lowering Price to Maximize Utilization

Hospital Cuts ER Charges, Ends Deposit Requirement

A Chicago hospital has cut basic emergency room charges in half and is eliminating its cash deposit requirement to boost hospital utilization. "Because of the economy and resulting unemployment, we are concerned that emergency room charges and cash deposit requirements may become barriers to good medical care for persons who need it," said Gerald W. Mungerson, executive director, Illinois Masonic Medical Center. IMMC on June 1 reduced the emergency room fee for minor illness and injury to $17 from $35 per visit. It also reduced "second level" fees for more serious cases, involving laboratory and X-ray services, to $48 from $65. The two categories have accounted for 68% of IMMC's emergency room visits since October 1. Emergency room admissions have dropped by 12% in the past year, Mr. Mungerson said, adding that the hospital expects the price reductions to boost admissions. IMMC eliminated the cash deposits after they caused several patients to cancel hospitalization for elective treatment. All non-emergency patients, before admission, had to pay the estimated part of their bills that insurance wouldn't cover.

SOURCE: Reprinted with permission from the July 1982 issue of *Modern Healthcare Magazine.* Copyright Crain Communications Inc., 740 N. Rush, Chicago, IL 60611. All rights reserved.

Family planners in India initially believed the distribution of free contraceptives would lead to the greatest level of usage. However, they discovered two flaws in the reasoning. Some potential consumers would interpret the zero price to imply low quality and avoid the free brand. In addition, many retailers would not carry it or display it prominently because it did not yield them profit, with the result that fewer units were ultimately available to consumers.

In many situations, a low price stimulates higher usage *and* may produce more revenue in the long run. However, the value offered by a low price must be weighed against the drawback of a low price being associated with low quality.

Market Disincentivization

Pricing might be undertaken with the objective of discouraging as many people as possible from purchasing a particular product or service. There are many reasons an organization might want to do this. It might consider the product to be bad for people; or it might want to discourage people from overtaxing a facility; or it might be trying to solve a temporary shortage; or it might want to discourage the patronage of certain classes of buyers.

One purpose of high government taxes on cigarettes and liquor is to discourage the use of these products. But the price is never raised high enough because the government has come to rely on the substantial revenue produced by these taxes. A tax that is truly disincentivizing would yield the government no revenue and might create a large black market.

Some HMOs use disincentive pricing to discourage nonemergency use of HMO services on weekends and evenings, when fewer clinical staff are available. They also may charge higher prices for nonappointment walk-in visits as a way to discourage walk-ins and to encourage appointment-setting behavior.

Public Relations Enhancement

An organization may choose to set prices based on a public relations objective. Hospitals often set daily room rate charges (prices) on the low side because room rates receive more publicity than charges for other services. Health care organizations, which increasingly operate in the public eye, must consider how their prices look to the public. If the room rate must be kept low because of its publicity value, then the organization may compensate by raising charges on services that do not receive such publicity. Even under conditions of prospective payment, where charges are irrelevant for accounting purposes, stated room rates still have a public relations value.

An interesting example of public relations pricing can be found in the emergency rooms and outpatient departments of urban hospitals. Set up decades ago to meet community demand and to provide care for the indigent, the emergency rooms and outpatient departments could never expect to collect much revenue because their primary users were poor. Therefore, their prices were set low. Then Hill-Burton money for hospital construction became available, carrying with it the requirement that the hospital provide a certain amount of free care. As a result, hospitals raised prices in emergency rooms and outpatient departments in order to look like they were providing more free care. The change in prices was made for public relations purposes, with little expectation that the higher prices would result in higher revenues.

Cross-Subsidization

A major pricing objective of many health care organizations is to balance the surpluses and losses of varying market segments and services through cross-subsidization. Services like the ambulatory care department, ICU, obstetric service, and pediatric service of a full service hospital generally produce a loss. However, for clinical, public relations, and other reasons, it is often important for a hospital to keep these services. Therefore, the hospital must cross-subsidize them using surpluses generated by "profitable" services such as the medical-surgical service. Under DRG's, many hospitals are seeking a balance between profitable and unprofitable DRG categories.

Health care organizations also cross-subsidize market segments. Medicare and Medicaid reimbursement often pays less than full costs for services. Health care organizations have been able to continue serving Medicaid and Medicare patients only by cross-subsidizing these segments through surpluses earned on Blue Cross and commercially insured patients. This is often referred to as "cost shifting" and has become the target of business and insurance companies nationally. Exhibit 13–3 is an advertisement designed to educate those who pay for health insurance about their unwitting role in cross-subsidizing Medicare and Medicaid patients. The advertisement's suggestion that all third party payers (government, Blue Cross, and commercial insurers) pay the same rates, a step being suggested or taken in a few states, is a major step toward removing cross-subsidization. Exhibit 13–4 discusses cross-subsidization under prospective payment.

CHOOSING A PRICING STRATEGY

After the organization has defined its pricing objective, it can consider the appropriate pricing strategy. Pricing strategies tend to be cost-oriented, demand-oriented, or competition-oriented. In the reimbursed health care market, an additional pricing strategy is maximum-reimbursement-oriented.

Cost-Oriented Pricing

Cost-oriented pricing refers to setting prices largely on the basis of costs. Most reimbursement formulas are cost-oriented. Even charges are usually determined on the basis of costs, with a small markup on the cost added to create the charge. Cost-oriented pricing is also used in settings where reimbursement is not an issue. The American Red Cross charges a price for its blood that covers the "irreducible cost of recruiting, processing, collecting and distributing the blood to hospitals." Many private social service agencies that deal with poor populations charge less than their costs; the remaining costs are covered by donations and interest on endowment funds.

The most popular form of cost-oriented pricing is known as *breakeven analysis.* The purpose of breakeven analysis is to determine, for any proposed price, how many units of an item would have to be sold to cover the costs fully; this is known as the *breakeven volume.* Perhaps the director of an agency for the hard of hearing wants to set a price to

EXHIBIT 13–3

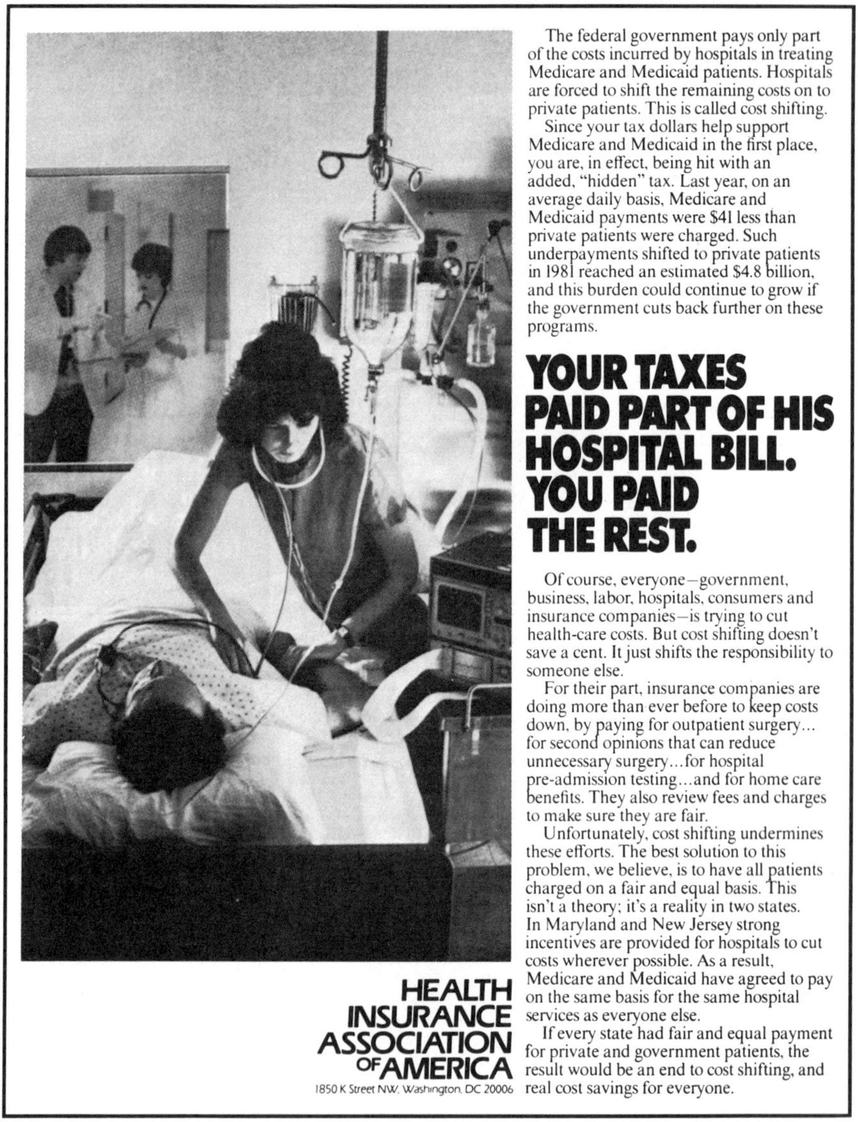

The federal government pays only part of the costs incurred by hospitals in treating Medicare and Medicaid patients. Hospitals are forced to shift the remaining costs on to private patients. This is called cost shifting.
Since your tax dollars help support Medicare and Medicaid in the first place, you are, in effect, being hit with an added, "hidden" tax. Last year, on an average daily basis, Medicare and Medicaid payments were $41 less than private patients were charged. Such underpayments shifted to private patients in 1981 reached an estimated $4.8 billion, and this burden could continue to grow if the government cuts back further on these programs.
YOUR TAXES PAID PART OF HIS HOSPITAL BILL. YOU PAID THE REST.
Of course, everyone—government, business, labor, hospitals, consumers and insurance companies—is trying to cut health-care costs. But cost shifting doesn't save a cent. It just shifts the responsibility to someone else.
For their part, insurance companies are doing more than ever before to keep costs down, by paying for outpatient surgery... for second opinions that can reduce unnecessary surgery...for hospital pre-admission testing...and for home care benefits. They also review fees and charges to make sure they are fair.
Unfortunately, cost shifting undermines these efforts. The best solution to this problem, we believe, is to have all patients charged on a fair and equal basis. This isn't a theory; it's a reality in two states. In Maryland and New Jersey strong incentives are provided for hospitals to cut costs wherever possible. As a result, Medicare and Medicaid have agreed to pay on the same basis for the same hospital services as everyone else.
If every state had fair and equal payment for private and government patients, the result would be an end to cost shifting, and real cost savings for everyone.
HEALTH INSURANCE ASSOCIATION OF AMERICA
1850 K Street NW, Washington, DC 20006

SOURCE: Courtesy of the Health Insurance Association of America.

businesses for the use of his agency's mobile hearing test van to test their employees' hearing that would cover the total costs of operating the van over the coming year. Suppose the fixed costs of the van—garage facilities, excise taxes, maintenance of the van and the equipment in it, and so on—are $30,000.

EXHIBIT 13–4 Cross-Subsidization under Prospective Payment

The ability to transfer costs is directly related to the percentage of revenue derived from nonregulated charge-based payers. The successful transfer of costs should moderate the revenue constraints of prospective payments. Thus, if hospitals respond to prospective payment by shifting costs, it is expected that transfers will be more pronounced in suburban hospitals, which typically have the greatest percentage of revenue derived from nonregulated, charge-based patients, than in inner-city hospitals that typically have the smallest percentage of revenue derived from charge-based, nonregulated patients.

Regarding (a) constraint on cross-subsidization, it is clear that all groups of patients cannot be used for this purpose. For example, in many areas, Blue Cross negotiates very "tough" cost-based reimbursement contracts in which their rate of reimbursement is even less than that for Medicare patients. Similarly, in many states hospital reimbursement for services provided to Medicare patients does not cover the cost of providing services. As a result, commercially insured patients represent the principal group which can be used for cross-subsidization of losses incurred in the provision of services to Medicare patients.

SOURCE: Michael D. Rosko and Robert W. Broyles, "Unintended Consequences of Prospective Payment," *Health Care Management Review* (Summer 1984), pp. 35–44. Reprinted with permission of Aspen Systems Corporation, copyright 1984.

The breakeven volume can be readily calculated for any proposed price by using the following formula:

$$\text{breakeven volume} = \frac{\text{fixed cost}}{\text{price} - \text{variable cost}} \qquad \textbf{(13–6)}$$

Using the numbers in the previous example, we get:

$$\text{breakeven volume} = \frac{\$30{,}000}{\$30 - \$20} = 3000$$

On the other hand, if the agency director thought of charging $25 per employee, Equation 13–6 indicates that he would have to attract 6,000 employees to break even.

Suppose the mobile van unit has the capacity to handle 6,000 employee hearing tests a year and the agency director would like to attract that number. He can try to estimate a demand curve showing how many employees would have their hearing tested at each price. Suppose Figure 13–1 shows the estimated demand curve. The $30 fee

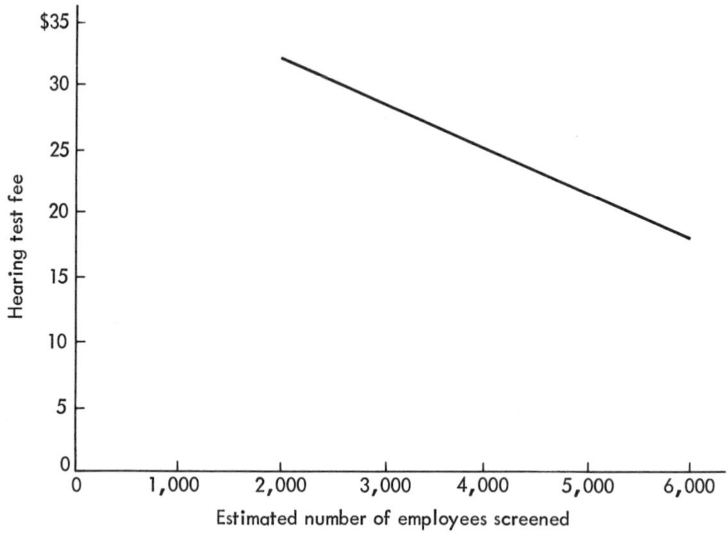

FIGURE 13–1 Estimated Demand Curve for a Mobile Hearing Test Van

would succeed in attracting 3,000 employees and allow the mobile van to break even. But the $25 fee would attract only 4,500 employees, not 6,000, and result in a loss. The agency director may decide to bear the loss and make it up through fundraising, in order to attract 4,500 employees. If he wants to attract 6,000 employees, a fee of $18 would be required according to Figure 13–1, thus spelling an even larger loss.

Cost-oriented pricing is popular for a number of reasons. First, there is generally less uncertainty about costs than about demand. By basing the price on cost, the organization simplifies the pricing task considerably; there is no need to make frequent adjustments as demand conditions change. Second, when all organizations in the industry use this approach, their prices are similar if their costs and markups are similar. Price competition can therefore be minimized. Third, there is the feeling that cost-markup pricing is socially fairer to buyers and sellers. Sellers do not take advantage of buyers when the demand becomes acute; yet sellers earn a fair return on investment. Thus the popularity of cost-oriented pricing rests on its administrative simplicity, competitive harmony, and social fairness.

Demand-Oriented Pricing

Demand-oriented pricing looks at the condition of demand rather than the level of costs to set the price. Demand-oriented sellers estimate how much value buyers see in the market offer and price accordingly. Thus a nursing home might charge $50 a day for a single room and $35 a day for a double room. The premise is that price should reflect the *perceived value* in the buyer's head. A corollary is that an organization should invest in building up the perceived value of the offer if it wants to charge a higher price. Thus a medical group practice that builds a reputation for excellent, quick, and responsive care can charge a higher fee than an average group practice.

A common form of demand-oriented pricing is price discrimination, in which a particular product is sold at two or more prices. Price discrimination takes various forms. Pricing that discriminates on a customer basis is illustrated when a neighborhood health center using a sliding scale charges a poor patient less. Pricing that discriminates on a product version basis occurs when the Massachusetts General Hospital charges more for the luxurious accommodations and service offered in its Phillips House than for patient rooms in the rest of the hospital. Product version price discrimination is not true price discrimination, which assumes an identical product. Thus, the Phillips House, while providing the same clinical product, is providing a different augmented product. Pricing that discriminates on a time basis occurs when a physician charges a patient more for a weekend than a weekday medical visit.

For price discrimination to work, the market must be segmentable, and the segments must show different intensities of demand.[5] Demand-oriented pricing also assumes that some segments of the market are both aware of and sensitive to price. This is often not the case in the health care field. Consumers are more likely to be aware of and sensitive to prices for health care services that are not well covered by third-party reimbursement and have low perceived risk. Children's dental checkups fall into this category. They call for repetitive outlays of cash for a service that has little risk associated with it. Therefore, parents are more willing to shop around for a low-cost dental provider for pediatric checkups than they would be for low-cost open heart surgery.

An interesting subset of a demand-oriented pricing strategy is one which recognizes that, in certain situations, consumers equate price with quality.[6] If they seek to assure themselves that they are receiving high-quality medical care, they may choose the higher-priced care. This is particularly likely to happen if the consumer is unable to judge the quality of the services by other characteristics, if the service is covered by a third party, and if the purchase of the service represents significant risk to the consumer. Thus, demand-oriented pricing need not necessarily mean that demand will increase as price falls, because of the price-quality equation. Examples of the effect of equating price with quality in health care settings are given in Exhibit 13–5.

Competition-Oriented Pricing

When a health care organization sets its prices chiefly on the basis of what competitors are charging, its pricing policy can be described as

EXHIBIT 13–5

The Price-Quality Equation of Demand

A medical group practice located in one of the poorest neighborhoods in Cleveland, Ohio promoted itself and its physicians by stating in its promotional literature that it "attracts health care professionals who are attracted by the program's objectives and are willing to earn less than what the market will bear." Consumers who read this assumed that, if the physicians were paid less than other physicians, they must be less competent than other physicians, leading the consumers to seek their health care elsewhere.

The outpatient department of a major teaching hospital employed salaried staff physicians full time to serve the medical needs of the department's patients, most of whom were indigent. Outpatient department charges were held at a reasonable level, in the hope that some of the patients would try to pay them. However, the staff physicians felt that charges for their services should be at a higher level, equal to the charges of their colleagues in private practice, even though the staff physicians received the same salary, regardless of what was charged. They felt that the charge was a reflection of their status and quality.

competition-oriented. It may choose to charge (1) the same as the competition, (2) a higher price, or (3) a lower price. The distinguishing characteristic is that the organization does *not* seek to maintain a rigid relation between its price and its own costs or demand. Its own costs or demand may change, but the organization maintains its price because competitors maintain their prices. Conversely, the same organization will change its price when competitors change theirs, even if its own costs or demand have not altered.

The most popular type of competition-oriented pricing is that under which an organization tries to keep its price at the average level charged by the competition. Called *going rate* or *imitative* pricing, it is popular for several reasons. Where costs are difficult to measure, it is felt that the going price represents the collective wisdom of the industry concerning the price that yields a fair return. It is also felt that conforming to a going price will be least disruptive of industry harmony. The difficulty of knowing how buyers and competitors might react to price differentials is still another reason for this pricing.

Physicians are encouraged by both their professional association and by commercial insurers to use a going-rate competition-oriented pricing strategy by charging "usual, customary and reasonable" fees.

Attempts to formalize going-rate fee structures among physicians were ruled by the Supreme Court to be in violation of the antitrust laws in 1982.[7] However, HMOs, PPOs, and companies in direct negotiation with physician groups have negotiated going-rate (or often lower than going rate) fee structures which the physicians accept in order to generate a continual flow of patients.

Many health care organizations engage in competition-oriented pricing by offering a service at a price lower than competitive prices. We see trade journal headlines such as "Same-day Surgery Competes with Flat Rate"[8] and "St. Louis Hospital Guarantees Rates for Outpatient Surgery: A St. Louis Hospital Is Guaranteeing Discounted Fixed-rate Prices for Outpatient Surgical Procedures through 1985."[9] Price advertising is usually engaged in by health care providers offering services at lower than average prices. And the competitive bidding required of California hospitals wanting a contract to serve Medi-Cal patients and of hospitals in the three counties surrounding Cleveland, Ohio, that wanted to serve Blue Cross/Blue Shield patients favored lower bids (although other criteria were considered as well).[10] The continued focus on cost containment by employers and insurers as well as the ongoing growth of HMOs and PPOs is likely to increase the amount and intensity of competitive bidding. This is true not only for hospitals, but also for physician groups, nursing homes, home health agencies, and other providers from which these organizations might want to contract for services.[11]

Maximum-Reimbursement-Oriented Pricing

Many health care organizations charge the maximum allowed by reimbursement agencies. This may be viewed as a perverted form of demand pricing, or "charging what the market will bear." It is only human nature that a provider will seek to charge as much as other organizations providing the same service. This strategy is described in an excerpt from an article on health care costs:

> In Massachusetts, . . . Blue Shield has established maximum fees for various medical procedures but so far has refused to tell doctors what the maximums are, lest everybody charge them. Many doctors do anyway. A Boston specialist's secretary explains: "Suppose we charge $45 for a service and then we learn that another doctor is being paid $65 for the same service. We then cannot ask $65 even though we may be as good or perhaps better. Blue Shield permits us to raise our prices by a small percentage from time to time, but we will never reach the maximum allowable. So the answer is to charge the insurance people well over the maximum. For a biopsy, we may put $110 on the insurance form. If the insurance company returns us $90, we know that is their maximum, and we then charge accordingly."[12]

There are four pricing strategies available to health care organizations. Now we will address some pricing issues specific to health care and social service organizations.

THE RELATIONSHIP OF PRICE AND DEMAND IN HEALTH CARE

Although pricing in other industries is not necessarily straightforward, we can at least usually assume in a gross sense that demand (D) is a function of price (P)—that is:

$$D = f(P) \tag{13–7}$$

However, in the health care field, it is safer to say that demand (D) is function of supply (S) and health insurance coverage (C):

$$D = f(S,C) \tag{13–8}$$

A classic study in 1961 by Roemer[13] was the first to demonstrate that health care demand expands to meet the supply, regardless of price. Roemer's study focused on the supply of hospital beds and services. Other studies have found the same demand response to the supply of physicians.[14] More recent studies, in *Scientific American* and *Health Affairs*,[15] stated that the number of physicians, their medical specialties, and styles of practice were primary determinants of health care demand. These and other studies have gone so far as to say that the health of those people being served by the physicians in the study had little if any relationship to the actual demand for health care services.[16] For example, in a study of 22 surgical procedures performed in one state, the rate of performance of certain procedures such as tonsillectomies, spinal fusions, and pacemaker insertions were found to show up to a fivefold variation from one community to the next (see Exhibit 13–6).

Thus, rather than being determined by price, demand for health care services appears to be heavily determined by suppliers. It is difficult for consumers to act in a price-sensitive manner when the control of health care purchase decisions is not usually in their hands:[17]

> Medicine is inherently a sellers' market. The customer (patient) has no bargaining power; he initiates only one decision—to see a doctor. The sellers (doctors and hospitals) then take over; they decide what services the patient needs, and do not ask but order him to buy. Unable to diagnose his own illness, the patient has little choice but meekly to obey.[18]

The provider decides what services are to be used, and the consumer, unable to make these medical decisions for himself, acquiesces

EXHIBIT 13–6

Variations in Medical Practice

A little more than two years ago, gynecologists in Lewiston, Maine, learned that they were removing women's uteruses four times more often than colleagues statewide. As one researcher put it, Lewiston gynecologists "kind of specialized in hysterectomies."

According to some accounts, the Lewiston specialists reacted to the new data with consternation, disbelief and anger. In the last two years, the hysterectomy rate in Lewiston has fallen by almost half, to about twice the statewide average. "It's probably still going down," one researcher said in an interview last week.

In Iowa, varicose vein surgery is performed up to 10 times more often in one community than another; hemorrhoid operations vary almost fivefold; and a child's chances of having his tonsils out by the age of 15 ranges from 7 percent to 70 percent depending on where he lives.

A child who lives in Waterville, Maine, for instance, is much more likely to be hospitalized for any reason than another child who lives next door in Augusta or downstate in Portland.

The residents of Ellsworth, Maine, are hospitalized for atherosclerosis (hardening of the arteries) 12 times more often than people living in Norway, Maine.

The newly appreciated disparities in hospital use "cannot be explained on the basis of difference in age or distribution of disease among populations" comments Dr. Philip Caper of Harvard University (due to the strength of the research methodology used to generate the data).

SOURCE: Richard A. Knox, "The Many Faces of Health Care," *The Boston Globe,* August 20, 1984, pp. 41–43. Reprinted courtesy of *The Boston Globe.*

with little thought to the alternatives or to the relative benefits versus monetary costs of the selected course of action. It is an interesting phenomenon in the health care field that the physician may be both the supplier and the demander (the one who determines demand) of health care services; in this situation, price cannot easily function to regulate demand.

Health care demand is also a function of health insurance or third-party coverage. Third-party reimbursement covers roughly 60 percent of physicians' fees and well over 90 percent of hospitalization costs. By lowering the economic barrier to use, it effectively makes many types of health care available at a zero or minimal price. Not surprisingly, the demand for services increases with increasing third-party coverage.[19]

Third-party coverage may be a determinant not only of demand, but also of price; that is

$$P = f(C) \tag{13–9}$$

Juba[20] suggests that, by lowering the real out-of-pocket price to the consumer, third-party coverage increases demand. Physicians, sensing an increase in demand, raise their price as traditional economic theory suggests should happen when demand increases without concomitant supply increases. On a more practical level, physicians and hospitals often find their "prices" set for them by third-party coverage. The prices, fees, or charges are set as a maximum, but the incentive of the health care provider is to charge the maximum allowed by the third party. Thus we find positive correlations between prices and third-party coverage.[21]

As a result of the relationship among demand, supply, coverage, and price, an interesting phenomenon in the health care field occurs infrequently elsewhere. In order to increase revenues, suppliers in other fields may raise their prices or attempt to increase their sales through gaining new customers or generating more sales from existing customers. However, health care providers and suppliers often do not have the freedom to raise prices as they choose because of third-party coverage fee or charge ceilings, negotiated per unit fees, or prospective payment systems. In addition, strong professional and peer norms against promotion and advertising have made it difficult for health care providers to develop strategies to attract new customers.

Yet the health care provider has until recently been in a uniquely desirable position to generate additional sales from existing customers. Since it is the provider who determines demand and usage of health care services, the provider may merely diagnose the need for additional services in order to increase revenues without increasing prices. While third-party coverage may limit price per unit of service, it has historically set no limits on volume of services. This is rapidly changing for hospitals in states where revenue caps exist, and for physicians under contract to PPOs. Hospitals, until recent reimbursement regulations caught up with them, would often run every new patient to be admitted through a series of high-charge diagnostic tests and might keep the patient hospitalized for extra days in order to build up total charges. In regulated situations, where provider fees or charges have been held constant, health care service volume has historically increased, generating greater revenues for providers[22] (see Exhibit 13–7).

The relationships between price, demand, supply, and third-party coverage suggest that, in the near term, price to the consumer may not have the power as a marketing tool it has in other industries. Moreover, the freedom health care providers (suppliers) have in setting price is

EXHIBIT 13–7 The Relationship between Fees and Volume

On Doctors Who Rush from Fee to Fee

The article on "Why Doctors are willing to freeze fees" (Regulators, March 5) missed one key element on remuneration. Physicians' fees may indeed have risen only by 148.5% in 10 years, but the missing element is frequency of service calls. Is there any person who has visited a surgery or general medicine ward in any hospital who has not seen attending physicians walking very briskly from room to room? This is not for their physical health. The usual dialogue with the patient is: "How are you today? Let's look at your chart. Your color is improved." Off they go. This costs Medicare, Medicaid, or someone $25 to $75 (per three minutes), depending on specialty. Neurologists do super well.

Unless this abuse is eliminated, fees could stay constant, or even decline, to no avail. Most doctors can walk faster or take to jogging.

Harold B. Reisman
Weston, Conn.

SOURCE: "Readers Report," *Business Week,* April 16, 1984, p. 10.

less than in other industries due to third-party reimbursement, cost-containment measures, and professional norms, thereby limiting price's usefulness as a marketing tool. On the other hand, the rapid rise in costs has caused the government and businesses (and, as a result, insurers) to become more sensitive to pricing. In addition, the health care market is heterogeneous. We would expect the role of price to vary according to the market segment in question. For example, let's look now at price in self-pay versus reimbursed markets.

THE SELF-PAY MARKET

The role price plays as a regulator of demand varies according to how well the consumer is covered for the services in question. Nationwide, patients self-pay only 6 percent of the hospital bills and 39 percent of the physician's fees. When patients are covered for the recommended service, they rarely ask how much the service costs. They are much more likely to ask, "will it cure me?" Patients are generally unaware of hospital charge rates, but have somewhat greater familiarity with office visit fees, since they are more likely to self-pay for office visits. Exhibit 13–8 provides an example of this contrasting orientation to price. The

EXHIBIT 13–8 Contrasting Price Sensitivities

Low Price Sensitivity

For most people, hospitals' price differences are not worth much attention. We show prices for three items—room and board in a semi-private room, room and board in an intensive care unit, and an hour in an operating room. These items comprise 30% to 50% of a typical hospital's billings.

On each of the items, some of the hospitals are more than twice as expensive as others. Although prices on items we do not report—X-rays, lab tests, drugs, etc.—in some cases tend to offset the differences the chart shows, the differences are still large.

But are these differences important to you? If you have little or no insurance, of course, they are. For a long hospital stay, they can mean thousands of dollars. On the other hand, if you have a policy like the federal employees' Blue Cross/Blue Shield plan, your hospital bills will be paid in full even at the most expensive of the hospitals. If your policy is a little less generous, and covers only 80 percent of hospital costs, the differences among hospitals in your out-of-pocket cost are still relatively small unless you have a rather long stay. For instance, although the price difference between Suburban and Howard University Hospital for a typical appendectomy is about $300, if you pay just 20 percent, the out of pocket difference is only about $60.

You may, of course, want to use a lower priced hospital as an act of public responsibility—your small contribution to controlling health care costs. But even this sort of decision is not simple. If you decide to take your hernia repair to Sibley instead of Georgetown because Georgetown is so much more expensive, at least be aware that Georgetown's high prices may reflect the fact that it is a university hospital, with a responsibility for training future doctors and dealing with complex cases.

SOURCE: Washington Consumers' Checkbook, II, 4 (Summer 1980), p. 35 (Washington, DC: Washington Center for the Study of Services).

High Price Sensitivity

When a surgeon tells a patient what he or she charges for a particular procedure (or, more typically, when the patient receives the surgeon's bill), the patient has no way of knowing how that surgeon's fee compares with fees charged by other surgeons doing the same procedure in the same community. The purpose of this directory is to inform patients about differences in surgical fees, which often are extremely large, and how a particular surgeon's fee compares to those of his or her colleagues. Patients can then take price into account choosing a surgeon or an operation. Consumer access to comparative surgical fee data is especially important, because, as will be discussed, we are aware of no evidence showing that more expensive surgeons are better surgeons.

To date, at least 33 directories of physicians, dentists and other health professionals and services have been compiled by consumer groups across the country. For the first time, consumers in these communities have objective, comparative information on which to base their choice of physician.

Most of the information in these directories concerned the training, credentials and practice setting of the doctor and the type and availability of services offered. Fee information was usually requested only for office visits and routine office tests, and even this limited data was not provided by many doctors. Thus, one of the most critical items of consumer information—price of service—was absent from the directories.

SOURCE: Ted Bogue, *Cutting Prices: A Guide to Washington Area Surgeons' Fees,* (Washington, DC: Health Research Group), March 1979, p. 1.

first excerpt assumes the reader has insurance. The second notes that Medicare pays only 80 percent of the "reasonable charges" for physicians' services, leaving Medicare recipients, many of whom are on fixed incomes, with hefty self-payments. These payments become even higher if the physician "refuses assignment," suggesting that price should influence demand.

Traditional marketing discussions about price assume the consumer pays for the purchases—that consumers self-pay. Health care consumers engage in many self-pay purchases, even if they are covered by a typical health insurance benefit package. These purchases may include dental care, psychiatric care, physician office visits, cosmetic surgery that is not medically required, nursing home care, and most homemaking/home health aide services. When consumers pay full price for a service—or even partial payment for a service, as is the case with co-insurance and deductibles—they are obviously more likely to be price sensitive than if they pay nothing at all out of pocket.

Yet even when the consumer self-pays, price may not act as a regulator of demand. There are at least four reasons for this. First, the price of health care services is often unknown or unknowable.[23] Most people, for example, do not know how much to expect to pay for nursing home care or homemaking services, and they often have only a rough idea of how much they will pay for a physician's office visit. Even the physician, hospital, or other health care provider cannot tell the patient in advance how much a visit will cost because the extent and type of health care services provided will depend upon the diagnosis. Thus, patients are not likely to choose providers based on price when prices are unknown.

Second, health care providers have traditionally had little price sensitivity.[24] Until quite recently, the financial implications of their professional behavior were not included in physicians' medical education. They were not taught to consider the costs versus the benefits of specific diagnostic tools or treatment. Instead, they were motivated to seek completeness of diagnosis and treatment, both for the quality of medicine such completeness produces and for the legal protection from malpractice it assures. Even when physician education programs on cost control are provided, physicians continue to display this insensitivity.[25] Health care providers (except those in organizations at financial risk, such as health maintenance organizations and preferred provider organizations) suffer no financial penalties for generating hefty costs nor have they been subject to peer pressure regarding such behavior until recently.[26] Thus, since health care providers generate much of the health care demand and yet are insensitive to price, demand is insensitive to price.

Third, many physicians charge "usual and customary" fees, meaning they charge approximately what other physicians charge. This means that consumers have little chance to choose on the basis of price, even if they know what the prices are, because all prices may be relatively similar. This pricing behavior tends to be found among physicians and other clinicians who act according to professional ethics. Some professional groups, such as dentists and optometrists, have begun to exhibit a breakdown in professional pricing norms, by offering unusually low prices and advertising these prices to the public. In these situations, consumers begin showing price sensitivity.[27]

A fourth reason why price may not regulate demand in what have traditionally been self-pay markets is due to the nature of the patients for certain self-pay services such as hospital outpatient services and the vast array of services offered by social service agencies. These services have catered primarily to the indigent, who use them without paying. Price therefore has no effect on usage. Any service with substantial use by the indigent population cannot expect an unpaid price to regulate demand.

One of the few self-pay hospital services in which consumers have exhibited price sensitivity (until it received better coverage) was obstetrics. It was not uncommon for pregnant women to call up local hospitals and ask how much it would cost to deliver a baby there (assuming an uncomplicated delivery). Because pregnant women are usually healthy, in contrast to most patients for hospital services, many of them were less dependent on physicians, needing little diagnosis or treatment. Delivering a baby is also considered a fairly routine procedure, meaning that the price of a maternity stay could be compared from one hospital to another. The recent extension of coverage to include maternity services is likely to lessen price's ability to regulate demand in this area. However, a significant segment which has no maternity coverage

EXHIBIT 13–9 An Advertisement for Obstetrics Directed to a Self-Pay Market

Total Care Short Stay Maternity Plans

at a discount

For couples with little or no medical insurance, here are two short stay, low cost plans.

Each covers normal, uncomplicated vaginal delivery utilizing the birthing room at The Waltham Hospital. Whether you intend to deliver at home or elsewhere, you can save money and be better protected by looking into these plans.

24-hour plan

Mother and baby spend a total of 24 hours in the hospital and then go home.

The charge is $650.

The charge includes:

* room and board for mother and infant for one day
* use of the birthing room
* Nursery care for one day for an infant
* all patient care items associated with a normal delivery

48-hour plan

Mother and baby spend a total of 48 hours in the hospital and then go home.

The charge is $1,080.

The charge includes:

* room and board for mother and infant for two days
* use of the birthing room
* Nursery care for two days for an infant
* all patient care items associated with a normal delivery
* steak and candlelight dinner for parents

Security, home style

The birthing room offers a home-like atmosphere with the security of a hospital-setting.

The bedroom-like suite is the nearest thing to a home-like setting while still providing mother and baby the security of a hospital site. With one nurse in attendance and a doctor present for the delivery, a mother shares her birth experience with a coach, usually her husband.

Low cost, top quality

Couples electing one of the plans can choose their physician from among the hospital's team of fully-trained, board certified doctors. The same physician will serve the family throughout prenatal care, delivery and post-partum care.

A mother will be encouraged to attend a course conducted at the hospital to prepare herself for childbirth. In order to use the birthing room, a couple must plan on utilizing natural childbirth.

A mother using the birthing room must meet certain criteria which necessarily screen out persons with a possible high risk.

Arrangements can be made, if the parents choose, for a visiting nurse or a home health aide to visit mother and child at home after the delivery. The cost is low and substantially lower than for a day of hospital care.

The plan rates are fixed and not subject to a sliding scale as they may be in similar programs offered elsewhere. Further, the rates are lower (by one-half to one-third) than the average charges for comparable maternity services.

What is not covered?

* Physician charges for anesthesia, pediatrics and obstetrics. Physicians participating in the plans will be pleased to provide their fee schedules in advance so you can budget your costs and make comparisons.
* Costs as a result of complications. If the delivery involves complications that require special procedures or a longer stay, naturally the full rate must be charged from the date of admission, less all charges prepaid.
* Additional days in the Nursery if an infant requires them.

Eligibility

* If you have a physician, that doctor must refer you. If you do not have a physician, please contact any of the hospital's obstetricians; (see accompanying list of names and telephone numbers).
* Anticipated uncomplicated vaginal delivery.
* Inability to pay regular hospital charges in full.
* Full payment of the rate for the plan you select no later than one month prior to the date of delivery.

SOURCE: Courtesy of the WalthamWeston Hospital & Medical Center.

still exists. It is for them that the advertisement in Exhibit 13–9 was developed.

Self-Pay Ambulatory Settings

Most self-pay health care services are ambulatory (seeing a physician or a dentist versus being an inpatient overnight in a hospital;

exceptions to this include nursing home and home health care for certain classifications of payment). In the ambulatory setting, additional considerations that lessen the role of price arise:

1. The patient-physician relationship is presumably based on trust and the belief that the physician is acting in the patient's best interests. Under this condition, it would be a rare patient willing to strain this trusting relationship by asking the physician, "Can you have me treated at a lower price? Is this medical diagnosis really worth what I'm going to have to pay for it?"
2. The canons of ethics of medical and clinical professionals have historically frowned upon advertising of any kind, but especially price advertising. If consumers cannot have access to comparative price information, then they cannot use price as a criterion in their purchase choice. This is changing rapidly, but price advertising behavior is primarily limited to the tangential professions (dentistry, optometry).
3. Consumers are unable to judge the quality of medical care.[28] In the absence of other ways to judge the quality of medical care, they are likely to rely on price as an indicator. Thus, if price does affect demand, it may do so in a manner contrary to classical economic theory, as noted by Shapiro:[29] Consumers may choose the higher-priced provider to assure themselves of quality.
4. Waiting time and convenience issues (nonmonetary prices) may outweigh and substitute for monetary prices in influencing demand. For example, a consumer may reasonably choose a higher-priced physician who always sees patients within ten minutes of appointment times vs. selecting a lower-priced physician for whom one must wait forty-five minutes or more.
5. Physicians' fees have been noted to be higher in areas where there are *more* physicians per population, contrary to economic theory.[30] Rather than using lower prices to generate demand, the explanation has been offered that physicians engage in income targeting.[31] With greater competition presumably lessening demand for each individual physician's service, the physician raises prices to compensate for the loss in demand. This allows the physician to maintain a target income, using price as a cost-oriented tool: cover costs and achieve a targeted rate of return.

THE REIMBURSED MARKET

In markets largely dependent on third-party reimbursement as opposed to self-payment, discussions of pricing (unrelated to demand) are vastly different. The similarities between the two markets are that the reimbursement agencies generally speak of charges and fees rather than prices, similar to most self-pay markets. And, like self-payers, reimbursed consumers are generally unaware of the prices of the services they use and are dependent on health care providers to determine which services are to be purchased. But the differences between pricing in the self-pay versus reimbursed markets are far greater than the similarities.

Health care charges are regulated by state-mandated rate-setting programs in some states. In other states, they may result from a negotiated settlement with Blue Cross and commercial insurers. And prospective payment, which appears to be a growing form of reimbursement, sets a flat fee for each diagnosis. Municipal providers, whose reimbursement agency may be a local government, often find charges must remain within strict limits. There may therefore be limited freedom in setting price (charges or fees).

Price setting under third-party reimbursement is also a complex process because different reimbursers have historically paid different prices, regardless of the stated price or charge. Consider a hospital that treats patients in the six common payment categories:

1. Self-payers who pay full charges and commercially insured patients, for whom the hospital is usually reimbursed full charges.
2. Blue Cross patients for whom the hospital might be reimbursed full charges, charges minus 2 percent, costs plus 2 percent, costs, or even less than cost.
3. Medicare patients for whom, until the advent of DRGs, the hospital was reimbursed by a complex set of formulas. For routine inpatient care, the hospital received:

$$\frac{\text{total costs of the hospital}}{\text{total patient days at the hospital}} \times \text{number of Medicare patient days}$$

   Interestingly, price or charges are nowhere to be found in this formula! For ancillary services, Medicare reimbursed according to this formula:

$$\frac{\text{total ancillary costs}}{\text{total ancillary charges}} \times \text{Medicare ancillary charges}$$

   Simple division cancels out "charges" from the numerator and denominator of the equation, leaving "costs" again as the primary determinant of reimbursement. DRGs are also based on costs, adjusted to reflect regional average costs and cost differences due to urban versus rural locations.
4. Medicaid patients for whom the hospital is reimbursed on the same basis as for Medicare patients, in many states. In other states, Medicaid reimburses on the basis of historical costs. Again, price or charges play little or no role in the amount paid to the hospital.
5. Patients for whom there is no coverage and who cannot pay—the no-pays.
6. HMO and PPO patients for whom the hospital is paid a rate often determined by competitive negotiations.

Of the six financial categories into which patients are generally divided, two (Medicare and Medicaid) and probably four (Blue Cross/Blue Shield and HMOs and PPOs) do not pay full price. Moreover, three (Medicare, Medicaid, BC/BS) generally pay on the basis of costs. And another category (the no-pays) pays little or nothing at all. Thus, the "price" set by the health care organization may be irrelevant for the majority of patients it serves.

THE FUTURE OF PRICING IN HEALTH CARE

Traditional reimbursement policies are currently changing, and it appears that they will continue to do so in the near future as reforms seek to slow the growth of health care costs. Past reforms include the development of HMOs for which the individual pays a fixed amount in exchange for unlimited access to specific health care providers at modest additional fees. The growth of HMOs during the 1980s has been quite high, with estimates as high as 20 percent for the market share they are expected to capture by 1990. Preferred provider organizations are also growing in numbers and in size. Like HMOs, preferred provider organizations limit the consumer's access to specific low-cost providers in exchange for lower insurance costs. However, unlike HMOs, which utilize a prepaid capitation system, preferred provider organizations operate on a traditional fee for service basis. HMOs and PPOs typically place the health care provider, who generates demand, at financial risk for excessive costs.

Other experiments include predetermining the overall annual revenue a hospital can earn, even if its costs or patient volume increase; preselection by state "czars" of specific low-cost providers who can then contract to serve certain financial categories of patients; negotiated bids with Blue Cross/Blue Shield, with employers, and even with school systems for contracts to provide services to their members (employees, students); DRGs or payment based on diagnosis; and mandates of equal payment by all reimbursement agencies to prevent the traditional cost-shifting in which many health care organizations engage.

Interestingly, many of these reforms do not address the issue of price, but of cost, volume, and type of coverage. The price of or charge for a specific service is so often irrelevant to both consumer and payer that any price-based reform for individual health services is likely to fail. However, the role price may play in regulating demand and controlling health care costs is being addressed on a higher level: the price of the total health insurance package. Consumers and their employers pay out-of-pocket for health insurance. As a result, it is at this level that price sensitivity does or has the potential to affect demand. Many HMOs and preferred provider organizations offer consumers the option of paying less for the total package of health care services in exchange for willingness to limit their health care patronage to specific low-cost providers. While consumers generally do not compare prices of a hernia operation at hospital A versus hospital B, they may be more likely to compare the total annual health insurance cost of a local HMO versus Blue Cross/Blue Shield or a commercial insurer.

California laws AB 799 and AB 3480, enacted in 1983, which allow Medi-Cal (California's name for Medicaid) and private health care insurers to preselect specific low-cost providers, work on a negotiated bidding process. While this type of pricing is foreign to, and causing great consternation within, the health care field, it is not unlike pricing behavior in many commercial industrial purchase situations. Currently under discussion are plans to offer varying levels of coverage at varying prices. The consumer wanting complete coverage for all health care needs would pay a heavy premium; the consumer willing to take the risk that he will not get sick or will pay out-of-pocket for most health care would pay a low price.

The traditional demand-regulating role played by price in other industries is not absent in the reimbursed health care market. Even though its effect is negligible on the demand for specific health services, price has the potential to reform the growth of health care costs when applied to annual health insurance coverage. Because some or all of the cost of (nongovernment-sponsored) health insurance comes out of the consumer's pocket, the insurance market more nearly approaches a free market situation in which price is traditionally a primary regulator of demand. Future attempts to control demand for services through price can be expected at the level of health insurance purchase, particularly if the consumer becomes better educated about the scope and nature of the services covered, the prices of the various types of coverage, and the extent to which each type of coverage requires further out-of-pocket payment.

To put the role of pricing in health care in perspective, we should remember that health care tends to be viewed as a right. Regardless of ability to pay, most people believe that a sick person should receive adequate and appropriate care. It is this belief that caused the passage of the bills creating Medicaid and Medicare. It is also this belief which has justified professional norms dictating that medical professionals serve all patients, regardless of ability to pay, and which suggests that price should not play a central role in regulating demand.

SUMMARY

Health care organizations may be guided by at least six pricing objectives: surplus maximization, cost recovery, usage maximization, market disincentivization, public relations enhancement, and cross-subsidization. Price setting in practice is normally oriented to cost, demand, competition or reimbursement considerations.

Price is an important but complex and difficult element to weave into the marketing strategy of health care organizations. Due to third-party reimbursement, to regulated pricing structures, and to consumer and provider price insensitivity and lack of price awareness, pricing's role in health care marketing is not as straightforward as it is in other industries. Unlike other industries, price may play little or no role in regulating demand for certain categories of care or patient. From the health care organization's perspective, the issue may not be price per unit as much as it is cost per unit, given the predominance of cost-based reimbursement. However, this too may change as opportunities for providers to negotiate contracts through competitive price bidding grow due to the increasing market shares of HMOs and PPOs, and to other cost-containment efforts.

NOTES

1. Joe M. Inguanzo and Mark Harju, "Are Consumers Sensitive to Hospital Costs?" *Hospitals* (February 1, 1985), pp. 68–69.

2. For a discussion of how marketers can reduce effort cost, see Karen F. A. Fox, "Time as a Component of Price in Social Marketing," paper presented at the American Marketing Association's Educators' Conference, Chicago, August 1980.

3. See "Pricing Strategy Found Vital for Hospitals," *American Medical News* (January 21, 1983), p. 17.

4. See T. R. L. Black and John Farley, "Retailers in Social Program Strategy: The Case of Family Planning," *Columbia Journal of World Business* (Winter 1977), pp. 33–43.

5. See George Stigler, *The Theory of Price,* rev. ed. (New York: Macmillan, 1952), pp. 215ff.

6. Benson P. Shapiro, "The Psychology of Pricing," *Harvard Business Review* (July 1968).

7. "Fee Arrangement Violaters Federal Antitrust Laws," *Hospital Week,* 18, 25 (June 25, 1982), p. 1.

8. "Same-day Surgery Competes with Flat Rate," *Hospitals* (November 1, 1984), p. 52.

9. "St. Louis Hospital Guarantees Rates for Outpatient Surgery," *Modern Healthcare* (March 1, 1985), p. 118.

10. For discussions of competitive bidding by hospitals and of the problems inherent in the bid process and selection, see "Blue Cross Hits a Nerve on Hospital Costs," *Business Week,* December 24, 1984, pp. 31–32; and Emily Friedman, "Medi-Cal Contracting: Model or Mayhem," *Hospitals* (August 1, 1984), pp. 74–78.

11. For an in-depth discussion of the future of competitive bidding in health care, see Jon B. Christianson, "The Challenge of Competitive Bidding," *Health Care Management Review* (Spring 1985), pp. 39–54.

12. "Health Costs: What Limit?" *Time Magazine,* May 28, 1979, p. 62.

13. Milton I. Roemer, M.D., "Bed Supply and Hospital Utilization," *Hospitals* (November 1, 1961), pp. 36–42.

14. See M. Redish, J. Gabel, and M. Blaxell, "Physician Pricing, Cost and Income," *Proceedings of the Western Economic Association Meeting,* Anaheim, CA, June 20, 1977; and V. E. Reinhardt, "A Production Function for Physicians' Services," *Review of Economics and Statistics* (February 1972).

15. See John Wennberg and Alan Gittelsohn, "Variations in Medical Care among Small Areas," *Scientific American* (April 1982), pp. 120–34; John E. Wennberg, "Dealing with Medical Practice Variations: A Proposal for Action," *Health Affairs* (Summer 1984), pp. 6–32. (The whole Summer 1984 issue of *Health Affairs* was a special issue dedicated to variations in medical practice.)

16. See "Update: Variations in Medical Practice," *Health Affairs* (Winter 1984), pp. 145–48.

17. Richard M. Bailey, "An Economist's View of the Health Services Industry," *Inquiry,* VI, 1 (1981), pp. 3–18.

18. "Health Costs: What Limit?" *Time,* May 28, 1979, p. 60. Copyright 1979 Time Inc. All rights reserved. Reprinted by permission from TIME.

19. Donald N. Muse, Darwin Sawyer, "The Medicare and Medicaid Data Book, 1981," *Health Care Financing Program Statistics,* published by the Health Care Financing Administration, U.S. Department of Health and Human Services, April 1982.

20. David A. Juba, "Price Setting in the Market for Physicians' Services: A Review of the Literature," *Health Care Financing Grants and Contracts Reports,* published by the Health Care Financing Administration, U.S. Department of Health, Education and Welfare, September 1979.

21. Marion Gornick, Marilyn Newton, and Carl Hackerman, "Factors Affecting Differences in Medicare Reimbursements for Physicians' Services," *Health Care Financing Review,* published by the Health

Care Financing Administration, Department of Health and Human Services, 1, 4 (Spring 1980).

22. J. Holahan, Junior Hadley, W. Scanlon, R. Lee, and J. Bluck, "Physician Pricing in California: Executive Summary," *Health Care Financing Grants and Contracts Report,* published by the Health Care Financing Administration, U.S. Department of Health, Education and Welfare, September 1979.

23. B. Ehrenreich and J. Ehrenreich, *The American Health Empire: Power, Profits and Politics* (New York: Vintage Books, 1974).

24. Alain C. Enthoven, "Cutting Cost without Cutting the Quality of Care," *New England Journal of Medicine* (June 1, 1978).

25. "Science Update: Doctors Flunk at Cost-Control," *The Boston Globe,* July 23, 1984, p. 38.

26. Eileen J. Tell, "Changing Physician Practices: A Key Piece in the Health Cost Management Puzzle," *Health Cost Management at the Community Level: Doctors, Hospitals and Industry,* Richard H. Egdahl and Diane Chapman Walsh, eds. (Cambridge, MA: Ballinger, 1983).

27. "Eyeglasses and Prices," *Advertising Age,* December 24, 1979, p. 52.

28. Joseph P. Newhouse, "A Model of Physician Pricing," *The Southern Economic Journal* (October 1970), pp. 174–83.

29. Shapiro, "The Psychology of Pricing."

30. J. R. Lave, "Forecasts of Physicians' Prices and Expenditures 1978," paper presented at Health Care for American Economy: Issues and Forecasts, a Blue Cross and Blue Shield sponsored conference, Miami, January 1978.

31. Kenneth J. Arrow, "Uncertainty and the Welfare Economics of Medical Care," *American Economic Review* (December 1963), pp. 941–73.

14

DISTRIBUTION DECISIONS

A community hospital examined its patient data and realized that it was attracting very few patients from three adjacent communities north of the hospital. Further probing indicated that none of the physicians practicing in the three communities had admitting privileges at this particular hospital. With the medical staff leadership, the hospital's top management sat down to decide how the hospital could place its "representatives" (physicians) in these three communities.

The Family Health and Counseling Agency (FHCA) in a major southwestern city hired a psychologist who had previously worked for the Mind and Spirit Center, another counseling center located at quite a distance from FHCA. The psychologist reported that the Mind and Spirit Center was attracting a large number of patients from FHCA's neighborhood to its evening and weekend sessions, in spite of the half-hour drive required to get there. Disturbed by this report, FHCA staff discussed the possibility of expanding hours, currently 9 A.M. to 5 P.M. weekdays, to include some evenings and weekends.

The Frisch Durable Medical Equipment Company (which provided medical equipment, supplies, and service to people who had been discharged from inpatient facilities) had long relied on the discharge planners of the three major hospitals in its area to send it most of its business. However, a large national durable medical equipment supplier had opened up an office two years ago and was slowly attracting referrals from the three hospitals away from the Frisch Company. Mr. Frisch began to consider developing contacts with discharge planners from other hospitals, developing relationships with nearby nursing homes, and advertising directly to the consumer as ways to attract additional referrals.

A multispeciality medical group practice in the town of Lyman realized that many of its patients came from the neighboring towns of Elkson and Canaan, where there are few practicing physicians. The group practice physicians believed that, if they did not set up a satellite practice in these communities, new physicians would set up practice there and provide unwelcome competition. The group practice physicians, after months of discussion, were torn between setting up a second full-fledged multispecialty medical group practice, two primary care two-physician practices, or an 8 A.M. to 8 P.M. walk-in health clinic.

A community hospital outside Boston was tangling with its architects on the cost of privacy for its patients. Noting that another nearby community hospital had built a new facility in which all the patient rooms were private, this hospital sought to have at least three-quarters of the patient rooms in its new inpatient wing private as well. The architects stated that, with the cost limitations set by the hospital, the goal of privacy for patients could be achieved only by cutting back elsewhere. Possibilities were to make the new lobby less spacious and well-appointed, or to modify the design of the inpatient floors in a way that might make the traffic flow more congested.

Every health care and social service organization should consider how it will make its products and services available and accessible to its target consumers. Marketers traditionally use the term *distribution* to cover this aspect of marketing. Most existing marketing literature on the subject of distribution deals with products rather than services. It raises issues of physical channels of distribution, of warehousing and inventory needs, of the flow of title to goods, of retailing and wholesaling institutions, and of reseller markets, among others. These considerations are largely irrelevant to health care institutions, since their "products" are for the most part services. But before dismissing this aspect of distribution, it is worth noting that there are expections. Pharmaceutical companies distribute drugs and other pharmaceutical products; durable medical equipment suppliers distribute and service wheelchairs, apnea monitors, and the like. Even service-producing organizations may produce and distribute tangible products on occasion[1] (see Exhibit 14–1 for an example).

Health care organizations whose primary products are services have three major distribution decisions. These involve (1) physical access (channels, location and facilities), (2) time access, and (3) informational and promotional access (including referral). The concept of access is not new to the health care field. While physical access to care has received some attention, most health care studies have focused on financial access to care and on having a regular source of clinical care, which is viewed as "having access." Marketers would view this latter type of access as a consumer behavior variable more than as a distribution variable.

EXHIBIT 14–1

A Service Organization Distributing Tangible Products

The Beth Israel Hospital (Boston, MA) Video Production Center is working on a marketing plan to produce and sell health-related videotapes to other hospitals. The tapes are divided into two categories: patient education and medical/clinical staff education, with the possibility of adding other content areas in the future. Among the issues under consideration for the marketing plan are the following:

Should the hospital distribute the tapes directly to other hospitals, or should it use channel intermediaries?

If it uses intermediaries, what characteristics should these intermediaries have? Should they have handled the distribution of health education material before? Need they have experience in distribution to hospitals? If so, with whom should they have established contacts in hospitals? What arrangement should be made for paying the intermediaries? Should they pay a commission for every tape sold? Should they discount the commission if the intermediary sells many tapes to one hospital, meaning that the intermediary's selling costs are less? Should the hospital maintain title to the tapes until another hospital purchases them? Or should the intermediary be expected to take the risk of purchasing and taking title to the tapes? How many intermediaries should the hospital use? Is it better to use one national intermediary exclusively, or to divide the country into regions and assign a different intermediary to each region?

If the hospital distributes the videotapes directly to other hospitals, what responsibilities must it assume? Must it develop its own salesforce to travel around the country, visiting hospital prospects?

If it develops its own salesforce, should it compensate them on the basis of salary, commission, or some combination of both? Whether or not it has its own salesforce, should the hospital rent a booth at hospital association meetings to promote and sell its videotapes? Should it undertake a mail, hospital journal or other type of advertising campaign? How much should it spend on this? Once a tape is purchased, should the tape be mailed by U.S. Post, UPS, or some other delivery service? How should the hospital deal with the return of damaged tapes?

SOURCE: Based on material found in an unpublished class paper by Paula Brody, Bobbi Fried, Stephanie Gay, Linda Harder, and Joanne Innesberger, "Marketing Study for Boston's Beth Israel Hospital Video Production Center," December 10, 1982.

Many of the "new" forms of care delivery that have raised the hackles of the industry are guilty of nothing more than providing different or better access to care. Dental offices in shopping malls operate in locations (physical access) that are more convenient for the consumer. They are also often open on weekends and evenings, providing better time access. And they rely on the traffic within the shopping mall (promotional access) rather than word of mouth or physician recommendation (referral) to generate demand.

Walk-in medical clinics and emergicenters are sometimes called "7-Eleven medicine" or "Doc-in-the-Box" by others in the medical field. However, the similarities actually lie in the realm of better access. Many are open seven days a week, often from 12 to 24 hours a day, and require no appointment. Waiting time is short. From the consumer's point of view, this is significantly more convenient than a private physician's office or the local hospital's emergency service.

We will now examine the three major distribution decisions facing health care and social service organizations: physical access, time access, and informational and promotional access.

Physical Access

Channels

A person wishing to have a sore throat examined could utilize one of many *channels:* a solo practice physician, a group medical practice, a neighborhood health center, a hospital-based nonemergency ambulatory care unit, a hospital-based emergency room, a free-standing walk-in clinic, and an HMO.

In the past decade there has been an explosion in the types of channels used to deliver medical care and health promotion; Figure 14–1 shows some hospital channels. Whereas surgery used to be performed only in a hospital on an inpatient basis, patients can now have surgery performed at the hospital on an inpatient or outpatient basis or in free-standing one-day surgicenters. Channel changes in obstetrics, some of which are not clinically accepted, have moved the birth process out of traditional labor and delivery rooms into hospital-based alternative birth centers, free-standing birth centers, and on occasion into the home. One of the "newest" channels of medical care delivery is a return to one of the oldest: house visits in some cities where an oversupply of physicians motivates a higher level of service to the patient. Home health care is also distinct from other forms of delivery by virtue of its channel of home delivery.

The channels used for health promotion and early disease detection have also expanded rapidly. The unexciting four basic foods chart

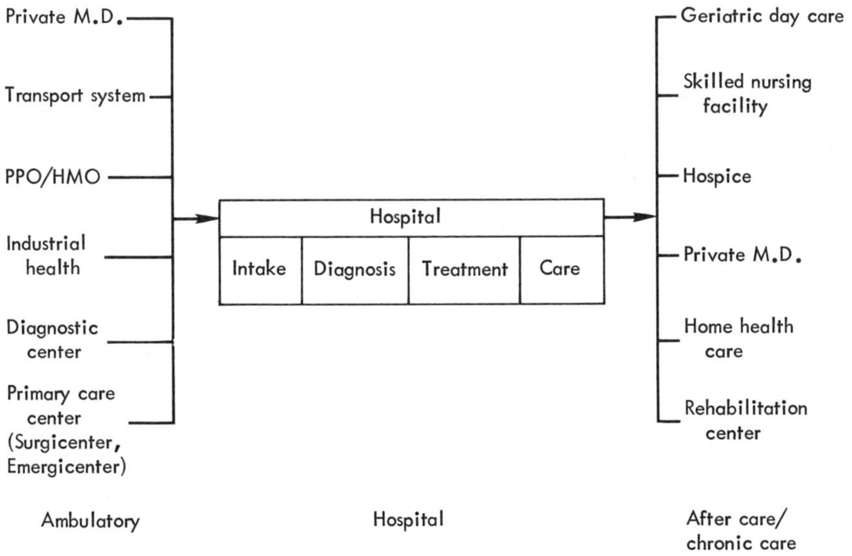

FIGURE 14–1 Controlling Channels into and out of the Hospital *Source:* Jeff Goldsmith, Health Futures, Chicago, Illinois. Provided by courtesy of Jeff Goldsmith.

that used to hang in every elementary school classroom has given way to health fairs in the community, computerized health information banks in public libraries, the Cable Health Network (a cable television network devoted exclusively to disseminating health-related information), health education videotapes to be rented for home use, hospital-based television systems providing patient education information, and telephone hotlines covering every conceivable aspect of health care, including Suicide Hotlines, Elder Health Hotlines, and Sexplanations ("Reach Out and Touch Someone").[2]

One noticeable trend in the use of new channels is the tendency to bring health care to the consumer, rather than forcing the consumer to come to the source of health care delivery. Mobile vans, such as the one advertised in Exhibit 14–2, now deliver medical care and health screening tests to shopping malls, schools, and worksites. One maternity hospital, located in an urban area but wishing to create a presence in nearby suburban communities, used the same channels suburbanites used for shopping: department stores. A story in the hospital's bimonthly bulletin was entitled "Boston Hospital for Women Brings the Pregnancy Experience to Bloomingdale's." Telephone lines, which bring the service right into the home, have been used not only for health promotion, but for billable diagnosis and treatment as well (see Exhibit 14–3).

EXHIBIT 14–2

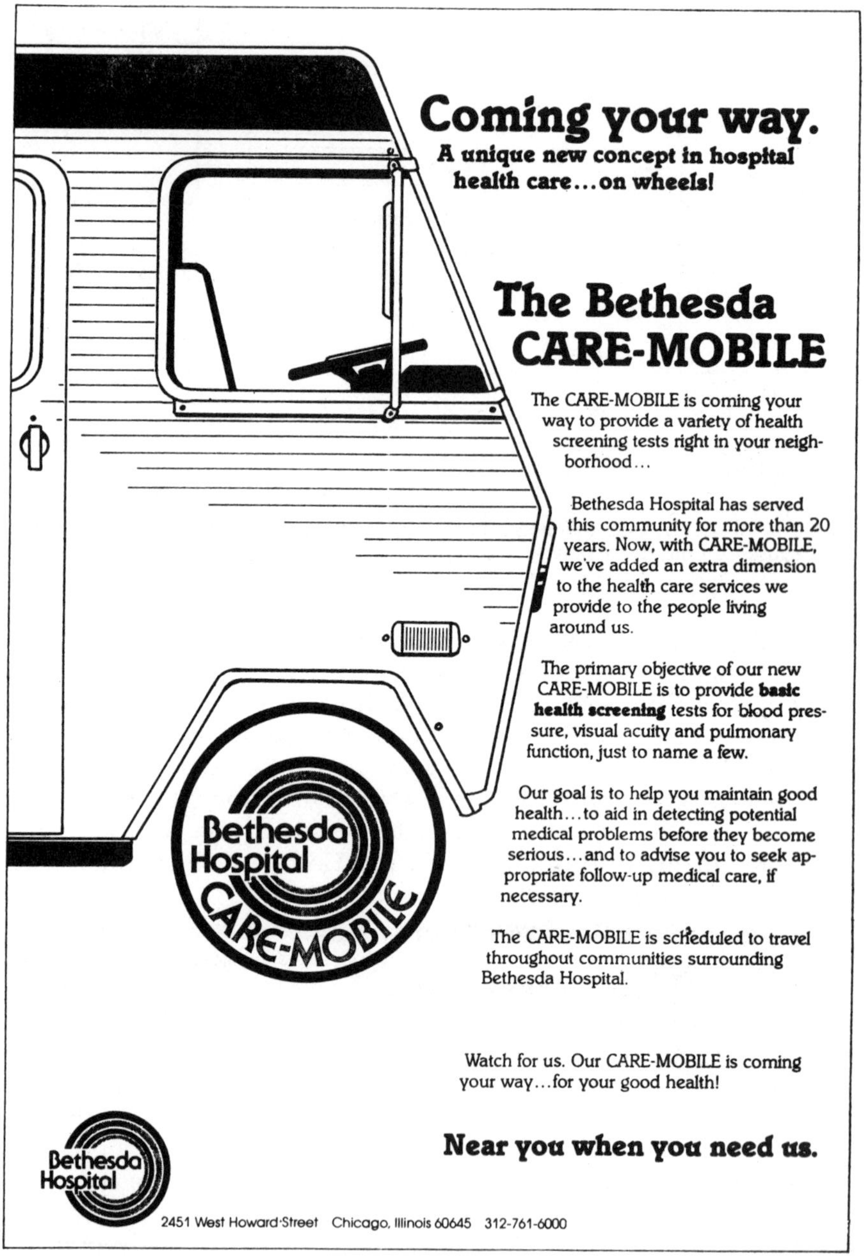
Coming your way.
A unique new concept in hospital health care...on wheels!
The Bethesda CARE-MOBILE
The CARE-MOBILE is coming your way to provide a variety of health screening tests right in your neighborhood...
Bethesda Hospital has served this community for more than 20 years. Now, with CARE-MOBILE, we've added an extra dimension to the health care services we provide to the people living around us.
The primary objective of our new CARE-MOBILE is to provide basic health screening tests for blood pressure, visual acuity and pulmonary function, just to name a few.
Our goal is to help you maintain good health...to aid in detecting potential medical problems before they become serious...and to advise you to seek appropriate follow-up medical care, if necessary.
The CARE-MOBILE is scheduled to travel throughout communities surrounding Bethesda Hospital.
Bethesda Hospital CARE-MOBILE
Watch for us. Our CARE-MOBILE is coming your way...for your good health!
Near you when you need us.
Bethesda Hospital
2451 West Howard Street Chicago, Illinois 60645 312-761-6000

SOURCE: Courtesy of Bethesda Hospital, Chicago, Il.

EXHIBIT 14–3 A New Channel for Health Care Delivery

New Call-In Service Enables People To Reach Out and Dial a Therapist

It's 9 p.m., you've been hit with a severe anxiety attack and your psychiatrist is nowhere to be found. Worry not. Just call Shrink Link.

This no-frills counseling service in New York is the latest of the budding dial-a-call services. From 10 a.m. to 10 p.m. weekdays, people can call Shrink Link from the privacy of their own couches and talk to a psychiatrist or psychologist. The cost: $15 for 10 minutes, payable through Visa, MasterCard or American Express.

CALL-IN SERVICE FOR EXECUTIVES

The idea was conceived by Dr. Sidney Lecker, an attending psychiatrist at Mount Sinai Medical Center, and Howard I. Glazer, an assistant attending psychologist at the Payne Whitney Psychiatric Center of Cornell University, both in New York. For the last five years they have also operated a call-in service for business executives who want to discuss emotional problems.

The pair maintain that the telephone has some distinct benefits. For one thing, Mr. Glazer says, it is a "user friendly instrument" that people "don't hesitate to pick up."

Consequently, problems are nipped in the bud. Mr. Glazer says that in many cases by the time people finally get around to arranging an office appointment, their problem has worsened considerably.

So far, calls have ranged from baby-boom-generation women bemoaning the lack of available men, to people who are so busy making money that they have to telephone a counselor to learn relaxation exercises, according to Kathryn Hahner, a psychologist and project director with Shrink Link.

"It's not exactly a crisis line or psycho-therapy, but an area in-between," explains Ms. Hahner. "They are people with daily life problems but who just don't want to talk to an untrained person."

FACIAL EXPRESSIONS

Dr. Robert J. Campbell, director of Gracie Square Hospital and a trustee of the American Psychiatric Association, admits to some reservations about such a service, such as the inability to evaluate facial expressions. "It's kind of risky," he says, adding, "Lord knows, it's an unusual form of care delivery." But he concludes, "I suppose that it's all ethical enough."

Open since October, Shrink Link gets about 10 calls a day. The average call is about 20 minutes, but some have lasted as long as 50 minutes.

Ms. Hahner, who used to host a radio call-in show in Albany, N.Y., dismisses that medium as competition. "You have to be entertaining," she says. "I can't tell you what it's like to talk to a depressive while the producer is waving to get rid of him, he's boring."

SOURCE: Paula Schnorbus, *The Wall Street Journal,* November 9, 1984, p. 33. Reprinted by permission of *The Wall Street Journal,*

Location

Physical access decisions also raise considerations of location. The majority of health care and social service organizations operate out of one facility. Those which do not encounter all the classic distribution problems faced by retail business firms: how many branches or outlets to operate, of what size, where located, and what specialization at each branch. These were the questions the Mayo Clinic, based in Rochester, Minnesota, had to address when it announced its decision in 1985 to open branches in Jacksonville, Florida, and Scottsdale, Arizona.

The location of a health care organization is often such a dominant factor that it dictates what the rest of the marketing mix looks like. A neighborhood health center in a lower-income neighborhood (location) usually attracts a poor clientele, so prices must be kept low. Because people from higher-income neighborhoods are unlikely to come to a poorer neighborhood for medical care, the health center limits its promotion to those who are likely to use the center. Low prices and the lower reimbursement rates paid by Medicaid probably result in there being little surplus available to keep the physical facility in top-notch condition. Also, lack of funds often means that professionals are paid low wages relative to their private practice peers. The result is usually high professional turnover, and thus poor continuity of patient care. Health care organizations locked into undesirable neighborhoods by virtue of major capital investment in physical plant are all too aware of the marketing repercussions of poor location.

Location decisions are made all the time in health care. Closed panel HMOs expand by adding centers in new locations. One HMO used its multiple locations as the key point in its advertising (see Figure 14–2). Group practices and hospitals set up satellite clinics. Physicians and dentists who are setting up practices must select office locations. Too frequently, these decisions are made with little consideration of relevant factors. These factors, formulated as questions, include: Is the area underserved medically? Or is there already significant competition in the area? Is the area anticipating population growth or decline? What is the current and projected demographic makeup of the community?

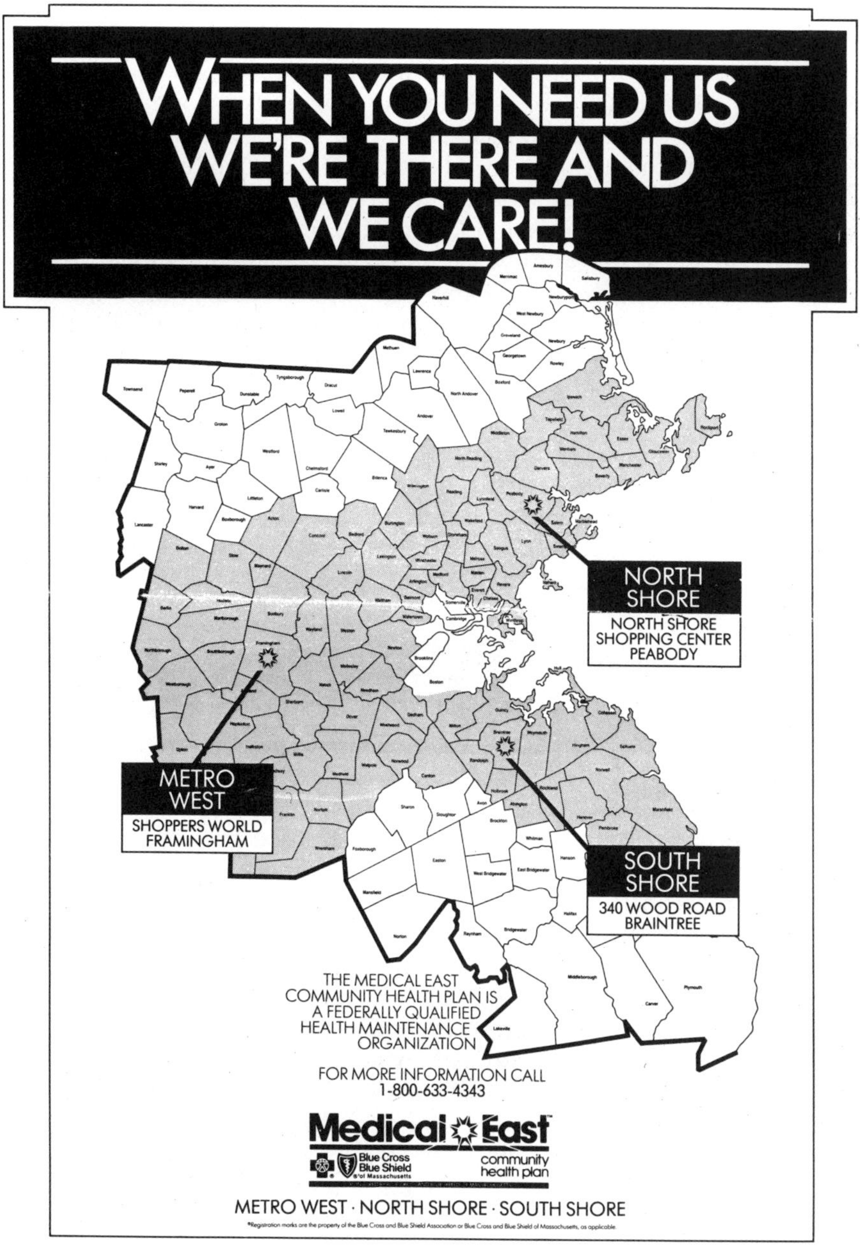

FIGURE 14–2 April 18, 1985 *Source:* Courtesy of Medical East Community Health Plan.

Does the location have to be in a high traffic area? Should it be accessible to public transportation or to parking facilities? Does it need to be near other medical facilities or near a referral base?

Some physicians have asked these questions prior to setting up practice and have chosen to locate in small towns where they face significantly less competition, a trend that is projected to increase over the next ten years. As reported by a Rand Corporation Study: "What we are saying is that doctors do respond to market forces. And with a 30 to 35 percent increase in the supply of physicians over the next ten years, we foresee a further diffusion of doctors in smaller and smaller towns."[3]

Choice of location is an important marketing decision because the patient market often segments itself according to proximity to the source of medical care.[4] One study found that the second most important reason for choosing a hospital is proximity to home (location).[5] This is most obvious in the choice of emergency room, where the most important factor is proximity. The importance of distance from the source of care lessens as the risk of the medical problem decreases, as the patient's level of education and income rises, and as the medical visit/admission moves from unplanned to planned.[6]

Facilities

A third physical access consideration is the design of the facilities. This issue may not arise if the channel of distribution does not call for the market to utilize the facility. A home health agency needs to consider the facility out of which it operates only insofar as it affects the staff, since the agency's market never sees its facilities.

Health care organizations that operate inpatient or ambulatory facilities or whose consumers use the facility in some other way have to make decisions on the "look" of their facilities, because the look can affect consumer attitudes and behavior. Consider how the "atmosphere" of a hospital can affect patients. Many older hospitals have an institutional look, with long narrow corridors, drab wall colors, and badly worn furniture, all contributing a depressed feeling to patients who are already depressed about their condition. Newer hospitals are designed with colors, textures, furnishings, and layouts that reinforce positive feelings. They may have circular or rectangular layouts with centralized nursing stations, permitting nurses to monitor the patients better. Single-care units are replacing the traditional semi-private rooms, based on the overwhelming preference for such units by both patients and physicians.

One of the most dramatic changeovers in atmosphere has occurred in abortion clinics.[7] When abortions were performed illegally, women would enter a depressing office with a single table on which the abortion would be performed. The sight of the office contributed to the patient's feeling of risk and sense of guilt and shame. Today's abortion clinics resemble normal doctors' offices, with a comfortable waiting room and a competent receptionist who shows great understanding in dealing with the patient's needs and fears. The patient feels that she is being professionally supported during a potentially traumatic moment in her life.

Marketers in the future will use atmospherics as consciously and skillfully as they now use price, advertising, personal selling, public relations, and other tools of marketing. *Atmospherics* describes the conscious designing of space to create or reinforce specific effects on buyers, such as feelings of well-being, safety, or comfort.[8]

Health care organizations designing service facilities face at least four major design decisions: (1) What should the facility look like on the outside? (2) What should be the functional and flow characteristics of the facility? (3) What should the facility feel like on the inside? (4) What materials, furnishings, and so on, would best support the desired feeling of the facility?

Each health care and social service facility has a look that may add to or detract from consumer satisfaction and employee performance. The latter point deserves special emphasis. Since employees work in the facility all day long, it should be designed to support them in performing their work with ease and cheerfulness. Granted, many health care organizations are financially weak and constrained by regulatory agencies. They cannot afford or are not allowed the facilities that would be desired in principle. But the organization should pay attention to the details of the present facility and take even minor steps to improve comfort or effectiveness. Every facility conveys something to users about the attitudes toward them felt by the service providers.

The risk in failing to attend to physical access issues is that the organization will create consumer dissatisfaction. If patients receive treatment in a rundown facility, they are likely to demean not only the facility, but the treatment as well. People often do not differentiate between tangible and intangible aspects of the services they receive.

TIME ACCESS

Time access deals with three distinct issues: (1) the hours during which services are provided, (2) the length of waiting time in the service provider's waiting area, and (3) the length of time between calling for and having an appointment. First we will address hours of operation.

Until the recent wave of new health care delivery forms provided better time access, health care organizations generally kept bankers' hours. Most physicians, dentists, neighborhood health centers, social service agencies, mental health clinics, and other ambulatory service providers were available from 8 A.M. to 5 P.M. on weekdays, with an occasional evening session that ran until 7 P.M. To receive care, those who worked had to take time off. Hospitals also had limited time access; surgical and diagnostic procedures were generally limited to weekdays, when operating room staff and medical technicians were available. Again, this meant that inpatient diagnostic and surgical care could be received only at the expense of the patient's work time.

Limited time access is often built into an organization for the convenience of providers and staff. X-ray technicians, physicians, social workers, dentists, nurses, understandably prefer to maintain a normal work week. In addition, the organizations that employ them are motivated to maintain normal working hours in order to avoid paying overtime and incurring additional overhead expenses such as heating and lighting.

However, these time access barriers have often been developed with little consideration for the needs of the consumer. When the consumer uses the health care system inappropriately due to being denied reasonable time access to proper care, the tendency is to blame the consumer rather than the health care delivery system. A classic example is the inappropriate use of hospital emergency services for primary care. Patients seeking primary care, if they wish to see physicians in private practice, must usually do so by advance appointment during working hours. If the patient cannot take time from work, has not made an appointment in advance because he became ill only that day, or does not believe the health problem justifies interrupting work time, he often has only two remaining choices (unless there is an emergicenter in town): Use the emergency services of a local hospital, which are available 24 hours a day, or seek no care at all. If the patient uses the emergency services, he has bypassed one time access barrier only to run into another one: justified but irritatingly long waits in the emergency service. Some hospitals' emergency service statistics indicate that as many as 10 percent of the people who visit the emergency room leave prior to receiving any medical care. Their unwillingness to stay is attributed to long waits in uncomfortable surroundings for minor health problems that do not justify the aggravation entailed.

Many new channels have developed to address this problem and older channels have modified their hours. The walk-in medical clinics and the 24-hour telephone information services and hotlines are further indications that health services are increasingly responding to time access barriers. Private practice providers have expanded their hours in order to remain competitive, and hospitals are operating the equivalent of walk-in medical clinics.

Women in Milwaukee can visit obstetricians and gynecologists in the evening at the Milwaukee County Medical Complex. The wom-

> en's evening Health Care Clinic is open on Tuesday evenings, making the program available to women who work outside the home as well as busy mothers. In operation since mid-April, the clinic averages 14 patients an evening, with a capacity of 18. Four female and one male ob/gyn residents and staff physicians service the clinic as part of their normal duties. The patients using the evening clinic pay the same rates as they would pay for ob/gyn services through the Medical Complex's outpatient department.[9]

Not all these responses are recent. Just as home health care has for decades distinguished itself by its physical access channel of home delivery, the Boston Evening Medical Center (a primary care service initially known as the Boston Evening Dispensary) has differentiated itself from its competitors for well over a hundred years by maintaining late evening hours.

Waiting time, whether in the health provider's waiting area or between the time of the call for the appointment and the appointment itself, is another area that is a potential source of great dissatisfaction and where some provider changes have already occurred. Walk-in medical service providers have done away with appointments, lessening one time access barrier. One walk-in clinic advertisement notes "The wait is short." A study of waiting times in different medical settings reported the following:

> How long people must wait for a physician appointment and how long they must wait in the physician's office or other medical setting to see the physician reflects the scheduling patterns of physicians and outpatient facilities and judgments about how quickly they should be seen. Waiting time for an appointment can be a source of dissatisfaction with the delivery of medical care if the patient's view of the appropriateness of the wait differs from that of the physician or the person scheduling the appointment. Waits in the office or outpatient department can likewise be a source of dissatisfaction if people must wait beyond their scheduled time, or if those making unscheduled or emergency visits wait longer than they consider reasonable.[10]

The potential for buyer alienation caused by waiting time cannot be underestimated. Exhibit 14–4 contains an article from one of the country's leading newspapers which advocates that the buyer (the patient) take a much more assertive approach to dealing with waiting times for health care services. It specifically recommends that no patient should have to wait more than 15 minutes beyond the time of the appointment. The availability of short waits at walk-in medical and dental clinics, plus the projected surplus of physicians and dentists in the next twenty years, suggests that health care providers who routinely make their patients wait long periods to be seen will find many of their

EXHIBIT 14–4 Reaction to Long Waiting Times

Demand the Right to Not Wait for a Doctor

A Physician Is a Businessman, Not a God; If He Wastes Your Time, Fire Him

See what you think of this arrangement:

You're a business executive. You engage a vendor—to whom you propose to pay thousands of dollars for services vital to the survival of your company—and not only does he not show the slightest gratitude for your custom, but keeps you waiting an hour or more every time you need to talk to him. Even though there are thousands of other vendors out there offering the same service, you are expected to accept this situation—and even be slavishly grateful for the opportunity.

Sounds pretty untenable, doesn't it? You might even be fired for cutting a deal like this to procure some highly technical and specialized product—say computers.

Yet, every day thousands of people calmly accept this arrangement from their physicians.

It's time to demystify the situation: Despite the subtle attempts of some physicians and dentists to create an aura around themselves, doctors are vendors. They are selling a service. And some have a better service to sell than others. It's that simple.

You have a right not to wait more than 15 minutes in the doctor's office.

* * *

A friend of mine sets 15 minutes as the limit. "It's as long as I'd wait if one of my vendors got stuck on long distance," he explains with a shrug.

In this as well as other life situations, you have to *teach* people how to treat you. The problem is that doctors and dentists are years ahead of the rest of us in this department.

How can you exercise your very real prerogatives as a paying customer of these specialized vendors? First, you have to give up your psychological security blanket. This person is going to be slicing into your vitals while you lie unconscious. Naturally, you would like to think he or she has special, even supernatural, qualities. One way to create that illusion is to accord him or her special privileges.

Why not give yourself a pat on the back instead? After all, you are a thoughtful, well-read, well-connected person, who located the best vendor for the job and evaluated what he or she had to say. *You* made the final decisions, *you* pay the freight and *you* will take the physical consequences for everything which is done. Your time, too, is worth money.

You have to define the relationship to include *you.* It doesn't have to be done rudely or crudely. You have several alternatives:

State to the nurse when you arrive that you have a policy of waiting only 15 minutes and ask if that means you should reschedule now.

If your care provider is a chronic over-scheduler, call ahead and see if he or she is running late. Your point will be made.

Offer overt little sallies, such as "Can I deduct this time from my bill? I make $100 an hour." Another friend of mine does this, but ends up ruining the effect ducking his head in sheepish obseisance. Use this method only if you can pull it off as an effective "teaching" approach. But beware—you probably can't follow through, because many professionals in Washington could legitimately bill the doctor more for waiting time than the doctor can bill them for care time.

Send this column to your doctor. If you're really getting the idea, you can even sign it.

Recognize that in education, age and experience you are your doctor's peer and that you deserve better treatment. Get another vendor. It's not the wrenching undertaking you might imagine. Tell the truth—isn't the respect or affection you feel for your doctor even slightly undercut by your regular irritation at being kept waiting?

* * *

If enough people start putting these relationships on a businesslike basis (I'm a doctor's daughter and, believe me, even the most warm and caring doctor isn't mulling over your problems all evening or coming to your house to urge you to get treatment like Dr. Welby), things may begin to change. Doctors will have to treat lost time from patients who don't show as a cost of doing business, as do other vendors. Doctors will have to begin appreciating our business and striving to keep it. They'll have to descend to earth.

I know it's heresy to suggest it, but you'll be doing your doctor, as well as yourself, a favor. They might start enjoying their work more if they can concentrate for a moment on that educated, accomplished patient in front of them instead of the packed waiting room at their back.

SOURCE: Jean Lawrence, "Demand the Right to Not Wait for a Doctor," *The Washington Post,* July 29, 1984, p. 33. Reprinted by permission.

patients leaving for providers organized to deliver care in a more timely manner.

The provision of health care does require some leeway in timing, because the time required for each visit or unit of service may not be able to be known in advance. A chest pain could be indigestion or a heart attack; one obviously requires more time than the other. Also, health care providers understandably will often double book in order to protect against last-minute cancellations and missed appointments. The disadvantage of double booking is that waiting times increase when all patients keep their appointments. One way in which health care providers deal with this is to identify those individual patients or categories of patients who are most likely to be "no-shows" and to double book only for them. Other providers send reminder letters or place reminder telephone calls to patients 24 hours in advance of the scheduled appointment. And still others charge partial or full fees for missed appointments and for appointments canceled less than 24 hours in advance.

Managing a health care service to minimize waiting time (but not at the expense of providing reasonably good care) involves not just actual waiting time, but also psychological waiting time. People may not mind waiting if they are enjoying themselves or are able to make productive use of the time. Techniques used by many shopping-mall-based health care providers—and now expanding to traditional physicians' and dentists' offices and to hospital emergency services—include having video equipment and tapes available for waiting patients, having a big toy box and play area for children, and having constantly updated magazines on nearby tables instead of the perennially dogeared *Time* announcing the news of two years ago. Another technique limited to shopping mall locations is discussed in Exhibit 14–5.

EXHIBIT 14–5 Lessening Psychological Waiting Time

In a suburban clinic of Kansas City, Mo., the patients carry the beepers, not the physicians.

The new Oak Park Medical Services clinic, located in the Oak Park mall shopping center in Overland Park, Kas., gives each patient a beeper, then lets them stroll off to shop or have lunch in the mall.

Then the patients are "beeped" about 10 minutes before the physician or dentist is ready to see them.

Sitting in the waiting room for what seems like hours is what people hate most about going to see a physician, said a spokesman for the Shawnee Mission Medical Center, which runs the Oak Park clinic. So the shopping-mall clinic removed that irritation by making the waiting time more pleasant and convenient.

Though the clinic's 20 beepers cost $170 each, the staff isn't worried about theft. Each patient has to give his name and address before getting one—and there isn't much reason to steal one, anyway. "All they do is beep," the spokesman said.

SOURCE: "Beepers Let Patients Cut Waiting Time," *American Medical News,* February 11, 1983, p. 61. Reprinted by permission.

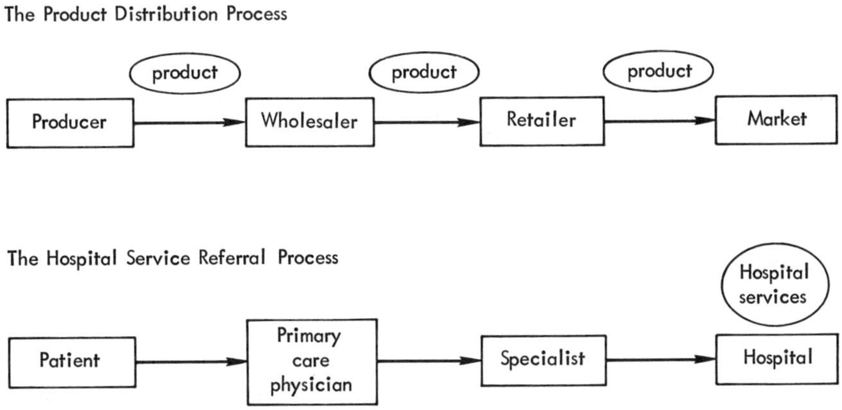

Note the chronological differences between the two processes:

1. The tangible product must exist before the physical distribution flow can start. The specific hospital services the patient will consume cannot be produced until the end of the distribution process.

2. The consumer of a tangible product does not get involved in the distribution process until the very end. The consumer of hospital services must initiate the referral flow and travel through the referral process if he or she is ever to receive hospital services.

FIGURE 14–3 Contrasting Distribution Flows of Products and Services

INFORMATIONAL AND PROMOTIONAL ACCESS

The distribution of tangible products usually addresses how to get the product to the consumer once it has been manufactured. In the case of most health care and social services, the distribution concern is the reverse: How to get the consumer to the service provider (manufacturer) so that the service can be produced (see Figure 14–3 for the difference in a hospital setting). The process of getting the service producer or provider and the consumer together so that the service can be delivered is called *referral.* The purpose of referral is to provide promotional and informational access to the consumer.

The process of referral involves the use of intermediaries who distribute information on and promote the organization. The most obvious intermediary in the health care industry is the physician. Hospitals rely on physicians to promote the hospitals' services to patients. This is evidenced by the proprietary interest hospitals exhibit in their medical staffs, particularly those responsible for heavy admissions. Physicians are also intermediaries for pharmaceutical companies, which rely on them to recommend and prescribe certain drug products to their patients.

Along with physicians, hospital discharge planners are the intermediaries for all the health care organizations populating the hospital aftercare market: nursing homes, home health agencies, homemaking services, rehabilitation centers, skilled nursing facilities, board and care homes, durable medical equipment, and so on. Alcoholism treatment services may rely on a broad array of people and organizations as intermediaries to promote their services: courts, schools, hospitals, clergy, and even bartenders.

The choice to use or not use intermediaries is encompassed by the choice between two strategies marketers commonly call *push* versus *pull.* A push strategy is one that relies on intermediaries to inform and promote—or push—the organization to the consumer. The essence of a push strategy is the use of personal selling. A pull strategy employs no middlemen, relying instead on substantial advertising and related promotion directed to pull the consumer in to use the organization's services. A pull strategy involves no personal selling and employs only impersonal promotion.

A classic business school case examines push versus pull strategies in the context of a floor wax producer. The producer can distribute the wax through hardware stores, using little advertising and relying on personal selling by the hardware store dealer (a push strategy), or he can distribute it through supermarkets, which will require a significant investment in advertising in order to gain brand recognition and to compete with the other well-advertised brands in the supermarket (a pull strategy). The latter tends to be more costly to initiate because of the heavy promotional investment required.

A health care organization that relies on referral and the use of intermediaries to generate demand is using a push strategy. It is the strategy traditionally used by health care and social service organizations, and it is likely to remain so. A push strategy is particularly appropriate for health and social services that are sensitive in nature and thus difficult to advertise, or for services for which the consumer must rely on an intermediary professional, clinician, or authority to decide on the appropriate purchase. There has been an increasing willingness to circumvent health care intermediaries and the whole referral process by advertising direct to the consumer; we will look at this further in Chapter 16.

Why should an organization relinquish any selling or supplying activities to intermediaries? Delegation usually means relinquishing some control over how and to whom products are sold. There are certain advantages to the use of intermediaries. Let us see what they are.

Many organizations lack the financial resources to carry out a program to direct marketing. The government of India adopted family planning as an official cause and set up a department to disseminate birth control information and contraceptives. The department's goal was to make contraceptives available to the smallest, remotest villages in that vast nation.[11] The solution took the form of engaging the distribution services of some of the largest packaged-goods companies in India because of their reach. For example, the government used the intricate distribution system of Lever Brothers of India and saved itself the tremendous cost of building its own pipeline to the final markets. In choosing types of retailers, the objective was to make contraceptives maximally available and accessible to target users. They eventually elected to work with the following retailers: (a) health clinics, (b) barbers, (c) field workers, (d) retail stores, and (e) vending machines. By placing contraceptives in these channels, the Indian government felt that potential users would have no difficulty finding the product.

Even if an organization has the funds to build its own distribution channel to the final markets, it might not be able to do it as cheaply as with an existing distribution system. The cost of distributing contraceptives throughout India is low because the intermediaries carry many other products that share in the cost of the distribution network. In a one-product distribution system, all the cost would be borne by that product.

Nor should the organization build its own distribution system if it can put its funds to better use. The number of births averted may be higher if the Indian government spends its funds to advertise family planning nationwide rather than using all the money to set up efficient distribution. On the other hand China, due to its tight social control system, used its own neighborhood health centers and "barefoot doctors" for distribution, needed little allocation of resources to promotion because of total media control by the government, and has been more successful.

The case for using intermediaries rests on their superior efficiency in the performance of basic marketing tasks and functions. Marketing intermediaries, through their experience, specialization, contacts, and scale, offer the producing organization more than it can usually achieve on its own. But the decision to use intermediaries involves the organization in a number of further decisions. The first is the problem of choosing the best intermediaries from the large number available. The Indian government had to decide which of several large packaged-goods companies could do the best job. It might decide to use only one of them (exclusive distribution), a few of them (selective distribution), or many of them (intensive distribution). It might also find that a desired intermediary is not willing to accept the assignment. Or the intermediary might handle the product only if given exclusive distribution. Or the intermediary might handle the product only if it receives better financial terms. Thus the first problem is to select and interest good intermediaries.

Suppose a community hospital has no pediatrician in one of the communities it serves, and wishes to attract to its staff the one pediatrician practicing in that community. That pediatrician might not be willing to switch her admitting privileges from another hospital. Or she might agree to switch on the condition that the hospital agree not to give privileges to any other pediatrician practicing in that community (exclusive distribution). Or she might demand that the hospital provide her with office space, a subsidized parking space, or some other extra benefit.

Hospitals are beginning to recognize their ability to implement marketing strategies involving physicians as intermediaries. Previously, the makeup of a hospital's medical staff was largely a function of the decision of individual physicians, who approached the hospital seeking privileges. To a great extent, the hospital's role was a passive one. Now, many hospitals actively seek to expand their medical staff in specialties in which additional patient volume is sought. They may also identify communities on the fringes of their service area from which they wish to attract patients and place physicians in practice there. This may be viewed as staking out territory, "protecting" it from competing hospitals with what militarists call a *border strategy* (protecting one's borders).

Effective use of referral requires recognizing that the intermediaries are a market. Not only do they serve the interests of the organization through the promotional and informational access they provide, but the organization must also provide value to them. Exhibit 14–6 identifies the market segment the hospital desires, the intermediaries (physicians) needed to reach that market segment, and the incentives offered to the intermediaries in order to involve them in the referral process. (The excerpt is not meant to address the ethical considerations involved, but to show the effective use of intermediaries in a consciously developed referral process.)

SUMMARY

Distribution, the third major variable of the marketing mix, deals with the availability and accessibility of products and services. Health care and social service organizations, whose products are primarily services, must consider three distribution decisions: (1) physical access, (2) time access, and (3) informational and promotional access.

Physical access can be broken into three decisions: channel selection, location selection, and facilities design. The recent dramatic expansion of channels bring greater convenience to the consumer.

EXHIBIT 14–6 The Effective Use of Intermediaries by Humana

Humana prefers to own facilities in suburbs where young working families are having lots of babies. Though young people use hospitals less than the elderly, they are more likely to be privately insured and in need of surgery, which makes the most money. The babies provide a second generation of customers.

In general, the shorter the stay, the more profitable the case. Diagnostic tests, operating-room services, and intensive-care facilities are used during the first few days of hospitalization and produce the highest revenues. After that, a hospital charges patients mainly for room and board. By attracting young, privately insured customers, Humana lowers the chance of having to deal with multisystemic or chronic diseases like leukemia or cancer that are four and five times more expensive to treat than a hernia.

To attract the "right" patients, Humana tries to sell the "right" doctors on its services. Doctors usually decide where patients are hospitalized. Family doctors are the first feeders: they see the most potential patients. Specialists are the second source, and Humana tries to influence the decisions of specialists with the greatest number of young, privately insured patients—gynecologists, neurologists, general surgeons, and so on. But choosing which specialists to attract can be tricky. By nosing around town, Humana discovers which orthopedists work with sports injuries (young patients apt to be privately insured) and which replace hips (older Medicare patients).

Humana often puts up office buidings next to its hospitals and offers doctors space at a discount—as much as a year's free rent. It readily approves doctors' requests for the latest diagnostic and therapeutic gadgetry and urges administrators to help physicians find office staff, furnishings, and even partners. Humana recruits doctors from Canada and all over the U.S., encouraging them to settle down near its hospitals and use the facilities. It guarantees them first-year incomes of up to $60,000; if a doctor earns less, Humana makes up the difference. Last year, 180 physicians recruited at an average cost of $19,000 were installed at rural Humana hospitals or posted to surrounding villages as satellite feeders.

Doctors subsidized by Humana are free to send their business wherever they like, but the company counts on their feeling beholden and acting accordingly. "If the patient has no preference," a doctor from Rochester, Illinois, says, "I refer him to Humana's hospital because Humana helped me get started." The company keeps records on every doctor's monthly admissions and the revenues these produce. "They let you know if you're not keeping up to expectations," says Dr. John Kreml, who has privileges at Springfield. "The pressure's a problem, but I've no contractual obligation to send them patients." Still, if the doctors don't produce for Humana, says Wendel Cherry, president and co-founder of Humana, "I'm damn sure I'm not going to renegotiate their office leases. They can practice elsewhere."

SOURCE Gwen Kinkhead, "Humana's Hard-Sell Hospitals," *Fortune*, November 17, 1980, pp. 68–81. Reprinted by permission.

Time access also is expanding in the delivery of health care services. Broken down into the hours during which services are provided, length of waiting time in the provider's waiting area, and length of time between calling for and having an appointment, time access, like physical access, has been changing in the direction of greater convenience for the marketplace.

Promotional and informational access may involve the use of intermediaries, whether individuals or organizations. Referral concerns the process of getting the consumer to the provider so that the service can be produced. A strategy that relies on referral is called a push strategy. It relies heavily on personal selling. A pull strategy circumvents the referral process and relies on the producing organization promoting directly to the consumer.

NOTES

1. For a more in-depth discussion regarding distribution decisions for tangible products, see Philip Kotler, *Marketing Management: Analysis, Planning, and Control,* 5th ed. (Englewood Cliffs, NJ: Prentice-Hall, 1984), chaps. 16, 17.

2. "Reach Out and Touch Someone," *Boston Magazine,* August 1982, p. 29.

3. Loretta McLaughlin, "Small-town Doctor Back Study Says," *Boston Sunday Globe,* May 9, 1982, p. 4.

4. Klaus J. Roghmann and Thomas R. Zastowny, "Proximity as a Factor in the Selection of Health Care Providers," *Social Science and Medicine,* 13D (Great Britain: Pergamon Press, 1979), pp. 61–69.

5. Joe M. Inquanzo and Mark Harju, "What Makes Consumers Select a Hospital?" *Hospitals* (March 16, 1985), pp. 90–94.

6. For more information on the role location plays in health care provider selection and usage, see Richard L. Morrill, Robert J. Earickson, and Philip Rees, "Factors Influencing Distances Travelled to Hospitals," *Economic Geography,* 26 (1970), pp. 161–71; Gary Shannon, Rashid Bashur, and Charles Metzner, "The Concept of Distance as a Factor in Accessibility and Utilization of Health Care," *Medical Care Review,* 26 (1969), pp. 143–61; Fortune Mannino, Herbert Rooney, and Ferdinand Hassler, "Distance and the Use of the Mental Health Clinic by Community Professionals," *Mental Hygiene* (January 1970), pp. 73–78; and Jon B. Christianson, "Evaluating Locations for Outpatient Medical Care Facilities," *Land Economics,* 52, 3 (August 1976), pp. 299–313.

7. Donald W. Ball, "An Abortion Clinic Ethnography," in William J. Filstead, ed., *Qualitative Methodology* (Chicago: Markham, 1970).

8. For more details, see Philip Kotler, "Atmospherics as a Marketing Tool," *Journal of Retailing* (Winter 1973–74), pp. 48–64.

9. Reprinted with permission from the July 1981 issue of *Modern Heathcare Magazine.* Copyright Crain Communications Inc., 740 N. Rush, Chicago, IL 60611. All rights reserved.

10. Judith A. Kasper and Marc L. Berk, "Waiting Times in Different Medical Settings: Appointment Waits and Office Waits," *National Health Care Expenditives Study,* Data Preview 6, U.S. Dept. of Health and Human Services Publication No. (PHS) 81–3296, March 1981, p. 1.

11. Nicholas J. Demerath, "Organization and Management Needs of a National Family Planning Program: The Case of India," *Journal of Social Issues,* 4 (1967), pp. 179–93.

15

SALES FORCE DECISIONS

Some health care facilities are using sales representatives to market their services to businesses.

West Suburban Hospital Medical Center, for example, uses professional sales reps to sell its occupational health services. Since January, the Oak Park, IL, hospital has signed up 40 companies, totaling 12,000 workers, for the program. West Suburban's goal is to add a company a week, said Robert A. Fey, director of marketing. The sales reps also sell radiology and other outpatient services through West Suburban's primary care center, called an immediate care center.

The 374-bed hospital has chosen to hire experienced salespeople rather than health professionals to market these services. "We take salesmen and teach them healthcare rather than taking master's (degree-holders) in public health and teaching them sales," Mr. Fey said. Sales reps are salaried for the first six months, then go to a commission-incentive pay system. Like sales staffs in other industries, West Suburban's has performance quotas, he added.

The sales reps study a company's size, location and type of business before approaching its safety director, industrial nurse or company physician, said Sherry Schmitter, West Suburban's marketing representative. Ms. Schmitter has experience both as a healthcare technician and salesperson.

West Suburban is in a highly industrial area with a proliferation of electronic manufacturing, waste management, baking and printing firms. Ms. Schmitter knows which local industries incur the most injuries and the most frequent types of injuries. That way, she can customize an occupational health program for each company, she said.

The hospital avoids formal contracts with its clients. In taking this informal approach, clients are ensured of getting what they want from the program, Ms. Schmitter said.

San Pedro (CA) Peninsula Hospital also uses a sales force to sell its alcoholism recovery services. The hospital is attempting to "reach a market that wasn't responsive to those services and wouldn't accept the normal admissions process," said Les Smith, president.

Four or five sales reps contact employee assistance program directors, personnel administrators and benefits managers at area companies. San Pedro offers treatment programs and employee education. The 238-bed hospital expects that these programs will generate referrals from companies.

Unlike West Suburban, San Pedro hires healthcare professionals—in this case, alcoholism counselors—to make its sales pitch. The sales rep is the "vital link between the client and the facility," said Ed Storti, director of marketing for health systems alternatives. San Pedro considers client contact as "going out to educate and make contacts," Mr. Storti said. "People will then (be) attract(ed) to us without us making the hard sales pitch."

SOURCE: "Sales Reps Sell Hospital Services," *Modern Healthcare,* May 1983, pp. 77, 80. Reprinted by permission.

We will concentrate in this chapter on sales personnel and the issues involved in running an effective sales force. *Sales personnel* are those whose major job is to sell something to others. In the health care and social service fields, until the mid-1980s rarely was anyone considered to be a salesperson. This is not because no personal selling took place, but because "selling" has traditionally been viewed as inappropriate. The feeling was that a health care organization did not *sell* its services; it *offered* them. The difference is primarily the choice of vocabulary.

Quite a bit of selling takes place in the health care field. People whose primary job it is to sell include physician and nurse recruiters, fundraisers and development officers, community outreach workers, liaison nurses, and government relations staff, as well as sales reps for hospitals, employee assistance programs, and the like. This list does not include the more obvious marketing representatives and commissioned agents for HMOs, preferred provider organizations, and health insurance companies, nor the detail people who sell for the pharmaceutical companies.

A distinction should be drawn between sales personnel and intermediaries for a health care organization's referral system. *Sales personnel* are generally employed by the selling organization and compensated for performing the selling function. Individuals and agencies that serve as referral *intermediaries* are not. The primary function of sales personnel is to sell, whereas the primary function of most health care and social service personnel is clinical and professional. Referral may be necessary in the performance of the intermediary's primary clinical or professional task. A salesperson's job entails pushing one specific organization or set of services above all others. A referral intermediary is free to refer to whatever service best suits the consumer's and the intermediary's needs. Very often, salespeople in the health care field are hired to sell to referral intermediaries. For a fuller discussion of the referral system and the intermediary's role in it, see Chapter 14.

Another area needing clarification is the role played by personal selling and other promotional tools. In discussing promotion mix decisions, Petit and McEnally point out that promotional tools, including advertising, sales promotion, public relations, and personal selling, are interchangeable within limits and that they are synergistic (the combined effect of the tools is greater than the effect of each tool individually). In addition, the choice of emphasis tends to dictate whether the organization is pursuing a pull strategy (relying heavily on advertising and sales promotion), a push strategy (relying heavily on personal selling), or a combination of both. And each tool performs somewhat different tasks:

> Suppose, for example, marketing management determines that the promotion objective of a marketing plan is to increase consumer awareness of the company's product. Working backwards, promotion specialists identify the following tasks: (1) to increase brand name recognition from 60 to 75 percent, (2) to increase trial of the product by nonusers by 10 percent, and (3) to open three new accounts in each sales territory within six months. The promotion specialists determine that the first task is best accomplished by advertising, the second by sales promotion, and the third by personal selling.[1]

Personal selling may be more effective than advertising in building preference, conviction, and action on the part of buyers because it has three distinctive qualities:[2]

1. *Personal confrontation.* Personal selling involves an alive, immediate, and interactive relationship between two or more persons. Each party is able to observe each other's needs and characteristics and make immediate adjustments.
2. *Cultivation.* Personal selling permits all kinds of relationships to spring up, ranging from a matter-of-fact selling relationship to a deep personal friendship. Sales representatives may use art to woo the buyer, may at times be tempted to use hard sell to close a sale, but must keep the customer's long-run interests at heart if they are to maintain a good selling relationship.
3. *Response.* Personal selling makes the buyer feel under some obligation for having listened to the sales talk or using up the representative's time. The buyer has a greater need to attend and respond, even if the response is a polite "thank you."

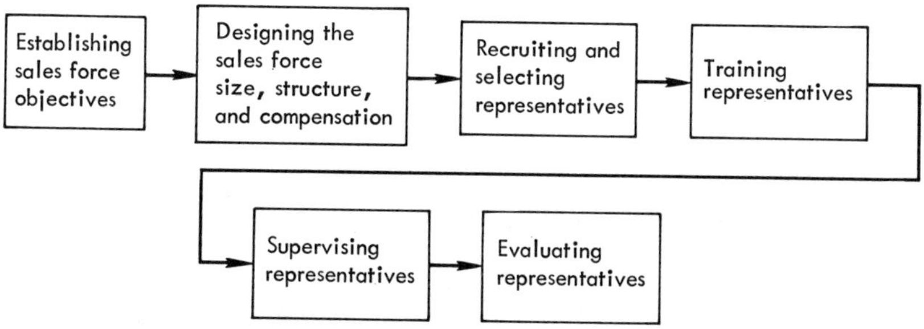

FIGURE 15–1 Major Steps in Sales Force Management

These distinctive qualities come at a cost: Personal selling is an expensive customer contact tool, costing commercial organizations an average of $60 a sales call in 1978.[3] By 1982, each visit to a physician's office by a pharmaceutical company detail person cost $75.[4] Even when the sales force consists of volunteers, there is the cost of recruiting, training, and motivating them. Thus, their time should be used wisely.

We will examine the major decisions in building and managing an effective sales force as part of the total marketing mix. These steps are shown in Figure 15–1 and examined in the following sections.

ESTABLISHING SALES FORCE OBJECTIVES

The sales force, as part of the marketing mix, is capable of achieving certain marketing objectives better than other tools. Sales representatives can perform as many as six tasks for an organization:

1. *Prospecting.* Sales representatives can find and cultivate new customers.
2. *Communicating.* Sales representatives can communicate useful information about the organization.
3. *Selling.* Sales representatives can be effective in the art of "salesmanship"—approaching, presenting, answering objections, and closing sales.
4. *Servicing.* Sales representatives can provide various services to customers—consultations on their problems, rendering technical assistance, and expediting service.
5. *Information gathering.* Sales representatives can supply the organization with useful market research and intelligence.
6. *Allocating.* Sales representatives can advise the organization on how to allocate scarce services to customers in times of service shortages.

The organization has to decide on the relative importance of these different tasks and coach its sales representatives accordingly. For example, home health agency liaison nurses spend most of their time prospecting, communicating, and selling. A hospital chain's government relationship officer, on the other hand, tends to emphasize communicating, servicing, and information gathering. Each organization normally gets its representatives to set specific goals for each of their activities so that their performance can be measured.

DESIGNING SALES FORCE STRATEGY

Given objectives, the health care organization has to make basic decisions on (1) sales force strategy, (2) sales force structure, (3) sales force size, and (4) sales force compensation.

Sales force *strategy* deals with determining how best to reach prospects and customers, given the marketing objectives. Suppose a regional consortium of home health agencies is seeking to increase contracts and referrals from HMOs, PPOs, and hospitals for its at-home hospice service. It wants to (1) "sell" these potential clients on some immediate contracts, and (2) build a stronger relationship with these clients for the future. The consortium can use one or more of five sales force strategies to meet its objectives:

1. *Sales representative to buyer.* A consortium salesperson talks to a manager in one of the client organizations in person or over the phone.
2. *Sales representative to buyer group.* A consortium salesperson makes a sales presentation to a group of managers from a client organization.
3. *Sales team to buyer group.* A team of people from the consortium (the consortium's CEO, vice-president of clinical services, director of nursing, and the salesperson) makes a sales presentation to a group of managers from a client organization.
4. *Conference selling.* A consortium salesperson arranges a meeting between people from the consortium and managers from one or more client organizations to discuss mutual problems and opportunities.
5. *Seminar selling.* A team of clinical experts from the consortium present an educational seminar to clinicians and managers in one of the client organizations about recent state-of-the-art developments. The consortium provides the seminar free to build or improve the relations with the client organization.

We see that the sales representative does not always do the whole selling job. The representative may act as the "account manager" who initiates and facilitates interactions between various people in the two organizations. Selling is increasingly becoming a matter of teamwork, requiring the support of other personnel: (1) Top management (here the CEO of the consortium) is increasingly getting involved in the sales process, especially when major sales are at stake. (2) Technical people (such as the clinicians and clinical managers) often work with the sales representative to supply expert information needed by the customer before, during, or after the purchase. (3) Service representatives provide information, clerical work, and other services to the customer.

Based on the type of selling it needs, the organization may choose (1) paid employees, (2) volunteers, and (3) temporary paid help. All three may be used to advantage. The blood bank of one hospital employs a small staff of professional salespeople who "sell" the concept of giving blood on a continuous basis; a volunteer auxiliary periodically runs campaigns in which the volunteers are responsible for all phases of the selling process; and when a blood shortage occurs, temporary help is hired to make phone calls and help the professional staff.

Sales Force Structure

Sales force strategy involves structuring the organization's sales force to achieve maximum market coverage and effectiveness. If the organization provides only one service to one type of customer who is found in many locations, the best structure would be a territorial-based sales force. If the organization sells many different services to many types of customers, it might have to develop product-structured or customer-structured sales forces.

Territorial Structure. In the simplest sales organization, each representative is given an assigned territory in which to sell the organization's services. The Spaulding Rehabilitation Hospital in Boston has divided up its liaison staff by region. Liaison workers are responsible for maintaining contact with the hospital discharge planners in their regions in order to get rehabilitation referrals. The Easter Seal Society raises money through regional, state, and local organizations, each responsible for fundraising in their respective territories.

A territorially structured sales force has a number of advantages. First, it results in a clear definition of the salesperson's responsibilities. As the only salesperson working the territory, he or she bears the credit or blame for area sales to the extent that personal selling makes a difference. This tends to encourage a high level of effort, especially when management is able to gauge the area's sales potential fairly accurately. Second, responsibility for a definite territory increases the incentive to cultivate personal ties those to whom representatives are selling. These ties tend to improve the quality of the sales representative's selling effectiveness and personal life. Third, travel expenses are likely to be relatively small, since each representative's travel takes place within the bounds of a small geographical territory.

Along with this structure may go a hierarchy of management positions if the sales force is large enough to warrant it. Several territories will be supervised by a district sales manager, several districts will be supervised by a regional sales manager, and several regions by a national sales manager or sales vice-president. This structure may be found in many of the national health care contract management companies. Each higher-level sales manager takes on increasing marketing and management work in relation to the time available for selling. In fact, sales managers are paid for their management rather than their selling skills.

Product Structure. Organizations that produce a large number of products and services often prefer to organize the selling activity by product line. Teaching hospitals and their affiliated medical schools usually allow each specialty or area of study to raise its own grant money—to identify sources of funds and develop contacts with them, even if this means that two or more are prospecting the same source of funds. Specialization by product is warranted where the organization's services are technically complex, highly unrelated, and/or numerous.

The major disadvantage is that of higher travel costs and possible redundancy. For example, the home health consortium, instead of sending one salesperson to a large HMO client to represent all the product and service lines it is selling, might send several salespeople, each representing a different product or service, such as durable medical equipment, parenteral nutrition, and hospice at-home services. Each will come with more knowledge of the relevant products or services at the cost of high salesforce expense.

Customer Structure. Organizations may also specialize their sales force according to customer type. For example, a health maintenance organization may assign its salespeople by customer category. One salesperson may specialize in government employee groups, another in unionized employee groups, a third in small business groups, and so on. By working full time to sell the HMO to, say, government employee groups, the HMO salesperson gets to know the relevant people in these groups well and uses his or her time more effectively.

The major disadvantage of customer-structured sales forces arises if the various types of customers are geographically dispersed. This means an overlapping coverage of territories, which is always more expensive.

Complex Structures. When an organization sells a wide variety of products to many types of customers over a broad geographical area, it often combines several principles of sales-force structure. This is still a rare situation in the health care field.

Sales Force Size

Once the organization clarifies its sales force strategy and structure, it is ready to consider the question of sales force size. Sales representatives are among the most productive and expensive assets in a company. Increasing their number will increase both sales and costs.

Most organizations use the *workload approach* to establish the size of their sales force.[5] The method consists of the following steps:

1. Customers are grouped into segments according to sales potential.
2. The desirable call levels (number of days spent on a customer account per year) are established for each segment.
3. The number of accounts in each segment is multiplied by the corresponding call level to arrive at the total workload in sales calls per year.
4. The average number of call days a sales representative has per year is determined, allowing for other tasks, holidays, and so on.
5. The number of sales representatives needed is determined by dividing the total number of call days required by the average annual number of calls a sales representative can make.

To illustrate, suppose a nursing school recruiting office determines that the recruitment target will require calling on 100 class A high schools, 80 class B high schools, and 40 class C high schools each year. To be effective, a recruiter will have to spend two days at a class A high school, one day at a class B high school, and a half day at a class C high school. Furthermore, each recruiter has only 60 call days available per year. The high schools will require 300 call days ($100 \times 2 + 80 \times 1 + 40 \times 1/2$), and the nursing school will require a staff of 5 recruiters (300 divided by 60).

A similar analysis can be undertaken in the case of fundraising. Given the campaign sales target and the potential of different donor groups, an organization can figure out how many fundraisers it needs. Most health care organizations tend to hire too few fundraisers rather than too many, because an additional competent fundraiser can usually add more money to the organization's coffers than he or she costs.

Sales Force Compensation

In order to attract the desired number of paid salespeople, the organization has to develop an attractive compensation plan that provides income regularity, reward for above-average performance, and fair payment for experience and longevity. An ideal compensation plan from management's point of view would emphasize control, economy, and simplicity.

Management must determine the level and components of an effective compensation plan. The level of compensation must bear some relation to the "going market price" for the type of sales job and organization. For example, the average earnings of the experienced salesperson in 1981 amounted to $30,444.[6] Many health care organizations tend to pay less than business firms, and this may result in attracting less skilled people and achieving lower results. Some health care organizations feel that they attract good people who are motivated by nonmonetary considerations and a belief in the value of their work. Others rely on clinically skilled personnel, such as nurses, occupational therapists, and medical technicians who no longer wish to be clinicians, and to whom a salesperson's compensation looks attractive in contrast to their former salaries.

The organization must also determine the components of compensation—a fixed amount, a variable amount, expenses, and fringe benefits. The *fixed amount,* which might be salary or a drawing account, is intended to satisfy the representatives' need for some stability of income. The *variable amount,* which might be commissions or bonus, is intended to stimulate and reward greater effort. *Expense allowances* are intended to enable the representative to undertake necessary selling costs, such as travel, taking prospects to lunch, and so on. And *fringe benefits,* such as paid vacations, sickness or accident benefits, pensions, and life insurance, are intended to provide security and job satisfaction.

Fixed and variable compensation taken alone give rise to three basic types of sales force compensation plans—straight salary, straight commission, and combination salary and commission. In industry, most plans are combination salary and commission, with 70 percent going to salary. In health care and social service organizations, the majority of salespeople are on straight salary, although this appears to be changing. See Exhibit 15–1 for one example of sales force issues.

RECRUITING AND SELECTING SALES REPRESENTATIVES

Having established the strategy, structure, size, and compensation of the salesforce, the organization has to manage the steps of recruiting and selecting, training, supervising, and evaluating sales representatives.

The Importance of Careful Selection

At the heart of a successful sales-force operation is the selection of effective representatives. The performance levels of an average versus a top sales representative are quite different. A survey of over 500 companies revealed that 27 percent of the sales force brought in over 52 percent of the sales.[7] Beyond differences in sales productivity are the great wasted costs in hiring the wrong persons. Of the 16,000 representatives who were hired by the surveyed companies, only 68 percent still worked for the company at the end of the year, and only 50 percent were expected to remain through the following year.

The financial loss due to turnover is only part of the total cost. The

EXHIBIT 15–1 Pill Purveyor

How a 'Detail Man' Promotes New Drugs to Tennessee Doctors

Merck's Ray Henderson Tells Merits and Gives Samples;
Are Colleagues as Candid?

'The Doctor's Psychiatrist'

KINGSPORT, Tenn.—Ray Henderson, beefy and amiable, presses a few orange pills into a doctor's hands. "Use it for mild to moderately severe pain," he says, in his characteristically soft, but fast-paced, drawl. "For sprains, strains, for backaches and post-surgical pain."

"Use it and let me know what you think," he adds.

Giving medicine to doctors is something Mr. Henderson does frequently. But he isn't a physician himself. Rather, he is a traveling salesman. Every day he drives the hills of northeast Tennessee, just west of the Appalachian Mountains, peddling his wares at doctors' offices and medical centers. The products he promotes are pharmaceuticals developed by his employer, Merck & Co. of Rahway, N.J.

In the prescription-drug trade, Mr. Henderson is known as a detail man. He is one of some 25,000 medical representatives who promote medicines to doctors and try to convince them to prescribe the drugs to their patients. Called detail men for the details they provide about new drugs, these salesmen—and increasingly women—have a profound influence on how doctors choose the drugs they prescribe. Indeed, whether a new drug becomes well-accepted by physicians can depend as much on the salesmanship of a man like Ray Henderson as on the qualities of the medicines themselves.

Frank W. Costner, vice president of sales for Merck, Sharpe & Dome, the pharmaceutical arm of Merck, describes detail men as "a link between the reasercher and the physician." He adds, "their role is vital to our marketing operation." In the past two years, Merck has increased its sales force by 55% to 1,400, largely to help promote the company's recent surge of new-product introductions.

Keeping up with so many introductions, and trying to determine the differences in the drugs, can be challenging for the busy physician.

"I know I should know about drugs before Ray tells me," says Chris Gillespie, a harried family physician in Johnson City, Tenn. "If it were physically possible to keep up with all the literature, I would. But family practice sees a lot of drugs. I shouldn't have to depend on it, but I must admit when a detail man tells me something I didn't know, I appreciate it."

Some physicians think that is a terrible way to learn about a drug. One young doctor who didn't want to be named says he thinks the whole practice of promoting pharmaceuticals this way isn't "ethical." Critics worry that patients wouldn't like the process much either—if they knew about it. Some doctors argue that these visits by detail men—which companies say cost about $75 each—add to the prices consumers pay for medicines.

A sales call can also help a doctor catch up on drugs a detail man considers competition for his own products. "If nothing else, it's a real fine way of finding out about the side effects of their competition's drugs," says William Pinsky, a Philadelphia internist. "They'll always tell you that."

While often uneasy, the relationship between the drug makers and doctors is also mutually beneficial. Detail men, for example, hear reports from doctors about previously unseen side effects, and can alert the producers. Also, detail men help organize medical symposiums. Of late, Mr. Henderson has been busy setting up meetings among local practitioners and bringing in guest lecturers from as far away as Boston. The meetings he says, "have done more for Merck's image than any single thing," he says.

Getting past a receptionist or nurse can often be Ray's toughest job, especially when the waiting room is crowded, the doctor is behind and the office personnel want to go home. At the Takoma Medical Building in Greeneville, Mr. Henderson runs up against a receptionist who at first gives him a stony glare. She smiles, however, when he piles a pack of writing pads on her desk. The name Clinoril, another Merck anti-arthritis drug, is stamped on top.

"I don't want those," she says, pointing to the pads. "I want the real thing."

After learning her mother uses the drug, Mr. Henderson slowly smiles and promises he will leave an extra box or two with the doctor in the Takoma building who is the mother's prescribing physician. At that, the receptionist cocks her head backward; Mr. Henderson marches past to the doctor's private offices.

Once Mr. Henderson is inside, doctors generally seem pleased to see him. Some use the time to discuss the finer points of pharmacology. Others see his visit as a chance to relax and chat. "Sometimes Ray or some other detail man will be the only normal person I'll see all day," says Gordon P. Hoppe, one of the physicians in the Takoma building. "I consider them the doctor's psychiatrist."

SOURCE: Excerpted from Michael Waldholz, "How a 'Detail Man' Promotes New Drugs To Tennessee Doctors," *The Wall Street Journal,* November 8, 1982, p. 1.

new sales representative who remains with the organization receives a direct income averaging around half of the direct selling outlay. If he or she receives $18,000 a year, another $18,000 may go into fringe benefits, expenses for travel and entertainment, supervision, office space, supplies, and secretarial assistance. Consequently, the new representatives should be capable of creating sales on which the amount left after other expenses at least covers the selling expenses of $36,000.

What Makes a Good Sales Representative

Selecting representatives would not be such a problem if we knew the characteristics of an ideal salesperson. The stereotype of the ideal salesperson is someone who is outgoing, aggressive, and energetic. But a review of the most successful representatives in any organization is likely to reveal a good number who are introverted, mild-mannered, and far from energetic.

The search for the magic combination of traits that spells sure-fire sales ability continues unabated. The number of lists that have been drawn up is countless, and most of them recite the same qualities. McMurry notes:

> It is my conviction that the possessor of effective sales personality is a habitual "wooer," an individual who has a compulsive need to win and hold the affection of others. . . . His wooing, however, is not based on a sincere desire for love because, in my opinion, he is convinced at heart that no one will ever love him. Therefore, his wooing is primarily exploitative . . . his relationships tend to be transient, superficial and evanescent.[8]

McMurry went on to list five additional traits of the super salesperson: a high level of energy, abounding self-confidence, a chronic hunger for money, a well-established habit of industry, and a state of mind that regards each objection, resistance, or obstacle as a challenge.[9]

Mayer and Greenberg offer one of the shortest lists of traits exhibited by effective sales representatives.[10] Their seven years of fieldwork led them to conclude that the effective salesperson has at least two basic qualities: (1) *empathy,* the ability to feel as the customer does; and (2) *ego drive,* a strong personal need to make the sale. Using these two traits, they were able to make fairly good predictions of the subsequent performance of applicants for sales positions in three different industries.

It may be true that certain basic traits may make a person effective in any line of selling. From the viewpoint of a particular organization, however, these basic traits are rarely enough. Each selling job is characterized by a unique set of duties and challenges. One only has to think about nursing school recruiting, the selling of hospital management

EXHIBIT 15–2

What Makes a Good HMO Marketing Representative

Marketing representatives and a Marketing Director should be selected with the same care devoted to finding a medical director or executive director. The kind of person a prepaid group practice plan might seek can be found in several different places. He might be a salesman who is not happy with the job he has, and is not entirely committed to standard selling techniques. He might have been selling a product connected to some service.

You might seek out recent college graduates who have had no experience but would be apt trainees. Or you might look beyond any professional places, perhaps to a local union for a competent union steward. A social worker with a sense of commitment or social reformer who is frustrated in his present job might be attracted to an innovative medical care delivery system.

The Harvard Community Health Plan hired a marketing staff consisting of a former commercial insurance company salesman, a former labor leader, and two women college graduates with little previous marketing experience. All four were trained to take responsibility for all types of the Plan's accounts, and subsequently worked interchangeably. As they developed confidence, each was able to make presentations to large and small groups within unions, social agencies, universities, etc.

SOURCE: Robert L. Biblo, "Marketing and Enrollment Strategies for Prepaid Group Practice Plans," DHEW Publications No. (HSA) 75-6207, *Marketing Prepaid Health Care Plans,* 1975, p. 36.

contracts, and fundraising for the multiple sclerosis society to realize the different educational, intellectual, and personality requirements that would be sought in the respective sales representatives.

How can an organization determine the characteristics its prospective sales representatives should possess? The particular duties of the job suggest some of the characteristics to look for in applicants. Is there a lot of paperwork? Does the job call for much travel? Will the person confront a high proportion of refusals? Exhibit 15–2 contains the thoughts of an HMO executive director and former HMO marketing director on how to identify a good marketing representative (the HMO term for a salesperson).

One question that constantly arises is whether the salesperson should be someone with a health care background who is then to be trained in selling, or someone with a successful selling record who then must be trained in health care and in the specific product or service. There are arguments to support either choice. Many organizations, unable to find health care people with selling experience, turn to experienced salespeople with the expectation that any good salesperson can learn about new industries, products, and services, but not anyone can become a successful salesperson. In addition, the perspective brought by someone with a different background is valued by many organizations.[11] Other health organizations specify that professionals or clinicians are not desirable as salespeople, but that people with health-related selling experience, such as in the pharmaceutical or medical equipment industries, are.[12] Still, many organizations take easily available clinicians and place them in sales positions because these individuals, knowledgeable about the industry and often the organization, appear to need the least training. The debate over which traits combine to make the best salesperson is not yet over.

Recruitment Procedures

After management develops general criteria for its sales personnel, it must attract a sufficient number of applicants. Recruiting is usually turned over to the personnel department, which seeks applicants through various means, including soliciting names from current sales representatives, using employment agencies, placing job ads both within and outside the organization, and contacting college students.

TRAINING SALES REPRESENTATIVES

Not too long ago, many organizations sent their new salespeople into the field almost immediately after hiring them. Nowadays a new representative can expect to spend from a few days to a few months in training (see Exhibit 15–3). Training has the following objectives:

1. The representative should know the organization's history, mission, and objectives and identify with them.
2. The representative should know the organization's products and services.
3. The representative should know customers' and competitors' characteristics.
4. The representative should know how to make effective sales presentations.
5. The representative should know the organization's systems and procedures.

Principles of Salesmanship

One of the major objectives of sales training programs is to train personnel in the art of selling. The sales training industry today in-

EXHIBIT 15–3 A Detail Man's Training

Mr. Henderson takes great satisfaction from the respect doctors give him. He ascribes much of this to his knowledge and preparation.* Though few detail men are formally schooled in science or medicine, all drug makers teach them about the medicines they sell, and the effects the medicines have. Merck's course of study is particularly rigorous. During a detail man's first year, he spends about 12 weeks of his time taking intensive courses, such as biology and pharmacology, and accompanying interns and residents on their rounds at a teaching hospital. Each year, Merck tests all its detail men four times on the characteristics of at least two drugs, and requires each to attend four regional tutorials at which medical experts lecture on various topics.

On his own, Mr. Henderson often studies late into the night. When Merck introduced its first antibiotic a few years back, he "had to learn a whole new vocabulary," he says. He studied hard. "My wife says it changed my personality."

His constant companion these days is a medical textbook on arthritis that he thumbs through whenever he is waiting to see a doctor or eating a quick lunch.

**See Exhibit 15–1 for background on Mr. Henderson.*

volves expenditures of hundreds of millions of dollars on training programs, books, cassettes, and other materials. Almost a million copies of books on selling are purchased every year, bearing such provocative titles as *How to Outsell the Born Salesman, How to Sell Anything to Anybody, The Power of Enthusiastic Selling, How Power Selling Brought Me Successes in 6 Hours, Where Do You Go From No. 1,* and *1000 Ways a Salesman Can Increase His Sales.* One of the most enduring is Dale Carnegie's *How to Win Friends and Influence People.*

All the sales training approaches are designed to convert a salesperson from being a passive order taker to a more active order getter. Order takers operate on the following assumptions: (1) Customers are aware of their needs; (2) they cannot be influenced or would resent any attempt at influence; and (3) they prefer salespersons who are courteous and self-effacing. An example of an order-taking mentality would be a charity fundraiser who phones prospects and asks if they would like to give any money.

In training salespersons to be order getters, there are two basic approaches—a sales-oriented approach and a customer-oriented approach. The first one trains the salesperson to be adept in the use of hard sell techniques. The techniques include overstating the product's merits, criticizing competitive products, using a slick canned presentation, selling yourself, and offering some concession to make the sale on the spot. The assumptions behind this form of selling are: (1) Customers are not likely to buy except under pressure; (2) they are influenced by slick presentations and ingratiating manners; and (3) they won't regret the purchase—or if they do, it doesn't matter. The director of an HMO recommends against this approach for HMO salespeople: "At all times, the marketing staff should avoid the image of high-pressure vacuum cleaner salesmen."[13] On the other hand, Homemakers Upjohn, a national proprietary home health care chain, is reported to be very successful using the hard sell approach to selling home health care.[14]

The other approach attempts to train sales personnel in customer need satisfaction. The salesperson studies the customer's needs and wants and tailors a proposal to meet these needs. An example would be a community hospital fundraiser who senses that a wealthy shoe manufacturer has a strong ego and need for recognition as a benefactor of the community. The fundraiser could propose naming a renovated inpatient wing after this person. The assumptions behind this approach are: (1) Customers have latent needs that constitute opportunities for the sales representative; (2) they appreciate good suggestions; and (3) they will be responsive to representatives who have their interests at heart. Certainly the need satisfier is a more compatible image for the salesperson under the marketing concept than the hard seller or order taker.

Most training programs view the selling process as consisting of a set of steps, each involving certain skills. These steps are shown in Figure 15–2 and discussed below.[15]

Prospecting and Qualifying. The first step in the sales process is to identify prospects. A hospital fundraiser could obtain the names of wealthy people in the following ways: (1) asking current wealthy donors for the names of other potential donors; (2) asking friendly referral sources, such as physicians, lawyers, accountants, and bankers; (3) join-

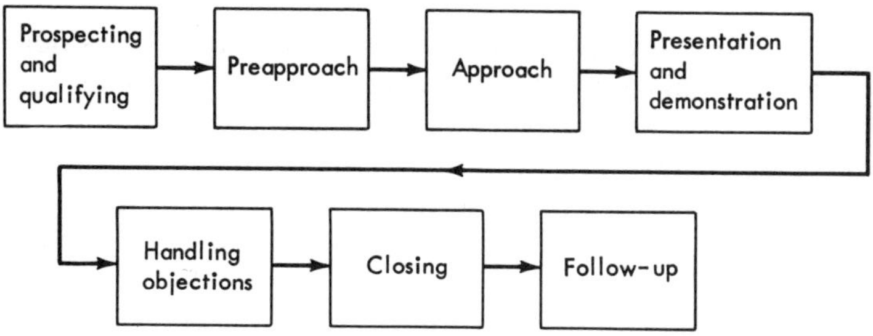

FIGURE 15–2 Major Steps in Effective Selling

ing organizations, such as country clubs, where there is a high probability of meeting wealthy people; (4) giving speeches or writing articles of interest to wealthy people that are likely to increase the salesperson's visibility; (5) examining various data sources (newspapers, directories) in search of names; and (6) using the telephone and mail to track down leads.

Sales representatives also need to know how to screen leads to avoid wasting valuable time. Prospects can be qualified by examining their financial ability, giving (or in nonfundraising situations, purchasing) history, personality, and location. The salesperson may use the phone or mail to qualify the prospects further.

Preapproach. This step involves the salesperson in learning as much as possible about each good prospect. The salesperson can consult reference sources, acquaintances, and others. The salesperson should determine call objectives, which may be to make an introduction, or gather information, or make an immediate sale. Another task is to decide on the best approach, which might be a personal visit (possibly with a respected intermediary), a phone call, or a letter. The best timing should be thought out, because many prospects are especially busy at certain times of the year. Finally, the salesperson should give thought to an overall strategy to use in the approach stage.

Approach. This stage involves the salesperson knowing how to meet and greet the prospect to get the relationship off to a good start. It consists of how the salesperson looks, the opening lines, and the follow-up remarks. The salesperson's looks include his or her appearance, manner, and mannerisms. The salesperson is encouraged to wear clothes similar to what the prospect usually wears, such as an open shirt and no ties in Texas; show courtesy and attention to the prospect; and avoid distracting mannerisms such as pacing the floor or staring. The opening line should be positive and pleasant, such as "Mr. Smith, I am Bill Jones from St. Luke's Hospital. My hospital and I appreciate your willingness to see me. I will be brief and do my best to make this visit worthwhile for you."

Presentation and Demonstration. After this introduction, the salesperson can make a brief statement about the organization and the purpose of the call. The salesperson will follow the AIDA formula: get *attention,* hold *interest,* arouse *desire,* and obtain *action.*

There are three contrasting styles of sales presentation. The oldest is the *canned approach,* which is a memorized sales talk covering the main points deemed important by the organization. It is based on stimulus-response thinking—that the buyer is passive and can be moved to purchase by the use of the right stimulus words, pictures, terms, and actions. An encyclopedia salesperson might describe the encyclopedia as "a once-in-a-lifetime buying opportunity" and show some beautiful four-color pages of pictures on sports, hoping these will trigger an irresistible desire for the encyclopedia on the part of the prospect. Canned presentations are used primarily in door-to-door and telephone canvassing. They may also be used by drug detail people because of FDA requirements on misleading statements. Otherwise, they have been pretty much abandoned by other companies in favor of more flexible approaches.

The *formulated approach* is also based on stimulus-response thinking, but attempts to identify the prospect's needs and buying style and then use an approach formulated for this type of prospect. The salesperson does some presenting at the beginning and attempts to draw the prospect into the discussion in a way that will indicate the prospect's needs and attitudes. As these are discovered, the salesperson moves into a formulated presentation that is appropriate to that prospect and shows how the transaction will satisfy that prospect's needs. It is not canned, but it does follow a general plan.

The *need satisfaction approach* does not start with a prepared presentation designed to sell the prospect, but with a search for the prospect's real needs. The prospect is encouraged to do most of the talking so that the salesperson can grasp the prospect's real needs and respond accordingly. This approach calls for good listening and problem-solving skills.

Sales presentations can be improved considerably with various demonstration aids, such as booklets, flipcharts, slides, movies, and samples. To the extent that the prospect can participate by seeing or handling the offer, he or she will better remember its features and benefits.

Handling Objections. Prospects will almost always pose objections during the presentation or when asked to sign up. Their sales resistance can take a psychological or a logical form. Psychological resistance includes:[16] (1) resistance to interference; (2) preference for established habits; (3) apathy; (4) reluctance to giving up something; (5) unpleasant associations with other person; (6) tendency to resist domination; (7) predetermined ideas; (8) dislike for making decisions; and (9) neurotic attitude toward money. Logical resistance might consist of objections to the terms or organization. To handle these objections, the salesperson uses such techniques as maintaining a positive approach, trying to have the prospect clarify and define the objections, questioning the prospect in such a way that the prospect has to answer his or her own objections, denying the validity of the objections, and turning the objection into a reason for buying. The salesperson needs training in the broader skills of negotiation, of which handling objections is a part.[17]

Closing. In this stage, the salesperson attempts to close the sale. Some salespeople never get to this stage, or do not do well in it. They lack confidence in themselves or their organization or product; or feel guilty about asking for the sale; or do not recognize the right psychological moment to close. Salespeople have to be trained to recognize specific closing signals from the prospect, including physical actions, statements or comments, and questions signaling a possible readiness to close. Salespersons can then use one of several closing techniques. They can ask the prospect for the sale; recapitulate the points of agreement; offer to help write up the agreement; ask whether the prospect wants A or B; get the prospect to make minor choices among possible variations; or indicate what the prospect will lose if the transaction is not completed now. The salesperson may offer the prospect specific inducements to close, such as a concession or gift item.

Follow-up. This last stage is necessary if the salesperson wants to ensure buyer satisfaction and repeat business. Immediately after closing, the salesperson should attempt to complete any necessary details. The salesperson should consider scheduling a follow-up call to make sure everything has gone smoothly. This call is designed to detect any problems, to assure the buyer of the salesperson's continuing interest and service, and to reduce any cognitive dissonance that might have arisen.

SUPERVISING SALES REPRESENTATIVES

The new sales representative is given more than an assignment, a compensation package and training—he or she is given supervision. Supervision is the fate of everyone who works for someone else. It is the expression of the employers' natural and continuous interest in the activities of their agents. Through supervision, employers hope to direct and motivate their sales forces to do a better job.

Directing Sales Representatives

Organizations differ in the extent to which they try to prescribe what sales representatives should be doing. Many health care organizations, it appears, do not do enough supervision.

Developing Customer and Prospect Call Levels. Many organizations classify their customers into account types, such as A, B, and C, that reflect the sales and growth potential of the different accounts. For example, a nursing home may classify different hospitals into groups. Then it establishes a certain desired call level per period that its liaison staff should make to each account type. The call levels depend upon competitive call norms and expected account response.

Organizations also like to specify how much time to spend prospecting for new accounts. Organizations like to set a minimum requirement for the canvassing of new accounts because salespeople, if left alone, will spend most of their time with current customers. Current customers are better-known quantities. The representatives can depend on them for some business, whereas a prospect may never deliver any business or deliver it only after many months of effort.

Using Sales Time Efficiently. Sales representatives should know how to schedule planned sales calls and use their time efficiently. One tool is the preparation of an annual call schedule showing which customers and prospects to call on in which months and which ancillary activities to carry out. The other tool is a time-and-duty analysis to determine how to use sales call time more efficiently. The sales representative's time is spent in the following ways:

> *Travel.* Travel time is the time spent in travel between rising in the morning and arriving at lodging in the evening. It can amount in some jobs to as much as 50 percent of total time. Travel time can be cut down by substituting faster for slower means of transportation, but this will increase costs.
>
> *Food and breaks.* Some portion of the sales force's workday is spent in eating and breaks. If this involves dining with a prospect, it will be classified as selling time; otherwise, as food and breaks.
>
> *Waiting.* Waiting consists of time spent in the outer office of the prospect. This is dead time unless the sales representative uses it to plan or fill out reports. Detail people for pharmaceutical companies report spending up to 35 percent of their time waiting in physicians' offices.
>
> *Selling.* Selling is the time spent with the prospect in person or on the phone. It breaks down into "social talk," which is the time spent discussing other things, and "selling talk," which is the time spent on the offer.
>
> *Administration.* This is a miscellaneous category consisting of time spent in report writing, attending sales meetings, and talking to others in the organization.

No wonder actual selling time may amount in some companies to as little as 15 percent of total working time! If it can be raised from 15 percent to 20 percent, this is a 33 percent improvement. Organizations are constantly seeking ways to help their sales representatives use time more efficiently. This takes the form of training them in the effective use of the telephone ("phone power"), simplifying recordkeeping, using the computer to develop call and routing plans, and supplying them with marketing research information on the prospect or customer.

Motivating Representatives

A small percentage of sales representatives in any sales force can be expected to do their best without any special prompting from management. To them, selling is the most fascinating job in the world. They are ambitious self-starters. But the majority of representatives on nearly every sales force require personal encouragement and special incentives to do their best. This is especially true for creative field selling, for the following reasons:

1. *The nature of the job.* The selling job is one of frequent frustration. Sales representatives usually work alone; the hours are irregular; and they are often away from home. They confront aggressive competing sales representatives; they have an inferior status relative to the buyer; they often do not have the authority to do what is necessary to win an account; they lose important sales they have worked hard to obtain.
2. *Human nature.* Most people operate below capacity in the absence of a special incentive. They won't "kill themselves" without some prospect of financial gain or social recognition.
3. *Personal problems.* The sales representative, like everyone else, is occasionally preoccupied with personal problems, such as sickness in the family, marital discord, or debt.

Management can affect the morale and performance of the sale force through its organizational climate, sales quotas, and positive incentives.

Organizational Climate. Organizational climate describes the feeling the sales force gets from the organization regarding the opportunities, value, and rewards for a good performance. Some organizations treat their salespeople, recruiters, and fundraisers as being of minor importance. Others treat them as critical to the organization's success. The company's attitude toward its representatives acts as a self-fulfilling prophecy. If they are held in low esteem, there is much turnover and poor performance; if they are held in high esteem, there is less turnover and high performance.

The quality of personal treatment from the sales representative's immediate superior is an important aspect of the organizational climate. An effective manager keeps in touch with the members of the sales force through regular correspondence and phone calls, personal visits in the field, and evaluation sessions. At different times the manager is the representative's boss, companion, coach, and confessor.

Sales Quotas. Many organizations, although not many health care organizations, set sales quotas for their representatives specifying objectives for the period. A preferred provider organization salesperson may be expected to sign up five new employee groups a month. Sales quotas are developed in the process of developing the annual marketing plan. The organization first decides on a sales forecast that is reasonably achievable. This becomes the basis of planning operations, workforce size, and financial requirements. Then management establishes sales quotas for all its regions and territories that typically add up to more than the sales forecast. Quotas are set higher than the forecast in order to stretch managers and salespeople to do their best. If they fail to make their quotas, the organization nevertheless may make its sales forecast.

Each manager takes the assigned quota and divides it among the representatives. Actually, there are three schools of thought on quota setting. The *high-quota school* sets quotas at levels above what most representatives will achieve, but that are possible for all. They are of the opinion that high quotas spur extra effort. The *modest-quota school* sets quotas a majority of the sales force can achieve. They feel that the sales force will accept the quotas as fair, attain them, and gain confidence from attaining them. The *variable-quota school* thinks that individual differences among representatives warrant high quotas for some, modest quotas for others.

Positive Incentives. Organizations use a number of positive motivators to stimulate sales force effort. Periodic sales meetings provide a social occasion, a break from routine, a chance to meet and talk with the organization's leaders, a chance to air feelings and to identify with a larger group. Organizations also sponsor sales contests, with the best performers winning a product or a trip somewhere. Other motivators include conferring honors and awards on high performers.

EVALUATING SALES REPRESENTATIVES

We have been describing the aspects of sales supervision reflecting the effort of management to communicate to representatives what they should be doing and to motivate them to do it. But good sales management also requires good feedback. And good feedback means getting regular information from and about sales representatives to evaluate their performance.

Sources of Information

Management gains information about its sales representatives in a number of ways. Probably the most important source of information is the representative's periodic reports. Additional information comes through personal observation, customer letters and complaints, and conversations with other sales representatives.

A distinction can be drawn between sales reports that represent plans for future activities and those that represent writeups of completed activities. The best example of the former is the *salesperson's work plan,* which most representatives are required to submit for a specified future period, usually a week or a month. The plan describes the calls they will make and the routing they will use. This report serves the purposes of encouraging the sales force to plan and schedule activities, informing management of their whereabouts, and providing a basis for comparing plans with accomplishments. Sales representatives can be evaluated on their ability to "plan their work and work their plan." Occasionally, management contacts individual sales representatives after receiving their plans to suggest improvements.

Organizations moving toward annual marketing planning in depth are beginning to require their representatives to draft an *annual marketing plan* in which they outline their program for developing new accounts and increasing business from existing accounts. Plan formats vary considerably; some ask for general ideas on account development and others ask for detailed sales volume and cost estimates. This type of report reflects the conception of sales representatives as market managers and cost centers. The plans are studied by sales managers and become the bases for rendering constructive suggestions to representatives and developing local sales quotas and estimates for higher-level management.

Several reports are used by sales representatives to write up completed activities and accomplishments. Perhaps the best known is the *call report,* on which the salesperson records pertinent aspects of dealings with a customer, including customer needs and wants, customer perceptions, best time for calling, and account promise. Call reports serve the objectives of keeping sales management informed of the salesperson's activities, indicating the status of the customers' accounts, and providing information that might be useful in subsequent calls. Representatives also report *expenses* incurred in the performance of their duties, for which they are partly or wholly reimbursed. The objective from management's standpoint is primarily to exercise control over the type and amount of expenses and then to have the requisite expense data for income tax purposes. It is also hoped that the representatives will exercise more care in incurring expenses when they must report them in some detail. Additional types of reports that some companies require from their sales representatives are: a report on new business secured and potential new business; a report on lost business; and a report on local, economic, and social conditions.

These various reports supply the raw data from which management can extract key indicators of sales performance. The key indicators they ordinarily watch are: (1) average number of calls per salesperson per day; (2) average call per contact; (3) average revenue per call; (4) average cost per call; (5) entertainment cost, if there is any, per call; (6) percentage of orders per hundred calls; (7) number of new customers per period; (8) number of lost customers per period; (9) sales force cost as a percentage of total sales. An analysis of these statistics will raise useful questions such as these: Are representatives making too few calls per day? Are they spending too much time per call? Are they spending too much on entertainment? Are they achieving enough sales per hundred calls? Are they producing enough new customers and holding old customers?

Formal Evaluation

The sales force's reports, along with other reports from the field and the manager's personal observations, supply the raw materials for evaluating members of the sales force. Formal evaluation procedures lead to at least three benefits. First, they lead management to develop specific and uniform standards for judging performance. Second, they lead management to draw together all its information and impressions about individual representatives and make more systematic, point-by-point evaluations. Third, they tend to have a constructive effect on representatives' performance. The constructive effect comes about because the sales representatives know they will have to sit down one morning with the sales manager and explain certain facets of their routing or call decisions or their failure to secure or maintain certain accounts.

Salesperson-to-Salesperson Comparisons. One type of evaluation frequently made is to compare and rank the performances of the various representatives. Such comparisons, however, must be done with care. Relative sales performances are meaningful only if there are no variations among assignments in market potential, workload, degree of competition, promotional effort, and so forth.

Furthermore, sales are not the only indicator of achievement. Management should be interested in how much each representative contributed to net surplus, and this cannot be known until the representatives' sales mix and expenses are examined. A possible ranking criterion would be the representative's *actual contribution to surplus as a ratio of his or her estimated potential surplus.* A ratio of 1.00 would mean that the representatives delivered the potential sales in his or her market segment. The lower a sales representative's ratio, the more supervision and counseling he or she needs.

Current-to-Past Sales Comparisons. A second common type of evaluation is to compare current with past performance. Each salesperson is expected to improve along certain lines, such as producing more sales, bringing down costs, opening new accounts, and so on. His or her progress can be measured and a judgment made about whether there is enough improvement, and if not, what the problem is.

Qualitative Evaluation. The evaluation usually extends to the salesperson's knowledge of the organization, products, customers, competitors, territory, and responsibilities. Personality characteristics can be rated, such as general manner, appearance, speech, and temperament. The sales manager can also consider any problems in motivation or compliance. Since an almost endless number of qualitative factors might be included, each organization must decide what would be most useful to know. It also should communicate these criteria to the representatives so they are aware of how their performance is judged and can make an effort to improve.

SUMMARY

Many organizations, including health care and social service organizations, utilize sales representatives and assign them a pivotal role in the creation of sales. The high cost of the sales resource calls for effective sales management, consisting of six steps: (1) establishing sales-force objectives; (2) designing sales-force strategy, structure, size and compensation; (3) recruiting and selecting; (4) training; (5) supervising, and (6) evaluating.

As an element of the marketing mix, the sales force is capable of achieving certain objectives effectively. The organization has to decide on the proper mix of the following sales attitudes: prospecting, communication, selling and servicing, information gathering, and allocating.

Given the sales force objectives, sales force strategy answers the question of what type of selling would be most effective (individual selling, team selling), what type of sales force structure would work best (territorial, product, or customer-structured), how large a sales force is needed, and how the sales force should be compensated.

Sale representatives must be recruited and selected carefully to avoid the high costs of hiring the wrong people. Their training should familiarize them with the organization's history, products, and policies, customer and competitor characteristics, and the art of selling. The art of selling itself calls for training in a seven-step sales process: prospecting and qualifying; preapproach; approach; presentation and demonstration; handling objections; closing and follow-up. The salesperson needs supervision and continuous encouragement because he or she must make a large number of decisions and is subject to many frustrations. Periodically, performance must be evaluated formally to help the representative do a better job.

NOTES

1. Thomas A. Petit and Martha R. McEnally, "Putting Strategy into Promotion Mix Decisions," *The Journal of Consumer Marketing* (Winter 1985), pp. 41–47. Reprinted by permission.

2. See Sidney J. Levy, *Promotional Behavior* (Glenview, IL: Scott, Foresman, 1971), pp. 65–69.

3. John Steinbrink, *Compensation of Salesmen: Dartnell's 19th Biennial Survey* (Chicago: Dartnell, 1978).

4. Michael Waldholz, "How a 'Detail Man' Promotes New Drugs to Tennessee Doctors," *The Wall Street Journal,* November 8, 1982, p. 1.

5. Walter J. Talley, "How to Design Sales Territories," *Journal of Marketing* (January 1961), pp. 7–13.

6. *Marketing News* (February 5, 1982), p. 1.

7. The survey was conducted by the Sales Executives Club of New York and reported in *Business Week,* February 1, 1964, p. 52.

8. Robert N. McMurry, "The Mystique of Super-Salesmanship," *Harvard Business Review* (March–April 1961), p. 117.

9. Ibid., p. 118.

10. David Mayer and Herbert M. Greenberg, "What Makes a Good Salesman?" *Harvard Business Review* (July–August 1964), pp. 119–25.

11. See Janet Plant, "Multis Import Business Talent," *Hospitals* (December 1, 1984), pp. M26–30.

12. R. L. Goldman, J. G. Reyes, G. T. Young, S. Barsamian, A. Thomas, and M. Thuss, "Marketing Employee Assistance Programs to Industry," *Health Marketing Quarterly* (Spring 1984), pp. 91–98.

13. Robert L. Biblo, "Marketing and Enrollment Strategies for Prepaid Group Practice Plans," DHEW Publication No. (HSA) 75–6207, *Marketing Prepaid Health Care Plans,* 1975, p. 15.

14. Robert N. Clarke, "Hospital/Home Health Care Agency," Harvard Business School Intercollegiate Case Clearing House, ICCH 9-577-065, 1977.

15. The following discussion draws in part from W. J. E. Crissy, William H. Cunningham, and Isabella C. M. Cunningham, *Selling: The Personal Force in Marketing* (New York: Wiley, 1977), pp. 119–29.

16. Crissy et al., *Selling,* pp. 289–94.

17. See Gerald I. Nierenberg, *The Art of Negotiation* (New York: Hawthorn Books, 1968); and Chester L. Karrass, *The Negotiating Game* (Cleveland: World Publishing, 1970).

16

ADVERTISING AND PROMOTION DECISIONS

"Ach-ooo! If you have a cold or the flu, come to St. Francis Hospital."

Radio advertisements with jingles such as this angered some physicians during an experimental four-week campaign in San Francisco to promote a clinic for commuters and tourists.

The San Francisco Medical Society charged that the radio spots debased the public's image of medicine, but hospital administrators, who have previously shunned advertising as unprofessional, predicted that the pilot's success in attracting new patients heralds an upswing of interest in hospital marketing.

Through advertising, St. Francis Memorial Hospital's Clinicare unit doubled its patient load. The public's awareness of the facility zoomed from zero to 18% throughout the Bay Area.

Because of its impact, physicians and hospital administrators think advertising probably will continue in San Francisco, giving hospitals which have money to spend a competitive edge over private physicians who cannot afford to mount a massive media blitz.

"A lot of doctors don't believe in advertising," said Ann Fyfe, marketing director for St. Francis.

"Our doctors had a lot of trouble with it, but they understood that if they were to keep the Clinicare program, it was their only alternative."

St. Francis opened Clinicare for people who previously had come to the emergency room with general medical complaints that did not require emergency treatment.

The hospital targeted the new service to tourists, commuters, and people who are new to the city and did not have their own physicians.

Patients are treated primarily for colds, the flu, infections and allergies, Fyfe said.

Located at the base of Nob Hill, St. Francis is the closest hospital to the financial district around Montgomery Street, where many commuters work.

For more than a year, Clinicare operated at a loss. The patient load refused to budge past 25 a day, while the hospital needed at least 50 patients a day to break even.

"That's how the idea of advertising came to us," Fyfe recalled. "We felt that we were informing rather than selling."

Before starting the campaign, she hired a research firm to conduct an "awareness survey" by telephone to measure the impact of the advertisements.

Marketing health care is "not like selling a shirt," Fyfe explained. "Unless people are sick, they're not going to use it. I wanted people to think of Clinicare when they get sick."

With the concurrence of the hospital board, Fyfe purchased commercial time on four popular radio stations, placed posters in commuter buses, and sent direct-mail solicitations to people living near the hospital.

The results were encouraging. "Direct mail to the area right around our hospital was definitely the most effective approach. We had, however, appealed to that market before, and we needed to expand our reach to the commuters in the financial district and to people who are new to the city.

"In that respect, radio was the most effective medium," she said. The largest group of new patients were commuters from Marin County.

Fyfe said St. Francis would continue to advertise, despite some criticism from the medical profession.

"It is a very sensitive subject. I was pleased and proud that our medical staff and our board stuck their necks out a little bit for the sake of the hospital."

"St. Francis and its programs have to survive. It would be selfish not to advertise," she added.

SOURCE: "Bay Area Hospital Takes Madison Avenue Approach," *American Medical News,* May 1, 1981, p. 3. Reprinted with permission from *American Medical News.*

Promotion and advertising are hot topics in health care marketing. The rejection of advertising and promotion as being imappropriate in the past led health care professionals to reject the whole field of marketing. Those who did this were mistakenly equating advertising and promotion with marketing, rather than seeing that they are only one part of marketing.

The opposition to advertising and promotion is based in the canons of ethics of physicians, dentists, psychologists, and other health care professionals. The canons contain rules that prohibit outright solicitation of patients. Health care and social service organizations, in deference to the professionals upon whom they rely, have also not actively promoted themselves and have maintained a similar antipromotion philosophy.

In recent years, the professional associations have run up against the law in their attempts to enforce ethical rules. In 1975 the Supreme Court ruled that professional associations were subject to federal antitrust laws, which are designed to protect competition. Accordingly, the AMA, among others, revised its code of ethics and loosened its advertising restrictions. Some restrictions remained, however, and an administrative law judge, siding with the FTC, concluded they deprived patients of the "free flow of information about the availability of health care services, including the offering of innovative forms of health care." He also stated that the AMA rules managed to "stifle the rise of almost every type of health care delivery that could . . . pose a threat to the income of . . . physicians in private practice." Subsequent decisions by the U.S. Court of Appeals in 1980 and the Supreme Court in 1982 upheld the FTC order. As a result, the AMA and similar professional associations cannot interfere in the advertising practices of their members unless the advertisements are clearly false and deceptive.

Many health care professionals and organizations, although in decreasing numbers, have continued to refrain from advertising and sales promotion. Professional group norms against advertising remain largely intact in spite of the change in the law. Uncertainty about the effect of advertising on consumer behavior makes potential advertisers wary. But in anticipation of a growth in advertising, many health professional associations have drawn up new guidelines intended to be responsive to the law. Exhibit 16–1 contains an example from the Council of Medical Specialty Societies, representing 24 national medical specialty societies, and is representative of most associations' guidelines.

Those who did choose to advertise, whether they were individual physicians or major health care organizations, still faced risks as recently as 1983. Two physicians who advertised their Computed Tomography Center, which had the first of its kind and the only fourth-generation CAT scanner in the State of Illinois, were ostracized by many of their colleagues. See Figure 16–1 for a copy of the advertisement and an anonymous note received by the president of the Chicago Radiological Society calling the ad "a big lie, outrageous and unethical," and demanding punitive action against the advertising physicians. The Maryvale Samaritan Hospital of Phoenix, Arizona, undertook an advertising campaign that aroused such hostility among its medical staff that the majority of the medical staff paid out of their own pockets for counteradvertising which stated:

> The following members of the Maryvale Samaritan Hospital Medical Staff wish to dissassociate themselves from the advertising campaign of Samaritan Health Services, Inc. We feel that hospital advertising is unprofessional, nonproductive and contrary to the best interest of patients and physicians. At a time when there is great pressure to reduce hospital costs, we find an advertising budget that approaches one-half million dollars is unacceptable and deplorable.

EXHIBIT 16–1 Advertising Guidelines of the Council of Medical Speciality Societies

According to the guidelines, ethical advertisements can include physician specialty, specialty residency, fellowships, professional society memberships, specialty board certification, and hospitals to which a physician admits patients. It can also state office hours and after-hours coverage, appointment requirements, office location and telephone number, a description of services, ranges of fees for specific services and tests, acceptance of Medicaid, Medicare and credit cards, and languages spoken. The CMSS cautions that this list is illustrative and does not exclude other relevant information consistent with ethical guidelines.

The Council is concerned that some physicians may unintentionally mislead the public by using statements which can be misunderstood. The guidelines include several cases in which advertising is considered false, fraudulent, deceptive, or misleading:

1. When it contains a misrepresentation of fact or omits a material fact necessary to prevent deception or misrepresentation.
2. When it contains a picture or facsimile of a person for the purpose of promising relief or recovery unobtainable by the average patient by the methods described.
3. When it contains a testimonial pertaining to the quality or efficacy of medical care or services that does not represent the typical experience of other patients.
4. When it is intended or is likely to create false or unjustified expectations of favorable results.
5. When it contains a claim that the physician possesses skills or provides services superior to those of other physicians with similar training, unless such claims can be factually substantiated.
6. When it takes improper advantage of a person's fears, vanity, anxiety, or similar emotions.
7. When it contains a claim that is likely to deceive or mislead the average member of the audience to whom it is directed.
8. When it contains a false or misleading prediction or implication that a satisfactory result or a cure will result from performance of professional services.
9. When it states or implies that a physician is a certified specialist unless he is certified by a board recognized by the American Board of Medical Specialties.
10. When it describes the availability of products or services which are not permitted by law.
11. When it is likely to attract patients by the use of exaggerated claims.
12. When it is not identified as a paid advertisement or solicitation, unless it is apparent from the context that is a paid announcement or advertisement.
13. When it contains a statement of the fees charged for specific professional services but fails to indicate whether additional fees may be incurred for related professional services which may also be required.

SOURCE: "CMSS Develops Guidelines for Physician Advertising," *Annals of Emergency Medicine*, 10, 12 (December 1981), p. 100. Reprinted by permission.

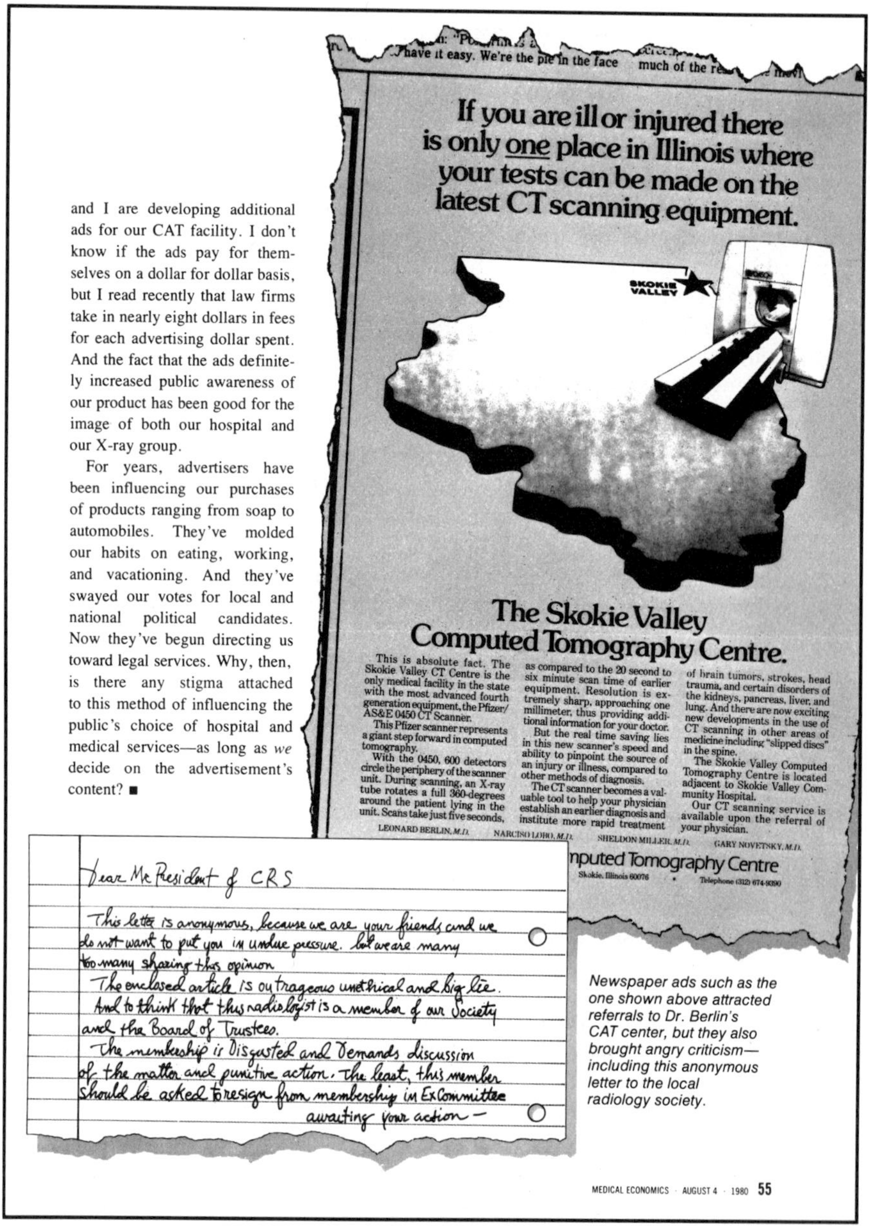

and I are developing additional ads for our CAT facility. I don't know if the ads pay for themselves on a dollar for dollar basis, but I read recently that law firms take in nearly eight dollars in fees for each advertising dollar spent. And the fact that the ads definitely increased public awareness of our product has been good for the image of both our hospital and our X-ray group.

For years, advertisers have been influencing our purchases of products ranging from soap to automobiles. They've molded our habits on eating, working, and vacationing. And they've swayed our votes for local and national political candidates. Now they've begun directing us toward legal services. Why, then, is there any stigma attached to this method of influencing the public's choice of hospital and medical services—as long as *we* decide on the advertisement's content? ■

If you are ill or injured there is only one place in Illinois where your tests can be made on the latest CT scanning equipment.

The Skokie Valley Computed Tomography Centre.

This is absolute fact. The Skokie Valley CT Centre is the only medical facility in the state with the most advanced fourth generation equipment, the Pfizer/AS&E 0450 CT Scanner.

This Pfizer scanner represents a giant step forward in computed tomography.

With the 0450, 600 detectors circle the periphery of the scanner unit. During scanning, an X-ray tube rotates a full 360-degrees around the patient lying in the unit. Scans take just five seconds, as compared to the 20 second to six minute scan time of earlier equipment. Resolution is extremely sharp, approaching one millimeter, thus providing additional information for your doctor.

But the real time saving lies in this new scanner's speed and ability to pinpoint the source of an injury or illness, compared to other methods of diagnosis.

The CT scanner becomes a valuable tool to help your physician establish an earlier diagnosis and institute more rapid treatment of brain tumors, strokes, head trauma, and certain disorders of the kidneys, pancreas, liver, and lung. And there are now exciting new developments in the use of CT scanning in other areas of medicine including "slipped discs" in the spine.

The Skokie Valley Computed Tomography Centre is located adjacent to Skokie Valley Community Hospital.

Our CT scanning service is available upon the referral of your physician.

LEONARD BERLIN, *M.D.* NARCISO LOBO, *M.D.* SHELDON MILLER, *M.D.* GARY NOVETSKY, *M.D.*

...nputed Tomography Centre

Skokie, Illinois 60076 • Telephone (312) 674-9390

Dear Mr President of CRS

This letter is anonymous, because we are your friends and we do not want to put you in undue pressure. But we are many too many sharing this opinion

The enclosed article is outrageous unethical and big lie.

And to think that this radiologist is a member of our Society and the Board of Trustees.

The membership is Disgusted and Demands discussion of the matter and punitive action. The least, this member should be asked to resign from membership in ExCommittee

awaiting your action —

Newspaper ads such as the one shown above attracted referrals to Dr. Berlin's CAT center, but they also brought angry criticism—including this anonymous letter to the local radiology society.

MEDICAL ECONOMICS · AUGUST 4 · 1980 55

FIGURE 16–1 Physician-sponsored Advertising and Resulting Critical Letter *Source:* Leonard Berlin, M.D . "Advertise—you'll need a thick skin," *Medical Economics,* August 4, 1980. pp. 53–55. Copyright © 1980 and published by Medical Economics Company, Inc., at Oradell, NJ 07649. Reprinted by permission.

> Maryvale Samaritan Hospital Medical Staff is on record as of March 23, 1981 as being in opposition to hospital advertising.

Yet in spite of reactions like these from professionals across the country, consumers appear to be accepting health care advertising. The Maryland Board of Dental Examiners, which had to deal with tremendous opposition to trade name advertising by dental clinics, admitted that "none of the complaints the board had received have come from patients. . . . All have come from dentists and dental associations."[1] The St. Francis Hospital Clinicare program described at the beginning of the chapter also found resistance to its advertising limited to health care professionals, specifically physicians.[2] And a study comparing the attitudes of physicians versus consumers toward health care advertising found that consumers were far more positively disposed toward it than were physicians.[3]

On the other hand, a survey of 1,000 consumers found that roughly 30 percent of the respondents felt that hospitals should not advertise because "people are already aware of hospital services," "advertising just adds to health care costs," "physicians are responsible for hospital promotion," "hospitals shouldn't advertise because they aren't really businesses," and "it's unethical for hospitals to advertise."[4] A second study found that "most individuals approve of advertising by hospitals." However, it also found that only half of the individuals surveyed reported noticing health care advertising, and of those, 25 percent could not remember the specific advertisement seen. Moreover, 75 to 80 percent of those surveyed indicated that advertising would not affect their choice of health care provider.[5] Thus, consumer acceptance and use of health care advertising are not as high as advertisers might wish.

Most health care advertising appears to be promoting self-referred services such as hospital-based primary care and emergency services, walk-in emergicenters, plastic surgery, optometry, general dentistry, alcoholism, eating disorders, and mental health services. These services are usually selected by a consumer with little input by medical professionals. Therefore, the advertising is not used as a substitute for expert opinion, but rather as one of the few pieces of information available to the consumer making what can be an important decision. One study of how people moving into a new neighborhood selected a pediatrician indicated heavy reliance on neighbors who were little more than acquaintances and upon the Yellow Pages.[6] The addition of advertising information to these limited sources could hardly be viewed as a drawback.

Some inpatient services have been advertised, even though inpatient usage generally relies on admission by a physician. Obstetrics is a common advertising theme because women increasingly select their obstetricians based on the hospitals to which they admit. Unlike patients for other inpatient services, maternity patients have nine months to shop around and, depending upon how well covered they are, may have a financial incentive to look for the least expensive obstetric package. Many hospitals advertise low-price maternity packages—"A flat $425 buys six prenatal classes, a one-day hospital stay, doctor services for an uncomplicated delivery and a post-delivery checkup" at University Hospital in Kansas City[7]—as well as a range of birth options such as birthing chairs, fathers and siblings at caesarean sections, and so on. General inpatient services have also been advertised. Sunrise Hospital in Las Vegas advertised "Win a once-in-a-lifetime cruise simply by entering Sunrise Hospital on any Friday or Saturday" in newspapers, and successfully spread its patient load more evenly through the seven-day week.

The pros and cons of health care advertising are numerous and in constant debate. Clearly, there will be more advertising in the future, given the legal loosening of restrictions, the increasingly competitive health care environment, and the greater acceptance of marketing techniques. One indication of this is the existence of *Healthcare Advertising Review,* a bimonthly publication of health care advertisements and commentary on those advertisements.

It is not clear what rules will govern health care advertising in the future. Will there be cooperative advertising, like the advertisement shown in Figure 16–2? Will advertisements contain coupons, such as First Stop Medical Clinic's coupon (in Racine, Wisconsin) of $100 toward a complete medical evaluation? Or Panorama Community Hospital's coupon for senior citizens offering no out-of-pocket Medicare deductible expense? Can testimonial advertising and comparison advertising be expected to continue? Will specialists advertise directly to consumers (Dr. Janis Smith, Neurosurgeon; initial appointment for $50), thus disrupting traditional referral patterns? Will health care organizations' advertising tend to be service-specific, institutional, or brand-name-specific for multi-organization systems, such as: "HCA. We care for America. We care for you."?

One type of advertising that seems likely to escalate in the near future is price advertising. Much price advertising appears to be directed toward employers and insurers, since they pay for most of the cost of health care. Thus, Methodist Hospital in St. Louis Park, Minnesota, advertised to local employers: "We care about people . . . AND your bottom line."[8] Other price advertising has been directed to consumers; such advertising has targeted Medicare recipients, offering them care without having to pay deductibles; maternity patients with limited or no coverage, and users of primary care services.

One factor that could have an impact on health care advertising is whether organizations will be reimbursed for it. In the past they have not been,[9] although some institutional advertising falls under accepted

THE AMERICAN EXPRESS
CARD BUYS YOU CARE
WHEN YOU NEED IT MOST.
AMERICAN EXPRESS
It's comforting to know there's someplace you can go in an emergency. And Boston's Beth Israel Hospital is just the place. It's one of the many outstanding medical facilities all across the country that welcome the American Express® Card.
Hospitals are just one example of the growing number of diverse businesses and organizations that welcome the American Express Card. All of which gives new impact to the phrase: Don't leave home without it.®

FIGURE 16–2 An Example of Cooperative Advertising
Source: American Express Travel Related Services Company, Inc. © 1984. All rights reserved. Reprinted with permission.

reimbursement guidelines. Under DRG or prospective reimbursement, these guidelines may not be relevant for certain third-party payors. Where health care services remain cost-based reimbursed, coverage of advertising expenses is relevant. If advertising is not to be reimbursed, then health care organizations must view it as an investment. And, as with any investment, there is always the risk of a poor payback. The health care industry's lack of experience in investing in advertising, coupled with probable lack of reimbursement for advertising, will probably be more powerful than peer pressure and professional norms in restraining the growth of health care advertising. Nonetheless, the use of advertising in the field is expected to grow, and managers must be prepared to incorporate advertising into their overall communications strategy. In the remainder of this chapter we will address the practical issues in advertising and sales promotion; publicity will be the focus of the following chapter.

PROMOTIONAL TOOLS AND THE COMMUNICATION PROCESS

In a broad sense, all the five tools of the marketing mix—product, price, place, promotion, and people—are communication tools. Messages are carried to the market by the product's styling and features, its price, and the places and times where and when it is available. Here we will confine our attention to the subset of marketing tools that are primarily promotional in nature—that are classified as promotion. These promotional tools are extremely numerous and varied. Examples include these:

Space and time advertising	Point-of-sale displays
Loudspeaker advertising	Sales literature
Mailings	Catalogs
Speeches	Films
Sales presentations	Trade exhibits
Demonstrations	Sales conferences
Trading stamps	Packaging
Contests	House organ publications
Premiums	Product publicity
Free samples	Corporate publicity and identification programs
Price specials	Endorsements
Coupons	Atmospheres
Posters and showcards	

In specific organizational settings, distinct promotional tools may evolve to serve the needs of that organization. Fundraising organizations make heavy use of benefit dinners and dances, auctions, bazaars, concerts, telethons, walkathons, door-to-door campaigns, plate passing, and direct mail. A private optometric practice might use mailed notices, store window displays, a large sign at the entrance to the practice, and local newspaper advertising. A state Medicaid office tends to use 8" by 11" letters, printed in wall-to-wall black and white print, in order to communicate information.

Classification of the various promotional tools is desirable to facilitate analysis and planning. These tools fall into four groups:[10]

Advertising. Any paid form of nonpersonal presentation and promotion of ideas, goods, or services by an identified sponsor.

Sales promotion. Short-term incentives to encourage purchase or sales of a product or service.

Personal selling. Oral presentation in a conversation with one or more prospective purchasers for the purpose of making sales or building goodwill.

Publicity. Nonpersonal stimulation of demand for a product, service, or business unit by planting commercially significant news about it in a published medium or obtaining favorable presentation of it on radio, television, or stage that is not paid for by the sponsor.

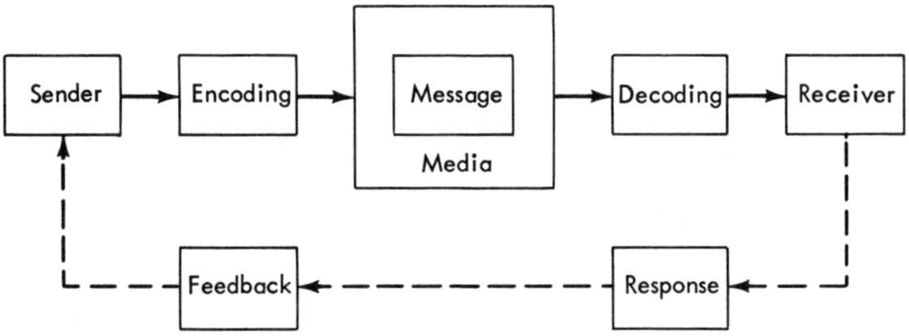

FIGURE 16–3 Elements in the Communication Process

To be used effectively, these tools should be viewed in a communication framework. Figure 16–3 shows the eight elements involved in every communication. There are two parties—a sender and receiver. One or both send a message through media. They also engage in four communication functions: encoding, decoding, response, and feedback:

Sender: The party sending the message to another party (also called the source or communicator)

Encoding: The process of putting thought into symbolic form

Message: The set of symbols the sender transmits

Decoding: The process by which the receiver assigns meaning to the symbols transmitted by the sender

Receiver: The party receiving the message sent by another party (also called the audience or destination)

Response: The set of reactions that the receiver has after being exposed to the message

Feedback: The part of the receiver's response that the receiver communicates back to the sender

The model underscores the key factors in effective communication. Senders must know what audiences they want to reach and what responses they want. They must be skillful in encoding messages that take into account how the target audience tends to decode messages. They must transmit the message over efficient media that reach the target audience. They must develop feedback channels so that they can know the audience's response to the message. Health care and social service marketers must also recognize that the importance of promotional tools varies when directed to a consumer and to an industrial market. The differences are shown in Figure 16–4.

Although advertising is less important than sales calls in industrial markets, it still plays a significant role. Advertising can build product awareness and comprehension, develop sales leads, offer legitimation, and reassure buyers.

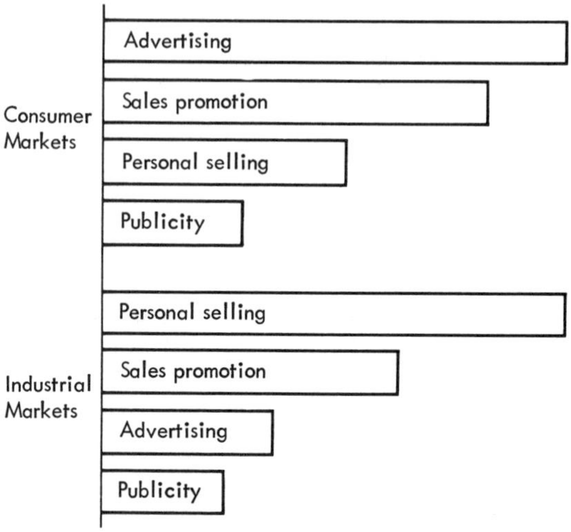

FIGURE 16–4 Relative Importance of Promotion Tools in Consumer versus Industrial Markets

Conversely, personal selling can and does make a strong contribution to the marketing of many health care services to consumers. Physicians engage in personal selling when recommending a specific hospital, physician specialist or pharmaceutical product to a patient. Discharge planners do personal selling when recommending specific nursing homes, care facilities, home health agencies, and rehabilitation centers.

All promotional tools have the potential to be of value in any marketing effort.

ADVERTISING

> **Advertising** consists of nonpersonal forms of communication conducted through paid media under clear sponsorship.

It involves such varied media as magazine and newspaper space; radio and television; outdoor (such as posters, signs, skywriting); novelties (matchboxes, calendars); cards (car, bus); catalogs; directories and references; programs; circulars; and direct mail. It can be carried out for such diverse purposes as the long-term buildup of a particular product (product advertising) or brand (brand advertising); information dissemination about a sale, service, or event (classified advertising); announcement of a special sale (sales advertising), and so on.

Total advertising dollars spent in the United States by health care organizations in 1983 amounted to over $200 million,[11] with forecasts

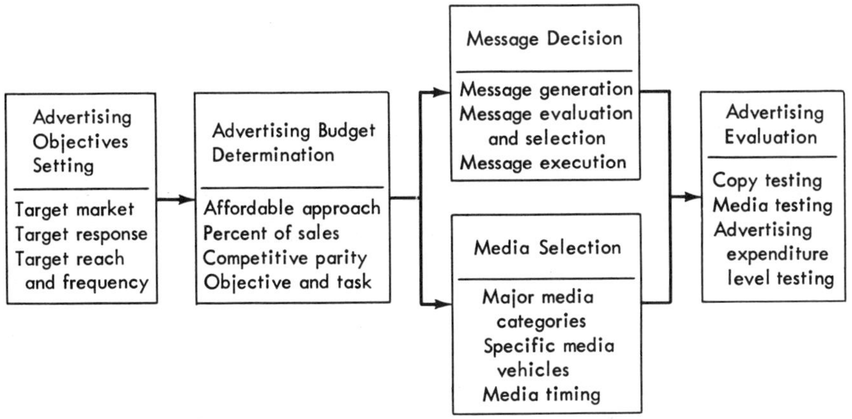

FIGURE 16–5 Major Decisions in Advertising Management

of great growth in expenditures in the future. This includes advertising for social causes, such as antismoking advertising; charitable advertising directed toward raising donations; government advertising, such as that promoting the use of carseats for babies; private nonprofit health care organization advertising, whether multi-organizational, institutional, or service-specific; and association advertising, like the American Dental Association's campaign directed toward encouraging people to get dental checkups.

In developing an advertising program, health care marketing managers must make five important decisions, as shown in Figure 16–5 and examined below.

Objectives Setting

Before an advertising program and budget can be developed, objectives must be set. These objectives must flow from prior decisions on the target market, market positioning, and marketing mix. The marketing mix strategy defines advertising's job in the total marketing mix.

Developing advertising objectives calls for defining the target market, target response, and target reach frequency.

Target Market. A market communicator must start with a clear target audience in mind. The audience may be potential buyers of the organization's services, current users, deciders, and/or influencers. The audience may consist of individuals, groups, particular publics, or the general public. The target audience will critically influence the communicator's decisions on *what* is to be said, *how* it is to be said, *when* it is to be said, *where* it is to be said, and *who* is to say it.

Consider this in terms of a home health agency named Qualicare.

Suppose it is seeking to expand its services into a new community, New Bedford, and it estimates that 4,000 people in the community might potentially want to use the agency's services. The home health agency must decide whether to aim its advertising primarily at HMOs, PPOs, and insurers, physicians, hospital discharge planners, or the patients themselves. Beyond this, it may want to develop communications to reach the families and other influentials in the home health care decision process. Each target market would warrant a different advertising campaign.

Target Response. Once the target audience is identified, the marketing communicator must define the target response. The ultimate response, of course, is purchase behavior. But purchase behavior is the end result of a long process of consumer decision making. The marketing communicator needs to know in which state the target audience is at the present time and to which state it should be moved.

Any member of the target audience may be in one of six *buyer readiness states* with respect to the service or organization. These states—awareness, knowledge, liking, preference, conviction, or purchase—are described below.[12]

1. *Awareness.* The first thing to establish is how aware the target audience is of the service or organization. The audience may be completely unaware of the entity, know only its name, or know one or two things about it. If most of the target audience is unaware, the communicator's task is to build awareness, perhaps even just name recognition. This calls for simple messages repeating the name. Building awareness takes time. The Qualicare home health agency has no name recognition among residents of the New Bedford community. The agency might set the objective of making 40 percent of the residents aware of Qualicare's name within one year.
2. *Knowledge.* The target audience may be aware of the entity, but may not know much about it. In this case, the goal will be to transmit some key information about the entity. Thus Qualicare may want its target audience to know that it offers 24-hour homemaker care and has a hospice program. After waging a campaign, it can sample the target audience members to measure whether they have little, some, or much knowledge of Qualicare, and the content of that knowledge. The particular set of beliefs that make up the audience's picture of an entity is called its *image.* Health care organizations are becoming more attuned to image issues, as measured by HCA's (Hospital Corporation of America) image enhancement campaign in which "HCA measured the awareness of consumers and HCA physicians and employees before, during, and after the campaign."[13]
3. *Liking.* If the target audience members know the entity, the next question is, How do they feel about it? We can imagine a scale covering dislike very much, dislike somewhat, indifferent, like somewhat, like very much. If the

audience holds an unfavorable view of Qualicare, the communicator has to find out why and then develop a communications program to build up favorable feeling. If the unfavorable view is rooted in real inadequacies of the agency, then a communications campaign will not do the job. The task would require first improving the agency and then communicating its quality. Good communications call for "good deeds followed by good words."

4. *Preference.* The target audience may like the entity, but may not prefer it to others. It may be one of several acceptable entities. In this case, the communicator's job is to build consumer preference for the entity. The communicator will have to tout its quality, value, performance, and other attributes. The communicator can check on the success of the campaign by surveying the members of the audience to see if their preference for the entity is any stronger.
5. *Conviction.* A target audience may prefer a particular entity, but may not develop a conviction about buying it. Thus, some New Bedford residents may prefer Qualicare to other agencies, but may not wish to go against the choice of the physician or discharge planner or may not wish to use an agency not covered by their HMO. The communicator's job is to build conviction that choosing Qualicare is the right thing to do. Building conviction that one should buy a particular entity is a challenging communications task.
6. *Action.* A member of the target audience may have conviction, but may not get around to making the purchase. He or she may be waiting for additional information, may plan to act later, and so on. A communicator in this situation must lead the consumer to take the final step, which is called "closing the sale." Among action-producing devices are offering the entity at a low price if bought now, offering a premium, indicating that the entity will soon be unavailable, or offering an opportunity to try it on a limited basis. The first three options had rarely been used by health care organizations until recently, but they are increasingly finding their way into health care promotional strategies.

The six states simplify to three stages known as the cognitive (awareness, knowledge), affective (liking, preference, conviction), and behavioral (purchase). The communicator normally assumes that buyers pass through these stages in succession on the way to purchase. In this case, the communicator's task is to identify the state most of the target audience is in and develop a message or campaign that will move them to the next stage. It would be nice if one message could move the audience through all three stages, but this rarely happens. Most communicators try to find a cost-effective approach to moving the target audience one stage at a time. The critical thing is to know where the audience is and what the next feasible stage is.

Some marketing scholars have challenged the idea that a consumer passes through cognition to affect to behavior in this order. Ray has suggested that some consumers pass from cognition to behavior to affect.[14] An example would be someone who has seen advertising about the wisdom of getting one's blood pressure checked, sees a hypertension mobile van, steps in without much feeling or thought about hypertension testing, and afterward decides that getting his blood pressure checked is a good idea. Ray has also suggested that sometimes consumers pass from behavior to affect to cognition. Thus, a new person in town may go to a physician about whom she knows nothing, but whose name was in the telephone book, develop a positive feeling toward the physician, and finally learn about the physician's training, background, and hospital and PPO affiliation. Each version of the sequence has different implications for the role and influence of communications on behavior. (See Chapter 10 for a more detailed discussion of these consumer behavior models.)

Clearly, this analysis can lead to many specific communication objectives for advertising. Colley has distinguished 52 possible advertising objectives in Defining Advertising Goals for Measured Advertising Results (DAGMAR).[15] The various advertising objectives can be sorted into whether their aim is to inform, persuade, or remind. The *inform* category includes such objectives as telling the market about a new service, informing the market of a price change, explaining how the service works, describing various available services, correcting false impressions, reducing consumer fears, and building an organizational image. The *persuade* category includes such objectives as building brand preference, encouraging switching to the advertiser's brand, trying to change the customer's perception of the importance of different product attributes, persuading the customer to purchase now, and persuading the customer to receive a sales call. The *remind* category includes such objectives as reminding customers that the service might be needed now or in the future, and reminding them where to obtain it.

Target Reach and Frequency. The third decision is to determine the optimal target reach and frequency of the advertising. Funds for advertising are rarely so abundant that everyone in the target audience can be reached, and reached with sufficient frequency. Health care managers must decide what percentage of the audience to reach with what exposure frequency per period. For example, Qualicare could decide to use direct mail and buy 20,000 advertising exposures. This still leaves many choices. It could try to expose Qualicare to 20,000 different New Bedford residents by sending one letter to each resident. Or it could try to reach 10,000 residents with two different letters a week apart, or it could try to reach 5,000 residents with four mailing to each. The issue is largely one of how many exposures are needed to create the desired response, given the market's state of readiness. One exposure might be enough to convert residents from being unaware to being aware. It would not be enough to convert them from awareness to preference.

It is unfortunately typical of health care and social service organizations to assume that one exposure per target audience member is enough. Rarely, with the exception of organizations relying on the advice of advertising agencies, do health care organizations set realistic target frequency objectives or engage in advertising other than in unassessed short bursts. Contrast this to Sears, Roebuck and Company's advertising campaign to introduce its new financial services. In one year, it spends $12 million to produce 11 billion exposures, or the equivalent of 50 exposures for every person in the United States.

Budget Determination

In Chapter 11 we reviewed the major ways organizations set their marketing budgets: affordable method, percentage-of-sales method, competitive basis method, and objective-and-task method. We prefer the last method. Suppose Qualicare wants to send two letters to each of 10,000 residents. The gross number of exposures is thus 20,000. Suppose the average mailing piece will cost $2 to cover design, production, envelop stuffing, and postage. Qualicare will need a rough advertising budget of $40,000 to accomplish its objectives.

In addition to estimating the total size of the required advertising budget, a determination must be made of how the budget should be allocated over different market segments, geographical areas, and time periods. In practice, advertising budgets are allocated to segments of demand according to their respective populations, sales levels, or some other indicator of market potential. It is common to spend twice as much advertising money in segment B than in segment A if segment B has twice as much of some indicator of market potential. In fact, however, the budget should be allocated to different segments according to their expected marginal response to advertising. A budget is allocated well when it is not possible to shift dollars from one segment to another and increase total market response.

Tied in with target frequency objectives which are unrealistically low are the insufficient advertising budgets characteristic of many health care organizations. Historically, the advertising allocation was burried in a public relations budget and was spent on brochures or other "acceptable" forms of advertising. This is changing as health care organizations reorganize the marketing function, the budgetary process, and overall marketing responsibility in an effort to remain competitive.

Nonprofit health care organizations especially have had difficulty moving to paid advertising, even though they may acknowledge its potential value. The ostensible reason is that they are the beneficiaries of donated or public service advertising which they fear will be withdrawn if they engage in paid advertising. For example, the American Red Cross has its advertising copy produced by a volunteer advertising agency (through the Advertising Council of America), and public service time and space are donated by the media. Unfortunately, the Red Cross has no control over when the ads are aired, and it is rarely prime time. Yet the Red Cross fears that if it started to buy media time, it would lose the free time it now gets.

As David Ogilvy, one of the patriarchs of modern advertising, pointed out in discussing public service advertising:

> Forty years ago, the advertising establishment in the United States set up the Advertising Council to provide free campaigns for US Savings Bonds, the Red Cross and other good causes. In 1979, the media gave $600,000,000 worth of free time and space to the Council's campaigns, and the agencies charged nothing for their services. This admirable system has one drawback: the success of each campaign depends on the generosity of the media, which cannot be predicted.[16]

Message Decision

Given the advertising objectives and the budget, management has to develop a creative message. An ideal message is one that manages to get *attention,* hold *interest,* arouse *desire,* and obtain *action* (known as the AIDA model). In practice, few messages will take the consumer all the way from awareness through purchase, but the AIDA framework still suggests some desirable qualities.

In making the message decision, advertisers and their agencies go through three steps: message generation, message evaluation and selection, and message execution.

Message Generation. Message generation involves developing a number of alternative messages (appeals, themes, motifs, ideas) that will conceivably help produce the desired response in the target market.

Message generation can be handled in a number of ways. One approach is to talk with members of the target market and other influentials to determine the way they see the service, talk about it, and express their desires about it. A second approach is to hold a brainstorming meeting with key personnel in the organization to generate advertising ideas. A third method is to use some formal, deductive framework for teasing out possible advertising messages.

One framework is to generate a set of possible themes falling into three categories: rational, emotional, and moral.

1. *Rational appeals* aim at passing on information and/or serving the audience's self-interest. They attempt to show that the service will yield the expected functional benefits. Examples would be messages discussing a service's quality, economy, value, or performance.
2. *Emotional appeals* are designed to stir up some negative or positive emotion that will motivate purchase. Communicators have worked with fear, guilt, and shame appeals, especially in connection with getting people to start doing things they should (brushing their teeth, having an annual health checkup) or stop doing things they shouldn't (smoking, excessive drinking, drinking and driving, drug abuse, overeating). Advertisers have found that fear appeals work up to a point, but if there is too much fear the audience will ignore the message.[17] Communicators have also used positive emotional appeals such as love, humor, pride, and joy. Evidence has not established that a humorous message, for example, is necessarily more effective than a stright version of the same message.[18]
3. *Moral appeals* are directed to the audience's sense of what is right and proper. They are often used in messages exhorting people to support such social causes as a cleaner environment, better race relations, equal rights for women, and aiding the disadvantaged. An example is the March of Dimes appeal: "God made you whole. Give to help those He didn't." Moral appeals are less often used in connection with everyday products and services.

Maloney proposed another deductive framework.[19] He suggested that buyers may be expecting any of four types of reward from a product: rational, sensory, social, or ego satisfaction. And they may visualize these rewards from results-of-use experience, product-in-use experience, or incidental-to-use experience. Crossing the four types of rewards with the three types of experience generates twelve types of advertising messages.

A third approach is to examine the product's actual and desired position in the product space and look for the themes that would shift the market's view of the product in the desired direction. The advertisement may try to change the belief about the product's level on some attribute, the perceived relative importance of different attributes, or introduce new attributes not generally considered by the market. See Exhibit 16–2 for an example of efforts to position competing HMO's through advertising.

Message Evaluation and Selection. The task of selecting the best message out of a large number of possibilities calls for evaluation criteria. Twedt has suggested that messages be rated on three scales: desirability, exclusiveness, and believability.[20] He believes that the communication potency of a message is the product of the three factors, because if any of the three has a low rating, communication potency will be greatly reduced.

EXHIBIT 16–2
The HMO Ad Campaign . . . It's Healthy, Hot and Heavy

Harvard Health is going for emotional testimonials.

Bay State wants people to choose between a bookkeeper and a doctor.

Tufts wants to be warm and cuddly.

And Multigroup pictures itself as the "class act" of the bunch.

The battle for the health care buck has never been fiercer.

This spring alone the state's big HMOs are expecting to spend $1 million–$1.5 million in advertising, each trying to position itself differently and capture a chunk of the burgeoning market with TV ads, radio spots and full-page newspaper spreads.

Harvard Community Health Plan, for example, went in for testimonials, filming four patients talking about their medical experiences. Knut Seeber, a 48-year-old heart transplant patient, praises Harvard Health for paying for his operation last year, and Opal Adams says how appreciative she is that the plan paid her medical costs in Delaware after she was in an automobile accident there with her daughter.

"We took a small part of the health issue and demonstrated it in very credible and human terms," said Michael Fortuna, a partner in Emerson Lane Fortuna Inc., Harvard Health's ad agency. The advertising, he said, was meant to be "very emotional."

Bay State Health Care Foundation opted, instead, to take not-so-subtle digs at Blue Cross/Blue Shield with the ads portraying a patient in bed trying to choose between a health plan "run by people who bill you" and another "run by people who cure you."

"We're positioning ourselves against Blue Cross/Blue Shield," said Terence M. Clarke of the Clarke Goward Fitts ad agency, which created the spot. And by calling itself "The Doctor's Plan," he said, "It pre-empts the rest of the HMOs from taking this position."

The Tufts Associated Health Plan has only one ad, a warm-and-cuddly spot featuring the little girl having a checkup and a friendly, smiling doctor who pronounces her "perfect."

James Walter, vice president of marketing at Tufts, wouldn't talk about his strategy but he did acknowledge that, "We're spending more money than ever before."

And animated characters in the Multigroup Health Plan Inc.'s TV spot try to understand the maze of disparate plans. In the end, the ad plugs a Multigroup booklet called "How to Choose a Health Plan."

"We regard ourselves as the class act in the field," said Dr. Thomas C. Peebles, a pediatrician and chairman and chief executive officer of Multigroup. "We want to promote HMOs."

Added Multigroup spokeswoman Marcia Breier, "We're trying to touch the consumer's feelings. Our TV ads are trying to help people choose. They say it's confusing out there. Well, just get our booklet. It's a soft sell."

SOURCE: Wendy Fox, "The HMO Ad Campaign . . . It's Healthy, Hot and Heavy," *The Boston Globe,* May 17, 1985, p. 82. Reprinted courtesy of *The Boston Globe.*

The message must first say something desirable or interesting about the product. This is not enough, however, since many brands will be making the same claim. Therefore the message must also say something exclusive or distinctive that does not apply to every brand in the product category. Finally, the message must be believable or provable. By asking consumers to rate different messages on desirability, exclusiveness, and believability, these messages can be evaluated for their communication potency.

For example, the March of Dimes was searching for an advertising theme to raise money for its fight against birth defects.[21] A brainstorming session led to over twenty possible messages. A group of young parents was asked to rate each message for interest, distinctiveness, and believability, assigning up to 100 points for each. For example, the message "Seven hundred children are born each day with a birth defect" scored 70, 60, and 80 on interest, distinctiveness, and believability, while "Your next baby could be born with a birth defect" scored 58, 50, and 70 (see Figure 16–6). The first message outperforms the second and would be preferred for advertising purposes. The best overall message was "The March of Dimes has given you: polio vaccine, German measles vaccine, 110 birth defects' counseling centers" (70, 80, 90).

Message Execution. The impact of a message depends not only upon what is said, but also upon how it is said. In fact, message execution can be decisive for products that are essentially the same. The advertiser has to put the message across in a way that will win the target audience's attention and interest. It is the task of the creative people to find a style, a tone, words, an order, and a format that make for effective message execution.

Any message can be put across in different *execution styles*. Suppose the local public health department is planning to launch an early morning jogging program (6:30 A.M.) and wants to develop a 30-second television commercial to motivate people to sign up for this program through their local hospital. Here are some major execution styles the department can consider:

1. *Slice-of-life.* A husband says to his tired wife that she might enjoy jogging in the early morning. She agrees, and the next frame shows her coming home at 7:45 A.M. feeling refreshed and invigorated.
2. *Life style.* A 30-year-old man pops out of bed when his alarm rings at 6 A.M., races to the bathroom, races to the closet, races to his car, races to the local track, and then starts racing with his companions with a "big kid" look on his face.
3. *Fantasy.* A jogger runs along a path and suddenly imagines seeing his friends on the sidelines cheering him on.
4. *Mood.* A jogger runs in a residential neighborhood on a beautiful spring day, passing nice homes, noticing flowers beginning to bloom, and neigh-

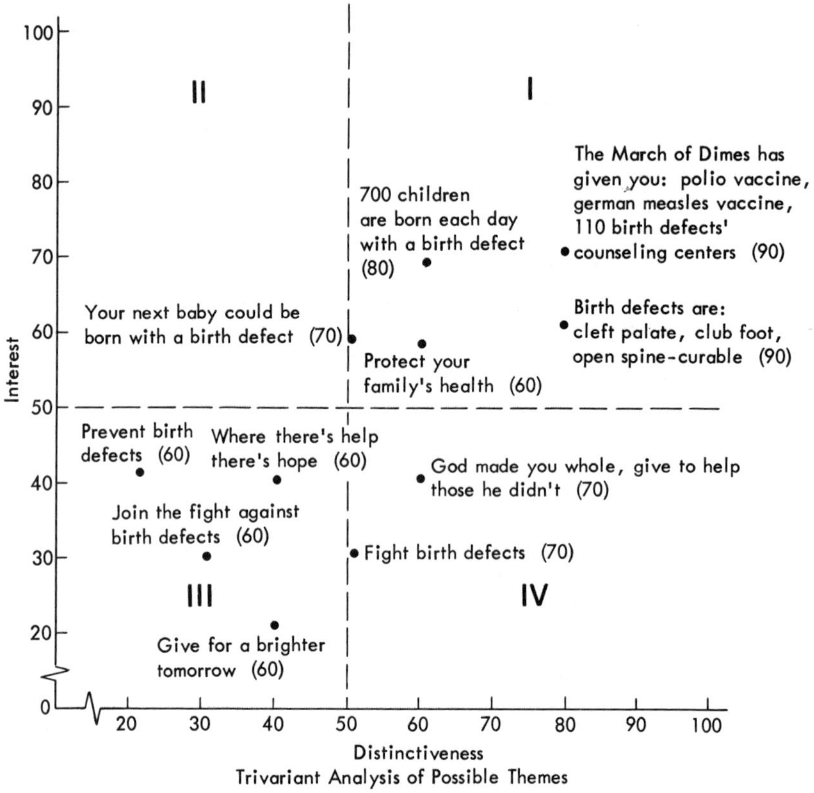

FIGURE 16–6 Advertising Message Evaluation *Source:* William A. Mindak and H. Malcolm Bybee, "Marketing's Application to Fund Raising," *Journal of Marketing* (July 1971), pp. 13–18.

bors waving to her. This ad creates a mood of beauty and harmony between the jogger and her world.

5. *Musical.* Four joggers run side by side wearing YMCA T-shirts and singing a song in barbershop quartet style about the joy of running.
6. *Personality symbol.* A well known sports hero is shown jogging with a smile on his face.
7. *Technical expertise.* Several sports medicine physicians are shown discussing the best time, place, and running style that will give the greatest benefit to joggers.
8. *Scientific evidence.* A sports medicine physician tells about a study of two matched groups of men, one following a jogging program and the other not, and the greater health and energy felt by the jogging group after a few weeks.
9. *Testimonial evidence.* The ad shows three members of a jogging group telling how beneficial the program has been.

Sometimes the execution belies the intent of the message.

The communicator must also choose a *tone* for the ad. The ad could be serious, chatty, humorous, and so on. The tone must be appropriate to the target audience and response desired. *Words* that are memorable and attention-getting must be found. This is nowhere more apparent than in the development of headlines and slogans. There are six basic types of headlines: *news* ("New Boom and More Inflation Ahead . . . and What You Can Do About It"); *question* (Have You Had It Lately?"); *narrative* ("They Laughed When I Sat Down at the Piano, But When I started to Play!"); *command* ("Save water—shower with a friend"); *1-2-3 ways* ("12 Ways to Save on Your Income Tax"); and *how-what-why* ("Why They Can't Stop Buying"). Look at the care airlines have lavished on finding the right way to describe their airline as safe without explicitly mentioning safety as an issue: "The Friendly Skies of United" (United); "The Wings of Man" (Eastern); and "The World's Most Experienced Airline" (Pan American).

The *order* of ideas in an ad can be important: The first issue is the question of *conclusion drawing,* the extent to which the ad should draw a definite conclusion for the audience or leave it to them. Experimental research seems to indicate that explicit conclusion drawing is more persuasive than leaving it to the audience. There are exceptions, such as when the communicator is seen as untrustworthy or the audience is highly intelligent and annoyed at the attempt to influence them.

The second issue is the question of *one- versus two-sided arguments*—that is, whether the message will be more effective if one or both sides of the argument are presented. Intuitively, it would appear that the best effect is gained by a one-sided presentation. This is the predominant approach in sales presentations, political contests, and childrearing. Yet the answer in advertising is not so clear-cut. The major conclusions are that one-sided messages tend to work best with audiences who are favorably disposed to the communicator's position, whereas two-sided arguments tend to work best with audiences who are opposed; two-sided messages tend to be more effective with better-educated audiences; and two-sided messages tend to be more effective with audiences likely to be exposed to counterpropaganda.

The third issue is the question of *order of presentation*—whether communicators should present the strongest arguments first or last. Presenting the strongest arguments first has the advantage of establishing attention and interest. This may be especially important in newspapers and other media, where the audience does not attend to the whole message. In a two-sided message, the issue is whether to present the positive argument first (primacy effect) or last (recency effect). If the audience is initially opposed, it would appear that the communicator would be smarter to start with the other side's argument. This will tend to disarm the audience and allow the speaker to conclude with the strongest argument.[22]

Format elements can make a difference in an ad's impact, as well as in its cost. If the message is to be carried in a print ad, the communicator has to develop the elements of headline, copy, illustration, and color. Advertisers are adept at using such attention-getting devices as novelty and contrast, arresting pictures and headlines, distinctive formats, message size and position, and color, shape, and movement. For example, large ads gain more attention, and so do four-color ads. But this must be weighed against the higher costs. If the message is to be carried over the radio, the communicator has to choose words, voice qualities (speech rate, rhythm, pitch, articulation), and vocalizations (pauses, sighs, yawns) carefully. If the message is to be carried on television or given in person, then all of these elements plus body language (nonverbal clues) have to be planned. Presenters have to pay attention to facial expressions, gestures, dress, posture, and hairstyle.

Media Selection

Media selection is another major step in advertising planning. Some thinking should take place before the message development stage and even before the advertising budget stage. It is essential to determine which media are used by the target audience and which are most efficient in reaching them. This information affects the advertising budget and even the type of appeal to use. The health care industry's historical reliance on brochures as the primary form of advertising was symptomatic of a failure to consider other media. The expansion of health care advertising into the vast array of other media has been quite dramatic in the past few years.

There are three basic steps in the media selection process: choosing among major categories, choosing among specific vehicles, and timing.

Choosing Among Media Categories. The first step is to determine how the advertising budget will be allocated among the major *media categories.* The media planner has to examine the major types for their capacity to deliver reach, frequency, and impact. Table 16–1 presents profiles of the major advertising media. In order of their advertising volume, they are newspapers, television, direct mail, radio, magazines, and outdoor. Media planners make their choice among these major media types by considering the following variables:

1. *Target audience media habits.* For example, radio and television are the most effective media for reaching teenagers.
2. *Product.* Media types have different potentialities for demonstration, visualization, explanation, believability, and color. For example, television is the most effective medium for demonstrating a complex product or service.

TABLE 16–1 Profiles of Major Media Categories

MEDIUM	*VOLUME IN BILLIONS (1983)*	*PERCENTAGE (1983)*	*EXAMPLE OF COST (1984)*	*ADVANTAGES*	*LIMITATIONS*
Newspapers	$20.6	27.1%	$20,974 one page, weekday *Chicago Tribune*	Flexibility; timeliness; good local market coverage; broad acceptance; high believability	Short life; poor reproduction quality; small "pass-along" audience
Television	16.1	21.2%	$6,000 for thirty seconds of prime time in Chicago	Combines sight, sound, and motion; appealing to the senses; high attention; high reach	High absolute cost; high clutter; fleeting exposure; less audience selectivity
Direct mail	11.8	15.5	$1,280 for the names and addresses of 34,000 veterinarians	Audience selectivity; flexibility; no ad competition within the same medium: personalization	Relatively high cost; "junk mail" image
Radio	5.2	6.8	$500 for one minute of prime time in Chicago	Mass use; high geographic and demographic selectivity; low cost	Audio presentation only; lower attention than television; nonstandardized rate structures; fleeting exposure
Magazines	4.2	5.6	$73,710 one page, four color in *Newsweek*	High geographic and demographic selectivity; credibility and prestige; high-quality reproduction; long life; good pass-along readership	Long ad purchase lead time; some waste circulation; no guarantee of position
Outdoor	0.8	1.1	$21,960 per month for 71 billboards in metropolitan Chicago	Flexibility; high repeat exposure; low cost; low competition	No audience selectivity; creative limitations
Other	17.2	22.7			
Total	$75.9	100.0%			

Miscellaneous media include media expenditures of the first six types that were not classified.

Source: Columns 2 and 3 are from *Advertising Age,* May 28, 1984. Reprinted with permission. Copyright © 1984. Crain Communications, Inc.

3. *Message.* A message announcing an emergency blood drive tomorrow will require radio or newspapers. A message containing a great deal of technical data might require specialized magazines or mailings.
4. *Cost.* Television is very expensive; newspaper advertising is inexpensive. What counts, of course, is the cost-per-thousand exposures rather than the total cost.

On the basis of these characteristics, the media planner has to decide how to allocate the given budget to the major media categories.

Selecting Specific Vehicles. The next step is to choose the specific vehicles within each media type that will produce the desired response in the most cost-effective way. Consider the category of male-oriented magazines, which includes *Playboy, Penthouse, Home Mechanics, Esquire,* and *Motorcycle.* The media planner turns to several volumes put out by Standard Rate and Data that provide circulation and costs for different ad sizes, color options, ad positions, and quantities of insertions. Beyond this, the media planner evaluates the different magazines on qualitative characteristics such as credibility, prestige, geographic editions, occupational editions, reproduction quality, editorial climate, lead time, and psychological impact. The planner makes a final judgment as to which specific vehicles will deliver the best reach, frequency, and impact for the money.

Media planners normally calculate the *cost per thousand persons* reached by a particular vehicle. If a full-page, four-color advertisement in *Newsweek* costs $30,000 and *Newsweek's* estimated readership is 6 million persons, then the cost of reaching each thousand persons is $5. The same advertisement in *Business Week* may cost $18,000 but reach only 2 million persons, at a cost per thousand of $9. A determining factor, then, is the extent to which *Business Week* better reaches the target market. Assuming equal reach, the media planner would rank the various magazines according to cost per thousand and would initially favor those with the lowest cost per thousand.

Deciding on Timing. The third step in media selection is *timing,* which breaks down into a macro and microproblem. The macroproblem is that of *seasonal timing.* For most products, there is a natural variation in intensity of interest at different times of the year. There is not much interest in flu shots except in the fall, or much interest in summer camp physicals except in late spring. Most marketers do not attempt to time their advertising when there is little or no natural interest. This would take much more money, and the effects would be dubious. Most marketers prefer to spend the bulk of the advertising budget just as natural interest is beginning to ripen in the product class and during the height of interest. For example, the HMO campaigns discussed earlier were all taking place in the spring because "most employers offering more than one kind of health plan allow employees to change only once or twice a year—July 1 and Jan. 1. Therefore, advertising picks up in the spring and again in late fall as HMOs vie for new group business."[23]

The other problem is the short-run timing. How should advertising be spaced during a short period, say a month? Consider three possible patterns. The first is called *burst advertising,* and consists of concentrating all the exposures in a very short space of time, say all in one day. Presumably this will attack maximum attention and interest. If recall is good, the effect will last for a while. The second pattern is *continuous advertising,* in which the exposures appear evenly throughout the period. This may be most effective when the audience buys or uses the product frequently and needs to be continuously reminded. The third pattern is *intermittent advertising,* in which intermittent small bursts appear in succession with no advertising in between. This pattern presumably is able to create a little more attention than continuous advertising, and yet has some of the reminder advantages of continuous advertising.

Advertising Evaluation

The final step in the effective use of advertising is that of advertising evaluation. The most important components are copy testing, media testing, and expenditure level testing.

Copy testing can occur both before an ad is put into actual media (copy pretesting) and after it has been printed or broadcast (copy posttesting). The purpose of pretesting is to make improvements in the copy to the fullest extent prior to its release.[24] There are three major methods of pretesting:

1. *Direct ratings.* A panel of target consumers or advertising experts examine alternative ads and fill out rating questionnaires. Sometimes a single question is raised, such as "Which of these ads do you think would influence you most to buy the service?" or a more elaborate form consisting of several rating scales may be used, such as the one shown in Exhibit 16–3. Here the person evaluates the ad's attention strength, read-through strength, cognitive strength, affective strength, and behavioral strength, assigning a number of points (up to a maximum in each case). The underlying theory is that an effective ad must score high on all these properties if it is ultimately to stimulate buying. Too often ads are evaluated only on their attention- or comprehension-creating abilities. At the same time, direct rating methods are judgmental and less reliable than harder evidence of an ad's actual impact on a target consumer. Direct rating scales help primarily to screen out poor ads rather than to identify great ads.
2. *Portfolio tests.* Respondents are given a dummy portfolio of ads and asked to take as much time as they want to read them. After putting them down,

EXHIBIT 16–3 Rating Sheets for Ads

Attention: How well does the ad catch the reader's attention?	____(20)
Read-through strength: How well does the ad lead the reader to read further?	____(20)
Cognitive strength: How clear is the central message or benefit?	____(20)
Affective strength: How effective is the particular appeal?	____(20)
Behavior strength: How well does the ad suggest follow-through action?	____(20)
Total	____

0	20	40	60	80	100
Poor ad	Mediocre ad	Average ad	Good ad	Great ad	

the respondents are asked to recall the ads they saw—unaided or aided by the interviewer—and to play back as much as they can about each ad. The results are taken to indicate an ad's ability to stand out and be understood.

3. *Laboratory tests.* Some researchers assess the potential effect of an ad by measuring physiological reactions—heartbeat, blood pressure, pupil dilation, perspiration—using such equipment as galvanometers, tachistroscopes, size-distance tunnels, and pupil dilation measuring equipment. These physiological tests at best measure the attention-getting and arousing power of an ad rather than any higher state of consciousness the ad might produce.

There are two popular posttesting methods, the purpose of which is to assess whether the desired impact is being achieved or what the possible weaknesses are:

1. *Recall tests.* These involve finding people who are regular users of the media vehicle and asking them to recall advertisers and products contained in the issue under study. They are asked to recall everything they can remember. The interviewer may or may not aid them in their recall. Recall scores prepared on the basis of their responses are used to indicate the power of the ad to be noticed and retained.
2. *Recognition tests.* Recognition tests call for sampling the readers of a given issue of the vehicle, say a magazine, asking them to point out what they recognize as having seen and/or read. For each ad, three different Starch

readership scores (named after Daniel Starch, who provides the leading service) are prepared from the recognition data:

Noted. The percent of readers of the magazine who say they had previously seen the advertisement in the particular magazine.

Seen/associated. The percent of readers who say they have seen or read any part of the ad that clearly indicates the names of the product (or service) of the advertiser.

Read most. The percent of readers who not only looked at the advertisement, but who say that they read more than half of the total written material in the ad.

All these efforts rate the communication effectiveness of the ad, and not necessarily its impact on attitude or behavior. The latter are much harder to measure. Most advertisers appear satisfied in knowing that their ad has been seen and comprehended and appear unwilling to spend additional funds to determine the ad's sales effectiveness.

Another advertising element that is normally tested is media. Media testing seeks to determine whether a given vehicle is cost-effective in reaching and influencing the target audience. A common way to test a vehicle is to place a coupon ad and see how many coupons are returned. Another testing device is to compare the ad readership scores in different vehicles as a sign of effectiveness.

Finally, the advertising expenditure level itself can be tested. Expenditure-level testing involves arranging experiments in which advertising expenditure levels are varied over similar markets to see the variation in response. A "high spending" test would consist of spending twice as much money in a similar territory as another to see how much more sales response (orders, outpatient visits, inquiries) this produces. If the response is only slightly greater in the high spending territory, it may be concluded, other things being equal, that the lower budget is adequate.

SALES PROMOTION

Sales promotion comprises a wide variety of tactical promotional tools of a short-term incentive nature designed to stimulate earlier and/or stronger target market response.

These tools can be subclassified into tools for consumer promotion (samples, coupons, money-refund offers, prices-off, gifts, contests, trading stamps, demonstrations), dealer-middleman promotion (free goods and services, merchandise allowances, cooperative advertising, push money, dealer sales contests), and salesforce promotion (bonuses, contests, sales rallies).

Although sales promotion tools are a motley collection, they have two distinctive qualities: (1) *Insistent presence.* Many sales promotion tools have an attention-getting, sometimes urgent, quality that can break through habits of buyer inertia toward a particular service. They tell the buyers of a chance that they may not have again or elsewhere to get something special. (2) *Product demotion.* Some of these tools suggest that the seller is anxious for the sale. If they are used too frequently or carelessly, they may lead buyers to wonder whether the product or service is desirable or reasonably priced. For two examples of sales promotion based product demotion, see Exhibit 16–4. Sales promotion tools are used by a large variety of health care organizations. Exhibit 16–5 lists a few.

Health care organizations have turned increasingly to sales promotions in recent years. One reason is because they are under greater pressure to obtain a quick response—the "quick fix." Other reasons include (1) increasing competition; (2) increasing use of promotion by competition; (3) consumer made more incentive oriented by recession and inflation;[25] and (4) for reasons previously discussed, a lingering resistance to using advertising.

No single purpose can be advanced for sales promotion tools, since they are so varied in form. Overall, sales promotion techniques make three contributions to exchange relationships: (1) *communication*—they gain attention and usually provide information that will, it is hoped, lead to trying the product; (2) *incentive*—they incorporate some concession, inducement, or contribution that is designed to represent value to the receiver; and (3) *invitation*—they include a distinct invitation to engage in the transaction now.

We will define **incentive** as something of financial or symbolic value added to an offer to encourage some overt behavioral response.[26] The decision by an organization to use incentives as part of its promotional plan calls for seven distinct steps.

The first is to specify *the objective* for which it is deemed necessary or desirable to undertake the use of incentives. Three objectives can be distinguished. Sometimes incentives are offered to create an immediate behavioral response because the organization has excess capacity. Many hospitals have used incentives to help fill empty maternity beds. Incentives may also be offered to promote trial of a product or service by groups that normally would not venture to try the product. Finally, incentives may be offered to win goodwill toward the organization, as when an organization offers to match its employees' contributions to a particular charity.

The second step is to determine the *inclusiveness of the incentive*—that is, whether it will be offered to individuals or to the groups to which the target individuals belong. Most incentives are offered to indi-

EXHIBIT 16–4 Sales Promotion-based Product Demotion

Choice Cuts

WASHINGTON—The latest news from the medical world is that hospitals are having more difficulty attracting patients. Occupancy rates are down and many institutions are now resorting to advertising and hiring people to get people to use their beds.

The competition is getting fierce, and no one can predict what kind of perks a hospital will offer to get a patient to use one of its rooms.

I visited a marketing consultant who works for one of the major hospitals in the Washington area.

He was very excited about a new idea. "What do you think of an Operation of the Month Club?" he asked me.

"It sounds good," I told him. "What do you get if you join?"

He showed a full-page layout he had designed. Across the top: "Save one thousand dollars on every operation. Join the Operation of the Month Club." Then there were photographs of different parts of the body and large type: "When you join, you are entitled to any one of these operations free." Then, in smaller type: "All you have to do is have four operations a year, and you will be entitled to another *at no cost to you.*"

"Wow," I said, "that's really a buy. How does it work?"

"Every month we will have a distinguished panel of surgeons choose the Operation of the Month," he said. "Let's say the main selection for April would be an appendectomy. You would get a notice in the mail that it is being offered. If you don't return the card within 10 days, we'll send an ambulance to your house and whisk you off to the hospital and perform the operation for one-half of what it would cost if you just went in and asked for one."

"Suppose I don't want an appendectomy?"

"Then you will have the choice of 30 alternative selections, anything from a tonsillectomy to implanting a pacemaker, at the same low prices. And remember, you only have to choose four a year, and you get a free one as a bonus."

My friend showed me the mockup of the Operation of the Month News Bulletin.

"When you become a member you'll receive 15 issues of this beautiful magazine outlining the various operations the hospital performs."

"You've got this all thought out," I said admiringly. "If the Operation of the Month Club catches on, hospitals will never have to worry about filling their beds again."

He seemed pleased with my reaction. "I'll tell you what. If you sign up as the first member I'll arrange a hernia operation for you for nothing."

"But I don't need a hernia operation," I told him.

"Then choose one of the alternates. It's all the same to us."

SOURCE: Art Buchwald, "Choice Cuts", *The Boston Globe,* April 8, 1984, p. A27. Reprinted with permission of the author.

> Top this, if you can. Owners of new North Hollywood medical clinic have announced an "Accident of the Month Award" for the survivor of the most unusual accident. "We'll give the prize to the person messed up the worst," Dennis Gilberg, a consultant to the owners of West Care Medical Center Inc., said. "All we're trying to do is make people cognizant that we exist." The winner will receive an all-expense paid weekend at the Hotel del Coronado near San Diego—upon recovery, that is.
>
> *SOURCE:* Dick Carpenter, "Names and Faces," *The Boston Globe,* July 11, 1983, p. 5. Reprinted by courtesy of *The Boston Globe.*

viduals for their direct benefit. A case of an incentive that is offered to a group is exemplified in communities that offer to provide free blood to all persons in the community if 4 percent or more of the residents make blood donations.

The third step is to specify the *recipient* of the incentive—that is, whether incentives should go to consumers, middlemen, or sales agents. For example, incentives to promote vasectomies in developing countries may be offered to the consumer, to the doctor, or to the canvasser who recruits prospects. At one time, canvassers in India were given so much incentive to find prospects that they brought in men who were too young to know better and men who were to old for it to matter.

The fourth step is to determine the *direction of the incentives*—that is, whether they should be positive (rewarding) or negative (punishing). Commercial or private organizations normally work with incentives rather than disincentives in promoting offers. Governments work with both with equal facility: They offer subsidies and special advantages to encourage certain types of behavior and impose taxes or costs on other types of behavior. In any particular problem area, either option may be available. Nations wishing to lower the birth rate reduce family allowances or disproportionately tax large families.

The fifth step is to determine the *form of the incentive*—that is, whether it should consist of monetary or nonmonetary value. Monetary incentives include price-off, cash, bonds, and savings accounts. Nonmonetary incentives include a whole variety of things such as food, free education, health care, lottery tickets, or old age security. The form of the incentive must be carefully researched, because its nuances may offend the target group. For exmaple, although cash is a very tangible incentive, it may be viewed as a corrupt consideration if it is used to influence the decision on how many children to have; an offer of better housing may be received more favorably. In the health care field, given its high public visibility, organizations must also be sensitive to the

EXHIBIT 16–5 Health Care Sales Promotion

Dr. Edward W. Hughes, a Northampton, Mass. psychiatrist, advertised a free 30 minute consultation. "I wanted to see what would happen," he said. But very little happened. Only two people called for appointments and they both later cancelled them.[27]

Hospitals are hotly competing for maternity patients. Many offer candlelight steak dinners for the new parents and T-shirts for the new babies. Sunrise Hospital in Las Vegas sells "baby bonds" to pregnant women who plan to deliver at Sunrise. When the baby is born, the principal and 25% interest are credited against the inpatient bill.

"Everyone at the hospital got the special chicken dish," said Terry Lowe, of Waukegan's Victory Hospital. The difference last week was that the chicken was served by bunnies—Playboy bunnies. Under a gourmet food program begun eight months ago for the hospital's 400 patients and 1,000 employees, well-known chefs donate their services to help the hospital's kitchen staff of 12 prepare gourmet treats. "This was the first time Playboy bunnies helped serve the patients. And they made a big hit," said Lowe. No doubt. "Of course," he said "the cardiac patients were examined and found to be able to take any extra excitement."[28]

The administrator of Westlake Hospital in Melrose Park, Illinois, took a physician with big admitting potential on a four day Colorado ski trip. Hospitals in California have offered leased luxury cars, paid vacations in the Bahamas, free office space and even cash bounties for maintaining a high volume of admissions.[29]

Family planners in many third world countries offer incentives such as transistor radios, cookware, etc. to potential adopters of birth control methods.

The New York City Department of Health offered souvenir giveaways of a note pad and a ballpoint pen in a simulated leather folder to stimulate usage of their chest X-ray mobile unit.[30]

A pharmaceutical company advertised its prescription antiarthritic drug directly to consumers, offered $1.50 rebate on every bottle purchased.

Health Stop, an organization with seventeen walk-in medical offices, offered free basketball game tickets and free ice cream from a local ice cream store chain in an advertisement that said: "This Saturday will be the most fun children (of all ages) ever had at the doctor's office. Health Stop is giving you the Boston Celtics and Brigham's ice cream to introduce you to the quality and convenience you told us you want in a family doctor's office. All 17 Health Stop offices will give everyone who stops in between 10 a.m. and 4 p.m., Saturday, June 30, a FREE gift from Brigham's Ice Cream. And while you are there, register to win SUPER CELTICS GIVEAWAY. . . ."

nuances incentives have for regulations and legislators. For example, the House Subcommittee on Health and Long-term Care investigated the sales promotion practices of intra-ocular lens (IOL) manufacturers targeted at physicians. Noting that IOL implants had become the most common Medicare-covered procedure in 1984, the subcommittee looked to IOL manufacturers' promotional tactics and found "some manufacturers have been offering ophthalmologists interesting incentives to use their product and/or buy in bulk. Examples: all-expense paid trips to "educational" seminars in warm climates and offers of updated equipment for the doctor's office.[31] This was not viewed positively by the legislators.

The sixth step is to determine the *amount of incentive.* An overly small incentive is ineffective and an overly large one is wasteful. If the incentive is nongraduated, the amount may seem too small for those in higher income brackets and too much for those in lower income brackets. This has led to interest in graduated incentives whereby the amount offered varies with the consumer's economic circumstances.

The seventh step is the *time of payment of the incentive.* Most incentives are paid immediately upon the adoption of the target behavior. In the family planning area, the adoption of sterilization is usually immediately followed by payment. But the agreement to use birth control pills may not be rewarded except on the basis of results each year.

In summary, incentives are an important means of promotion, but they require, as we have seen, several steps of analysis and research. Commercial companies tend to learn over time what incentives work best, and their optimal amounts and timing. In the area of family planning, several propositions are emerging about incentives and their effective use.[32] Similar knowledge is accumulating on the use of incentives in other health-related areas, such as nutrition, immunization, and self-medication practices. The outlook is one of increasing use of incentives in social service and health care marketing.

SUMMARY

Recent changes in the law plus an increasing willingness to use marketing techniques have led health care organizations to consider advertising and sales promotion. Due to long-held beliefs that any form of promotion constitutes solicitation and therefore is inappropriate, most health care organizations have historically refrained from all but the most timid use of advertising and sales promotion. However, the field has changed dramatically in the past few years in its orientation toward advertising and promotion, and appears to be preparing for greater activity in this area.

All health care organizations engage in communications and promotion activity. This activity can be considered as the fourth major component in the marketing mix. Promotion is defined as the development of persuasive communications. The main tools of promotion fall into four categories: advertising, sales promotion, personal selling, and publicity. This chapter discusses the first two.

Advertising calls for skill in setting objectives and budgets; in developing effective messages, media, and timing; and in evaluating results. Sales promotion consists of incentive tools designed to stimulate early product trial or to win customer goodwill. The organization has to decide on such issues as the incentive's inclusiveness (individual or group), the recipient (middleman or final consumer), the direction (negative or positive), the form (monetary or nonmonetary), the amount (large or small), and the timing of payment (immediate or deferred).

NOTES

1. "Dental Clinic advertising attacked in Maryland," *American Medical News,* April 16, 1982, p. 24.

2. Judith D. Berger, "The Ethical Side of Advertising," *Hospital Forum* (November–December 1981), pp. 35–39.

3. John A. Miller and Robin Waller, "Health Care Advertising: Consumer vs. Physician Attitudes", *Journal of Advertising* (Fall 1979), pp. 20–29.

4. Bill Jackson and Joyce Jenson, "Majority of Consumers Support Advertising of Hospital Services," *Modern Healthcare* (April 1984), pp. 93–97.

5. "Hospital Advertising Has Few Critics: Study," *Hospitals* (April 16, 1985), p. 30.

6. Rick Markello and Carol Vorhous, "Selecting a Pediatrician," Graduate student project for the Boston University Health Care Management Program, December 1978.

7. "Have I Got an Appendectomy for You," *The Wall Street Journal,* April 9, 1981, p. 1.

8. Julie Franz, "Hospital Advertises Cost Comparisons to Impress Employers, Physicians," *Modern Healthcare* (February 15, 1984), p. 72.

9. Roberta N. Clarke, "Health Care Marketing: Problems in Implementation," *Health Care Management Review* (Winter 1978).

10. These definitions, with the exception of the one for sales promotion, came from *Marketing Definitions: A Glossary of Marketing Terms* (Chicago: American Marketing Association, 1960).

11. "Competition Heightens Healthcare Ads," *Healthcare Marketing Report,* July 1984, p. 1.

12. There are several models of buyer readiness states. See, for example, Robert J. Lavidge and Gary A. Steiner, "A Model for Predictive Measurements of Advertising Effectiveness," *Journal of Marketing* (October 1961), pp. 59–62.

13. "HCA Launches Houston Ad Campaign Pilot That Could Lead to National Program," *Hospitals* (Multis Special Section), December 1, 1984, p. M12.

14. Michael L. Ray, *Marketing Communication and the Hierarchy of Effects* (Cambridge, MA: Marketing Science Institute, November 1973).

15. See Russell H. Colley, *Defining Advertising Goals for Measured Advertising Results* (New York: Association of National Advertisers, 1961).

16. David Ogilvy, *Ogilvy on Advertising* (New York: Crown, 1983), p. 150.

17. Michael L. Ray and William L. Wilkie, "Fear: The Potential of an Appeal Neglected by Marketing," *Journal of Marketing* (January 1970), pp. 55–56; and Brian Sternthal and C. Samuel Craig, "Fear Appeals: Revisited and Revised," *Journal of Consumer Research* (December 1974), pp. 22–34.

18. See Brian Sternthal and C. Samuel Craig, "Humor in Advertising," *Journal of Marketing* (October 1973), pp. 12–18.

19. See John C. Maloney, "Marketing Decisions and Attitude Research," in *Effective Marketing Coordination,* ed. George L. Baker, Jr. (Chicago: American Marketing Association, 1961).

20. Dick Warren Twedt, "How to Plan New Products, Improve Old Ones, and Create Better Advertising," *Journal of Marketing* (January 1969), pp. 53–57.

21. See William A. Mindak and H. Malcolm Bybee, "Marketing's Application to Fund Raising," *Journal of Marketing* (July 1971), pp. 13–18.

22. See C. I. Hovland, A. A. Lumsdaine, and F. D. Sheffield, *Experiments in Mass Communication* (Princeton, NJ: Princeton University Press, 1948), Vol. III.

23. Wendy Fox, "The HMO Ad Campaign . . . It's Healthy, Hot and Heavy," *The Boston Globe,* May 17, 1985, p. 82.

24. Novelli reports that many public service announcements, especially those containing health messages, are dull and ineffective. New ads should be pretested. His firm has devised a Health Message Testing Service that has already tested and analyzed messages on high blood pressure, breast self-examination, childhood immunization, smoking cessation, drug abuse prevention, physical fitness, and offers for telephone assistance and printed materials on cancer. See William D. Novelli, "Copy Testing Messages on Health," a presentation to the Advertising Research Conference on the American Marketing Association, New York chapter, May 16, 1978.

25. See Roger A. Strang, "Sales Promotion—Fast Growth, Faulty Management," *Harvard Business Review* (July–August 1976), pp. 115–24.

26. This definition, and the following discussion, relies largely on two sources: Edward Pohlman, *Incentives and Compensations in Birth Planning* (University of North Carolina: Carolina Population Center, 1971); and Everett M. Rogers, "Effects of Incentives on the Discussion of Innovations: The Case of Family Planning in Asia," in *Processes and Phenomena of Social Change,* ed. Gerald Zaltman (New York: Wiley, 1973).

27. "Doctor Advertising: Here to Stay," *Medical World News* (February 2, 1982), pp. 61–70.

28. "Newsnotes," *Chicago Tribune,* July 29, 1980, p. 1.

29. Joann S. Lublin, "Hospitals Turning to Bold Marketing to Lure Patients and Stay in Business," *The Wall Street Journal,* September 11, 1979, p. 28.

30. Teresa J. Katz and Martin Svigir, "Effect of Souvenir Giveaways on Response to Offers of Free Chest X-rays," *Public Health Reports,* 82, 8 (August 1967), pp. 735–38.

31. "Implant Manufacturers Investigated for Sales and Marketing Tactics," *Hospitals* (April 16, 1985), p. 76.

32. Ibid.

17

PUBLIC RELATIONS DECISIONS

Judith Rice has been director of public affairs for Chicago's 265-bed Children's Memorial Hospital for 2½ years. She previously was in hospital public relations at Northwestern Memorial Hospital in Chicago for seven years. We asked her what her job involves.

> When I began the newly-formed Public Affairs department, our responsibilities were broadened beyond the traditional public relations functions to include—in addition to media relations, publications and support for the hospital's fund-raising function—community relations, governmental relations and marketing communications. The public affairs function has progressed in two short years from being a "publicity office" to being a staff function that is a part of institutional decision-making and plays an important role in implementing the strategic plan of the hospital.
>
> Being in the unique position of starting a department from scratch with a totally new staff presented tremendous opportunities and challenges. Our first step was to establish a public relations plan and to draft the policies we needed to carry it out. The plan was based on the short- and long-range objectives of the hospital:
>
> 1. To strenthen the public's perception of Children's as the major pediatric medical center in the Midwest.
> 2. To emphasize the expertise of the hospital and its staff as a leader in patient care, research and education.
> 3. To assist in the development and implementation of a hospital marketing program as an important component of the marketing function.
> 4. To increase referrals to private-pay patients to Children's physicians.
> 5. To develop consistent, high-quality publications for all departments that

require them and to take responsibility for quality control over all printed communications with patients, families, the public, and physicians in the community.
6. To create avenues by which the hospital becomes active in the affairs of its community, and establish consistent, positive contact and communications with its neighbors.
7. To recognize and support the achievements and contributions of the hospital staff and family.
8. To keep hospital family members fully informed as to institutional priorities, objectives and major accomplishments so as to build pride in the hospital among members of its family.
9. To provide communications support to the development office in fund-raising, special events, telethon, support group activities.

To achieve those objectives, we made media relations a top priority, particularly with national media and community media throughout Illinois and northern Indiana, areas from which we receive many patient referrals. We also developed *Carousel,* a community magazine which is mailed to families within the hospital's immediate community, donors, corporations, governmental officials, Chicago opinion leaders, and the media.

We collaborate extensively with the hospital's marketing director to develop direct mail campaigns directed to both referring physicians and consumers. We serve as an in-house advertising agency on all advertising projects, with assistance from a graphic design firm. We have developed new patient information materials and brochures used to recruit employees, physicians, and nurses. One brochure, which we informally refer to as our "marketing brochure," is the centerpiece of our recruitment materials and also accompanies fund-raising proposals and is given to individuals and organizations requesting information about the hospital.

We have developed attractive new publications for employees, which we also target to our physicians and volunteers; for nurses; and for auxiliary groups.

An important function of our department has been to upgrade the graphic "look" of the hospital through drafting a publications policy that requires that all printed materials be produced through Public Affairs. We use one design firm to achieve a consistent, high quality look, and we plan to begin a corporate identity program this year which formalizes the graphic look which has evolved over the last two years, fast on the heels of a corporate restructuring which created a parent company and seven subsidiaries.

Community relations responsibilities include staffing a school which we "adopted" under the Chicago school system's "Adopt-a-School" program; staffing community meetings and smoothing relations when the hospital embarks on changes in physical plant which affect the community—building a helipad on the hospital roof is the current example.

Governmental relations activities include influencing legislators, locally, statewide and nationally, on legislation which affects hospitals specifically and the health and welfare of children in general.

I'm sure that Children's is not unique in the broadening of its public relations function and the importance placed on it by its board and administration. A survey of CEOs of Illinois hospitals taken by the Illinois Hospital Association two years ago showed that their number one concern was the image Illinois consumers have of hospitals and the importance of improving that image through public relations efforts. The last several years have seen enormous changes in non-profit public relations, and I can't think of a more exciting and challenging career choice that carries the opportunity for making a major impact on one's organization.

SOURCE: Courtesy Judith M. Rice, Director of Public Affairs, Children's Memorial Medical Center, Chicago, IL. June 1985.

Public relations (PR) is a well-established function in health care and social service organizations that fulfills a number of needed functions for the organization. In the course of performing its basic tasks, an organization will seek the attention of certain publics and unavoidably attract the attention of other publics. The local community, news media, medical professional associations, business roundtables, regulators and government policymakers, social action groups—all may take an active or reactive interest in the organization's activities. The organization's managers may handle these publics in the course of carrying on their other duties. But sooner or later the organization recognizes the advantages of consolidating or coordinating these activities in the hands of a public relations manager. In employing a public relations manager, the organization can gain several advantages: (1) better anticipation of potential problems; (2) better handling of these problems; (3) consistent public-oriented policies and strategies; and (4) more professionally formulated communications.

The public relations function will be of high or low influence in the organization depending on the board and chief officer's attitude. In some health care organizations where the potential of the public relations function is recognized, the public relations manager is a vice-president and sits in on all meetings involving sensitive information and actions. He or she not only puts out fires, but also counsels management on actions that will avoid starting future fires. In many more organizations, especially those where the function is undervalued and receives poor resource support, public relations is a middle-management function charged with getting out publications and handling news and special events. The public relations people are not involved in policy or strategy formulation, only tactics.

The emergence of marketing as a "hot topic" in health care circles has raised a major question in the minds of top-level management and public relations managers as to the relation between marketing and public relations in health care organizations. Clearly, the two functions

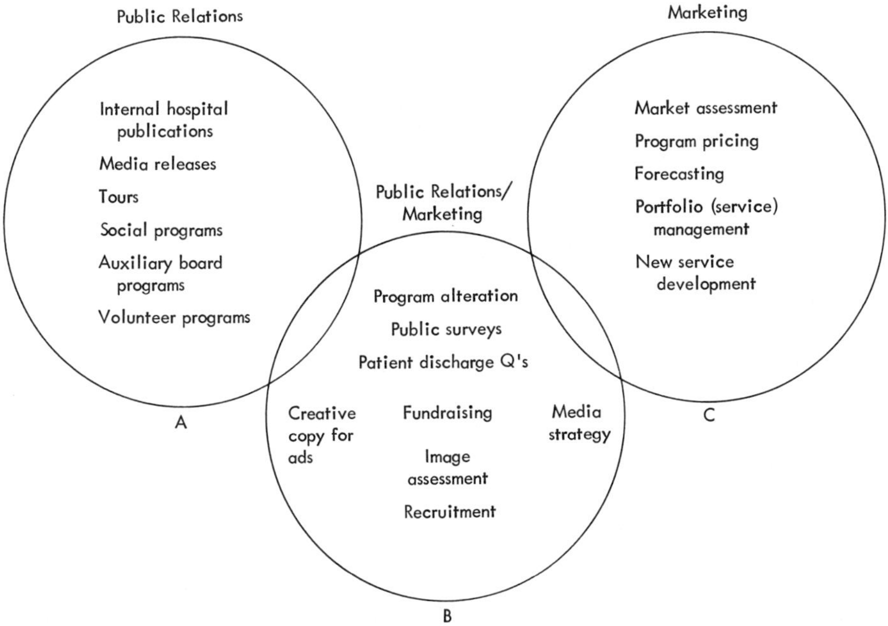

FIGURE 17–1 Spheres of Responsibility for Marketing vs. Public Relations *Source:* Eric N. Berkowitz, Steven Hillestad, and Pamela Effertz, "Marketing/Public Relations—A New Arena for Hospital Conflict," *Health Care Planning and Marketing* (January 1982), p. 7. Reprinted with permission of Aspen Systems Corporation. Copyright 1982.

work well together in business firms, with marketing focusing on the development and implementation of plans to market the company's products and services to customers, while public relations takes care of relations with other publics. In health care and social service organizations, the relationship is less clear. Both functions are involved in promotional activity, and both may undertake market research. Both are concerned with achieving results with various publics.

There is enough overlap between the two functions for some people to assume they are redundant. But Berkowitz, Hillestad, and Effertz make the argument that marketing and public relations are distinct, encompassing different objectives and tasks.[1] Specifically, they identify distinct as well as overlapping spheres of responsibility (see Figure 17–1). Others, defining the spheres of responsibility differently, have alternatively suggested that public relations handles all promotional activity, handles only nonpaid media promotion plus direct mail, or manages all image-creating activities, including those affecting governmental and regulatory bodies.

This chapter advances the thesis that public relations is most effective when viewed and conducted as part of the marketing mix being used by the health care organization to pursue its marketing objectives. We will look at the following questions:

1. How did the public relations function evolve?
2. What is the relationship between public relations and marketing in health care organizations?
3. What are the main tools of the public relations practitioner?

THE EVOLUTION OF PUBLIC RELATIONS

Public relations, like marketing, is a relatively new corporate function, although its roots go back in history.[2] Edward L. Bernays, one of the fathers of modern public relations, posited that the three main elements of public relations are as old as society: informing people, persuading people, and integrating people with people.[3] Bernays traced public relations from primitive society—in which leaders controlled by force, intimidation, and persuasion—to Babylonia, where kings commissioned historians to paint favorable images of them. In Europe the Reniassance and the Reformation freed men's minds from established dogmas, thus leading institutions to develop more subtle means to influence people. In America, historical milestones for public relations include:

Samuel Adams's use of the press to unite the colonists against the British.

The abolitionist movement's use of public relations as a political tool to rally support for blacks in the North, including the publication of *Uncle Tom's Cabin.*

P. T. Barnum's use of public relations to generate interest in an event—the arrival of his circus—by placing articles in newspapers.

Corporate public relations first emerged in the late nineteenth century and passed through the five stages shown in Figure 17–2. In the first stage, corporations established a *contact* function to influence legislators and newspapers to support positions favorable to business. The legislative contact function became known as *lobbying,* and the newspaper contact function became known as *press agentry.* George Westinghouse is credited with the formal establishment of public relations when in 1889 he hired two men to fight the advocates of direct current electricity and to promote instead alternating current.[4]

The next stage occurred when companies began to recognize the positive value of planned *publicity* to create customer interest in the company and its products. Publicity entailed finding or creating events, preparing company- or product-slanted news stories, and trying to interest the press in using them. Companies recognized that special skills are needed to develop publicity and began to add publicists to their ranks.

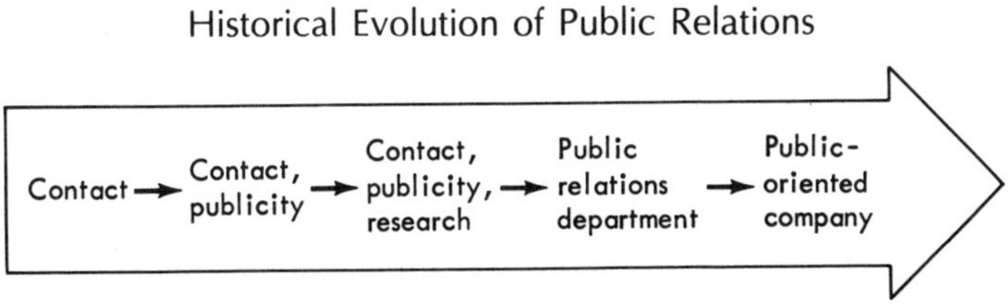

FIGURE 17–2 Historical Evolution of Corporate Public Relations

Somewhat later, public relations practitioners began to recognize the value of conducting *research* into public opinion prior to developing and launching public relations campaigns. The emerging sciences of public opinion measurement and mass communication theory permitted more sophistication in the conduct of public relations. Forward-looking firms added specialists who could research public opinion.

These functions—contact, publicity, and research—were uncoordinated in the typical firm. The lobbyists had little to do with the publicists; the publicists had little to do with the researchers. This led finally to the concept of a *public relations department,* which integrated all the work going on to cultivate the goodwill of different publics of the company. In larger organizations, public relations departments grew to encompass subspecialties to deal with each public—stockholders, neighbors, employees, customers, government agencies—and each tool—publications, press relations, research, and so on.

The establishment of a public relations department did not ensure that the organization as a whole acted like a *public company.* The vice-president of public relations had limited influence over other departments and needed the backing of top management to press for public-oriented actions by all departments. Organizations were facing growing challenges in the form of consumerism, environmentalism, energy conservation, inflation, shortages, employment discrimination, and safety. Public relations people wanted a more active role in counseling the organization and its departments on how to act as public citizens. PR practitioners emphasize that their job is not just to produce "good words," but to produce "good deeds followed by good words." Unless they can get the organization to act like a good citizen, good words alone will not be enough.

The development of the public relations function in most health care and social service organizations appears to have evolved quite differently. Historically, the organizations producing health care or social services were not-for-profit; they were by definition viewed as performing good deeds. For them, the first stage of public relations activity consisted of seeking publicity in order to gain recognition for their good works and deeds. The formation of public relations departments followed, in order to coordinate publicity-seeking activity as well as press agentry. Only more recently have some public relations departments undertaken public opinion research. Many health care and social service organizations do little lobbying. In organizations undertaking aggressive lobbying activity, it is often the planning department or top management, and sometimes the public affairs department, which is involved in the lobbying effort. And many health care organizations have historically tried to act as public citizens. However, the extent to which health care organizations can be classified as public companies is debatable, particularly in light of the growing orientation toward financial survival rather than good deeds.

Certain health-related organizations have followed the evolution of corporate public relations more closely than the traditional not-for-profit organization. Starr points out how the forerunners of the American Medical Association first engaged in public relations by lobbying to outlaw other forms of medical practice, such as homeopathy and Thomsonian medicine.[5] The AMA has since evolved through all the stages of the public relations function.

PUBLIC RELATIONS AND MARKETING

Public relations is often confused with one of its subfunctions, such as press agentry, company publications, lobbying, complaint handling, and so forth. Yet it is a more inclusive concept. The most frequently quoted definition is the following:

> Public relations is the management function which evaluates public attitudes, identifies the policies and procedures of an individual or an organization with the public interest, and executes a program of action to earn public understanding and acceptance.[6]

Sometimes a shorter definition is given which says that PR stands for *performance* (P) plus *recognition* (R).

Most of today's public relations people have come out of English departments and journalism schools. Management thinks of PR as essentially a communication tool. Journalism training adds the advantage that the PR person will know how the press thinks and probably know a lot of press people, thus ensuring greater access to the media.

When marketing has been proposed as a useful function to install in health care organizations, public relations people have reacted in different ways. Some PR people feel that they are doing the organization's marketing work and that there is no need to hire a marketing person. Others feel that they could quickly learn whatever is involved in marketing and that there is no need to add a marketer. Still others see marketing and PR as separate but equal functions and do not feel threatened. Finally, some PR people see marketing as the dominant function to which they will one day have to report.

The Marketing Task Force of the American Society for Hospital Public Relations recommended that the marketing and public relations functions should be structured to enhance each other without having one function necessarily report to the other. The task force recognized that an overlap between the two functions exists in the area of communications. Even within communications, however, public relations was viewed as more image-oriented, while marketing was perceived as service-, management-, or demand-oriented. And the task force recommended that PR people become better educated about marketing even if they intend to remain focused on public relations.[7] Other task forces and organizations have come to different conclusions. For our purposes, we will view public relations as primarily a communication tool to advance the marketing objectives of the health care organization. We see the following three important differences between public relations and marketing:

1. Public relations is primarily a communication tool, whereas marketing also includes need assessment, product development, pricing, and distribution.
2. Public relations seeks to influence attitudes, whereas marketing tries to elicit specific behaviors, such as purchase, joining, utilization, and so on.
3. Public relations does not define the goals of the health care organization, whereas marketing is intimately involved in defining the organization's mission, customers, and services.

THE PUBLIC RELATIONS PROCESS

PR practitioners view themselves as the caretakers and enhancers of the organization's image. At various times they are assigned the task of forming, maintaining, or changing attitudes. In this connection, they carry out the five-step process shown in Figure 17–3.

Identifying the Relevant Publics

Health care organizations would like to have the goodwill of every public that they affect or are affected by. This is usually not possible, especially without an active program to communicate with and relate to each public. Given limited public relations resources, health care organizations have to concentrate on certain publics more than others. Most organizations will distinguish between primary and secondary publics.

An organization's *primary* publics are those that it relates to on an active and continuous basis. Losing the support of a primary public

The Public Relations Process

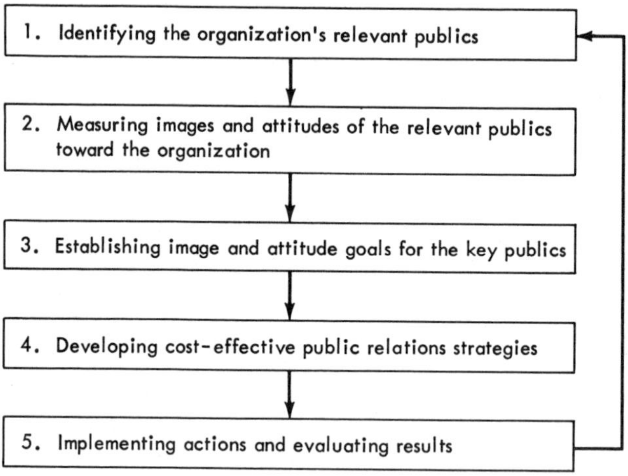

FIGURE 17–3 The Public Relations Process

could deal a death blow to the organization. The primary publics of health care provider organizations are its patients, employees, referral intermediaries, health insurers and employer group puchasers, directors, and the community. The patients receive the services of the organization. The employees provide the services. The referral intermediaries provide patients to the organization and are sometimes involved in providing the services. The insurers and purchasers buy significant quantities of the organization's services. The directors govern the organization. And the community provides the setting and location where the organization carries on its activities. If the goodwill of any of these groups disappears—patients stop coming, employees start quitting, intermediaries stop referring, insurers and purchasers stop buying, directors lose their interest, or the community becomes hostile—the organization is in deep trouble.

An organization also deals with secondary publics that it must monitor and relate to on a fairly continuous basis. These include suppliers, government groups, competitors, and general and special purpose groups. Suppliers provide the organization with equipment, office materials, fuel, and other inputs needed to carry on daily operations. Government groups include regulatory agencies, funding agencies, legislators, jurists, and others who set policy, provide services or funds, define and enforce the law, and collect taxes. Competitors are direct and indirect groups representing alternative sources for the same goods, services, or satisfactions provided by the organization. General purpose groups are those that seek to advance the interests of their members, such as labor unions, professional associations, and clubs. Special purpose groups are those that exist to carry out some purpose outside of themselves, such as charitable organizations and social action groups. The organization may contribute resources to a number of these groups because their cause is worthwhile in itself (charitable groups) or will benefit the organization directly (trade association). Other special purpose groups may take on a confrontation role toward the organization (a hostile labor union or social action group), and the organization must choose between appeasement and counterattack.

The publics are related not only to the organization, but also to each other. A particular public may have a great deal of influence on the attitudes and behavior of other publics toward the organization. Consider a health maintenance organization (HMO) whose members are highly satisifed. Their enthusiasm will be transmitted to co-workers and friends who might be potential members. Their enthusiasm will have a reinforcing effect on the HMO medical provider staff, who will feel that their care is competent and appreciated. They may pass on their enthusiasm to the employer benefits officers who arranged to offer the HMO option. Their enthusiasm will affect the future level of support they will give to the HMO in terms of reenrollment. The satisfaction felt by HMO members will influence the attitudes and behavior of other HMO publics.

Likewise, the dissatisfaction of a particular public will affect the attitudes of other publics. Suppose current HMO members are highly dissatisfied with the HMO over some policy. If the members choose to act, they have several recourses, as suggested in Figure 17–4. First, they may go directly to the HMO (administration, trustees, or board) and try to negotiate a better policy. Second, they may attempt to win the support of their employers' benefits officers to bring pressure on the HMO. Third, they may attempt to get the government to intervene. Fourth, they may solicit the support of various social action publics. Fifth, they might give up, leave the HMO, and join a competitive health insurance plan. Thus, publics that are passive in one period might suddenly be spurred into action in another period because of sympathy with the grievance of a particular public.

From the organization's point of view, it is important to set up relations with its valued publics that produce satisfaction. A health care organization's task is to consider what benefits to offer each of its valued publics in exchange for their valued resources and support. Once an organization begins to think about cultivating the support of a public, it is beginning to think of that public as a market, a group to whom it will attempt to offer benefits in exchange for valued resources.

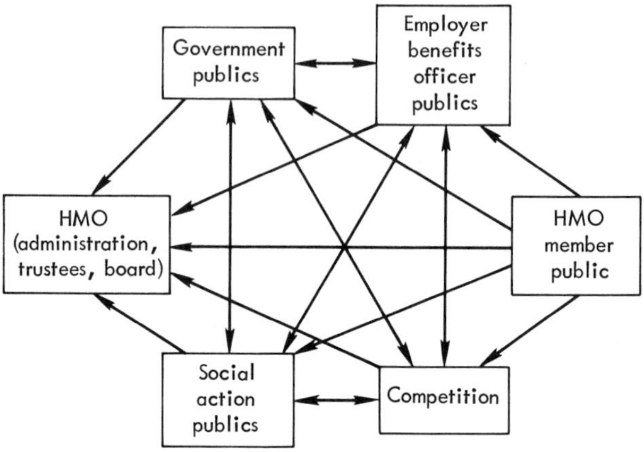

FIGURE 17–4 Dynamic Relations Between an HMO and its Publics

Measuring Images and Attitudes of the Relevant Publics

Once a health care organization has identified its various publics, it needs to find out how each public thinks and feels about the organization. Management will have some idea of each public's attitude simply through its regular contacts with members of that public. But impressions based on casual contact cannot necessarily be trusted. In the middle 1970s, a hospital wanted to build a new facility and tear down the old one. While the venture received government approval and adequate financing, it was stopped dead in its tracks by local neighborhood groups that organized to prevent the new structure from being built. They attacked the hospital, calling it arrogant and insensitive. They complained that the hospital never even contacted residents who lived in neighboring areas. Had it done so, the hospital would have learned that the neighborhood was concerned about issues of disruptive traffic patterns, the esthetics of a new concrete structure in an older neighborhood with historic houses nearby, and speeding ambulances on streets where young children played. A large number of the residents harbored deep-seated negative attitudes toward the hospital that needed only an issue in order to surface. In the end, while it was allowed to build the new facility, the hospital was forced to make many compromises with the neighborhood, many of which worked to the hospital's disadvantage.

To really know the attitudes of a public, a health care organization needs to undertake some formal marketing research. A good start is to organize a focus group consisting of six to ten members of that public and lead a discussion to probe their knowledge and feelings about the organization. While the observations of the focus group are not necessarily representative, they normally contribute interesting perspectives and raise interesting questions which the organization will want to explore more systematically. Eventually, the organization may find it worthwhile to conduct formal field research in the form of a public opinion survey. The public opinion survey measures such variables as awareness, knowledge, interest, and attitude toward the organization.

Establishing Image and Attitude Goals for the Key Publics

Through periodically researching its key publics, the health care organization will have some hard data on how these publics view the organization (see Chapter 2). The findings can be assembled in the form of a scorecard such as the one illustrated for a nursing home in Table 17–1. The scorecard becomes the basis for developing a public relations plan for the coming period. The nursing home's scorecard shows that hospital discharge planners have a medium amount of knowledge about the nursing home and a negative attitude. Since discharge planners are important in influencing the nursing home choice decision, the organization needs to develop a communication program that will improve discharge planners' knowledge of and attitudes toward the nursing home. The goals should be made even more specific and measurable, such as "80 percent of the discharge planners should know at least four key things about the nursing home and at least 60 percent should report having a positive opinion about the nursing home, within two years." Making the goals concrete means that the necessary activities can be planned on the right scale, the necessary budget can be estimated to finance these activities, and the results can be measured later to evaluate the success of the plan.

Looking at the next item on the scorecard, we see that communication also has to be directed at local physicians to increase their knowledge and improve their attitude toward the nursing home. As for patients and their families, their knowledge and attitude are ideal; the nursing home's job is simply to maintain their enthusiasm. As for the general public, the nursing home may decide to do nothing. The general public's knowledge and attitude are not that important in attracting

TABLE 17–1 Scorecard on a Nursing Home's Publics

PUBLIC	*KNOWLEDGE*	*ATTITUDE*	*PUBLIC'S IMPORTANCE*
Hospital discharge planners	Medium	Negative	High
Local physicians	Low	Neutral	High
Patients and their families	High	Positive	High
General public	Low	Neutral	Low

patients, and the cost of improving the situation would be too high in relation to the value gained.

Developing Cost-Effective Strategies

A health care organization usually has many options in trying to improve the attitudes of a particular public. Its first task is to understand why the attitudes have come about so that the causal factors can be addressed by an appropriate strategy. Let us return to the hospital that found that it had weak community support when it wanted to build a new facility. In digging deeper into the negative citizen attitudes, the hospital discovered that many local citizens harbored a history of resentment against the hospital, including (1) the hospital never consults citizens or citizen groups before taking action; (2) the hospital made no special effort to hire local neighborhood residents for jobs they were qualified to perform; (3) the hospital does not inform the local community about hospital-sponsored events and programs; and (4) the hospital owns local property that is tax-free and raises the taxes of the citizens. Essentially, the community feels neglected and exploited by the hospital.

The diagnosis suggests that the hospital needs to change its ways and establish stronger contacts with the community. It needs to develop a *community relations program.* Here are some of the steps it might take:

1. Identify the local opinion leaders—prominent business people, news editors, city council people, heads of civic organizations, school officials—and build better relationships through inviting them to hospital events, consulting with them on hospital/community issues, and placing a few of them on the hospital's board of trustees.
2. Encourage the hospital's management and staff to join local organizations and participate more strongly in community campaigns such as the United Way and American Red Cross Blood Bank program.
3. Develop a speaker's bureau which offers the public service of speaking to local groups such as the Kiwanis, Rotary, and so on.
4. Make the hospital's facilities and screening programs more available to the community. Auditoriums and meeting rooms can be offered to local organizations for meetings.
5. Arrange open houses and tours of the hospital for the local community.
6. Participate in community special events such as parades, holiday observances, and so on.
7. Establish a community advisory board of leaders to act as a sounding board for issues facing the hospital.

Each project involves money and time. The organization will need to estimate the amount of expected attitude improvement with each project in order to arrive at the best mix of cost-effective actions. This issue of the cost effectiveness of a public relations strategy was often noted in discussions of Humana's well-publicized support of artificial heart transplants (see Exhibit 17–1). The public relations strategies health care organizations pursue for the purpose of increasing awareness and improving attitudes are likely to go well beyond local health fairs and special events, if Humana's actions are any indication. They are also likely to be far more complex and more costly, in many cases, than traditional public relations efforts. This suggests that health care organizations will need to be far more cognizant than in the past of the costs and payoffs of public relations efforts.

Implementing Actions and Evaluating Results

Specific public relations actions have to be assigned to individuals within the organization, along with concrete objectives, time frames, and budgets. The public relations department should oversee the effort and monitor the results. Evaluating the results of public relations activities, however, is not easy, since they occur in conjunction with other marketing activities and their contribution is hard to separate.

Consider the problem of measuring the value of the organization's publicity efforts. Publicity is designed with certain audience-response objectives in mind, and these objectives form the basis of what is measured. The major response measures are exposures, awareness, comprehension, attitude change, and sales. The easiest and most common measure of publicity effectiveness is the number of exposures created in the media. Most publicists supply the client with a "clipping book" showing all the media that carried news about the organization and a summary statement such as the following:

> Media coverage included 3,500 column inches of news and photographs in 35 publications with a combined circulation of 49.4 million; 2,500 minutes of air time on 290 radio stations and an estimated audience of 65 million; and 660 minutes of air time on 160 television stations with an estimated audience of 91 million. If this time and space had been purchased at advertising rates, it would have amounted to $1,047,000.[8]

The purpose of citing the equivalent advertising cost is to make a case for publicity's cost effectiveness, since the total effort must have cost less than $1,047,000. Furthermore, publicity usually creates more reading and believing than ads. Still, this measure is not very satisfying. There is no indication of how many people actually read, saw, or heard the message, and what they thought afterward. Furthermore, there is no information on the net audience reached, since publications and other media reach overlapping audiences.

A better measure calls for finding out what change in public

EXHIBIT 17–1 The Cost Effectiveness of a Public Relations Strategy

The way to become famous now is not through the social columns, but through the medical annals, and not as a performer but as a patient.

Just look at the record, the hospital record. Barney Clark was a superstar for 112 days. Baby Fae for 20 days. Now it's Bill Schroeder's turn. He couldn't be a better health-care star if he came from central casting.

We know about his taste for beer and his choice of basketball teams. We know about his phone call from the President and his Social Security hassles. We've watched him ask people to feel his artificial heart, and read about the effects of his stroke. We have seen him up and seen him down, and rooted for him. Like the others in this peculiar medical lineup, he has become famous for what's been done to him.

My colleague at the Globe, Otile McManus, calls this the era of celebrity medicine, and I think she is right. We take our hi-tech medicine personalized now. We prefer our innovations with a shot of hype. The latest in medical technology comes attached to a name and a story. It makes it much more interesting.

I confess to being uncomfortable with all this. It not only makes celebrities out of patients but turns medical researchers into publicity hounds. *Would Humana Hospital have volunteered to pick up the bill for a hundred hearts if it did not believe that its patronage would pay off?*

The company spokesman was not ashamed to admit his hope that the artificial-heart program will make Humana a "household word in health care."

SOURCE: Ellen Goodman, "Celebrity Medicine," *The Boston Globe,* December 20, 1984, p. 23. © 1984, The Boston Globe Newspaper Company/Washington Post Writers Group, reprinted with permission.

The sight of William Schroeder joking with his family last week was the best possible advertisement not just for the miracles of science, but for Humana, the investor-owned medical conglomerate. . . . Humana's heart program is an example of how a corporation can use its resources to develop a new field of medicine. Its Heart Institute had been open less than a year when the company decided in June to work on the mechanical heart. Institute Director Allan Lansing, an open heart surgeon, had told Jones (founder of Humana) that Dr. William DeVries, who performed the first permanent artificial-heart implant on Barney Clark at the University of Utah in 1982, might be willing to come to Louisville to pursue his research. With Jones' support, Lansing courted DeVries as ardently as any coach ever wooed an All-Stars pitcher or a Super Bowl quarterback.

Says (Princeton economist Uwe Reinhardt): "Hiring big names is good business and good academics. It's one way to achieve a certain luster.

DeVries and the artificial heart give Humana legitimacy in the medical world and put its name before prospective patients."

SOURCE: "Earning Profits, Saving Lives," *Time,* December 10, 1984, pp. 84–85. Reprinted with permission.

The market value of Humana, Inc., Louisville, will not be significantly affected by the recent media blitz the company received following the second artificial heart implant. . . . In the short run, Humana Hospital-Audubon may see an increase in the number of cardiovascular patients who want to receive care at the facility. In addition, Humana's activities may help to eradicate the stigma that investor-owned hospital management companies are not committed to research.

SOURCE: "Media Blitz Won't Boost Humana Market Value: Analyst," *Hospitals,* Vol. 59, No. 1, January 1, 1985, p. 23. Copyright 1985, American Hospital Association.

In offering to pay the hospital expenses of additional clinical trials of the artificial heart, Humana was making what its own officials described as "a shrewd investment," anticipating that the long-term commercial value of the publicity would be worth many times the cost of the subsidized hospital care.

SOURCE: Arnold S. Relman, "Letters to the Editor: Privatizing Artificial-Heart Research," *The Wall Street Journal,* December 26, 1984, p. 11. Reprinted by permission of *The Wall Street Journal,* © Dow Jones & Company, Inc., 1984. All rights reserved.

awareness/comprehension/attitude occurred as a result of the campaign (after allowing for the impact of other promotional tools). This requires the use of survey methodology to measure the before and after levels of these variables. The best measure is utilization, sales volume, or the equivalent.

Certain PR activities may be found to be too costly in relation to their impact and might be dropped. Or the PR goals might be recognized as too ambitious and require modification. Furthermore, new problems will arise with certain publics and require redirection of the public relations resources. As the public relations department implements these actions and measures the results, it will be in a position to return to the earlier steps and take a new reading of where the organization stands in the mind of specific publics and what improvements in attitudes or awareness it needs to pursue.

Unfortunately, even though public relations has historically been one of the most sophisticated marketing functions in health care organizations—in that it has been a recognized function, often with someone hired to perform it—the overall sophistication of public relations in health care organizations is quite variable. While some PR people measure their organization's image, and the awareness and attitudes of the relevant publics, many do not. Even fewer health care PR people establish goals and measure the cost effectiveness of their strategies. And the vast majority of PR strategies are either not evaluated at all or are evaluated with crude measures.

For example, many organizations have held health fairs, sometimes at substantial cost, because it is a "neat idea" or because a competing organization held one the previous year. While a health fair, or other public relations activity, is unlikely to hurt the sponsoring health care organization, the relevant question is not "Is this doing any good?" but rather "Is the effort worth the cost? Exactly what is it doing for us? How do we measure this and whom do we measure? Would some other form of public relations activity be more cost effective, more efficient, or have a greater impact?" Until public relations people can answer these questions about every activity they undertake, they are not fulfilling the terms of good PR management.

PUBLIC RELATIONS TOOLS

Here we want to examine the major public relations media and tools in more detail. They are: (1) written material, (2) audiovisual material, (3) corporate identity media, (4) news, (5) events, (6) speeches, and (7) telephone information service.

Written Material

Health care organizations rely extensively on written material to communicate with their target publics. For example, a hospital will use such written material as an annual report, brochures, employee newsletters, physicians newsletters, quarterly community publications, flyers, and so on. Because printed material is often less costly to use than other media forms, and because it is less likely to fly in the face of clinicians' resistance to promotion, much public relations activity in health care consists of printed material. Printed material by itself is not a medium. Once it is printed, a way must be found to distribute the printed material to the target audience. Unfortunately, anecdotes abound in the health care field about brochures which lie around on tables in the organization's facility because no distribution strategy was developed for them.

Also, in preparing each publication, the public relations department must consider *function, esthetics,* and *cost.* For example, the function of a community health center's annual report is to inform interested publics about the organization's accomplishments and community service during the year, as well as about its financial status, with the ultimate purpose of generating confidence in the organization and its leadership. Esthetics matter, in that the annual report should be readable, interesting, and professional. If the annual report is published in mimeograph form, it suggests a poor and amateur organization. If the annual report is high gloss and extremely fancy, the public may ask why a nonprofit health care organization is spending so much of its money on graphics instead of on needed services. Cost acts as a constraint, in that the organization will allocate a limited amount of money to each publication. The public relations department has to reconcile considerations of function, esthetics, and cost in developing each publication.

Audiovisual Material

Audiovisual material, such as films, slides-and-sound, and video and audio cassettes, are coming into increasing use as communication tools. The cost of audiovisual materials is usually greater than the cost of printed materials, but so is its impact. Some health care organizations are videotaping their annual reports or organization-sponsored health promotion series, and having them shown over local cable television channels as well as on in-hospital cable systems. As video technology becomes less expensive and more widespread in both business and residential environments, the use of video material can be expected to grow. Other organizations are using 16 mm full-color films or a combination of slides and recorded voiceover, at a lower cost, for purposes such as to recruit nurses, explain a pending change to relevant publics, or introduce a new alcoholism and mental health program to bartenders.

In all cases, visual materials should be put together with care. Audiences can be impressed negatively as well as positively by audiovisual materials. Too many slides accompanied by a rambling discourse or an out-of-focus film with a mumbling background speaker can be a disservice to the sponsoring organization.

Organizational Identity Media

Normally, each of the health care organization's separate materials takes on its own look, which not only creates confusion, but also misses an opportunity to create and reinforce an *organizational identity*. In an overcommunicated society, organizations have to compete for attention. They should at least try to create a visual identity the public immediately recognizes. The visual identity is carried by the organization's permanent media—logos, stationery, brochures, signs, business forms, business cards, buildings, uniforms, and rolling stock.

The organizational identity media become a marketing tool when they are attractive, memorable, and distinctive. The task of creating a coordinated visual identity is not easy and can be done only if all these media are coordinated by one office, presumably the public relations office. If each department designs its own public relations material, the chance for organizational identity is lost. The organization should select a good graphic design consultant who will get management to identify the essence of the organization, and then will try to turn it into a concept backed by strong visual symbols. The symbols are adapted to the various organizational media so that they create immediate brand recognition in the minds of various publics.

News

One of the major tasks of the public relations department is to find or create favorable news about the organization and promote it to the appropriate media. The ability to recognize what makes a news story is a great skill and requires creativity. Breakthrough medical research efforts and breathtaking surgical procedures are not the only stories meriting media attention (see Exhibit 17–2).

The appeal of publicity to many organizations is that it is viewed as "free advertising"—that is, it represents exposure at no cost. As someone said: "Publicity is sent to a medium and prayed for, while advertising is sent to a medium and paid for." However, publicity is far from free. Good publicists cost money; special skills are required to create good publicity, and to cultivate good long-term relationships with the press.

Publicity has three qualities that make it a worthwhile investment. First, it may have higher veracity than advertising because it appears as normal news and not as sponsored information. Second, it tends to catch people off guard who might otherwise actively avoid sponsored messages. Third, it has high potential for dramatization in that it arouses attention in the guise of a noteworthy event.

Consider a hospice suffering from low visibility that adopts the objective of achieving more public recognition through news management. The public relations director will review the hospice's various components to see whether any natural stories exist. Are any of the hospice patients noteworthy or well-known in the community? Are the services offered by the staff members in some way unusual? Is there a

EXHIBIT 17–2 News About Chicken Soup

Sure, Chicken Soup Is Good for You, But It's Even Better for Mount Sinai

While chicken soup has been proven to be effective for the common cold, it has also helped Mount Sinai Medical Center, Miami Beach, FL.

In December, the medical center began selling 10-ounce cans of kosher chicken soup produced by Manischewitz Food Products Corp., Jersey City, NJ, bearing the Mount Sinai label. Since then, Mount Sinai has received more publicity nationwide on the soup than any other function or item it has offered, says Judy Stanton, public relations director for Mount Sinai. Despite the fact that Mount Sinai has not advertised its "liquid gold," there have been over 200 newspaper articles nationwide written about the soup. "We're getting a lot of name visibility," Stanton remarks.

Mount Sinai had no intention of becoming a soup manufacturer, according to Stanton. However, she notes, the medical center has been approached by retailers and other soup manufacturers. The response to the soup was so successful that Mount Sinai is working on a licensing agreement that would allow Manischewitz to use the Mount Sinai label and market soup outside of the facility. In addition, Mount Sinai is contacting other Mount Sinai facilities across the country to work out agreements for selling the soup. "With such an arrangement, we could tell out-of-town callers that the soup is available at their local Mount Sinai," Stanton says.

The idea behind the soup began in October 1978, when the pulmonary disease journal *Chest* published research conducted by Marvin Sackner, M.D., director of medical services at Mount Sinai. The study showed that chicken soup, more than hot or cold water, clears the respiratory system of congestion.

SOURCE: Suzanne Powills, "Sure, Chicken Soup Is Good for You, But It's Even Better for Mount Sinai," *Hospitals,* May 1, 1985, p. 50. Reprinted by permission from HOSPITALS, Vol. 59, No. 9, May 1, 1985. Copyright 1985, American Hospital Publishing, Inc.

story in the doctor's perspective on the hospice versus the patient's perspective? Usually a search along these lines will uncover stories that can be fed to the press with the effect of creating much more public recognition of the hospice. Ideally, the stories should symbolize the kind of image the hospice wants to have; they should support its desired market position.

Getting media organizations to accept press releases and press conferences calls for marketing and interpersonal skill. A good media relations director understands the press's needs for stories that are interesting and timely, and for press releases that are well written and eye-catching. The PR director should make a point of knowing as many news editors and reporters as possible and helping them interview the organization's leaders when news breaks. The more the press is welcomed by the organization, the more likely it is to give it more coverage and good coverage. This means welcoming the press, even when it is pursuing information about the organization that could be viewed negatively (see Exhibit 17–3). It also means "fighting back" when the media are wrong: "Believe it or not, candor works in press relations. So does the growing tendency for companies to fight back when they think the press got it wrong."[9]

EXHIBIT 17–3 Public Relations Under Adverse Circumstances

Mr. James King, former assistant vice president of corporate communications for a major Harvard teaching hospital in Boston, had been anticipating devoting enormous resources to his hospital's pending name change. The hospital, whose new facility was nearing completion in 1981, was in fact a merger of three hospitals: the Peter Bent Brigham Hospital, the Robert Breck Brigham Hospital, and Boston Hospital for Women. And the Boston Hospital for Women was better known by previous names it had held, such as the Boston Lying-In and the Free Hospital for Women, than it was by its current name. To further add to the name confusion, the three hospitals had organizationally merged and assumed the name, Affiliated Hospitals Center, years before the new building physically unifying the three were built. Now, Mr. King had to develop a strategy which would effectively wipe out the use of all the previous hospital names, substituting the new name, Brigham and Women's Hospital.

In the early fall of 1980, three physicians practicing at the Brigham and Women's Hospital were accused of raping a Brigham and Women's Hospital nurse. The hospital was on the front page of major New England newspapers for months, as well as on the television and radio, as the media followed the story through the indictment, trial, conviction and sentencing of the three physicians. Realizing that the media were going to cover this story, whether the hospital cooperated or not, Mr. King chose to be as open and helpful to the media as possible. All he requested in return was that, in addition to fair and truthful reporting, they get the name of the hospital (as Brigham and Women's Hospital) correct. Otherwise, reporters would have been likely to use one of the hospital's previous names. Because of the heavy continuous coverage of this story in the media, and the constant reference to the Brigham and Women's Hospital name, Mr. King estimates that the hospital saved $100,000 in public relations efforts which would have been directed to effecting the name change.

EXHIBIT 17–4 Humana's Sophistication in Handling the Press—The Artificial Heart Implant

Humana handled Bill Schroeder's implant with far more candor and professionalism than did the doctors and officials who attended the ill-fated Baby Fae; at times they dissembled or avoided the press entirely. Humana also seems to have learned from the bitter experiences of the University of Utah officials in the case of Barney Clark, the first recipient of an artificial heart at De Vries's skilled hands. They were so stingy with information that some journalists took to impersonating doctors, stealing records, and even breaking into the Clark house. Nothing like that occurred in Louisville, thanks to Humana's solicitous ministrations to the press. These included a rehearsal of the operation so the official photographer could practice getting good pictures, opening a cafeteria-sized press center, twice-a-day briefings by the well-informed Dr. Allan Lansing, head of the Humana Heart Institute, and prompt updatings of Schroeder's condition.

SOURCE: Frederic Golden, "Surgery as Spectacle," © *Discover Magazine,* Time Inc., February 1985, p. 94.

Humana prepared for its first artificial implant with a promotion campaign as elaborate as one that General Motors might use for launching a new model. Before the Schroeder operation, Humana public relations specialists consulted with officials at the University of Utah on the press interest that might be expected. The company rented space for a press headquarters in the Commonwealth Convention Center in downtown Louisville and produced seven informational videotapes about the operation.

SOURCE: "Earning Profits, Saving Lives," *Time,* December 10, 1984, p. 85.

The sophistication necessary to "welcome the press" and handle press conferences grows as the news story takes on a more national perspective, and as the media come to expect better conference facilities and news management by its subject facilities (see Exhibit 17–4).

Events

Organizations can increase their newsworthiness by creating events that attract the attention of target publics. The Humana artificial heart transplants have been treated as national news events. On a lesser scale, health care organizations often hold health fairs, which may feature well-known local personalities; charities sponsor fundraising events; and all organizations may celebrate anniversaries of important events and hold press conferences. Each well-run event may not only impress the immediate participants, but also serve as an opportunity to develop a multitude of stories directed to relevant media vehicles and audiences.

Event creation management is a particularly important skill in running fundraising drives. Fundraisers have developed a large repertoire of special events, including anniversary celebrations, art exhibits, auctions, benefit evenings, bingo games, book sales, cake sales, contests, dances, dinners, fairs, fashion shows, parties in unusual places, phonothons, rummage sales, tours, and walkathons. For example, the American Cancer Society distributes a brochure to local units in which it outlines the following ideas for special events:

> Dramatic special events attract attention to the American Cancer Society. They bring color, excitement, and glamor to the program. Well planned, they will get excellent coverage in newspapers, on radio and TV, and in newsreels . . . A Lights-On-Drive, a one-afternoon or one-night House-to-House program have such dramatic appeal that they stir excitement and enthusiasm . . . Keep in mind the value of bursts of sound such as fire sirens sounding, loud-speaker trucks, fife and drum corps . . . A most useful special event is the ringing of church bells to add a solemn, dedicated note to the launching of a drive or education project. This should be organized on a division or community basis, and the church bell ringing may be the signal to begin a House-to-House canvass. Rehearsals of bell ringing, with community leaders tugging at ropes, offer good picture possibilities.[10]

Speeches

Speeches are another tool through which health care organizations can communicate with target publics. The public relations director will look for effective spokespersons for the organization and will try to arrange speaking engagements. If a physician or other clinician is articulate and attractive, the public relations director will try to line up appearances on talk shows, at meetings and conventions. Physicians, recognizing the increasingly competitive environment they face, sometimes arrange for speech appearances for themselves, often with the help of public relations firms (see Exhibit 17–5).

A spokesperson's impact will be further enhanced by engaging a good speech writer and coach and providing audiovisual aids. The public relations director can set up a speakers' bureau to deliver appropriate talks to community organizations. This form of promotion is generally well accepted by clinicians:

EXHIBIT 17–5

If the Doc's on TV, Maybe It's Because He Takes the PR Rx

Daniel Silver is one of many orthopedic surgeons who now use a technique of inserting miniature TV cameras in bone joints while operating on them. But unlike a lot of the others, he has been featured in several magazine articles on the technique and has described it on a number of television and radio talk shows.

The media attention isn't a coincidence. The 39-year-old Los Angeles specialist pays a public-relations firm $1,500 a month to publicize his practice.

Stuart Berger, a 30-year-old psychiatrist and nutritionist in Manhattan, has also made numerous TV and radio appearances, discussing everything from his work with teenagers who have drug problems to a test for food allergies. That isn't a coincidence, either. Dr. Berger pays a PR firm $2,500 a month to get him on the air.

Doctors didn't use to do that sort of thing. Many still criticize it, and most of those who do use PR firms don't want their colleagues to know they do. Yet despite the criticism, the benefits of publicity are luring a growing number of doctors, especially those with unusual or controversial cures. Dr. Silver (whose bone-joint technique isn't controversial though it is relatively new) says his patient load quadrupled as a result of the publicity. And Norman Stahl, a Bellmore, N.Y., ophthalmologist who hired a PR firm several years ago, confesses that the attention tickles doctors' egos. "There is a certain amount of ham in people who do this. It's a bit of a thespian thing."

PHYSICIANS AS CELEBRITIES

No one knows just how many doctors have press agents, but many press agents say their doctor business is booming. Some, like Kip Morrison & Associates, whose firm represents Dr. Silver, are beginning to specialize in representing physicians. For a price ($50,000 to $150,000 a year at one firm), they seek media coverage for their doctors, groom them for talk shows and send out slick press kits touting their specialties. In effect, the publicists turn ordinary physicians into celebrities.

Doctors can even legally advertise now, though few do. They find PR more credible—and less easily identifiable by critical colleagues.

Such critics remain legion. "I think PR is abhorrent," says John Burkhart, a Knoxville, Tenn., family physician and past chairman of the AMA's judicial council. "If you give good service, you don't have to get up on the rooftop and beat your breast and proclaim it."

Defenders of publicity-seeking argue that it often brings valuable information on advances in medicine to the public's attention. Dr. Stahl, the Bellmore, N.Y., ophthalmologist, says: "The practice of medicine has changed like everything else. We can't live in the 20th century and live by the codes of the 18th century."

But as much as the defenders disagree with the critics, they still take them seriously. A urologist who uses a PR firm says he keeps it a secret because his business depends on referrals from other physicians. Many of them would send patients elsewhere if they knew he used a PR firm. "Other physicians know I'm getting publicity, but they don't know how I'm getting it."

SOURCE: Jennifer Bingham Hall, "If the Doc's on TV, Maybe It's Because He Takes the PR Rx," *The Wall Street Journal,* August 23, 1983, p. 1. Reprinted by permission of *The Wall Street Journal,*

In central New Jersey, for example, a group of orthopedists, while declining to advertise, "market" their expertise in sports medicine by giving educational talks before groups of high-school coaches and athletic directors—and before athletes and their parents as well. These talks, which often feature slide presentations on first aid and managing athletic injuries, are bound to remind some viewers of the experts giving them, when they need orthopedic care.

Several years ago, such activities might have prompted censure from their colleagues and the local medical society and accusations of "soliciting," members of the group note. But in today's changed climate, the same activity is termed "marketing." It's not condemned when done under the aegis of a hospital, they say, and many hospitals with sports-medicine departments regularly hold "clinics" for the public, with similar goals in mind.

The real change, observes one member of the group, is in attitude. "Before, we would have waited for the schools and the coaches to call us," he says. "Now, we call them."[11]

Telephone Information Service

A newer public relations tool is a telephone number through which members of the public can get information about the organization and its services. Various health organizations have set up telephone numbers that provide health messages about specific symptoms and diseases. Child abuse and drug abuse hotlines have been set up to take emergency calls, provide on-the-spot counseling, and make referrals to local service agencies. Many hospitals have physician referral telephone services in order to promote their medical staffs to people needing a physician. These telephone services suggest that the organization cares about the public and is ready to serve them.

SUMMARY

Public relations is a well-established but changing function in health care organizations. The introduction of marketing into health care organizations has raised the question of marketing's relation to public relations.

There are conflicting views on the subject. Public relations and marketing are seen by various people as separate but equal functions; or equal and overlapping functions; or with public relations as the dominant function; or with public relations and marketing as the same function. We assume that public relations is a tool used to advance the marketing purposes of the organization.

The task of public relations is to form, maintain, or change public attitudes toward the organization and/or its services. The process of public relations consists of five steps: (1) identifying the organization's relevant publics; (2) measuring the images and attitudes held by these publics; (3) establishing image and attitude goals for the key publics; (4) developing cost-effective strategies; and (5) implementing actions and evaluating results.

Public relations practitioners have to be skilled communicators and adept at developing written material, audiovisual material, corporate identity media, news, events, speeches, and telephone information services.

NOTES

1. Eric N. Berkowitz, Steven Hillestad, and Pamela Effertz, "Marketing/Public Relations—A New Arena for Hospital Conflict," *Health Care Planning and Marketing* (January 1982), p. 1–10.

2. Some of the material in this chapter is adapted from Philip Kotler and William Mindak, "Marketing and Public Relations," *Journal of Marketing* (October 1973), pp. 13–20.

3. Edward L. Bernays, *Public Relations* (Norman: University of Oklahoma Press, 1952).

4. Scott M. Cutlip, "The Beginning of PR Counseling," *Editor and Publisher,* November 26, 1960, p. 16.

5. Paul Starr, *The Social Transformation of American Medicine* (New York: Basic Books, 1982).

6. *Public Relations News,* October 27, 1947.

7. Based on a report of the Marketing Task Force, Kenneth G. Trester, chairman, to the American Society for Hospital Public Relations, July 1982.

8. Arthur M. Merims, "Marketing's Stepchild: Product Publicity," *Harvard Business Review* (November–December 1972), pp. 111–12.

9. Walter Guzzardi, Jr. "How Much Should Companies Talk?" *Fortune,* March 4, 1985, pp. 64–68.

10. *Public Information Guide* (New York: American Cancer Society, 1965), p. 19.

11. "Doctor Advertising: Here to Stay," *Medical World News,* HEI Publishing, Inc. February 2, 1981, p. 68. Reprinted by permission.

PART V
Supporting the Marketing Effort

18

RECRUITMENT MARKETING: ATTRACTING PEOPLE

The Parental Stress Line is a 24-hour telephone counseling service designed to offer anonymous counseling and referral to people who abuse or might potentially abuse their children. It was started by the Parents' and Children's Services of the Children's Mission, a Boston-based social service agency that was able to raise sufficient funds to cover the first two years' expenses for the line. These expenses included the cost of the telephone lines, including a statewide line, the cost of rent, salary for a full-time supervisor, plus other related incidental expenses. The funds were not sufficient to pay salaries to professionals to staff the telephones.

But they were never intended to be. The Parental Stress Line was to be staffed by volunteers. Otherwise, the agency stated, the cost of paying for 24-hour telephone coverage would be too great. Also, the use of volunteers permitted the agency to avoid a legal predicament; Massachusetts state law mandated that employed professionals report all instances of suspected child abuse. If callers feared they would be reported, they might never call the Stress Line. Volunteers did not fall under the same statute and therefore could not be required to report.

A few months prior to the initiation of the Parental Stress Line (PSL) service, the agency had to determine policies and set strategies to attract volunteers. This raised a number of issues:

1. What sort of training would be required of the PSL volunteers? Since they would be dealing in such a sensitive area, the agency believed that at least 60 hours of intensive training was necessary. Some of the agency's social workers believed that even more training would be necessary.

2. How would they screen those who volunteered for PSL? The agency clearly wanted to weed out "weirdos" and those whose motivations or style seemed inappropriate. They also wanted people with good verbal skills. They questioned whether or not volunteers should have had children, so that they would be familiar with the stress parents experience. This could weed out college students, who represent a major source of volunteers in the Boston area. They also wondered if the elderly were too far removed from the experiences of parents with young children, and might scold the parent instead of being, as their advertising would say, "a sympathetic listener."
3. Should they seek volunteers who already had training as social workers, teachers, nurses, guidance counselors, and so forth? This would allow the agency to cut back on training or to direct it to a higher level of performance. There were many women living in the suburbs, who had chosen not to work while raising their children, with these qualifications. However, the agency also wanted to recruit minority volunteers and thought it would have a difficult time doing so if it maintained these standards.
4. How much supervision would the volunteers need? While it was easy to have a supervisor available during business hours, it was less clear how they could provide supervision at night.
5. What did the agency have to offer that would attract volunteers? It was not paying them, and was asking them to donate four hours of their time every week. The training and supervision were viewed as attractions to women who might later want to resume working in related jobs. The opportunity to do good, to help other people, and to be with other volunteers like themselves were considered as possible but less salient attractions.
6. What methods should they employ to promote the PSL volunteer opportunity? Television, radio, and newspaper advertising were possibilities, as was promotion through church groups, donor groups, or other organizations such as the Kiwis (retired airline stewardesses).
7. What steps should the agency take to assure retention of volunteers once they had been attracted and trained? The site which had been rented by PSL had been selected with its attractiveness to volunteers in mind. Were recognition awards also called for? Or a newsletter to volunteers? Or periodic parties to introduce all the PSL volunteers to each other?

SOURCE: "The Parental Stress Line," written by Naomi J. Banks, under the supervision of Professor Roberta Clarke, Boston University, 1979.

Every health care organization faces a resource attraction problem. Organizations need to attract people, funds, and so on. In this chapter, we will examine the problem of attracting people; in the next chapter, the problem of attracting funds.

All organizations, whether commercial or nonprofit, whether producing products or services, must attract employees. This is generally considered a personnel function. Marketing principles can be applied to this personnel issue, but there is sufficient literature in the commercial personnel field about employee attraction that it need not be addressed here.

Unlike commercial organizations, some health care and social organizations may seek to attract two other groups of people: members and/or volunteers. This chapter will study these two people-attraction tasks from a marketing point of view.

MEMBERSHIP DEVELOPMENT

Certain health care organizations, such as trade and professional associations and various types of alternative delivery systems, have membership as a core or ancillary component of their operation:

> **Members** are people who join an organization and support it with dues, payments, or other forms of energy.

Members have a more permanent relationship with an organization than patients or consumers, who come and go. Yet they are not paid employees who work under contract. They may volunteer to do unpaid work, although this is not typically a condition for membership.

Membership organizations exist to serve their members, who are also, in fact, their major consumers. In some organizations, such as hospitals, visiting nurse associations, and charitable organizations, membership is an ancillary feature designed primarily to raise money and volunteer services in order to serve a separate group of consumers. We should be aware that some organizations use the term membership in a slightly different sense; HMOs, for example, have members who pay a premium for coverage (rather than dues) and are unlikely to engage in volunteer work for the HMO. HMOs, PPOs, and other alternative delivery systems can be considered membership organizations, but because they engage in a direct exchange of money for services, they fit less neatly into the membership organization category we will be discussing.

Membership organizations typically face a number of problems, such as too few members, a poor mix of members, too many inactive members (or too many active members in the case of HMOs), and too many nonrenewing members. *Membership development* is the general name given to the task of creating a healthy membership situation. Here we will examine, from a marketing point of view, the four major problems of a membership organization: membership definition, membership attraction, membership motivation, and membership retention.

Membership Definition

Every membership organization needs to define membership qualifications, membership classes, and member benefits. These decisions will critically affect the ability of the organization to attract and retain members.

Organizations vary in the qualifications they place on membership. At one extreme are the professional associations, which will accept only licensed or "schooled" practitioners into their ranks. The American Medical Association (AMA) will accept only licensed physicians as members, while excluding osteopaths, chiropractors, and others who claim medical knowledge and status. Furthermore, they may drop members who violate its professional code of ethics. At the other extreme are charitable organizations that will accept anyone as a member who is willing to pay the annual dues, without any attention to the moral character or other aspects of the person.

Membership qualifications can become a divisive issue within the current membership ranks. Certain nursing associations have experienced extreme internal conflict over qualifications for membership. Some members want only those with a four-year B.S. degree in nursing to qualify. Others think that three-year nursing program graduates should qualify. And a few are willing to admit graduates of two-year programs as well.

Various membership organizations also define classes of membership. The American Occupational Therapy Association, Inc., has three classes of membership: registered occupational therapists, certified occupational therapy assistants, and occupational therapy students. In organizations that use membership primarily as a fundraising device, new members can "buy" into any level of membership through the size of their gift or dues. For example, people can join the Vision Foundation, a service for those losing their sight (Watertown, Massachusetts), at any of eight membership levels:

Benefactor	\$250
Sustaining membership	\$100
Life membership	\$50
Family membership	\$25
Couple membership	\$15
Single membership	\$10

All members are entitled to a core set of benefits. Members of the Vision Foundation receive *Vision Views,* a newsletter in large print telling of news about the organization and services available to those losing their sight. Higher classes of members may receive additional benefits, such as invitations to office openings. Clearly, a major task of a membership organization is to define the benefit mix that will achieve the desired mix of members. The more generous the benefits, the greater the organization's ability to attract members.

Membership Attraction

An organization can view itself as having too few, enough, or too many members. Here we deal with the former problem, which is the most common. For example, AMA membership dropped from 62 percent of the nation's physicians in 1968 to 47 percent in 1980. The AMA is quite disturbed about this, since it hurts its revenue and its power in Washington as a spokesperson for the medical profession.

Attracting new members calls for carrying out the normal marketing steps of (1) defining and locating prospects, (2) determining their attitudes toward the organization, and (3) developing a plan to sell them on membership.[1]

Defining and Locating Prospects. Organizations with a strict membership definition, such as professional and trade associations, ususally have little or no trouble defining and locating prospects. Thus, the AMA knows the name and address of every U.S. physician, since all are listed in a registry. Those physicians who are not AMA members constitute the prospect pool, and it is relatively easy to reach them.

Organizations that have open membership have a tougher problem defining their prospect pool. For a prepaid group practice HMO seeking to add individual members to its employed group members, the prospect pool, in principle, includes every adult living in or near the HMO facility. In practice, many of these people will not be interested in and/or willing to join the HMO. The HMO must therefore grade its prospects from those who would show the most interest and financial ability to those with somewhat less interest and/or ability to pay. The HMO could "buy" the names and addresses of people who are self-supporting and do not belong to an employer group. Depending on the quality of its prospect list, the HMO could direct appropriate and cost-effective communications.

Determining Prospects' Attitudes toward the Organization. The organization should interview some prospects to learn various reasons they give for not joining the organization. Each reason becomes something the organization may want to refute or counterclaim. These reasons usually lead to a segmentation of prospects into three groups: resistors, indifferents, and uninforms.

Resistors are those who do not join an organization because they dislike it. Among the reasons they may give are: "I disagree with the organization's principles"; "The organization doesn't do any good"; "The membership is self-serving and hypocritical." If these beliefs are unfounded, the organization can offer evidence that refutes these views and attract some resistors. But where these views are well founded, the organization will gain little by pursuing this group.

Indifferents are prospects who do not see much net benefit to joining the organization. They will give as reasons for not joining: "The dues are high in relation to the benefits"; or "I don't like to join organizations." The best approach to indifferents is to try to demonstrate that the organization's value is higher in relation to the cost than the indifferents believe.

Uninforms are prospects who have little information on which to base a judgment about the value of belonging to the organization. They say: "I guess I don't know what it really does"; or "I have no idea what the dues are, but I think they are high." The best approach to the uninformed is to send them information to increase their knowledge of the organization.

Developing a Plan to Sell Membership. An organization can pursue membership building along three lines. The first is *normal membership recruitment,* in which printed pieces are developed and sent through the mail, distributed at meetings, and handed out personally on appropriate occasions. The second is *person-to-person solicitation* by members or field staff, often directed to very desirable prospects. The third is the *major membership drive* waged at conventions and other meetings through the use of speakers, visual aids, testimonials, and sign-up booths. Each approach is discussed below.

For a professional organization, normal membership recruitment boils down to developing printed material that communicates an effective case for the value of membership in relation to the cost. The organization must first take stock of the real benefits it offers members and whether they are sufficient in number and quality. For example, the AMA offers to its physician members the following benefits:

1. Various journals and newsletters
2. Insurance programs
3. Seminars on medical, social, and political topics
4. Placement services
5. Services of one of the nation's largest medical libraries
6. A 32 percent discount at Hertz car rentals
7. Lobbying for physician interests

The AMA should research prospects with respect to how important they regard each benefit. The results can be used to identify a set of *benefit segments.* Some prospects will be motivated by personal nonmedical benefits such as insurance, Hertz discounts, chance for better placement, and collegial-social relations. Others will be motivated by the opportunity to improve their medical competence through seminars, journals, and library services. Still others will be motivated by seeing the AMA as a political instrument to protect and advance the interests of the medical profession. By identifying these different segments, different brochures could be developed and mailed that would maximize the appeal to each segment. In addition, prospects should be asked for their ideas about new benefits that would motivate them to join the AMA.

The professional association should also research prospects' (and members') opinions about the appropriateness of the dues level and structure. Hit with two successive dues increases (in which annual dues rose from $110 to $250), AMA membership continued its downward decline. Physicians, who have to pay another $200 for membership in their state and county medical associations, in many cases thought that another $250 for AMA membership was too much. Clearly, the AMA must either do a better job of selling the benefits of membership or think twice about passing on dues increases to the membership.

Among the prospects an organization seeks to attract are usually some VIPs who would make especially valuable members. For example, the AMA might consider it a real coup to attract a well-known physician to membership who had previously been publicly critical of the organization. Obviously, this "conversion sale" won't be accomplished simply by mailing an attractive brochure. This physician requires a tailored marketing approach that relies heavily on personal selling.

The process consists of taking the prospect through the following four stages designed to bring about growing commitment to the organization:

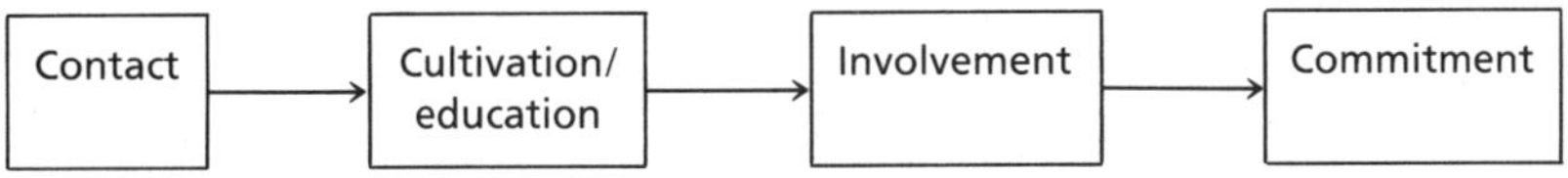

The first stage is *contact,* in which the organization's representative makes an appointment to see the physician and describes the strong interest the organization has in his or her membership. The purpose of the meeting is simply to get acquainted and to offer information. The second stage is *cultivation/education,* in which the organization mails interesting material about its activities in the hope of increasing the physician's interest. The representative may take the physician to lunch or dinner in order to build the relationship. The third stage is called *involvement.* The representative asks the physician to join the organization and get involved. A specific high-minded type of involvement that the physician cannot easily refuse is usually proposed. The fourth stage is *commitment,* in which the physician, having joined, begins to meet new people and serve on committees and begins to feel a commitment to the organization.

From time to time, an organization may undertake a major *membership drive.* It will set a high goal, substantially increase its membership-building budget, engage the services of advertising and marketing experts, and blitz prospects with literature and appeals. The major membership drive derives part of its effectiveness through "turning on" the staff and current members to becoming more active recruiters, and it may derive another part of its effectiveness through the offering of special incentives for joining at that time, such as half-price memberships, premiums, public recognition of new members, and so on.

Membership Motivation

Ideally, membership organizations (excluding HMOs and other prepaid provider organizations) would like every member to be active, proud, and ready to serve the organization whenever called upon. In practice, only a small percent of the membership of any organization shows enthusiasm and takes a real interest in its affairs. An allied health professional association reported that about one-half of its members are *inactives,* who may or may not attend the one major association conference each year; one-quarter are *moderate actives* who attend three to four regional events as well as the national conference; and one-quarter are *high actives,* who contribute most of the time, money, and other things that make it possible to run the association. In other words, a small fraction of the membership of any organization will do most of the work involved in running it.

The first step for an organization is to determine the proportion of inactives, moderate actives, and high actives. A high or growing number of inactives is a sign that the organization is not creating value for these members, and this could eventually spell the demise of the organization. The organization should then proceed to survey the three groups to find out what aspects of the organization are satisfying and dissatisfying to them. Exhibit 18–1 shows two key questions that can reveal areas of dissatisfaction and their relative importance. By monitoring the feelings of members, the organization can learn what steps would improve member satisfaction.

The organization should supplement its surveys with focus group discussions in which a sample of members are invited to consider new ways to create involvement and excitement. Members want to feel that they are worthwhile members of a worthwhile organization. They need evidence that they are personally highly regarded in the organization (need for response and recognition), an expectation of new experiences (need for variety), and a sense that the organization itself is accomplishing important things for the members and the society. Too often organizations are run without change from year to year, and then member interest begins to flag.

EXHIBIT 18–1 Survey Instrument Measuring Members' Dissatisfaction

1. HOW OFTEN DO YOU FIND ANY OF THE FOLLOWING PROBLEMS OR ANNOYANCES OCCURRING WHEN DEALING WITH THE SOCIETY?

	Often	Sometimes	Seldom	Never
Lack of experienced staff				
Returns calls late				
Impersonal service				
No advisory assistance				
Poor meetings				

2. HOW MUCH DOES THE PROBLEM BOTHER YOU?

	Extremely bothered	Very bothered	Just a little bothered	Not at all bothered
Lack of experienced staff				
Returns calls late				
Impersonal service				
No advisory assistance				
Poor meetings				

Membership Retention

The ultimate indicator of a failure to satisfy members is a high or growing nonrenewal rate. This is the annual "market test," where each member votes on whether the "product" is worth the cost. This is why many membership organizations put a lot of effort into the task of membership renewal. Instead of sending a plain renewal notice as in the past, they send printed material (letter and/or brochure) listing all the benefits and accomplishments of the organization, along with "won't you please renew your membership, Jon Jones." If no renewal is forthcoming in the first few weeks, another letter is sent, and eventually a phone call might be made to encourage the member to renew.

The central need is to determine various reasons why members do not renew. An HMO found four reasons accounting for 70 percent of its membership dropout:

1. Move to a new community (20 percent)
2. Change of employment to a new employer who did not offer the HMO (15 percent)
3. Reported dissatisfaction with access to physicians (15 percent)
4. Reported dissatisfaction with emergency care procedures (20 percent)

The HMO cannot do anything to stop members from moving out of the community or changing their place of employment, but clearly it can do something about perceived access to its own physicians and about emergency care policies. In the short run, the HMO may have to sell members on other benefits of membership; in the long run it will have to improve its product to compete more successfully with other health care coverage alternatives.

VOLUNTEER RECRUITMENT

One of the common features of many health care and social service organizations is their use of volunteers—both to keep down expenses and to provide a channel for high-minded people to contribute time to a cause they believe in. The core concept of voluntarism is that individuals participate in spontaneous, private, and freely chosen activities that "promote or advance some aspects of the common good, as it is perceived by the persons participating in it."[2] These activities are not coerced by any institution in society, and the behavior "is engaged in not primarily for financial gain. . . ."[3] Between 50 and 70 million Americans act as volunteers each year. In 1974, the economic value of volunteer time exceeded $34 billion. In recent years, however, the number of volunteers has been declining due to the rise in the proportion of working women. Organizations now have to give increased attention to the problem of volunteer attraction and satisfaction.[4]

Volunteers may seem to be a free "good" to the organization, but this is not entirely true. Some cost is incurred in recruiting, training, and motivating volunteers. Further cost is incurred when volunteers fail to show up when needed, or show up late, or work at a slow pace. Some managements believe that competent paid staff members are ultimately better for the organization than unpaid volunteers. Each organization has to determine the optimal ratio of volunteers to staff to get its work done.

The proper way to attract and motivate volunteers is to recognize them as a distinct market segment with certain needs and expectations with whom the organization exchanges benefits. These needs and expectations have been changing over time. Years ago, volunteers talked about the gratification they derived from helping others, and how volunteering enhanced their sense of self-worth. In some cases, volunteering allowed them to repay obligations. Volunteering also provides stimulation and socialization. Investigation in the 1950s began to reveal more self-serving gratifications: Volunteering conveyed and validated a higher social status.[5] The 1970s brought other motives to light. Training and work experience is a major motivation for many types of volunteers, especially students and women volunteers who have been homemakers but intend to reenter the workforce. Also, volunteering provided social ties in a world where mobility, an increasingly nuclear family, and social conflict are rising. The 1980s have brought a return of some of the earlier motives (the gratification from helping others, enhancing a sense of self-worth). American Express recognized this in advertising targeted at Yuppies (young urban professionals); they pictured their target market in volunteer situations such as coaching a Little League team.

Volunteer Attraction

New volunteers must constantly be attracted as others leave. Organizations need a systematic procedure to attract volunteers. One method is to ask current volunteers to recruit among their friends and acquaintances. If this method fails to produce enough qualified volunteers, a notice or advertisement might be distributed to members of the organization inviting them to volunteer. Beyond this, the organization can place ads in other media announcing the strong need for volunteers and the benefits volunteers enjoy.

Not all volunteers can be accepted or assigned to tasks they want to perform. People with undesirable characteristics and/or who do not mix well with others may be turned down on some excuse. Volunteers who want to handle specialized tasks, such as publicity or fundraising, must show the necessary qualifications. If Mr. Tedious volunteers to call on important donors, he may have to be told that this job is being well handled and that the organization really needs volunteers for other tasks, such as letter writing and envelope stuffing.

Volunteer Motivation

Volunteers need recognition and occasional challenge. Since they are giving their time freely, they are especially sensitive to slights from management, such as being ordered to do something undesirable, like working extra long hours, and so on. The tasks assigned to them must also reflect their sense of status and value. While stuffing envelopes may be appropriate for some groups of volunteers, it is not for others, such as board members of a major academic medical center. While board members volunteer their time, they expect it to be applied to tasks similar to what they do at work. They would feel demeaned being asked to do what they would consider their secretary's job if they were at work. Managing a volunteer force, therefore, calls for a manager who is sensitive to the needs and feelings of volunteers. The supervisor must be friendly and appreciative of the services and open to suggestions and complaints. Competent volunteer managers will normally arrange special benefits and recognitions for the contributions of volunteers. Thus, a hospital may do the following things for its auxilliary volunteers: give special pins and ranks to recognize 10, 15, and 25 years of service; sponsor an annual dinner for its volunteers in which one or more staff physicians speak on a subject of interest; give free passes to plays to its volunteers; and so on.

SUMMARY

Health care and social service organizations, in addition to recruiting employees as all organizations and companies must do, may also seek to attract members and volunteers. Membership development is a function of organizations like professional and track associations, charitable organizations, and, in a slighty different sense, prepaid provider organizations. Membership organizations face a number of problems, such as too few members, a poor mix of members, too many inactive members, and too many nonrenewing members. Membership development calls for defining the characteristics of desirable members and preparing programs to attract members, motivate them, and ensure their renewal. To attract important new members, the process consists of contact, cultivation/education, involvement, and commitment.

Volunteer attraction and development is a problem for organizations that depend on volunteers to do much of the work. Volunteers pose certain problems in that, being unpaid, they tend to be less reliable and more sensitive to slights and lack of supervision. As the pool of volunteers diminishes because of increasing number of working women, organizations have to improve their approaches to attracting, motivating, and rewarding volunteers.

NOTES

1. Readers interested in membership attraction and development should contact the American Society of Association Executives, 1101 16th Street, NW, Washington, DC, which publishes useful materials and runs seminars.

2. Gordon Manser and Rosemary H. Cass, *Voluntarism at the Crossroads* (New York: Family Service Association of America, 1976), p. 14.

3. Jon Van Til, "In Search of Voluntarism," *Volunteer Administration,* 12, 2 (Summer 1979), p. 9.

4. The interested reader should contact the National Center for Voluntary Action, 1214 16th Street, NW, Washington, DC, 20036, for extensive publications and information on voluntarism.

5. David L. Sills, *The Volunteers—Means and Ends in a National Organization* (Glencoe, IL: Free Press, 1957).

19

DONOR MARKETING: ATTRACTING FUNDS

A substantial portion of its community thought that Roosevelt Hospital, in New York, was a mediocre, city-run hospital—used primarily by low-income ethnic groups, and offering little to the higher income residents who were its best fundraising prospects. How, then, did Roosevelt Hospital raise $2,000,000 from its catchment area—enough to buy a new emergency room without a single penny of government money?

To find out, *PROFILES* interviewed Tom Rosenberg, of the PR/Marketing firm that devised the research and implemented the one-year program that ended with groundbreaking last month.

"We had to program fundraising to generate the money," Mr. Rosenberg states, "and concurrently, we had to educate the residents of Manhattan's West Side. People needed to learn that Roosevelt's ER is just as good as any ER anywhere."

The program began with a comprehensive market research study, which not only included the standard demographic data, but also uncovered the community's attitudes toward the hospital and its ER, their propensity for contributing to hospitals and other non-profit organizations, and the appeal strategies that would be most successful in reaching them. Further information included data on community radio listenership habits.

From the research came a program designed to reach new audiences, consisting in part of parents whose children attended private schools in the area. Other groups—new residents, corporate giants headquartered in area office buildings, and restaurants and other small businesses whose customers might require access to Roosevelt Hospital—were also revealed.

A major education and publicity campaign included extensive media interviews with physicians; topics discussed dealt with current community activities, like jogging information and roller skating injuries. Volunteer nurses and doctors staffed nearby Lincoln Center, on hand for urgent problems. Local restaurant employees went to class to learn the "Heimlich Maneuvers." And personnel at Rockefeller Center studied CPR.

Industry, too, became involved. A Hotline was established between Gulf and Western and the ER, for example. And corporate gifts increased substantially—because they were motivated by services that Roosevelt offered them, rather than being just the usual token donations. Through cooperation with the West Side Chamber of Commerce, information about the project was also circulated to local merchants.

All materials associated with the media campaign were specific to the potential market, as determined by the market research. Radio spots, written by a professional who donated his time, ran on the station with the highest area listenership. Placards appeared on buses that traveled to and from the West Side. In addition, several direct-mail appeals were addressed to specific audience segments.

Cost consciousness was a factor throughout the program, according to Mr. Rosenberg. For example: an existing 64-page emergency handbook was selected as a giveaway in return for contributions. Only a change of cover was necessary to customize this stock booklet for Roosevelt's ER . . . and avoid any special production expenses.

Recently, Roosevelt has merged with St. Luke's Hospital, to become Roosevelt-St. Luke's Medical Center. Although the institutions are mutually supportive, they maintain separate Emergency Rooms. And the Roosevelt unit's new facility is busier than ever. Solvent, too.

"Sure, we're pleased," confirmed Mr. Rosenberg. "We made all that money by ourselves."

SOURCE: "ER Development Campaign," *Profiles in Hospital Marketing,* 1st Quarter, 1981, p. 8. Reprinted by permission.

Many health care and social service organizations rely on external funds to support their activities. These external funds include individual donations, corporate donations, foundation grants and government funds, whether grants or tax allocations. The organizations receiving these funds are usually nonprofit. For these organizations, revenues generated by usage of their services may not be sufficient to keep it operating in the long term. Fundraising strategy is therefore an essential component of these organizations. For other health care organizations, fundraising is helpful but not necessary; and for yet others, it is irrelevant.

The role of philanthropy has declined considerably in recent years for health care organizations. In his article pointing out how the decline of philanthropic funds has led to the "monetarization of medical care," Ginzberg notes that philanthropy accounted for 24 percent of the total operating budget of nonprofit hospitals in New York City in 1940, for 17 percent by 1948, and for barely 1 percent in 1984.[1]

Yet the total amount of charitable money raised by organizations is significant; in 1983; $60.39 billion was donated to more than 300,000 charities listed as being tax-exempt by the IRS. Over 84 percent of all contributions came from individuals, with the remainder coming from bequests (5 percent), foundations (5 percent), and corporations (5 percent). Almost 50 percent of the money was raised by religious organizations and the rest by education, health and hospitals, social welfare, arts and humanities, civic and public, and other. About one out of every three dollars was raised by mail or mail-assisted campaigns, and the rest by personal contact campaigns.[2]

The art of fundraising has passed through various stages of evolution. Its earliest form was begging, where needy people and groups would implore more fortunate people for money and goods. Beggars perfected many techniques to gain the attention and sympathy of their target audience, such as simulating pain or blindness, or showing children with bloated stomachs. The next stage consisted of collection, where organizations such as churches would regularly collect contributions from a willing and defined group of supporters. In recent times campaigning emerged as a concept and involved organizations appointing a specific person or group to be responsible for soliciting money from every possible source through a systematic fundraising campaign. Most recently, fundraising has been reinterpreted as development: The organization systematically builds up different classes of loyal donors who give consistently and receive benefits in the process of giving. Today's health care and social service organizations vary considerably in their concept of raising money, some seeing it as begging, others as collection, others as campaigning, and still others as development.

Organizations that raise money tend to pass through the following three stages in their thinking about how to carry on fundraising effectively.

1. *Product stage.* Here the prevailing attitude is "We have a good cause; people ought to support us." Money is raised primarily by the top officers through an "old boy network." The organization relies on volunteers to help raise additional funds. A few loyal donors supply most of the funds.
2. *Sales stage.* Here the prevailing attitude is "There are a lot of people out there who might give money, and we must find them." The institution appoints a development director who eventually hires a staff. This staff raises money from all possible sources, using typically a "hard sell" approach. The fundraisers have little influence on the institution's policies or personality since their job is to raise money, not improve the organiza-

tion. Unfortunately, too many health care organizations are still in this stage.

3. *Marketing stage.* Here the prevailing attitude is "We must analyze our position in the marketplace, concentrate on those donor sources whose interests are best matched to ours, and design our solicitation programs to supply needed satisfactions to each donor group." This approach involves carefully segmenting the donor markets; measuring the giving potential of each donor market; assigning executive responsibility for developing each market through using research and communication approaches; and developing a plan and budget for each market based on its potential. Some larger and more sophisticated health care organizations have moved into this stage, and it is attracting increased attention as fundraisers become aware of the difference between a sales and a marketing approach.

This chapter will analyze fundraising from a marketing perspective. The first section will examine four major donor markets: individual givers, foundations, corporations, and government. The next section will examine how organizations organize their fundraising effort internally. Section three will consider the important task of setting fundraising objectives and strategies, while section four will take a look at the multiplicity of fundraising tactics. The final section will consider how health care and social service organizations can evaluate and improve their fundraising effectiveness.

ANALYZING DONOR MARKETS

An organization can tap into a variety of sources for financial support. The four major donor markets are individuals, foundations, corporations, and government. Small health care and social service organizations often solicit funds primarily from one source—often wealthy individuals or one particular foundation—to meet their needs. Larger organizations tend to solicit all sources, and a few are able to make specific executives responsible for each market. Ultimately they seek to allocate the fundraising budget in proportion to the giving potential of each donor market. Here we will examine the institutional and behavioral characteristics of each donor market.

Individual Givers

Individuals are the major source of all charitable giving, accounting for some 83 percent of the total. Almost everyone in the nation contributes money to one or more organizations each year, the total amount varying with such factors as the giver's income, age, education, sex, ethnic background, and other characteristics. Relatively more money is contributed by high-income people, people in their middle years, and people of high education. At the same time, giving levels vary substantially within each group. Some wealthy individuals give little and some lower-income individuals give a lot. Among wealthy people, for example, physicians tend to give less than lawyers, but according to one hospital fundraising executive, neither physicians nor lawyers are as willing to part with their money as successful business executives.

Charitable causes vary in their appeal to individuals. In a study sponsored by Save the Children Foundation, the public was asked: "Which of the five (categories of charity) would rate as the most worthwhile?" The ranking turned out to be: (1) needy children; (2) disaster victims; (3) medical research; (4) aid to handicapped; and (5) religious organizations.[3] That is, Americans would be most ready to give to a cause involving needy children, followed by disaster victims, and so on. Paradoxically, they give relatively small amounts to these causes in relation to the amounts they give to their religious organizations.

Within each category of charity, the appeal levels also vary greatly. For example, within medical charities people give most readily to the American Red Cross ($381.5 million), American Cancer Society ($139.7 million), Easter Seals ($99 million), American Heart Association ($87 million), March of Dimes ($68.5 million), Muscular Dystrophy Association ($68.5 million), and Mental Health Association ($20.9 million) (figures as of 1978). Some of the difference in the amounts raised is due to the fact that organizations have different life spans and different degrees of effectiveness at fundraising. But a larger part of the difference in giving levels is due to the opinions people hold about specific diseases, particularly about the disease's severity, prevalence, and remediability. Thus, heart disease and cancer are severe diseases—they kill—whereas arthritis and birth defects are considered less serious, since they do not kill. Cancer has a higher prevalence than muscular dystrophy and therefore attracts more support. Finally, people believe that cures or preventions are possible for heart disease and less so for birth defects, and this leads to more giving. Figure 19–1 shows the hypothetical positions of three diseases on the three variables. If the March of Dimes wants to attract more funds for its cause—birth defects—it must try to increase the perceived severity, prevalance, and remediability of birth defects.

Why do individuals give to charity? Health care organizations dependent on external funds need a good understanding of giving motives in order to be effective at fundraising. The answer called "altruism" tends to mask the complex motives that underlie giving or helping behavior. The best working hypothesis is that the individual "gives" in order to "get" something back. In other words, donations should not be viewed as a *transfer*, but as a *transaction*. The question is: What does the donor get? Table 19–1 lists several motives underlying giving behavior. People give to get response or recognition, reduce fear, meet social pressure, or feel "altruistic."

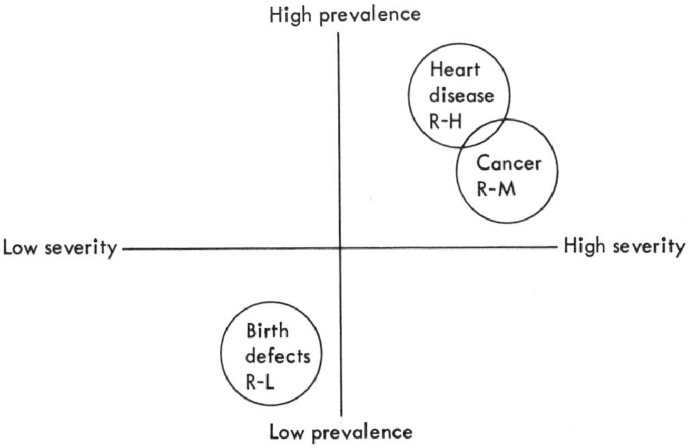

Note: The third variable, remediability (R), is shown next to each disease with an indication of low (L), medium (M), and high (H).

FIGURE 19–1 Public Perception of Different Medical Conditions

TABLE 19–1 Individual Giving Motives

1. *Need for self-esteem.* Person attempts to build self-esteem through self-image, playing God, or feeling good from giving. Opposite of this would be shame or guilt.
2. *Need for recognition from others.* Person attempts to build social status or enhance prestige in the eyes of others. There is a strong need to belong.
3. *Fear of contracting disease.* This need centers around an insecurity in people that they will contract the disease or that a member of their family will. They hope in some sense for immortality.
4. *The habit giver.* This person gives out of habit for no real reason other than a desire not to be embarrassed by not contributing to the cause. These people are very indifferent to contributions but feel that they must give to someone because everyone else does.
5. *Nuisance giver.* This person gives only to get rid of the caller. He feels he is contributing to a cause of no real significance, but would rather donate a few dollars than be troubled by others.
6. *Required to give.* These people are required to give at work; they are under pressure from superiors to donate part of their checks to a fund. Future job promotions and evaluations may depend on their giving.
7. *Captive givers.* These people feel real sorrow for someone they know who might have contracted the disease. They are other-centered in that they earnestly would like to aid the victim in some way. Givers in this category may contribute at the death of a friend, rather than sending flowers, etc.
8. *People to people givers.* These people have a real feeling of the "commonness of man"—a solidarity with other people. This group of people has internalized the idea of helping others because they want to.
9. *Concern for humanity.* This segment of givers is concerned about others for religious reasons and because they are "God's children." They feel a moral obligation to contribute to charity. They have accepted the love for humanity idea because it is a requirement of their faith.

Is there such a thing as giving without "getting"? Some people give and say that they expect nothing back—but actually they have "expectations." They expect the organization to use the money efficiently; they expect the organization to show gratitude; and so on. Even the anonymous giver, while wanting no acknowledgment, may privately enjoy the self-esteem of being "big enough" to give money without requiring recognition.

The various motives for giving provide clues to marketing strategy for fundraising executives. Harold Seymour has suggested that in many mass donor markets, one-third of the people are *responsible* (they donate without being solicited), one-third are *responsive* (they donate when they are asked), and one-third react to *compulsion* (they donate because of pressure).[4] Closely allied to these motives is the motive, of *recognition by one's peers.* Making use of this motive entails peer solicitation rather than solicitation by a paid fundraising executive. Each market can be investigated further to discover the specific motive segments that exist.

Too many organizations ask people to give to them as a needy organization rather than to give to them to support promising programs. The latter is more effective. People respond to what they sense as the relevance, importance, and urgency of a giving opportunity. Seymour suggests that the issue on which the giving is focused must be bigger than the institution. And it must be presented in a way that catches the eye, warms the heart, and stirs the mind.

Another important principle for segmentation is the donor's "giving potential." Fundraisers distinguish between small, medium, and large donors. Some fundraisers prefer to concentrate all or most of their energy on large potential donors, feeling that attracting a few large gifts would produce more funds than attracting many small gifts. Other fundraisers believe that they need to concentrate on small givers as much as large givers, because the future large givers often come from the ranks of the small givers.

Nonetheless, seeking the large gift is still the most important part of fundraising for many organizations. Fundraisers use a five-step approach: *identification, introduction, cultivation, solicitation,* and *appreciation.* They first identify wealthy individuals who could conceivably have a strong interest in the organization. They identify others who might supply information and arrange an introduction. They cultivate the person's interest without asking for any money. By asking too early, they may get less than is possible. Eventually they do ask for money and upon receiving it, express their appreciation.

Large individual gift fundraising is most effective when the organization develops a "wish list" of exciting projects and lets the prospective donors see the list. Boston's Beth Israel Hospital pursued this strategy in a forthright fashion for THE PROJECT, a five-year program to

EXHIBIT 19–1 Fundraising Brochure of Boston's Beth Israel Hospital

Opportunities Available for Naming by Donors

In addition to the facilities listed below (some facility names have been shortened for this listing), there are other rooms and areas in a wide range of price categories, many of which are available for naming.

Charles A. Dana Research Building

Subscribed
$2,500,000

Surgical research laboratory
$600,000

Renal research laboratory
$400,000

Gastroenterology research laboratory
$400,000

Reisman Cardiovascular Research Laboratory
Subscribed

Anesthesia research laboratory
$300,000

Hematology research laboratory
$300,000

Neurology research laboratory
$300,000

Obstetrics-gynecology research laboratory
$300,000

Orthopedics research biomechanics laboratory
$300,000

Radiology research laboratory
$300,000

Infectious diseases research laboratory
$200,000

Hemostasis-thrombosis research laboratory
$200,000

Oncology-virology research laboratory
$200,000

Conference center
$150,000

Conference rooms (3)
$60,000

Robert and Eleanor Leventhal Research Library
Subscribed

Altschuler Research Laboratory
Subscribed

West Tower

To name the building
$2,500,000

Labor and delivery suite
$1,000,000

Brezner Respiratory-Surgical Intensive Care Unit
Subscribed

Pulmonary-general intensive care unit
$500,000

Patient floors (2)
$600,000

Wings on patient floors (6)
$250,000

Neonatal special care unit
$200,000

Roof patio/helicopter port
$150,000

Waiting rooms/solaria (3)
$100,000

Nursing stations (4)
$75,000

Individual labor and delivery rooms (10)
$75,000

Elevators (2)
$75,000

Patient rooms, Brezner Respiratory-Surgical Intensive Care Unit (12)
$50,000

Patient rooms, pulmonary-general intensive care unit (12)
$50,000

Northeast Building

To name the building
$2,500,000

Radiation therapy unit
$1,000,000

Morse Medical Intensive Care Unit
Subscribed

Berenson Emergency Unit
Subscribed

Clinical laboratory floor
$200,000

Linear accelerator unit
$150,000

Markell Shock-Trauma Room
Subscribed

Shock-trauma room
$100,000

Walk-in unit suite
$100,000

Medical record department
$100,000

Waiting room, Morse Medical Intensive Care Unit
$100,000

Chemistry, bacteriology, hematology laboratories
$75,000

Special procedure room, Morse Medical Intensive Care Unit
$75,000

Nursing stations, Berenson Emergency Unit and Morse Medical Intensive Care Unit
$50,000

Patient rooms, Morse Medical Intensive Care Unit
$50,000

Exam rooms, Berenson Emergency Unit
$50,000

Elevator
$50,000

Charles A. Dana Research Building

Facilities to be designated

Edward C. and Bertha Rose

The Kresge Foundation

Permanent Charity Fund

Related research facilities

Pathology research laboratory
$500,000

Electron microscopy laboratory
$250,000

West Tower

Related clinical facilities

Ultrasound laboratory
$100,000

Cystoscopy suite
$100,000

Ambulatory surgery operating rooms (2)
$100,000

Nurseries, newborn (2)
$100,000

Northeast Building

Related clinical facilities

Evelyn K. and Daniel E. Price Cardiac Clinical Center
Subscribed

Computer medicine laboratory
$350,000

SOURCE: Courtesy Beth Israel Hospital, Boston, MA.

build facilities needed for the hospital to meet its goals in patient care, teaching, and research. The fundraising brochure, which was part of a larger, more complex development strategy targeted at prospective major givers, listed various giving opportunities (see Exhibit 19–1); for example, if a donor gave $350,000, he could get a computer medicine library named for him; $100,000 would "buy" you an untrasound laboratory, $50,000 an elevator, and $2,500,000 a whole building. Organizations may classify their wished-for gifts in several financial sizes in order to attract different classes of donors.

One of the most powerful appeals is offering donors the opportunity to have their names (or the names of loved ones) attached to physical facilities, research funds, distinguished medical school chairs, and the like. In addition, fundraisers can offer these individuals all kinds of ways to make their gifts, including direct cash payment, gifts of stock and other property, and bequests where they will assign part or all of their estate to the organization upon their death. One life insurance company developed a Charitable Life policy, to be promoted by and sold through health care organizations' development departments, which made giving more attractive by substituting smaller payments spread out over time for one lump-sum donation.[5] Previous changes in the laws opened up tax advantages to medium-sized gift donors. Proposed changes in the laws in 1985 limit tax advantages to almost all donors. Through planned giving methods, fundraisers can provide tax counseling services to any donor with sufficient resources to consider estate planning.

Foundations

Currently there are over 26,000 foundations in the United States, all set up to give money to worthwhile causes. They fall into the following groups:

1. *Family foundations,* set up by wealthy individuals to support a limited number of activities of interest to the founders. Family foundations typically do not have permanent offices or full-time staff members. Decisions tend to be made by family members and/or counsel.
2. *General foundations,* set up to support a wide range of activities and usually run by a professional staff. General foundations range from extremely large organizations such as the Ford Foundation and the Rockefeller Foundation, which support a wide range of nonprofit organizations and which tend to give most of their money to large well-established organizations, to more specialized general foundations that tend to give money to a particular cause, such as health (Johnson Foundation) or education (Carnegie Foundation).
3. *Corporate foundations,* set up by corporations and allowed to give away up to 5 percent of the corporation's taxable income.
4. *Community trusts,* set up in cities or regions and made up of smaller foundations whose funds are pooled for greater impact.

With 26,000 foundations, it is important for the fundraiser to know how to locate the few that would be most likely to support a given project or cause. Fortunately, there are many resources available for researching foundations. The best single resource is known as The Foundation Center, a nonprofit organization with research centers in New York, Washington, and Chicago as well as other cities, which collects and distributes information on foundations. In addition, many libraries around the country also carry materials describing foundations. The most important are these:

1. *The Foundation Grants Index,* which lists the grants that have been given in the past year by foundation, subject, state, and other groupings. The fundraiser, for example, could look up children's disease research and

discover all the grants made to support children's disease research and identify the most active foundations in this area of giving.

2. *The Foundation Directory,* which lists over 2,500 foundations that have assets of over $1 million or award grants of more than $500,000 annually. The Directory describes the general characteristics of each foundation, such as type of foundation, types of grants, annual giving level, officers and directors, location, particular fields of interest, contact person, and so on. The Directory also contains an index of fields of interest, listing the foundations that have a stated interest in each field and whether or not they gave money to this field last year.
3. *The Foundation News,* which is published six times a year by The Council on Foundations and describes new foundations, new funding programs, and changes in existing foundations.
4. *Fund Raising Management,* which is a periodical publishing articles on fundraising management.

The key concept in identifying foundations is that of *matching.* The health care or social service organization should search for foundations matched to its interests and scale of operation. Too often a small organization will send a proposal to the Ford Foundation because it would like to get the support of this well-known foundation. But Ford accepts about 1 out of every 100 proposals and may be less disposed toward helping small organizations than more regional or specialized foundations would be.

After identifying a few foundations that have a high interest in the project area, the organization should try to qualify their level of interest before investing a lot of time in grant preparation. Most foundations are willing to respond to a letter of inquiry, phone call, or personal visit regarding how interested they are likely to be in a specific project. The foundation officer may be very encouraging or discouraging. If the former, the organization can then make the investment of preparing an elaborate proposal for this foundation.

Writing successful grant proposals has become a fine art, with many guides currently available to help the grant seeker.[6] Each proposal should contain at least the following elements:

1. A *cover letter* describing the context of the proposed project, and who has been contacted, if anyone, in the foundation.
2. The *proposal,* describing the project, its uniqueness, and its importance.
3. The *budget* for the project.
4. The *personnel* working on the project with their resumes.

The proposal itself should be compact, individualized, organized, and readable. In writing the proposal, the organization should be guided by knowledge of the "buying criteria" the particular foundation uses to choose among the many proposals that it receives. Many foundations describe their criteria in annual reports or memos; or their criteria can be inferred by looking at the characteristics of the recent proposals they have supported, or by talking to knowledgeable individuals. Among the most common rating criteria used by foundations are these:

1. The importance and quality of the project
2. The neediness and worthiness of the organization
3. The organization's ability to use the funds effectively and efficiently
4. The degree of benefit the foundation will derive from supporting the proposal

If the proposing organization knows the relative importance of the respective criteria, it can do a better job of selecting the features of the proposal to emphasize. For example, if the particular foundation is influenced by who presents the proposal, the organization should send its highest-ranking officials or most persuasive speakers to the foundation. On the other hand, if the foundation attaches great importance to the credentials of the project personnel, the organization should enlist highly qualified people to participate in the project.

Organizations should not contact foundations only on the occasion of a specific proposal. Each organization should cultivate a handful of appropriate foundations in advance of specific proposals, much as public relations officers cultivate the media in advance of seeking to generate publicity. This is called "building bridges" or "relationship marketing." If an organization sees a particular foundation as a "key customer account," the development officer will arrange for various people within the organization to get to know people at their corresponding level within the foundation. One or more of the organization's top managers and/or best-known researchers may arrange to see board members of the foundation each year. The organization's CEO or board chairperson may also visit the foundation's president each year for a luncheon or dinner. One or more members of the organization's development staff may cultivate relations with foundation staff members at their level. When the organization has a proposal, it knows exactly who should present it to the foundation and to whom. Furthermore, the foundation is more favorably disposed toward the organization because of the ongoing relationship and special understanding. Finally, the organization is able to do a better job of following up the progress of the project as it is being considered by the foundation.

Corporations

Business organizations represent another distinct source of funds for health care and social service organizations. Corporations have historically been especially supportive of such causes as health care and social services, as well as of higher education, United Way, and civic and cultural causes. In 1979 American business contributed $2.3 billion of the $43.3 billion received in total charity. This amounted to slightly less than 1 percent of business's pretax income. Since business organizations are allowed by law to give up to 5 percent of their pretax income to charity, considerable potential for more corporate giving exists.

Corporate giving differs from foundation giving in a number of important ways. First, corporations regard gift giving as a minor activity; at foundations, it is the major activity. Corporations will vary their giving level with the level of current and expected income. They have to be sensitive to the feelings of their stockholders, to whom they have the first obligation both in terms of how much to give to charity and what particular charities to support. Corporations are therefore more likely to avoid supporting controversial causes than are foundations. Corporations typically handle the many requests for support they receive by setting up a foundation so that corporate officers are not personally drawn into decision making.

Second, corporations pay more attention than foundations to the personal benefit any grant or gift might return to them:

> Few corporations engage in philanthropy because others need money, as though a corporation were a well-heeled uncle who should spread his good fortune around the family. For the most part, corporations give because it serves their own interests—or appears to.[7]

If they can show that a particular grant will increase community goodwill (as a grant by a cigarette company to the cancer research foundation) or train more manpower that they need (as a grant by a national nursing registry to a nursing school), these grants will set better with their board of directors and stockholders (see Exhibit 19–2).

In the third place, corporations can make more types of gifts than foundations can. A health care organization can approach a business for money, securities, goods, (asking a furniture company for some furniture), services (asking a printing company for some free printing or printing at cost), trained personnel (asking a software bureau for ten hours of a programmer's time), and space (asking a company for the use of its auditorium for a program). In the extreme, the health care organization should be able to get office equipment, marketing research, advertising, and so on free or at cost if it can identify the right corporate prospects to approach.

Effective corporate fundraising requires the health care organization to know how to identify good corporate prospects efficiently. Of the millions of business enterprises that might be approached, relatively few are appropriate to any specific organization; furthermore, the organization ordinarily does not have the resources to cultivate more than a

EXHIBIT 19–2

Editorial on Health Care Fundraising

Nonprofit hospitals that depend on philanthropists to pay for new plant and equipment face major new challenges and opportunities under the Economic Recovery Tax Act of 1981.

The biggest challenges, as outlined last month, involve changes in the tax code that will make it less attractive for high-income wage earners and for people with large estates to make big contributions to nonprofit hospitals and charities. These changes will cost nonprofit institutions some $18 billion in contributions over the next five years, according to one study. That forecast obviously is based on the assumption that much of today's giving is done to shelter income and estates from the tax collector. Many dispute that assumption. But only time will tell, and hospitals can't afford to wait to see what happens before they respond to such a major threat to their fund raising capabilities.

At the same time the Congress made giving less economically attractive for high-income wage earners and extremely wealthy individuals, it made philanthropy more attractive to lower income workers and, most important, corporations.

Obviously, mass marketing techniques, including advertising and direct mail, will become much more important weapons in fund raiser's arsenals, if small individual contributors are turned on by the tax law changes as predicted. Advertising and direct mail will work, however, only if based on marketing research designed to identify the contributors most likely to give to hospitals and the programs and services that will attract their contributions. The American Hospital Assn. is developing programs that will enable small hospitals to cooperate in fund drives aimed at entire communities, according to President J. Alexander McMahon. Perhaps a few major multi-institutional healthcare providers and the super groups of nonprofit hospitals and hospital chains should also launch national and regional fund raising drives.

At the same time that hospitals and other fund raisers are becoming more skilled in their marketing, however, corporate contributors are becoming much more concerned about putting their money where it will do them the most good. Corporations are most concerned about looking good in the eyes of their employees, and they are paying more attention to nonprofit organizations that involve their employees. *They are particularly generous to hospitals in their communities, according to the Sept. 22 issue of Fortune.* Indeed, "For most corporations, even better than doing good is to be seen doing good," *Fortune* says. (One caveat: It is unethical and unprofessional for purchasing agents or anyone else to tap suppliers for contributions.)

The nonprofit hospitals' challenge will be to *get employees of large local employers more involved in their institutions; the next step will be to get those workers to appeal to their companies for substantial contributions.* Their success will help ensure the future of nonprofit hospitals; their failure could mean capital starvation for nonprofit institutions.

We think the changes in the tax law offer new opportunities to solve the capital gap being forecast by executives of many nonprofit institutions. All that's needed is a little ingenuity, and the nonprofit hospital industry has shown that its managers, trustees and volunteers have it.

SOURCE: "Fund Raising" editorial, *Modern Healthcare* (October 1981), p. 7. Reprinted with permission from the October 1981 issue of MODERN HEALTHCARE MAGAZINE.

handful of corporate givers. The best prospects for corporate fundraising have the following characteristics:

1. *Local corporations.* Corporations located in the same area as the health care organization are excellent prospects. A hospital, for example, can base its appeal on the health care it offers to the corporation's employees. Corporations find it hard to turn away worthwhile organizations that provide direct services to their employees.
2. *Kindred activities.* Corporations located in a kindred field to the health care organization's field can be excellent prospects. An organization serving people losing their sight may effectively solicit funds from an optometric products company. However, it is considered unethical for health care organizations to tap suppliers or pharmaceutical companies; this raises the concern that health care organizations will feel the need to reciprocate by endorsing the corporate donor's products.
3. *Declared areas of support.* Health care and social service organizations should target corporations that have a declared interest in supporting that type of organization. Thus, a preventive health care organization might approach the Kimberley-Clark Corporation because of the latter's publicly stated active support of health maintenance and disease prevention activities.
4. *Large givers.* Large corporations and those with generous giving levels are excellent prospects. Yet fundraisers must realize that these corporations receive numerous requests and favor those organizations in the local area or kindred field. Regional offices of major corporations are often not in a position to make a donation without the approval of the home office.
5. *Personal relationships or contacts.* Organizations should review their personal contacts as a clue to corporations they might solicit. An organization's board of trustees consists of influential individuals who can open many doors for corporate solicitation. Corporations tend to respond to peer influence in their giving.

6. *Specific capability.* The fundraiser may identify a corporation as a prospect because it has a unique resource needed by the health care organization. Thus, a nonprofit skilled nursing facility might solicit a paint manufacturer for a donation of paint to repaint the rooms in an old wing of the facility.

These criteria will help the health care or social service organization identify a number of corporations that are worth approaching for contributions. Corporations in the organization's geographical area or field are worth cultivating on a continuous basis ("relationship marketing"), aside from specific grant requests. However, when the organization is seeking to fund a specific project, it needs to identify the best prospects and develop a marketing plan from scratch. We will illustrate the planning procedure in connection with the following example:

> An internationally known teaching hospital was seeking to raise $5 million to build a cardiac rehabilitation center. Its current facility was wholly inadequate, the cardiac rehabilitation center was a logical outcome of the hospital's cardiac diagnostic and treatment services, and all indications were that it would receive regulatory approval. The hospital was willing to name the new center after any major corporate donor who would supply at least 60 percent ($3 million) of the money being sought. This donor would be the "bell cow" that would attract additional corporate donors to supply the rest.

The first step called for the hospital to identify one or more major corporations to approach. The fundraisers recognized that major prospects would have two characteristics: They would be wealthy corporations, and they would have a high interest in this project. The fundraisers developed the matrix shown in Figure 19–2 and proceeded to classify corporations by giving potential and interest potential. In classifying corporations, they realized that certain companies fell in the upper left cell because they had very high profits (giving potential) and a high interest in health care causes (interest potential). These companies also wanted to give money to good causes to win public goodwill.

Which company? Here the hospital applied additional criteria. One company located in the same geographical area had already given a major donation to this hospital for another project; it was ruled out. The hospital considered whether it had any good contacts with some of the other companies. The hospital identified one corporation whose top executive had had open heart surgery at the hospital. In addition, a member of the hospital's board of trustees—a major bank president—knew the chairman of the company. It was decided on the basis of this and other factors to approach this company for support.

The next step called for preparing a prospect solicitation plan. As a

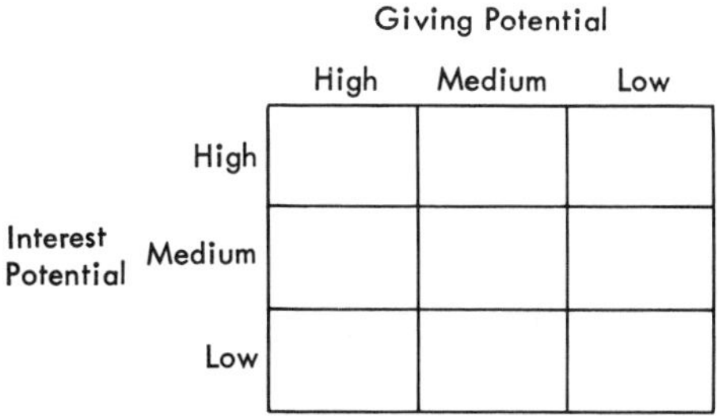

FIGURE 19–2 Classifying Prospective Corporate Donors by Level of Interest and Giving Potential

start, the hospital development office researched the company's sales, profits, major officers, recent giving record, and other characteristics. This information was useful in deciding whom to approach at the corporation, how much to ask for, what benefits to offer, and so on. A decision was made to approach the corporation's chairman, ask for $3 million for the new cardiac rehabilitation center, and offer to name the center after the corporation.

The final step called for plan implementation. The bank president arranged an appointment to visit the corporation's chairman, who was an old friend. He was accompanied by the hospital's president and also the vice-president of development. When they arrived, they met the chairman and the company's foundation director. They made their presentation, and the chairman said the proposal would be given careful consideration. A subsequent meeting was held at the hospital, and ultimately the corporation gave the money to the hospital.

The company responded positively to this solicitation because the proposal stood high on its major criteria. The company foundation rated each proposal on four criteria:

1. The proposal had to be worthwhile from a societal point of view. In this case, the cardiac rehabilitation center would contribute toward furthering the care and life expectancies of heart patients, presumably lessening acute care costs as well.
2. The corporation had to feel that the soliciting institution was worthwhile and would handle the grant well. Here, the company had full confidence in the teaching hospital because of its trustees and management.
3. The proposal should create some direct benefit, if possible, for the company. In this case, the company would memorialize its name in the hospital, and it would get good publicity for supporting the hospital.
4. The company foundation placed value on the personal relations involved. The fact that an important bank president had taken the time to present personally the proposal to the company chairman was an important factor in considering the proposal.

In general, corporations pay attention to these criteria in considering whether to "buy" a particular proposal, and therefore the seller (fundraiser) should weave them into its planning and presentation.

Government

Another major source of funds are government agencies at the federal, state, and local levels which have been established specifically to fund worthwhile causes. Various agencies of the National Institutes of Health, the Health Care Financing Administration, and so on grant hundreds of millions of dollars to health care organizations annually. Health care organizations interested in pursuing government grants will assign a staff person to concentrate on cultivating opportunities in this sector. The staff person—and often key medical researchers themselves—will monitor announcements of government grant opportunities that might have potential for the organization, as well spend time in Washington and elsewhere getting to know officers at these various agencies. In many ways, attracting grants from the government is not significantly different than attracting them from foundations.

Government agencies normally require the most detailed paperwork in preparing proposals. On the other hand, the agencies are very willing to review proposals, and place the main weight on the proposal's probable contribution to the public interest and on the credentials of the participants. Certain topics become "hot," such as AIDS research, osteoporosis, child abuse, and so on. The granting agencies look for the best proposals they can find on these topics. They pay less attention to agency benefit or to personal relations with the requesting organizations.

The recent cutback in government grants demonstrates the problems of organizations that had come to rely on government grants. The decrease in government funding through grants is now causing some organizations to attend to other fundraising markets for the first time. A wise strategy includes doing other types of fundraising from the beginning, rather than relying on only one source of funds.

ORGANIZING FOR FUNDRAISING

Organizations must develop an organized approach to fundraising. They cannot simply rely on money coming over the transom; this would make funding too erratic. Small organizations normally rely on one person to be responsible for fundraising; this person may be the organization's CEO or development director. Sometimes the same person is also responsible for public relations. He or she will be responsible for identifying fundraising opportunities and activating others—management, employees, trustees, volunteers—to assist when possible.

Large organizations—such as the American Cancer Society and American Heart Association—will have entire departments of development consisting of dozens of staff members plus volunteers numbering in the thousands. In these large organizations, development staff members take responsibility for specific donor markets, services, marketing tools, or geographical areas.

An ideal model for fundraising in a large organization is shown in Figure 19–3; a national religious-based nonprofit hospital and health care system is used for this example. The board of trustees has the ultimate responsibility for overseeing the financial health of the organization. To the extent that board members are involved in fundraising strategy and activities, they do this by making personal and company contributions, arranging donor contacts, and suggesting new fundraising ideas. The CEO or president is usually the chief fundraiser when it comes to meeting important people and asking for money. The vice-president of development is the chief planner of the fundraising strategy for the organization and also personally asks for money from potential donors. Day-to-day management is often handled by a director of development to free the vice-president of development for strategic planning and outside travel. The remaining development staff carry out specialized activities. Some staff are specialized to donor markets—there are directors of patient giving, foundations, corporate giving, and so on. Other staff members manage marketing functions, such as public rela-

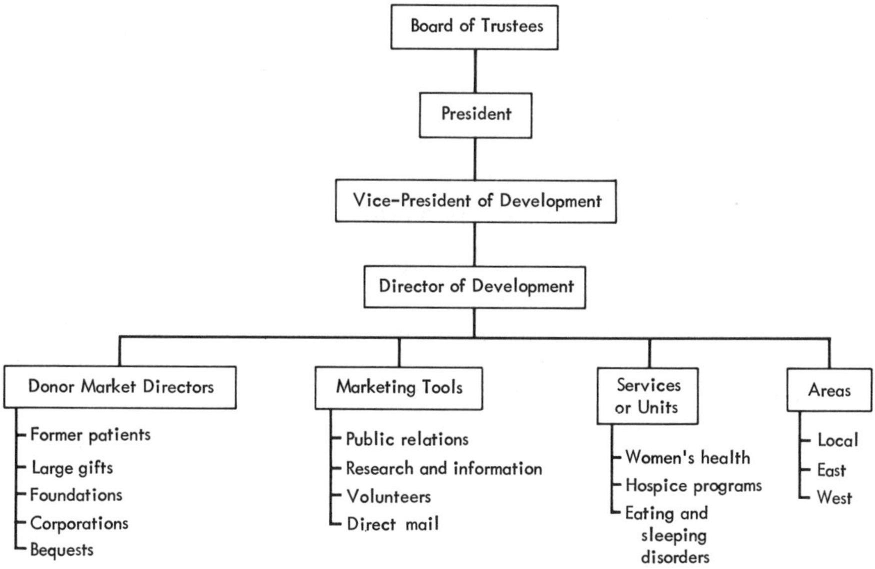

FIGURE 19–3 The Fundraising Organization of a National Nonprofit Health Care System

tions, research, and volunteers. Still other staff members handle various medical services, departments, or organizational units, where they get to know fundraising needs and opportunities. Finally, some staff members may manage regions of the country.

The organization's effectiveness may be amplified by managing a large number of volunteers—such as trustees, auxiliary groups, former patients or clients, and so on. Many health care organizations rely on professional development staff to manage large numbers of volunteers who are responsible for contacting potential donors. In this case, the staff functions to activate the volunteers, who are the main fundraising arm of the organization.

The organization's fundraising effectiveness is also affected by the quality of its information system. The development office needs to maintain up-to-date and easily accessible files on donors and prospects (individuals, foundations, corporations) so that past and/or potential giving can be identified and previous solicitations can be reviewed. To the extent that these files are computerized and data can be retrieved by year, relationship to the organization, giving level, and other key variables, the fundraiser is in a much better position to allocate effort effectively.

FUNDRAISING GOALS AND STRATEGY

Organizations must set annual and long-range goals for fundraising. As an example, the March of Dimes set the following goals:

To become the leading charitable organization in the area of birth defects

To increase annual contributions received each year by an average of 10 percent

To keep the expenses-to-contributions ratio below 20 percent

To increase the median size contribution

To increase grants from the government

Presumably these goals would have to be checked for consistency and ranked in terms of importance.

Every organization tends to set an annual contributions goal because this allows the organization to (1) know how much to budget for fundraising, (2) motivate staff and volunteers, and (3) measure fundraising effectiveness. Organizations arrive at their fundraising goal in different ways:

1. *Incremental approach.* Here the organization takes last year's revenue and increases it to cover inflation and then modifies it up or down depending on the expected economic climate. Thus the American Heart Association

may decide to raise about 15 percent more than it did in the preceding year.

2. *Need approach.* Here, the organizational goals determine program and building goals. From this, the organization forecasts its financial needs and sets a goal based on its needs. Thus a social service agency's management will estimate future building needs and costs, staff salaries, energy costs, and so on, and set the portion that has to be covered by fundraising as its target.
3. *Opportunity approach.* Here the organization makes a fresh estimate of how much money it could raise from each donor group with different levels of fundraising expenditure. It sets the goal of maximizing the net surplus. This approach is illustrated in Figure 11–2. The sales response function shows the gross revenue that would be raised with different levels of fundraising expenditure. Nonmarketing expenditures can be subtracted to reveal the gross surplus before marketing expenditures. The 45° line shows the marketing expenditures on fundraising. The vertical distance between the last two curves shows the net surplus associated with various fundraising marketing expenditures. The highest point on the surplus curve shows the marketing expenditure level that will maximize net surplus.

The incremental approach is the weakest of the three. The opportunity approach is the most sound. The vice-president of development would be responsible for preparing this analysis by analyzing the potential of each donor group. If this goal is accepted, the vice-president of development knows how much staff effort to allocate to each donor group.

After setting its fundraising goal, the organization has to develop an overall strategy. It must decide how to present its case to the donors. For example, the American Heart Association has to decide whether to base its case on hope, fear, or some other major motive for giving. It has to decide how to allocate scarce staff time to different donor groups and geographical areas.

The role of the fundraising executive in influencing the organization's objectives and strategies varies greatly among organizations. Most health care organizations treat the fundraiser as a technician rather than a policymaker. The CEO and/or board decides how much money is needed, selects the broad fundraising strategy, and then assigns its implementation to the fundraiser. This, unfortunately, robs the organization of a valuable contribution the fundraiser can make.

Some organizations grant more scope to the fundraising executive. These individuals coordinate closely with public and community relations departments, and they help develop the organization's positioning and personality. Fundraising depends upon good communications and a positive image to legitimate the organization and its need for external funding.

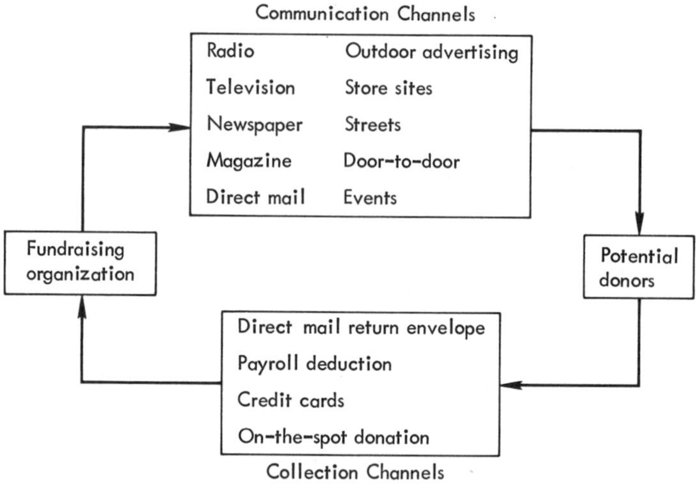

FIGURE 19–4 Communication and Collection Channels for Fundraising

FUNDRAISING TACTICS

Fundraising strategy sets the overall parameters for the effort which the development officer must fill in with specific actions. The organization's job is to send messages to potential donors through the most effective channels and allow the donors to return money through the most efficient collection channels. This view of the channel options is shown in Figure 19–4.

The various channel opportunities give rise to a whole set of specific, well-known fundraising tactics. Table 19–2 lists the major tactics that are effective in four markets: mass anonymous small gift market, members and friends market, affluent citizens market, and wealthy donors market.

The *mass anonymous small gift market* consists of all citizens who might be induced to contribute a small sum (say under $50) to a cause. The key idea is to use low-cost methods of fundraising, since the contributions from noninvolved individuals are expected to be low. One of the oldest forms of mass fundraising is to use volunteers for street and sidewalk solicitation. The volunteers stand in high-traffic areas holding out a can (Crippled Children), offering tags (Veteran's Day), ringing bells (Salvation Army), or distributing religious materials (Hare Krishna). Somewhat more costly is door-to-door solicitation, because more time is involved and many people won't be home. Yet door-to-door canvassing is the preferred method of the American Heart Association (AHA), which has a massive army of volunteers organized by city,

TABLE 19–2 Fundraising Methods

Mass anonymous small gift market
Charity cans in stores
Direct mail
Door-to-door solicitation
Street and sidewalk solicitation
TV and radio marathons
Thrift shops
Yearbooks
Members and their friends market
Anniversary celebrations
Art shows
Auctions
Benefits (theater, movies, sports events)
Bingo games
Book sales
Cake sales
Dances
Dinners, suppers, lunches, breakfasts
Fairs
Fashion shows
Parties in unusual places
Phonothons (also called telethons)
Plate passing
Raffles
Rummage sales
Sporting events
Tours
Walkathons, readathons, bikeathons, danceathons, jogathons, swimathons
Affluent citizens market
Convocations
Dinners (invitational and/or testimonial)
Letters from high-status individuals
Parlor meetings
Telephone calls from high-status individuals
Wealthy donors market
Bequests/estate planning
Celebrity grooming
Committee visit to person's home, office
Memorials
Testimonial dinner for wealthy individuals
Wealthy person invited to another's home or club

neighborhood, and block who ring doorbells once a year for the AHA. Block volunteers are typically homemakers (although, with the advent of working women, decreasingly so) who solicit their neighbors for money and make a substantial contribution themselves. Some charities enlist retailers to keep donation cans in their establishments near the cash register where people can deposit their spare change.

In recent years, direct mail has become a major fundraising tool. Organizations buy mailing lists of people who are likely to contribute and send persuasive letters asking for support. The advent of "intelligent" word processors has made it possible to vary the content of these letters by the recipients' demographic characteristics, giving history, and other characteristics, thus allowing tailor-made strategies for each segment. Organizations can calculate the response rate required to break even on the mailing cost in advance and usually do substantially better than this rate. There is also a multimedia approach which involves, for example, a letter followed within a week by a phone call, as promised by the letter.

The *members and their friends market* consists of the people who belong to the organization and their friends, who have a personal interest in supporting the organization. This market can be tapped for donations in a number of ways. For example, many health care and social service organizations have auxiliaries whose members run theater benefits, dinners, and tours. The auxiliaries also raise money by sponsoring Bingo games, rummage sales, cake sales, and raffles. Each of these fundraising methods requires careful planning in order to maximize its potential revenue. Fashion shows, for example, have to be planned and promoted far in advance; the same can be said of dances and fairs. Fundraising consultants can be found who specialize in each method and know how to stage it for maximal effectiveness. These consultants can recommend the most effective and appropriate fundraising method to an organization. Furthermore, they continue to invent new approaches each year.[8] No sooner had walkathons become popular than other organizations created readathons, bikeathons, and jogathons. Each organization seeks to give a special or distinctive twist to its events.

The *affluent citizens market* consists of persons whose income and interest in the organization or cause could lead them to give anywhere from $50 to several hundred dollars as a donation. The affluent citizen's market is worth pursuing with more than direct mail. A highly effective technique is to issue invitations for special dinners or events at $100 or $500 a plate. Or the dinner might be free, with donations solicited after a round of enthusiastic speechmaking and drinking, both calculated to loosen the purse strings. Another popular method is letter writing and/or phone calls from supporters of the organization to their affluent friends asking for donations.

The *wealthy donors market* consists of those whose wealth and potential interest is such that they might be induced to contribute anywhere from $1,000 to several million dollars to a cause or organization. These wealthy donors are usually well known in the community and solicited by many organizations for financial support. Many of them set up foundations to handle these solicitations so that they do not have to be bothered personally.

All these fundraising tactics can be organized under the umbrella concept of a *campaign:*

> a **campaign** is an organized and time-sequenced set of activities and events for raising a given sum of money within a particular time period.

We can distinguish between an *annual campaign* and a *capital campaign*. Hospitals, social service agencies, and charitable organizations will plan an annual campaign to raise a target amount of money each year. The campaign plan will spell out their "case," the breakdown of their goals, their events, and so on. A well-known person may be invited to be the campaign chairperson to energize and symbolize that year's campaign.

Various institutions will also run a *capital campaign* from time to time to raise a much larger amount of money needed to provide capital for major undertakings or expansions. These campaigns require the most careful planning. Here are some of the major considerations:

1. An organization cannot run a capital campaign too often. After one Jewish chronic care facility ended its five-year capital campaign, it did not launch another capital campaign for nine years. This "spacing" is necessary if the capital campaigns are to retain their specialness in the minds of the donors.
2. The organization has to make decisions on the capital campaign's goal and duration. The goal should be achievable, for there is nothing more embarrassing than failing to reach the goal. And the campaign should not last too long because it will eventually lose its momentum.
3. The organization should try to add a matching gift feature to the campaign, where some wealthy donors promise to match, say $1 for $1, the money raised. Early in the planning the organization has to find and cultivate challenge grants.
4. The organization should prepare an attractive booklet showing the main items the money will buy (called a *wish list*).
5. The campaign strategy calls for approaching various potential donor groups in a planned sequence. First, board members should be asked for large gifts to be in hand even before the campaign begins. Next, large potential donors should be approached. These steps will create the impression that the campaign is generating much support and enthusiasm so that others will want to join the bandwagon.

An issue in designing a campaign is to decide whether potential donors should be "coached" in how much to give, or whether this should be left to their judgment. In fact, there are three possibilities:

1. Don't specify any amount.
2. Suggest a specific dollar amount on the low side.
3. Suggest a specific dollar amount on the high side.

The first approach is the most common. People differ in what they can give, and it is felt that this is best left to their individual judgments. Suggesting a specific amount on the low side is seen as accomplishing two things. It helps prospects know what is considered a minimum proper amount to give. And the "low-amount feature" allows people to get into the habit of giving ("foot-in-the-door").[9] The problem is that many people who might have given more will take this as an adequate amount to give. Suggesting a high amount to give works on the theory of "door-in-the-face."[10] It stretches people's ideas of the appropriate amount to give. As a result, they might give this much or something close to it. Thus, the United Way might suggest that citizens give 1 percent of their income. Most people regard this as too high, but end up giving more than they normally would.

EVALUATING FUNDRAISING EFFECTIVENESS

Each organization must make a continuous effort to improve its effectiveness through evaluating its recent results, especially in the face of increasingly sophisticated competition, greater vigilance among donors, and scarce funds. Organizations use several methods to evaluate their overall fundraising effectiveness.

Percentage of Goal Reached. For organizations that set an annual goal, the first thing to look at is how close they came to achieving the goal. Every organization wants to achieve at least its goal or better. This creates a temptation to set the goal low enough to be achieved. Often the fundraising executive favors a low goal so that he or she can look good. The organization's CEO, however, is tempted to set a higher goal to induce the fundraising office to work hard.

Composition of Gifts. The organization should examine the composition of the money raised, looking at trends in the two major components:

$$\text{gifts} = \text{number of donors} \times \text{average gift size}$$

Number of Donors. Each organization hopes to increase the number of donors each year. The organization should pay attention to the number of donors in relation to the potential number of donors. Many organizations have a disappointing "reach" or "penetration." For example, 9 percent of one hospital's former patients gave the year after being hospitalized. The question raised is not why the hospital has 9 percent penetration, but why 91 percent of its former patients did not give. The fundraiser should interview a sample of nongivers and identify the importance of such reasons as: "did not think the medical care was good," "did not think the hospital cared about the patients," "prefer to give to a newer hospital," "couldn't care less," "was never asked," and so on. Some of these reasons may stem from misperceptions the hospital could correct.

Average Gift Size. A major objective of the fundraising organization is to raise the size of the average gift. The development office should review the size distribution of gifts. It should estimate the potential number of additional gifts that might be obtained in each size donor class against the current number to determine the size classes of gifts that deserve targeted effort in the next period.

Market Share. For some organizations, share or rank in fundraising among comparable organizations can be a revealing statistic about whether the organization is doing a competent job. For example, one of the large Visiting Nurse Associations (VNAs) compared its results to the results of other large VNAs and found it was trailing in the number of givers and in the amount raised. This led to more effort in these directions. As another example, the Chicago Lung Association found that while it managed to raise more dollars each year, its rank among charitable causes had slipped from third to eighth place. It was losing its "share of heart" in the giving community and needed to find ways to reverse this relative decline.

Expense/Contribution Ratio. The fundraising organization is ultimately interested in its net revenue, not gross revenue. At one time it was found that the American Kidney Fund spent $750,000 to raise $779,434, thus creating a scandal. It is more normal for expense-to-contributions to run 10 to 30 percent, and the public generally accepts this. The American Red Cross runs its expenses at 5 percent of its contributions. Many large donors look up this key ratio before they decide whether to support an organization (see Exhibit 19–3 for a discussion of ways in which donors are recommended to evaluate charities).

SUMMARY

Some health care and social service organizations rely on fundraising for survival. Others find funds raised externally helpful, although not necessary. Organizations are shifting from a product orientation to a sales orientation to a marketing orientation in their fundraising efforts. A marketing orientation calls for carefully segmenting donor markets,

EXHIBIT 19–3

Not All Charities Are Particularly Charitable; There Are Some Ways to Check Before You Give

A variety of organizations and governmental agencies exist to help people (choose between charities). On request, they will mail you an analysis of a charities program, information on how it is governed and a breakdown of its expenses and revenue. Some of these organizations have established standards and will tell you if a charity meets them.

Yet, even with this data, a contributor may find it hard to know where each charitable dollar will end up. The financial statements are complicated, and accounting standards are chaotic. As Joseph G. Shea, the chief of the New York State charities registration office, says, being an informed contributor takes some effort.

"You could compare it to being a stockholder," he says. "If you had some money to invest, it would take a little work to find out what would give you the best return. The $2 contributor does it on a whim. But if someone wants to give several hundred dollars or make a bequest, it would certainly behoove him to do this research."

One way is to send for the charity's annual report. . . . Another way is to send for evaluation reports prepared by two watchdog agencies: National Information Bureau, Inc., 419 Park Ave. South in New York and the BBB's Philanthropic Advisory Service, 1515 Wilson Blvd., Arlington, VA. Both agencies have standards for charities and publish lists of those that do and don't meet them.

Of special importance in evaluating a charity is the share of revenue it spends on programs and the portion it allocates for fundraising and administration. NIB says at least 60% of money raised should go to programs. PAS says 50% is acceptable, but no more than 35% should go for fundraising.

But that can be hard to determine since charities account for their expenses in some creative and interesting ways. "Even if you have a financial statement, there is real uncertainty as to where the funds are allocated because there are no uniform accounting rules for charitable organizations," explains Larry W. Campbell, California's registrar of charitable trusts. "There isn't any comparability from one organization to another."

Some, for example, divide the cost for a mailing between fundraising and public education, arguing that part of the message is designed to inform the public. Mr. Campbell says that many charities are reluctant to publicize the amount of money that actually goes to programs because it may raise questions about the rest.

Those who frequently deal with charities say you shouldn't be afraid to demand information. "I think you just have to ask very specific questions," say Robert H. Gudger, a vice president of the Xerox Foundation. He says he always tries to determine how effective a group will be in carrying out its program, and one way is to visit the charity's offices. "We wouldn't give a cent if we didn't visit," he says.

SOURCE: Excerpted from Lynn Asinof, "Not All Charities Are Particularly Charitable; Here Are Some Ways to Check Before You Give," *The Wall Street Journal,* November 28, 1983, p. 60. Reprinted by permission of *The Wall Street Journal,* © Dow Jones & Company, Inc., 1983. All rights reserved.

measuring their giving potentials, and assigning responsibility and resources to cultivate each segment. Marketers assume that the act of giving is really an exchange process in which the giver also gets something that the organization can offer.

The first step in the fundraising process is to study the characteristics of each of the four major donor markets; individuals, foundations, corporations, and government. Each donor market has its own giving motives and criteria.

The second step is to organize the fundraising operation in a way that covers the different donor markets, organization services or units, marketing tools, and geographical areas.

The third step is to develop sound goals and strategies to guide the fundraising effort. Goals are set on incremental, need, or opportunity bases.

The fourth step is to develop a mix of fundraising tactics for the various donor groups. Different tactics are effective with the mass anonymous small gift market, the members and their friends market, the affluent citizens market, and the wealthy donors market.

The fifth step is to conduct regular evaluations of fundraising efforts. A macro evaluation consists of analyzing the percentage of goal reached, the composition of the gifts, the average gift size, the market share, and the expense/contribution ratio.

NOTES

1. Eli Ginzberg, "The Monetarization of Medical Care," *The New England Journal of Medicine* (May 3, 1984), p. 1162.

2. For additional information, see *Giving USA—1979 Annual Report: A Compilation of Facts and Trends on American Philanthropy for the Year 1979* (New York: American Association of Fundraising Councils, Inc., 1980).

3. "How Do We Choose the Charities We Support?" *Chicago Tribune,* July 30, 1972, Sec. 5, p. 9.

4. Harold J. Seymour, *Designs for Fund-Raising* (New York: McGraw-Hill, 1966).

5. "'The Quiet Company' Sells New Fundraiser," *Hospitals* (June 1, 1985), p. 37.

6. Here are some useful books on grantsmanship: Virginia P. White, *Grants: How to Find Out about Them and What to Do Next* (New York and London, Plenum Press, 1975); Lois DeBakey and Selma DeBakey, "The Art of Persuasion: Logic and Language in Proposal Writing," *Grants Magazine,* 1, 1 (March 1978), pp. 43–60; F. Lee Jacquette and Barbara J. Jacquette, *What Makes a Good Proposal* (New York: The Foundation Center, 1973); and Robert A. Mayer, *What Will a Foundation Look for When you Submit a Grant Proposal?* (New York: The Foundation Center, 1972).

7. Lee Smith, "The Unsentimental Corporate Giver," *Fortune,* September 21, 1981, p. 121. Reprinted by permission.

8. For examples, see Suzanne Seixas, "Getting More from Givers," *Money,* September 1976, pp. 79–82.

9. In a study by Freedman and Fraser, the experimenters asked subjects to comply with a small initial request. Two weeks later, they were contacted and asked to comply with a large request. It was found that 76 percent of the experimental participants agreed to comply with the large request compared to a 17 percent compliance rate by those subjects approached with only the large request. See J. L. Freedman and S. Fraser, "Compliance with Pressure: The Foot-in-the-Door Technique," *Journal of Personality and Social Psychology,* 4 (1966), pp. 195–202.

10. For a description of "door-in-the-face" and "foot-in-the-door" techniques, see R. B. Cialdini et al., "Reciprocal Concessions Procedure for Inducing Compliance: The Door-in-the-Face Technique," *Journal of Personality and Social Psychology,* 31 (1975), pp. 206–15; and W. DeJong, "An Examination of Self-perception Mediation of the Foot-in-the-Door Effect," *Journal of Personality and Social Psychology,* 37 (1979), pp. 2221–39.

INDEX

B

C

D

E

F

S

Z